FLORIDA GULF COAST

JOSHUA LAWRENCE KINSER

Contents

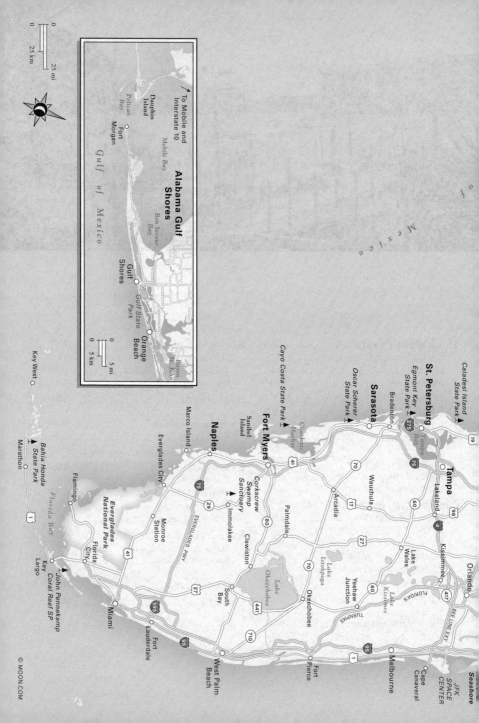

Alabama Gulf Shores

Gulf of Mexico

To Mobile and
Interstate 10

Dauphin Island

Pelican Bay

Fort Morgan

Mobile Bay

Bon Secour Bay

Gulf Shores

Gulf State Park

Orange Beach

Bayou St. John

0   25 mi
0   25 km

0   5 mi
0   5 km

Gulf of Mexico

Caladesi Island State Park

St. Petersburg

Egmont Key State Park

Tampa Bay

Tampa

19

275

75

Bradenton

Sarasota

Oscar Scherer State Park

Cayo Costa State Park

Sanibel Island

Charlotte Harbor

Fort Myers

Naples

Marco Island

Everglades City

Flamingo

Everglades National Park

Corkscrew Swamp Sanctuary

Immokalee

Monroe Station

Florida City

41

29

75

41

EVERGLADES PWY

27

Clewiston

Palmdale

Lake Okeechobee

South Bay

441

710

80

70

Okeechobee

Lake Istokpoga

Yeehaw Junction

27

Lake Wales

60

Lakeland

4

Kissimmee

Orlando

417

BEE LINE EXPY

JFK SPACE CENTER

Cape Canaveral

Melbourne

1

95

Fort Pierce

West Palm Beach

Fort Lauderdale

Miami

95

595

John Pennekamp Coral Reef SP

Key Largo

Florida Bay

1

Marathon

Bahia Honda State Park

Key West

70

Wauchula

Arcadia

17

Lake Kissimmee

FLORIDA'S TURNPIKE

98

60

Seashore

Lake Okeechobee

Bayou St. John

© MOON.COM

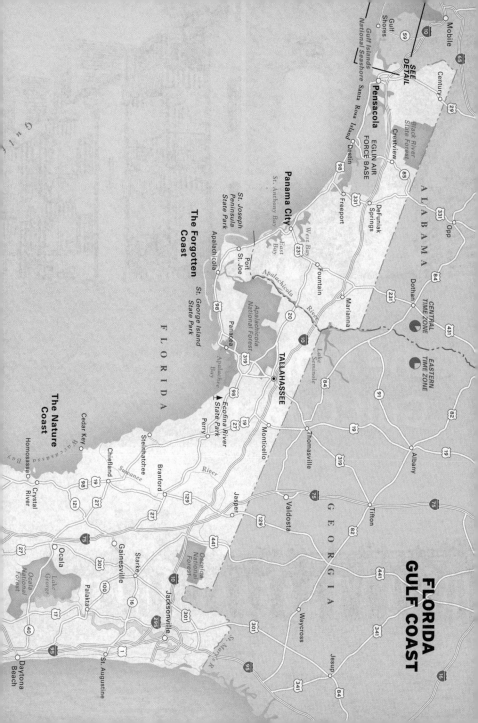

DISCOVER

the Florida
Gulf Coast

Crystal quartz beaches fade into the emerald waters of the Gulf of Mexico, luring millions each year to Florida's Gulf Coast. There isn't anywhere else in Florida where the name "sunshine state" feels truer than on the Gulf Coast, where sandals, shorts, and sunglasses are the local attire.

Beyond the sandy beaches and tropical bungalows, cities like Tampa, Pensacola, Sarasota, and Naples provide all the excitement and amenities you could ask for. In Tampa you'll find a modern skyline of glass skyscrapers gleaming in the sun, while in Pensacola, Old Florida charm and Southern hospitality still exist. And what would a trip on the Gulf Coast be if you didn't spend the day screaming down 100-foot drops on a Busch Gardens roller coaster?

But the best place to be on the Gulf Coast is out on the water. Bodysurf alongside a giant winged manta ray. Collect fresh scallops in the spring-fed waters of Apalachicola Bay. Explore the winding maze of mangrove islands in Everglades National Park. Sail a yacht through the canals of Tampa. Sit down to a dinner of fresh crab cakes, raw oysters, and a bowl of seafood gumbo.

Experience the life that so many have come to love: a life with sand between your toes and sunshine on your shoulders, in a state whose true borders extend deep into the dark blue waters of the Gulf.

Clockwise from top left: the St. George Island Lighthouse; a row of condos on Santa Rosa Beach; view from the Ritz-Carlton Sarasota; Tarpon Lodge on Pine Island; a palm frond in the Everglades; Naples Pier at sunset.

8 TOP
EXPERIENCES

1 **Hit the Beach**: A diverse array of beaches stretching from Pensacola to Naples makes finding your own personal paradise easy (page 24).

2 **Kayak and Canoe in the Everglades:** Paddle your way through the lush network of rivers, mangroves, and swamps that make up the exotic landscape of Florida's largest national park (page 64).

3 **Root for your Team at Baseball Spring Training:** Enjoy America's favorite game in the pre-season (mid-February to late-March), when the tickets are cheaper, the crowds are smaller, and you can see big league players up close (pages 121 and 169).

4 **Go Fish:** Enjoy the astounding variety of fish, crabs, and mollusks that can be harvested from the surrounding waters (page 23).

5 **Experience Thrills and Spills:** The warm weather makes Florida the ideal location for roller coasters, log flumes, and water slides, so this is where theme parks were perfected. On the Gulf Coast, **Busch Gardens Tampa** is one of the best (page 158).

6 **Spot Birds:** Hundreds of native and migratory species, concentrated in reserves and refuges, make scanning the horizon with binoculars addictive. Hardcore enthusiasts should follow the Great Florida Birding Trail (page 26).

7 **Golf:** Pick up your clubs and find your bliss where the sun shines on the green almost all year long (page 42).

>>>

8 **Go Camping:** The diversity of the landscape, from beaches to pine forests and freshwater lakes, means you can find the best place for you to sleep under the stars (page 27).

>>>

Planning Your Trip

Where to Go

Naples, the Everglades, and the Paradise Coast

At the southwestern tip of Florida's Gulf Coast, **Naples** is full of upscale resorts, high-end restaurants, cultural amenities, and more **golf courses** per capita than anywhere on the Gulf Coast. **Marco Island,** just south, similarly boasts resort hotels and condos rising on a long crescent of **white-sand beach. Everglades City** provides a paddler's and outdoors enthusiast's paradise at one end of the Everglades backcountry, the famous **Wilderness Waterway** route linking Everglades City to Flamingo.

Fort Myers, Sanibel, and Captiva

Fort Myers is the largest and oldest city in southwest Florida, set on the banks of the Caloosahatchee River. **Sanibel Island** is a casual low-rise beach town with just enough to do (visit the **J. N. "Ding" Darling National Wildlife Refuge** and the **Bailey-Matthews Shell Museum**) to keep the whole family entertained. There's less to do on neighboring **Captiva Island,** and that's just the way residents and visitors like it. The superlatives heaped on it include "exclusive," "romantic," and "tranquil."

Sarasota County

Sarasota has been recognized as **Florida's cultural capital,** home to a professional symphony, a ballet, and an opera. There are theaters, art galleries, the **John and Mable Ringling Museum of Art,** and the **Van Wezel Performing Arts Hall.** A chain of narrow barrier islands sits offshore to the west. Lido and St. Armands Keys are fairly urban extensions of downtown Sarasota, connected by a causeway. Destinations in their own right, **Longboat Key** to the north is lined with upscale resort hotels and condominiums, and **Siesta Key** to the south is a more casual and fun low-rise beach getaway.

Tampa

Busch Gardens, Ybor City, the Florida Aquarium, professional football, baseball, and ice hockey—notice I didn't mention the beach? Tampa fronts **Tampa Bay,** not the Gulf of Mexico. A huge **port city**—the largest pleasure and industrial port in the Southeast—it doesn't have any beaches to speak of, but it's an excellent **family vacation destination.** There's a perfect convergence of warm weather, affordable accommodations, professional sports, kids' attractions, and upscale shopping to suit every taste.

St. Petersburg and Pinellas County

Easygoing and relaxed, the city of **St. Petersburg** exerts its pull with a vibrant downtown of pastel art deco buildings and cultural attractions like the **Salvador Dalí Museum,** the symphony at Ruth Eckerd Hall, and theater at American Stage. On the Gulf side of the peninsula, **Clearwater Beach** and **St. Pete Beach** are welcoming shores of Gulf water lapping at white sand, backed by restaurants, souvenir shops, and boogie-board-and-bikini stores. Caladesi Island, Honeymoon Island, and Fort De Soto Park are all favored Pinellas beaches.

The Nature Coast

The Nature Coast includes Homosassa and Crystal River in the south, both famous for their **tarpon fishing** and **manatee habitat.** South of that, and worth a day's excursion, is **Weeki Wachee Springs,** with its historic mermaid show and incredibly productive spring. To the

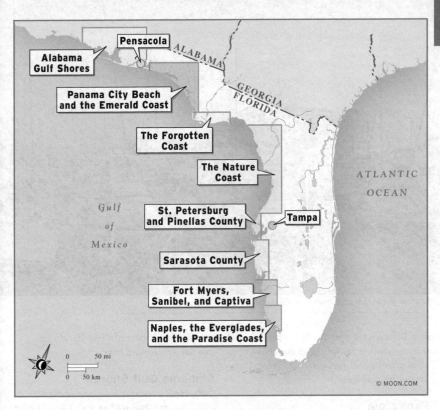

north, the **small fishing communities** of Cedar Key and Steinhatchee require a little extra effort to get to, but the payoff is big. Each is a look into Florida's past, populated by anglers, some great bars, relaxed motels, and plenty of guides eager to take you out into the beauty of the Nature Coast.

The Forgotten Coast

With 200 historic homes and buildings on the National Register, and a downtown of repurposed 1850s brick cotton warehouses, Apalachicola has charm galore. With the **Apalachicola National Estuarine Research Reserve,** historic **Grady Market,** and the very "cool" **John Gorrie State Museum,** which celebrates the inventor of modern refrigeration, there's enough here to occupy visitors for at least a couple of days. Top it off

with incredible nearby beaches and camping on **St. George Island** and **St. Joseph Peninsula** or a view into Franklin County's dwindling **oystering business** in Eastpoint.

Panama City Beach and the Emerald Coast

The Emerald Coast—Fort Walton Beach and Destin, Beaches of South Walton, Panama City Beach—got its name from the deep green color of its water that laps against its glinting white-sand beaches. But this is basically all that these coastal communities have in common. Its easternmost section, **Panama City Beach,** is a densely populated beachside playground, especially favored by college kids on spring break. Farther west, the **Beaches of South Walton** feature quieter, more luxurious beachside enjoyments. And still farther

boats on the waterfront in downtown Pensacola

west, fishing is what put **Destin** on the map, and that continues today with anglers arriving from all over the planet to get a crack at the local marlin, sailfish, and spearfish.

Pensacola

For a relaxed, fun, and casual place to explore beautiful beaches and be welcomed with Southern hospitality, Pensacola is the place to go. Its long stretches of white beaches are a popular summer destination for Floridians and tourists from across the country. It's known as the **City of Five Flags,** having been administered at different times by Spain, France, England, the Confederacy, and the United States; and as the Cradle of Naval Aviation, home to the **Naval Air Station Pensacola;** and even America's first

European settlement (the Spanish attempted to colonize Pensacola in 1559).

Alabama Gulf Shores

Considered a natural extension of the Florida Gulf Coast, the **Orange Beach** and **Gulf Shores** coastline offers 32 miles of sugar-white beaches pretty enough to rival the more popular vacation destinations of Pensacola and Destin to the east. Known as **"Pleasure Island,"** this stretch of Alabama coastline is booming with newly developed vacation properties and classic Gulf Coast hangouts that are remarkably family-friendly. For something more low-key, take the ferry across Mobile Bay to **Dauphin Island** and explore this easygoing Gulf Coast community teeming with history and Southern charm.

When to Go

Florida is a year-round destination, but each broad geographical area along the Gulf Coast has its own peak season, off-season, and in-the-know in-between times.

Southwest Florida sees a huge influx of "snowbirds" in the **winter months.** These northerners come after Thanksgiving and stay just through Easter, generally speaking, bumping up the populations in Naples and Fort Myers through Sarasota and Bradenton. The timing isn't arbitrary—**March-April** along much of the Gulf Coast is magical: temperatures are in the high 70s, there's a little breeze, low humidity, little rain, and Gulf water just warm enough for swimming. That said, if you visit before the snowbirds arrive in the fall or after they depart in the spring, you'll find plenty of accommodations, unoccupied tables in restaurants, and room to roam the beaches.

The **Central West** region encompasses the southern portion of Florida's Nature Coast, as well as the popular vacation destinations of Tampa, St. Petersburg, and Clearwater. Again, **Thanksgiving to Easter** is the peak visitor time, but it's less clear-cut here. A huge family draw, partly because of its proximity to Orlando and Walt Disney World, the area is at its busiest during school vacations, including the hot, steamy summer one.

On the **Panhandle,** which has colder winters and more moderate summers than elsewhere on the Gulf Coast, it's busiest during **summer.** Many of the summer-season visitors here are Florida residents from elsewhere hoping to improve on the high temperatures and humidity of their hometowns.

For college kids, the time to visit the Gulf Coast, and specifically Panama City Beach, is **spring break,** during March-April.

the Venice train station

Road Tripping the Florida Gulf Coast

The entire length of the Florida Gulf Coast covered in this guide is just under 700 miles long. If you were to drive from Pensacola to Everglades City without stopping for a break, it would take just under 11 hours. Over 10 days, you can explore the entire Gulf Coast and hit many of the best attractions with about three hours of driving per day. It's also possible to pick any of the three regions described for a shorter trip.

Day 1
TAMPA AND ST. PETERSBURG

Fly into **Tampa** and spend the day riding roller coasters, exploring recreated African savannas, and splashing down log flume rides at **Busch Gardens.** Cross the bridge to **St. Petersburg** for an evening baseball game with the **Tampa Bay Rays** at **Tropicana Field,** with the required dinner of ballpark hot dogs and cold beer. For something a little fancier, stay in Tampa and have a nice seafood dinner at an outdoor fireside table at **Oystercatchers** alongside Tampa Bay at the Grand Hyatt, or head to **Shula's Steak House** at the Westshore Grand if you want a sizzling-good steak.

Finish off the evening with wine and dessert at **Armani's** rooftop bar, also in the Grand Hyatt, with the best views of Tampa all lit up at night. Spend the night in Tampa at the **Renaissance Tampa International Plaza Hotel** or the **Grand Hyatt Tampa Bay.**

Day 2
SARASOTA COUNTY
60 MILES, 1 HOUR

Get on I-75 and take the hour-long drive south to **Sarasota.** Spend the morning shopping at the luxurious **St. Armands Circle** before popping over to **Marie Selby Botanical Gardens** for a short tour through the fabulous orchid exhibit and gardens. Take the John Ringling Causeway

(Hwy. 789) over Sarasota Bay. Pass through **Longboat Key,** stopping for a walk on **Coquina Beach.**

Continue on Highway 789 until you arrive on **Anna Maria Island.** Enjoy dinner at the **Beach Bistro,** one of Florida's most award-winning restaurants. Make sure to have the lobster tail and seafood bouillabaisse and then the decadent chocolate truffle for dessert. Spend the night on Holmes Beach at the **Mainsail Beach Inn** and enjoy the rest of the evening relaxing on Holmes Beach or by the inn's pool and hot tub surrounded by palm trees.

Day 3
FORT MYERS, SANIBEL, AND CAPTIVA
76 MILES, 1.25 HOURS

Drive south on I-75 for a little more than an hour to **Fort Myers.** Eat breakfast at **First Watch Restaurant** downtown, and then spend the morning walking the grounds and exploring the museums at the **Edison & Ford Winter Estates.** Drive out to the barrier islands of **Sanibel** and **Captiva** and spend the rest of the day enjoying the beautiful beaches and driving down the mansion-lined roads. Have lunch at the **Island Cow** and make sure to be on the beach at the **Mucky Duck** on Captiva to watch the sunset and have dinner. Spend the night on Captiva at the **South Seas Island Resort** or at **'Tween Waters Inn Beach Resort.**

Days 4-5
NAPLES, THE EVERGLADES, AND THE PARADISE COAST
61 MILES, 2 HOURS

Drive south on I-75 for two hours to **Naples Municipal Beach and Fishing Pier** and spend a few hours in the sun. Walk down 2nd Street to 5th Avenue and admire the spectacular homes along the stroll that leads to one of

Big Cypress National Preserve in the Everglades

the Gulf Coast's most upscale shopping districts. Spend the afternoon exploring the shops, cafés, and gelato along **5th Avenue South.** Have dinner at **Trulucks** for steak and seafood within walking distance of the Inn on Fifth, or at **Pazzo Cucina Italiana** on 5th Avenue for Italian fare in a more intimate setting. If upscale Naples isn't really your style, drive farther down to **Everglades City** and enjoy the eco-centric atmosphere at the **Ivey House Inn Bed and Breakfast.** Spend the night in Naples at **The Inn on Fifth** for some truly fancy accommodations or the **Lemon Tree Inn** for a more laid-back experience.

The next morning, enjoy the scenic drive through **The Everglades** on your way to **Chokoloskee Island** for breakfast on the delightful back porch of the **Havana Café.** Get Cubano sandwiches and fresh fruit to go before taking an airboat ride with **Wooten's** through the swamps for a high-adrenaline adventure. Spend the day spotting wildlife and spectacular scenery as you drive down Turner River Road in **Big Cypress National Preserve.** It's a place where you can venture into the heart of Florida's wildlands yet remain in the safety of your own car. Take a sunset paddle in the **Ten Thousand Islands** of **Everglades National Park** and then have dinner at the **Camellia Street Grill.** Spend the night in **Everglades City** at the **Ivey House Bed and Breakfast** and relax for the evening by the impressive indoor pool. Enjoy the first-class breakfast in the morning.

Day 6
THE NATURE COAST
281 MILES, 4 HOURS

Drive north on I-75 for three hours to **Crystal River** and spend a few hours swimming and snorkeling with the manatees. Have lunch at the **Plantation on Crystal River** and then take the very scenic hour-long drive to **Cedar Key.** Spend the evening exploring **Dock Street** and eating fresh seafood at the **Island Hotel and Restaurant.** Stay the night at the charming **Cedar Key Bed and Breakfast.**

Day 7
THE FORGOTTEN COAST
198 MILES, 3.5 HOURS

Continue west on U.S. 98 for about three hours and pass through the town of **Carrabelle,** and the oystering town of **Eastpoint.** Continue west to **Apalachicola** and try a dozen oysters on the half shell. Then take the **Self-Guided Historic Walking Tour** around downtown Apalachicola for a tour of antebellum, Greek Revival, and Victorian homes on wide tree-lined streets.

Head over to St. George Island Bridge to **St. George Island.** Word of its first-class fishing and fabulous beaches has not been widely disseminated, which means much of the year you'll be walking alone in the 1,900-acre beachfront **St. George Island State Park.** Spend the night in a rented small cottage on St. George Island or camping at St. George Island State Park.

Day 8
PANAMA CITY BEACH AND THE EMERALD COAST
113 MILES, 3 HOURS

Stay on U.S. 98 and follow the coastline for three hours west to Highway 30A, and then take the short and scenic drive past the picturesque towns of **Santa Rosa Beach, Seaside, Blue Mountain Beach,** and **WaterColor.** Explore the quaint town squares and superb beaches tucked away along the Emerald Coast. Have a drink or a small plate at the rooftop bar at **Bud and Alley's Restaurant** in Seaside.

Spend the day at the public beach in Seaside and then drive to **Destin** for a dinner of peel-and-eat shrimp and fresh oysters at **AJ's Seafood and Oyster Bar.** Sit on the back deck, watch the sunset, and enjoy the excellent view of Choctawhatchee Bay, East Pass, and the Gulf of Mexico. Spend the night at the phenomenal **Henderson Park Inn** bed-and-breakfast in Destin, and don't miss their delectable complimentary breakfast in the morning.

the beach at Seaside on the Emerald Coast

From sea bass to billfish, stone crabs to blue crabs, and redfish to red snapper, there are many popular species of fish to hook in the Gulf and surrounding waters. You can fish for some species year-round in Florida, but most fish generally run during specific months, and the peak fishing season shifts from summer into the spring, fall, and winter the farther south you go. In north Florida, from Pensacola to Cedar Key, the best season for fishing runs April-October. Once you reach the Everglades, the peak season runs October-March.

PENSACOLA

Fish offshore for snapper, grouper, triggerfish, and amberjack or head into deeper waters in search of blue marlin, white marlin, tuna, wahoo, and mahimahi. For exceptional **pier fishing,** try your luck at the **Pensacola Beach Fishing Pier.**

DESTIN

Offshore **deep-sea fishing** dominates the Destin area. Known as the **"World's Luckiest Fishing Village,"** Destin is lucky indeed—its position on the Gulf Coast places it closest to the **100-Fathom Curve,** where the sea shelf abruptly drops and provides habitat for deep-sea species. Red snapper, grouper, amberjack, king mackerel, sailfish, and blue marlin are the favorite targets from Destin.

APALACHICOLA

The **oyster** is king in the Apalachicola area. A combination of nutrient-rich and spring-fed waters has made Apalachicola Florida's oyster harvesting capital. Charter services, primarily embarking from downtown Apalachicola, offer oyster harvesting trips as well as exceptional **flats fishing** in Apalachicola Bay and **offshore fishing** in the Gulf of Mexico. Speckled trout, flounder, tarpon, and redfish are popular catches in the flats and bays. Cobia, mahimahi, and snapper are easy to hook in the Gulf of Mexico, and **scallops** are harvested around Apalachicola July-September.

CEDAR KEY

Redfish and **speckled trout** are abundant in the shallow waters surrounding **Cedar Key.** The island-dotted bay is not very well marked and can

fishing charters at the Orange Beach Marina

be hard to navigate without a guide, but the fishing in this area is legendary. **Cobia, mackerel, grouper,** and **snapper** are the usual suspects when fishing offshore in the Gulf.

SARASOTA

There's not much need to go offshore when the inshore fishing for **snook,** redfish, trout, pompano, and bluefish around **Siesta Key, Longboat Key,** and **Sarasota** is so good. The narrow and winding mangrove channels in this area give inshore **fly-fishing** and light-tackle trips a wilderness backcountry feel. Offshore trips mostly target grouper, amberjack, and snapper.

THE EVERGLADES

Fishing the sheltered waters and mangrove islands throughout **Everglades National Park** and surrounding **Everglades City** is one of the most rewarding and unique fishing experiences to be had in the entire state of Florida. Snook, redfish, trout, and tarpon are popular targets in the Everglades, and Everglades City is regarded as the capital for harvesting **stone crabs.** The season for collecting the juicy clawed crabs runs October-May.

Day 9
PENSACOLA
50 MILES, 1.25 HOURS

Drive west for an hour on U.S. 98 and cross the Beach Causeway Bridge to Navarre. Follow Gulf Boulevard west to the pristine stretch of beach at **Gulf Islands National Seashore,** between Pensacola and **Navarre Beach.** Stop at one of the public beach accesses along the way and spend a few hours hiking through the impressive dunes on the **Seashore Trail.** Grab a grouper sandwich for lunch at **Peg Leg Pete's** in Pensacola Beach, and then cross the Pensacola Bay Bridge to historic downtown **Pensacola,** the westernmost city on the Florida Gulf Coast.

Tour the historic homes surrounding **Seville Square,** and then watch the sun go down and have dinner at the back deck of **The Fish House** on Pensacola Bay. Finish the night with cocktails at historical **Seville Quarter** in downtown Pensacola. Spend the night at the **Margaritaville Beach Hotel** on Pensacola Beach so you can watch the sunrise from your balcony overlooking the Gulf of Mexico.

Day 10
RETURN TO TAMPA
467 MILES, 7 HOURS

If you're flying home from Tampa, the drive back will take you about seven hours. Take I-110 North from Pensacola for 5.6 miles, and then take exit 6 onto I-10 east toward Tallahassee. Follow I-10 east for 283 miles to exit 296A, and merge onto I-75 south. Follow I-75 south toward Tampa for 161 miles. Merge onto I-275 south for 21 miles, and then take exit 39 onto Highway 589 to **Tampa International Airport.**

Best Beaches

Some people say, "If you've see one beach, you've seen 'em all." Well, not here—most Gulf Coast beaches are entirely unique. There is a diverse amount of sand types, sealife, and natural settings, and an equally wide range of waterside activity. You'll also find an extremely large number of barrier islands off the coast of the mainland. Many times these barrier islands are very thin, and in a few minutes' time you can walk from the beaches of the Gulf Coast to the beaches on the bayside, two very different but equally interesting and beautiful environments. Here's a list of the Florida Gulf Coast's most "sandsational" top picks.

Naples, the Everglades, and the Paradise Coast

- **Naples Municipal Beach and Fishing Pier:** Take a break from the shopping on 5th Avenue and walk a few blocks toward the sound of waves to sit on one of the most beautiful beaches on the Florida Gulf Coast. Nestled amid an upscale neighborhood, this beach and pier are known for superb people-watching, excellent swimming, and proximity to some of the best fine dining and fancy boutiques in the city (page 38).

Fort Myers, Sanibel, and Captiva

- **Fort Myers Beach:** Head to Bowditch Point Regional Park on the northern tip of Estero Island and enjoy the excellent beaches that border both the Gulf and Hurricane Bay (page 80).

- **Lovers Key State Park:** This very secluded beach park is spread out among four stunning barrier islands. The state park's pet-friendly policy brings beach lovers and their pets to the 2.5 miles of shore (page 81).

- **Captiva Beach:** Hands down the best beach for sunsets on the Gulf Coast. Search for shells or just enjoy the rolling dunes and clear water of the Gulf, perfect for swimming (page 99).

Venice Beach

Sarasota County

- **Siesta Key Beach:** This beach always draws praise for its superior white sand. It gets crowded in the summer, but the exceptional size of this beach leaves sun seekers with plenty of spots to spike a shade-supplying umbrella or spread out a supersize beach towel (page 139).

- **Turtle Beach:** Tucked among villas and a residential district on Siesta Key, this family-oriented beach has excellent picnic facilities and is much less crowded than the more popular Siesta Key Beach to the north, yet it still has that special sugar-white sand that makes this barrier island a big draw for beach hunters (page 140).

- **Venice Beach:** Famously regarded as the place to go to hunt for fossilized sharks' teeth, this beach is in a convenient location close to the heart of Venice, just a bike ride from the popular inns and villas. A great beach for families, it has nice picnic pavilions and shower facilities (page 140).

St. Petersburg and Pinellas County

- **Clearwater Beach:** Go to this urban beach surrounded by seaside hangouts and hotels during the day to find the epicenter of oceanfront activity around Tampa. Sunsets from the beach pier are phenomenal, and by night the beach transforms into a fun spot with a nice mix of family fun and beach-bar nightlife (page 202).

- **Fort De Soto Park:** Take a break from the city and explore the seven miles of pristine, preserved beaches at this beautiful park. You can also camp, hike, fish, launch a boat, and explore the historic fort on the southwest tip if you get tired of lounging and swimming (page 202).

The Forgotten Coast

- **St. Joseph Peninsula State Park:** Do you love long, quiet walks on the beach? White sand and exceptionally tall sand dunes stretch down this preserved peninsula for more than seven miles. Combine that with one of the best oceanfront campgrounds in the state of Florida

a roseate spoonbill at J. N. ``Ding`` Darling National Wildlife Refuge

It's an exciting time for birders in Florida. The **Great Florida Birding Trail** (GFBT, www.floridabirdingtrail.com) is a 2,000-mile trail through the state of numerous sites selected for their excellent bird-watching or bird-education opportunities. The trail is split into four sections—the east, the west, the Panhandle, and south Florida—and trail maps can be downloaded from the GFBT website. Even if you focus on the western or Panhandle sections of the trail, there's too much to cover in a single trip. Pick a smaller section, or play it fast and loose and hit a few spots in each, like these.

LOWER SUWANNEE NATIONAL WILDLIFE REFUGE

One of the largest undeveloped river delta-estuarine systems in the United States, the **Lower Suwannee National Wildlife Refuge** extends north and south along the Gulf Coast from the Nature Coast town of Suwannee. The refuge headquarters is 16 miles west of U.S. 19 on Highway 347, with a nearby river trail and boardwalk from which to see migratory songbirds. Citrus County is home to 250 bird species, with red-cockaded woodpeckers, Bachman's sparrows, American white pelicans, and Florida scrub jays among the rarer sightings. The county has its own birding website at (www.citrusbirdingtrail.com).

CEDAR KEY SCRUB STATE RESERVE

You can see a denser concentration of Florida scrub jays at **Cedar Key Scrub State Reserve**, which protects one of the fastest-disappearing habitats in Florida. The park has 12 miles of marked walking trails. Also in Cedar Key, the **Cedar Keys National Wildlife Refuge** is accessible only by boat but is worth the effort—you're likely to see egrets, white ibis, cormorants, herons, pelicans, and anhingas.

SANIBEL ISLAND

Once you're on this island in Lee County, you can do a little birding warm-up, looking for some of the many resident bird species. Find rare white pelicans hanging out in Pine Island Sound and ospreys and eagles nesting on telephone poles above the bike paths and along Sanibel-Captiva Road. The lighthouse area of Sanibel is a good place to see birds, as are the mangrove islands off Pine Island Sound, as is Tarpon Bay.

You're going to hit pay dirt at **J. N. "Ding" Darling National Wildlife Refuge,** which takes up half of Sanibel Island. It's serious birder territory—everyone is equipped with high-powered binoculars and huge camera lenses. There's a naturalist-led tram ride on which you're bound to see rare, colorful, and important life-list species. There are more than 238 species in the refuge, among them tricolored and little blue herons, black-crowned night herons, ibis, wood storks, peregrine falcons, roseate spoonbills, and anhingas. The best time to go is early morning, about an hour before or after low tide.

and you've found a special slice of paradise. If you only go to one beach in Florida, go here (page 263).

The Emerald Coast

- **Panama City Beach:** Known as the headquarters for spring break mania, this town also has pretty beaches, if you can look past the short-sighted development. The oceanfront has the same wonderfully white sand as the more upscale destinations like Destin to the west, and the rock-bottom hotel and motel prices draw a large number of tourists each year. It's the place to party, with more beach bars, dance clubs, and all-day-breakfast diners than anywhere else on the Gulf Coast (page 294).

- **Grayton Beach State Park:** It's a favorite beach for those visiting the idyllic and affluent beach communities like Seaside and WaterColor along Highway 30A. The tranquil vibe of this preserved beach makes it a perfect spot to camp or find yourself in beautiful beach bliss (page 321).

Pensacola

- **Pensacola Beach and Fishing Pier:** Just follow the three-mile bridge to the iconic beachball water tower and you'll find yourself at the center of Pensacola's beach activity.

Surrounded by beach bars and restaurants, the beach and fishing pier are a favorite among surfers, sun seekers, and swimmers (page 342).

- **Gulf Islands National Seashore:** This preserved beach is managed by the National Park Service and is a wonderful choice for beach lovers looking to shore fish, swim, or just lounge on the beach in an undeveloped setting away from all the hubbub of Pensacola Beach. Hikers can also explore a section of the Florida Trail that traverses the large rolling dunes on the sound side of the park (page 342).

Alabama Gulf Shores

- **Gulf Shores Public Beach:** Surrounded by beach hangouts, restaurants, and beach shops, this beautiful beach with excellent picnic pavilions is popular among tourists and young folks looking for a beach party (page 365).

- **Bon Secour National Wildlife Refuge:** Whether you drive or hike in to the preserved beaches at the refuge, you'll find miles of secluded rolling dunes and white-sand beaches. Enjoy hiking the inland trails around Little Lagoon for some excellent fishing and bird-watching in this beautiful sanctuary for wildlife (page 367).

Coastal Camping

Florida has some of the best campgrounds in the country, and a few of them are right on the Gulf. So whether you're a tent-staking, fire-making, s'mores-eating, backcountry-camping purist or a modern-day road warrior coasting in a 40-foot RV with a hot tub and a gourmet kitchen, these campgrounds will accommodate and appease you with their range of amenities, natural beauty, and proximity to some of the best beaches on the Gulf Coast.

Grayton Beach State Park

This beautiful campground puts you right in the heart of the incredible beaches of Walton County.

You won't have to rough it out here, because the idyllic New Urbanist villages of **Seaside** and **WaterColor** are right down the road. After spending the day **sunbathing and relaxing** on the perfect bright-white beaches of the state park, you can meander over to Seaside for an escape to a casual pedestrian wonderland of upscale seafood restaurants, high-fashion shopping, and coastal nightlife fun. If you're not into including all that comfort and city life in your camping trip, the park has miles of **hiking trails** and **beaches** to explore. The campground has 34 sites that can accommodate tents or RVs.

camping at Fort de Soto Park near St. Petersburg

St. Joseph Peninsula State Park

This is one of my favorite parks in the state. The two campgrounds at the park are right on the Gulf. The extensive **boardwalk** that connects the two allows exploration of all the ecosystems here, and the **miles of beach** that stretch to the tip of the peninsula can keep you intrigued for days. The park has some of the largest **sand dunes** anywhere on the Gulf Coast, and the **fishing, crabbing,** and **scalloping** in Apalachicola Bay are out of this world. The park has backcountry camping throughout the peninsula and 119 campsites. I recommend camping in the **Shady Pine Campground,** which offers private campsites surrounded by stands of pine trees, separated by strips of thick shrubs and palmetto ferns.

Turtle Beach Campground

The golden rule of real estate is location, location, location, and the same should be said for campgrounds on the Gulf Coast. And for location, Turtle Beach Campground has all the competition beat. It is right on the Gulf in incredibly beautiful **Siesta Key.** What more could you ask for? The campground may be small, but the 40 campsites are **well designed** with fences providing a bit of privacy and noise reduction between the sites. About a block away is the **public beach** access point, and the campground is a short drive to the city center, with plenty of fun restaurants, bars, and shops to keep you entertained. The park even has Wi-Fi for all the sites.

Fort De Soto Park

As you get past Tampa, finding a decent place to camp becomes increasingly difficult. There are places you can get to by ferry or boat, but this isn't helpful for RV campers. One exceptional anomaly is Fort De Soto Park, run by Pinellas County, with a whopping 236 campsites, 86 of them for tent, van, or pop-up campers only. The park is 1,136 acres on five interconnected islands. It has miles of **beautiful white-sand beaches** and **hiking trails,** a sprawling fort area to explore, 13 artificial reefs to dive and snorkel, and a large network of **paddling trails.** The park is just off the coast of **St. Petersburg,** if you find yourself in need of an escape to the city, and just south of all the urban beach excitement of **St. Pete Beach.**

Everglades National Park

The Everglades is the granddaddy of camping on the Gulf Coast. The **Flamingo Campground** is a little isolated from anything else on the coast, 38 miles from the entrance to the park in Everglades City, but it is the best choice for RV and tent camping in the area. It gives you access to the surrounding national park from its 234 drive-in sites and 64 walk-in sites. The campground is open all year, but I recommend visiting October-March; other parts of the year are too hot and buggy. Park ranger-guided **canoe and kayak tours** launch from the campground, equipped with showers and restrooms, a marina store and gas station, bike rentals, and a visitors center with a museum.

Family Vacation

A family vacation on the Gulf Coast should start in Tampa—first because it boasts a big easy airport with lots of flights; second because it's only an hour away from Walt Disney World and all the other excitement in Orlando; and third because it's where Busch Gardens is.

Day 1

Tampa really has family fun dialed. The first stop must be a day at **Busch Gardens** for a ride on the Cheetah Hunt, or the Cobra's Curse, Montu, the SheiKra, the Kumba, and the Python, in descending order of priority. It's a park for all ages, with a mix of big scary coasters and cool animal attractions.

Day 2

Right across the street from Busch Gardens is Tampa's **Museum of Science & Industry (MOSI),** probably the best science museum on the Gulf Coast. It's nearly impossible to see this the same day as Busch Gardens, so visit MOSI on

West Indian manatee

the second day, and spend the other half of the day wandering at either the **Florida Aquarium** (with a stop for lunch across the street at the **Sparkman Wharf** portside dining and entertainment complex) or the **ZooTampa at Lowry Park.** Both attractions are midsize and thus walkable, requiring less than four hours to fully explore. Before you get out of Tampa, take the aquarium's **Wild Dolphin Cruise** out into the bay to eagle-eye dolphins, manatees, and migratory birds.

Day 3

Head north along the coast on U.S. 19. Stop and visit the mermaids at **Weeki Wachee Springs** (about an hour north of Tampa on U.S. 19). The show is brief, and afterward the family can cool off at the attached **Buccaneer Bay Waterpark,** fed by a natural spring. This is a warm-up for the manatees, another 30 miles north on U.S. 19.

Day 4

You may need to stay overnight in **Homosassa** or **Crystal River** to get a jump on the day.

Mid-October-March, you'll find hundreds of endangered **West Indian manatees** swimming in the warm waters of Kings Bay in the Crystal River and the Blue Waters area of the Homosassa River. **Manatee Tour & Dive** or **Bird's Underwater** will take whole families out for snorkel trips with these huge and playful herbivores. When manatees aren't in season on the Nature Coast, **scalloping in Steinhatchee** is lots of fun July-September 10.

Day 5 and Beyond

So far, this family vacation has been action-packed. You'll need a few extra days to cool down—keep driving north up and around the Big Bend for 300 miles on U.S. 19/98. Head over the St. George Island Bridge for a few days of fishing, beachcombing, and relaxing on **St. George Island.** It's very family-focused, with comfortable beach houses (many with bunk-bed rooms and private pools), biking paths the length of the island, and a tremendous 1,900-acre state park that encompasses the whole eastern end of the island.

ZooTampa at Lowry Park offers 56 acres of rides, animals and fun.

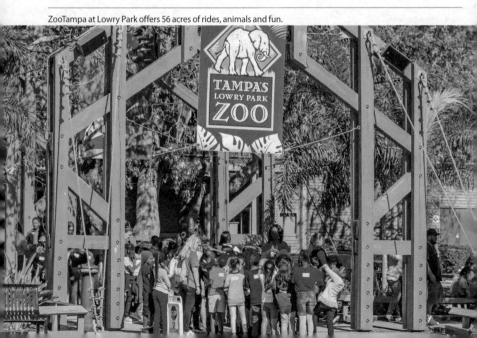

Naples, the Everglades, and the Paradise Coast

This beautiful region is known as the Paradise

Coast, but one person's paradise can be another person's episode of *Survivor*. Let's explore the three cities that make up this exceptionally diverse part of the Florida Gulf Coast and discover the sights and fun adventures that fit your definition of paradise, whatever that may be.

Drive the entire length of the Paradise Coast, from Naples to the Everglades, and you'll experience nearly the full spectrum of the Florida Gulf Coast experience in one short, beautiful, 54-mile drive. It takes less than an hour to drive this section of coast by car, and the journey begins in Naples. As its name implies, the founders modeled the new Naples on the cultured Italian seaport. Today, the town has the look of other moneyed American cities, like Santa Barbara and

Highlights

Look for ★ to find recommended sights, activities, dining, and lodging.

★ **The Baker Museum:** Beyond its 15 galleries, the building itself is a work of art in its own right, showcasing spectacular chandeliers by acclaimed glass artist Dale Chihuly (page 37).

★ **Naples Zoo:** Kids enjoy the gator-feeding show, the panther kittens, and monkey islands. Parents will appreciate the park's impressive collection of native and exotic plants (page 38).

★ **Naples Municipal Beach and Fishing Pier:** Walk the 1,000-foot fishing pier, the beautiful beach and Millionaires' Row, the classy group of jaw-dropping mansions that line the Naples waterfront (page 38).

★ **Corkscrew Swamp Sanctuary:** Fascinating wood storks and resilient resurrection ferns are among the wonders in this serene swamp sanctuary (page 41).

★ **3rd Street South:** Enjoy the upscale boutiques, galleries, and restaurants on Naples's most impressive shopping thoroughfare. (page 47).

★ **Tigertail Beach:** Against a backdrop of resort hotels, this beach draws a crowd that likes to have fun, which means Jet Skis, paddleboards, and lively games of beach volleyball (page 56).

★ **Boat Tour to Calusa Shell Mounds:** Explore the tiny mangrove isles near Marco Island by searching for artifacts of the Native Americans that once inhabited this region (page 58).

★ **Everglades Eco Adventures:** Paddle

through mangrove tunnels where you'll see beautiful birds, rare orchids, and gators of all sizes in their natural habitat (page 65).

★ **Everglades Island Airboat Tours:** Zoom around this majestic ecosystem in an exhilarating and high-speed tour of mangrove islands, swamps, waterways, and see the wildlife that call it home (page 65).

Palm Springs, complete with palm tree-lined boulevards, ritzy resorts, and first-class golf courses.

Travel 17 miles south to tuck your toes in the sand on Marco Island, a top choice for families and those seeking a less formal holiday hideaway. On the beaches along Collier Boulevard are resort hotels and condos. Vacationers often never see much of the island, spending most of their time on the beach to enjoy the gorgeous water of the Gulf and the views of mangrove islands.

Drive 37 miles south to complete your journey from the ultra-civilized to the wildly primitive when you arrive at Everglades National Park. This vast wilderness preserve is dotted with pine groves and rainforest landscapes where beautiful orchids are found in the wetlands. Prehistoric creatures such as alligators still lurk among the tall green swamp grasses, and on its north edge you'll discover Everglades City and Chokoloskee, the end of civilization before you run into the wilderness beyond.

PLANNING YOUR TIME

So how do you pack for this type of place? This little stretch of coast has every type of landscape that Florida has to offer. Cities and towns range from formal to flip-flops. To travel down the Paradise Coast and comfortably enjoy it all, you'll need a diverse wardrobe. Pack formal wear for the Naples area, resort casual for Marco Island, an old pair of sneakers and durable outdoor-activity clothing to keep the bugs at bay in the Everglades, and swimsuits and sandals for the entire coast, since there are beaches and places where you may get wet throughout the area. Bring plenty of bug spray, especially for Everglades City and the surrounding wilderness, as well as sunscreen and an excellent pair of sunglasses.

Where to stay depends on what you're looking to do. Most of Naples's accommodations are upscale and expensive, and the others are generally overpriced for what you get compared to the surrounding areas, as are those on Marco Island. Regardless, most visitors choose to stay in the Naples area, and the fancy 5th Avenue is preferred, since it's close to the upscale shopping, fine dining, and entertainment and is within walking distance of the best beaches. Family travelers set their sights on Marco Island, with many of the large hotels offering programs for kids. Everglades City attracts outdoors enthusiasts, and most of the accommodations are simple, less expensive, and lean toward the rustic.

The most affordable options are the campgrounds and backcountry camping in and around Everglades National Park. Big Cypress has some excellent spots to camp that accommodate RVs and campers as well as tents. Many of these are fairly primitive, but several have electricity, running water, showers, and restrooms. Paddling and boating are popular in the Everglades. If you rent a kayak or a canoe, prepare to paddle against strong winds and dramatic tides. In the backcountry of the national park you can escape to the wild and paddle to private islands or pitch a tent on a platform raised atop the swamp, where it'll be just you, the gators, more mosquitos than you've ever seen in your life, a team of stealthy and resourceful raccoons trying to eat all your food, and the beautiful stars above.

Peak season in Naples is December-March. Rates for hotels reflect this, and you may save a bundle visiting in late spring or early fall, when the weather in Naples and on Marco Island is very nice. Everglades City, on the other hand, is best to visit November-February. During the hotter months in the Everglades, the heat, humidity, and mosquitoes are unbearable, and this keeps most visitors away.

If you plan to explore all of the Paradise Coast, you'll want a car, especially in the

---

Previous: airboat in the Everglades; an alligator in the Everglades; sunset at Tigertail Beach on Marco Island

Naples, the Everglades, and the Paradise Coast

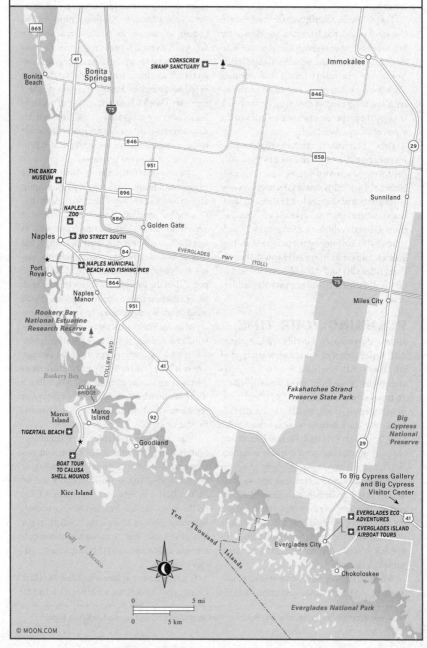

Everglades, where there is no real community transportation, and most of the popular destinations are separated by long miles of backcountry roads. I-75 is the main artery into the region, with Davis Boulevard the connector to Naples and U.S. 41 serving the coastline. Collier Boulevard gets you out to Marco Island, while U.S. 41, the Tamiami Trail, leads south to the Everglades. Highway 29 ventures to Everglades City, the Everglades National Park Gulf Coast Visitor Center, and Chokoloskee Island.

By air, the closest large airport is **Southwest Florida International Airport** (RSW, 11000 Terminal Access Rd., Fort Myers, 239/590-4800, www.flylcpa.com), 40 minutes north in Fort Myers. There is a little commuter airport in Naples, the **Naples Municipal Airport** (APF, 160 Aviation Dr., 239/643-0733, www.flynaples.com).

Naples

With nearly 90 golf courses, Naples has been dubbed the Palm Beach of Florida's Gulf Coast. It has one of the highest ratios of greens to golfers in the United States. Beyond the links are world-class shopping, dining, and a preponderance of wealthy beautiful people. Although a stroll of trendy 5th Avenue is reminiscent of the upscale Atlantic Coast resort, the analogy breaks down at Naples's tranquil beauty, which begins just five miles out of town at the Rookery Bay National Estuarine Research Reserve to the south, with sprawling mangroves and a high diversity of rare birds; Big Cypress National Preserve to the east; and the untamed wilderness of Everglades National Park.

And then there are the nine miles of sun-soaked white-sand beaches. Boosters describe Naples as the crown jewel of southwest Florida, and the jewel that sparkles brightest is the downtown beach, arguably the finest city beach in Florida and within walking distance of 5th Avenue's high-end hotels, restaurants, and shopping.

SIGHTS
Trolley Tours
A good place to start and orient yourself in Naples is with a long ride aboard a **Naples Trolley Tour** (1010 6th Ave. S., 239/262-7300, hourly 8:30am-5:30pm daily, $27 adults, $13 ages 5-13, free under age 5). The open-air trolley has a narrated tour of more than 100 local places, including historic Naples Pier, Tin City, and the Port of Naples Marina. The tour itself lasts two hours, but you can hop on and off whenever you want and then explore each area, catching the next trolley when you're ready to go to the next stop. Trolleys arrive at each destination every hour, and a simple-to-use schedule is provided. Tickets are available at all boarding stops, but the best way to get familiar with the area is to start at the Experience Naples Visitor Information Center, the welcome center for the Naples Trolley. This is also where you board the Everglades van tours offered by Naples Transportation as well as the Segway Tours by Segway Tours of Naples.

Galleries
At last count Collier County had nearly 200 commercial art galleries, mostly wedged among the downtown shops along **3rd Street South,** called "Gallery Row." You'll also find more galleries on Broad Avenue off 3rd Street South, and along **5th Avenue,** many between the 600 and 800 blocks.

Naples was selected the number-one small art town in America by author John Villani in his fourth edition of *The 100 Best Art Towns in America.* He cited the area's "amazing range of natural splendor," along with its "sophistication and serious art galleries," art fairs, community arts centers and theaters, and the Philharmonic Center complex. *AmericanStyle*

Naples

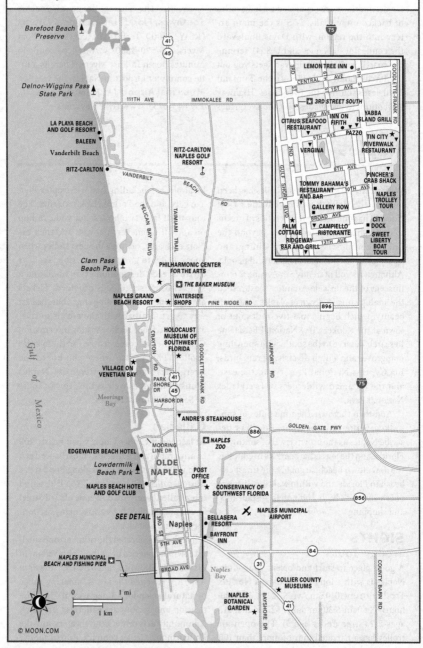

Barefoot Beach Preserve

Delnor-Wiggins Pass State Park

LA PLAYA BEACH AND GOLF RESORT

BALEEN

Vanderbilt Beach

RITZ-CARLTON

RITZ-CARLTON NAPLES GOLF RESORT

VANDERBILT BEACH RD

PELICAN BAY BLVD

TAMIAMI TRAIL

111TH AVE

IMMOKALEE RD

Gulf of Mexico

Clam Pass Beach Park

PHILHARMONIC CENTER FOR THE ARTS

THE BAKER MUSEUM

NAPLES GRAND BEACH RESORT

WATERSIDE SHOPS

PINE RIDGE RD

HOLOCAUST MUSEUM OF SOUTHWEST FLORIDA

CRAYTON RD

GOODLETTE-FRANK RD

AIRPORT RD

VILLAGE ON VENETIAN BAY

Moorings Bay

PARK SHORE DR

HARBOR DR

ANDRE'S STEAKHOUSE

GOLDEN GATE PWY

MOORING LINE DR

NAPLES ZOO

EDGEWATER BEACH HOTEL

Lowdermilk Beach Park

OLDE NAPLES

POST OFFICE

CONSERVANCY OF SOUTHWEST FLORIDA

NAPLES BEACH HOTEL AND GOLF CLUB

SEE DETAIL

Naples

3RD ST

5TH AVE

BROAD AVE

BELLASERA RESORT

BAYFRONT INN

NAPLES MUNICIPAL AIRPORT

NAPLES MUNICIPAL BEACH AND FISHING PIER

Naples Bay

COLLIER COUNTY MUSEUMS

NAPLES BOTANICAL GARDEN

BAYSHORE DR

COUNTY BARN RD

0   1 mi
0   1 km

© MOON.COM

Detail

LEMON TREE INN

3RD ST

CENTRAL AVE

1ST AVE

9TH ST

GOODLETTE-FRANK RD

3RD STREET SOUTH

3RD AVE

INN ON FIFTH

YABBA ISLAND GRILL

CITRUS SEAFOOD RESTAURANT

2ND ST

5TH AVE

PAZZO

TIN CITY

RIVERWALK RESTAURANT

VERGINA

GULF SHORE BLVD

6TH AVE

PINCHER'S CRAB SHACK

TOMMY BAHAMA'S RESTAURANT AND BAR

10TH AVE

NAPLES TROLLEY TOUR

GALLERY ROW

BROAD AVE

PALM COTTAGE

CAMPIELLO RISTORANTE

CITY DOCK

RIDGEWAY BAR AND GRILL

13TH AVE

SWEET LIBERTY BOAT TOUR

magazine also named Naples in the top 25 arts destinations in the United States. Most of the galleries are downtown, and to see the work of many local artists, stop at the **Von Liebig Art Center** (585 Park St., next to Cambier Park, 239/262-6517, 10am-4pm Mon.-Sat., free). It houses the Naples Art Association and features changing exhibitions in five galleries.

★ The Baker Museum

The Baker Museum (formerly Naples Museum of Art, 5833 Pelican Bay Blvd., 239/597-1111, www.artisnaples.org, 10am-4pm Wed.-Sat., noon-4pm Sun., $10 adults, $5 students and military, free under age 17, more for special exhibitions) is the crown jewel of Naples's cultural attractions at the incredible **Artis—Naples campus.** The visual arts center is a three-story, 30,000-square-foot museum with 15 galleries. Exhibits are varied and expertly curated, such as a small antique walking stick show, the underwater-phantasmagorical blown glasswork of Dale Chihuly, an Andy Warhol print show, and one of the largest collections of Mexican art in the Southeast. Beyond the permanent collection and visiting shows, the space itself is a work of art, with a huge glass-domed conservatory, entrance gates by metal artist Albert Paley, and an impressive Chihuly chandelier. Educational programs and art lectures are held at the museum, and many of them sell out, so buy tickets early on the museum's website.

Collier County Museums

Five minutes east of downtown Naples, history enthusiasts flock to the **Collier Museum at Government Center** (Collier County Government Center, 3331 Tamiami Trail E., 239/252-8476, 9am-4pm Mon.-Sat., free). This museum is one of five locations in the Naples area known collectively as the Collier County Museums. The four others are the Museum of the Everglades in Everglades City, the Immokalee Pioneer Museum at the Robert Roberts family ranch, and the Naples Depot Museum, a historic train station on

5th Avenue South, and the Marco Island Historical Museum on Marco Island—but this is the main museum and worth the most time. Established in 1978, interpretive exhibits that illuminate the history, archaeology, and development of the area along with a five-acre botanical park with a native plant garden, an orchid house, two early Naples cottages, a logging locomotive, swamp buggies, and a World War II Sherman tank. The museum holds the **Old Florida Festival** ($10 adults, $5 ages 5-12, free under age 5, free parking) every year in March—a good time for people who like historical reenactments.

Palm Cottage

On the National Register of Historic Places, **Palm Cottage** (137 12th Ave. S., 239/261-8164, 1pm-4pm Tues.-Sat., $13, free under age 11) is the oldest house in Naples, built for Walter N. Haldeman, the then editor and owner of the *Louisville Courier-Journal.* The house is one of the few remaining tabby mortar structures in the area—a concrete-like building material made from seashells mixed with sand and seawater. The 3,500-square-foot cottage is decorated to reflect the 1900s era, filled with antiques, art, and tools, and the home gardens are worth exploring.

Holocaust Museum of Southwest Florida

Growing out of an exhibit created by Golden Gate Middle School students in Naples, the **Holocaust Museum of Southwest Florida** (4760 Tamiami Trail N., 239/263-9200, www. holocaustmuseumswfl.org, 1pm-4pm Tues.-Sat., $10 adults, $5 ages 12-18, under age 12 and museum members free) is another small history museum. Students collected more than 300 death camp and Holocaust artifacts, which constitute the bulk of the exhibit. Docents lead tours for individuals as well as local school groups. The museum has also embarked on an oral history project with local survivors, liberators, and others, and it installs traveling Holocaust exhibits in local schools as well.

★ Naples Zoo

Adults will enjoy the sophisticated dining, shopping, and arts of Naples, but kids must be entertained with regularity, or mutiny is assured. The single most mutually agreeable family attraction in Naples is **Naples Zoo at Caribbean Gardens** (1590 Goodlette-Frank Rd., 239/262-5409, www.napleszoo. com, 9am-5pm daily, $23 adults, $22 over age 64, $15 ages 3-12, free under age 3, $18 military, free parking).

It began as a botanical garden, founded by botanist Henry Nehrling in 1919, and was expanded in the 1950s. The Tetzlaff family introduced the rare animals in 1969. In 2004 the zoo acquired nonprofit status after local taxpayers opted to tax themselves to save the zoo land from being sold to a developer. Since then this quickly expanding zoo has been able to add a new exhibit every year.

The greatly increased number of species in the presentations now includes raptors and dozens of native and exotic venomous reptiles, from diamondback rattlesnakes and Gila monsters to an African puff adder and a Komodo dragon, as well as South American poison dart frogs and bushmaster snakes. Other notable exhibits are the Panther Glade and Leopard Rock, which separate you from the big cats with a thrillingly thin sheet of glass, and the three rare and beautiful Malayan tigers, the only such cats in Florida. New residents include black and white colobus monkeys and a Florida panther kitten.

Kids will prefer the baby alligator-feeding shows and the fossa exhibit, instantly recognizable from the movie *Madagascar*. Zookeepers hand-feed alligators from an elevated deck, adding excitement and up-close action to the feedings. Be sure to catch the Planet Predator and Meet the Keeper live animal shows. Seeing these animals up close inspires awe, and the keepers' banter keeps the shows entertaining. There's also a wonderful short boat ride past a bunch of tiny islands to view various species of primates. For $5 you can hand-feed the seven giraffes from an elevated deck.

Family-Friendly Attractions

If the weather is nice, which it usually is in Naples, kids can enjoy a round of mini golf at **Coral Cay Adventure Golf** (2205 Tamiami Trail E., 1 mile east of Tin City, 239/793-4999, 10am-11pm daily, $9.50 adults, $8.50 ages 5-11, $3.50 under age 5), with its exotic tropical setting featuring caves, reefs, and a waterfall. There's a snack bar, slushies, and ice cream as well as a game room.

North Collier Regional Park (15000 Livingston Rd., 239/252-4000, 6am-10pm daily, free) is a great destination for families, with eight soccer fields, five softball fields, an interactive playground, a fossil-dig play area for children, an exhibit hall with ranger-led tours, and a recreation center. The outstanding part is the **Sun-N-Fun Lagoon Water Park** (239/252-4021, 10am-5pm daily summer, 10am-5pm Sat.-Sun. spring and fall, $13 over 48 inches tall, $6 under 48 inches tall, $9 over age 59, free under age 4), with one million gallons of good times for children and their handlers. The water park features three waterslides, a lazy river, a family pool, a "tadpole" pool for kids under age 7, Turtle Cove for kids over age 6, and a lap and diving pool, as well as water-dumping buckets and water pistols.

BEACHES
★ Naples Municipal Beach and Fishing Pier

For an urban beach experience, stroll along **Naples Municipal Beach and Fishing Pier** (25 12th Ave. S., access at 12th St. and Gulf Shore Blvd., just south of downtown, 239/213-3062, 24 hours daily, free, metered parking near entrance). Known locally as the Pier, the 1,000-foot structure juts into the Gulf and attracts anglers. The best fishing months and May-July and September-October. There's a bait house, fish-cleaning tables, a chickee shelter, restrooms, and concessions on the pier, built in 1888 as a freight and passenger dock. Damaged repeatedly by fire and hurricanes

---

1: Naples Fishing Pier **2:** Corkscrew Swamp Sanctuary

and rebuilt in 1910, 1926, and 1960, the pier is a symbol of the locals' tenacity and civic pride. It is perhaps the most photographed spot in Naples, with the emerald-green Gulf water and wide swath of beach on either side.

Proximity to downtown and the stretch of fancy houses known as Millionaires' Row makes it ideal for a moonlit stroll after dinner or a sandy escape after an afternoon in the city. The beach can be accessed at the Gulf end of each avenue—downtown is a grid, with streets running north and south, avenues east and west—with ample metered parking. Many of the parking meters on the roads near the beach are $2.50 per hour and take quarters only; if you don't mind walking five blocks or more, you can park downtown for free and walk to one of the beach access points. New parking-meter stations that take credit and debit cards have also been installed at several of the beach parking areas, so you don't always need a roll of quarters to spend the day at the most popular stretch of beach in the city. You may find a loggerhead sea turtle nest or a swirl of prehistoric-looking pelicans.

Clam Pass Beach Park

At the south end of Naples is **Clam Pass Beach Park** (465 Seagate Dr., end of Seagate Dr., 239/252-4000, 8am-sunset daily, $8 parking fee or beach parking pass required). Clam Pass consists of 35 acres of mangrove forest, rolling dunes, and 3,200 feet of white-sand beach. There's a 0.75-mile boardwalk from a high-rise development through the mangroves and out to the beach. It's easily walkable, and you'll likely see eagles, ospreys, and waddling armadillos, but you can also take a fun free tram that runs continuously throughout the day. Once at the beach, there are kayak, canoe, sailboard, and catamaran rentals. The water is shallow and the surf mild, a perfect combination for a family day at the beach. Clam Pass also has a concession area and picnic pavilions.

Delnor-Wiggins Pass State Park

At the north end of the city, **Delnor-Wiggins Pass State Park** (11135 Gulfshore Dr., 5 miles west of I-75, exit 17, 239/597-6196, 8am-sunset daily, $6 parking in 5 parking areas) regularly makes Dr. Beach's (a.k.a. Dr. Stephen Leatherman of the University of Maryland) top-20 list of America's best beaches. On Delnor-Wiggins you'll find the white-sand swath framed by picturesque sea oats, sea grapes, and cabbage palms. Delnor-Wiggins is on a narrow barrier island separated by a maze of mangrove swamp and tidal creek, and it boasts a nature trail and observation tower from which to spy on the abundant wildlife. It's a superior shelling beach, and Wiggins Pass generates much enthusiasm among anglers. The water is shallow, with a gentle slope and calm surf suitable for swimming. There are picnic facilities, a lifeguard on duty, and a boat ramp. Stay out of the dunes and don't pick the sea grass, which is protected due to its important role as a sand stabilizer.

Other Beaches

Other beaches in the area would be star attractions anywhere but here, but the wealth of possibilities make **Lowdermilk Beach Park** (1301 Gulf Shore Blvd. N., 239/213-3029), **Vanderbilt Beach Park** (near the Ritz-Carlton, end of Vanderbilt Dr., 239/252-4000), and **Barefoot Beach Preserve,** also known as **Lely Barefoot Beach** (take U.S. 41 to Bonita Beach Rd. and head west, 239/591-8596), less popular here. All have restrooms and picnic facilities, are open sunrise-sunset daily, and charge for parking. In addition, Lowdermilk has fun sand-volleyball courts, and Vanderbilt offers exceptional bird-watching. Barefoot boasts a learning center with exhibits on sea turtles and shorebirds, as well as a nature trail.

SPORTS AND RECREATION

★ Corkscrew Swamp Sanctuary

The Naples area offers several outstanding opportunities to explore the exotic and wild natural world of the Gulf Coast—easily accessible to those with disabilities, seniors, or the stroller-bound.

In Collier County, huge swaths of bald cypress forest stood until logging in the 1940s quickly decimated it, with just one virgin stand of cypress left in southwest Florida—the Corkscrew Swamp near Immokalee, now **Corkscrew Swamp Sanctuary** (375 Sanctuary Rd. W., 239/348-9151, 7am-5:30pm daily, $14 adults, $6 students, $10 Audubon Society members, $4 ages 6-18, free under age 6). It provides visitors with a 2.25-mile raised boardwalk—there's also a 1-mile trail if the longer one sounds daunting, and benches and rain shelters along the way—through four distinct local environments: a pine upland, a wet prairie, a cypress forest, and a marsh. Interpretive signs along the boardwalk give you the basics, but the guide-led tours are tremendous, and there's a field guide and a kids' activity book that you can pick up at the admissions desk. There's a birders' checklist and a whiteboard for birders to jot down what they've seen for the benefit of those who've just arrived. It's also a great place to spot gators, wood storks, resurrection ferns, and rare orchids. To get here, take I-75 to exit 111, go approximately 15 miles, and turn left onto Sanctuary Road.

Rookery Bay National Estuarine Research Reserve

Another worthwhile day trip is about 13 miles south of Naples at **Rookery Bay National Estuarine Research Reserve** (300 Tower Rd., 239/530-5940, 9am-4pm Mon.-Fri. May-Oct., 9am-4pm Mon.-Sat. Nov.-Apr., $5 adults, $3 ages 6-12, free under age 6). The Rookery Bay and Ten Thousand Islands estuarine ecosystem is one of the few pristine mangrove estuaries in North America, with 110,000 acres of forest, islands, bays, interconnected tidal embayments, lagoons, and tidal streams that are home to bald eagles, pink roseate spoonbills, and lots of other birdlife. Explore the estuary on your own by kayak or with a guided kayak excursion through Rookery Bay's mangrove estuary (offered once per month on average, check the website). There are also occasional boat tours (Nov.-Apr.) that take a closer look at the marine habitat within the Estuarine Reserve. A 16,500-square-foot Environmental Learning Center has interactive exhibits and a visitors center, four marine research laboratories, a coastal training center, and five aquariums along with an authentic Seminole chickee and an observation bridge over Henderson Creek. The big fish at the entrance, by the way, is a polka-dot batfish.

The coolest part of the center is the climb-in "bubble" that allows visitors to observe the many creatures that live among the roots of a 14-foot mangrove in the center aquarium, including the unwelcome highly invasive lionfish that is decimating native aquatic life. An aggressive eradication program has begun in the park, and classes on how to catch and handle the fish are frequently held. Do your part to protect Florida's aquatic environment and learn how to remove these fish.

Conservancy of Southwest Florida

In the center of town, the 13 acres of the **Conservancy of Southwest Florida** (1450 Merrihue Dr., 239/262-0304, 9:30am-4:30pm daily, $13 adults, $9 ages 3-12) provide opportunities for canoe tours and nature hikes, as well as aviaries and a serpentarium (that's a snake house). Its **Naples Nature Center** (1495 Smith Preserve Way, 239/262-0304, www.conservancy.org/nature-center, 9:30am-4:30pm daily Jan.-Apr., 9:30am-4:30pm Mon.-Sat. May-Dec., $15 adults, $10 ages 3-11) has education programs and lectures on the common area's deck (11am-3pm Mon.-Sat.), talks about the aquatic life found in the area's bays and the Gulf at the touch tank (every half hour

Tee Time

Naples isn't called the golf capital of the world for nothing. Here are the courses available to visitors, plus the driving ranges and pro shops. All of the greens fees quoted fluctuate seasonally and by time of day; call ahead.

THE COURSES

ArrowHead Golf Club
2205 Heritage Greens Dr., 239/596-1000
Public, 18 holes, 6,832 yards, par 72, course rating 73.1, slope 130
Greens fees: $105 7am-11:52am, $95 noon-2:22pm, $59 2:30pm-3:52pm, $39 after 4pm

Cypress Woods Golf and Country Club
3525 Northbrook Dr., 239/592-7860
Semiprivate, 18 holes, 6,330 yards, par 72, course rating 71.7, slope 136
Greens fees: $35-70 7am-noon, $28-79 noon-2pm, $28-52 2pm-close, cart included

Eagle Lakes Golf Club
18100 Royal Tree Pkwy., 239/732-0034
Public, 18 holes, 7,150 yards, par 71, course rating 71.1, slope 122
Greens fees: $39-89 for 18 holes

Hibiscus Golf Club
5375 Hibiscus Dr., 239/774-0088
Public, 18 holes, 6,476 yards, par 72, course rating 71.7, slope 128
Greens fees: $45-95

Flamingo Island Club
8004 Lely Resort Blvd., 239/793-2223
Classics Course: private, 18 holes, 6,805 yards, par 72, course rating 72.4, slope 128
Flamingo Course: resort, 18 holes, 7,171 yards, par 72, course rating 73.9, slope 135
Mustang Course: resort, 18 holes, 7,217 yards, par 72, course rating 75.3, slope 141
Greens fees: $49-162, depending on the month, cart included

Marco Island Marriott Beach Resort, Golf Club, and Spa
400 South Collier Blvd., Marco Island, 239/389-6600
Resort, 18 holes, 7,152 yards, par 72, course rating 75.2, slope 145
Greens fees: $99-205

Naples Beach Hotel & Golf Club
851 Gulf Shore Blvd. N., 239/261-2222
Resort, 18 holes, 6,488 yards, par 72, course rating 71.2, slope 129
Greens fees: $55-95, cart included

Naples Grande Golf Club
7335 Premier Dr., 239/659-3700
Resort, 18 holes, 7,102 yards, par 72, course rating 75.1, slope 143
Greens fees: $39-99

Quality Inn and Suites Golf Resort
4100 Golden Gate Pkwy., 239/455-1010
Resort, 18 holes, 6,564 yards, par 72, course rating 70.8, slope 125
Greens fees: $25-75, cart included

Riviera Golf Club of Naples
48 Marseille Dr., 239/774-2011
Public, 18 holes, 4,090 yards, par 62, course rating 60.4, slope 95
Greens fees: $45-60, cart included

golf bags at Naples Grande Golf Club

Tiburon Golf Club
2620 Tiburon Dr., 239/593-2200
North Course: resort, 9 holes, 3,693 yards, par 36, course rating N/A, slope N/A
South Course: resort, 9 holes, 3,477 yards, par 36, course rating N/A, slope N/A
West Course: resort, 9 holes, 3,500 yards, par 36, course rating N/A, slope N/A
Greens fees: $60-225, depending on season

Valencia Golf Course
1725 Double Eagle Trail, 239/352-0777
Public, 18 holes, 7,145 yards, par 72, course rating 74.3, slope 130
Greens fees: $55-90, cart included

DRIVING RANGES

Coral Isle Golf Center
4748 Championship Dr., 239/732-6900

PRO SHOPS

Fix Up Stix
1101 Sun Century Rd., 239/591-3743

For the Love of Golf
9765 Tamiami Trail N., 239/566-3395

Golf Balls Galore & More
2181 J&C Blvd., 239/597-6528

Golf Galaxy
6428 Hollywood Dr., 239/254-0483

Naples Golf Co.
5091 Tamiami Trail E., 239/643-5577

PGA Tour Superstore
2135 Tamiami Trail N., 239/384-6380

10:30am-3:30pm Mon.-Sat.), and electric boat cruises through the mangrove habitat on the Gordon River (hourly 10am-noon Mon.-Sat.). Make sure to check the Nature Center's website for up-to-date schedules for talks and programs. Newly added to the center is the Dalton Discovery Center, where visitors can view 125 animals in their natural habitat, and the Von Arx Wildlife Clinic, where animals are cared for and released back into the wild.

Big Cypress National Preserve

Midway between Naples and Miami on U.S. 41, the Big Cypress National Preserve (Oasis Visitor Center, 52105 Tamiami Trail E., Ochopee, 239/695-2000, www.nps.gov/bicy, welcome center 9am-4:30pm daily, preserve 24 hours daily, free), contiguous with Everglades National Park and just about as big, was the first national preserve. It encompasses 720,000 acres of the Big Cypress Swamp of southwest Florida, with swamp, freshwater marshes, forests of slash pine and palmetto, and wet prairies containing abundant wildlife. Explore this vast area on the network of roads that crisscross the preserve, or get deeper into the backcountry hiking or in a canoe.

HIKING

There's a public boardwalk at the Kirby Storter roadside pullout that allows you to walk into a cypress dome without getting your feet wet. A longer walk with wonderful hiking is the Florida Trail, which stretches across the state from Gulf Islands National Seashore through the Big Cypress National Preserve. The three sections include Part 1, the Loop Road to U.S. 41 (7.8 miles one-way), which begins at Loop Road 13 miles from its east end on U.S. 41. The other end is across from the Big Cypress Visitors Center (53 miles east of Naples on U.S. 41). The easy path meanders through dwarf cypress and prairies and crosses through Robert's Lake Strand (can be very wet during rainy months). Part 2, for seasoned backpackers, is U.S. 41 to I-75 (30 miles one-way), with trailheads on U.S. 41 near Big Cypress Visitors Center and

on I-75 at the rest area at mile marker 63. A more difficult hike (you'll need to pack in all your own water), it runs through hardwood hammocks, pinelands, prairies, and cypress. High-ground camping is at the 13-mile mark. Part 3, I-75 to Preserve North Boundary (7.6 miles one-way) follows an old oil road through hardwood, prairie, and pine forest.

CANOEING

The park's main canoe trail begins at U.S. 41 and follows the Turner River until it ends in Chokoloskee Bay (a 5-hour paddle). You can also put in at the Everglades National Park Gulf Coast Visitor Center. There's another trail called the Halfway Creek Canoe Trail; put in at Seagrape Drive and paddle south past Plantation Island.

CAMPING

Eight campgrounds accommodate tent and RV camping across the preserve. From Naples and heading east, the campgrounds are: Bear Island, Gator Head, Pink Jeep, Burns Lake, Monument Lake, Midway, Mitchell Landing, and Pinecrest. The most popular sites for RVs are at the Midway campground. The Gator Head and Pink Jeep campgrounds cater exclusively to tent campers for those of you looking for a more authentic wilderness experience. The best camping season is between December and January when the weather is cooler and the mosquito population is tolerable. Before camping in the reserve you'll need to go to a visitors center (or visit the National Park Service website at www.nps.gov/bicy) to see an informative 15-minute movie about the preserve, view a small wildlife exhibit, and pick up a permit ($10-30, depending on location) and literature about the preserve. Reservations can be made and are highly suggested for all campgrounds with the exception of Pink Jeep, Mitchell Landing, Gator Head, and Bear Island campgrounds, which are all walk-in only. Backcountry

1: a gator at Big Cypress National Preserve 2: Midway Campground in Big Cypress Preserve

Walking Trees

This area owes much of its landmass to the **mangrove tree,** often called walking trees because they hover above the water, their arching prop roots resembling many spindly legs. The mangrove is one of only a handful of tree species on Earth that can stand having its roots in ocean water, immersed daily by rising tides, and that thrives in little soil and high levels of sulfides. The mangrove's hardiness is just one of its many idiosyncrasies.

Mangroves are natural land builders. Seed tubules about the heft and length of a cigar sprout on the parent tree, drop off, and bob in the brackish water until they lodge on an oyster bar or a snag in the shallows. There the seed begins to grow into a tree, its leaves dropping and getting trapped along with seaweed and other plant debris. This organic slurry is the bottom of the food chain, supplying food, breeding areas, and sanctuary to countless tiny marine creatures. In addition, it is the foundation on which a little island, or key, begins to take shape, this buildup of sediment and debris creating a thick layer of organic peat upon which other plant species start to grow. This first tree drops more seed tubules,

mangrove trees in the Everglades National Park

which get stuck in the soft mud around the base of the parent tree and send up shoots. Soon there's an impenetrable tangle of trees and roots extravagant enough to support birdlife and other animals.

Three types predominate in the Everglades and Ten Thousand Islands: The red mangrove forms a wide band of trees on the outermost part of each island, facing the open sea. The red mangrove encircles the black mangrove, which in turn encircles the white mangrove at the highest, driest part of each mangrove island (they are the least tolerant of saltwater). The mangroves' leathery evergreen leaves fall and stain the water a tobacco-colored tannic brown, but in fact mangroves and all the species dependent upon them do much to keep the waters clean and pure.

For all these reasons, mangrove trees are protected by federal, state, and local laws. Do not injure, spindle, mutilate, or even taunt a mangrove, or face steep penalties.

---

camping is permitted in Big Cypress, allowing visitors to car camp, backpack or tent camp anywhere among the 729,000 acres with a few exceptions. There is no fee to backcountry camp in the preserve and to receive a permit you will need to visit one of the two visitor's centers. Please be aware that backcountry camping is not permitted in some areas during archery season, muzzle loading season, general gun season, and spring turkey season.

Naples Botanical Garden

To experience all the incredible plantlife of the Big Cypress Preserve in a more cultivated setting, the **Naples Botanical Garden** (4820

Bayshore Dr., 239/643-7275, 8am-2pm daily, $15 adults, $10 ages 4-14, free under age 4) is a 220-acre living botanical museum, within minutes of downtown and with 2.5 miles of walking trails. Spot gopher tortoises and bald eagles among the native plants and wildlife in the 90 acres of native preserve. Don't miss the butterfly house, history exhibitions, the wonderful lecture series, and the exceptional garden store.

Boat Tours

Cruise the Gulf and Naples Bay, wind through the Ten Thousand Islands, or idle along one of the area's many rivers on a boat tour. These are just a sampling. The *Sweet Liberty* (Naples City Dock, 880 12th Ave. S., 239/793-3525) is a 53-foot sailing catamaran available for public tours and private charters. Departing from Crayton Cove in Naples Historic District are shelling tours (9:30am-12:30pm, $40 adults, $20 ages 5-12), sightseeing tours (1:30pm-3:30pm, $30 adults, $20 ages 5-12), and two-hour sunset tours (sunset, $34 adults, $21 children). On all the cruises, the boat is usually trailed by a playful pod of dolphins, and you'll have an opportunity to see the large homes of Port Royal.

The *Lady Brett* (departing from Tin City, 1146 6th Ave. S., 239/263-4949, departure times vary, $99 over age 5) offers deep-sea fishing tours for up to 20 people, and the double-decker *Double Sunshine* (departing from Tin City, 1200 5th Ave. S., 239/263-4949, 10am, noon, 2pm, 4pm, and 1 hour before sunset daily, $39 adults, $19.50 under age 13) does sunset and sightseeing cruises aboard a 45-foot vessel equipped with restrooms. If you want to wet a line in the Ten Thousand Islands (think snook, sheepshead, redfish, snapper, and trout), **Captain Paul Luciano** (departing from the Naples City Dock, 880 12th Ave. S., 239/450-4870, 7:30am and 12:45pm daily, $100 pp) takes people on half-day bay fishing trips on a comfortable pontoon boat.

A fancier experience, the *Naples Princess* (departing from Port-O-Call Marina, 550 Port-O-Call Way, 239/649-2275, www. naplesprincesscruises.com, $16-62) has narrated lunch cruises and sunset buffet dinner cruises on a 93-foot air-conditioned luxury yacht that can accommodate 149 passengers.

ENTERTAINMENT AND EVENTS

The *Naples Daily News* (239/213-6000, www.naplesnews.com) is the best way to find out about local events and entertainment. News kiosks are pretty much everywhere.

The **Artis Naples** (5833 Pelican Bay Blvd., 239/597-1900, www.artisnaples.org, box office 10am-5pm Mon.-Fri., 10am-4pm Sat., noon-4pm Sun., prices vary), formally the Naples Philharmonic Center for the Arts, is an outstanding venue hosting 800 events a year, including world-class dance, opera, classical and popular music, and traveling Broadway musicals. The center contains a 1,425-seat main hall and a 283-seat black-box theater. The **Naples Philharmonic Orchestra** (239/597-1111) performs more than 120 concerts per year, including classics, pops, chamber orchestras, and numerous educational performances.

For professional theater, see plays and performances by the **Gulfshore Playhouse** (The Norris Center, 755 8th Ave. S., 239/261-7529, www.gulfshoreplayhouse, $20-65), the first professional theater company in Naples. Around six productions a year range from comedies to mysteries and serious dramas. The **Sugden Community Theatre** (701 5th Ave. S., 239/434-7340) is home to the 40-year-old **Naples Players,** a community theater troupe that stages 14 musicals, comedies, dramas, and children's productions annually. It also hosts a program called KidzAct, with musical theater workshops for kids.

SHOPPING

Along the Gulf Coast of Florida, Naples stands out as a top-notch shopping destination. Comparisons are often made to Beverly Hills's Rodeo Drive, but Naples has an original style and a widely diverse collection of shops.

★ 3rd Street South

Start at **3rd Street South,** with exquisite clothing and giftware stores, chic restaurants, and dozens of art galleries. It's just a couple of blocks from the beach and Naples Pier, making it easy to shop and sun all in one afternoon. Don't know where to begin? Consult the **street concierge** (1203 3rd St. S., 239/434-6533, 10am-6pm Mon.-Sat., noon-5pm Sun.), just opposite the Fleischmann Fountain in Camargo Park, for help navigating the area's storefronts.

5th Avenue South

Not far from there, **5th Avenue South**

(239/692-8436) is another huge draw. The Seminole people once sold their crafts from a stand on 5th Avenue, and before that the Calusa people used this area as a canal connecting Naples Bay with the Gulf. In 1923 the Ed Frank Garage was the first commercial building, and later the birth of the mall heralded the death of downtown.

In 1996 the Florida Main Street Program saw 5th Avenue South's dilapidated one-story storefronts replaced with sleek Mediterranean-style two- and three-story buildings with residences above. Today, 5th Avenue encompasses 12 blocks and 50 buildings, including the Bayfront and the Tin City shopping-and-dining complexes. Find a wonderful mix of shops, dining, and nightlife possibilities that keep the street busy most hours. The second Thursday of the month, don't miss the free street entertainment **Evenings on Fifth** (7pm-10pm), where you'll enjoy music and entertainment at several spots along the beautiful avenue, masterfully landscaped with banyan trees and colorful tropical plants.

Village on Venetian Bay

Equally fancy is the **Village on Venetian Bay** (4200 Gulf Shore Blvd., 239/261-6100), with a kind of Venetian canal-side vibe. You'll find lots of independent clothing boutiques, plus familiar faces like Tommy Bahama and Chico's; a couple of high-end shoe stores; a handful of restaurants, plus Ben & Jerry's; and some home interior shops.

Tin City

More overtly touristy, but fun, **Tin City** (1200 5th Ave. S., 239/262-4200, www.tin-city.com), at the eastern end of downtown, was built on the site of a 1920s clam- and oyster-processing plant. It incorporated the crusty waterfront buildings, with oodles of rustic maritime charm, into a shopping emporium (surf shop, bikini shop, and plenty of Jimmy Buffett-themed items) with a few restaurants

(Riverwalk Restaurant, Pincher's) worthy of your time. The Naples Trolley drops you right here, and it's an easy walk from 5th Avenue.

Waterside Shops

The **Waterside Shops** (5415 Tamiami Trail N., Pelican Bay, 239/598-1605, www.watersideshops.com, 10am-7pm Mon.-Sat., noon-6pm Sun.) are anchored by Saks Fifth Avenue, Nordstrom, Tiffany & Co., Gucci, Pottery Barn, Banana Republic, Barnes and Noble, and the like. It's a classic high-end mall with covered walkways and restaurants like California Pizza Kitchen.

Other Shopping Areas

Before you get shopping fatigue, let me put in a word for the boutiques along the **Dockside Boardwalk** (1100 6th Ave. S., at 11th St., 239/384-2186) and **Crayton Cove** (City Dock, 1187 8th St. S., 239/404-5014). If you need a good old-fashioned JCPenney or Sears to offset all the glitz, the **Coastland Center Mall** (1900 Tamiami Trail N., 239/262-2323), has Macy's, Dillard's, and restaurants that include Chick-fil-A, Starbucks, and the Cheesecake Factory.

FOOD

Naples takes dining seriously, with an excellent and continually evolving restaurant scene. Top chefs open up branches of their namesake kitchens, and chefs fresh out of culinary college come to cut their teeth. Competition is fierce, which means only great restaurants can stay open in Naples. Despite the abundance of choices, in high season you need to make reservations at the most popular spots.

At the beginning of May, visit the annual **Taste of Collier** (Bayfront Naples, 1221 5th Ave. S., 239/331-7371, www.tasteofcollier.com, $5 pp, free under age 10) to sample the top restaurants in the area as they showcase their best flavors in a one-day family-friendly festival.

5th Avenue South

There are a few exceptionally dense

1: 3rd Street in Naples 2: Pazzo! in Naples 3: the colorful shops of the Village on Venetian Bay concentrations of wonderful restaurants in downtown Naples; 5th Avenue has the greatest embarrassment of riches, between 9th Street and 3rd Street. The gamut is impressive, from trendy to fancy continental, covering a range of prices and ethnicities. The best are listed here from east at 9th Street (the beginning of downtown) to the west as it reaches the Gulf.

Pazzo! Cucina Italiana (853 5th Ave. S., 239/434-8494, 5:30pm-8:30pm Sun.-Thurs., 5:30pm-9pm Fri.-Sat., $15-30) presents diners with a conundrum—sit in the lovely modern dining room with its open bar and kitchen, or one of the sidewalk tables through the open French doors and watch the world stroll by? Pazzo makes a mean Bellini—champagne and peach-nectar cocktails that are the height of festivity—and lots of elegant spins on familiar Italian dishes. Worth trying are the grouper piccata and the house-made gelato.

Practically next door is one of downtown's most happening places, **Chops City Grill** (837 5th Ave. S., 239/262-4677, 6pm-9pm Sun.-Thurs., 5:30pm-9:30pm Fri.-Sat., $20-40). The menu might sound a bit schizophrenic, but it all works. Try the pan-seared black grouper served with wild mushroom risotto and a spicy rock shrimp sauce, or an order of addictive roasted candy-cane beets drizzled in oil infused with Indian River orange juice and aged balsamic vinegar. Singles: Dine at the long food bar and you won't be alone for long. Everyone's friendly, and the look of the place is hip.

A block down you'll find the other hippest waitlist-for-miles place, **Yabba Island Grill** (711 5th Ave. S., 239/262-5787, 5:30pm-8:30pm Sun.-Thurs., 5:30pm-9pm Fri.-Sat., $15-30). It's no coincidence as Pazzo, Chops, and Yabba are all owned by the same folks. Yabba has a menu that's centered on seafood and steak entrées that have an inventive Asian or island-fusion spin in an upbeat and island-inspired atmosphere.

Take your appetite to the more upscale **Vergina** (700 5th Ave. S., 239/659-7008, 8:30am-11:30pm daily, $15-30). Wonderful outdoor seating is in a sheltered plaza, and a soaring indoor space has a long inviting bar. The food is familiar Italian, with a bold caesar salad and hearty seafood pastas. They started serving breakfast recently with a perfect mix of American and Mediterranean-inspired favorites. Try classic pancakes with two eggs, maple bacon, sausage, and roasted potatoes ($18); New York strip with two eggs and roasted potatoes ($18); or the caprese omelet with fresh mozzarella, pesto, and tomatoes ($13).

The ★ **Citrus Seafood Restaurant** (455 5th Ave. S., 239/435-0408, 11:30am-10pm daily, $11-32) is an exceptional seafood restaurant with small and large plates, salads, and an excellent wine list. There is a wonderful outdoor seating area where diners can enjoy 5th Avenue. Try the crab cakes, snapper, whole hogfish, or Macadamia grouper.

There are plenty of other fine choices along 5th—walk and peer in, reading menus as you go. For ice cream, try **Regina's Ice Cream Pavilion** (824 5th Ave. S., 239/434-8181, 11:30am-10:30pm Mon.-Thurs., 11:30am-11pm Fri.-Sat., noon-10pm Sun.).

3rd Street South

Once the central business district of Old Naples, these days 3rd Street South is overrun with galleries, high-end boutiques, and antiques shops. There aren't as many restaurant choices as on 5th, but a few of Naples's absolute best restaurants line up along 3rd.

★ **Campiello Ristorante** (1177 3rd St. S., 239/435-1166, 11:30am-3pm and 5pm-10pm Sun.-Thurs., 11:30am-3pm and 5pm-11pm Fri.-Sat., $20-40) is a favorite with a healthy and fresh Cal-Ital bistro approach to the menu, but the atmosphere reminds you of power-lunch restaurants of the 1980s. Bite into a spit-roasted turkey sandwich with smoked bacon, red onion, and avocado, or sample the crab linguini with heirloom tomatoes. The food is good, and presentations are simple. The produce is fresh and well selected, and the slow-roasted meats steal the show.

A totally different vibe but equally popular is **Tommy Bahama's Restaurant and Bar**

(1220 3rd St. S., 239/643-6889, 11am-10pm daily, $15-30), the same company as the "purveyor of island lifestyles" clothing line, with upscale island cuisine—great macadamia-crusted grouper, tropical fruit cocktails—served under slowly rotating bamboo-blade fans and a palm frond-thatched roof. Tommy Bahama's also has live music most nights, so it's a good place to relax and listen to musicians performing tunes that often have island vibes.

A longtime Naples institution, **Ridgway Bar & Grill** (1300 3rd St. S., 239/262-5500, 11:30am-9:30pm Mon.-Fri., 10am-9:30pm Sat.-Sun., $15-30) is owned by Tony Ridgway, a legend in Naples, having brought one of the first restaurants using a traditional gourmet approach 30 years ago. The menu is focused on excellent seafood and steak dishes such as pan-roasted shrimp, crab cakes, pan-seared grouper and shrimp, and a delicious center-cut filet. Ridgeway also owns a small cooking school as well as **Tony's Off Third** (1300 3rd St. S., 239/262-7999, 7am-9pm daily), a gourmet deli and wine shop next door; the Ridgeway Bar and Grill's wine offerings reflect this close proximity, with more than 600 bottles on the list. The food is mostly American with a bit of French flavor.

Tin City

Tin City Waterfront Marketplace is a waterside indoor shopping center with about 40 mostly nautical-theme upscale shops and several good restaurants. The complex is on U.S. 41 at Goodlette Road. A little more upscale is the lively **Riverwalk Restaurant at Tin City** (1200 5th Ave. S., 239/263-2734, 11am-9pm Mon.-Sat., 10:30am-9pm Sun., $15-30), serving local seafood and classic American grill selections. And then there's **Pincher's Crab Shack** (1200 5th Ave. S., Suite 8, 239/434-6616, 11am-10pm daily, $10-25), a part of the southwest Florida family of restaurants as famous for their fresh-caught Gulf grouper and snapper as for their cheesy crab dip. Right across from Tin City is a casual joint called **Kelly's Fish House Dining Room**

(1302 5th Ave. S., 239/774-0494, 4:30pm-10pm daily, $15-25). It's one of the oldest restaurants around here, and where you'll find the city's best stone crabs.

Downtown and Vicinity

The rest of the area's top restaurants are spread out, although there's a dense concentration north of downtown on the Tamiami Trail (U.S. 41) between about Golden Gate Parkway and Pine Ridge Road. **Andre's Steakhouse** (2800 Tamiami Trail N., 239/263-5851, 5pm-9pm daily, $20-40) falls squarely in the luxury American steak house idiom. Try the porterhouse for four people, like something from the *Flintstones,* with a bottle from the wine list that contains 4,000 options.

If you love French food and the French way of life, visit chef Claudio Scaduto's **Cote D'Azur** (11224 Tamiami Trail N., 239/597-8867, 5pm-10pm Tues.-Sun., $18-36). It's an intimate restaurant, great for a date night, with dishes like *loup de mer Antibois* (Mediterranean sea bass) and *noisettes d'agneau peillois* (roasted spring lamb loins).

Back downtown, next to Sugden Theater, **Trulucks** (698 4th Ave. S., 239/530-3131, 5pm-9pm Sun.-Thurs., 5pm-10pm Fri.-Sat., $15-35) is part of a small Texas chain, but the seafood is great. Especially the crab, and there's lots of it: northwest Dungeness crab, Florida stone crab, and red king crab.

Hotel Restaurants

These are all upscale and expensive restaurants, suggesting reservations and dressy attire. Starting at the top, **The Grill** (Ritz-Carlton, 280 Vanderbilt Beach Rd., 239/598-6644, 6pm-10pm daily Sept. 4-June 24, $30-55), formerly Artisans in the Dining Room, features "aged prime meats, chops and fresh seafood paired with rare vintages." Nightly entertainment and a cozy fireplace are attractions.

Baleen (LaPlaya Beach & Golf Resort, 9891 Gulf Shore Dr., 239/598-5707, 7am-10pm daily, $25-40) is a favorite among visitors and locals. The dining room has wonderful indoor-outdoor seating that overlooks a perfect swath of beach and the Gulf of Mexico. The menu contains a variety of dishes: seared sea scallops, broiled lobster risotto, filet mignon with blue cheese polenta, ceviche, and lamb gnocchi.

ACCOMMODATIONS
$100-200

My favorite mid-range hotel in Naples is the ★ Lemon Tree Inn (250 9th St. S., 239/262-1414, www.lemontreeinn.com, $89-199). Most of the 35 recently remodeled rooms have four-poster beds. There's a cute little gazebo and swimming pool, surrounded by lush tropical landscaping, where breakfast is served each morning. It has an Old Florida charm married to a sophisticated Naples aesthetic and an ideal location in the heart of downtown. Just around the corner is the upscale dining and shopping district of 5th Avenue. A short walk past the galleries, boutiques, and beautiful homes will take you to the happening beach hangout surrounding the Naples Municipal Pier. There's free lemonade in the office, thirst-quenching after a long day at the nearby beach.

The Bayfront Inn on Fifth (1221 5th Ave. S., 239/649-5800, $100-300) has spacious rooms, tropical decor, a central location, and a full-service marina. Hampton Inn (2630 Northbrooke Plaza Dr., 239/596-1299, $95-175) is off I-75's exit 111, closer to Corkscrew Swamp Sanctuary.

$200-300

Naples is full of luxury hotels—the Ritz-Carlton boasts two properties in town. In the luxury price range, where to stay depends largely on your priorities. If you want an urban experience, so you can roll out of bed and be wandering the downtown shops within minutes, consider ★ The Inn on Fifth (699 5th Ave. S., 239/403-8777, www.innonfifth.com, $175-400), a boutique hotel with Mediterranean charm. The 87 rooms are beautiful, with sliding French doors to a balcony or terrace. The common space

features splashing fountains, courtyards, and nice gardens. The inn features the full-service Spa on Fifth. The club-level suites range 550-1,160 square feet and have sleek, modern furnishings. The separate building has its own check-in desk and access to a private rooftop hot tub with a sunbathing area and excellent views of 5th Avenue. Breakfast is served daily for club-level guests, as well as an assortment of fresh fruits, snacks, evening cocktails, and appetizers throughout the day. The 750-square-foot conference and event center is equipped with state-of-the-art technology.

On a residential street downtown, the Trianon Old Naples (955 7th Ave. S., 239/435-9600, www.trianonoldnaples.com, $150-400) is another small luxury hotel with a pool, a lounge, off-street parking, and complimentary continental breakfast served in the lobby (although there's no on-site restaurant, and thus no room service). The 55 spacious guest rooms and three large one-bedroom suites have fine amenities, balconies, and easy access to Tin City and 5th Avenue South.

The Naples Grande Beach Resort (475 Seagate Dr., 239/227-2182, www.waldorfastorianaples.com, $164-869) has a sweeping granite lobby leading to the Aura restaurant and bar, complete with a South Beach-style draped lounge. The resort is surrounded by 200 acres of tropical mangrove preserve, with beach access and three swimming pools. The newest additions are the Naples Grande Spa and The Catch of the Pelican seafood restaurant.

Over $300

The Bellasera Resort (221 9th St. S., 888/205-7322, www.belaseranaples.com, $250-500) features 100 luxurious studios and one- to three-bedroom suites with kitchens and spacious living and dining areas, all with bold Tuscan-style architecture and decor. It's a AAA Four Diamond award winner that's far enough removed from the bustle of 5th

1: the Lemon Tree Inn 2: The Inn on Fifth 3: the Ritz-Carlton Naples

Avenue to seem restful. A heated outdoor pool, a fitness center, the Zizi Restaurant & Lounge, a meeting space, and a business center round out the amenities.

If you love tee time, there are several golf wonderlands. The **Naples Beach Hotel & Golf Club** (851 Gulf Shore Blvd. N., 239/261-2222, www.naplesbeachhotel.com, $400-600) is a 125-acre beachfront resort with 317 guest rooms and suites, championship golf, an award-winning tennis center, a large beachside swimming pool, a fitness center and spa, a complimentary kids program, four restaurants, an open-air beach bar, and lovely boutiques. The $5 million pool-complex includes a secluded oval-shaped pool for adults.

LaPlaya Beach & Golf Resort (9891 Gulf Shore Blvd. N., 239/597-3123, $300-700) is one of the best properties in the area. The 189 spacious guest rooms and suites offer marble baths with jetted tubs, goose-down pillows, and twice-daily maid service. You have to drive three miles from the hotel, but enthusiasts say the Bob Cupp-designed course is worth it. It has a championship layout with a driving range, and 12,000-square-foot clubhouse.

Not to be outdone, the **Ritz-Carlton Naples Golf Resort** (2600 Tiburon Dr., 239/593-2000, $350-700) has received kudos from *Golf Digest* as one of the best golf resorts in North America. All 295 guest rooms look out on the sweeping vistas of the Greg Norman-designed Tiburon Golf Club. Guests can enjoy the amenities at the sister Ritz-Carlton in town.

If your aim is to have the beach within walking distance, there are several wonderful luxury hotels, including the **Edgewater Beach Hotel** (1901 Gulf Shore Blvd. N., 239/403-2000, $250-600), an intimate 126-suite boutique hotel right on the beach. Two large palm tree-lined pools are steps from the Gulf. It's a AAA Four Diamond property, with a deliciously edgy lobby restaurant, Coast, that's definitely worth a visit.

The other **Ritz-Carlton Naples** (280 Vanderbilt Beach Rd., 239/598-3300, $400-800) is a Mobil Five-Star, AAA Five Diamond resort; all 463 rooms have stunning views of the Gulf. There are seven on-site restaurants, tennis courts, a 33-treatment-room spa with a fitness center, two pools, championship golf nearby at Tiburon, and white sand as far as the eye can see.

Vacation Rentals

Reflecting the Naples demographic, most of the rental homes and condos in the area tend toward the upscale. The cost depends on the location. A large majority of rental homes are on golf courses, while the more expensive homes are the luxurious mansions in the beachfront districts. During the heat of summer you can find exceptional deals on vacation rentals. Most of the year a spectacular five-bedroom, four-bath house on the beach will run $1,000 per night, $6,000 per week; a more modest two- or three-bedroom home with a pool on a golf course $200-500 per night; and a one- or two-bedroom condo near the beach $150-400 per night. The top rental agencies in the area are **Marco Naples Vacation Rentals** (239/774-1273, www.marconaplesvacationrentals.com) and **Naples Rentals** (www.naplesrentals.com). Both have an extensive variety of homes available and exceptional websites. **Airbnb** (www.airbnb.com) allows home and condo owners to list and rent their properties to visitors through an easy-to-use online hub.

TRANSPORTATION
Car

From I-75, you can take exit 101 to Highway 84, which leads to downtown Naples for shopping or dining along 5th Avenue South or 3rd Street South or an amble along the Naples Pier. Exit 105 is best to reach Naples Zoo and Naples Municipal Airport. Exit 107 (Pine Ridge Rd.) leads directly to U.S. 41, the Tamiami Trail, and is the best exit to reach Clam Pass and Vanderbilt Beach parks and beaches. The National Audubon Society's Corkscrew Swamp Sanctuary is most easily accessed by exit 111 (Immokalee Rd.), which also takes you to North Naples.

From Miami, take U.S. 41 the whole way. The Tamiami Trail is a little slower than I-75, but it offers more sightseeing, as it has been designated a National Scenic Byway and a Florida Scenic Highway. The route takes you through the Everglades and Big Cypress National Preserve.

Air

There is a little commuter airport in Naples, the **Naples Municipal Airport** (APF, 160 Aviation Dr., 239/643-0733, www.flynaples. com), with charter jet service to Key West and other nearby destinations. Private jets constitute much of this airport's daily traffic. From the Naples Municipal Airport, there is a convenient **Naples Airport Shuttle** (239/430-4747).

Private planes can also fly into Marco Executive Airport, Immokalee Regional Airport, and Everglades Airpark in Everglades City.

Bus

Greyhound (239/774-5660) provides regular bus service to Naples, and **Collier Area Transit** (239/252-7777, www.colliercountyfl.gov) operates a network of city buses (day pass $4).

One of the most pleasant sightseeing opportunities in Naples is the **Naples Trolley** (1010 6th Ave. S., 800/592-0848, www. naplestrolleytours.com, day pass $27 adults, $13 ages 5-13, free under age 5). The narrated tour covers over 100 local points of interest and offers a nice historical overview. You can disembark whenever something captures your interest and then hop the next trolley that comes by.

Marco Island

Marco Island has lots going for it—less-expensive lodging and restaurants than Naples, gorgeous sunsets, gentle Gulf breezes, subtropical lushness, and easy access to Naples (to the north) and the Everglades National Park (to the south). Much of the island is given over to a luxury-resort paradigm, with most of the residents living in the low-rise ranch-style homes on the bridge end of the island. High-rise hotels line most of the coast, so there's a serious lack of public beach access and parking. However, the positive side is that resort and hotel beaches are much less crowded and much more private, making it a great choice for families.

Marco is a perfect base to day-trip to Naples and avoid the hustle-and-bustle and high expense. Its average annual high temperature of 85°F and average low of 65°F means it's enjoyable all year long. There are beautiful beaches; excellent golf courses; good snook, redfish, and pompano fishing; and access to hundreds of tiny wonderful islands, most

only accessible by boat. During high season, the island becomes a beach retreat for 14,000 people.

SIGHTS

History enthusiasts have a couple of small yet illuminating museums on the island. At the **Marco Island Historical Museum** (180 S. Heathwood Dr., 239/252-1440, www.themihs. info, 9am-4pm Tues.-Sat., free), the focus is on archaeological finds with an emphasis on Calusa culture. There's even a sweet life-size diorama of a Calusa household, and the grounds of the museum are beautifully landscaped with native plants and ponds.

The **Key Marco Museum** (lobby of the Board of Realtors office, Waterway Court, 9am-4pm Mon.-Fri., free) covers some of the same ground, with Calusa treasures displayed prominently. It also captures pioneer history and early island industries into the 20th century. Both museums are unstaffed, but a guided tour can be arranged by calling ahead. There are also maps at the museums for a self-guided tour of Marco Island's 13 historical markers, including the Cushing Archaeological Site from 1895, one of the most historically significant excavations in North America, where the renowned statue known as the Key Marco Cat was unearthed. It doesn't take long to zip through the tour, either by car or bike, and it's a good orientation to the island.

BEACHES
★ Tigertail Beach

Marco Island boasts a four-mile crescent of white sandy beach. Not far from the long stand of tall condominiums and resort hotels, **Tigertail Beach** (entrance at Spinnaker Dr. and Hernando Dr., 8am-sunset daily, parking $8 per day, $1.50 per hour) is pretty much all things to all people. There's a rental stand for water sports and toys, umbrellas, and chairs; volleyball nets that see heavy action; a concession stand, showers, and restrooms; and a children's play area. Out across the lagoon is little Sand Dollar Island, not long ago a sandbar. It's a perfect place for shelling and sand castle-building at low tide. The 32-acre beach park is also a birder's favorite for

shorebirds (but the nearby bird sanctuary is off-limits to visitors).

Marco South Beach

Marco South Beach (walkway access from Collier Blvd., north of Cape Marco, sunrise-sunset daily, parking $8 per day, $1.50 per hour) is a residents' beach with public access and parking. This beach has no facilities but is a good place to beachcomb for Florida sand dollars, whelks, fighting conchs, lion's paws, calico scallops, and 400 other types of sea-shells found on the island. Be sure to leave all live shells on the beach. Pets are prohibited on Marco Island beaches.

SPORTS AND RECREATION
Fishing

Island visitors and locals surf-cast for black drum and sheepshead; they take boats out in the backcountry mangrove flats to fish for tarpon, snook, and redfish; or they head into deeper water offshore for grouper, amberjack, snapper, and kingfish. A number of species in the area have game fish status and are thus more exotic and often the most sought after. This means redfish, snook, tarpon, bonefish, and sailfish are illegal to buy or sell (that's

Marco Island coastline

The Stingray Shuffle

It's not a dance, exactly. It's strictly anecdotal, but Marco Island seems to have more than its share of flat, seafloor-living stingrays. Visitors occasionally step on these creatures, their winglike fins hidden in the sandy shallows. When trod upon, a stingray flips up its tail in self-defense and delivers a nasty stinging puncture with its barb. To avoid this, drag your feet along the sandy bottom instead of stepping up and down. The "shuffle" may not look too swift, but it alerts stingrays to your approach. They hang around the shallows to catch shellfish and crustaceans, and they'd rather not waste their time stinging you.

If you are unlucky enough to be stung, clean the wound with freshwater immediately (other bacteria in seawater can infect the area). As soon as you can, soak the wound in the hottest water you can stand for up to 90 minutes to neutralize the venom. The pain can be severe, often accompanied by weakness, vomiting, headache, fainting, shortness of breath, paralysis, and collapse in people who are allergic to the venom. You may want to see a doctor, who might add insult to injury with a tetanus shot. Always report stingray injuries to the lifeguard on duty.

why you don't ever see them on restaurant menus), and many of them have low catch limits and specific seasons. For instance, in the Gulf of Mexico and the Everglades, open season (the period of time you are allowed to harvest a fish) for snook is now limited to March-April and September-November. Fish must be 28-33 inches to keep, with one snook allowed per person. If you catch a snook during December-February or May-August, the fish must be released alive. Don't wet a line until you've studied up on what you can catch, how many, and when.

To head out fishing with an expert, Marco Island, as with much of the Gulf Coast, has specialists willing to show you the way. Specializing in light tackle and fly-fishing,

Captain Gary Eichler (239/642-9779, www. doublersfishingandtours.com, $400-800) has a number of boats to choose from and lots of experience in the area. He does individual private charters (no split charters) with six passengers at most.

Captain Bill Walsh takes visitors out with his **Dawn Patrol** (239/394-0608, www. dawnpatrolcharters.com, half-day $325 for 4 people), known for fishing the nearshore artificial reefs and ledges. Dawn Patrol specializes in family trips and will tailor a fishing trip to include a mix of shelling, fishing, and sightseeing so even the nonanglers in your group are entertained.

Specializing in fly-fishing and light tackle angling is **Naples Fishing Charters** (1500 Danford, Naples, 239/450-9230, www. naplesfishingcharters.org, $400-800). Captain Mike Ward used to run the Everglades Angler Fly Shop. He has lots of experience in the area and is Orvis endorsed.

If you want to go it alone, **Marco River Marina** (951 Bald Eagle Dr., 239/394-2502) rents out the largest array of boats on the island, including center consoles, deck boats (half-day $200, full-day $300), and pontoons. Boats at **Walker's Hideaway Marina** (705 E. Elkcam Circle, 239/394-9333, www. walkersmarine.com) all come equipped with a bimini (sun top), a plastic cooler stocked with ice and drinks, a VHF radio, Coast Guard equipment, and an easy-to-navigate color chart of the local waters. They're endlessly patient with beginners. The Marco River Marina is also the debarkation point for *Key West Express* (239/463-5733, 8:30am daily Jan.-May, 8:30am Thurs.-Mon. June-Dec., round-trip $155 adults, $145 over age 61, $102 ages 5-12, $72 under age 5), a three-hour cruise to Key West; this is an affordable way to explore Key West without flying.

Golf

Guidebooks all point out that Naples has more golf courses per capita than anywhere else. Many of these are in East Naples, and many are private. On Marco Island there are several notable private courses—**Hideaway Beach Club** (250 Beach Dr. S., 239/394-5555), **The Island Country Club** (500 Nassau Rd., 239/394-6661), and others—but only a couple of public courses. The Marco Island Marriott's **Rookery at Marco** (3433 Club Center Blvd., 239/389-6600), designed by Joe Lee, is an 18-hole, par-72, Scottish links-style course built on 240 acres of rolling terrain and featuring several mounds in play around the greens. The signature hole is No. 16, a 165-yard par-3, requiring a tee shot over water to a peninsula green. Swing tune-ups for experienced players as well as beginners' lessons are available at the Marriott's Faldo Institute located at The Rookery at Marco.

Despite its name, the **Marco Shores Country Club** (1450 Mainsail Dr., Naples, 239/394-2581) is in Naples. The course has long, wide fairways and well-maintained greens blended seamlessly into the native mangroves and waterways of the Ten Thousand Islands. With four separate tees, Marco Shores accommodates all skill levels.

★ Boat Tour to Calusa Shell Mounds

The Calusa people lived on the coast and along the inner waterways in this area. They were tall and fierce and regularly battled with neighboring nations. They did not farm but rather fished and hunted for their sustenance from the bays, rivers, and Gulf, so bountiful that as many as 50,000 Calusas may have been living here. They controlled much of the southwest coast of Florida, and many other nations justifiably feared their aggression. Spanish settlers ran them off or killed them, both actively and passively with the introduction of smallpox and other diseases, starting soon after the Spanish arrived in the 1500s. By the 1700s the Calusas were essentially wiped out, with the remaining handful of people purportedly migrating to Cuba when the Spanish turned Florida over to the British in 1763.

The impact of the Calusas on the area and their unique way of life are still

Chickees

What is a chickee, you ask? You'll see the term a lot here. It's a Seminole word for an open, handmade structure of cypress poles and a roof of palm fronds. Historically there was an art to erecting chickees, with the cypress stripped in a process called "draw knife" and the fronds nailed in a particular pattern to keep out the area's heavy rains. A chickee is now more broadly defined as any open-air structure, but usually those in which boozing and general merriment occur.

apparent today. They built homes on stilts with palmetto-leaf roofs and no walls and fashioned nets from palm-tree fiber to catch mullet, catfish, and pinfish. Their most ingenious work was with shells. Shellfish were a staple in the Calusa diet, and once the meat was removed, the shells were used to make jewelry, utensils, spearheads, other tools, and vast heaps upon which other things could be built. Little mangrove keys, uninhabitable on their own, became homes or sacred places with the addition of a few thousand carefully piled shells.

These shell mounds are literally the building blocks for Marco Island and many of the Ten Thousand Islands. Spend a day exploring the remnants of Calusa mounds on an ecotour with **Florida Saltwater Adventures** (239/595-7495, 2.5-hour trip $380 for up to 6 people). Captain Alex Saputo takes small groups on his 24-foot boat, weaving in and out of the Ten Thousand Islands while pointing out wildlife and explaining in detail the horticultural and local history. He's extremely knowledgeable about the Calusa and Seminole peoples and history, and his enthusiasm is infectious as you tramp around a shell mound, crouching to see a fat whelk shell once used as a hammerhead or other tool. On the way back, watch for dolphins leaping in the wake of the boat—they're either playing or drafting off the boat's speed (even dolphin experts disagree about why they do it)—but it's about as close as you'll get to dolphins outside of Sea World.

Ecotour

The *Dolphin Explorer* (Marco River Marina, 951 Bald Eagle Dr., Marco Island, 239/642-6899, www.dolphin-study.com, departures 9am and 1am daily, $64 adults, $45 ages 3-12, $59 over age 59, $10 under age 3) is a 30-foot catamaran that takes up to 28 passengers out for a laid-back dolphin-watching cruise that is actually part of the Ten Thousand Islands Dolphin Project, an ongoing scientific dolphin research study, the only one in the country that involves the public on a daily basis. Passengers work with a naturalist on board to identify the resident dolphin population and catalog their activities. Dolphins are identified by their dorsal fins, as unique as human fingerprints, and if a passenger spots a dolphin not already cataloged in the study, he or she gets to name it. Cruises include a stop at a barrier island for shelling and beach walking.

SHOPPING

Marco doesn't have as many upscale shops as Naples to the north, but it certainly has more shopping than you'll find in Everglades City to the south. There are a few concentrated areas: The **Esplanade** (740-760 Collier Blvd. N., 239/394-6333) is a newer development with clothing and home decor stores, a few restaurants, and a nice day spa. There's a collection of shops at the **Marco Town Center Mall** (1017 Collier Blvd. N., at Bald Eagle Dr., 239/394-7549). Adjacent to the Olde Marco Island Inn at the northern tip of the island, the **Shops of Olde Marco** (100 Palm St., 239/475-3466) complex has a couple of boutiques, gourmet food shops, and the inn's spa and fitness center.

For the big kahuna of shopping, drive north, just off the island, to **Naples Outlet Center** (6060 Collier Blvd., 239/259-9033, 10am-8pm Mon.-Sat., 11am-6pm Sun.), with more than 40 stores, most of them big-name designer clothes and shoes, books, and housewares at up to 70 percent off retail prices.

FOOD

All the open hours listed below are for peak season. Dining during the off-season, it's best to call for hours.

Casual

Originally called the Snook Hole for the wealth of snook you could catch right off the dock, the **Snook Inn** (1215 Bald Eagle Dr., 239/394-3313, 11am-10pm daily, $10-25) was first a sprawling casual restaurant that catered to construction workers in the 1960s. Right on the Marco River, the Snook Inn is a fun indoor-outdoor joint with live music and long lines. Locals and visitors seem to come for the grouper and the vast salad bar with a neat old-fashioned pickle barrel. The garden courtyard is a great locale to get creamy seafood chowder or tackle a pile of peel-and-eat shrimp (if you aren't wild about seafood, try the island chicken with grilled pineapple rings). There's docking available for more than 20 boats near the chickee.

Most of the island's other restaurants are lined up along Collier Boulevard. You'll see locals tucking into a thick-crust pizza at **Joey's Pizzeria and Pasta House** (257 Collier Blvd. N., 239/389-2433, 11am-10pm daily, $10-15).

Browse the range of possibilities at the Marco Town Center Mall: **Crazy Flamingo** (1035 Collier Blvd. N., 239/642-9600, 11am-2am daily, $10-20) is a lively raw bar with good fish entrées, and **Doreen's Cup of Joe** (267 Collier Blvd., 239/394-2600, 7:30am-2pm daily, $7-15) is a favorite for breakfast and lunch. They have embraced the healthy farm-to-table concept and offer locally produced sausage, coffee, and dairy. Their orange juice is made from fresh-squeezed Florida oranges, and they have an exceptional variety of breakfast options such as pancakes, waffles, French toast, omelets, oatmeal, and yogurt. At lunch it's salads, sandwiches, and burgers.

Upscale

Marek's Collier House (1121 Bald Eagle Dr., 239/642-9948, 5pm-10pm Tues.-Sat., $20-35) gets the nod from local publications nearly every year for upscale and romantic continental dining, partly due to the setting—the restaurant is nestled in Captain Bill Collier's beautiful historic home—and partly because of chef-owner Peter Marek's tasteful take on rich seafood dishes. Marek is a triple gold medalist at the World Culinary Olympics. Try the filet mignon in cabernet reduction or the shrimp pasta alfredo with shaved parmesan.

The **Bistro Soleil** (100 Palm St., 239/389-0981, 5pm-10pm daily, $25-35) restaurant at the Olde Marco Island Inn is another expensive favorite in the area for a nice bottle of wine and perfectly prepared steak, seafood, and more. There are five individual dining rooms, each with a slightly different feel, so try to wander through each before settling on a table (there's also an upper dining deck that looks out over the inn's gardens).

Marco Prime Steaks and Seafood (599 S. Collier Blvd., 239/389-2333, 4:30pm-10pm Sun.-Thurs., 4:30-10:30 Fri.-Sat., $20-35) serves a range of steaks and seafood cooked to perfection, paired with an extensive wine list. Try the steak, charred salmon, or herb-crusted tuna.

Dining with a Twist

Dine one of several ways aboard the 74-foot *Marco Island Princess* (departs from the marina, 951 Bald Eagle Dr., 239/642-5415, www.themarcoislandprincess.com, $39-52), sister ship to the *Naples Princess*. There's the Sea Breeze lunch buffet cruise, a sunset hors d'oeuvres cruise, or a sunset dinner cruise. Head out on the luxury yacht as it glides along the scenic Marco River into the Gulf of Mexico with leaping dolphins in hot pursuit. The ship itself is beautiful, as is the scenery, either by day or with sunset casting its warm glow. The food is pretty good, but the cash bar is expensive. The ship gets busy for Valentine's Day, Mother's Day, and New Year's Eve, and is often rented out for private parties, so reserve early.

Marco boasts another unusual dining experience. An evening at **Marco Movie Theater** (599 S. Collier Blvd., Suite 103, 239/642-1111, $8-15) is the oldest date-night one-two punch in the books: dinner and a movie, but at the same time. The small family-owned four-screen theater shows first-run movies (there's always at least one family-appropriate pick) and serves food and alcoholic beverages. A sampling of the menu includes Greek salad, good sweet-potato fries, several tortilla-wrapped sandwiches, pizzas, banana splits, beer, wine, cocktails, and, of course, popcorn.

ACCOMMODATIONS
Under $100

There's not much on Marco Island for the budget traveler, but a couple of minutes away is Goodland, a little town adjacent to Marco Island that boasts a few hundred residents, mostly fisherfolk, and a bunch of down-home bars. There has been a shift toward more upscale development in recent years, but you can still find casual and reasonably priced accommodations at the **Pink House Motel** (310 Pear Tree Ave., Goodland, 239/394-1313, $59-99), a historic family-owned waterfront motel with boat docking, efficiency kitchens, laundry facilities, and the Marker 7 Marina and Tackle Shop.

$100-200

On Marco Island, the **Boat House Motel** (1180 Edington Place, 239/642-2400, www.theboathousemotel.com, $120-290) is a little more glamorous—two stories with a gazebo and boat docks—and a little pricier than Pink House Motel, but it's still a straightforward low-rise motel.

Marco Island Lakeside Inn (155 1st Ave., 800/729-0216, $120-300) has 10 one-bedroom and 2 two-bedroom units and 7 studio efficiencies located on Marco Lake, one mile from the beach. There is a pool area with a thatched-roof gazebo and gas grill overlooking the lake, an Italian steak house, and a full bar on-site.

Over $300

If you're going to stay on Marco Island, you

might as well pony up the dough and stay at one of the big three. Three beachfront resorts dominate the most coveted piece of shoreline, each with lots of amenities, good restaurants on-site, and a broad price range to accommodate different budgets.

The Marco Island Marriott Beach Resort, Golf Club, and Spa (400 Collier Blvd. S., 239/394-2511, www.marcoislandmarriott.com, $250-1,000) may be best suited to a romantic golf-and-pampering getaway, with more than 700 rooms and lavish resort activities and facilities, the 24,000-square-foot Balinese-themed spa, a tiki pool, and the Rookery at Marco—the resort's wonderful golf course.

The Marco Beach Ocean Resort (480 Collier Blvd. S., 239/393-1400, www.marcoresort.com, $250-1,000) opened in 2001 with 98 one- and two-bedroom suites, a spa, upscale Italian restaurants, and a stunning rooftop swimming pool with a panoramic view of the Gulf.

The 25-year-old Hilton Marco Island Beach Resort (560 S. Collier Blvd., 239/394-5000, www.marcoisland.hilton.com, $200-1,000) is a luxury resort that consistently wins four-diamond status for its large guest rooms with Gulf-view private balconies, lighted Har-Tru tennis courts, vast amoeba-shaped pool, and other amenities. An incredible luxury spa opened in 2008 with spacious massage and relaxation rooms in a stylish and bold Greco-Roman theme.

Right out the back door of all three hotels, you can rent aqua trikes and personal watercraft with Marco Island Ski & Watersports (239/642-3377), which also offers parasailing, shelling trips, WaveRunner tours, sunset cruises, and dolphin-watching tours on the Gulf.

For a more historic, small-inn experience, try Olde Marco Island Inn & Suites (100 Palm St., 239/394-3131, www.oldemarcoinnandsuites.com, $250-600), a 116-year-old Victorian in the historic district. It features one- and two-bedroom suites with roomy screened lanais. There are six luxurious penthouses and a much-lauded restaurant. It's a convenient location near beaches, shopping, and golf, and guests enjoy complimentary use of the inn's 38-foot catamaran.

Vacation Rentals

There are hundreds of vacation rental homes and condominiums on Marco Island. Many of these rent only by the week, especially in high season, and most work out to less than $150 per night. Several rental companies have websites to peruse properties: Coldwell Banker (239/394-6121, www.marcoislandvacations.net) seems to rent largely in high-rise condos, Holiday Homes of Marco Island (239/389-9940, www.marco-island.com) represents a number of single-family homes, and Prudential Florida Realty (239/642-5400, www.prudentialfloridarealty.com) offers a wide range, from fancy high-rise condos to individual homes on a golf course.

TRANSPORTATION

To get to Marco Island, take exit 101 from I-75, then follow Collier Boulevard (Hwy. 951) west to the island, crossing Jolley Bridge on the way. From Naples, the drive is 18 miles, which usually takes about 30 minutes. From Everglades City, drive north on County Road 29, then take U.S. 41 north to San Marco Road (County Rd. 92), and drive to Marco Island. The 30-mile drive will take you about 40 minutes.

Everglades City

Everglades City is a locus of ecotourism, with canoe tours, airboat rides, fishing guides, and other nature-based businesses capitalizing on the mystery and majesty of the million acres of mangrove jungle just to the south. It's significantly more rustic than swanky Naples to the north—there are no Ritz-Carltons, tuxedo-clad waiters, or turndown service, but Everglades City is a must for adventure seekers.

SIGHTS

Everglades National Park

Everglades National Park (305/242-7700, www.nps.gov; Gulf Coast Visitor Center, 815 Oyster Bar Lane, 239/695-3311, 8am-4:30pm daily mid-Nov.-mid-Apr., 9am-4:30pm mid-Apr.-mid-Nov., no entrance fee on this side of the park) is the third-largest park in the continental United States and has been designated a World Heritage Site, an International Biosphere Reserve, and a Wetland of International Importance. It's the only subtropical preserve in North America containing both temperate and tropical plant communities. It's also the only everglade in the world.

The Seminole people called the park "grassy water," because it is essentially a wide shallow river with no current, falls, or rapids that flows slowly southward along the subtle slope of the land, eventually meeting open water in Florida Bay 100 miles away. This river flows along sawgrass prairies, mangrove and cypress swamps, pinelands, and hardwood hammocks. Everywhere there are wading birds, alligators, and dense and exotic tropical plantlife.

Still, I don't think any of this conveys what's so cool. A couple of days of paddling Everglades National Park will have you gliding past 12-foot gators, beautiful orchids and epiphytes (air plants) dotting the swamp with color, and birds engaged in a strenuous call-and-response—it's an exceptionally wild and beautiful park, best explored by kayak or canoe, that is well worth extensive exploration.

The Everglades region is mild and pleasant December-April, rarely reaching freezing temperatures, and mostly without a drop of rain. Summers are hot and humid, with

Everglades City

0   300 yds

0   300 m

To Stan's Idle Hour Seafood Restaurant and Goodland

DUPONT ST

EVERGLADES CITY BRIDGE

EVERGLADES ISLAND AIRBOAT TOURS

IVEY HOUSE INN BED AND BREAKFAST

EVERGLADES ECO ADVENTURES

CAMELLIA STREET GRILL

CAMELLIA ST

COLLIER AVE

TRIAD SEAFOOD MARKET AND CAFE

W SCHOOL DR

COPELAND AVE

EVERGLADES HISTORICAL BED AND BREAKFAST

ROD AND GUN CLUB

BROADWAY

MUSEUM OF THE EVERGLADES

Lake Placid

JASMINE ST

SHORTER AVE

COPELAND AVE

PLANTATION PWY

Gulf of Mexico

To Everglades National Park Gulf Coast Visitors Center

To Havana Cafe, Chokoloskee and Turner River

© MOON.COM

One Day in the Everglades

a heron in the Everglades

For this trip, you'll want strong bug spray, plenty of water, sunglasses, shoes you don't mind getting wet or muddy, comfortable clothes (preferably quick-dry lightweight pants and a long-sleeved shirt), and a hat to protect you from the sun.

MORNING

Start the morning off with breakfast at **Havana Café of the Everglades** (191 Smallwood Dr., Chokoloskee, 239/695-2214, www.myhavanacafe.com, 7am-3pm daily, call for summer hours, $6-15), and then take a sunrise paddle through **Everglades National Park.** It's a wonderful place to observe birds, alligators, and other native wildlife. Then do something a bit more thrilling and take an airboat ride with **Everglades Island Airboat Tours** (239/695-2591, www.airboatusa.com, 1-hour ride $50). The tours are offered on a first-come, first-served basis. Be cautious around wildlife when adventuring in the Everglades, and do not feed the alligators!

AFTERNOON

Drive to Turner River Road in the **Big Cypress National Preserve** (3 miles east of the Big Cypress Welcome Center, U.S. 41) and spend the rest of the afternoon spotting wildlife and enjoying the scenery. Return to Everglades City and have lunch at **Triad Seafood Market and Cafe** (401 School Dr., 239/695-0722, 10:30am-5pm daily, call for summer hours, $7-15).

EVENING

Stay the night at the **Ivey House Inn Bed and Breakfast** (107 Camellia St., 239/695-3299, $100-200), a relaxing inn built in 2001 that's beautifully landscaped, and has an excellent screened pool and waterfall area. Have dinner at the waterfront **Rod and Gun Club Restaurant** (200 Broadway, 239/695-2101, 11am-2:30pm and 5pm-9:30pm Mon.-Sat., $12-25, no credit cards).

temperatures hovering around 90°F and humidity at a fairly consistent steamy 90 percent. As with most places along the Gulf Coast, there are tremendous afternoon thunderstorms in summer.

CANOEING AND KAYAKING

Everglades National Park is America's only subtropical wilderness, a third of it given over to marine areas and shallow estuaries easily paddled by rookie or seasoned kayakers or canoers (in my experience, a kayak seems easier to navigate through these sometimes-tight quarters). The mangroves form canopied tunnels through the swamp, through which you navigate in a peculiar way: Often the flat of your paddle is used to gently push off from the tangle of mangrove roots when it's too tight to actually dip the paddle into the water. In this way you pole through the tight spots, the nose of your craft sometimes hitching up in the roots, necessitating backward paddling to disengage.

Mosquitoes, surprisingly, are not a big problem until summer, when you probably don't want to be paddling anyway due to the heat and humidity. Still, you'll need bug spray, water, sunglasses, a flotation device (required by law), shoes you don't mind getting wet or muddy, comfortable clothes, a hat—and a plan.

Check at the **Gulf Coast Visitor Center** (815 Oyster Bar Lane, 239/695-3311, 8am-4:30pm daily mid-Nov.-mid-Apr., 9am-4:30pm mid-Apr.-mid-Nov.) for maps and directions. You can rent canoes downstairs from the visitors center at **Everglades National Park Boat Tours** (239/695-2591, $37 adults, $19 ages 5-12, free under age 5). It's fairly daunting to head off by yourself the first day, so the visitors center and Everglades National Park Boat Tours both offer guided tours on a first-come, first-served basis ($40 adults, $20 ages 5-12, free under 4).

After that, if you want to push off on your own, put in at the canoe ramp next to the visitors center or the ramp next to Outdoor Resorts on Chokoloskee Island. As everyone will tell you: Don't overestimate your abilities, and time your trip with the tides (a falling tide flows toward the Gulf of Mexico; a rising tide flows toward the visitors center). If you want to pick up a nautical chart, No. 11430 covers the Chokoloskee Bay area. There are also detailed descriptions to be had at the visitors center and other local shops of how to traverse the **Wilderness Waterway,** a 99-mile canoe trail that winds from Everglades City over to the Flamingo Visitor Center at the southeast entrance to the national park. It's about an eight-day excursion, to be undertaken only after plenty of diligent preparation.

Collier County has completed Phase I of the **Paradise Coast Blueway,** a system of GPS-marked paddling trails in the Ten Thousand Islands region that will eventually extend north to Bonita Springs. There is a main trail route from Everglades City to Goodland, as well as six day-trip routes ranging 2-10 hours of paddling. If you only have time to do one section of the trail, I highly recommend reserving a campsite at Rabbit Key through the Everglades National Park visitors center and camping out on the sandy, palm-lined, private beach for the night. The paddling trip embarks from the Outdoor Resorts center on Chokoloskee Island and is about five miles to Rabbit Key. It can easily take an entire day, depending on your skill level, strength, and the speed and weight of your kayak or canoe. It is especially important to check the tides when paddling in the Ten Thousand Islands region of the Everglades, as they are dramatic and can leave you stranded in water too shallow to paddle in, with nowhere to camp. You should also bring a GPS receiver and use the GPS waypoints posted on the Paradise Coast Blueway website for ease of navigation, as it is easy to get lost among the literally thousands of mangrove islands that look extremely similar. Visit www.paradisecoastblueway.com for more information and detailed downloadable route maps.

★ EVERGLADES ECO ADVENTURES

Everglades Rentals & Eco Adventures (Ivey House Inn, 107 Camellia St., 239/695-4666, Nov.-Apr., $89-99) offers spectacular three- and four-hour tours led by naturalist guides who have a clear passion for the abundant natural beauty of the area. They offer paddling tours in the morning, afternoon, and at sunset. One trip launches at the old Turner River Canal, quickly passing into narrow mangrove tunnels, out into lagoons, past sawgrass prairies, and into Turner Lake. The company offers a range of specialty tours for small groups, from photography workshops to night paddles. It also rents equipment if you prefer to explore the area on your own.

★ EVERGLADES ISLAND AIRBOAT TOURS

Lots of airboat companies offer competent tours with nature-focused narration, but the most historically significant is **Everglades Island Airboat Tours** (929 Dupont St., just before the Everglades City Bridge, 239/695-2333, 30-minute, 1-hour, and 1.5-hour tours $30-50).

Loren "Totch" Brown, author of *Totch: A Life in the Everglades* (a must-read if you are interested in the crusty taciturn folks who've eked a living out of the Everglades over the past 100 years), grew up on an island near Chokoloskee during the Depression. He fought in World War II before going home to work as a pompano fisher and stone crabber (legally) and an alligator poacher and marijuana smuggler (illegally). You can see a picture of the local legend in Smallwood Store, a tiny museum on Chokoloskee Island (150 acres made entirely of shells by the Seminoles), or catch a glimpse of him in the 1955 film *Wind Across the Everglades* with Christopher Plummer.

Totch died in 1996, but his tour company comprises his family members and a number of fourth- and fifth-generation Everglades residents who will take you out either in the backcountry or open water to Totch's Island to see his rustic family cottage on a tiny mangrove island. Along the way, you'll be trailed by pelicans, catch glimpses of manatees lumbering along the brackish shallows beneath you, and see big alligators, wild pigs, ospreys, and incredible plantlife.

OTHER BOAT TOURS

You've seen these embodiments of Newton's Third Law—those tall boats propelled by air whooshing through their giant fans. With no outboard motor or rudder for propulsion and control, these boats can scoot through extreme shallows on their flat bottoms, perfect for swamp exploration. It's an Everglades cliché, and a loud one, but fun. They are not allowed in Everglades National Park, but they scoot around the edges in the Ten Thousand Islands.

One successful airboat company is **Everglades City Airboat Tours** (907 Dupont St., 239/695-2400, www.evergladescity-airboattours.com, $42 adults, $22 under age 11). The tour groups are small, and the tour is one hour of meandering through the mangrove forest backcountry and a sawgrass wetland. Tours depart at 9am, 10am, 11am, 12:30pm, 1:30pm, 2:45pm, 4pm, and 5pm.

My favorite place to take a thrilling airboat ride is five miles south of Everglades City at **Wooten's Everglades Airboat Tours** (32330 Tamiami Trail E., Ochopee, 239/695-2781, www.wootenseverglades.com, 9am-4:30pm daily, $32.50 adults, $20 ages 4-10, $7 under age 4, $9 animal sanctuary and alligator show, free with airboat ride), also known as Wooten's. It's a little farther afield but the airboat rides explore a diverse section of wetland while the narrators and captains deliver an overview of the history of the Everglades with an overtly environmental and libertarian message. You may also want to take one of the 30-minute swamp tours on the swamp buggy ($27.50 adults, $20 ages 4-10, $7 under age 4). You'll travel through spooky cypress swamp and spot alligators as well as North American crocodiles (the Everglades is the only place

you'll find these guys in the United States), deer, snakes, and tons of birds. Wooten's small zoo with native Florida wildlife gives you an opportunity to get as close to a Florida panther as you will ever want to be.

A quieter ride can be found on the **Everglades National Park Boat Tour** (815 Oyster Bar Lane, at the ranger station on the causeway between Everglades City and Chokoloskee Island, 239/695-2591, every 30 minutes 9:30am-4:30pm, $37 adults, $19 ages 5-12), a wonderful 1.5-hour motorboat tour departing from the Gulf Coast Visitor Center. The cruise is slower, following a loop through a dizzying number of the Ten Thousand Islands. Along the way, tour-goers are likely to see manatees, frisky bottlenose dolphins, bald eagles, and loads of smirking alligators.

Everglades Area Tours (238 Mamie St., Chokoloskee Island, 239/695-3633, www.evergladesareatours.com, from $59) provides year-round, half-day, guided kayak ecotours assisted by a motorboat shuttle that carries kayaks and up to six passengers. Aptly named the Yak Attack, the tour strategy allows you to quickly get to the remotest and most beautiful paddling areas. All tours are guided by experienced naturalists. Motorboat ecotours, sea kayaking and camping trips, backcountry charter boat and kayak fishing trips, bicycle tours, and aerial tours in the winter season are also offered.

Museums

The dire economic climate after the Civil War prompted some robust families to move to the southwest Florida frontier. They came, cleared the land on little islands (many of them now named after the family inhabiting them), built rough-hewn cabins of pine and cypress, and hunted, fished, and farmed. Stoically, they made do in the wilderness. Then Ted Smallwood opened Chokoloskee Island's first general store in 1906. There, settlers and the remaining Seminole people would bring in their hides, furs, and produce in exchange for sugar, coffee, ammunition, and other essentials.

Today, **Smallwood Store** (360 Mamie St., Chokoloskee, 239/695-2989, 10am-5pm daily, $4), three miles south of Everglades City, is preserved as a 1920s-era general store with its original structure and its last stock of merchandise. The small museum provides stirring insight into the hard lives of the pioneers who settled at the edge of this vast wilderness, and the isolation born of living on tiny remote mangrove islands. The store was placed on the National Register of Historic Places in 1974 and reopened as a museum by Ted Smallwood's granddaughter in 1989.

Just off the circle in the center of Everglades City, the little **Museum of the Everglades** (105 W. Broadway, 239/695-0008, 9am-4pm Mon.-Sat., $2) is in the town's Old Laundry, a building that dates to the 1920s when Everglades City was Barron Collier's company town during the construction of the Tamiami Trail. The focus is more on the area's Seminole people and other indigenous nations before the settlers arrived. The building is of note for the history buff—listed on the National Register of Historic Places, it's the only unaltered original building in town. Don't just visit the museum, though; make sure to get a sense of the area's unique history by chatting with the locals or gliding through the mangroves in a canoe. If it's a rainy day, put aside an hour or two for the museum.

Big Cypress Gallery

East of Everglades City, famous black-and-white landscape photographer Clyde Butcher has a photo gallery worth the drive. **Clyde Butcher's Big Cypress Gallery** (52338 Tamiami Trail, Ochopee, 239/695-2428, 10am-5pm daily) features Butcher's own work on local themes—he is to Big Cypress and the Everglades what Ansel Adams was to Yosemite—as well as the work of other nature-inspired photographers. Around Labor Day, the gallery sponsors a huge party with a naturalist-led swamp walk, music, and more.

1: Wooten's Everglades Airboat Tours **2:** kayaking through a mangrove forest

FESTIVALS AND EVENTS

The annual **Everglades Seafood Festival** (239/695-2277, www.evergladesseafoodfestival.org) in Everglades City draws thousands in early February with the promise of stone crabs (Everglades City is the world's capital, with more than 400,000 pounds of crab claws harvested Oct. 15-May 15), fish chowder, gator nuggets, fresh Gulf shrimp, grouper, and fish of all local vintage, along with live country music, rides, and arts and crafts.

SHOPPING

There's a squat nondescript building in the middle of nothing, near where the road ends in the Everglades. You can buy ice, bait, gas, and a small assortment of groceries here. It's called the Chokoloskee Mall. I'm sure it's a joke the locals play on travelers, but that sums up the shopping options in this edge-of-the-wilderness area. Head back up into Naples if the retail bug bites.

FOOD

Dining in Everglades City is uniformly casual, but with no fast food and few international restaurants. The open hours listed reflect peak season. During the off-season, it's best to call for hours.

Several spots are outstanding for the food and the convivial ambience. ★ **Havana Café of the Everglades** (191 Smallwood Dr., Chokoloskee, 239/695-2214, www.myhavanacafe.com, 7am-3pm daily, call for summer hours, $6-15) has the best breakfast and lunch in town, specializing in Cuban and American food with a bent toward fresh seafood and classic sweets. It's the best spot to grab an omelet and a cup of authentic Cuban-style *café con leche* as well as delicious Cuban sandwiches, fish platters, peel-and-eat shrimp, and key lime pie. The best seats are out on the back patio, surrounded by hibiscus and other tropical plants. The place is as charming and upbeat as they come in the Everglades, and the owners are extremely friendly. Even if you're not hungry, stop in for a cup of Cuban coffee and some friendly banter with owners Carlos and Dulce Valdez.

The **Camellia Street Grill** (202 Camellia St., 239/695-2003, 9am-5pm Mon.-Tues., 11am-9pm Wed.-Sat., $10-20) is a fun and colorful place on the water with Florida and fishing memorabilia decor and nice outdoor seating on the back deck. They have seafood platters and stone crabs, fish tacos, salads, and other usual choices. It's a casual place, and the seafood is very fresh. Try the peanut butter pie for desert.

At the **Rod and Gun Club Restaurant** (200 Broadway, 239/695-2101, 11am-2:30pm and 5pm-9:30pm Mon.-Sat., $12-25, no credit cards), set your sights on the conch fritters, gator nuggets, hush puppies, or blue crab claws. At **Triad Seafood Market and Cafe** (401 School Dr., 239/695-0722, 10:30am-5pm daily, call for summer hours, $7-15), try the crab cake sandwiches, grouper sandwiches, fried shrimp platters, and homemade peanut butter pie. If you've worked up an appetite after a day of Everglades adventure, order up the all-you-can-eat stone crab.

Anyplace that's known for a dance called the Buzzard Lope and that throws the biggest annual party around in honor of mullet is worth some investigation. ★ **Stan's Idle Hour Seafood Restaurant** (221 Goodland Dr. W., Goodland, 239/394-3041, 11am-10pm Tues.-Sat., 11am-7pm Sun., $14-25) is on the tiny island of Goodland, between Marco Island and Everglades City, connected by causeways. Sunday afternoons are the time to go to Stan's, when a fair percentage of the island's 200 or so residents show up for live music, pitchers of beer, peel-and-eat shrimp, and fried oysters. (For fisherfolk, Stan's also has a "you caught 'em, we cook 'em" policy.) The weekend after the Super Bowl every January brings the Mullet Festival to Stan's, with lots of rowdy fun and festivities to enjoy.

1: house built in 1920, now the Museum of the Everglades 2: Smallwood Store, built in 1917

ACCOMMODATIONS
$100-200

There are three wonderful places to stay in Everglades City, all significant pieces of local history. The white clapboard **Rod and Gun Club** (200 Broadway, 239/695-2101, www.evergladesrodandgun.com, $95-140, no credit cards) was built in 1850 on the first homestead site in Everglades City. A long, low lodge, it contains 17 comfortable rooms, a waterfront restaurant, and dock space. It has hosted U.S. presidents and celebrities needing to get away from it all.

The ★ **Ivey House Inn Bed and Breakfast** (107 Camellia St., 239/695-3299, $100-200) has three lodging options: the historic Ivey House, a large rustic house with seven rooms; the Ivey House cottage, a two-bedroom, fully equipped bungalow; and the Inn, a 17-room lodge with a beautifully landscaped pool area. A delicious breakfast is served in the morning. The inn earned Florida Green Lodge certification, and they offer eco-tours and boat rentals.

Just outside Everglades City and closer to the expansive Fakahatchee Strand Preserve and Big Cypress National Preserve is the **Port of the Islands Everglades Adventure Resort** (2500 Tamiami Trail E., 844/884-8567, $120-150). This canal-side hotel with a marina offers 32 one-bedroom and studio suites, some fully equipped with kitchens. Sit out on your private balcony or patio and enjoy the waterfront views of the adjacent marina, where boaters can dock.

Camping

Camping opportunities are abundant in this area, but you may want to stay indoors during the hot wet season, June-October, and in April-May, when temperatures can climb above 90°F. The best time to camp the Everglades is November-February, with the park and surrounding wilderness getting the most visitors during the week between Christmas and New Year's. If you're looking for tolerable weather, fewer bugs, and fewer people, visit mid-October-mid-November or the last week in January, before the spring breakers arrive.

Camping in **Everglades National Park,** you'll need to visit the Gulf Coast Visitor Center for an overnight pass. Two campgrounds are accessible from the Homestead entrance of the park: The **Long Pine Key Campground,** six miles from the Ernest Coe Visitor Center in Everglades City, and the **Flamingo Campground,** near the Flamingo Visitor

Rod and Gun Club

Center near the shores of Flamingo Bay. Both accommodate RV and tent campers and offer a limited number of group sites; both cost $20 per site and are first come, first served.

The nearby **Big Cypress National Preserve** also offers many campgrounds that are generally closed during the wet season, June-October. More information on these sites and a listing of open campgrounds can be found through the **Oasis Visitor Center** (239/695-1201) or at the Big Cypress website (www.nps.gov/bicy).

RV campers have an appealing option at **Outdoor Resorts of America** (entrance to Chokoloskee Island, 239/695-3788, $69-89).

Tent camping is prohibited, but the RV campsites are pleasant, offering canoe rentals ($35 per day), 16-foot skiff rentals ($150 per day), showers, laundry, and a small convenience store. It may be the quickest way from under the covers to steering through the magical Ten Thousand Islands. Pets are welcome.

TRANSPORTATION

To reach Everglades City from Naples, continue south on U.S. 41. The 36-mile drive takes about 50 minutes. From Miami, take I-95 north for 2 miles, and then take I-75 north for 117 miles to exit 105. The 125-mile drive takes about 2.5 hours.

Information and Services

Naples and environs are located in the **eastern time zone.**

VISITOR INFORMATION

For visitor information in Naples, stop in at the **Chamber of Commerce Visitors & Information Center** (2390 Tamiami Trail N., Naples, 239/262-6141, 10am-4pm Mon.-Fri.) to pick up brochures, maps (there's a good city one that's worth the couple of bucks it costs), and lots of coupons.

Marco Island events and information can be found in a copy of *Marco Island Sun Times* (239/394-4050, www.marconews.com), the widely distributed free community paper.

For Everglades City information, call the **Everglades Area Chamber of Commerce** (239/695-3941, www.evergladeschamber.org, 9am-4pm daily), or visit it at the junction of U.S. 41 and Highway 29, where there's a little gift shop and lots of good books on the area.

POLICE AND EMERGENCIES

In an emergency, call 911. For a nonemergency police need, call or visit the **Naples Police Department** (355 Riverside Circle, 239/213-4844, www.naplesgov.com/police). The **Marco Island Police Department** can be reached at 239/389-5050, and the sheriff in **Everglades City** can be reached at 239/695-2301.

In the event of a medical emergency, go to the **Naples Community Hospital** (350 7th Ave. N., 239/624-5000) or **Marco Urgent Care Center** (40 S. Heathwood Dr., Marco Island, 239/624-8540, 8am-7:30pm daily). To fill a prescription there are nine CVS pharmacies in the Naples area, with one near downtown (294 9th St. S., 239/261-8610).

Fort Myers, Sanibel, and Captiva

The Fort Meyers area and nearby barrier islands

are known for their long stretches of beach with spectacular sand, birds, sunsets, and shells. Lightning whelks are abundant in the area, and shell hunters are seen searching for perfect conchs along the shoreline.

The city of Fort Myers, in large measure due to its most famous residents, Thomas Edison and Henry Ford, is culturally rich, with attractions spread along the banks of the Caloosahatchee River. It is the oldest and largest city in southwest Florida and is dense with history.

Nearby, the barrier islands offer tropical island getaways. The best-known of this group are Sanibel and Captiva, siblings that bear a family resemblance but have vastly different personalities. Both cater to mostly wealthy winter visitors, but Sanibel is more physically and financially

Highlights

Look for ★ to find recommended sights, activities, dining, and lodging.

★ **Edison & Ford Winter Estates:** Tour the fascinating estates of lifelong friends Thomas Edison, considered one of the most inventive men who ever lived, and Henry Ford, founder of the Ford Motor Company. (page 76).

★ **Lovers Key State Park:** With 2.5 miles of beautiful beach and 5 miles of bike trails, this park is a great place for recreation, shelling, and bird-watching (page 81).

★ **Bailey-Matthews Shell Museum:** Take a crash course in Neptune's treasures, a must if you want to know which species you're unearthing along the shoreline (page 89).

★ **J. N. "Ding" Darling National Wildlife Refuge:** Occupying more than half of Sanibel Island, this refuge is home to a tremendous variety of birdlife (page 91).

★ **Palm Island:** Spend a soul-refreshing day or two on this unbridged barrier island paradise (page 106).

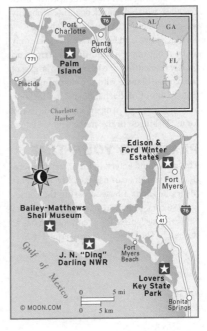

accessible, with miles of bike paths and low-rise independently owned inns and smaller hotels. A tremendous wildlife refuge takes up half of the island, with white-sand beaches on the Gulf and picturesque mangrove forests on the eastern side. Captiva, to the north and connected by a causeway, is the playground of the even more affluent. The many homes on Captiva are tucked down driveways shielded by lush foliage. There's less to do on Captiva, fewer places to stay, and fewer amenities. But that's how people on Captiva like it.

Each of the other barrier islands has its own character. Fort Myers Beach is on the long strip of coast-hugging land known as Estero Island, the closest thing this area has to a spring break-type beach, with affordable motels and crowded family-friendly beaches. Gasparilla Island calls itself the tarpon capital and has hosted presidents and a wide array of fish-seeking celebrities. Its town of Boca Grande is worth the quick boat ride or slightly longer car ride on the causeway. Cabbage Key, North Captiva, and Useppa are accessible only by boat but make a beautiful day trip. And mostly residential Pine Island is the largest of the barrier islands, with the charming maritime towns of Matlacha, Bokeelia, Pineland, and St. James City. Anglers know Pine Island for its "Fishingest Bridge in the United States."

PLANNING YOUR TIME

This area could entertain for a week or more. Budget travelers can use Fort Myers or Fort Myers Beach as a base, crossing the causeway ($6 cars, $2 motorcycles, free bicycles) to Sanibel and Captiva for a rejuvenating day at the beach. The Edison and Ford estates in Fort Myers will occupy much of a day, as will the J. N. "Ding" Darling National Wildlife Refuge on Sanibel. The rest of the area's attractions are more fleetingly entertaining, although the beach never gets old. Families can spend time at the kids water park and attractions north in Cape Coral; history buffs can occupy themselves at one of several Calusa museums; and outdoors enthusiasts can choose fishing, canoeing, sailing, or all of the above. The Great Calusa Blueway Paddling Trail is a truly remarkable newly charted route for beginning or advanced paddlers—well worth a half day's exploration even for the most timid.

The **Calusa Blueway Paddling Festival** (www.fortmyers-sanibel.com, late Oct.-early Nov.) is nine days of festivities, including competitive canoe and kayak races, a kayak fishing tournament, paddling clinics, and other activities along the Great Calusa Blueway.

Fall is beautiful here, while summers are extremely hot and humid. In winter, it's cheaper to visit in the first two weeks of December. Rates increase for high season during the third week of December, and the large crowds arrive in February-March. In early December, you'll find lots of accommodations and nominal traffic, which can be frustrating on Sanibel and Captiva in March.

Lee County is along southwest Florida's Gulf Coast between Naples and Sarasota. The biggest north-south driving routes are I-75 and U.S. 41. East-west major arteries include Alligator Alley (I-75) and U.S. 41 (where it jogs east at around Naples). By air, the area is served by **Southwest Florida International Airport** (RSW, 11000 Terminal Access Rd., Fort Myers, 239/590-4800, www.flylcpa.com).

Previous: the ferry to Cabbage Key and surrounding islands; statue of Thomas Edison at Edison & Ford Winter Estates; birdwatching at the J. N. "Ding" Darling National Wildlife Refuge

75

Fort Myers, Sanibel, and Captiva

FORT MYERS, SANIBEL, AND CAPTIVA

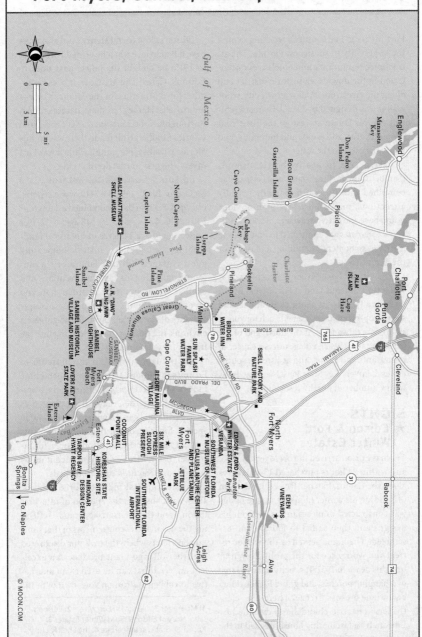

© MOON.COM

Fort Myers

Fort Myers is Lee County's working center, the largest city in southwest Florida. The attractions, restaurants, and hotels are concentrated in the downtown historic district and along the riverfront. A downtown city renovation was designed by New Urbanist architect Andrés Duany to restore the riverfront shopping area, add ponds and fountains, and increase access to the water.

Easy access to nearby barrier islands (Sanibel, Captiva, Pine Island, and Gasparilla), combined with its wealth of family-friendly attractions, makes Fort Myers an obvious home base for active travelers. Several full-service marinas are connected to hotels along the river, so boaters can pull up and dock for the night.

The city of Fort Myers is beachless, but you'll find sun and sand at Fort Myers Beach on Estero Island—its gentle slope and lack of steep drop-offs make it a safer beach for young swimmers or waders. At the north end of the island, a casual beach village offers a cluster of restaurants and shops, and at Estero's southern end, Lovers Key State Park is a huge draw, with a number of nearby resort hotels.

SIGHTS
★ Edison & Ford Winter Estates

Thomas Edison arrived in Fort Myers in 1885, and within 24 hours purchased 13-plus acres along the Caloosahatchee River with the aim of building his winter home. Seminole Lodge was constructed in pieces in Maine from his designs and then sailed to Florida and assembled. The home served as the winter retreat and workplace for the prolific inventor until his death in 1931. It's encircled with large overhanging porches, and grand French doors encourage a cross-breeze. There are "electroliers" (electric chandeliers) designed by Edison. It's a fascinating house, deeded to the city for $1 by Edison's widow, Mina.

Edison's close friend Henry Ford also must have fallen in love when he visited Fort Myers in 1915; he bought the house next door to Edison's. Called The Mangoes, it became another top destination for the country's elite—industrialist Harvey Firestone, naturalist John Burroughs, Nobel laureate Alexis Carrel, and Charles Lindbergh all made their way to this Florida paradise. For quite a while it was Fort Myers's biggest tourist destination.

Edison & Ford Winter Estates (2350 McGregor Blvd., 239/334-7419, www.efwefla. org, 9am-5:30pm daily, combined estates tour $30 adults, $25 ages 13-19, $18 ages 6-12, free under age 6) are 14 acres of botanical landscaping, the two titans' historic homes and guest cottages, Edison's laboratory, a museum containing his famous inventions and exhibits, a museum store, a garden shop, and an outdoor café. It's worth at least a couple of hours of wandering through the gorgeous environs, but the real draw is looking into the lives of these fascinating men.

See the laboratory and the museum of Edison's inventions and artifacts, spend time in Ford's garage, then walk through the tropical botanical garden that Edison planted as an experimental garden with more than 1,000 species, focusing on the byproducts of plants (rubber for his friend Firestone's tires, for instance). Later, Mina Edison prettied it up by adding roses, orchids, and bromeliads.

In the painstakingly restored houses, 1929 was chosen as the "period of interpretation," and the interiors accurately reflecting the decor and accoutrements of that time. Edison's lab is where the inventor discovered that the solidago plant produces an excellent material that can be used as an alternative to rubber. It's fun on your own with the

1: McGregor Boulevard in Fort Myers **2:** Edison's laboratory at Edison & Ford Winter Estates **3:** Koreshan State Historical Site **4:** the Shell Factory & Nature Park

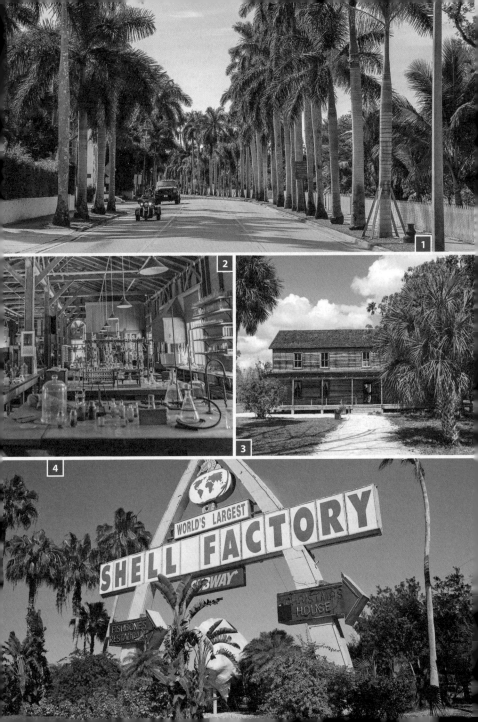

electronic audio tour, but the staff-led tours give the place context and depth. A combined **tour of the estates** (9am-5:30pm daily, included with admission) has the last tour leaving promptly at 4pm. **Botanical tours** (10:30am Wed., $40 adults, $25 ages 13-19, $15 ages 6-12, free under age 6) are also offered.

You can dispel Edison myths (alas, the lightbulbs burning in the estate are not Edison's originals), hear funny stories (Henry Ford imprudently stuffed the seats of his first Model T with local Spanish moss, which prompted the first automotive recall when little chiggers started crawling out and biting drivers on the butts), or just learn a little about the quirks of these American legends (Edison hated paparazzi, so he disembarked from the train before the station and walked the rest of the way).

The very young may be underwhelmed by all the memorabilia, but everybody feels a sense of awe when navigating the huge banyan tree out front. Its circumference spans more than 400 feet, making it one of the largest in the country, a gift to Thomas Edison from Harvey Firestone.

McGregor Boulevard

Fort Myers is sometimes called the "City of Palms": Edison and Ford's estates are poised at the edge of **McGregor Boulevard**, which is lined on both sides by 60-foot-tall royal palms. The original 200 trees, from Cuba, were gifts from Thomas Edison to the city. The idea caught on, and now more than 2,000 palms flank the stately roadside. Drive the length of the 15-mile boulevard, and the city's nickname seems fairly apt.

Museums

Southwest Florida Museum of History (2031 Jackson St., 239/321-7430, www. fortmyers-sanibel.com, 10am-5pm Tues.-Sat., $9.50 adults, $8.50 seniors, $5 students) features the history of the Calusa and Seminole people, as well as this area's Spanish explorers, and more broadly the history of Fort Myers. Set in a restored Atlantic Coastline railroad depot, built in 1924, the museum houses photographs and memorabilia; there's an 84-foot-long Pullman railcar built in 1929 and a replica of a late 1800s Cracker house. A changing exhibit lends a different flavor to the museum every few months. The museum also runs 90-minute architectural and historical downtown Fort Myers **walking tours** (10am Wed. and Sat., $12, reservations required).

Koreshan State Historical Site

Hands-down winner of Weirdest Attraction in the Area prize is the **Koreshan State Historical Site** (3800 Corkscrew Rd., Estero, 239/992-0311, 8am-5pm, $5 per car with 2-8 passengers, $4 per car with one passenger, $2 pedestrians or bicyclists, $32.70 camping, canoe rentals $5-7 per hour). It commemorates an eccentric religious sect begun by Dr. Cyrus Teed in 1894 after he had a spiritual "great illumination." It seems he and his followers believed the world is a hollow globe, with humankind residing on the inner surface, gazing into the universe below. The Koreshan followers (at its peak there were 250) gave their commune to the state on the condition it would be maintained as a historic site in perpetuity. Now the site is a compound of buildings and a theater, but visitors also avail themselves of the park's fishing, camping, nature study, and picnicking. There's a boat ramp and canoes for rent, and guided walks and campfire programs are offered seasonally.

Family-Friendly Attractions

Cape Coral, north of Fort Myers, isn't among the area's biggest draws for adults. As soon as children get a say, however, you may find yourself driving north with regularity. On a hot day, navigate to **Sun Splash Family Waterpark** (400 Santa Barbara Blvd., 239/574-0557, www.sunsplashwaterpark. com, 10am-5pm Fri.-Sun. mid-Mar., 10am-5pm daily late Mar. and late May-early Aug., 10am-5pm Sat.-Sun. Apr.-late May and late Aug.-late Sept., $20 adults, $18 seniors and ages 2-12), on the shore of Lake Kennedy. It's not huge, but there are two tall water flume

Excursion to Key West

Something to think about: If you have an extra day, why not go to Key West? Explore the country's southernmost city just for the day. There are high-speed shuttles from Fort Myers, a welcome alternative to driving (7 hours) or flying. *Key West Express* (1200 Main St., 239/463-5733, $155 adults, $145 seniors, $92 ages 5-12, $60 under age 5) departs from Fort Myers; look for coupons in local papers. The company operates the 140-foot *Atlanticat* catamaran, the 155-foot *Big Cat* catamaran, and the 170-foot *Key West Express* catamaran. The ferry zips to Key West in 3.5 hours.

Most seating on the boat is in contoured airplane-like chairs, but there are also plush couches with tables. Although the floor-to-ceiling windows provide plenty of entertainment (and there's a full outdoor deck upstairs), there are six plasma-screen TVs showing movies, sports, and more. The *Key West Express* catamaran features two enclosed cabins, a sundeck, satellite TV, slot machines, and a full galley and bar. The ships depart Fort Myers Beach at 8:30am, arriving at Key West at noon; depart Key West at 6pm, arriving at Fort Myers Beach at 9:30pm. That gives you five hours to explore the town. Alternatively, find a hotel or inn, stay overnight, and come back on the next day's ferry for no additional fare. This tiny 3-by-5-mile island, 100 miles from the coast, has the only living coral reef in the United States, not to mention great restaurants and nightlife.

rides, a big family pool, a tot playground, a "river" tube ride, a café, and a super-fast ride called the Electric Slide, which is an enclosed tube in which you twist and turn at high speed. Not far away is **Mike Greenwell's Family Fun Park** (35 NE Pine Island Rd., Cape Coral, 239/574-4386, 10am-10pm Sun.-Thurs., 10am-11pm Fri.-Sat., miniature golf $7.50-9.50, batting cages $2 for 24 pitches, plus $1 equipment rental, go-karts $5-7.50). It fills in the activity gaps with miniature golf, batting cages, four go-kart tracks, a Ferris wheel, an arcade, and a fish-feeding dock that's much more fun than it sounds.

In downtown Fort Myers, another bad-weather delight for little kids is the **Imaginarium Hands-On Museum** (2000 Cranford Ave., 239/321-7420, www.imaginariumfortmyers.com, 10am-5pm Tues.-Sat., noon-5pm Sun., $14 adults, $12 seniors, $10 ages 3-12, free under age 3), a calm hands-on museum in which kids can fly and be free. A hurricane simulator, a fossil dig, a miniature TV weather studio—it's hard not to get engrossed. There's also an aquarium, with cool moray eels and a lively coral reef tank.

Bigger kids have similar options, with science and nature centers more suited to school-age kids and adults. The **Calusa Nature Center & Planetarium** (3450 Ortiz Ave.,

239/275-3435, www.calusanature.com, museum and trail 10am-4pm Mon.-Sat., 11am-4pm Sun., $10 adults, $5 ages 3-12, free under age 3) enables people to learn about southwest Florida's natural history. Nature trails on boardwalks run through pine flatwoods and cypress wetlands, on which you'll pass a Seminole village replica, a live bobcat, and a native birds-of-prey aviary for permanently injured birds. Inside the nature center are live animals and exhibits about their habitats. The best parts of the center are the regularly scheduled guided walks and animal lectures on snakes, gators, and Florida's endangered species. The center also has a planetarium, in which you can learn about the Hubble Telescope and the night sky or just chill out while watching a laser light show.

The kind of Old Florida tourist draw people get nostalgic for, the **Shell Factory & Nature Park** (2787 Tamiami Trail N., North Fort Myers, 239/995-2141, www.shellfactory.com, free admission, miniature golf $5 adults, $4 children and seniors, boat rides $5, zip line $8.50, trampolines $3) has had a something-for-everyone approach since the 1950s. There's a lot of kitschy shell-themed merchandise to check out while kids get into the miniature golf, bumper boats, batting cages, and a video arcade. Supposedly it has the world's largest collection of rare shells and coral, but the glass-blowing artisans are more entertaining to watch; there's also a funny little History of Glass Museum on-site. Outdoors is the nature park ($13 adults, $10 seniors, $8 ages 4-12, free under age 4) with a petting zoo (camels, llamas, donkeys, potbellied pigs, goats), trails, and a botanical garden. This is the kind of place where you have to give in and consume a batter-dipped hot dog followed by a pound of fudge.

After the fudge, get the blood flowing at Fort Myers's **Skatium** (2250 Broadway, 239/321-7509, www.cityftmyers.com, public skating 8pm-9:50pm Fri., 1pm-2:50pm and 7pm-8:50pm Sat., noon-1:50pm Sun., closed Sun. summer, $7, skate rentals $3), a 72,000-square-foot facility with an ice-skating rink, an in-line rink, a laser tag arena, and a video arcade. Most of the time, the rink is used for youth hockey and figure skating.

BEACHES

Fort Myers Beach is actually on the island of Estero, connected to Fort Myers by a causeway. There are several worthwhile beaches here. The 17-acre **Bowditch Point Regional Park** (50 Estero Blvd., 239/765-6794, parking $2 per hour) fronts the Gulf and the bay at the northern tip of Estero Island, with a boardwalk to a beach with beautiful views of nearby barrier islands. Ten boat slips accommodate boats up to 28 feet for day use, and a paddle craft launch provides access to the Great Calusa Blueway Paddling Trail. Parking is available behind the bathhouse, with nice showers and changing rooms. Just south on the Gulf side, **Lynn Hall Memorial Park** (950 Estero Blvd., 239/765-6794, parking $2 per hour) is a great family beach and teen hangout. There's also a fishing pier here, frequented by opportunistic pelicans. If you happen to hook a pelican or other bird while fishing, reel the bird in slowly, cover its head with a towel to calm it, cut the line close to the hook and remove all monofilament from wings and body, then call **Clinic for the Rehabilitation**

Fort Myers Beach

Ferry to Key West

Bodwitch Point Park

ESTERO BLVD

San Carlos Island

SAN CARLOS BLVD

To Cape Coral and Fort Myers

MAIN ST

EMILY LN

Lynn Hall Memorial Park

MATANZAS INN

CRESCENT ST

FISHING PIER

KEY WEST EXSPRESS

BEACH PIERSIDE GRILL

VIRGINIA AVE

DIAMONDHEAD BEACH RESORT

Matanzas Pass

ISLAND PANCAKE HOUSE

LOVERS LN

Matanzas Pass Preserve

ESTERO BLVD

WILLIAMS DR

DAKOTA AVE

SANDPIEPER GULF RESORT

CHARLEY'S BOATHOUSE

FLAMINGO ST

OUTRIGGER BEACH RESORT

CURLEW ST

GULL WING BEACH RESORT

EGRET ST

ALBATROSS ST

POINTE ESTERO BEACH RESORT

BAY BEACH LN

ESTERO BLVD

0   1mi

0   1km

© MOON.COM

To LOVERS KEY STATE PARK

of Wildlife (CROW, 239/472-3644, www. crowclinic.org), a local nonprofit bird rescue organization.

★ Lovers Key State Park

Lovers Key State Park (8700 Estero Blvd., Fort Myers Beach, 239/463-4588, 8am-sunset daily, $8 per car up to 8 people, $4 per car single occupancy and motorcycles, $2 pedestrians and bicyclists) occupies four small barrier islands (Black Island, Long Key, Inner Key, and Lovers Key) between Fort Myers Beach and Bonita Beach to the south. The park contains a 2.5-mile stretch of beautiful beach and 5 miles of bike trails, including the Black Island Trail through a maritime hammock. Bike, canoe, and kayak rentals are available on-site. There are excellent picnic facilities at the New Lovers Key Bayside area on Estero Boulevard, and free tram service to the beach (9am-5pm daily).

In addition to roseate spoonbills, snowy egrets, and American kestrels, birders will see active osprey nests and a couple of bald eagle nests. The park offers two-hour paddling **sunset ecotours** (239/765-7788, $60-85) Friday and Saturday nights, and there is a **full moon tour** ($60-85) offered once or twice a month depending on weather and tides.

SPORTS AND RECREATION
Six Mile Cypress Slough Preserve

The **Six Mile Cypress Slough Preserve** (7751 Penzance Crossing, 239/533-7550, www. leegov.com, sunrise-sunset daily, parking $1 per hour, maximum $5) is a fabulous wild spot in south Fort Myers, easily accessible to those on the way to or from the airport. You'd never know you were in a county of half a million people. There are ongoing free guided **nature walks** (9:30am and 1:30pm daily January-March) along a 1.5-mile fully accessible boardwalk trail through a wooded wetland, as well as monthly nature programs in which children and adults learn to identify animal tracks, evening moon walks, summer camps for kids, and wilderness exploration camps for teens.

Manatee-Watching

Spend a little time on the Orange and Caloosahatchee Rivers and chances are you'll see a West Indian manatee. Take a guided kayak tour with **Gaea Guides** (239/694-5513, www.gaeaguides.com, $40-95) and the odds get even better that you'll see these mammals, related biologically to the elephant and, unlikely though it may seem, the aardvark. The narrated ecotour provides insight into the life of the area's most famous species, as well as information about how they are threatened by outboard motors and habitat destruction. Manatees seem to congregate in the Orange River in the winter, basking in waters warmed by the outflow of the nearby power plant. This is a good family adventure.

Manatee Park (10901 Hwy. 80, North Fort Myers, 239/690-5030, 7am-sunset daily, parking $2 per hour Dec.-Apr., $1 per hour May-Nov., maximum $5, kayak rentals $15 per hour), 1.5 miles east of I-75 has three observation decks for viewing and hydrophones so you can listen in (I don't speak manatee, but even scientists are unsure how they make these chirps, whistles, and squeaks). A cow and her calf are especially talkative, vocalizing back and forth. The park rents kayaks in winter and on summer weekends, with kayak clinics (2nd Sat. of the month) and free guided walks through the native plant habitats (9am Sat.).

Golf

The Fort Myers area has 100 public and semi-private golf courses, the egalitarian nature of which makes the city proud; the city itself maintains two professionally designed golf courses. **Fort Myers Country Club** (3591 McGregor Blvd., 239/321-7488, public, 18 holes, 6,414 yards, par 71, course rating 70.5, slope 118, greens fee $25-70) was designed by the great Donald Ross and opened in 1917, making it one of the oldest courses on the Gulf Coast. It hosts the pro-am Coors

Open tournament every year in January and is only a mile from downtown. **Eastwood Golf Course** (4600 Bruce Herd Lane, 239/321-7485, public, 18 holes, 6,772 yards, par 72, course rating 73.3, slope 130, greens fee $30-70) includes 84 bunkers, 54 tee grounds, and a driving range. Golfers will also enjoy the $2 million clubhouse.

Spring Training

When the regular season just isn't enough, Boston Red Sox fans can take in a **Boston Red Sox Spring Training** (JetBlue Park, 11500 Fenway South Dr., 866/800-1275, www.mlb.com, $10-46) game at the $77.9 million ballpark, a near exact replica of the classic Fenway Park in Boston, complete with the famed Green Monster in the outfield, the triangle, Pesky's pole, and the lone red seat that marks the spot of the longest home run in the history of Fenway. This outfield wall has seats carved into the middle and a net to protect fans from deep fly balls. The stadium also has a roof that shades spectators from the Florida sun. The ballpark is quickly becoming a favorite of Grapefruit League fans. Spring training games are at 1:05pm or 7:05pm daily in March.

Minnesota Twins Spring Training (CenturyLink Sports Complex, 14400 Six Mile Cypress Pkwy., 239/768-4210, www.fortmyers.miracle.milb.com, $16-18) is at the Lee County Sports Complex, recognized as one of baseball's top-five spring training facilities. Games are at 1:05pm daily during March, and in April, fans can watch the Miracle League, a minor-league affiliate of the Minnesota Twins and member of the Florida State League.

ENTERTAINMENT AND EVENTS

Music and Theater

The **Barbara B. Mann Performing Arts Hall** (Edison College, 13350 FSW Pkwy.,

1: a great white egret and American osprey in Lovers Key State Park 2: Six Mile Cypress Slough Preserve

239/481-4849, www.bbmannpah.com) is the center of arts activity for Fort Myers. The full-size fully equipped stage hosts traveling Broadway musicals, popular music, and **Southwest Florida Symphony** (8290 College Pkwy., 239/418-1500, www.swflso.org) concerts in classical and pops series. Its chamber orchestra series takes place in Schein Hall at BIG Arts on Sanibel Island.

The **Florida Repertory Theatre** (Arcade Theater, 2268 Bay St., 239/332-4488, www.floridarep.org) is a 21-year-old ensemble-based company with a year-round season. Split between musicals, comedies, and serious dramas, the professional repertory's season features nine productions, staged in a restored 1908 Victorian movie house.

Broadway musicals and family-friendly comedies are the mainstay at **Broadway Palm Dinner Theatre** (1380 Colonial Blvd., 239/278-4422, www.broadwaypalm.com), which has a main stage as well as a more intimate black-box theater where Off Broadway Palm stages smaller-scale comedies and musical revues as well as children's theater. Some of the performers are local, and they occasionally bring in talent from farther afield. Performances are accompanied by cocktails, a salad bar, and a buffet.

Visual Arts

Lee County isn't the visual arts smorgasbord of Naples to the south, but there are several nice galleries and the local arts center, the **Alliance for the Arts** (10091 McGregor Blvd., 239/939-2787, www.artinlee.org, 9am-5pm Mon.-Fri., 9am-1pm Sat., free). On a 10-acre campus, the organization contains the Frizzell Cultural Center, with galleries, classrooms, a 175-seat indoor theater, and an outdoor amphitheater. The adjacent Charles Edwards Building houses local artists and arts groups. Local, regional, and national art and crafts are displayed in the public galleries, and the theaters host live performances and festivals throughout the year. Locals use the facility for adult and youth art classes of all kinds, from glass fusing to acrylics.

The densest concentration of crafts and fine arts is on the main drag of Matlacha on Pine Island. Many of the galleries are in little houses painted in a variety of sunset colors. Leoma Lovegrove's work is on display at **Lovegrove Gallery & Gardens** (4637 Pine Island Rd., 239/938-5655, call for hours), and you'll find the metal sculptures of Peggy McTeague next door at **Wild Child Art Gallery** (4625 Pine Island Rd., 239/283-6006, 10am-5pm Tues.-Sun.). A dozen other whimsical galleries are within walking distance of the Matlacha drawbridge. Tour these small galleries on **Art Night** (2nd Fri. of the month Nov.-Apr.), with the artists on hand to discuss their work.

SHOPPING

Downtown Fort Myers is the city's entertainment district, but east of **Centennial Park** is a strip of nice shops, galleries, and cafés perfect for exploring on a walk. Strictly a driving route, the **Tamiami Trail** (U.S. 41) is lined with the basic businesses that cater to locals. You'll find chain restaurants of all stripes along the busy road.

Serious shoppers head to **Sanibel Outlets** (20350 Summerlin Rd., 239/454-1974), with more than 60 shops stocking deeply discounted clothing, housewares, and gifts. It's nothing you haven't seen before, including Polo Ralph Lauren, Under Armour, Gap, Coach, Guess, Calvin Klein, Brook Brothers, and Banana Republic. A more pleasant shopping experience, capitalizing on the area's glorious weather, is the **Bell Tower Shops** (13499 U.S. 41 SE, 239/489-1221), an outdoor mall anchored by Bed Bath and Beyond and The Fresh Market, with the usual upscale chains (Chico's, Ulta Beauty) and a 20-screen movie theater.

Edison Mall (4125 Cleveland Ave., 239/939-5464) is more a workhorse mall serving the local community, with Macy's, Dillard's, JCPenney, Sears, and lots of little mall stores. It's the biggest mall in southwest Florida. **Fleamaster's** (4135 Martin Luther King Blvd., 239/334-7001, www.fleamall.com, 9am-5pm Fri.-Sun. fall-spring, 9am-3pm Fri., 9am-5pm Sat.-Sun. summer) is a serious hoot: a vast 400,000-square-foot indoor flea market with 900 vendors, perfect for rainy-day exploration. From hardware to bath soap, this place sells some of everything.

The **Miromar Design Center** (10800 Corkscrew Rd., Estero, 239/390-5111, www.miromardesigncenter.com) is an interior design resource for fine furniture, accessories, fabrics, wall coverings, lighting, kitchen and bath products, flooring, and antiques. More than 80 internationally known showrooms (Ralph Lauren Home, Flexform, Poggenpohl, and Casa Italia, for example) anchor the three-story center.

Another newcomer in Estero, **Coconut Point** (23106 Fashion Dr., at U.S. 41 and Coconut Rd., 239/992-9966, www.simon.com) is an open Main Street-style shopping destination with Mediterranean architecture. Find an Apple Store, Dillard's, GNC, Chico's, White House/Black Market, Pacsun, Hollywood Theatres, and restaurants like Starbucks, Ruth's Chris Steakhouse, California Pizza Kitchen, and Panera Bread.

Gulf Coast Town Center (9903 Gulf Coast Main Center Dr., 239/267-5107, www.gulfcoasttowncenter.com) is another new shopping center with some of the usual suspects, but its calling card is the hugely buff **Bass Pro Shops Outdoor World** (www.basspro.com), a 75,000-square-foot retail center that includes the Islamorada Fish Company Restaurant and a boat showroom along with outdoor gear, clothing, and accessories for hiking, backpacking, wildlife-viewing, camping, outdoor cooking, and hooking those bass. Kids will be entertained by the indoor aquariums and water features stocked with native fish species.

FOOD

Fort Myers is awash in chains. You have to look a little to find the unique independent gems.

Breakfast

For traditional American breakfast, **Mel's Diner** (4820 Cleveland Ave., 239/275-7850, 6:30am-10pm Mon.-Thurs., 6:30am-10:30pm Fri.-Sat., 6:30am-9pm Sun., $8-12) has all the diner staples. Mel's biscuits and sausage gravy will give you the get-up-and-go for a day at the beach, and kids love it here. It's a regional chain. A delicious short stack of banana nut pancakes can be had for an affordable price at **The Island's Pancake House** (Seagrapes Plaza, 2801 Estero Blvd., Fort Myers Beach, 239/233-8188, 6am-2pm daily, $5-10), along with a wide variety of essential pre-kayaking breakfast foods. Fort Myers residents swear by the hangover special at **Oasis Restaurant** (2260 Martin Luther King Jr. Blvd., 239/334-1566, 7am-3pm Mon.-Fri., 8am-2pm Sat.-Sun., $8-12) of three fluffy eggs enfolding cheese, sausage, and sautéed veggies. It serves breakfast all day—very casual—and is near the Edison and Ford estates.

Casual

At the Bell Tower shopping center, stop at **Blue Pointe Oyster Bar & Seafood Grill** (13499 S. Cleveland Ave., 239/433-0634, www.bluepointerestaurant.com, 11:30am-10pm Mon.-Thurs., 11:30am-11pm Fri.-Sat., noon-9pm Sun., $15-35), a New England-style fish restaurant with excellent grilled swordfish and Florida black grouper, a nice crab cake, and slightly pricey oysters on the half shell.

Also at the Bell Tower, **Bistro 41** (13499 S. Cleveland Ave., 239/466-4141, 11:30am-9pm Mon.-Thurs., 11:30am-9:30pm Fri.-Sat., 11am-8pm Sun., $15-35) is a local business favorite, upscale with an American seafood-and-steaks menu. Beware the daily specials, which can run close to $40. Otherwise it's a pleasant, something-for-everyone place with a nice outdoor patio.

On Fort Myers Beach on Estero Island, lots of casual beachfront restaurants make great use of the location and purvey mostly seafood-centric cuisine. **Matanzas Inn Restaurant** (416 Crescent St., 239/463-3838, 11am-10pm daily, $15-25) has a great deck and a good fried grouper plate. Make sure to check out the daily frozen drink special. Next to the pier, **Beach Pierside Grill** (1000 Estero Blvd., 239/765-7800, 11am-11pm daily, $12-20) is more family-friendly, featuring ribs, fried seafood platters, and the fat beach burger.

Fine Dining

A favorite fancy restaurant in Fort Myers is ★ **Veranda** (2122 2nd St., 239/332-2065, 11am-9pm Mon.-Fri., 5:30pm-9pm Sat., $25-35), set in two stately 100-year-old homes joined by publishing heir Peter Pulitzer in the 1970s for his buddy Fingers O'Bannon, who ran the restaurant. The menu at this happening place is traditional but with contemporary touches, meaning pan-seared local grouper with wilted spinach, New York steak covered in gorgonzola, and artichoke fritters stuffed with blue crab.

The Coconut Point Mall in Estero has a number of upscale eateries, including the ubiquitous **Ruth's Chris Steakhouse** (23151 Village Shops Way, Suite 101, 239/948-8888, 4:30pm-10pm Mon.-Sat., 4:30pm-9pm Sun., $15-30)—worth a visit if you're at the mall anyway. Otherwise, check out a selection from the huge salad bar and then the slow-roasted prime rib at **Charley's Boat House Grill** (6241 Estero Blvd., Fort Myers Beach, 239/765-4700, 5pm-9:30pm daily, $15-30).

One of my personal favorites for seafood, located in the Bonita Springs Hyatt Regency Coconut Point Resort & Spa, is ★ **Tarpon Bay** (5001 Coconut Rd., Bonita Springs, 239/390-4295, 5:30pm-10pm daily, brunch 10:30am-2:30pm Sun., $15-35). Start with a sampler of the ceviche, or order a platter of oysters on ice. Don't miss out on the decadent lobster mac-and-cheese before treating yourself to the whole fried snapper, the signature entrée. The wine list is geared toward seafood pairings. Try the chocolate and hazelnut torte. There are excellent views of Estero Bay from many tables, and on cooler nights the best seats are out on the back deck, which extends over the water. Reservations are recommended, and attire is resort-casual.

ACCOMMODATIONS
Under $100
Budget travelers should consider **Rock Lake Resort** (2937 Palm Beach Blvd., 239/332-4080, www.rocklakeresort.com, $69-145). The 18 units in nine little cottages encircling a small lake were built in 1946. It features canoeing, lighted tennis courts, a nature trail, barbecue facilities, and comfortable porches overlooking the water. Rock Lake isn't fancy, but it's just a short drive to the beach and 0.5 miles from downtown. Pets are welcome, and it's wheelchair accessible.

$100-200
At Matlacha Pass, right near the drawbridge on Pine Island, is the funky **Bridge Water Inn** (4331 Pine Island Rd., Matlacha, 239/283-2423, www.bridgewaterinn.com, $140-200). Some multitasking enthusiasts have been known to throw a line right out the motel window into the water off the west deck below—fishing and catching the football game simultaneously. You can watch the late-night snook anglers battling catfish for their bait right outside.

$200-300
The **Outrigger Beach Resort** (6200 Estero Blvd., Fort Myers Beach, 239/463-3131, www.outriggerfmb.com, $160-330) is a casual, tropical-themed high-rise hotel that's a great choice for families and couples. On a wide stretch of beach, all rooms are efficiencies, with a king or two double beds, an additional sleeper sofa, and a full kitchen. A living room adjoins a dining room with a private balcony. Thatched-roof cabanas and a tiki bar surround the pool.

On Fort Myers Beach, a natural family destination, are lots of mid-priced hotels and motels. **Sandpiper Gulf Resort** (5550 Estero Blvd., 800/584-1449, www.sandpipergulfresort.com, $200-400) is a low-rise hotel in a few buildings, with 63 large guest suites. The big pool is surrounded by tropical gardens, and the beach is just beyond.

Over $300
Gull Wing Beach Resort (6620 Estero Blvd., Fort Myers Beach, 239/873-5527, www.gullwingfl.com, $250-600) is a high-rise hotel on the quiet south end of Estero Island. There are 66 comfortable and spacious one- to three-bedroom family suites, with a lovely Gulf-side swimming pool, tennis courts, an outdoor spa, barbecues, and a gazebo area. Its parent company, **SunStream Hotels & Resorts** (888/568-9330, www.sunstream.com), is headquartered in Fort Myers Beach and has a number of other luxury properties locally.

The **DiamondHead Beach Resort** (2000 Estero Blvd., Fort Myers Beach, 844/652-3693, www.diamondheadfl.com, $250-500) offers one-bedroom, one-bath suites with Gulf, island, or pool views. All suites are 700 square feet and feature a private balcony, fridge, and microwave, an additional queen-size sofa sleeper, and an interactive computer with room service and concierge services. The resort has a large heated pool, two hot tubs, and a fitness facility on-site.

The **Pointe Estero Beach Resort** (6640 Estero Blvd., Fort Myers Beach, 855/923-8075, $250-550) is a great choice for families and large groups. The resort offers one and two-bedroom suites with wraparound balconies, excellent Gulf views, spacious kitchens, a dining room, two full baths, marble jetted tubs, and a spacious living room. The resort has tennis courts, a heated pool, trolley service, and water-sports rentals on the beach.

North of Estero Island is **The Westin Cape Coral Resort at Marina Village** (5951 Silver King Blvd., Cape Coral, 259/541-5000, $250-500). The resort offers studio to three-bedroom suites up to 2,225 square feet. Dock your boat at the on-site Tarpon Point Marina, grab drinks at the tiki bar, or enjoy fine dining at Marker 92. The pool area includes beautiful

---

1: the signature whole fried snapper at Tarpon Bay
2: the Bridge Water Inn

fountains and a hot tub, and the spa and fitness center are excellent.

Sanibel Harbour Marriott Resort & Spa (17260 Harbour Pointe Dr., Fort Myers, 239/466-4000, www.sanibel-resort.com, $200-600) is a big place, with 240 hotel rooms, 107 elite and more private accommodations complete with concierge services at Grande Bay, and waterfront condominiums as well. It's the most luxurious resort-style spot in Fort Myers, with two gorgeous pools, several restaurants (including an excellent steak house), a pool-side bar, and a spa.

The destination-style ★ **Hyatt Regency Coconut Point Resort & Spa** (5001 Coconut Rd., Bonita Springs, 239/444-1234, $200-600) is in Bonita Springs, halfway between Fort Myers and Naples, with 454 elegantly appointed guest rooms, a Raymond Floyd-designed championship golf course, a day spa, poolside waterslides, several excellent restaurants, a private water taxi that transports guests to the resort's private beach, and grounds landscaped with fountains and tropical plants. Golf packages are often available.

Vacation Rentals

Fort Myers has more opportunities to find relatively affordable beachfront homes than in Naples. Prices run the gamut, but a two- or three-bedroom house on the Gulf is generally $1,500-4,000 per week or $200-600 per night, a bargain compared to Naples. The prices go down from there for condos and homes outside of the beach area, which run $800-3,000 per week or $150-400 per night. For an exceptional website to view copious photos of a large selection of vacation rentals, see **VIP Vacation Rentals** (239/472-1613, www.vip-vacationrentals.com), which also serves Sanibel and Captiva.

TRANSPORTATION
Car

To get to Fort Myers, take either I-75 or U.S. 41. In town, McGregor Boulevard (Hwy. 867) runs alongside the Caloosahatchee River. Highway 865, also known as Hickory

Boulevard, Estero Boulevard, and San Carlos Boulevard, depending on where you are, is the route south to Fort Myers Beach on Estero Island. Driving into Florida from the north via Jacksonville, take I-95 south to I-4 to I-75. The drive is 317 miles via I-75 and will take about five hours.

Air

In 2005, **Southwest Florida International Airport** (RSW, 11000 Terminal Access Rd., Fort Myers, 239/590-4800, www.flylcpa.com) was one of the first in the United States to be built with new security equipment and procedures incorporated into the design. The project focused on passenger convenience, with a lovely subtropical look and a permanent collection of works by Florida photographer Alan Maltz. Major domestic airlines serve the airport, and there are international flights from Germany and Canada. Current routes are with Air Canada, American, Delta, Eurowings, Frontier, JetBlue, Silver, Southwest, Spirit, Sun Country, United, and Westjet.

Alamo (800/327-9633), **Avis** (800/230-4898), **Budget** (800/227-5945), **Dollar** (800/800-3665), **Enterprise** (800/736-8222), **Hertz** (800/654-3131), **National** (800/227-7368), and **Thrifty** (800/847-4389) provide rental cars from Southwest Florida International Airport. Enterprise and Thrifty offices are directly across the street from baggage claim.

Bus and Train

LeeTran (239/275-8726, www.leegov.com/leetran, $1.50, $0.75 seniors, students, and disabled, day pass $4) serves Lee County, with most stops in the Fort Myers region. The south Fort Myers routes serve the beach areas. LeeTran has hourly service 6am-10pm daily to a transfer point at Daniels Parkway and U.S. 41, with connections to other routes.

Greyhound (239/774-5660) offers bus service to the Fort Myers station, but from here you really need to rent a car; public transportation to and between the islands is limited to taxis and limousines.

Sanibel Island

More than 100 small barrier islands flank the coastline of the Fort Myers area. Of these, Sanibel stands out—literally because it lies east-west in a gentle shrimp-shaped curve, and figuratively because it is so well known and widely trafficked. The island's biggest draw is that the island's orientation, coupled with the fact that there are no offshore reefs, means that more than 400 varieties of shells have been found along the 16 miles of white-sand beaches. Expect crown conch, lion's paw, angel wings, alphabet cones, and sand dollars to wash up whole at your feet.

The birding on Sanibel is impressive for breadth as well as sheer numbers. More than half the island is encompassed by the J. N. "Ding" Darling National Wildlife Refuge, 6,354 acres of preserved subtropical barrier island habitat for Florida's native wetland, part of the largest undeveloped mangrove ecosystem in the country. On foot, biking, canoeing, or with a narrated tram ride, naturalists and sightseers can observe wading birds, wetland birds, and the array of other Sanibel wildlife.

Connected to the mainland by a three-mile-long scenic drive across a causeway, Sanibel is a comfortable island that welcomes families and couples with friendly, easy charm and fairly reasonable prices. There are no gigantic resort hotels, and most accommodations are low-rise; buildings can only be as tall as the tallest palm. There are no traffic lights, no street lamps, and no motorized water sports such as Jet Skis.

Sanibel's main street is Periwinkle Way, a picturesque thoroughfare. Shops, small inns, and casual restaurants punctuate the road from the Sanibel Lighthouse to Tarpon Bay Road. There are things to do here beyond beach walking, with friendly restaurants and a great shell museum.

SIGHTS
★ Bailey-Matthews Shell Museum

Slippersnail. White baby ear. Ponderous ark. All of these are the beautiful names of shells. The **Bailey-Matthews Shell Museum** (3075 Sanibel-Captiva Rd., 239/395-2233, www.shellmuseum.org, 10am-5pm daily, $15 adults, $9 ages 12-17, $9 ages 5-11, free under age 5) will make a shell collector out of most people. It's not a vast museum—it will occupy a pleasant 90 minutes or so—but it equips you to go out there and get yourself some of Neptune's treasures. Shells are arranged in thematic groupings from around the world, with an emphasis on the local offerings, and there are anthropological exhibits on humanity's relationship to shells (did you know that Native Americans' use of conch shells as weapons was the origin of the expression "conk on the head"?). There's also a video called *Mollusks in Action* shown five times each day.

Sanibel Historical Village and Museum

Sanibel Historical Village and Museum (950 Dunlop Rd., 239/472-4648, 10am-4pm Tues.-Sat., $10 adults, free under age 18) is a celebration of the local history of the island. This little cluster of historic buildings moved from all over the island includes pioneer Clarence Rutland's original island home from the early 1900s, the Burnap Cottage built in 1898, Miss Charlotta's Tea Room restored to its 1930s look, Bailey's General Store, the original Sanibel post office, an old schoolhouse, an antique Model T, a Sanibel Lighthouse display, archived newspaper articles, and photos. The on-site town historian is a wealth of information and a wonderful storyteller.

Sea Turtles

May to October, the beaches of Sanibel play host to a different kind of visitor. Loggerheads, the most common sea turtles in Florida, make their way out of the Gulf and up the beaches to lay their eggs. An estimated 14,000 females nest in the southeastern United States each year, many of them from the northern tip of Fort Myers Beach to the Lee-Collier border of Bonita Beach. Called loggerheads because of their big heads, they can reach 200-350 pounds and measure about three feet long.

Female loggerheads return to the beaches where they were born to lay their own eggs. They painstakingly dig nest cavities with their rear flippers, deposit about 100 golf ball-size eggs, cover them up, and head back out to sea. Two months later the two-inch hatchlings break out and flap their way toward the moonlit sea. Sanibel has a lights-out policy on beaches so the little turtles aren't confused in their mission, stumbling toward a brightly lit condo instead.

According to the Florida Fish and Wildlife Research Institute, the number of known nesting loggerheads between 1998 and 2010 declined by 25 percent, but the most recent data shows a dramatic recovery: The 2015 census shows that between 2010 and 2015, the number of nests nearly doubled, from 3,500 in 2010 to 6,000 in 2015.

What you can do to help:

- Pack up your beach trash, monofilament fishing line, and especially plastic bags and plastic six-pack holders. Turtles mistake this stuff for tasty sea creatures undulating in the water, and they often get snarled in fishing line.

- Observe nesting turtles only from a distance. That goes for your curious pets too. Dogs must be leashed on Sanibel, and do so even at night when no one's around to enforce the regulation.

- Stack up beach chairs or other items that might impede the baby loggerheads' progress toward the water.

- If you're staying in a beach house, close your drapes or blinds after dark. If you use exterior lights, make sure they are 25-watt yellow bug lights. Don't use flashlights, fishing lanterns, or flash photography on the beach.

- Leave nest identification markers in place. To report a wandering hatchling or a dead or injured turtle, call the Florida Fish and Wildlife Conservation Commission (888/404-3922) or the volunteer organization Turtle Time (239/481-5566).

Old Town

For more historical sightseeing, the East End village of Old Town was originally a fish camp built by Cuban fishers in the 1860s, prior to construction of the lighthouse in 1884. The Sanibel Historical Society has a walking and biking tour map of 19 historic sites along a stretch of about 2.5 miles. You can pick up a copy of the map at the chamber of commerce (1159 Causeway Rd.) or at the Sanibel Historical Village and Museum.

BEACHES

Sanibel is unusual among barrier islands due to its east-west orientation. Because of this, the surf is gentle and the shells arrive whole and pristine. The beaches along East, Middle, and West Gulf Drive slope gradually, making the shallows vast and safe for young waders and beachcombers. There are some beach rules to follow: Pets must be on leashes and cleaned up after (no pets are allowed on Captiva beaches); no alcoholic beverages on the beaches November-May; no open fires; and no collecting live shells. All public beach access areas on the island have restrooms, some with concessions and picnic tables. Beach parking is $5 per hour.

If you have to pick two beaches to visit from among the 14 miles of sand, start with Lighthouse Beach & Fishing Pier (turn left on Periwinkle Way, the first stop sign as you enter the island, and follow Periwinkle Way, which terminates at the parking lot for the boardwalk) and **Bowman's Beach** (off Sanibel-Captiva Rd., turn left on Bowman's Beach Rd.). The heart of Lighthouse Beach is the **Sanibel Lighthouse Boardwalk** (1 Periwinkle Way), the most frequently photographed landmark on the island. It's been here since 1884 on the eastern tip of the island, near the bay side. The beach has a lovely T-dock fishing pier and a boardwalk nature trail through native wetlands. Bowman's Beach is remoter and quieter. Park in the lot and walk over a bridge to the secluded white beach. It offers showers and barbecue grills.

Beyond these, **Gulfside City Park** (mid-island on Algiers Lane, off Casa Ybel Rd.), **Tarpon Bay Beach** (mid-island at the south end of Tarpon Bay Rd. at W. Gulf Dr.), and the **Causeway Beaches** (adjacent to the causeway on both sides) are inviting.

Shelling

Beaches are the most magnetic draw on Sanibel, with wide lengths of white-sand beach and some of the best shelling in the world. Some say 400 species of seashells dot the beaches here, from polka-dotted junonia to lacy apple murex and fat lightning whelks.

The most fruitful time to shell is early morning, at low tide, and after a storm, especially after the big-wave coastal storms in January and February. Other experts say the peak season for shelling is May-September. Walk slowly and look for seashells hidden just beneath the surface of the sand where the surf breaks, about where the water comes up to your knee. Wear polarized sunglasses so you can see into the water, bring a bag or fanny pack for your treasure, and don't take any shell that's inhabited.

The south side of Sanibel has a wide shallow beach that seems to attract shells without battering them—they stay whole and perfect. You're more likely to find good ones where the competition isn't too fierce—the less populated the stretch of beach, the better. The beaches of North Captiva and Cayo Costa Islands are known, among aficionados, for their lack of people and wealth of starfish, conchs, and sand dollars. Generally, smaller shells are found closer to the Lighthouse Beach end, with larger shells the closer you get to Captiva. Common shells include lightning whelk, cockle, scallop, murex, tulip, olive, little coquina, and conch. If you find a junonia, hang on to it for the bragging rights.

If you're coming up empty-handed, turn it over to the professionals, with one of the local shelling charters. **Captain Mike Fuery's Shelling Charters** ('Tween Waters Marina, 239/466-3649, www.sanibel-online.com/fuery, $250 for a 3-hour private charter for up to 4 passengers) is a famous shelling outfit, with its tours featured in *National Geographic, Southern Living, Martha Stewart,* and other magazines. Shelling trips for romantic couples are a specialty.

SPORTS AND RECREATION

★ J. N. "Ding" Darling National Wildlife Refuge

J. N. "Ding" Darling National Wildlife Refuge (1 Wildlife Dr., 239/472-1100, www.fws.gov/dingdarling, 7am-sunset Sat.-Thurs., $5 per vehicle, $1 pedestrians or bicyclists) takes up more than half of Sanibel Island. The refuge was named for Pulitzer Prize-winning cartoonist Jay Norwood Darling, the first environmentalist to hold a presidential cabinet post (during FDR's administration), and it is an absolute marvel. It contains a visitors center, a five-mile driving-tour route, hiking trails, canoe and kayak rentals, and guided interpretive programs.

The 6,354-acre refuge is made up of a variety of estuarine and freshwater habitats. You'll see mudflats and mangrove islands, wide swaths of sea grass and open water, West Indian hardwood hammocks and ridges, and places poetically described as spartina swales. But the real draw is birds.

Ordinarily I'd advise walking or biking through a refuge like this, 2,825 acres of it designated as wilderness area, to go at your own

pace and get a close-up look. But then you'd miss out on the naturalist-narrated tram ride full of competitive birders.

An up-close look at birders is half the fun of a day at "Ding" Darling. On the tram ride, listening to these birders, you can learn to recognize black-crowned night herons and immature ibis, and see wood storks, peregrine falcons, and a wealth of the 238 bird species that hang out in the refuge. The best birding time is early morning, about an hour before or after low tide, when you'll see birders equipped with cameras set up on tripods. Watch what they're watching and ask questions. You'll see things rare and magnificent. The wildlife observation tower is a superb place to hang out any time of the day, and the **education center** (9am-4pm daily) provides a little guidance to the rookie.

Tarpon Bay Explorers (900 Tarpon Bay Rd., 239/472-8900, www.tarponbayexplorers. com), which runs a tram tour through the refuge ($13 adults, $8 children), also offers a 90-minute kayak trail tour ($30 adults, $20 children) along the Commodore Creek water trail and a sunset paddle ($30 adults, $20 children) out to the rookery islands in the refuge. You'll see hundreds of egrets, herons, anhingas, and ibis, all bedded down in the treetops for the night.

Kayaking

The **Great Calusa Blueway Paddling Trail** (www.greatcalusablueway.com) is a 100-mile mapped and marked route for paddlers of all skill levels. Following the trail of the area's early fishers, the Calusa people, it runs along Lee County's coastal waters from Cayo Costa and Charlotte Harbor south through Pine Island Sound and Matlacha Pass to Estero Bay and the Imperial River in Bonita Springs. Even if you're not an outdoorsy type, you can enjoy a couple of days of easy kayaking with stops for lunch and bird-watching, and a comfy bed at the end of each day.

The website gives details on the routes, what you'll see along the way, where to launch or stop, maps, GPS coordinates, and more, but you need to pick up a kayak or canoe. Outfitters offer guided trips, including moonlight excursions, and there are numerous rentals and launch areas if you want to head out on your own.

Start the first day on the Pine Island Sound-Matlacha Pass section of the paddling trail. Crunching over the gravel at the Fish House Marina, find your way to **Gulf Coast Kayak** (4120 Pine Island Rd., Matlacha, 239/283-1125, www.gulfcoastkayak.com, 9am-5pm daily, single kayak $35 half-day, $50 full-day). You get paddles, life jackets, trail maps, and kayaks, and put in just at the drawbridge at Matlacha Pass.

The second segment to be mapped, the Pine Island Sound trail is gentle and sheltered. See small black crabs scoot along red mangrove trunks and great blue herons wade in their shade as you meander through backwaters and mangrove tunnels from marker 84 to marker 89. A few hours later, you realize paddling makes you hungry.

Head back down through Buzzard Bay until you reemerge at the Old Fish House. Lunch here is local shrimp quesadillas, local smoked mullet, and a novelty food: fried mullet gizzard. The mullet is like a chicken in that it has no stomach but a crop and a gizzard. Order at the counter, eat at picnic tables, and watch the snook and needlenose gar churn the water down below.

On day two, put in at Fort Myers Beach, which is on Estero island, connected to Fort Myers by a causeway. There are several worthwhile beaches here (Bowditch Point Regional Park, Lynn Hall Memorial Park), but **Lovers Key State Park** (8700 Estero Blvd., 239/463-4588, 8am-sunset daily, $8 per car up to 8 people, $4 per car single occupancy, $2 pedestrians and bicyclists) is another key embarkation point on the Great Calusa Blueway.

From here, head to **Lovers Key Adventures** (8700 Estero Blvd., 239/765-7788, single kayak $38 half-day), pick up paddles and

---

1: beach on Sanibel **2:** the Sanibel Lighthouse **3:** J. N. "Ding" Darling National Wildlife Refuge

gear, and then head to the launch spot to put in. Using a Blueway map, you can make your way from marker 8 to markers 13 and 22. In parts the water as shallow as a foot deep, and you quietly make your way out to congregations of ibis, egrets, and herons. If you keep paddling, you can make it to **Mound Key** (Estero Bay, 239/992-0311, sunrise-sunset daily, free), a complex of Calusa mounds made of shells, fish bones, and pottery. Thought to be a sacred ceremonial center for the indigenous people, in 1566 it was settled by the Spanish and became the site of the first Jesuit mission in the Spanish New World. It didn't last long, as the Calusa weren't welcoming of the settlers.

The shell construction contains mounded platforms, ceremonial mounds, ridges, substantial carved-out canals, and open water courts—evidence of an elaborate community 2,000 years ago. There are not a lot of interpretive markers or signs here, but it's a nice place for a picnic.

Adventure Sea Kayak ('Tween Waters Marina, 15951 Captiva Dr., Captiva, 239/822-3337, www.captivaadventures.com, $40 adults, $30 children) conducts kayak tours. Its specialty is interactive trips that focus on the wildlife, ecology, and history of the barrier islands. Also based in Captiva, **Captiva Kayaks** (McCarthy's Marina, 11401 Andy Rosse Lane, Captiva, 239/395-2925, www.captivakayaks.com, 9am-5pm daily) offers rentals, instruction, and sunrise, sunset, and starlight tours. On Sanibel, **Tarpon Bay Explorers** (900 Tarpon Bay Rd., Sanibel, 239/472-8900, www.tarponbayexplorers.com, 8am-6pm daily, $15-180) has a range of services, from canoe, kayak, and bike rentals to guided tours. Farther south, **Estero River Canoe & Tackle Outfitters** (20991 S. Tamiami Trail, Estero, 239/992-4050, www.esteroriveroutfitters.com, 7am-6pm daily) offers a large variety of canoes, kayaks, stand-up paddleboards, and paddling accessories.

Sea School

Sanibel Sea School (1451 Middle Gulf Dr., 239/395-7236, www.sanibelseaschool.org) is dedicated to teaching children and adults about marine ecosystems. It uses the setting of the barrier island habitats of Sanibel and Captiva as an opportunity to touch, feel, and understand. Adult classes might focus on bivalves, gastropods, local history, and natural history, with field trips to study mollusk distribution, fish seining, investigating the mangroves at Blind Pass, and exploring the island on Indigo Trail and the Bailey Tract hikes. Call for a schedule of classes and drop-in events.

Biking

It's an island pastime partly because it's relatively safe (there are 25 miles of wide paved biking paths) and partly because you can cover serious ground on these pancake-flat islands. You can take an extremely enjoyable bike ride from the eastern tip of Sanibel to the northern tip of Captiva, stopping occasionally to take a swim in the Gulf. You can also bike on the main drags, Sanibel-Captiva Road and Periwinkle Way, or swing through a stretch of the J. N. "Ding" Darling National Wildlife Refuge, or skirt the water's edge along Gulf Drive. The **Sanibel-Captiva Islands Chamber of Commerce** (1159 Causeway Rd., Sanibel, 239/472-1080) has a free bike-path map.

Many inns on Sanibel and Captiva offer complimentary use of bikes to their guests—ask before you set up a rental elsewhere. The oldest bike shop on Sanibel is **Billy's Rentals** (1470 Periwinkle Way, 239/472-5248, www.billysrentals.com, 8:30am-5pm daily, $5-10 for 2 hours). Billy's offers regular hybrids but also a range of unique stuff, from adult trikes to recumbent bikes, Segways, and cool multi-person surreys. You can even rent jog strollers and motor scooters. **Finnimores Cycle Shop** (2353 Periwinkle Way, 239/472-5577, www.finnimores.com, 9am-4pm daily, $9-24 for 4 hours) is another wonderful shop, with no charge for delivery and pickup for a multi-day rental. It also has in-line skates (with free helmet and pad rentals), umbrellas, fishing equipment, boogie boards, and most other essential fun-in-the-sun beach gear.

Birding

Birds like it here. Some live here year-round, while migrating species stop over. J. N. "Ding" Darling National Wildlife Refuge is a wealth of avian splendor, but the rest of the island is a birder's paradise too. Sanibel boasts so many habitats—freshwater wetlands, brackish mangrove estuaries, beaches, woodlands—that 240 different species live here. The ornithologically inclined have websites and chat groups devoted entirely to Sanibel. One of the local papers has a regular bird column, and traffic stops fairly regularly for recalcitrant crossing herons or egrets.

Part of the thrill is the chase: tramping around with your binoculars trained on the treetops or water's edge at low tide. Here's where to look: Rare white pelicans hang out in Pine Island Sound; ospreys and eagles nest on telephone poles above the bike paths and along Sanibel-Captiva Road; wood storks troll for snacks in roadside ditches in the winter; burrowing owls dig tunnels in shopping center parking lots; sandhill cranes walk gracefully across expanses of lawn in groups of three; great blue herons search the Gulf's shoreline for an easy meal. The lighthouse area of Sanibel is a good place to see birds, as are the mangrove islands off Pine Island Sound and Tarpon Bay on Sanibel. The little clumps of island off the causeway area attract lots of species as well. For an absolute sure thing, Periwinkle Park has an aviary for lovebirds, toucans, flamingos, and talking birds.

ENTERTAINMENT AND EVENTS
Theater

The **Big Arts Strauss Theater** (2200 Periwinkle Way, 239/472-6862, www.bigarts.org, 8pm Mon.-Sat., $42-30 adults, $5 under age 17), is where you can enjoy music, theater, movie, and dance performances. The restored 1896 one-room schoolhouse that used to house the theater has been moved to the Sanibel Historical Village and Museum; performances are held in a newer 160-seat venue.

Festivals and Events

The biggest festival in the area is in March, when Sanibel hosts an annual **Sanibel Shell Festival** (www.fortmyers-sanibel.com), usually held at the **Sanibel Community House** (2173 Periwinkle Way, 239/472-2155). The largest and longest-running shell festival in the country, it draws serious shell collectors from around the world.

SHOPPING

Sanibel's shopping is as low-key as the island itself. **Periwinkle Place** (2075 Periwinkle Way, 239/395-1914, www.periwinkleplace.com) boasts 28 attractive shops, a wonderful restaurant called The Blue Giraffe, and the enjoyable Sanibel Day Spa, all connected by covered walkways and shaded by banyan trees. Its clothing shops are mostly geared to beachwear and sportswear; there are nice toy and swimsuit shops. **Olde Sanibel Shoppes** (630 Tarpon Bay Rd., 239/472-2792) is another cluster of gift, clothing, and jewelry shops, with a couple of casual restaurants. The **Village Shops** (2340 Periwinkle Way) has a similar lineup, and the 15 shops arrayed in the low pink buildings of **Tahitian Gardens** (1975-2019 Periwinkle Way) sell artisanal candles, bright cotton clothing, jewelry, bathing suits, T-shirts, and giftware. This center also contains one of the island's best breakfast spots, the Sanibel Café.

None of these will rock your world, but for a real one-of-a-kind island shopping experience, browse **She Sells Sea Shells** (1157 Periwinkle Way, 239/472-6991, www.sanibelshellcrafts.com). The funky shop contains shells from all over, but many are the same species you'll see stooped enthusiasts mining for (some even wear lighted miners' hats in the early morning) along Sanibel beaches. If you need a regular old grocery store, **Bailey's** (2477 Periwinkle Way, 239/472-1516, 7am-9pm daily) is the biggest local market.

Galleries

Sanibel has some galleries worth

investigating. It attracts residents of artistic temperament, many of them opening shops that feature their work. **Tower Gallery** (751 Tarpon Bay Rd., 239/472-4557, www.towergallery.net, 10am-9pm daily) is a good place to start, and it's hard to miss in an electric-blue and green building. It's a cooperative of 23 local artists in all media and a real mix of styles; the work is all juried. Nearby is another small cooperative called the **Hirdie Girdie Gallery** (2490 Library Way, 239/395-0027, www.hirdiegirdiegallery.com, 9am-5pm Mon.-Sat.).

Sanibel's **BIG Arts** (Barrier Island Group for the Arts, 900 Dunlop Rd., 239/395-0900) is a community cultural arts organization that has a center for island arts. It has two galleries (9am-4pm Mon.-Fri. Oct.-Dec. and Apr., 9am-4pm Mon.-Fri., 9am-1pm Sat. Jan.-Mar., 9am-3pm Mon.-Fri. May-Sept.), a sculpture garden, and performance space. Exhibits change monthly, and there are frequent workshops, lectures, films, and concerts.

FOOD

The restaurants of Sanibel are mostly fun, casual locations for delicious seafood. Expect prices to be slightly higher than elsewhere on the Gulf Coast. You're paying for the view and the expensive location, but you can cut the cost by doing the early-bird special, before 6pm, offered at many restaurants, and happy hour at the bars. There are also a few great deals on the island.

Breakfast

Lighthouse Cafe (362 Periwinkle Way, 239/472-0303, 7am-3pm daily year-round, 5pm-9pm daily Dec.15-Apr., $8-15) usually beats the early-morning competition, whether you're a fan of the seafood benedict or the blueberry whole-wheat hotcakes.

Lunch

Novelist Randy Wayne White is about the biggest booster this area has. When he was young he was a light-tackle fishing guide in this neighborhood. I'm not sure how often he's in residence at the restaurant named for the main character of many of his books, set in these parts. Wayne White is actually purported to be a good cook, with a seafood cookbook to his name. Regardless of who's cooking, **Doc Ford's Sanibel Rum Bar & Grille** (2500 Island Inn Rd., 239/312-4275, 11am-10pm daily, $12-25) is a blast, with lots of TVs blaring the game, good sandwiches, and great drinks. The food—panko-breaded fried shrimp, Cuban sandwiches, pulled pork—is better than you might expect for such a laid-back setting. **Sanibel Café** (2007 Periwinkle Way, 239/472-5323, 7am-2:30pm daily, $8-17) is an unpretentious and friendly local hangout. Go for the fat blue-cheese hamburgers.

Dinner

The **Island Cow** (2163 Periwinkle Way, 239/472-0606, 7am-9pm daily, $8-16) occasionally has a mooing contest for guests, the winner of which gets a T-shirt in addition to deep and abiding respect. There's also live music, a wonderful outdoor patio, and generous seafood baskets with fries. They serve a great breakfast too. It's a wonderfully fun restaurant, with excellent food, where you can save a lot of "moo-lah."

The **Mad Hatter Restaurant** (6467 Sanibel Captiva Rd., 239/472-0033, 5pm-9pm Tues.-Sun., $20-35) serves steaks, seafood, and salads in an eccentric Alice in Wonderland-themed dining room complete with a mural depicting the fictional characters from the story. It may not seem to be the type of setting for a romantic dinner, but somehow it works, perhaps since the food is exceptional and the coastal view at sunset beautiful.

Matzaluna (1200 Periwinkle Way, 239/472-1998, 4:30pm-9:30pm daily, $10-20) is a traditional Italian restaurant. The wood-fired pizzas get top honors, with hearty baked pasta dishes (lasagna, stuffed

1: outdoor patio at the Island Cow 2: one of the cottages at the Island Inn on Sanibel Island

shells) a close second. Like many island spots, it offers excellent drink specials during happy hour.

ACCOMMODATIONS

There's little on Sanibel Island that's dirt-cheap. On the other hand, nothing is extremely upscale. It's the kind of place where you get a sweet apartment, hotel, or motel a few steps from the beach and don't worry about luxurious amenities because you have the Gulf of Mexico at your doorstep.

To stay for a whole week, rent a condo or cottage. **Cottages to Castles of Sanibel & Captiva** (2427 Periwinkle Way, 239/472-6385, www.cottages-to-castles.com) has a number of intimate and affordable one-week rentals; it also offers the enormous seven-bedroom pink house called Sandhurst that was once featured as the MTV Summer Beach House. The rates on the condos ($700-1,750 per week) are reasonable off-season.

My two favorites on the island have a subtle Old Florida nostalgia to them, with nice interiors and modern amenities like Wi-Fi as well as a historical feel—the kinds of places you could imagine visiting for decades. The ★ **Island Inn on Sanibel Island** (3111 W. Gulf Dr., 239/472-1561, www.islandinnsanibel.com, $150-500) opened in 1895. Look at the scrapbook of clippings to get a sense of who has roamed this compound of lovely little cottages and larger lodges on 10 acres, with 550 feet of unobstructed beachfront. Draws include shuffleboard, table tennis, and bike rentals, but it's the warmth of the staff and other guests that seems anachronistic.

The same can be said of ★ **West Wind Inn** (3345 W. Gulf Dr., 239/472-1541, www.westwindinn.com, $200-400), a beachfront place on the quiet part of the island. Rooms have a touch of Old Florida styling and include kitchenettes, but don't skip breakfast at its Normandie Seaside Restaurant. West Wind's 500-foot stretch of beach is a marvel for stargazing. The lush landscaping surrounding the large heated pool captures the essence of this tropical destination.

Shalimar Resort (2823 W. Gulf Dr., 239/472-1353, www.shalimar.com, $300-500) is another favorite getaway, with 33 one- and two-bedroom cottages, apartments, and motel efficiencies spread around a huge property right on the Gulf. All units have full kitchens, and the pool is beautiful. **Sundial Beach Resort and Spa** (1451 Middle Gulf Dr., 239/472-4151, www.sundialresort.com, $200-700) has 270 one- and two-bedroom suites that all have a condo vibe, complete with full kitchens. It sits in 33 acres of tropical landscape right along the beach and has a tremendous weekday camp for children ages 4-11.

Sanibel Inn (937 E. Gulf Dr., 239/472-3181, www.sanibelinn.com, $200-600) is smaller, with 94 hotel rooms and one-bedroom suites. The inn sits in the shade of more than 600 palms, with gardens and complimentary guest use of the inn's bikes. Inside, bamboo flooring and shades of green, blue, and light brown give the rooms a relaxed style. The Sanibel Inn also offers a wonderful children's program. For adults, the Dunes Golf & Tennis Club is nearby.

TRANSPORTATION

To get to Sanibel from I-75, take the new exit 131 or the old exit 21 (Daniels Pkwy.) west to Summerlin Road, approximately seven miles. Turn left onto Summerlin Road and drive approximately 15 miles to the Sanibel Causeway ($6 toll). Drive across onto Sanibel Island. At the four-way stop at Periwinkle Way, either a right or a left turn will lead you to beaches, shops, and accommodations. Sanibel Island has a couple of main roads that parallel each other: Periwinkle Way, the main business route; and Gulf Drive, segmented into East, Middle, and West Gulf Drive. Tarpon Bay Road connects Sanibel-Captiva Road with Periwinkle Way at its west end. And Sanibel-Captiva Road—most folks call it San-Cap—goes by most of Sanibel's attractions before crossing over a short bridge at Blind Pass, where it becomes Captiva Drive on Captiva Island.

Captiva Island

Sanibel's northern neighbor, Captiva Island, is smaller, at a half-mile wide and five miles long. It is at once more laid-back and more exclusive, perfect for a solitary getaway or a romantic escape. Captiva has less commerce, fewer hotels and inns, and fewer people in general. A fair percentage of the island's houses, all recessed behind dense pines and thick foliage, are the beach retreats of wealthy and often absentee owners, contributing to the island being quieter than Sanibel.

Captiva, with Captiva Drive running its length, has a relaxed downtown area of beach bars, restaurants, and gift shops that draw their inspiration from the beaches of Key West and the lyrics of Jimmy Buffett tunes. Captiva Village uses colorful upbeat pastels, and some of the restaurants (such as the Bubble Room) adopt a fun and eccentric approach to decorating. Things are casual without being run-down—which lets much more upscale accommodations seem proper on Captiva. The South Seas Island Resort dominates a whole section at the northern tip of Captiva, where it breaks before the island of North Captiva (once attached). Its sprawling charm and incredible beach set a tone for the island.

There are few attractions on the island, although much to do. Walk, run, fish, canoe, sit and read, or just sit. Anne Morrow Lindbergh was so inspired by Captiva's tranquility that it's where she wrote her best-selling book *A Gift from the Sea*.

SPORTS AND RECREATION
Beaches

Captiva's beaches are less populated than those on Sanibel for a couple of reasons. First, there are more private homes on Captiva, visited sporadically by their affluent owners, and thus there are just fewer feet to churn the sand and rustle the waterbirds. Second, the shelling is better on Sanibel. But Captiva's waters are clearer and the swimming slightly better. Captiva Beach (at the end of Captiva Dr., parking $5 per hour) has beautiful sand, lovely clear water, and only a few people in sight, a great place to watch the sunset. Because of fairly swift currents, don't count on swimming at Turner Beach (Sanibel-Captiva Rd. at Blind Pass Bridge), but it's still a favorite among fisherfolk and shell collectors. Gulf-side beach erosion has been a problem in recent years, exacerbated by recent storms. Private and public funds have been raised to restore beaches by pumping in sand from offshore.

Fishing

The South Seas Island Resort hosts the annual Caloosa Catch & Release Tournament on Captiva each June. This one is known as the largest single-site public flats tournament in Florida. People here are serious about fishing, and not just about the seasonal giant tarpon.

What are you likely to catch? Redfish is pretty steady, some over 10 pounds. The species has rebounded since the New Orleans blackening craze made them a hot commodity. They can be fished on the flats. Snook is best in the springtime, and the season is closed December 15-January 31 and June-August. You'll catch lots of speckled trout in the winter when they're especially large; they tend to hang out in three to five feet of water near the edges of the grass flats and sand holes. The area's biggest draw is tarpon, huge fish that range 100-150 pounds with lots of fight in them. Some say the first tarpon taken on rod and reel was in southwest Florida, near Punta Rassa across San Carlos Bay from Sanibel, in 1885. Tarpon season, recently changed to catch-and-release only, runs late April-August. Then there are cobia (Feb.-July, but best Apr.-May), tripletail, and jacks for much of the year on the flats, and black grouper far out in the Gulf. Commercial catches of grouper have been limited recently, so sportfishers might benefit from increased numbers.

Fishing charters start at around $250 for a half-day trip, and the charter captain provides the boat, fishing license, fishing gear, equipment, and bait. Sometimes the client pays an additional fee for gas—ask about this. As a matter of etiquette, a tip of $25-50 is customary, as is buying your captain and crew a meal or drinks at the end of your fishing trip. Many guides will clean and fillet your edible catch—if you don't want all the fish, give it to whomever seems interested dockside. As for mounting and taxidermy: Big fish are largely catch-and-release, so have a picture taken of yourself with your catch before you release it. Then, one of the new breed of high-tech taxidermists will create a lifelike plastic model of your prize.

Figure out whether you want to do deepwater fishing, cast in the flats, or maybe take a fly-fishing lesson, and then visit the marinas to ask around about charter captains, rates, what people are catching, and where. **Santiva Fishing Charters** ('Tween Waters Marina, 15951 Captiva Dr., 239/472-1779, www.sanibelcaptivafishing.com, fishing $250-450, sightseeing $150 per hour) does back-bay fishing; **Capt. Joe's Charters** (Castaways Marina, Sanibel-Captiva Rd., Sanibel, 239/472-8658, www.captainjoescharters.com, $250-450) does back-bay and fly-fishing.

Sailing

Take the three-day certification program with **Offshore Sailing School** (16731 McGregor Blvd., Fort Myers, 239/454-1700, www.offshoresailing.com), with courses for beginners, racers, and cruisers and a basic keelboating class ($895), held at the Pink Shell Beach Resort & Spa in Fort Myers Beach and the South Seas Island Resort on Captiva. It's a tremendous amount of fun—three days on the water with an instructor and three other students, plus hours of classroom time learning all the sailing jargon, parts of the boat,

and points of sail. At the end of the class you take a fairly difficult 80-question test, then get out and show your sailing chops to your teacher, complete with man-overboard demonstrations and a quick stop by "shooting" into the wind.

If you're a goal-oriented person, it's a great activity to build a vacation around. You learn on a midsize daysailer, a Colgate 26, designed specifically for training and chosen by the U.S. Naval Academy to replace its training fleet. From here, you can take any number of other courses designed for more advanced sailors—performance sailing, live-aboard cruising, or a camp for racing sailors. At the very least you'll be able to tie nautical knots as a party trick.

SHOPPING

Hand-painted souvenirs and shell trinkets can be found along Sanibel-Captiva Road and in the Captiva Village area along Andy Rosse Lane, at the only four-way stop on Captiva. A popular shop here is **Jungle Drums** (11532 Andy Rosse Lane, 239/395-2266), a collection of wildlife, island, and environmental art in a variety of media.

FOOD

Most of the restaurants are casual and reasonably priced, set in pastel-colored cottages with outdoor seating. There's a fun beachy style and funky charm.

The ★ **Bubble Room** (15001 Captiva Dr., 239/472-5558, 11:30am-3pm and 4:30pm-9pm daily, $15-28) is definitely fun and entirely eccentric. Waiters and bartenders are in scouting uniforms, with patches of their own devising meticulously sewn on. They wear neckerchiefs and mischievous grins. The interior is like something out of Santa's workshop, with toy trains and elves and hobbyhorses, with 2,000 movie stills and glossies, lots of Betty Boop memorabilia, and a long list of other stuff. The food is definitely good,

1: the Bubble Room 2: 'Tween Waters Inn Island Resort 3: Captiva Island

Tropical Fruit

Jackfruit, carambola, mamey sapote, sapodilla, lychee, longans, pineapple, and papaya are the kinds of fruits you imagine eating on a far-away tropical island. A little closer is Pine Island, just west of Cape Coral, the largest along the southwest coast of Florida and the producer of some of the state's most exotic fruits. Not the usual Florida orange, Pine Island's king of fruits is the mango. Its reign is so celebrated that there is an annual two-day festival, the **Pine Island MangoMania Tropical Fruit Fair** (239/283-0888, July) with mango-inspired foods, entertainment, and lots of fragrant fruits and plants for sale.

Late May to Labor Day, enthusiasts can also stop into the tent-covered **Pine Island Tropical Farmer's Market** (10am-4pm daily June-Aug., 10am-4pm Mon.-Sat. Sept.-May) in Bokeelia for a wide array of tropical fruits. The **Fort Myers Downtown Farmers Market** (7am-1pm Thurs.) in Centennial Park offers a fair sampling of the local exotic fruits. Even local winemakers applaud the local fruits by making wine from carambola.

Carambola is another word for starfruit, a light-yellow, ribbed, ovoid fruit that, when sliced, has star-shaped cross sections. The flesh is yellow, crisp, juicy, and not fibrous, ranging from sour to mildly sweet.

Mamey sapote is a large football-shaped fruit that grows on an ornamental evergreen. The brown skin has a rough texture—rougher than a kiwi. The flesh is either a creamy pink or salmon color, and it has a big avocado-like pit. The flavor is described as a combination of honey, avocado, and sweet potato. Closely related, the **sapodilla** has soft brown flesh that tastes a little like sweet root beer. The sapodilla tree is also the source of chicle, a chewing gum component.

Lychee are nubby red fruits with pearly white flesh and the texture of a grape. The flesh is sweet but tart, and with a strong scent. Experienced lychee eaters bite lightly through the skin of the top and then squeeze the fruit out. The **longan** is known as the little brother of the lychee. They look alike, but the longan is smaller. The flesh is whitish and translucent like the lychee, but less strong-smelling and a little muskier.

Jackfruit is for the intrepid. It is the largest tree-borne fruit in the world, at up to 80 pounds, and the unopened fruit has a strong disagreeable smell. The exterior is spiky and green, and the inside has large edible bulbs that taste like a cross between banana and papaya. You may not want to bother with jackfruit, but do check out the rest of Lee County's tropical bounty.

from fried shrimp to grilled fish cooked with a pineapple-ginger marinade.

Andy Rosse Lane, the area often called Captiva Village, has a cluster of fun places. The **Keylime Bistro** (Captiva Island Inn, 11509 Andy Rosse Lane, 239/395-4000, 8am-10pm daily, lounge until 1am, $15-30) offers live entertainment daily—it's a great place to hear musicians performing island music such as Jimmy Buffett. The kitchen serves an excellent grouper sandwich as well as a delicious sausage sandwich with onions and peppers; at dinner, choose shrimp scampi or grouper piccata. There are good margaritas, and a Bloody Mary bar for Sunday brunch.

RC Otter's Island Eats (11506 Andy Rosse Lane, 239/395-1142, 8am-10pm daily, $8-20) is right across the street, with a vast menu of accessible American staples, and care put into vegetarian options. It serves wine as well as a house-made beer. Depending on the weather, you can sit indoors, on the covered veranda, or out on the patio, where there's usually live island music. **Mucky Duck** (11546 Andy Rosse Lane, 239/472-3434, 11:30am-3pm and 5pm-9:30pm daily, $18-28) has an English pub vibe, but set right on the beach. The only thing on the menu that might be construed as English is fish-and-chips, but the seafood platter is good. Every night at sunset, revelers convene on the beachside patio to watch the colorful sunset.

The **'Tween Waters Inn Beach Resort** (15951 Captiva Rd., 239/472-5161) is something of an institution, stretching from the bay side to the Gulf side across the island and with a couple of restaurants on-site. I'd skip the fine dining at **Captiva House** (7am-11am and 5:30pm-9:30pm daily, $18-34) and head for the ★ **Crow's Nest Beach Bar and Grille** (4pm-11pm daily, cocktails until late, $8-15). Not that Captiva House isn't good—it often wins Florida's Golden Spoon Award, with swordfish saltimbocca, jerk grouper, seafood jambalaya, and key lime pie served in an intimate special-occasion kind of space (sit in the Sunset Room). It's more that the Crow's Nest is so much fun, with good drink specials, fine bar staples, and a band on many nights. Don't miss the hermit crab races, 6pm for families, 9pm for adults. Pick your hermit crab, the one who looks most like Dale Earnhardt Jr. or Jeff Gordon, and line him up. The competition is an ESPN-worthy drama. For lunch at 'Tween Waters, opt for the **Oasis Pool Bar** (11am-6pm daily, $7-10) on-site, where you can eat a fat sandwich, a cold salad, or a fruity drink while watching the commotion around the resort's pool.

When you're looking for a cocktail and a place to watch the sun go down, the **Green Flash Bayside Bar & Grill** (15183 Captiva Dr., 239/472-3337, 11:30am-3:30pm and 5:30pm-9:30pm daily, $13-20) is another top choice. The two-story restaurant is on Roosevelt Channel and overlooks Buck Key and Pine Island. The menu offers wide choices, including seafood, steak, and burgers. The barbecue shrimp and lobster bisque are favorites.

ACCOMMODATIONS
$100-200
Jensen's Twin Palm Cottages (15107 Captiva Dr., 239/472-5800, 1-bedroom $110-180, 2-bedroom $125-190) are spread out along the bayside marina and fishing action. You can rent a boat right here, grab some bait, and be out on the water before your pajamas have had time to miss you. The 14 cheerful tin-roofed cottages have kitchens and screened porches.

$200-300
If you want to be where the action is, ★ **Captiva Island Inn** (11509 Andy Rosse Lane, 239/395-0882, www.captivaislandinn.com, $150-300) is a wonderful bed-and-breakfast in the middle of teeny Captiva Village. There are traditional B&B rooms, one- and two-bedroom cottages, a loft, and a suite. The owners also have a four-bedroom house with 4½ baths for big gatherings. **Jensen's on the Gulf** (15300 Captiva Dr., 239/472-4684, www.gocaptiva.com, motel suites $150-300, apartments $175-400, houses $300-600) has nine units directly on the Gulf.

Over $300
The biggest game in town is ★ **South Seas Island Resort** (5400 Plantation Rd., 239/472-5111, www.southseas.com, $250-1,200) at the northern tip of the island. Set in 330 acres of mangroves, it's casual but spectacular, with beautiful rooms, a popular children's program, world-renowned sailing, pools, kayaking, a fishing pier, 2,100 feet of dockage for boats up to 130 feet long, and Gulf-edge golf. The main pool area at the resort offers sleek cabanas for rent with a private attendant and spa services. The Point restaurant offers casual Caribbean fare, and an upscale bar upstairs provides views of Pine Island Sound.

'Tween Waters Inn Island Resort (15951 Captiva Dr., 239/472-5161, www.tween-waters.com, $150-600) is another excellent choice, with a huge resort complex that stretches from the bay side to the Gulf side. There are 137 water-view rooms, suites, and cottages; Olympic-size and children's pools; tennis courts; a day spa; four restaurants; and a full-service marina. The rooms are attractive, and there's a nice complimentary breakfast.

TRANSPORTATION
You have to drive through Sanibel to reach Captiva. From Sanibel, turn right onto Periwinkle Way, drive two miles, turn right onto Tarpon Bay Road, and at the next left turn onto Sanibel-Captiva Road. Drive for approximately eight miles, cross Blind Pass Bridge, and you're here.

Charlotte Harbor and the Barrier Islands

From Charlotte Harbor south past Fort Myers is an incredible number of great little islands in the waters of Lee County and Charlotte County. A long line of curves and dots on the map between the Gulf waters and the Intracoastal Waterway, some of these islands are accessible by causeway, others just by boat. What unifies them is unbelievable natural beauty and romanticized pirate-related histories. Sailboating outfits, fishing charters, regularly scheduled ferries, and water taxis head out to these barrier islands. One of the area's first visitors was Spanish explorer Ponce de León, who ended up taking a Calusa arrow and dying in these waters. The locals are friendlier now.

CHARLOTTE HARBOR

Most people hadn't heard of Florida's Charlotte Harbor and Punta Gorda until Hurricane Charley blew through in 2004. Punta Gorda took one of the category 4 storm's worst beatings, with loads of people months later still trying to decide whether to renovate or rebuild. The area rebounded and added 500 new hotel rooms, a new terminal at Charlotte County Airport, and a rebuilt and expanded sports arena, **Charlotte Sports Park,** which now hosts the Tampa Bay Rays for spring training.

The whole area is worth exploring, especially for the eco-traveler. Charlotte Harbor is the second-largest estuary in the state, encompassing 270 square miles, and has 190 miles of saltwater canals and 175 miles of freshwater canals. Most of the area bordering the harbor is preserved land, with parks, 57 blueway trails, and the largest undisturbed pine flatwoods in southwest Florida. To reach Charlotte Harbor from Fort Myers, follow U.S. 41 north for 24 miles, which takes 30 minutes. Once you cross the Peace River,

you're here. The area has been featured on *Sail* magazine's list of the "10 Greatest Places to Sail in the United States" and was ranked by *Golf Digest* as the "Third Best Place to Live and Play Golf in America."

Visiting Lee County, don't skip **Punta Gorda.** It's worth the drive north from Fort Myers to visit **Babcock Wilderness Adventures** (8000 Hwy. 31, 800/500-5583, tours by reservation 9am-3pm, $24 adults, $23 seniors, $16 ages 3-12) for an exhilarating 90-minute tour through the Babcock Ranch, Telegraph Cypress Swamp, and the 90,000-acre Crescent B Ranch. Guides offer narration on birds, animals, plants, and the cattle and horses raised on the ranch. You'll see Florida panthers (not in the wild), big gators, white-tailed deer, wild turkeys, and ornery-looking Florida Cracker cattle that are raised on the ranch. It's thrilling, especially for kids.

Out of Fisherman's Village in Punta Gorda, **King Fisher Fleet** (1200 W. Retta Esplanade, 941/639-0969, www.kingfisherfleet.com, cruises $12-23 adults, $6-12 ages 3-11, free under age 3, back-bay fishing $350-700 per day, deep-water $900 per day) pays equal attention to sightseers and anglers with sightseeing cruises to the out islands, ecotours, full- and half-day cruises, sunset cruises, and harbor tours. After a day of fishing, you can visit one of Punta Gorda's two excellent day spas, **Spa One** (115 Taylor St., 941/506-6111) and **E'lan Salon and Spa** (1801 Shreve St., 941/637-8786). At Christmastime, all the houses and boats along the canals in Punta Gorda are decorated lavishly. King Fisher offers a charming evening cruise along the canals to check out the lights and holiday festivities.

The little town of **Englewood,** west of

1: Charlotte Sports Park 2: fishing off Punta Gorda

Charlotte Harbor and north of Cape Haze, is definitely worth the drive. A great place for an evening barbecue is the covered pavilion on the downtown beachfront at **Chadwick Park.** There's also the 135-acre **Oyster Creek Regional Park** in Englewood, on the greenway-waterway corridor known as the Oyster Creek-Lemon Bay Aquatic Preserve-Ainger Creek waterway.

Lemon Bay is at the north end of the Cape Haze peninsula, where evidence suggests early Floridians lived well from about 1000 BC to AD 1350. You can see their faint evidence at **Paulson's Point** (210 Winson Ave., 941/861-4000, dawn-dusk daily, free), also known as the Sarasota County Indian Mound Park. The tall shell-mound park features helpful interpretive markers and a beautiful easy walkway around and through the Native American mound.

In Manasota Key, **Turtle Bay Condos** (2375 N. Beach Rd., Manasota Key, 941/473-2335, www.myturtlebaycondos.com, $150-230, $795-1,420 per week) has eight two-bedroom condo units that are fully furnished, spacious, and have fully equipped kitchens, making them a good choice for families and extended stays. Each unit has beach chairs, beach towels, a private back deck, and a washer and dryer. The heated pool is surrounded by palms, and across the street is public access to the Gulf.

Food

Worthwhile eateries include **Amimoto Japanese Restaurant** (2705 Tamiami Trail, Punta Gorda, 941/505-1515, 5pm-9pm Mon.-Sat., $15-22), serving sushi presented artistically. It's a great lunch spot. Also popular in Punta Gorda are the restaurants of **Fisherman's Village** (1200 W. Retta Esplanade, www.fishville.com, 10am-6pm Mon.-Sat., noon-6pm Sun.), including **The Captain's Table** (941/637-1171, 11:30am-3pm and 5pm-9pm Sun.-Thurs., 11:30am-3pm and 5pm-10pm Fri.-Sat., $16-25), **Village Fish Market** (941/639-7959, 11am-9pm Mon.-Sat., 11:30am-8pm Sun., $10-25), and

Harpoon Harry's (941/637-1177, 11am-10pm daily, $8-15). In the town of Englewood, classy water-view dining can be had at **The Waverly Restaurant and Bar** (2095 N. Beach Rd., 941/475-3500, 11am-9pm daily, $12-32). Get the stone crab claws if they're in season.

Undoubtedly the best restaurant in the area is **The Perfect Caper** (121 E. Marion Ave., Punta Gorda, 941/505-9009, 11:30am-2pm and 4:30pm-9pm Tues.-Thurs., 11:30am-2pm and 4:30pm-10pm Fri., 5pm-10pm Sat., 5pm-9pm Sun., $20-45), where James and Jeanie Roland take a fresh approach to California-Asian fusion. Jeanie, a Culinary Institute of America grad, is strict about the ingredients. Her passion for the season's best can be seen in starters like fried jumbo prawns wrapped in phyllo and served with avocado relish and blood-orange vinaigrette, and entrées of grilled venison tenderloin with roasted purple potatoes.

★ PALM ISLAND

Almost everything on Palm Island revolves around **Palm Island Resort** (7092 Placida Rd., Cape Haze, 800/824-5412, www.palmisland.com, $400-1,200), one of the best places to stay on the entire Gulf Coast. Start by driving to Cape Haze, for which the directions are a little tricky: Take I-75 for 29 miles north from Sanibel. Take the exit for County Road 768 west (exit 161) toward Punta Gorda. Almost immediately, turn right onto Taylor Road (County Rd. 765A), which runs into the Tamiami Trail (U.S. 41) north. Follow this nine miles, then turn left onto El Jobean Road (Hwy. 776) west. Follow this eight miles, turn left onto Gasparilla Road (County Rd. 771), and drive another eight miles. Turn right onto Placida Road (County Rd. 775), go two miles, and you're there. Then you wait in line in your car for the car ferry. Drive on, and about 60 seconds later the ferry lands on Palm Island. Then you're in paradise. Nice young men in shorts greet you, take all your stuff, and tell you where to ditch your car; you get your own golf cart, and you motor over to your unit along gravel roads.

The island is due north of Boca Grande, with 200 private homes, plus 15 more private homes within the resort. Resort guests stay in 154 one- to three-bedroom villas right on the Gulf. In clusters of low-rise buildings, spacious units reflect a real range of tastes, from beachy casual to swanky contemporary—be specific about your tastes and needs when you call, or make sure and browse through the photos of each on the website before making reservations. There are several pools, tennis courts, a comfy restaurant called the Rum Bay, children's programs, and kayak rentals. Make sure to bring your own groceries from the mainland, as the prices at the little on-island market are exorbitant. Beautiful beaches, green-blue waters, amazing sunsets—it's all worth the rates, making Palm Island a perfect getaway.

GASPARILLA ISLAND

Named for the infamous pirate José Gaspar, who may have hidden out (and buried his treasure, never to be found) on this island in the 1700s with his band of adventurous men, Gasparilla Island has had a much more upscale recent history. Connected to the mainland by a short causeway near Punta Gorda, the island was founded as a vacation retreat and fishing spot by the DuPont family in the late 1800s. Its town of **Boca Grande,** at the mouth of Charlotte Harbor, is filled May-mid-July with tarpon fishers; the opening between Cayo Costa and Gasparilla Island has been called the "Tarpon Fishing Capital of the World." Tarpon are sparser in the pass and the estuarine waters of Pine Island Sound these days, but during peak season, the dense cluster of fishing boats still pulls into port to try their luck. There is driving access to the island via the Boca Grande Causeway, the causeway at County Road 775, and at Placida.

Boca Grande is on the southern tip of Gasparilla Island and has a quaint fishing village feel that appeals to anglers and is complemented by a number of upscale shops and restaurants (George W. Bush has been a regular guest). Walk around **Boca Grande**

Lighthouse Park (Gasparilla Island State Park, 880 Belcher Rd., 941/964-0375, 8am-sunset daily, $3 per car). The wooden Boca Grande Lighthouse was built in 1890 and is a maritime landmark. The lighthouse is open to the public (10am-4pm last Sat. of the month), and there's a little lighthouse museum, a gift shop, and the Armory Chapel. The waters in these parts have strong currents—not great for swimming, but you'll see people sailboarding.

The **Gasparilla Inn and Club, Boca Grande** (500 Palm Ave., 941/964-4500, www.the-gasparilla-inn.com, $245-2,000) is designated a Historic Hotel of America. The Victorian-style resort has a main hotel surrounded by cute cottages. With a major Old Florida feel, it sits on 156 acres with great views of the Gulf of Mexico and Charlotte Harbor. A Pete Dye-designed golf course, a croquet lawn, two pools, fishing, a spa, and a 200-slip marina have made it a favorite over the years.

USEPPA ISLAND

Across from Cabbage Key is Useppa Island. Pirate José Gaspar supposedly named the place for one of his more favored captives, a Mexican princess named Joseffa. Calusa people may have lived here as far back as 5000 BC, discarding their oyster and clam shells to create a greater amount of dry land. Barron Collier, for whom Collier County is named, bought the 100-acre island in 1912 and built a resort there in his own name that lured fishing enthusiasts from all over. The island is really a private residential club called the Useppa Island Club, with a couple of places on-island for visitors to stay. The **Collier Inn** (8115 Main St., 239/283-4443, $150-300) offers seven stylishly decorated suites, and there are also a number of cottages for rent. The **Useppa Marina** accommodates visitors' boats, and the **Tarpon Lodge Restaurant** is only a short drive away.

The Useppa Island Historical Society's little **Useppa Museum** (239/283-9600, noon-2pm Tues.-Fri., 1pm-2pm Sat.-Mon., $5) is a worthwhile museum, full of an odd assortment of things. There are uniforms from Cuban leaders who participated in the doomed invasion of the Bay of Pigs. These leaders were chosen in secrecy on Useppa by the CIA. And there's a forensic restoration of the "Useppa Man," taken from a skeleton unearthed during an archaeological dig in 1989. Other finds reflect the Paleolithic nomadic hunter-gatherer people who were here 10,000 years ago when the island was part of the mainland.

Useppa Island is only accessible by water taxi or private boat. Water taxis run every day from Pine Island, Captiva Island, and Punta Gorda. **Captiva Cruises** (239/472-5300, www.captivacruises.com, 10am-3pm Tues.-Sun., $40 adults, $25 children, plus $2 park admission) has a luncheon cruise to Useppa that includes a visit to the museum.

CABBAGE KEY

The **Cabbage Key Inn** (Intracoastal Waterway, marker 60, Pineland, 239/283-2278, www.cabbagekey.com, $134-460, transient dockage available), built by writer Mary Roberts Rinehart and her son in 1938, has many tempting draws for the visitor. It was here that Jimmy Buffett drew his inspiration for "Cheeseburger in Paradise." And indeed, the inn serves a great burger, as well as some of the best seafood and stone crab claws in the area. The **Dollar Bill Bar,** located in the inn, rides atop a 38-foot Calusa shell mound. The pub is lined with dollar bills, a custom that began in 1941 when a fisherman autographed and taped his last dollar to the wall for safekeeping (ensuring a beer on his return). Since then, people sign and date a buck, and tack them up—more than 30,000 dollar bills are taped to the walls, ceilings, and woodwork, providing a historical collage. (It's illegal to deface currency, but no one in this live-and-let-live bar will tell on you.)

Cabbage Key is accessible only by boat, helicopter, or seaplane, located directly across from mile marker 60 on the Intracoastal Waterway. It doesn't really have sandy beaches, but there is an impressive network of walking trails to explore, you can climb the historic water tower for an awesome aerial view of the island, and there are several excellent rental cottages on the island available through the Cabbage Key website. Make this your base, and rent or charter a boat and explore surrounding islands of Sanibel, Captiva, Cayo Costa, and Pine Island. **Captiva Cruises** (239/472-5300, www.captivacruises.com, 10am-3pm Tues.-Sun., $40 adults, $25 children) offers a narrated cruise to Cabbage Key, and there are regularly scheduled water taxis daily from Pine Island, Captiva Island, and Punta Gorda.

CAYO COSTA

It's one of the quietest unbridged barrier islands in the chain but one of the largest. Immediately west of Cabbage Key, stretching from Boca Grande Pass to Captiva Pass, it offers eight miles of pristine beach and unspoiled beauty. **Cayo Costa State Park** (4 nautical miles west of Pine Island, 941/964-0375, www.floridastateparks.org, 8am-sunset daily, $2) is the least-visited state park in Florida, but that's because there are no cars, no electricity, and no hot water, not because it's not worthy. Cayo Costa is accessible only by passenger ferry or private boat. Call **Tropic Star of Pine Island** (239/283-0015, $35 adults, $25 children) to make reservations.

The Calusa people lived on the island for hundreds of years. In the early 1800s Cuban fishers landed here, and in 1848 the U.S. government started managing the land. There are 20 private homes on the island, only a few lived in year-round. It's a place to tent camp ($22) or overnight in one of 12 rustic cabins ($40), all on the northern end of the island. There's a small pioneer cemetery as well as a fair number of wild pigs, along with sea creatures, birds, and swaths of sun-warmed sand.

1: stone crab claws at Cabbage Key Inn **2:** the Cabbage Key sign **3:** the Boca Grande Lighthouse **4:** Tarpon Lodge in Pineland

NORTH CAPTIVA ISLAND

Once part of Captiva Island, this island was severed during a hurricane in 1926. The right eye wall of 2004's Hurricane Charley passed over North Captiva Island and severed it into two parts; not surprisingly, folks call it Charley Pass. The island has maintained a reputation as a remote retreat for the super wealthy. There are four miles of state-owned beaches—the state bought 350 acres, almost half of the island, in 1975. At the turn of the 20th century, the island contained a vast tomato plantation; after that it was the processing plant for the Punta Gorda Fish Company. In recent years there have been about 50 year-round residents, most of them on the northern part in an enclave known as the Island Club, with the rest of the island given over to affluent vacationers driving golf carts and strolling the sparsely populated beaches. North Captiva Island is only accessible by private boat, water taxi, or seaplane. Water taxis leave daily from Pine Island and Captiva Island.

PINE ISLAND

Pine Island is one of the largest off the Gulf Coast of Florida and consists of Matlacha (mat-la-SHAY), Pine Island Center, Bokeelia (bo-KEEL-ya), Pineland, and St. James City. Unlike many of the barrier islands, you don't need a boat to get here. Take Pine Island Road from U.S. 41 to find this great fishing retreat (the tarpon fishing craze started here in the 1880s), a lovely place to observe wildlife, such as the bald eagle nesting sites.

Matlacha is a funky fishing village with a drawbridge over Matlacha Pass that has seen a lot of fishing action in its day. If you want to wet a line, there are plenty of bait and tackle shops and boat rentals at the Olde Fish House Marina and Viking Marina. The island's commercial district is Pine Island Center, where shopping, the school, the fire station, ball fields, and a community pool are located.

Bokeelia is the home port for many of the island's commercial fishing boats and the agricultural part of the island; you'll see mangoes and other tropical fruits such as carambola, longan, and loquat. This part of the island contains a few historic buildings, including the Museum of the Islands (5728 Sesame Dr., 239/283-1525, www.museumoftheislands.com, 11am-3pm Tues.-Sat., 1pm-4pm Sun. Nov.-Apr., 11am-3pm Tues.-Thurs. May-Oct., $2 adults, $1 under age 13), with exhibitions on Pine Island pioneers.

Pineland is home to the Randell Research Center (13810 Waterfront Dr., 239/283-2157, www.floridamuseum.ufl.edu, $7 adults, $5 seniors, $4 children), one of the main historic sites of Calusa mounds. You can spend a day paddling the Calusa route and explore the Calusa Heritage Trail, a series of artistic signs interpreting the Calusa way of life and religious beliefs. There are also guided tours (10am Wed.) from Pineland Marina (13921 Waterfront Dr., Bokeelia, 239/283-3593). Also in Pineland you'll find one of the country's smallest post offices, and boat rentals and fishing charters at the marina.

The Randell Research Center is near celebrated Florida author Randy Wayne White's house and across the street from Tarpon Lodge (13771 Waterfront Dr., Pineland, 239/283-3999, $110-350), which has 12 rooms in the charming waterfront Island House and 8 rooms in the on-site Historic Lodge. Ask for a water-view room with a private balcony overlooking the Gulf. For more privacy, stay in the one-bedroom cottage or two-bedroom boathouse. Both have kitchenettes. Enjoy wonderful seafood at the Tarpon Lodge Restaurant (11:30am-4pm and 5pm-9pm daily, $30-60); try the crab chowder and grilled snapper. The four-star restaurant is open to non-guests. The lodge is an excellent location if you're looking to rent a boat or charter and travel to Cabbage Key, Cayo Costa, Sanibel, or Captiva.

St. James City is Pine Island's residential community, with about two-thirds of the island's population. Most homes are located on canals with easy access to Pine Island Sound, San Carlos Bay, and the Gulf of Mexico.

Information and Services

Lee County is located in the **eastern time zone.**

VISITOR INFORMATION

The **Sanibel & Captiva Islands Chamber of Commerce** (1159 Causeway Rd., Sanibel, 239/472-1080, www.sanibel-captiva.org, 9am-5pm daily) maintains a visitors center on Causeway Road as you drive onto Sanibel from Fort Myers. The chamber gives away an island guide and sells a detailed street map ($3).

POLICE AND EMERGENCIES

In an emergency, call 911 or the local **Emergency Management Office** (239/533-3622). For a nonemergency police need, call the **Lee County Sheriff's Office** (239/477-1000), **Florida Highway Patrol** (239/278-7100), **U.S. Coast Guard** (239/463-5754), or **Florida Poison Information Center** (800/222-1222).

Sanibel and Captiva medical facilities serve the local community during business hours. For emergency medical needs, **HealthPark Care and Rehab Center** (16131 Roserush Court, Fort Myers, 239/343-7300) and **Lee Memorial Hospital** (2776 Cleveland Ave., Fort Myers, 239/343-2000) are full-service hospitals on the mainland with 24-hour emergency service. For your pharmacy needs on the islands, **CVS** (2331 Palm Ridge Rd., Sanibel, 239/472-1719) is convenient. If your pet has a medical problem, there's **Coral Veterinary Clinic** (1530 Periwinkle Way, Sanibel, 239/472-8387).

FISHING LICENSES

Fishing licenses are sold at all county tax collectors' offices and at many bait and tackle shops, or by phone (888/347-4356). On Sanibel, you can buy a license at the **Bait Box** (1041 Periwinkle Way, 239/472-1618); at **Bailey's** (2477 Periwinkle Way, Sanibel, 239/472-1516), at the corner of Tarpon Bay Road; at **Tarpon Bay Explorers** (900 Tarpon Bay Rd., 239/472-8900, www.tarponbayexplorers.com, 8am-6pm daily); and at all the marinas. Also pick up the Florida Marine Fisheries Commission's publication about size and bag limits. You do not need a license if you are fishing from a boat that has a valid recreational vessel saltwater fishing license, if you are under 16, or if you are a Florida resident fishing from a pier, a bridge, or on shore.

Sarasota County

Today, Sarasota is an undisputed cultural center, with theater, opera, symphony, ballet, art museums, and restaurants to rival those in much bigger cities. But it took a while for the city to get here. An influx of wealthy socialites settled the area from around 1910, among them circus magnate John Ringling. He scooped up property all around Sarasota, moving the circus's winter home here and building himself a winter residence, art museum, circus museum, and college.

The population doubled in the Florida land boom of 1924-1927, with hotels, tourist attractions, and a causeway over the bay sprouting up to accommodate the surge in interest. Tourists gradually settled their sights on the keys, noticing the 35 miles of glistening white-sand beaches that fringe their Gulf side. Each of the keys maintains its own identity, with

Highlights

Look for ★ to find recommended sights, activities, dining, and lodging.

★ **Marie Selby Botanical Gardens:** You don't have to be a master gardener to enjoy a day here. In 11 bay-front acres, the open-air and under-glass museum has more than 6,000 orchids and 20,000 other plants (page 116).

★ **John and Mable Ringling Museum of Art:** This museum is a must-see for fans of Flemish and Italian baroque art, with room after room of canvases, the most impressive of which is Peter Paul Rubens's *The Triumph of the Eucharist* (page 117).

★ **Spring Training at Ed Smith Stadium:** Visit the spring home of the Baltimore Orioles, where all the Grapefruit League teams cycle through in preparation for the summer season. Tickets are cheap, and the hot dogs are good (page 121).

★ **Film Festivals:** Time a trip to Sarasota to catch one of the city's two film festivals, the Sarasota Film Festival in April and the Cine-World Film Festival in November. Both are a citywide excuse for a party, in between two-hour popcorn-eating stints (page 130).

★ **Siesta Key Beach:** Despite other world-class contenders, Siesta Key Beach, with its powdered-sugar sand, usually gets top honors (page 139).

abundant beach access the unifying theme. Lido and St. Armands are really just extensions of downtown Sarasota, connected by a causeway, and are fairly urban. Longboat Key is extremely upscale, with tall resort hotels and condos and an abundance of golf courses. Siesta Key is more low-rise, with a personality to match. It's relaxed, laid-back, and definitely the most youthful spot on this part of the Gulf Coast. Casey Key is less a tourist draw, dotted with single-family homes. Anna Maria Island is a popular vacation spot, with an exceptional fishing pier and beach, a picturesque shopping district, plenty of lodging choices from casual to upscale, and a surprising number of excellent restaurants for the island's size.

PLANNING YOUR TIME

A typical vacation in this area is about a week, because there's about a week's worth of things for most people to do. Many of the beach houses and condos rent only by the week, especially in high season, but using sites like Airbnb, you can find nightly rentals year-round. Staying downtown in Sarasota is a little cheaper than staying beachside. Downtown streets and roads run east-west; avenues and boulevards run north-south.

The area's peak season, when the average temperatures around 75°F, begins in February and continues until Easter. During that time, prices are hiked and reservations are necessary for accommodations. What travel agents call "the value season" is summer in Sarasota, June-September, when Gulf waters are bath temperature and as gentle and safe to swim in as your bathtub. On a hot summer day (meaning 90°F with high humidity), the water temperatures aren't refreshing, but the beaches are peaceful and sparsely populated. Many of Sarasota's cultural institutions (symphony, ballet, opera, theaters) take a hiatus during the summer months, another drawback to visiting then.

Sarasota-Bradenton International Airport (SRQ, 6000 Airport Circle, at U.S. 41 and University Pkwy., Sarasota, 941/359-2770) is the closest airport. Another option is to fly into **Tampa International Airport** (TPA, 4100 George J. Bean Pkwy., 813/870-8700, www.tampaairport.com), with more flights and often better fares and rental car rates. Tampa International Airport is 53 miles north of Sarasota County via I-75 or I-275. Flights to **St. Petersburg-Clearwater International Airport** usually aren't as frequent or as cheap as to Tampa. Private planes can use the **Venice Municipal Airport** in the city of Venice, just down U.S. 41 from Sarasota.

Sarasota

The circus built Sarasota. Sure, the 361 days of sun each year and the exotic subtropical plants and animals brought people to the area, but when circus impresario John Ringling snapped up real estate, others started giving this rural orange grove and celery farm another look. In the 1920s, as Ringling began amassing baroque paintings in his new mansion, Ca' d'Zan, so too did his cohorts begin assembling collections of their own for winter rest and relaxation. Soon the opera, theater, and symphony orchestras took root.

Beyond Ringling's generous gift of his house and museums to the city, the Circus King gave Sarasota a tradition of arts patronage. Sarasota's population of 54,000, with help from twice that number of winter visitors, supports a vast number of arts events along with an equally strong restaurant and shopping scene. The striking thing is that it's all in

Sarasota County

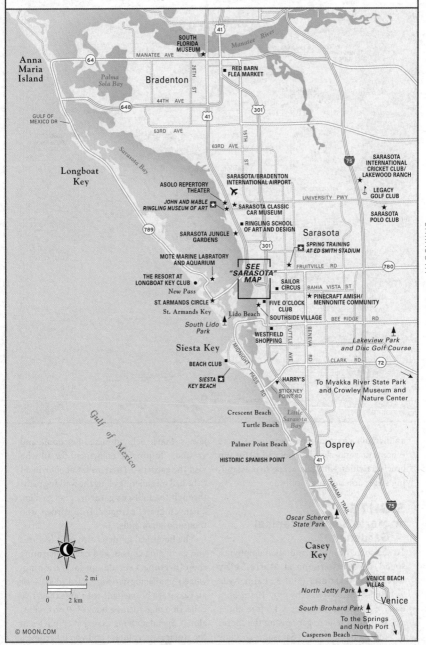

Anna
Maria
Island

**SOUTH
FLORIDA
MUSEUM** ★

MANATEE AVE

64

Palma
Sola Bay

Bradenton

26TH ST

41

RED BARN
FLEA MARKET ■

Manatee River

44TH AVE

648

301

GULF OF
MEXICO DR

53RD AVE

41

63RD AVE

15TH ST

Longboat
Key

Sarasota Bay

75

SARASOTA
INTERNATIONAL
CRICKET CLUB/
LAKEWOOD RANCH

LEGACY
GOLF CLUB

**SARASOTA/BRADENTON
INTERNATIONAL AIRPORT** ✈

UNIVERSITY PWY

ASOLO REPERTORY
THEATER ★

**SARASOTA CLASSIC
CAR MUSEUM** ★

SARASOTA
POLO CLUB

**JOHN AND MABLE
RINGLING MUSEUM OF ART** ★

**RINGLING SCHOOL
OF ART AND DESIGN** ■

Sarasota

789

**SARASOTA JUNGLE
GARDENS** ★

301

**SPRING TRAINING
AT ED SMITH STADIUM**

**MOTE MARINE LABRATORY
AND AQUARIUM** ★

**SEE
"SARASOTA"
MAP**

FRUITVILLE RD

780

**THE RESORT AT
LONGBOAT KEY CLUB** ●

New Pass

★

**SAILOR
CIRCUS** ■

BAHIA VISTA ST

St. Armands Key

ST. ARMANDS CIRCLE ★

Lido Beach

**FIVE O'CLOCK
CLUB** ■

**PINECRAFT AMISH/
MENNONITE COMMUNITY** ★

*South Lido
Park*

SOUTHSIDE VILLAGE

BEE RIDGE RD

Siesta Key

**WESTFIELD
SHOPPING** ■

TUTTLE AVE

BENEVA RD

*Lakeview Park
and Disc Golf Course*

MIDNIGHT PASS RD

CLARK RD

72

BEACH CLUB ★

**SIESTA
KEY BEACH** ✚

HARRY'S ■

STICKNEY
POINT RD

To Myakka River State Park
and Crowley Museum and
Nature Center

Gulf of Mexico

Crescent Beach

*Little
Sarasota
Bay*

Turtle Beach

Palmer Point Beach ★

Osprey

HISTORIC SPANISH POINT

41

TAMIAMI TRAIL

*Oscar Scherer
State Park*

75

Casey
Key

0   2 mi

0   2 km

**VENICE BEACH
VILLAS**

North Jetty Park

South Brohard Park

Venice

To the Springs
and North Port

Casperson Beach

© MOON.COM

Sarasota

an incredible natural environment. Sarasota is home to world-class beaches and all the fun beach activities, with easy access to outstanding state parks and outdoor fun.

SIGHTS
★ Marie Selby Botanical Gardens

To see some beautiful and alien epiphytes, spend a long afternoon at **Marie Selby Botanical Gardens** (900 S. Palm Ave., 941/366-5731, www.selby.org, 10am-5pm daily, $20 adults, $10 ages 4-17, free under age 4). The nine-acre gardens on the shores of Sarasota Bay are one of Sarasota's absolute

jewels. Marie Selby donated her home and grounds "to provide enjoyment for all who visit the gardens." There's a lot of enjoyment to be had meandering along the walking paths through the hibiscus garden, cycad garden, a banyan grove, a tropical fruit garden, and thousands of orchids.

The botanical gardens also host lectures and gardening classes, and have a charming shop (beginners should opt for a training-wheels phalaenopsis—very hard to kill—or an easy-care bromeliad) with an exhaustive collection of gardening books (80 on orchids alone). Spend an hour gazing at epiphytes in the tropical greenhouse and you'll become a

Hope Springs Eternal

Nine million gallons of warm mineral water flow daily at the Warm Mineral Springs Park (12200 San Servando Ave., North Port, 941/426-1692, 9am-5pm daily, weather permitting, $15 adults, $11.25 ages 6-17, free under age 6), with a higher mineral content than any other spring in the United States, believed by some to have healing powers. At 87°F year-round, it's said to be Ponce de León's fabled Fountain of Youth.

North Port isn't a tourist destination but rather a rural town where the big draw is this natural wonder, an hourglass-shaped springhead, 1.4 acres around and 230 feet deep. You'll learn quickly upon exiting your car that the water has a sulfurous smell similar to rotten eggs, and the mineral content makes it somewhat slimy-feeling. Russians and other international visitors come from across the globe to splash around in this water. The snack bar is the proof: It's an all-Russian menu—goulash, something called Russian ravioli, pictured with descriptions beneath, written in Russian.

Because the spring contains no dissolved oxygen, organic matter that gets into the springs stays more or less intact. In 1973, a scientist named Wilburn A. Cockrell brought up a nearly complete skeleton of an adult Paleo-Indian male that was 11,000 years old. Dated to nearly the same time period, part of a saber-toothed cat was also found. If you enjoy mineral springs, a trip to this impressive site will keep you fulfilled for half a day.

fan, I promise. Kids get fairly bored here, with a brief flurry of interest around the koi pond and butterfly garden. I recommend not bringing them unless they're really into plants or stroller-bound.

★ John and Mable Ringling Museum of Art

John Ringling's lasting influence on Sarasota is remarkable, but the John and Mable Ringling Museum of Art (5401 Bay Shore Rd., 941/359-5700, www.ringling.org, 10am-5pm daily, $25 adults, $23 seniors, $5 students, $15 active military, $10 teachers, $5 ages 6-17) makes it simply undeniable. A 2007 renovation made it one of the 20 largest art museums in North America, with four new buildings as well as the restored Historic Asolo Theatre.

The museum complex is spectacular, but the art museum is worth its hefty admission price. Built in 1927 to house Ringling's pathological accretion of 600 paintings, sculptures, and decorative arts, including more than 25 tapestries, the Mediterranean-style palazzo contains a collection that includes five extremely large paintings by Peter Paul Rubens, many Spanish works of art, and the music room and dining room of Mrs. William B.

Astor (Ringling bought all this in 1926 when the Astor mansion in New York was scheduled to be demolished). The permanent collection is spectacular, with Van Dycks, Poussins, and lots of other baroque masters. There are exhibitions such as a recent one on surrealism and another on the photos of Ansel Adams and Clyde Butcher that cover up to the 20th century.

The complex also houses the Museum of the Circus, a peek into circus history. The museum's newspaper clippings, circus equipment, parade wagons, and colossal bail rings creates nostalgia for a time most people today never knew. The single most impressive thing about the museum, which causes loitering and inspired commentary like "Whoa, cool," is the Howard Bros. Circus model. The world's largest miniature circus, it is a three-quarter-inch-to-the-foot scale replica of Ringling Bros. and Barnum & Bailey Circus at its largest. The model takes up 3,800 square feet, with eight main tents, 152 wagons, 1,300 circus performers and workers, 800 animals, a 57-car train, and a zillion wonderful details.

Also open to the public is John Ringling's home on the bay, Ca' d'Zan (House of John), an ornate structure evocative of Ringling's

1

2

3

two favorite Venetian hotels, the Danieli and the Bauer Grunwald. Completed in 1926 and fully restored in 2002, the house is 200 feet long with 32 rooms and 15 baths. It is truly a magnificent mansion.

Sarasota Classic Car Museum

What's your dream car? DeLorean? Ferrari? Mini Cooper? The **Sarasota Classic Car Museum** (5500 N. Tamiami Trail, 941/355-6228, www.sarasotacarmuseum.com, 9am-6pm daily, $13 adults, $11 seniors, $7.25 ages 6-12, free under age 6) has examples of everyone's favorite wheels in a collection of more than 100 vehicles, from muscle to vintage to exotic cars. You'll see a rare Cadillac station wagon, one of only five ever made, and the gift shop has collectibles for most automotive preoccupations. The museum rents out some of its cars if you want to make a grand entrance somewhere, and the cars are also available for photo ops.

Historic Spanish Point

History buffs may want to visit **Historic Spanish Point** (337 N. Tamiami Trail, Osprey, 941/966-5214, www.historicspanishpoint.org, 9am-5pm Mon.-Sat., noon-5pm Sun., $12 adults, $10 seniors and military, $5 ages 5-12), operated by the Gulf Coast Heritage Association. Bordered on its western edge by Little Sarasota Bay and by pine flatlands to the east, the 30-acre site tells the story of life in Sarasota going back many generations. Interpretive markers and an "Indian village" show how early indigenous Floridians fished and hunted here, building middens, or shell mounds, and a burial mound (an archaeology exhibit in the main hall gives the background on this). Then there's a restored pioneer home and chapel, revealing the story of the Webb family of early settlers. After that, stroll the gardens of heiress Bertha Matilde Honore Palmer's winter

estate on Osprey Point. The site has a butterfly garden, showing the larval and nectar plants for monarch, zebra longwing, swallowtail, and other butterflies native to the area.

South Florida Museum

The **South Florida Museum** (201 10th St. W., Bradenton, 941/746-4131, 10am-5pm Tues.-Sat., noon-5pm Sun., $19 adults, $17 seniors, $14 ages 4-12) is worth a short drive north to Bradenton. There are ice-age dioramas with animals and natural history exhibits that trace the state's ancient history. The Spanish explorers are covered in detail, and the museum houses the Tallant Collection of artifacts, an assemblage of loot from Floridian archaeological sites. Included in admission is access to the Bishop Planetarium, with a modern digital projection system, and the Parker Manatee Aquarium, a nearly 60,000 gallon aquarium used as a rehabilitation center for manatees.

Downtown Farmers Market

Despite the fact that Florida is a huge agricultural state that produces citrus, sugarcane, tomatoes, and strawberries, much of the Gulf Coast doesn't have serious farmers markets. Sarasota is an exception: Every Saturday morning year-round are the sights and smells unique to the local Florida farmers market: stacked produce; the cookie lady; a band of musicians passing the hat; babies in strollers smiling around a mouthful of gummed peach; wind chimes and handicrafts; and bromeliads, orchids, and cut flowers filling the bulging bags of nearly every shopper. The **Downtown Farmers Market** (Lemon Ave. at Main St., 7am-1pm Sat.) has been going on for 30 years with the tents and tables of 50 or so vendors. It used to be located on South Pineapple Avenue, but now it sets up each week on Lemon Avenue.

Sightseeing Tours

One of the more popular tours in the area is a two-hour guided tour of downtown Sarasota on a Segway with **Sarasota by Segway**

1: close-up of Ca' d'Zan, John Ringling's mansion 2: Mote Marine Laboratory and Aquarium 3: John and Mable Ringling Museum of Art

Tours (1370 Boulevard of the Arts, Suite C, 941/312-2615, www.sarasotabysegway.com, minimum age 12, 10am, 1pm, and 5:30pm daily, 1.5-hour tour $55, 2-hour tour $65), zipping along the bay front and arts community. The two side-by-side wheels (as opposed to a bike or motorcycle, in which the two wheels are in a line) are self-balancing, and you stand above the wheels on a little platform, steering the electric-powered vehicle with the handlebars. With speeds of up to 12 mph, they can be used in pedestrian areas and are a perfect way to cover serious ground at a pace slow enough to really appreciate things. Tours are limited to 12, and there are weight limitations.

If your passion is architecture, you won't need to be told that Sarasota is the birthplace of a certain strain of American modernism. (If this is news to you, pick up a copy of the excellent *The Sarasota School of Architecture, 1941-1966,* by John Howey.) The Sarasota Architectural Foundation (941/487-8728, www.sarasotaarchitecturalfoundation.org) hosts architectural tours, educational events, film screenings, exhibits, and parties for architecture lovers who travel to Sarasota to see its architecture up close and personal. A list of tours is posted on the website.

Family-Friendly Attractions

My favorite family attraction in Sarasota is Sarasota Jungle Gardens (3701 Bay Shore Rd., 941/355-5305, 10am-5pm daily, $18 adults, $17 seniors, $13 ages 4-16, free under age 4), but then I'm a sucker for quirky Old Florida attractions. Once part boggy banana grove, part universally agreed-upon "impenetrable swamp," the subtropical forest was purchased in the 1930s by newspaperman David Lindsay. He brought in tropical plants, trees, and bird species. It opened in 1940 as a tourist attraction. Every elementary student within 100 miles has made the trek by school bus to sit and watch the short birds of prey show and then wander along the paths through the lush formal gardens, the farmyard exhibit, the tiki gardens, and the flamingo area. The zoological gardens are home to about 100 animals,

many of them abandoned pets, so it's an odd assortment. Another section of the park, however, has nothing to do with plants or animals—in one back corner you'll find the Gardens of Christ. It's a series of eight two-dimensional dioramas by Italian-born sculptor Vincent Maldarelli depicting important events in the life of Jesus Christ.

The Mote Marine Laboratory and Aquarium (1600 Ken Thompson Pkwy., City Island, 941/388-4441, 10am-5pm daily, $22 adults, $16 ages 3-12, free under age 3) is an enjoyable small aquarium that also serves as a working marine laboratory. For kids, the coolest parts are the 135,000-gallon shark tank and the "immersion cinema" state-of-the-art theater with a 40-foot-wide high-definition screen. Visitors get their own interactive consoles that change the outcome of the game or movie on the screen. Children will also like the underwater microphone in the Marine Mammal Center, which allows visitors to hear the resident manatees chirping at each other and methodically munching the heads of romaine lettuce that bob at the top of their tank. There's a touch tank, where you'll see parents cajoling their small ones to feel up a sea urchin, starfish, horseshoe crab, or stingless stingray, as well as nicely interpreted exhibits of eels, puffer fish, sea horses, and extraterrestrial-looking jellies.

The more impressive part of the Mote is not open to the public—the Mote Marine Laboratory is known internationally for its shark research and more locally for its research on red tides, or algal blooms, which occasionally adversely affect Sarasota's summer beach season with fish kills.

Sarasota Bay Explorers (941/388-4200, www.sarasotabayexplorers.com) works in conjunction with Mote Marine Laboratory and runs their science boat trips from the facility. They offer several wonderful styles of ecotours, all perfect for a fun yet educational family outing. There are narrated Sea Life Encounter Cruises ($29 adults, $25 ages 3-12, free under age 3), backwater guided kayak tours ($55 adults, $45 children),

Sunset Cruises ($29 adults and ages 3-12, free under age 3), Nature Safari ($45 adults, $40 children), and private charters aboard the 24-foot Sea Ray Sundeck *Miss Explorer* (3-hour trip $345, 4-hour trip $420, 5-hour trip $495).

BEACHES

North Lido Beach is just northwest of St. Armands Circle, off John Ringling Boulevard on Lido Key (which is just a 2.5-mile spit of beach from Big Sarasota Pass to New Pass). It's a short walk from shops or restaurants, and fairly secluded. There are no lifeguards, swift currents, nor amenities. In the other direction from St. Armands Circle, southwest, you'll run into Lido Beach, which has parking for 400 cars, cabana beach rentals at the snack bar, playground equipment, and restrooms. It's a good hang-out-all-afternoon family beach, but is more crowded than North Lido. The third beach on Lido Key is called South Lido Park, on Ben Franklin Drive at the southern tip of Lido Key. The park is bordered by four bodies of water: the Gulf, Big Pass, Sarasota Bay, and Brushy Bayou. It has a nature trail, and the beach offers a great view of the downtown Sarasota skyline. There's a nice picnic area with grills as well as volleyball courts. Kayakers use this area to traverse the different waterways.

SPORTS AND RECREATION

Golf

Sarasota is Florida's self-described "Cradle of Golf," home to the state's first course, built in 1905 by Scottish colonist John Hamilton Gillespie. The nine-hole course was at the center of what is now Sarasota's downtown. That first course is long gone, but there are more than 1,000 holes to play at public, semiprivate, and private courses in Sarasota, at all levels of play and most budgets. Of the top Southwest regional courses as voted by the readers of *Florida Golf News* (a good resource, www. floridagolfmagazine.com), many are in the Sarasota area.

★ Spring Training at Ed Smith Stadium

Sarasota's Ed Smith Stadium has been an exciting part of the Grapefruit League's spring training program for years. The New York Giants arrived in 1924, followed by the Red Sox and then the White Sox. These days, Sarasota's Ed Smith Stadium (2700 12th St., at Tuttle Ave., 941/893-6300, box seats $22-36, reserved $16-30, general $8-14, parking $10) is the spring training home of the Baltimore Orioles (the Boston Red Sox now train a bit to the south in Fort Myers, and the Pittsburgh Pirates play in nearby Bradenton). To reach the stadium from I-75, take exit 210, Fruitville Road.

The 8,500-seat stadium provides intimate access to big-league play in a small-time venue. A 2010 renovation replaced all the seats, moved the bullpens, and added a Mediterranean-style facade. Cheap tickets and up-close seats make for a perfect outing on a warm Sarasota spring evening, even if baseball's not your sport. Day games start at 1:05pm and night games at 7:05pm; practices begin at 9am. Many spring training games sell out, so buy tickets in advance. For more information, visit www.baltimore.orioles.mlb.com.

Polo

There are scads of spectator sporting opportunities in Sarasota, but polo trumps many of them. Games are enormous fun, with horses racing around tearing up the lush sod of the polo grounds while their riders focus fiercely on that pesky little ball. Polo is amazingly physical and exciting to watch, whether you're in your fancy hat or your weekend jeans. Sarasota Polo Club (Lakewood Ranch, 8201 Polo Club Lane, 941/907-0000, www. sarasotapolo.com, 1pm Sun. mid-Dec.-early Apr., $12 adults, free under age 13) has been in operation since 1991, with professional-level players coming from around the world to play on the nine pristine fields. Bring a picnic or buy sandwiches and drinks once you're here.

Gates open at 10am, and dogs on leashes are welcome. You can also take polo lessons at Lakewood Ranch.

Cricket

Polo's not the only game in town. Cricket, anyone? The **Sarasota International Cricket Club** (Lakewood Ranch, 7401 University Pkwy., just east of Lorraine Rd., 941/726-6814, www.sarasotacricket.com) was founded in 1983 and has 40 active members who play 35 matches a year with clubs from around the Southeast. The season runs weekends mid-September-May, and watching is free. Call for a game schedule.

Lawn Bowling

Are you starting to see a theme? Vast expanses of perfect grass, a ridiculous number of beautiful sunny days—people in Sarasota clearly love to spend their time outside. The **Sarasota Lawn Bowling Club** (809 N. Tamiami Trail, at 10th St., 941/316-1123, 9am Mon.-Fri. May-Nov., 12:50pm Mon.-Fri. Nov.-Apr., $8 per day to play) is the oldest sporting club in Sarasota, with three greens, $1 *boule* (ball) rentals, and free lessons. Wear flat shoes if you want to play.

Pétanque

Similar to lawn bowling but a little more obscure, pétanque is played at **Lakeview Park** (7150 Lago St., 941/861-9830, 9am Sun., free to watch). Players toss and roll a number of steel balls as close as possible to a small wooden ball called the *cochonet* (the piglet). Pronounced PAY-tonk, it's a great spectator sport, especially when accompanied by a wide blanket, a bottle of wine, and a picnic. The Sarasota Club de Pétanque has 30 members of all skill levels, from beginners to the national singles champion, and they bring extra *boules* and are happy to give instructions. Lakeview Park, adjacent to Lake Sarasota, also contains an enclosed dog park (6am-dark daily)—even

if Rover stayed at home, visitors find it fun to just watch all that canine enthusiasm.

State Parks and Nature Preserves

If you want to spend a day outdoors, the 28,875-acre **Myakka River State Park** (13208 Hwy. 72, 941/361-6511, 8am-sunset daily, $6 per vehicle for up to 8 people, $4 per vehicle single occupant, $2 motorcycles, bicycles, and pedestrians), nine miles east of Sarasota, has a lot of activities: hiking, off-road biking, horseback riding, fishing, boating, canoeing, camping, and airboating. Both part of Florida Division of Forestry's Trailwalker Program, the North Loop (5.4 miles) and South Loop (7.4 miles) are fairly easy but scenic marked trails. Beyond these, there are 35 miles of unmarked trails open to hikers, mountain bikers (rentals $15 for 2 hours, or rent cool 4-person tandems for $30 for 1 hour), and equestrians (BYOH—that's bring your own horse). If you just want to breeze in for a few hours, a ride on the **Myakka Wildlife Tours Tram Safari** (10151 Sommers Rd., Sarasota, 941/377-5797, Dec.-May, $12 adults, $6 ages 6-12, free under age 5 if held in lap) takes visitors on a whirlwind tour of the park's backcountry, through shady hammocks, pine flatwoods, and lush marshes.

The 14-mile stretch of the scenic Myakka River has fairly easy-to-follow canoe trails (bring your own or rent at the Myakka Outpost; $20 for first hour, $5 each additional hour). Canoes and kayaks can be launched at the bridges, fishing area, other picnic areas, or at the boat ramp. During periods of low water (winter and spring), you'll have to portage around the weir at the south end of the Upper Lake. If you don't want to travel under your own paddle power, the park has a **boat tour** (941/365-0100, $20 adults, $12 ages 3-12, free under age 3) that runs every 1.5 hours, and a couple of the world's largest airboats, the *Gator Gal* and the *Myakka Maiden,* are available for guided one-hour tours on the

1: Ed Smith Stadium, home of the Orioles' spring training. 2: a rider at the Sarasota Polo Club

Sarasota's Golf Courses

Call for tee times and greens fees, as they vary wildly by time of day and time of year.

Bobby Jones Golf Club
1000 Circus Blvd., Sarasota, 941/365-4653
6,039 yards, par 71, course rating 68.4, slope 117

Greens of Manatee Golf Course
101 Cortez Rd. W., Bradenton, 941/755-8888
3,521 yards, par 61, course rating 58.6, slope 96

Moccasin Wallow Golf Club
9680 Buffalo Rd., Palmetto, 941/755-8888
7,019 yards, par 72, course rating 73.9, slope 136

Legacy Golf Club at Lakewood Ranch
8255 Legacy Blvd., Bradenton, 941/907-7067
Semiprivate, 7,069 yards, par 72, course rating 73.8, slope 130

The Links at Green Field Plantation
10325 Greenfield Blvd., Bradenton, 941/747-9432
6,719 yards, par 72, course rating 72, slope 130

Manatee County Golf Course
6415 53rd Ave. W., Bradenton, 941/792-6773
6,747 yards, par 72, course rating 71.6, slope 122

Peridia Golf & Country Club
4950 Peridia Blvd., Bradenton, 941/758-2582, www.peridiagcc.net
3,344 yards, par 60, course rating 55.0, slope 76

mile-wide and 2.5-mile-long Upper Myakka Lake (serious gator territory).

One unique park feature opened in 2004 in conjunction with Marie Selby Botanical Gardens. The Canopy Walkway, the first of its kind in North America, is an 85-foot-long observation deck suspension bridge that hangs 25 feet in the air in the midst of a sub-tropical forest canopy. Perched in the tops of live oaks, laurel oaks, and cabbage palms, your perspective on birdlife and animal life is unparalleled.

The park offers primitive camping ($5) and more equipped campsites ($26, including water and electric), but the neatest option might be one of the five palm log cabins (800/326-3521, reserve far in advance, $70 for up to 4 people) built in the 1930s. They're pretty comfortable, with two double beds, linens, blankets, and kitchen facilities.

Adjacent to the state park you'll find the Crowley Museum and Nature Center (16405 Myakka Rd., 941/322-1000, www. crowleyfl.com, 10am-5pm Sat.-Sun., $5 adults, $2 ages 3-12, free under age 3), a 190-acre wildlife sanctuary and education center. A couple of hours here goes nicely with time spent hiking or paddling in Myakka River State Park—there's a short nature trail, a boardwalk across Maple Branch Swamp, and an observation tower overlooking the Myakka River. To give more historical context, the Crowley's core is a pioneer museum with a rustic one-room cabin, a restored 1892 Cracker house, a working blacksmith shop, and a little sugarcane mill. The museum sponsors Pioneer Days every December, an annual antiques fair, a folk music festival in October, and a yearly stargazing night with high-powered telescopes.

Pinebrook/Ironwood Golf Club
4260 Ironwood Circle, Bradenton, 941/792-3288
3,706 yards, par 61, course rating 59.9, slope 101

The River Club
6600 River Club Blvd., Bradenton, 941/751-4211
7,026 yards, par 72, course rating 74.5, slope 135

River Run Golf Links
1801 27th St. E., Bradenton, 941/708-6331
5,825 yards, par 70, course rating 67.9, slope 115

Rosedale Golf and Country Club
5100 87th St. E., Bradenton, 941/753-6200
6,779 yards, par 72, course rating 72.9, slope 134

Terra Ceia
2802 Terra Ceia Bay Blvd., Palmetto, 941/729-7663
4,001 yards, par 62, course rating 67.9, slope 99

Timber Creek Golf Course
4550 Timber Lane, Bradenton, 941/794-8381
2,086 yards, par 27 (9 holes), course rating 35.1, slope 117

University Park Country Club
7671 Park Blvd., University Park, 941/355-3888
4,914-7,247 yards, par 72, course rating 67.8-74.4, slope 113-138

Waterlefe Golf & River Club
1022 Fish Hook Cove, Bradenton, 941/744-9771
6,908 yards, par 72, course rating 73.8, slope 145

Birders and families who want to spend an afternoon in nature without a lot of hassle will enjoy **Oscar Scherer State Park** (1843 S. Tamiami Trail, Osprey, 941/483-5956, 8am-sunset daily, $5 per vehicle 2-8 occupants, $4 per vehicle 1 occupant, $2 pedestrians, bicycles, and motorcycles, $4 sunset entry). Much of it is a classic Florida flatwoods (scrub pine and sawtooth palmetto populated by animals like scrub jays, gopher tortoises, and indigo snakes). The park has several marked trails open to hikers and bikers (it's sandy terrain, most suitable for mountain bikes), and kayakers paddle around South Creek (bring your own canoe or kayak, or rent canoes from the ranger station for $15 per hour, $60 per day), launched from the South Creek Picnic Area. The park also has a 104-site campground with tent and RV sites ($26, $13 seniors or disabled) equipped with electricity and water. The restrooms have hot showers, and the maximum RV length is 36 feet.

Guided Tours

Several companies offer boat tours on Sarasota Bay and into the Gulf of Mexico. **Key Sailing** (2 Marina Plaza, 941/346-7245, www.siestakeysailing.com, $60 pp for 2 hours, $80 pp for 3 hours) offers charters and sailing instruction aboard a sleek 41-foot Morgan Classic II. **LeBarge Tropical Cruises** (2 Marina Plaza, U.S. 41 at Marina Jack, 941/366-6116, www.lebargetropicalcruises.com, 9am-6pm daily, $27 adults, $22 ages 4-12) offers two-hour cruises of Sarasota Bay. Choose from a dolphin and manatee watch narrated by a marine biologist, a narrated sightseeing cruise, a tropical sunset cruise, or a full moon cruise when available. Check their website for cruise times.

ENTERTAINMENT AND EVENTS

Sarasota describes itself as the "cultural coast" of Florida.

Theater

Asolo Repertory Theatre (5555 N. Tamiami Trail, 941/351-9010, www.asolorep. org, Nov.-June) is a professional company that performs primarily in the 500-seat Mertz Theatre at the Florida State University Center for the Performing Arts, originally built as an opera house in 1903 in Dunfermline, Scotland. There's a second smaller 161-seat black-box theater on-site for performances of the conservatory season and smaller productions. Students at the FSU Asolo Conservatory for Actor Training also present a series of works and a variety of other special events and performances. Currently, the Asolo Rep and the Conservatory perform one show each in the Historic Asolo Theatre, located in the Ringling Museum's Visitors Pavilion.

Because the Conservatory's graduate-level program yields so many newly minted thespians in Sarasota, the whole theatrical playing field has been elevated. Worthwhile community and professional theater troupe efforts include the contemporary dramas and comedies at **Florida Studio Theatre** (1241 N. Palm Ave., 941/366-9000). Enjoy six annual musical productions with **The Players Center for Performing Arts** (838 N. Tamiami Trail, 941/365-2494, www.theplayers.org), and even the small community productions on two stages of the **Venice Theatre** (140 W. Tampa Ave., Venice, 941/488-1115).

Music and Dance

The oldest continuously running orchestra in Florida, **The Sarasota Orchestra** (Beatrice Friedman Symphony Center, 709 N. Tamiami Trail, box office 941/953-3434, www.sarasotaorchestra.org) offers an array of 100 classical, pops, chamber, and family concerts per year. It also hosts the internationally recognized Sarasota Music Festival each June, an intense three-week event of chamber music, master classes, and concerts, with the coaching and performance of chamber music as its primary priority. Several Masterworks programs are presented by the symphony throughout the season, as well as a collection of Great Escapes programs of light classics and pops.

Presenting a range of Broadway productions, world-class dance, music, comedy, and popular acts, as well as being the home base for many of the local arts organizations, local landmark **Van Wezel Performing Arts Hall** (777 N. Tamiami Trail, 941/953-3368, www. vanwezel.org). Designed by William Wesley Peters of the Frank Lloyd Wright Foundation, the building riffs on a seashell found by Frank Lloyd Wright's widow, Olgivanna, near the Sea of Japan. It has an eye-popping lavender-purple color scheme, and it looks accordion-folded, like a scallop shell, supposedly to maximize the space's acoustical possibilities.

The **Sarasota Ballet of Florida** (5555 N. Tamiami Trail, 941/359-0099, www. sarasotaballet.org) splits its performances between the Van Wezel, the Asolo, and the FSU Center for the Performing Arts, offering treasured classical works and contemporary and modern dance. The ballet was founded in 1987 by Jean Allenby-Weidner, former prima ballerina with the Stuttgart Ballet and works collaboratively with other local arts organizations on productions, such as a ballet with Circus Sarasota that tells the story of John Ringling's life, complete with aerialists and clowns. The Sarasota Ballet also runs the Sarasota Ballet Academy; The Next Generation, an award-winning scholarship program for youth at risk; and an international summer school.

The **Sarasota Opera** (61 N. Pineapple Ave., 941/328-1300, www.sarasotaopera.org) presents concerts year-round, but its much anticipated, often sold-out repertory season is February-March, housed in the beautifully restored 1926 Mediterranean Revival-style

---

1: Van Wezel Performing Arts Hall 2: sand sculpting contest 3: Asolo Repertory Theatre

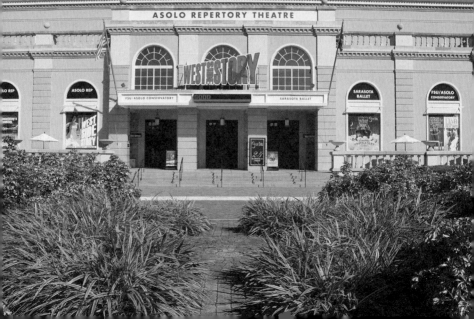

Edwards Theatre. The opera offers youth out-reach, and Sarasota Youth Opera receives all kinds of recognition for its productions.

An endurance event that takes grit and a good pair of opera glasses is the Sarasota Opera's **Winter Opera Festival,** which draws opera buffs from all over the country for a compact season of four productions that can be enjoyed nearly at one sitting for the especially enthusiastic. The festival provides a good program of obscure operas as well as the big crowd-pleasers. While you're hanging around in the striking art deco lobby during intermission, look up: The chandelier is from the movie *Gone with the Wind.*

Sarasota has an annual chamber music fes-tival each April, **La Musica International Chamber Music Festival** (rehearsals at Mildred Sainer Pavilion of New College of Florida, performances at Edwards Theatre, 61 N. Pineapple Ave., 941/366-8450, ext. 7, www.lamusicafestival.org, $40, rehearsal pass $75). Before the evening performances are short lectures about the pieces.

Circuses

Five of the seven sons of August and Marie Salomé Ringling of Baraboo, Wisconsin, ran away and joined the circus—or, rather, invented their own. In 1870 they premiered their show and charged a penny admission, building it year by year from a modest wagon show (its first "ring" a strip of cloth staked out to form a circle) to a major national show that traveled via rail from town to town. Meanwhile, circus titans P. T. Barnum and James A. Bailey teamed up in 1888 to create "The Greatest Show on Earth," blowing away the competition with their glitz, animals, and death-defying acts. It was Bailey's untimely death in 1906 that led the "Greatest Show" to be bought out by the Ringling brothers. The two circuses ran separately until 1919, when they were joined to form the **Ringling Bros. and Barnum & Bailey Circus.**

In the 1920s, John Ringling and his wife, Mable, built a spectacular Venetian-style es-tate on Sarasota Bay called Ca' d'Zan (House of John in Venetian dialect). They built an art museum to house their bursting-at-the-seams collection of 17th-century Italian paintings, Flemish art, and works by Peter Paul Rubens. In 1927 Sarasota became an official circus town—the Ringling Bros. and Barnum & Bailey Circus's winter quarters were moved here, giving the sedate Florida town a first-hand look at the oddity, eccentricity, and glamour that is the circus.

Many of the circus performers who acted in the *Wizard of Oz* and that ultimate non-PC film *Terror of Tiny Town* (a musical western starring all little people) called Sarasota home, with specially built homes in a section of town called, unsurprisingly, **Tiny Town** (you can visit this area on Ever-Glide guided tours).

Today visitors get a sense of Sarasota's cir-cus history at the **Museum of the Circus,** housed in the **John and Mable Ringling Museum of Art** (5401 Bay Shore Rd., 941/359-5700, 10am-5pm Fri.-Wed., 10am-8pm Thurs., $25 adults, $23 seniors, $15 military, $5 students and ages 6-17) on the Ringling grounds, but during February-March the circus comes alive with **Circus Sarasota** (140 University Town Center Dr., 941/355-9335, $15-55). Founded in 1997 by Ringling Bros. alums Pedro Reis and aerial-ist Dolly Jacobs, a second-generation circus performer—her father was the famous clown Lou Jacobs—it's a single-ring European-style circus that changes every year. Reis and Jacobs often perform an aerial pas de deux, and there are tightrope acts, trained horses, aerial ac-robats from China, clowns, tumbling, con-tortionists, and so forth, all performed in an intimate setting.

Despite the fact that Ringling Bros. per-formed their last show in 2017, Sarasota is still training the next generation of circus per-formers. **PAL Sailor Circus** (2075 Bahia Vista St., 941/361-6350, $20 adults, $15 children) has been thrilling audiences for more than 50 years, educating kids 8-18 in the circus arts and then letting them put on a show. In 2004, the Police Athletic League took over the Sailor Circus as one of its after-school programs.

Clowning Around

tiny statues in the Museum of the Circus

Ringling Bros. and Barnum & Bailey Circus, the oldest—in addition to being the greatest—show on earth, reinvents itself every two years with two totally different traveling units. The Red Unit and the Blue Unit each tour North America 11 months of the year for two years before going back to winter quarters (now in Tampa, but historically in Sarasota) and preparing a new edition. The Red Unit presents the odd-numbered editions, the Blue Unit presents the even-numbered editions (so, for instance, if you see the 140th edition Blue Unit this year, you'll see the 141st edition Red Unit next year).

One year the show's centerpiece might be the Living Carousel, an assemblage of 105 people, 27 animals, and more gold lamé than a Liberace concert, with something like two million rhinestones and elephant blankets inset with 81,000 mirrors, turning the whole arena into a disco-ball fantasy. Or the Globe of Steel, a 16-foot steel globe, into which ride eight members of the Torres Family on a complicated routine of loops around the interior, reaching speeds of 65 mph, and then someone gets in and stands there, daring one of them to flub up. Talk about extreme sports. Maybe you'll see sixth-generation circus performer Taba (no last names please), the tiger whisperer, who quietly persuades four different types of Bengal tigers to romp around the center ring. Then there are the high-wire acts, the classic Clown Alley, and an incredible live band performing zany circus music.

These days Ringling Bros. and Barnum & Bailey Circus is not the only show in town. Even with the pageantry and death-defying acts, it has to lure audiences from other popular traveling shows like Cirque du Soleil and persuade them to choose the big top over the big screen. To get a sense of how much the magic of the circus means, visit the **Museum of the Circus** at the **John and Mable Ringling Museum of Art** (5401 Bay Shore Rd., 941/359-5700, 10am-5pm Fri.-Wed., 10am-8pm Thurs., $25 adults, $23 seniors, $15 military, $5 students and ages 6-17). John Ringling brought the circus to Sarasota from Bridgeport, Connecticut, in 1927, thus changing this part of Florida forever. The museum documents, preserves, and exhibits the history of the circus with props, rare handbills, parade wagons, tent poles, and memorabilia.

About 90 students participate in the twice-annual training sessions, where they learn circus skills like clowning, tumbling, high-wire, flying trapeze, unicycling, juggling, rigging, and costuming. Then, in March and the end of December, the students perform for the public in an exciting four-ring circus.

Festivals and Events

February is not a bad time to visit because you can catch the monthlong annual run of the European-style **Circus Sarasota.** Music lovers may want to come in February or March for the repertory season of the **Sarasota Opera,** although in April there's **La Musica International Chamber Music Festival.** April brings the weeklong **Florida Wine Fest & Auction.**

If you're visiting the area strictly for the white powdery sand, come in May for the pro-am **Sand Sculpting Contest** on Siesta Key Beach. **Fourth of July** fireworks over the Gulf are also wonderful from the vantage spot of Siesta Key Beach.

★ FILM FESTIVALS

Sarasota supports two film festivals. By far the more famous is the **Sarasota Film Festival** (multiple venues, box office 332 Cocoanut Ave., 941/364-9514, www.sarasotafilmfestival.com) every April. The fastest-growing film festival in the country, it showcases 180 independent feature, documentary, narrative, and short films. The event usually includes a Shorts Fest, a couple of family-oriented events, and lots of panel discussions with industry leaders and symposiums with guest stars. Every November is the Sarasota Film Society's 10-day **Cine-World Film Festival** (Burns Court Cinemas, 506 Burns Lane, 941/955-3456), which showcases Florida film artists and the best of the preceding Toronto, Cannes, New York, and Telluride film festivals.

NIGHTLIFE

Bars

Downtown has a few nightspots that stand out. For a more rarefied experience, head to the **Jack Dusty Lounge** (Ritz-Carlton, 1111 Ritz-Carlton Dr., 941/309-2000, 5pm-midnight Mon.-Thurs., 5pm-2am Fri.-Sat., 1pm-midnight Sun., $10-25). A 2018 remodel made it brighter, sleeker, and more modern with a restaurant serving steaks and seafood and an outstanding outdoor seating area on the water where you can sip specialty drinks and socialize.

If you have a passion for beer, the **Mandeville Beer Garden** (428 N. Lemon Ave., 941/312-1961, 5pm-11pm Tues., 11am-11pm Wed.-Thurs., 11am-1am Fri.-Sat., 11am-9pm Sun., $5-10) will quench your thirst for cold brews. They have 30 beers from all over the world on tap and more than 100 bottled varieties. An excellent outdoor area has seating and games like corn hole and Ping-Pong. They promote a family-friendly environment, and dogs are welcome.

Drinks and good times are to be had at many places, including the **Beach Club** (5151 Ocean Blvd., Siesta Key, 941/349-6311, www.beachclubsiestakey.com, noon-2am daily) in Siesta Key Village and **Sharky's** (1600 Harbor Dr. S., Venice, 941/488-1456, www.sharkysonthepier.com, 11:30am-10pm Sun.-Thurs., 11:30am-midnight Fri.-Sat.), beachfront on the Pier in Venice. Go to **8 Ball Lounge** (3527 Webber St., 941/922-8314, noon-2am daily) when you feel like working on your own game.

Dance and Music Clubs

When you're ready to get on the dance floor, the **Five o'clock Club** (1930 Hillview St., 941/366-5555, noon-2am Mon.-Fri., 3pm-2am Sat.-Sun., happy hour noon-8pm daily, cover charge varies) in Southside Village has what the mechanic ordered. There's live music seven nights a week, with national and local rock, blues, and pop bands taking the stage at 10pm. The 5-O draws a 30s and 40s crowd and just a smattering of college kids. The **Gator Club** (1490 Main St., 941/366-5969) is another longtime nightlife haunt. There's live music every night, often of the Jimmy Buffett cover variety, plus pool tables upstairs and an impressive single-malt selection.

For something totally different and un-booze-centric, track down the **Siesta Key Drum Circle** on Sunday evenings, a drop-in party in which everyone adds their own beat. It gets under way about one hour before sunset, just south of the main pavilion between lifeguard stands 3 and 4.

SHOPPING

The shops of **St. Armands Circle** on Lido Key have been a primary retail draw in Sarasota for a long time, historically for high-end boutiques. These days the shops cover familiar ground—chains like **Chico's** (443 St. Armands Circle, 941/388-1393), **Tommy Bahama** (300 John Ringling Blvd., 941/388-2888), **Fresh Produce** (1 N. Blvd. of the Presidents, 941/388-1883), and **White House/Black Market** (317 St. Armands Circle, 941/388-5033)—and a handful of up-scale independent boutiques. Explore the circle's novelty and giftware shops **Fantasea Seashells** (345 St. Armands Circle, 941/388-3031) or **Kilwin's** (312 John Ringling Blvd., 941/388-3200), offering ice cream and fudge.

Towles Court Artist Colony (1938 Adams Lane) in downtown Sarasota is a collection of 16 quirky pastel-colored bungalows and cottages that contain artists working furiously and the art they've been working on. Watch them in action and buy their work (11am-4pm Tues.-Sat.).

Palm Avenue and **Main Street** downtown are lined with galleries, restaurants, and cute shops, and historic **Herald Square** in the SoMa (south of Main Street) part of downtown on Pineapple Avenue has a dense concentration of antiques shops and up-scale housewares stores. Also on Pineapple is **Artisan's World Marketplace** (128 S. Pineapple Ave., 941/365-5994, 10am-5pm Mon.-Fri., 9am-2pm Sat.), which promotes self-employment for low-income artisans in developing countries worldwide by selling their baskets, clothing, and handicrafts.

Westfield Siesta Key (3501 S. Tamiami Trail, 941/955-0900) is a standard mall, with Macy's as its anchor store and many of the usual suspects (Talbots, Bare Minerals, GNC, Chico's). When you need to make those credit cards sizzle, head north on I-75 to the **Ellenton Premium Outlets** (5461 Factory Shops Blvd., Ellenton, 941/723-1150). There are more than 130 stores (Ralph Lauren, Gap, Guess, Tommy Hilfiger, Nike, Nautica) with deep discounts.

If your mantra is "reduce, reuse, recycle," you'll find all kinds of used goods at the more than 400 covered booths of the **Red Barn Flea Market** (1707 1st St. E., Bradenton, 941/747-3794), in Manatee County to the north. Go on the weekend for the greatest number of vendors and the widest variety of things, from collectibles and antiques to out-and-out junk.

FOOD

Strips of chain restaurants pop up on the Gulf Coast of Florida like mushrooms after the wet season. In fact, many chains, such as Outback Steakhouse and Hooters, call the Gulf Coast home, and new chains are often market-tested first in the urban areas in this part of Florida. Why, I ask myself? Demographics. In an area that has a dense concentration of retirees, the newest growth segment is young families. What do the elderly and young families have in common? They like to eat out, but they want things to be familiar. They want to go to Chili's and eat the same thing they ate last time. Even though Sarasota is awash with chain restaurants, the city still has an abundance of unique restaurants and the diners who love them.

Downtown

★ **Bijou Café** (1287 1st St., 941/366-8111, 11:30am-2pm Mon.-Fri., 5pm-9pm Mon.-Thurs., 5pm-10pm Fri.-Sat., 4pm-8pm Sun., $20-40) has been a local gem since 1986, making everyone's top 10 list and bringing praise from *Zagat, Bon Appétit,* and *Gourmet.* It's what you'd call continental-American fare, presided over by chef Jean-Pierre Knaggs and his wife, Shay. A couple of blocks from Ritz-Carlton Sarasota in a 1920s gas station turned restaurant, the vibe is special-occasion dining, with a bar, a lounge, a private room, and outdoor dining courtyards. The wine list features a number of French, American, and Italian wines, and the menu contains shrimp and crab bisque, roast duck with orange or sherry sauce, and crab cakes with Louisiana rémoulade. And don't miss the crème brûlée. Opened in 2003, **Mattison's City Grill** (1 N. Lemon Ave., 941/330-0440, www. mattisons.com 11am-11pm Tues.-Thurs., 11am-midnight Fri., 9:30am-midnight Sat., 11am-10pm Sun.-Mon., $17-25) is casual and hopping, with Italian-ish small plates and pizzas. More urban than many of the other downtown restaurants, it has great outdoor seating, cool wine events, cigar dinners, and live music nightly. It has been so successful that owner Paul Mattison has a virtual empire in the area: Mattison's Riverside, Mattison's Forty One, Mattison's Bayside at Van Wezel, and a catering business—all fun, fresh dining experiences.

Marina Jack's (2 Marina Plaza, 941/365-4232, www.marinajacks.com, 11am-10pm Sun.-Thurs., 11am-11am Fri.-Sat., $10-35) is a longtime downtown favorite with nightly live music. It's all about casual waterside dining, with differently priced ways to eat with the water in view. Choose from the second-level Bayside Dining Room, the Blue Sunshine Patio, or a cocktail at the Deep Six Lounge and Piano Bar. If you still don't feel aquatic enough, there's the *Marina Jack II* yacht to wine and dine on the bay. Back on land, the menu leans to crowd-pleasers like crab-stuffed mushrooms, conch fritters, and steaks.

A fun, casual seafood joint with no water views, **Barnacle Bill's** (1526 Main St., 941/365-6800, 11:30am-9pm Mon.-Thurs., 11:30am-10pm Fri.-Sat., 4pm-9pm Sun., $15-25) is the chain's white-tablecloth establishment, with choices like crab cakes, fried popcorn shrimp, or stuffed flounder. Its other location is at 5050 North Tamiami Trail (941/355-7700).

Any list of important downtown restaurants has to include ★ **Michaels On East** (1212 East Ave. S., 941/366-0007, 11:30am-2pm and 5pm-9pm Mon.-Thurs., 5pm-10pm Fri.-Sat., $15-30), slightly south of downtown. It has won best-of-Florida accolades from nearly everyone since opening in the 1990s and has kept up with the newcomers, consistently pushing the envelope and wowing diners with New American takes and a lavish interior. During the day it's a power-lunching crowd; at night, romantic dinners include grilled duck breast paired with Bermuda onion and shiitake fondue and fig and pecan risotto, all flavors showcased with a nice selection of wine.

When you're tired of fish, ★ **Patrick's** (1481 Main St., 941/955-1481, 11am-10pm Mon.-Thurs., 11am-11pm Fri.-Sat., 11am-9pm, $10-20) gets top honors for Sarasota's best burger. It's a casual spot, with no reservations accepted, and the bar scene is fun. Patrick's has an extensive lunch and dinner menu with an exceptional variety of burgers, steaks, seafood, salads, and traditional bar-fare favorites like chicken wings and jalapeño poppers. The burger selection is creative and original—try the Bronx burger with grilled onions, swiss cheese, and barbecue sauce. The wine list contains 20 well-selected wines, and the beer selection focuses on stout ales and Irish varieties.

For a quick, inexpensive bite, head to downtown's **Café Epicure** (1298 N. Palm Ave., 941/366-5648, 11am-10:30pm daily, $5-25). It's a cool bistro, deli, and market and an easy place to hang out on the patio and write postcards while having a drink and enjoying a great sandwich, salad, or pizza.

Best breakfast? It's a chain, but this location is without a doubt the best of the breed. **First Watch Restaurant** (1395 Main St., 941/954-1395, 7am-2:30pm daily, $7-15) serves Sarasota's finest quick, no-fuss, inexpensive breakfasts with bottomless coffee and cheery service. Investigate the Inspired Italian

---

1: a beach boardwalk leads to the ocean at Lido Beach **2:** Bijou Café **3:** St. Armands Circle on Lido Key

omelet (roasted red peppers, tomatoes, mozzarella cheese, and Italian sausage, topped with fresh herbs) or the carrot-cake pancakes. Lines can be long, but they move quickly. If you just can't wait, walk south along Central Avenue and stop into one of the sidewalk coffeehouses.

St. Armands Circle and Lido Key

In 1893, a Frenchman named Charles St. Amand bought a little mangrove island off Sarasota, homesteading with fishing, hunting, and growing a little produce. In the land deeds his name was misspelled, so it stuck when circus magnate John Ringling bought the property in 1917 (it's rumored he won it in a poker game). He planned for St. Armands Key to be a residential and shopping development laid out in a circle, bringing people over first by steamer and then via the John Ringling Causeway completed in 1926 (the major lifting was done by circus elephants). The area has had a consistent commitment to becoming as upscale as possible since Ringling wheedled it away from Charles St. Amand. It's often compared to Rodeo Drive and other famous shopping districts.

There are a variety of shops, from upscale clothing stores to tourist souvenirs, and some of the city's best restaurants around the circle; you can explore the shops and go to dinner. Two of the oldest on the stretch are **Café L'Europe** (431 St. Armands Circle, 941/388-4415, 11:30am-9pm Sun.-Thurs., 11:30am-10pm Fri.-Sat., $25-40) and the **Columbia Restaurant** (411 St. Armands Circle, 941/388-3987, 11am-10pm daily, $10-25). Close together, both feature beautiful dining rooms and wonderful sidewalk dining. The Columbia opened in 1959, making it the oldest restaurant in Sarasota. Its sister restaurant in Tampa is the oldest restaurant in Florida. The Cuban food is authentic, and dishes include the red snapper Alicante and 1905 Salad with chopped cheese, olives, and vinaigrette. The black bean soup and stuffed pompano in parchment are excellent choices.

Table-Hopping

In the off-season, Sarasota's many culinary pearls are yours for the plucking—and during June that plucking gets all the more delicious with a 14-day **Savor Sarasota restaurant week.** In a city with one of the highest concentrations of *Zagat*-rated restaurants in Florida, dozens have banded together to offer value-priced three-course prix-fixe menus.

It's definitely a bargain, but what's in it for the restaurants? According to Michael Klauber, proprietor of Michaels on East and one of the instigators of the restaurant week, "The original idea came from the local convention and visitors bureau. They got a few of us restaurateurs together to talk about it. We thought this would be a great way to showcase the restaurants, and it gives the restaurants an opportunity to explore something different with a special menu. I hope it can become a destination event, and that hotels and resorts will see an influx of people."

Some restaurants include interactive cooking demonstrations; others feature live music. Many of the restaurants offer several choices for appetizer, entrée, and dessert, some with suggested wine pairing flights. At the core, though, it's not complicated: Pick a participating restaurant, make a reservation, dine, and pay ($16 lunch, $32 dinner). Repeat. For more information about participating restaurants, events, and pricing, visit www.savorsarasota.com.

Columbia is also known for its fruity sangria. Café L'Europe has a broad collection of culinary influences that are hard to pin down: The kitchen does an equally good job with a New England lobster roll, wild mushroom ravioli, and herb-crusted lamb with mint sauce.

15 South Ristorante Enoteca (15 S. Blvd. of the Presidents, 941/388-1555, 4:30pm-1am Fri.-Sun., 4:30pm-10:30pm Mon.-Thurs., $15-35) seems to be the place to go in the area for northern Italian, and the upstairs nightclub features an excellent martini bar and diverse music nightly (Latin acts, belly dancing, Caribbean tunes, a big band, you name it). The restaurant's menu will be familiar, but dishes like grilled veal chop and garlic bruschetta are exceptional.

It's a chain, but **Tommy Bahama Tropical Café & Emporium** (300 John Ringling Blvd., 941-388-2888, 10am-10pm daily, $20-30) is just plain fun, the food is excellent, and the drinks are too good for common sense to kick in. The store downstairs carries Tommy Bahama's signature mix of tropical leisurewear and cool housewares—you have to take a flight of stairs off to the side to reach the upstairs restaurant, which has huge windows that look out on the circle. Salads and drinks are pricey but good.

Cha Cha Coconuts (417 St. Armands Circle, 941/388-3300, 11am-11pm Sun.-Thurs., 11am-midnight Fri.-Sat., $10-15) is a good place to go for a drink or island-inspired dishes like coconut shrimp or a burger topped with mango chutney. **Blue Dolphin Cafe** (470 John Ringling Blvd., 941/388-3566, 7am-2pm daily, $7-15) is for cheap diner-style breakfasts with a twist (crab benedict, raspberry blintzes). When you're ready for some great fudge, head to **Kilwin's** (312 John Ringling Blvd., 941/388-3200, 9am-11pm Sun.-Thurs., 9am-11:30pm Fri.-Sat.).

Southside Village

You may be driving through Southside Village, and before you have time to ask, "Hey, why are all these beautiful young professional types drinking glasses of red wine at sidewalk tables in the middle of a Tuesday afternoon?" you've passed right through it on your way downtown. Visitors don't hit this little shopping-restaurant area with frequency, which is a shame. A few of Sarasota's most contemporary restaurants are here. Southside Village is centered on South Osprey Avenue between Hyde Park and Hillview Streets, about 15 blocks south of downtown.

The best place in Sarasota to pick up the ingredients for a picnic is in the same block: **Morton's Gourmet Market** (1924 S. Osprey Ave., 941/955-9856, www.mortonsmarket. com, 8am-8pm Mon.-Sat., 10am-7pm Sun.)

has the kind of fresh salads, deli items, fancy specialty sandwiches, and cooked entrées that make you press your nose up against the glass case, leaving an embarrassing smudge. Most items are cheap, and you can eat on the premises or take it out.

Pacific Rim (1859 Hillview St., 941/330-8071, www.pacificrimsarasota.com, 11:30am-2pm and 4:30pm-9:30pm Mon.-Thurs., 11:30am-2pm and 4:30pm-10:30pm Fri., 5pm-10:30pm Sat., 5pm-9pm Sun., $10-20) takes you on a pleasant pan-Asian romp, from Thai basil curries to expertly rolled tekka maki sushi and beyond. Play chef here and select your combinations of meats and veggies to be grilled or cooked in a wok.

Libby's Café and Bar (1859 Hillview St., 941/330-8071, www.pacificrimsarasota.com, 11:30am-2pm and 4:30pm-9:30pm Mon.-Thurs., 11:30am-2pm and 4:30pm-10:30pm Fri., 5pm-10:30pm Sat., 5pm-9pm Sun., $10-20) specializes in steaks and seafood, and also offers a nice variety of New American comfort-food favorites with a twist such as kobe meatloaf, rotisserie half chicken, and a short-rib burger. It's a stylish place with white table cloths, dark-wood paneling, and a large copper bar. The outdoor seating area under the palms is a little more casual if the weather is nice.

International District at Gulf Gate

Many of the better less-expensive restaurants can be found at the **Gulf Gate neighborhood,** a tiny international district that spans a three-block area from Gulf Gate Drive to Superior Avenue, and from Mall Drive around the block to Gateway Avenue. It's where to go for a quick meal, takeout, or just something that won't break the bank. At Gateway Avenue is **Rico's Pizzeria** (6547 Gateway Ave., 941/922-9604, 11am-10pm daily, $6-15). Just down the road, get your pizza fix late into the night at **Solorzanos Late Night Pizza** (6670 Superior Ave., 941/924-5800, 10am-4am daily, $6-15), popular with the party crowd. Once you hit Gulf Gate Drive, there are a couple of Chinese and sushi takeout places, a Russian joint, and a British tearoom.

Pinecrest and Beyond

Amish cuisine—if that looks like a typo, recall that Sarasota is a huge Amish and Mennonite winter resort. Both groups come from Pennsylvania and the Midwest looking for sun and good Amish food, with luck on both counts. The locus of Amish activity is in Pinecrest, where you'll see the bearded men in suspenders and wide straw hats, the women in long skirts and bonnets, all enjoying the Florida weather. They eat at **Yoder's** (3434 Bahia Vista, 941/955-7771, 6am-8pm Mon.-Thurs., 6am-9pm Fri.-Sat., $7-15), a Sarasota institution since 1975, with wholesome rib-sticking country ham and corn fritters, turkey and gravy, meat loaf and mashed potatoes, and pies, pies, pies. Note especially the peanut butter cream pie. **Troyer's Dutch Heritage** (3713 Bahia Vista, 941/955-8007, 7am-8pm Mon.-Thurs., 7am-9pm Fri.-Sat., $5-12) is even more venerable, dating to 1969, with sturdy accessible buffet-style meals and a gift shop on the second floor.

ACCOMMODATIONS

There are plenty of condos and beachfront rentals in the Sarasota area, but most rent only by the week. If that's your time frame, the weeklong rentals are a financially prudent choice. If you're only here for a few days, hotels and motels run the gamut from moderately priced and no-frills to truly luxurious. Generally speaking, beachside places are pricier than mainland or downtown accommodations, and winter rates are highest, dropping usually by a third in summer. Listed here are Sarasota and Lido Key accommodations; Longboat Key, Siesta Key, and Venice are covered in *The Keys* section of this chapter.

Under $100

Less than a mile from Siesta Key, a bargain and unique fun experience is **Tiny House Siesta** (6600 Ave. A, 941/474-3782, $95-270), with several tiny houses that start at a very tiny 152 square feet. Each tiny house has its own full kitchen, bath, and outdoor area to enjoy. The location is exceptionally convenient, a very short drive to Siesta Key and the beaches and a five-mile drive to downtown Sarasota. If you've ever wondered what it's like to stay in a tiny house or are thinking of building one, this is a great place to experience tiny house living for yourself.

$100-200

Business travelers enjoy **Springhill Suites by Marriott** (1020 University Pkwy., 941/358-3385, $149-200), a moderately priced all-suites hotel close to the airport. All rooms have a king or two double beds with separate sleeping, eating, and working areas. There's a pull-out sofa bed, a pantry area with mini fridge, a sink, and a microwave, and a big desk. The included continental breakfast isn't an afterthought, offering items like sausage, eggs, oatmeal, and make-your-own waffles.

$200-300

The three-story **La Quinta Inn & Suites Sarasota** (1803 Tamiami Trail N., 941/366-5128, $145-300) is not far from the Ringling School of Art and Design, a few minutes' drive from downtown. Rooms are midsize, some with sofa beds, and those on interior hallways have desks. There's an outdoor pool, a pleasant complimentary breakfast, and free parking, and pets under 30 pounds are accepted.

Courtyard by Marriott (850 University Pkwy., 941/355-3337, $149-250) is a mostly business three-story hotel across from the airport, convenient to both Bradenton and Sarasota. This hotel has a hot breakfast buffet and is an excellent choice for business trips or family vacations.

Over $300

The **Ritz-Carlton Sarasota** (1111 Ritz-Carlton Dr., 941/309-2000, www.ritzcarlton.com, $500-1,000), is a 266-room, 18-story luxury hotel right downtown, convenient to restaurants and attractions. Rooms are spacious with balconies and marble baths, and there's a lovely pool, three lighted tennis courts, two excellent restaurants, and the Jack Dusty Lounge. The Ritz has an excellent spa with a sauna, a steam room, and a whirlpool to help you relax. A section of the hotel will be under construction until 2020, but you can escape the noise at the nearby Beach Club and pool on Lido Key. For a pampered experience, Club Level gives you access to spa amenities and the wonderful Club Level Lounge, which includes five meals a day and offers a full open bar, wine, champagne, and snacks. The Tom Fazio-designed course is 13 miles from the hotel, but it is immaculately maintained and the clubhouse serves food and drinks. The hotel offers shuttle service.

Lido Beach Resort (700 Benjamin Franklin Dr., 941/388-2161, www.lidobeachresort.com, $200-600) is a favorite among families, featuring one- and two-bedroom suites with kitchens. Two beautiful free-form pools and three hot tubs are right on the beach, along with one of Sarasota's few beachside tiki bars. It's a brief walk out the door to Lido Beach and St. Armands Circle shopping and dining area, 10 minutes to downtown, and 20 minutes to the airport.

The 12-story **Hyatt Sarasota** (1000 Blvd. of the Arts, 941/953-1234, $300-600) is a big convention hotel downtown with easy access to Van Wezel Performing Arts Hall, the Municipal Auditorium, and other attractions. It's in the downtown business district and waterside, with its own private marina, a floating dock, and a beautiful lagoon-style pool. The 294 guest rooms have bay or marina views, most with little balconies.

One of the trendiest and hippest hotels in the area is the ★ **Hotel Indigo** (1223 Blvd. of the Arts, 941/487-3800, www.hotelindigo.com, $250-400). Guest rooms have wall-size murals and fabrics in bold blues and greens—a fun, contemporary alternative right in the thick of things. The H2O Bistro is the on-site café and wine bar. They have a fitness center and two wading pools (one hot and one cool) to relax in.

Vacation Rentals

Try giving **Argus Property Management** (941/951-4034, www.argusmgmt.com) a call, or visit **Vacation Rentals by Owner** (www.vrbo.com) or **Airbnb** (www.airbnb.com). There are also golf resort condo communities, such as **Heritage Oaks Golf and Country Club** (4800 Chase Oaks Dr., 941/926-7602) and **Timberwoods Vacation Villas & Resort** (7964 Timberwood Circle, 941/312-5934), that rent by the week.

sunset at the Beach Club, Ritz-Carlton Sarasota

TRANSPORTATION
Car

Sarasota is along I-75, a major corridor for the southeastern United States. Sarasota County is south of Tampa and north of Fort Myers, 223 miles from Miami (4 hours' drive), 129 miles from Orlando (2 hours' drive), and 5-6 hours from the Florida-Georgia line. If you prefer I-95, take it to Daytona Beach, then follow I-4 to I-75 before heading south.

U.S. 301 and U.S. 41 (Tamiami Trail) are the major north-south arteries on the mainland; Gulf of Mexico Drive (County Rd. 789) is the main island road. The largest east-west thoroughfares in Sarasota are Highway 72 (Clark Rd.); County Road 780; University Parkway; and to the islands, Ringling Causeway, which takes you to Lido Beach.

Air

Sarasota-Bradenton International Airport (SRQ, 6000 Airport Circle, at U.S. 41 and University Pkwy., Sarasota, 941/359-2770) is the closest, with commuter flights and half a dozen major airlines or their partners, including Air Canada, American, Delta, JetBlue, and United.

Alamo (800/327-9633), **Avis** (800/831-2847), **Budget** (800/527-0700), **Dollar** (800/800-4000 domestic, 800/800-6000 international), **Enterprise** (800/736-8222), **Hertz** (800/654-3131), and **National** (800/227-7368) provide rental cars from Sarasota-Bradenton International Airport. **Diplomat Taxi** (941/777-1111) is the taxi provider at the airport.

Bus and Train

Sarasota County Area Transit, or **SCAT** (941/861-5000), runs scheduled bus service (6am-7pm Mon.-Sat.). A $1.25 fare takes you to stops in Sarasota and St. Armands, Longboat, and Lido Keys. **Greyhound** (5951 Porter Way, Sarasota, 941/342-1720) offers regular bus service to Sarasota from Fort Myers and points north, and Miami to the southeast; **Amtrak** (800/872-7245) provides shuttle buses between the Tampa rail station and Sarasota.

The Keys

These barrier islands off the Sarasota coast are where you'll find the best beaches in the area. They also offer the relaxed atmosphere that most vacationers desire. Go into Sarasota for a taste of the city and to listen to the symphony—then head to the keys to put your toes in the sand and listen to the waves of the Gulf of Mexico lapping the shore.

The northernmost of Sarasota's stretch of keys, **Longboat Key** is a 12-mile barrier island populated mostly by extremely upscale private residences, most down long driveways behind tall hedgerows. There are only about 8,000 full-time residents, but in high season (Dec.-Mar.), Longboat Key is where the rich and famous come to play golf and get a little sun away from the public. If you are interested in seeing celebrities,

hang around at the Longboat Key Club or on the golf courses. The island hasn't always been so swanky. The Arvida Company laid the foundation for development in the late 1950s, enabling construction on previously loose, shifting soil. Generally speaking, visitors stay in the high-rises that line the well-landscaped Gulf of Mexico Drive; residents live on the bayside in discreet, shielded estates.

Siesta Key is something else—a similar eight-mile-long barrier island with beaches just as beautiful as those of Longboat Key, but Siesta is mostly casual and fun family-owned accommodations, none extremely upscale, with easy access to the beach, fishing, boating, kayaking, snorkeling, scuba diving, and sailboarding. And at night, unlike on Longboat,

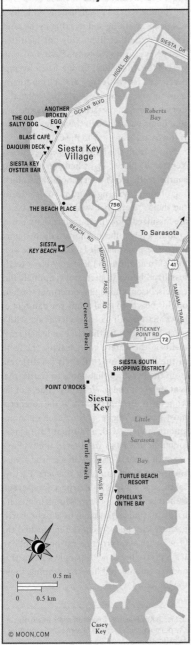

Siesta Key

THE OLD SALTY DOG

ANOTHER BROKEN EGG

BLASÉ CAFÉ

DAIQUIRI DECK

SIESTA KEY OYSTER BAR

OCEAN BLVD

HIGEL DR

SIESTA DR

Siesta Key Village

Roberts Bay

THE BEACH PLACE

758

BEACH RD

To Sarasota

SIESTA KEY BEACH

MIDNIGHT PASS RD

41

TAMIAMI TRAIL

Crescent Beach

STICKNEY POINT RD

72

SIESTA SOUTH SHOPPING DISTRICT

POINT O'ROCKS

Siesta Key

Little Sarasota Bay

Turtle Beach

BLIND PASS RD

TURTLE BEACH RESORT

OPHELIA'S ON THE BAY

0   0.5 mi

0   0.5 km

© MOON.COM

Casey Key

these people like to party. Siesta Key Village has the area's most lively nightlife.

Farther south, **Casey Key** is eight miles long, stretching from Siesta Key on the north to Venice at the southern tip. It is almost exclusively single-family homes with just a few low-rise Old Florida beach motels. Two bridges provide access to the key, including a cool old swing bridge dating to the 1920s. Parts of the key are only 300 yards wide.

The town of **Venice** is more like a real place than a tourist destination, in good and bad ways. The residents seem to be mostly sociable and active retirees. The downtown is quaint—a handful of upscale shops and galleries, a couple of restaurants, a place to get ice cream, a couple of coffee shops, and a good wine bar. There's a little community theater, of which the residents are extremely proud. But the biggest draw in Venice is teeth. Every April, Venice holds the **Shark's Tooth Festival,** with arts, crafts, food stalls, and lots of little pointy black fossils. Sharks of all species have 40 or so teeth in each jaw, with seven rows of teeth waiting to mature behind the first one. The average tiger shark produces 24,000 teeth in 10 years, shedding them continually. To find them when they wash up on Venice beaches, stop by one of the gift shops downtown and ask for a shark tooth shovel.

BEACHES
★ Siesta Key Beach

In 1987, scientists from the Woods Hole Oceanographic Institution in Woods Hole, Massachusetts, convened to judge the Great International White Sand Beach Challenge, comparing more than 30 beaches around the world. Siesta Key Beach remains the world champ. Named America's Best Sand Beach and ranked in Florida's Top Ten Beaches multiple years on the Travel Channel, Dr. Beach named it in his top 10 in America numerous times, as has *National Geographic Traveler*. In the 1950s a visitor from New York, Edward G. Curtis, sent a pickle jar of Siesta's sand to the Geology Department of Harvard University for analysis. The report came back: "The sand from Siesta Key is 99 percent pure quartz grains, the grains being somewhat angular in shape. The soft floury texture of the sand is due to its fine grain size. It contains no fragments of coral and no shell. The fineness of the sand, which gives it its powdery softness, is emphasized by the fact that the quartz is a very hard substance, graded at 7 in the hardness scale of 10."

Lie on the sloping strand, run the warmed granules through your fingers, sniff the salt air, and listen to a plaintive gull overhead. The water is shallow and the beach incline gradual, making it perfect for young swimmers. There are 800 parking spots, which tend to fill up, and the lifeguard stands are painted different colors as points of reference. The Siesta Key beaches south of a rock outcropping called Point of Rocks are grayer and shellier.

Other Beaches

The Sarasota area has lots of beaches to recommend. Those described here run north to south.

Longboat Key has 10 miles of white powdery beach, but most of it is accessible only to residents. **Longboat Key Beach** is accessible at several points—Longview Drive, Westfield Street, Mayfield Street, and Neptune Street. It's mostly underpopulated and often offers incredible sand-dollar collecting. **Beer Can Island Beach,** at the very north end of Longboat Key and accessible by boat or from North Shore Road off Gulf of Mexico Drive, attracts a fair number of anglers and sun worshippers.

Turtle Beach, on Midnight Pass Road near the south end of Siesta Key, is prized for its private feel, large picnic shelter, and good shelling opportunities. Separating Siesta Key from Casey Key, there used to be a small inlet called Midnight Pass that was filled in, amid great controversy, in 1983. There have been disruptive environmental consequences to this choice, but for visitors it means you can walk all the way on **Palmer Point Beach** from Siesta Key to Casey Key. The northern

part of the beach was the former home of Mote Marine Laboratory. These days it's a quiet dune-backed beach, usually with just a few people walking and relaxing in the sand. There are neither lifeguards nor facilities. Casey Key also has **Nokomis Beach,** directly west of the Albee Road Bridge, a nice average beach, and **North Jetty Park** at its southernmost tip, one of the few Gulf Coast spots that draws surfers; anglers seem to congregate here too. Boats pass through the jetties from the Intracoastal Waterway to the Gulf.

South from the jetties are the beaches of Venice, the place to go when you're hunting sharks' teeth. Don't worry about sharks lurking offshore waiting to gum you to death; the sharks' teeth that wash up on the beach are fossilized, floating in from a shark burial ground a few miles offshore, a deep crevice where these cold-blooded predators once went to die. In addition to these gray-black teeth, fossilized bones of prehistoric animals like camels, bison, and tapirs sometimes wash up on this beach. In local shops you can rent or buy a shark-tooth scooper, a wire rake with a mesh box that sifts the sand and shell fragments at the water's edge, leaving the teeth in the basket. **Venice Beach** (so different from the beach of that name in California) is at the west end of Venice Avenue, not far from town. **Brohard Park,** at the southernmost part of Venice, is the beach of choice among anglers, with a 740-foot fishing pier for public use. Dogs are allowed at **Paw Park** at South Brohard Park, with a fenced area, a small dog beach, and dog showers. Farther south, near Venice's little airport, **Caspersen Beach** is the locus of shark's tooth mania. It's harder to find teeth than it used to be, partly because city boosters have replenished the beach with sand from an offshore sandbar. It's a pretty beach with people surf casting and red-shouldered hawks swooping above the shorebirds.

1: Siesta Key Beach 2: fossilized shark tooth on Caspersen Beach 3: Snook Haven Fish Camp 4: Lido Beach

SPORTS AND RECREATION

Golf

In the early 1920s, John Ringling purchased major acreage on the south end of Longboat Key, where he constructed a golf course and planted Australian pine trees along Gulf of Mexico Drive; he eventually abandoned the construction of a luxurious Ritz-Carlton. With this legacy, the **Resort at Longboat Key Club** (220 Sands Point Rd., 941/383-8821, resort courses, greens fees $55-160) offers several remarkable golfing experiences to guests (and their guests). Opened in 1960, the Bill Mitchell-designed Islandside Course (par 72, 6,792 yards, course rating 73.8, slope 138) features 18 holes of crisp up-and-down shot-making through a 112-acre bird sanctuary filled with 5,000 palm trees and flowering plants. Water appears on 16 of its 18 fairways. The resort also has three 9-hole courses with a more country-club feel (and where more of the private members play), played in three 18-hole combinations: blue-red (par 72, 6,709 yards, course rating 72.6, slope 130), red-white (par 72, 6,749 yards, course rating 72.7, slope 131), and white-blue (par 72, 6,812 yards, course rating 73.1, slope 132).

Fishing

Venice is a well-known fishing destination—people wet a line at the Venice jetties, Sharky's Pier, or Caspersen Beach. Expect to catch snook, redfish, Spanish mackerel, sheepshead, sea trout, and flounder, depending on the time of year. Lots of charter companies can take you deep-sea fishing out in the Gulf (grouper and snapper most of the year; kingfish, cobia, greater amberjack, and mahimahi seasonally). At the end of East Venice Avenue on the Myakka River, **Snook Haven Fish Camp** (5000 E. Venice Ave., 941/485-7221) has a fun riverside restaurant, boat rides, and fishing. **Reel Tight Fishing Charters** (941/444-9749, sunset cruise $500 for up to 6 people, $500 for 4 hours, $750 for 6 hours, $1,000 for 8 hours) takes groups out fishing as well as on non-fishing sunset cruises. **Sarasota Fishing Charters** (941/587-9852, $375 for 4 hours, $525 for 6 hours, $650 for 8 hours for up to 4 people) takes small groups from the Ken Thompson Boat Ramp on Lido Key for light-tackle fishing. Captain Jack Hartman also offers specials for Tarpon fishing and single-angler trips.

Waterway Park

The **Venetian Waterway Park** (sunrise-sunset daily, free) in Venice is a mixed-use linear park that features a recently completed 10-mile running trail that parallels the Intracoastal Waterway, ending on Caspersen Beach, one of the most beautiful on the Gulf. It's a long, winding, wheel-friendly park, good for in-line skaters, bikers, and even jogging strollers.

While in Venice, visit the **Historic Venice Train Depot** (303 E. Venice Ave.) downtown. The Mediterranean-style depot was constructed in 1927 and is listed on the National Register of Historic Places. The depot also serves as a trailhead for the Legacy Trail, 10 miles of paved paths that run from just south of the city of Sarasota to Venice following the former CSX rail bed.

SHOPPING

Shopping on Longboat Key is limited: On the lush, tropically landscaped Avenue of the Flowers is a little shopping center (525 Bay Isle Pkwy.) where you'll find a large Publix grocery and a drugstore; at the **Centre Shops of Longboat Key** (5370 Gulf of Mexico Dr., 941/387-3135), about mid-island, is a small collection of galleries, shops selling T-shirts and resort wear, and little restaurants.

On Siesta Key are two main shopping areas: **Siesta Key Village** on the northwest side of the key, about one block from the Gulf, and **Siesta South shopping area,** beginning at the Stickney Point Bridge and going south along Midnight Pass Road. Both have plenty of T-shirt-and-sunglasses shops, the shell-themed beachy giftware shops, and a few other stores not quite as touristy.

Neither area boasts high-end galleries, antiques, or clothing.

FOOD
Longboat Key

Sarasota's has a long-term love affair with **Euphemia Haye** (5540 Gulf of Mexico Dr., 941/383-3633, $22-43). Dine in the restaurant (6pm-10pm Sun.-Fri., 5:30pm-10pm Sat.), dessert room (6pm-11pm Sun.-Fri., 5:30pm-11pm Sat.), or HayeLoft (5pm-11pm daily) on far-reaching food in a tropical setting. It's won top honors from national food magazines, and you need only try the smoked salmon on buckwheat crepes or pistachio-crusted Key West snapper to see why. The wine list is broad, food prices are high, and dishes are rich in the restaurant; try the lighter and cheaper fare upstairs in the HayeLoft. Chef-owner Raymond Arpke offers cooking classes at the restaurant ($65 pp).

At the south end of the key in the Boathouse Marina, **Dry Dock Waterfront Grill** (412 Gulf of Mexico Dr., 941/383-0102, 11am-9pm Sun.-Thurs., 11am-10pm Fri.-Sat., $15-25) has excellent views of Sarasota Bay and one of the best grouper sandwiches in town. The outdoor seating area is casual, relaxing, and exceptionally comfortable. There is an assortment of tables, or simply order drinks and relax on the comfy couches and chairs that surround the waterfront fire pit. The best views of the bay are up on the second floor. Try the lobster bisque, grouper sandwiches, or lobster rolls. Dogs are welcome.

Siesta Key

Like everything else on Siesta Key, restaurants are more casual than on Longboat Key. Ocean Boulevard runs through Siesta Key Village, which is lined with loads of fun, laid-back, beachy bars and restaurants. Most places have outdoor seating, and many have live music at night.

Looking for that special romantic restaurant, only one place on Siesta Key will do. ★ **Ophelia's on the Bay** (9105 Midnight Pass Rd., 941/349-2212, 5pm-10pm Mon.-Sat.,

11am-2pm and 5pm-10pm Sun., $20-40), at the southern tip of the key, has a waterfront terrace that the moon favors with an extra luminous show over Sarasota Bay and the mainland. The interior of the restaurant is stylish and romantic, but sit outside. Try the coconut- and cashew-crusted corvine drum fish with tropical fruit jam or the jumbo shrimp scampi with capellini pasta. The distinctive dishes are accompanied by a unique wine list. The oyster bar next door to Ophelia's is a wonderful place to kill time, and appetite, if you have to wait for a table at Ophelia's.

Siesta Key Oyster Bar (5238 Ocean Blvd., 941/346-5443, 10am-midnight Mon.-Thurs., 11am-2am Fri.-Sat., 9am-midnight Sun., $6-15) has the acronym SKOB on the sign out front. The sandwiches are called skobwiches, and the grouper or fried shrimp skobwich is mighty fine washed down with a house margarita while listening to a live rock band. Margaritas seem to find their foothold in Siesta Key, but if rum is more your drink, right down the road you'll enjoy the **Daiquiri Deck** (5250 Ocean Blvd., 941/349-8697, 11am-2am daily, $6-17). One of the better drinks is the Siesta Tea, a mix of raspberry liqueur, light rum, gin, vodka, raspberry juice, and melon mix—tangy yet sweet, and strong.

For a great beer batter-dipped hot dog, head to **The Old Salty Dog** (5023 Ocean Blvd., 941/349-0158, 11am-9:30pm Sun.-Thurs., 11am-10pm Fri.-Sat., $5-15), an institution among locals who come for that treat or a bowl of clam chowder and a beer. It's open-air, with great views, good burgers, and saucy waitstaff. The beer bar is fashioned from the hull of an old boat, which adds a nautical tilt. There's another location with the same hours at 1601 Ken Thompson Parkway (941/388-4311).

Best breakfast? That's the easiest call on Siesta Key. ★ **Another Broken Egg** (140 Av. Messina, 941/552-8320, 7am-2pm daily, $7-12) is such a cheery and busy scene most mornings that they opened a second location at Lakewood Ranch (6115 Exchange Way, 941/388-6898, 7am-2pm daily). Try the Floridian omelet (three eggs filled with cream cheese and topped with crabmeat, monterey jack, and onions) or cinnamon-roll french toast. The well-landscaped and shady patio is the place to sit.

Blasé Café (5263 Ocean Blvd., 941/349-9822, 4pm-midnight Wed., 5pm-10pm Thurs.-Sun., $7-23) reinvented itself from a well-loved breakfast spot to an even more well-loved lunch and dinner favorite with a martini bar that's hopping most nights. They serve burgers, sandwiches, soups, salads, and a variety of entrées that feature steaks and seafood. Be sure to ask for outside seating on the wooden deck with the big palm tree in the middle; if you're just stopping in for a drink, the bar is the seat of choice.

Casey Key

On Casey Key, eat at Casey Key Fish House (801 Blackburn Point Rd., 941/966-1901, 11:30am-9pm daily, $5-15). This shambling restaurant and tiki bar does a brisk business, with diners navigating peel-and-eat shrimp while watching the sunset over picturesque Blackburn Point Marina. Casual seafood is the mainstay, and the fancier white wine-steamed mussels and almond snapper are brilliant.

Venice

Along Nokomis Avenue (the main drag downtown) are shops, diners, coffeehouses, and lunch spots—the best of which is Venice Wine and Coffee Co. (201 W. Venice Ave., 941/484-3667, 8am-8pm Mon.-Thurs., 9am-5pm Fri., 10am-4pm Sat.), a coffee shop by day and wine bar at night. To find Venice's Old Florida dining possibilities—all fun, all casual—you'll have to go farther afield. The Crow's Nest, Marina Restaurant and Marina (1968 Tarpon Center Dr., 941/484-9551, 11:30am-9pm daily, $15-30) has been feeding locals since 1976, with a fun tavern and great views of the marina, Venice Inlet, and the Intracoastal Waterway. The wine list is extensive, and the food is fried oysters, fried shrimp, and steamed clams. Happy hour in the tavern is 4pm-6pm daily. Marina hours are 8am-7pm daily.

The Snook Haven Restaurant and Fish Camp (5000 Venice Ave. E., past River Rd., 941/485-7221, 11:30am-8pm daily, $10-20) has a down-home and bayou-style vibe, right on the Myakka River (rent a pontoon boat or kayak before you eat). The burgers are good, and you can count on some entertaining fellow customers and occasional live entertainment.

Sharky's on the Pier (1600 S. Harbor Dr., 941/488-1456, 11:30am-10pm Sun.-Thurs., 11:30am-midnight Fri.-Sat., $12-24) is closer to civilization, with beach views and the day's catch offered broiled, blackened, grilled, or fried. Sit outside on the veranda and enjoy a margarita finished off with triple sec and blue Curaçao for that dark-blue water look.

ACCOMMODATIONS
Longboat Key

Longboat Key is mostly dotted with expensive high-rise condos and resort hotels that loom over the beaches. If you like a more modest scale, the Wicker Inn (5581 Gulf of Mexico Dr., 941/387-8344, www.wickerinn.net, cottages $1,199-3,296 per week) is more like it. There are 11 casual and fun Key West-style cottages around an inviting pool and landscaped with purple hibiscus and oleander. There's a private beach just steps away, and a 16-acre public park.

★ The Resort at Longboat Key Club (220 Sands Pointe Rd., 941/383-8821, www.longboatkeyclub.com, from $500) is where serious golfers come for the 45 holes of the private Longboat Key Golf Club, but there are lots of other reasons to settle into one of the 210 suites with full kitchens or one of 20 hotel rooms. There's a fine restaurant on-site, 38 tennis courts, bike and beach-gear rentals, great pools, and a private stretch of white-sand beach with cabana rentals and beachside service. Despite the fact that this is an extremely upscale resort, the people who work here are friendly and personable.

1: a relaxing view at Casey Key Fish House 2: Venice Beach Villas 3: Turtle Beach Resort on Siesta Key

Siesta Key

Not many chain hotels and no huge resorts are on Siesta Key, which means you're more likely to have a memorable time in one of the modest mom-and-pop house rentals or small hotels. The warm independent spirit of many of these hoteliers is apparent in the relaxed decor and easy beachside pleasures. Many accommodations on Siesta Key adopt an efficiency approach, with little kitchens, essential for keeping vacation costs down (have a quick breakfast in the morning, then prepare yourself a great picnic lunch for the beach).

Rented by the week, the tropical garden beach cottages of **The Beach Place** (5605 Av. Del Mare, 941/346-1745, www.siestakeybeachplace.com, $400-1,700 per week) make a nice romantic or family beach getaway. There's a pool (but the beach is 30 seconds away), a tiki cabana with a wet bar, beachside barbecue facilities, lounge chairs, beach cruiser bikes, and free laundry. The cottages themselves are modest but recently repainted and pleasant, whether it's the one-bedroom Coquina or Seahorse, the two-twin-bed Starfish, the large one-bedroom Sand Dollar, or the huge studio cottage called the Dolphin.

★ **Siesta Holidays** (1015 Crescent St., 941/312-9882, $700-1,400 per week) is a similar place with two options. The Siesta Sea Castle, directly on Crescent Beach, consists of a large two-bedroom, two-bath apartment and four one-bedroom efficiency apartments. The ground-level units have patios directly on the beach. The Siesta Holiday House, a little farther from the beach, has two one-bedroom apartments on the ground floor, with a big private screened pool, and two two-bedroom, two-bath apartments on the second floor. Pets are allowed in the Holiday House.

The **Tropical Breeze Resort of Siesta Key** (140 Columbus Blvd., 941/349-1125, www.tropicalbreezeinn.com, $200-400) also offers a range of choices, spreading across four blocks of an attractive neighborhood between the village and the shoreline. There are one- to three-bedroom efficiencies and suites on the beach as well as more privately located units

in lush tropical gardens. Each building comes with its own pool, and the property has a centrally located yoga deck. Everything is within walking distance of Siesta Key Village.

On the south end of the island, ★ **Turtle Beach Resort** (9049 Midnight Pass Rd., 941/349-4554, www.turtlebeachresort.com, from $300) is one of the area's best-kept secrets. Reservations are hard to get, but the 10 clapboard cottages, each individually decorated with its own porch and featuring a private hot tub, are worth waiting for. There are views of Little Sarasota Bay, Turtle Beach is a short walk away, and guests have free use of bikes, hammocks, canoes, kayaks, paddleboats, and fishing poles. Paddle a kayak from the dock of the resort to the quiet and secluded beach at Midnight Pass to enjoy the sunset. Then paddle up an appetite on the way back and eat at Ophelia's next door. Pets are welcome.

Just down the road a few blocks from the resort, pull up your RV or stake out your tent and camp at the wonderful **Turtle Beach Campground** (8862 Midnight Pass Rd., 941/861-2267, www.scgov.net/turtlebeachcampground, $32-60). The 14-acre park has 40 small, well-planned sites on the Gulf shore. A sandy path leads down to the beach, and the campground offers a boat ramp, a volleyball net, horseshoe pits, and a playground. The city center of Siesta Key is a short drive down the road and has plenty of fun shops, restaurants, and bars to keep you from having to rough it too much.

Venice

If you've come to the Sarasota area with the express purpose of collecting sharks' teeth, it makes sense to stay in Venice. Otherwise, Venice lacks the amenities found in Sarasota, Lido Key, Longboat Key, or Siesta Key, and the downtown closes up at night. However, a bike ride or walk along the Venetian Waterway Park trails that lead to Caspersen Beach is fun, and exploring the park and beach is the perfect reason to spend a day or two. The inexpensive **Inn at the Beach** (725 W. Venice Ave., 941/484-8471, $150-250) and a **Best Western** (400 Commercial Court, 941/480-9898, $175-250), are both good options. My favorite place to stay in Venice is the **Venice Beach Villas** (501 W. Venice Ave., 941/488-1580, $75-250, $500-1,700 per week), charming efficiencies, studios, and one- and two-bedroom units equipped with full kitchens. The two locations, within blocks of one another, let you choose from a variety of rooms around beautiful pools and artfully landscaped tropical grounds.

Vacation Rentals

In the Siesta Key and Longboat Key area, contact **A Paradise Rentals** (5201 Gulf Dr., 800/237-2252, www.aparadiserentals.com); in Sanibel and Captiva, contact **Sanibel Holiday** (239/472-6565, www.sanibelholiday.com); and on Longboat Key, contact **Emerald Kite** (941/932-8428, www.emeraldkite.com).

TRANSPORTATION
Air

From downtown Sarasota, go east across the John Ringling Causeway to access St. Armands Circle and Lido Key, then continue north on Gulf of Mexico Drive (County Rd. 789) to Longboat Key. The drive from Sarasota to Longboat Key is 12 miles and takes 30 minutes in normal traffic. To reach Siesta Key from Sarasota, head south on U.S. 41 (Tamiami Trail), then take a right onto Siesta Drive to the northern residential section of the key, or Stickney Point Road to the funky Siesta Key Village. The 6.6-mile drive takes 20 minutes in normal traffic.

To reach Casey Key from Sarasota, drive south on U.S. 41, then take a right onto Blackburn Point Road. The 15-minute drive takes 40 minutes in normal traffic. To reach Venice Beach from Sarasota, drive south on U.S. 41, then turn right onto West Venice Avenue. The 19-mile drive takes 40 minutes in normal traffic.

Bus and Train

Sarasota County Area Transit, or **SCAT** (941/861-5000), runs scheduled bus service (6am-7pm Mon.-Sat.). A $1.25 fare takes you to stops in Sarasota and St. Armands, Longboat, and Lido Keys.

Anna Maria Island

Stand at the northern end of Longboat Key and look north to see a seven-mile-long strip of sandy barrier island that couldn't be more different from Longboat. Manatee County's Anna Maria Island is far enough south of Tampa to be removed from the city's urban hustle and bustle, and far enough north of Sarasota to escape being just another key. It's the northernmost of the string of barrier islands that extend down to the Florida Keys, with three distinct towns: **Anna Maria** at the northern end, **Holmes Beach** in the middle, and **Bradenton Beach** at the southern end—all of them linked by a sweet laid-back atmosphere. Three drawbridges access the island, from Longboat Key and from the mainland (Hwy. 64 and Hwy. 684).

The little island community owes its existence to the Fig Newton. The inventor of the "oo-ee, gooey, rich and chewy" Newton, Charles Roser, sold the recipe to Nabisco, made a fortune, bought up Anna Maria land, and started building. These days there's an active year-round community and a robust tourist trade reinvigorated by new upscale development that retains the Old Florida nostalgia. Tourists mostly come for the boating, sailing, scuba, snorkeling, and fishing. Parking is the only hassle on the island, so park your car where you're staying and walk across to the beach—Holmes Beach, Anna Maria Beach, Coquina Beach, Cortez Beach, and Manatee Beach are all equally lovely stretches of white sand and blue-green water, although Manatee has the most parking and a nice picnic area. None have lifeguards or restrooms.

Anna Maria is the kind of island where it's easy to do nothing because the pace is one of easy relaxation. If your work ethic forces you to do something, I recommend a sunset sailing cruise with **Spice Sailing Charters** (departures next to Rotten Ralph's Restaurant, Anna Maria Island, 941/704-0773, $40 pp for 2.5 hours, $60 pp for 4 hours). The captain has a wealth of information about Florida history, fishing, and the area's recent environmental challenges.

Also worth checking out are Bradenton Beach and its municipal pier complex, with a restaurant, a 220-foot floating dock for free day docking, a bait house, and public bathing facilities. The 660-foot fishing pier and boater-related facilities sit at the bayside end of Historic Bridge Street in Bradenton Beach. Visitors can take advantage of watercraft transportation to the dock, but new bike lanes, sidewalks, a multiuse nature path along the beach, and a free trolley system add some other options for navigating the area.

FOOD

Romantic, cozy, and noncorporate, ★ **Beach Bistro** (6600 Gulf Dr., Holmes Beach, 941/778-6444, www.beachbistro. com, 5pm-10pm daily, $35-80) beats fancier restaurants, according to the likes of *Zagat* and *Wine Spectator*. Chef Sean Murphy serves food that lives up to his superstar reputation; a more casual bar-café on-site is a good pick for a tasty burger. The formal dining room has spectacular views of the Gulf, and single long-stemmed roses adorn the center of each table. Although geared toward romantic dining, the Beach Bistro welcomes children. It isn't outlandishly pricey if you opt for the small plates, adequate if you include an appetizer. Start with the blue cheese and plum tomato soup or a side of fingerling potatoes roasted in duck fat and garlic. For the entrée, dive into their signature seafood bouillabaisse chock-full of mussels, jumbo shrimp,

premium fish, and lobster tails, or enjoy an herb-rubbed rack of Colorado lamb finished with a demi-glace of port and rosemary. Ask about recommended pairings from the impressive wine list. For dessert, try the chocolate truffle terrine served with berries and drizzled in a delectable caramel sauce. Chef Murphy has said, "What we do must be done perfectly, and we must be relentless in the pursuit of that perfection."

A favorite on the north end of the island is the **Sandbar Waterfront Restaurant** (100 Spring Ave., 941/778-0444, noon-9pm Mon.-Thurs., noon-10pm Fri., 11am-10pm Sat., 10am-9pm Sun., $10-25). It's the place to go for a sunset cocktail, lunch, dinner, or jazz brunch on the beach (10am-1pm Sun.). The covered deck has unimpeded views of the Gulf, and their signature grouper sandwich is excellent. They also serve excellent grouper tacos and a variety of seafood, steak, and pasta dishes.

Oma's Pizza (201 N. Gulf Dr., Bradenton Beach, 941/778-0771, 11am-midnight daily, $8-15) serves seriously delicious, big, and cheesy pizza with a thin crust. The lasagna is good. For more everyday dining, it's hard to go wrong with the barbecue at **Mr. Bones BBQ** (3007 Gulf Dr., Holmes Beach, 941/778-6614, 11am-9pm Mon.-Sat., noon-9pm Sun., $7-15), and unexpectedly, it also has good Indian and Greek food.

ACCOMMODATIONS

The best place to stay on Anna Maria is the ★ **Mainsail Beach Inn** (101 66th St., Holmes Beach, 888/849-2642, www. mainsailbeachinn.com, $250-500). The Gulf of Mexico is a stone's throw from the stunning vaulted-ceiling lobby. The two- and three-bedroom condos have full kitchens, spectacular Gulf views from the private balconies, and spacious master baths. Spend the day on Holmes Beach or relax by the heated pool and hot tub. At night, walk across the

1: Sandbar Waterfront Restaurant 2: Mainsail Beach Inn

street to the Beach Bistro, one of Florida's top-ranked restaurants. No detail is overlooked at this hidden gem.

For something a little more affordable, stay at **Palm Tree Villas** (207 66th St., Holmes Beach, 941/778-0910, www.palmtreevillas.com, $150-250), an inviting warm haven for honeymooning couples or families. The low-rise Old Florida-style motel, with well-appointed units clustered around a central courtyard and swimming pool, has been nicely refurbished. There's a great packet of literature in each villa.

Another favorite on the island is **Harrington House Beachfront Bed &** **Breakfast** (5626 Gulf Dr., Holmes Beach, 941/778-5444, www.harringtonhouse.com, $199-749), a converted 1925 coquina-brick beachfront house. Most rooms feature French doors opening onto balconies that overlook the heated swimming pool, the beach, and the Gulf beyond. The breakfasts are legendary, and the sweet little beach gazebo is the perfect spot to watch the sunset.

GETTING THERE

To reach Anna Maria Island from Sarasota, drive north on U.S. 301, then turn left onto County Road 64 (Manatee Ave. W.). The 22-mile drive takes 50 minutes in normal traffic.

Information and Services

Sarasota and vicinity are in the **eastern time zone.**

VISITOR INFORMATION

The Sarasota Convention and Visitors Bureau's official **Visitor Information Center** (1945 Fruitville Rd., 941/706-1253, www.visitsarasota.com, 10am-5pm Mon.-Fri., 10am-2pm Sat., 11am-3pm Sun.) offers heaping piles of reading material on the area.

POLICE AND EMERGENCIES

In an emergency, dial 911 for immediate assistance. If you need the police in a non-emergency, contact the **Sarasota Police Department** (2099 Adams Lane, 941/366-8000). For medical emergencies, the nicest facilities are at the emergency care center at **Sarasota Memorial Hospital** (1700 S. Tamiami Trail, 941/917-9000).

Tampa

Tampa is a family-friendly town with plenty of upscale restaurants and shopping. The University of South Florida (USF), University of Tampa, and Hillsborough Community College lend a bit of youth and liveliness.

Centrally located on the Florida Gulf Coast, Tampa has an exceptional airport, making it ideal to fly into for trips to the region. It is home to Busch Gardens, a large cruise ship port, a great zoo and aquarium, professional sports, and affordable accommodations and restaurants. Since Tampa isn't that old, it's not the best place for history lovers. The railroad came to Tampa in 1884, when a steamship line from Tampa to Key West and Havana spurred the city's growth. Tampa's first residential suburb, Hyde Park, is still the residential area

Highlights

Look for ★ to find recommended sights, activities, dining, and lodging.

★ **Florida Aquarium:** This 152,000-square-foot aquarium focuses on Florida's relationship to the Gulf, estuaries, rivers, and other waterways, with a strong environmental message (page 153).

★ **Ybor City:** Once known as the Cigar Capital of the World, Tampa's Latin Quarter offers historic shops by day and the city's best nightlife and dining when the sun goes down (page 156).

★ **Bayshore Boulevard:** These five miles of sidewalk are bordered by historic homes on one side and panoramic views of the wide-open bay on the other (page 158).

★ **Busch Gardens Tampa:** This theme park is a thrilling mix of rides, animal attractions, and entertainment (page 158).

★ **Spring Training:** See the New York Yankees train at George M. Steinbrenner Field or watch Tampa's own Rays at Charlotte Sports Park (page 169).

★ **Tampa Theatre:** Ornately decorated to resemble an open Mediterranean courtyard, this theatre features 1,446 seats, 99 stars in the auditorium ceiling, and 1,000 pipes in its mighty Wurlitzer theater organ (page 170).

of choice, and the Old Hyde Park Village boutiques and restaurants is one of the city's biggest draws.

A mix of historic buildings, artisanal shops, restaurants, authentic Cuban food, hand-rolled cigar shops, and nightclubs are in the vivacious Latin community of Ybor City. Davis Islands and Harbour Island, the two little islands off downtown Tampa, where the Hillsborough River empties into Hillsborough Bay, are home to an airport, Tampa General Hospital, and more than 100 of the original homes.

Tampa hasn't been buoyed by tourism dollars to the degree other Gulf Coast cities have, and so it has been less susceptible to the ups and downs of the Florida travel economy. Unlike other urban centers along the Gulf, in Tampa there are no beaches; for those, drive over the causeway to St. Pete or Clearwater, 30 minutes from downtown Tampa.

PLANNING YOUR TIME

How long you spend vacationing in Tampa depends on whether you have kids in tow. Tampa is a paradise for children, and the big kahuna is Busch Gardens, but that's just day 1. Four or five other attractions are worthy of a day of family focus.

Many people visit Orlando's Disney attractions and then tack on a day or two at Tampa's Busch Gardens. Orlando is only an hour away, but it may be too much of a good thing. Busch Gardens is different from Disney, with more focus on thrill rides and wildlife. If you love theme parks, visit Busch Gardens while you're in the area. If you are already spending a few days at Disney, consider coming to Tampa and renting a canoe, going to the zoo, visiting the science museum, and then heading over to Clearwater for a day of leisurely beach time.

On the Gulf Coast the fall and early spring are the most enjoyable weather-wise, with very dry days in the low 80s. The summer is unrelentingly hot and humid through each afternoon's huge thunderstorm. The best beaches are Clearwater Beach, Fort De Soto Park, Honeymoon Island and Caladesi Island, St. Pete Beach, Madeira Beach, Sand Key County Park, and Egmont Key State Wildlife Preserve.

The best way to see the Tampa area is with a car, especially if you want to explore some of the surrounding barrier islands. The area is served by **Tampa International Airport** (TPA, 4100 George J. Bean Pkwy., 813/870-8700, www.tampaairport.com). If you plan on staying downtown with occasional trips to Clearwater and Busch Gardens, you can manage with community transportation and taxis. I-75 runs to Tampa from the north, and I-4 from Orlando. I-275 and Gandy Boulevard both lead north to St. Pete, while West Courtney Campbell Causeway is the primary thoroughfare to Clearwater.

Sights

DOWNTOWN TAMPA
★ Florida Aquarium

The 152,000-square-foot **Florida Aquarium** (701 Channelside Dr., 813/273-4000, www.flaquarium.org, 9:30am-5pm daily, $27 adults, $25 seniors, $23 ages 3-11, parking $6) is smart, focusing on the waters of Florida. It doesn't contain an exhaustive catalog of the world's aquatic creatures, but it tells a compelling story about Florida's relationship to the Gulf, estuaries, rivers, and other waterways. There are some exotic exhibits (otherworldly sea dragons, like sea horses mated with philodendrons), but the best parts are the open freshwater tanks of otters, spoonbills, gators, Florida softshell turtles, and snakes.

Tampa

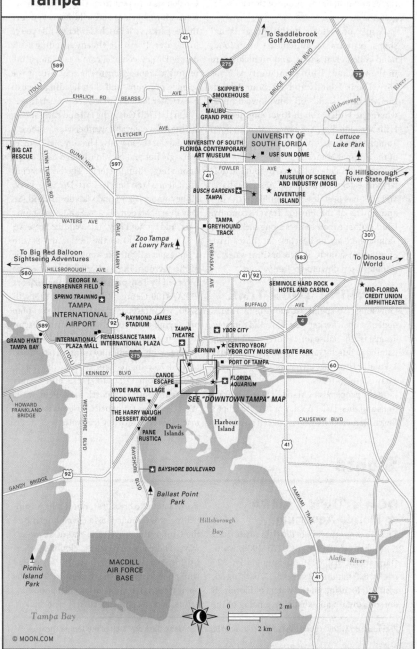

To Saddlebrook Golf Academy

SKIPPER'S SMOKEHOUSE

MALIBU GRAND PRIX

BIG CAT RESCUE

UNIVERSITY OF SOUTH FLORIDA CONTEMPORARY ART MUSEUM

UNIVERSITY OF SOUTH FLORIDA

USF SUN DOME

Lettuce Lake Park

To Hillsborough River State Park

MUSEUM OF SCIENCE AND INDUSTRY (MOSI)

BUSCH GARDENS TAMPA

ADVENTURE ISLAND

Zoo Tampa at Lowry Park

TAMPA GREYHOUND TRACK

To Big Red Balloon Sightseeing Adventures

To Dinosaur World

SEMINOLE HARD ROCK HOTEL AND CASINO

MID-FLORIDA CREDIT UNION AMPHITHEATER

GEORGE M. STEINBRENNER FIELD

SPRING TRAINING

TAMPA INTERNATIONAL AIRPORT

RAYMOND JAMES STADIUM

TAMPA THEATRE

YBOR CITY

GRAND HYATT TAMPA BAY

INTERNATIONAL PLAZA MALL

RENAISSANCE TAMPA INTERNATIONAL PLAZA

BERNINI

CENTRO YBOR/ YBOR CITY MUSEUM STATE PARK

PORT OF TAMPA

HOWARD FRANKLAND BRIDGE

CANOE ESCAPE

HYDE PARK VILLAGE

CICCIO WATER

FLORIDA AQUARIUM

SEE "DOWNTOWN TAMPA" MAP

THE HARRY WAUGH DESSERT ROOM

PANE RUSTICA

Davis Islands

Harbour Island

CAUSEWAY BLVD

BAYSHORE BOULEVARD

Ballast Point Park

Hillsborough Bay

Alafia River

Picnic Island Park

MACDILL AIR FORCE BASE

Tampa Bay

0   2 mi

0   2 km

© MOON.COM

Downtown Tampa

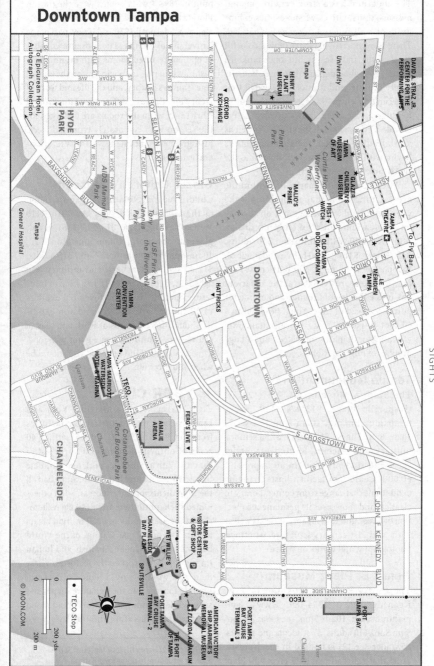

Map labels: DAVID A. STRAZ JR. CENTER FOR THE PERFORMING ARTS, HENRY B. PLANT MUSEUM, OXFORD EXCHANGE, University of Tampa, Plant Park, TAMPA MUSEUM OF ART, GLAZER CHILDREN'S MUSEUM, FIRST WATCH, Curtis Hixon Waterfront Park, MALIO'S PRIME, TAMPA THEATRE, OLD TAMPA BOOK COMPANY, LE MÉRIDIEN TAMPA, To Fly Bar, DOWNTOWN, HATRICKS, TAMPA CONVENTION CENTER, USF Park on the Riverwalk, Jannus Park, TAMPA MARRIOTT WATERSIDE HOTEL & MARINA, TECO, AMALIE ARENA, FERG'S LIVE, Cotanchobee Fort Brooke Park, CHANNELSIDE, WET WILLIE'S, CHANNELSIDE BAY PLAZA, SPLITSVILLE, TAMPA BAY VISITOR CENTER & GIFT SHOP, FLORIDA AQUARIUM, PORT TAMPA BAY CRUISE TERMINAL - 2, AMERICAN VICTORY SHIP MARINER'S MEMORIAL MUSEUM, THE PORT OF TAMPA, PORT TAMPA BAY CRUISE TERMINAL 3, PORT TAMPA BAY, Streetcar, TECO, Ybor Channel, HYDE PARK, AIDS Memorial, Tampa General Hospital, To Epicurean Hotel, Autograph Collection

TECO Stop

© MOON.COM

The aquarium has a strong environmental message in its natives-versus-exotics exhibits, but it's all fun and never heavy-handed. There's a wonderful big shark tank, a colorful coral grotto, and a sea-urchin touch tank. It's a small enough aquarium that three hours is plenty of time, and it's not so crowded that kids can't do a little wandering on their own. Regularly scheduled shows involve native Florida birds and small mammals, as well as shark feeding (in fact, the aquarium offers "swim with the fishes" wetsuit dives into the shark tank for the stalwart).

After perusing the marinelife within the eye-catching shell-shaped building, take your newfound knowledge out on the bay on an aquarium-run **Wild Dolphin Cruise** (813/273-4000, with admission $50 adults, $45 seniors, $41 ages 3-11, free under age 3). Tampa Bay is home to 400 bottlenose dolphins. Tickets are available at the aquarium box office the day of the tour and online for purchase ahead of time. You'll head out in a 64-foot 49-passenger Caribbean catamaran, watching for dolphins, manatees, and a huge number of migratory birds.

Tampa Museum of Art

The **Tampa Museum of Art** (120 W. Gasparilla Plaza, 813/274-8130, www.tampamuseum.org, 10am-5pm Fri.-Wed., 10am-8pm Thurs., $15 adults, $7.50 seniors, military, and teachers, $5 students, under age 7 and students free), in an impressive 60,000-square-foot facility, hosts changing exhibitions that range from contemporary to classical and showcases its permanent collection of Greek and Roman antiquities as well as 20th- and 21st-century sculpture, paintings, photography, and works on paper.

Henry B. Plant Museum

The **Henry B. Plant Museum** (401 W. Kennedy Blvd., 813/254-1891, www.ut.edu/plantmuseum, 10am-5pm Tues.-Sat., noon-5pm Sun., $10 adults, $7 students and seniors, $5 under age 12) is housed in the dramatic hotel that railroad magnate Henry B. Plant built in 1891. Its 511 rooms were the first in Florida to be outfitted with electricity. It operated as a hotel until 1930 and is now part of the University of Tampa. The museum consists of opulent restored rooms with original furnishings that provide a window on the Gilded Age, Tampa's history, and the life and work of Henry Plant. The best time to see it is around Christmas, when the rooms are bedecked for the season with elaborately trimmed trees, lush greenery, antique toys, and Victorian-era ornaments.

Glazer Children's Museum

Children up to age 10 will enjoy an afternoon at the **Glazer Children's Museum** (110 W. Gasparilla Plaza, 813/443-3861, www.glazermuseum.org, 10am-5pm Mon.-Fri., 10am-6pm Sat., 1pm-6pm Sun., $15 adults, $12.50 seniors, teachers, and military, $10 ages 1-12, free under age 1). In a kind of miniature outdoor city, it has over 170 exhibits in 12 themed areas with hands-on exhibits about different kinds of work and play (a cruise ship, a mini theater, a giant telescope, a grocery store). Find out what you should be when you grow up.

★ YBOR CITY

Cigar makers Vicente Martinez Ybor and Ignacio Haya moved their cigar factories from Key West to Tampa in 1886, settling 40 acres of uninviting scrubland northeast of the city. With a railroad, a port, and a climate that acted as a natural humidor, Tampa had all the ingredients for cigar success. Soon others joined them until there were 140 cigar factories in the area producing 250 million cigars a year. The new Cigar Capital of the World became home to Cuban, Spanish, and Italian immigrants who worked the factories. These men and women would hand-roll several kinds of tobacco into the signature shapes and sizes while listening to "lectors" read aloud great works of literature and the day's news.

1: Ybor City **2:** Henry B. Plant Museum **3:** the Florida Aquarium in downtown Tampa

For a window into this world, read Nilo Cruz's Pulitzer Prize-winning drama, *Anna in the Tropics,* which depicts a Cuban American family of cigar makers in Ybor City in 1930.

The area flourished until the early 1960s, when embargoes against Cuban tobacco and declining cigar consumption (coincident with the ascendance of the cigarette as the smoke of choice) caused the market to decline. Today Ybor City is one of only three National Historic Landmark Districts in Florida, with redbrick streets, wrought-iron balconies, and old-timey globe street lamps.

During the day visitors can still see cigars being hand-rolled and enjoy an authentic Cubano sandwich (invented here, some say), while at night Ybor is the city's nightlife district, drawing 40,000 visitors on weekends to dine at sidewalk cafés and drink and dance at nightclubs. Day or night, park your car in one of the many parking lots or garages (metered parking is strictly enforced 24 hours daily) and walk around, or take the Ybor City trolley. You can still see little cigar shops and Latin social clubs mixed in with tattoo parlors and restaurants along La Setima (7th Ave.).

Centro Ybor (1600 E. 8th Ave., 813/242-4660, www.centroybor.com, shops 10am-8pm Mon.-Wed., 10am-10pm Thurs.-Sat., 11am-7pm Sun., restaurant hours vary) is a shopping, dining, and entertainment complex at the pulsing heart of the neighborhood. The trolley runs through the center, so it's easy to get here from anywhere in the area. Along with the shops, there is a comedy club, a large movie theater, an arcade, several bars, a salon, and plenty of great places to eat. Prices tend to be higher than elsewhere in town.

The **Ybor City Museum State Park Garden** (1818 E. 9th Ave., 813/247-6323, www.ybormuseum.org, 9am-5pm Wed.-Sun., $4 adults, free under age 6) contains photographs, cigar boxes, and other artifacts of the neighborhood's rich history. A more three-dimensional look at Ybor comes from walking: Walk by the **La Union Marti-Maceo mural** (226 7th Ave.), pick up a copy of *La*

Gaceta (the neighborhood's Spanish-language weekly for the past 95 years), and walk by the restored former cigar workers' casitas on your way to get a Cubano sandwich, or buy a cigar at **Metropolitan Cigars** (2014 E. 7th Ave., 813/248-3304, 10am-8pm Mon.-Fri., 10am-4pm Sat.-Sun.), a 1,700-square-foot walk-in humidor.

SOUTH TAMPA AND HYDE PARK
★ Bayshore Boulevard

Bayshore Boulevard is one of the world's longest continuous sidewalks. It borders Tampa Bay for nearly five miles without a break in the gorgeousness. Joggers, walkers, skaters, and bikers dot its length, which goes from downtown through Hyde Park. Lined with the fanciest homes in Tampa, the boulevard was named one of AAA's Top Roads for its panoramic views. If you don't feel like walking it, it's Tampa's signature drive. **Tampa Preservation** (813/248-5437, www.tampapreservation.org) also has an excellent driving tour of Hyde Park and a walking tour of part of the neighborhood geared for young children.

BUSCH GARDENS AND NORTH TAMPA

TOP EXPERIENCE

★ Busch Gardens Tampa

How many people can say they rode on a Cheetah and a Congo River Rapid in one day? You can join the ranks of the thrill-seeking elite with a quick trip to **Busch Gardens Tampa** (10165 N. Malcolm McKinley Dr., 888/800-5447, www.buschgardens.com, 9:30am-6pm daily winter 9am-10pm daily summer, $89 adults, yearly pass $168, free under age 3). Busch Gardens is half high-energy amusement park and half first-class zoo. With something of a personality disorder,

---

1: Cheetah Hunt coaster at Busch Gardens **2:** Busch Gardens Serengeti Safari

this is the only park I know where you can alternate between petting zoos and twisting, turning, high-speed roller coasters.

RIDES

The amusement park has a huge section geared to **children** ages 2 to 7 in a Sesame Street-centric part of the park, to the far left when you're looking at the map, near **Stanleyville,** as well as in sections near the **Congo** and in **Timbuktu.**

Major coasters are the biggest draw for those over 42 inches tall (48 inches for Cheetah Hunt and 54 inches for Montu, SheiKra, and Kumba). The rides at Busch Gardens are either little-kiddie or startlingly huge. The roller coasters, in descending order of excellence: The **Cheetah Hunt** is the longest ride in the park and reaches 60 mph after climbing a nearly vertical 102-foot hill. The **SheiKra** has an incredible 90-degrees-straight-down thrill at the beginning, an underground tunnel, speeds of 70 mph, and water features late in the ride. The ride is a little short, but it's floorless, which adds another level of thrill. **Kumba** offers a full three seconds of weightlessness, an initial 135-foot drop, and cool 360-degree spirals. It offers good speed, a long ride, and one of the world's largest vertical loops. The **Cobra's Curse** reaches a top speed of 40 mph after climbing a 70-foot hill and then plunging down for a bit of heart-in-your-throat fun. **Montu,** at the far right side of the park, is one of the tallest inverted roller coasters in the world. You are strapped in from above, so your feet dangle while you travel at 60 mph through 60-foot vertical loops. Beyond the coasters, the **Stanley Falls** and **Congo River Rapids** boat ride are guaranteed to fully saturate you, so time them for the hottest part of the day.

ANIMAL ATTRACTIONS

Busch Gardens contains more than 2,700 animals. Colorful lorikeets will land on your shoulder in the aviary called **Lory Landing.** The fun-filled **Opening Night Critters** show features rescued dogs, cats, a horse, and even a kangaroo. The best animal attraction is the **Serengeti Plain,** which takes up the whole right half of the park—you can see it all by getting on the **Serengeti Express Railway** (or the **Skyride,** or a **Serengeti Safari**). Ostriches may race the train, and there are big cats and huffing rhinos. It's thrilling as well as a wonderful opportunity to sit down and regroup. **Jungala,** set in the Congo area, is a four-acre attraction that has guests mingling with exotic creatures, exploring a village hidden deep in the jungle, and connecting with the inhabitants of the lush landscape through up-close animal interactions, multistory family play areas, rides, and live entertainment.

PLANNING YOUR VISIT

A Few Tips: To minimize walking, take the **Skyride** at the entrance (near the Cheetah Run exhibit) all the way to the back of the park (the Jungala area) and start there, making your way to the front again. For the best value on food, eat at the **Dragon Fire Grill and Pub** (Pantopia area in the middle of the park). They offer a large range of cuisines, including American, Chinese, Mexican, and Italian. There's also a nice selection of salads, a full bar, and a Starbucks inside. There's a remarkable amount of seating, so it's usually easy to find a good seat.

The Details: Busch Gardens is expensive, so is it worth it? Definitely. It is a wonderful full-day extravaganza for any age. If you don't like rides, go to Beer School, where you can learn about the process of making beer, and then get what you really came for—free samples. Busch Gardens can entertain for two full days, but if you do just one day, everyone will be clamoring for more. A 14-day, four-park **FlexTicket** ($169 over age 2) is a good deal if you have the stamina to hit SeaWorld Orlando, Adventure Island, Aquatica, and Busch Gardens.

The park hours change seasonally. If you visit in the summer, count on heavy rains in the afternoon. Restrooms are plentiful and clean, there are plenty of strollers to rent, the food is better than it needs to be (Zambia Smokehouse also serves good ribs and chicken), and there's even a dog kennel to watch your pet while you enjoy the park. The park is eight miles northeast of downtown Tampa. Parking is an irritating additional $20, with a free shuttle that takes you from the 5,000-spot parking lot to the park's entrance.

ZooTampa at Lowry Park

This zoo has recently made the overt decision to take it to the Big Time, going mano a mano with San Diego and the other big zoos. To this end, it imported four African elephants and created a huge habitat for them. The previous elephant program was curtailed years ago when a trainer was killed by a panicked pachyderm.

At the **ZooTampa at Lowry Park** (1101 W. Sligh Ave., 813/935-8552, www.zootampa. com, 9:30am-5pm daily, $35 adults, $26 ages 3-11), habitats are naturalistic and nicely landscaped, but still designed for maximum viewing. All told there are around 2,000 native and exotic animals (white tiger cubs are a big draw), organized into reasonable housing developments, such as Wallaroo Station and Safari Africa. Lots of shade provided by big tropical plants seems to keep all the species comfortable, even in the substantial summer heat. One of the zoo's highlights is its Manatee and Aquatic Center, one of only three hospitals and rehabilitation facilities in Florida for sick sea cows.

Adventure Island

Adjacent to Busch Gardens but closed in winter is **Adventure Island** (10001 N. McKinley Dr., 888/800-5447, www.adventureisland. com, hours vary mid-Mar.-Oct., $60 at gate, $25 in advance, free under age 3), a 30-acre water park with slides, corkscrews, waterfalls, a monstrous 17,000-square-foot wave pool, and a children's play area. There are 50 lifeguards on duty, but it's still only appropriate for the water-safe. There's also a championship white-sand volleyball complex. If you buy a ticket to Busch Gardens, you can combine it with a ticket here for a discount.

University of South Florida Contemporary Art Museum

University of South Florida is an enormous institution, casting its imposing shadow on the cultural scene of Tampa. Visitors have little reason to walk around the less-than-picturesque campus, but a visit to the **University of South Florida Contemporary Art Museum** (3821 USF Holly Dr., 813/974-4133, 10am-5pm Mon.-Wed., 10am-8pm Thurs., 10am-5pm Fri., 1pm-4pm Sat., free) is a good excuse to drive around the university before parking at the small gallery. USFCAM maintains the university's art collection, comprising more than 5,000 artworks. There are exceptional holdings in graphics and sculpture multiples by internationally acclaimed artists, such as Roy Lichtenstein, Robert Rauschenberg, and James Rosenquist, who have worked at USF's Graphicstudio. Contemporary photography and African art are also represented. The museum hosts USF student art shows and oversees public art projects on campus.

Museum of Science & Industry (MOSI)

You spent a day on the rides at Busch Gardens, then a day at the aquarium. What next? The third day is Tampa's **Museum of Science & Industry** (4801 E. Fowler Ave., 813/987-6000, www.mosi.org, 10am-5pm Mon.-Fri., 10am-6pm Sat.-Sun., $13 adults, $11 seniors, $8 ages 3-12), a wonderful resource for local schools, family vacationers, or local parents. It's a sprawling modern structure that contains 450 hands-on activities grouped into learning areas. There's some unique and fun stuff like the Virtual Reality Simulator, which allows you to experience a spacewalk on the International Space Station, and the Sky Trail Ropes Course, a 36-foot-high multilevel course. The Look Inside exhibit teaches all about the human body. The museum has an IMAX dome and—get this—the admission price to the museum includes one free viewing of an IMAX film. The museum hosts traveling exhibits as well. Through interactive exhibits, film, and immersion experiences, guests explore the principles of simple mechanics, optics, electromagnetism, math, and psychology.

Malibu Grand Prix

If they've been really good, take the kids to **Grand Prix** (14320 N. Nebraska Ave., 813/977-6272, www.grandprixtampa.com, noon-9pm Mon.-Thurs., noon-midnight Fri., 10am-midnight Sat., 10am-9pm Sun., $3-50). It has excellent miniature golf with lots of windmills, pagodas, and water play, Grand Prix-style go-kart racing, batting cages, and a frenetic game room with a wide variety of video games.

GREATER TAMPA

Big Cat Rescue

The world's largest accredited sanctuary for big cats, **Big Cat Rescue** (12802 Easy St., 813/920-4130, www.bigcatrescue.org), across from Citrus Park Town Center and down a dirt road next to the McDonald's, provides a permanent retirement home to over 200 animals. The center offers regular tours (over age 9, 3pm Mon.-Wed. and Fri., 10am and 3pm Sat.-Sun., $39), a children's tour (noon Sat.-Sun., $39 adults, $29 under age 10), and feeding tours (9am Fri.-Sun., $65) as well as outreach presentations, animal interaction, and the opportunity to spend an evening in the heart of the sanctuary on the last Friday of each month on the Wild Eyes at Night tour (dusk, $65), in which guests roam the grounds equipped with flashlights that illuminate the hundreds of shining eyes in the cat enclosures.

Dinosaur World

For the dinosaur-obsessed, drive half an hour east of Tampa to an agricultural town called Plant City. It is known as the Winter Strawberry Capital of the World, but amid the strawberry fields lurks **Dinosaur World** (5145 Harvey Tew Rd., Plant City,

813/717-9865, www.dinosaurworld.com, 9am-5pm daily, $17 adults, $15 seniors, $12 ages 3-12, free under age 3). There are 150 huge models of prehistoric beasts arrayed in a huge subtropical garden. Having recently spent time in the dinosaur exhibit at the Museum of Natural History in New York, I have a sneaking suspicion that Dinosaur World isn't preoccupied with strict accuracy; for instance, we don't really know about dinosaur coloring, but these ones all sport the mottled green-brown made popular in movies. In addition to the dinosaurs, there are spooky fake caves to explore and an archaeological dig-sandbox area. This is best for kids under age seven.

Big Red Balloon Sightseeing Adventures

Big Red Balloon Sightseeing Adventures (8710 W. Hillsborough Ave., 813/969-1518, www.bigredballoon.com, 8am-8pm daily year-round, weather permitting, by reservation, $185 adults, $160 children) takes you up, up, and away in a beautiful hot-air balloon, and all you have to bring is a camera. Meet before dawn at a restaurant on the commercial strip of Dale Mabry at **Black Rock Bar and Grill** (11702 N. Dale Mabry Hwy.), where you are whisked into the Red Balloon van and taken to your agreed-on launch site (there are more than 30 in the area). Once inflated, the solid red balloon, the largest in the southeastern United States, is 8.5 stories tall and contains 210,000 cubic feet of air. The balloon, which comfortably accommodates eight passengers, takes a one-hour sunrise flight up to 1,000 feet, drifting over New Tampa, southeast Pasco County, Lutz, and Land O' Lakes. A champagne toast followed by a hearty breakfast back at Mimi's is included in the price.

After landing in a field, the pilot makes the champagne toast and recites a traditional balloonist prayer, "The winds have welcomed you with softness, the sun has left you with warm hands, you have flown so high, and so well, that God has joined you in your laughter, and set you gently back again into the loving arms of Mother Earth." Feel free to join in.

Pasco County Excursion

Naked people. That got your attention. The sleepy, mostly residential county to Tampa's north, Pasco County has at least a day's worth of a unique brand of fun that is definitely worth a side trip, a couple of meals, and even an overnight at one of the area's upscale spa, golf, and tennis resorts.

Lake Como Family Nudist Resort in the town of Land O' Lakes is the area's original nudist community, started in 1947. Since then, Pasco County has become a hotbed of naturist activity, with six all-ages nudist communities and recreational activities. These days the biggest player is the 120-acre Caliente Club and Resorts (21240 Gran Via Blvd., Land O' Lakes, 813/996-3700).

Another Pasco original requiring a bit of courage is Skydive City (4241 Skydive Lane, off Chancey Rd., 813/783-9399, www.skydivecity.com, 13,500-foot jump $199, 10,500-foot jump $179, plus $95 if you want a video documenting your experience) in Zephyrhills. The town has been a world-famous drop zone since the 1960s. Why here? According to owner T. K. Hayes, "It's in the middle of nowhere. It's really about the people—Zephyrhills is the largest skydiving place in the world." Tandem jumping, where a rookie jumps physically harnessed to an instructor, has opened skydiving up to people who never would have had the opportunity—the elderly, people with disabilities—really, anyone can do it.

If jumping out of an airplane sounds doable, it takes about an hour to prepare, with a 20-minute briefing. The whole experience is a three- to four-hour adventure, with free fall at 120 mph for about a minute from 13,500 feet, followed by up to six minutes of steering with the parachute open. Hayes says he's never had a student fatality or serious injury.

After that, take it down a notch and enjoy a walking tour of downtown Dade City. In the rolling hills of eastern Pasco County, the town has more than 50 antiques stores, gift shops, and boutiques. Stop into the historic 1909 Pasco County Courthouse and look at the sweet collection of artifacts from the turn of the 20th century. Have a slice of pie at Lunch on Limoges (14139 7th St., 352/567-5685, www.lunchonlimoges.com, $12-18). It's a charming throwback to an era of structured and unhurried lunching, with a daily-changing menu served on Limoges china by waitresses in nurses' uniforms.

Not far from downtown and usually taking about an hour, the Pioneer Florida Museum (15602 Pioneer Museum Rd., 352/567-0262, www.pioneerfloridamuseum.org, 10am-5pm Tues.-Sat., $10 adults, $8 seniors, $5 students and ages 6-18, free under age 6 and military) consists of nine period buildings dating back to 1878. There's the John Overstreet House, the Lacoochee School, and the Enterprise Methodist Church, all displaying period furniture, clothing, toys, and tools.

If there's time, take a tour around New Port Richey's Main Street (walking tour maps at www.nprmainstreet.com) and then board a boat and ride the Pithlachascottee River to see historic homes once owned by Gloria Swanson, Thomas Meighan, and Babe Ruth. Then walk around Centennial Park, which contains the Pasco Fine Arts Council, the Centennial Library, and the 1882 Baker House, one of the oldest structures in Pasco County. If you're hungry, stop in at the waterside Catches (7811 Bayview St., 727/849-2121, 11:30am-9pm Sun.-Thurs., 11:30am-10pm Fri.-Sat., $15-30).

If you're thinking about bed, Saddlebrook Resort & Spa (5700 Saddlebrook Way, 813/907-4419, $180-450) is Tampa's nicest four-star resort hotel, in the sleepy Pasco town of Wesley Chapel. It has 800 guest rooms, all beautiful, as well as pools, tennis, the Palmer and the Saddlebrook golf courses and the Saddlebrook Golf Academy, and a variety of dining options (if you eat on the Tropics Terrace, you can see nesting wood storks).

For more information about Pasco County, visit www.visitpasco.net.

TAMPA
SIGHTS

Sports and Recreation

LETTUCE LAKE PARK

To get out in nature, head to **Lettuce Lake Park** (6920 E. Fletcher Ave., near the I-75 exit, 813/987-6204, 8am-7pm daily spring-summer, 8am-6pm daily fall-winter, $2 per vehicle), just east of the University of South Florida. It's a stone's throw from urban sprawl, but the dense wilderness shelters a 3,500-foot-long raised boardwalk and a recently rebuilt tower overlooking the Hillsborough River, a perfect place from which to spy on tall wading birds, gators lurking among cypress knees in the swamp, or even delicate orchids and other epiphytes nestled in the trees' crooks. Rent a canoe for a closer look at the creatures that call this tannin-tinged water home, hike the fully accessible boardwalk or dirt trails (dogs are not allowed on the boardwalks), then settle in for a picnic at one of the waterfront shelters, equipped with barbecues. A kids playground, restrooms, and water fountains make this wilderness park much more comfortable.

FISHING AND BOATING

The 400 square miles of Tampa Bay offer an abundance of excellent fishing and boating spots. You'll catch snook, spotted trout, redfish, flounder, and sheepshead, to name a few. May is the peak season for tarpon, an exciting fish to catch. They tend to congregate near the bridge and rock structures of the bay. For all types of fishing, you need a **Florida fishing license,** available at most bait shops, outdoor stores, and Walmarts throughout the state.

If you're looking to fish from the shore, one of the best spots is **Upper Tampa Bay Park** (8001 Double Branch Rd., 813/855-1765, 8am-6pm daily, $2 per vehicle, kayak rentals $25 for 4 hours). The park also has enjoyable nature trails that explore the mangrove forest and tidal ecosystems. Fish from the shoreline or launch a canoe or kayak and cast a line in the creek for red drum and snook. In South Tampa, the pier and shoreline provide excellent fishing at **Ballast Point Park** (5314 Interbay Blvd., 813/274-8615, park sunrise-sunset daily, pier 24 hours daily, free). Other good spots are the piers at **E.G. Simmons Park** (2401 19th Ave. NW, 813/671-7655, 7am-7pm spring-summer, 7am-6pm fall-winter, $2 per vehicle), and **Picnic Island Park** (7409 Picnic Island Blvd., 813/274-8615, 7am-6pm daily, $2 per vehicle).

Rent a charter to have an expert to take you out by hiring **Tampa Fishing Charters** (401 Channelside Walk Way, 813/245-4738, www.tampafishingcharters.com, $425 half-day, $625 full-day), **Captain Chet Jennings Fishing Charters** (611 Destiny Dr., 813/477-3576, www.fishintampa.com, $499 half-day for 2 people, $749 full-day), or **Tampa Flats and Bay Fishing Charters** (10913 N. Edison Ave., 813/727-8843, www.flatsandbay.com, $425 half-day for 2 people, $700 full-day for 2 people).

Explore the bay and surrounding creeks on your own with a powered boat from **Tierra Verde Boat Rentals** (100 Pinellas Bayway, Tierra Verde, 727/867-0077, www.tvboatrentals.com, 22-foot center console $298 for 4 hours, $369 full-day, Jet Ski $75 per hour). Closer to downtown Tampa near the Convention Center, you can motor around the bay by renting a covered power boat that can hold up to 12 people from **eBoats Tampa** (333 S. Franklin St., 813/767-2245, www.eboatstampa.com, $75 per hour).

SAILING

Climb aboard the SV *Lionheart*, a 44-foot Caribbean sailing yacht, for a sightseeing sailing tour in Tampa Bay with **Olde World Sailing Line** (97 Columbia Dr., 888/989-7245, www.oldeworldsailing.com, $96 sunset sail, $396 sunset dinner cruise for 2).

A less intimate but more affordable sunset cruise and sightseeing tour is found aboard the **Tampa Bay Fun Boat** (333 S. Franklin

Tampa Golf

Tampa has several dozen public and semiprivate courses for visitors, many of them in Tampa's swankier northeast residential developments. Here are a handful of the area's top public courses:

Babe Zaharias Golf Club
11412 Forest Hills Dr., 813/631-4375, www.babezahariasgolf.net
18 holes, 6,244 yards, par 70, course rating 68.9, slope 121
Greens fees: $9.35-20.56

Heritage Isles Golf & Country Club
10630 Plantation Bay Dr., 813/907-7447, www.heritageislegolf.com
18 holes, 6,976 yards, par 72, course rating 73.2, slope 132
Greens fees: $12-35

Rocky Point Golf Course
4151 Dana Shores Dr., 813/673-4316, www.rockypointgolf.net
18 holes, 6,444 yards, par 71, course rating 71.7, slope 122
Greens fees: $10-26

Rogers Park Golf Course
7910 N. 30th St., 813/356-1671, www.rogersparkgc.com
18 holes, 6,802 yards, par 71, course rating 72.3, slope 125
Greens fees: $10-32

TPC Tampa Bay
5300 W. Lutz Lake Fern Rd., Lutz, 813/949-0090, www.tpctampabay.com
18 holes, 6,898 yards, par 71, course rating 73.6, slope 135
Greens fees: $89-189, $20 juniors

University of South Florida Golf Course ("The Claw")
4202 E. Fowler Ave., 813/632-6893, www.theclawatusfgolf.com
18 holes, 6,863 yards, par 71, course rating 74.2, slope 132
Greens fees: $10-35

Westchase Golf Club
11602 Westchase Golf Dr., 813/854-2331, www.westchasegc.com
18 holes, par 72, 6,699 yards, course rating 72.0, slope 136
Greens fees: $29-59

St., 727/204-9787, www.tampabayfunboat.com, $18 adults, $10 ages 3-12, free under age 3). They operate a 35-passenger deck boat that takes one-hour fun cruises (noon, 2pm, 4pm, 5:30pm, and 7pm daily). Depart from the Convention Center downtown and take a slow ride around the bay, where you will probably see some dolphins and have a stunning view of downtown. It's a great way to spend a few hours with the family.

CANOEING

You want to see big gators? Great blue herons, river otters, turtles, and more fish than you can string on a lifetime of lines? Paddle down the gently flowing Hillsborough River in a 16,000-acre wildlife preserve called **Wilderness Park.** You can rent canoes or kayaks and head out on your own, choosing from six different self-guided day trips. All paddling adventures start at **Canoe Escape** (12702 U.S. 301, Thonotosassa, 813/986-2067, www.canoeescape.com), 4.5 miles east of I-75. Whether you go on a guided tour or on your own, call ahead. Staff will equip you, give you maps and paddling pointers, then take you over to your debarkation point (all paddles are downstream) and establish a pickup time.

The Sargeant Park to Morris Bridge Park trip is a 4.5-mile, two-hour paddle, with 70 percent shade and alternating sun and shade. Morris Bridge Park to Trout Creek Park is a 4-mile, two-hour paddle, with 80 percent shade and a little full sun at the end. From Trout Creek Park to Rotary Park it's 5 miles and two hours of full-sun paddling, and Sargeant Park to Trout Creek Park is a longer 8.5-mile paddle with the first 75 percent in the shade. Morris Bridge Park to Rotary Park is a long 9-mile route, and Sargeant Park to Rotary Park is for experienced paddlers only, with 14 miles of river to paddle.

Self-guided rentals are $49-69 pp for a tandem canoe or kayak depending on the trip (a child under 12 can usually fit as a center passenger). A solo kayak rents for $46-56. Prices include the shuttle fee, paddles, and life vests. If solo paddling seems daunting, Canoe Escape offers a 4.5-mile interpreted guided tour ($75 pp) for solo kayakers and $50 pp for tandem canoes. I'd recommend this for newcomers, because the guides' vast knowledge of the local flora and fauna enrich the trip immeasurably.

GOLF

If you are thinking about picking up the sport, the **Saddlebrook Golf Academy** (5700 Saddlebrook Way, Wesley Chapel, 813/973-1111, www.saddlebrook.com, $1,495) at the Saddlebrook Resort teaches golfers of all skill levels. Classes combine classroom and practice time with course play. The package includes accommodations for six nights, 18 holes of golf a day, instruction, meals, video analysis, and use of resort facilities. There are two 18-hole Arnold Palmer-designed championship courses on the property, as well as 45 tennis courts in the four Grand Slam surfaces. The resort is also home to the Harry Hopman Tennis Academy.

SPECTATOR SPORTS

Tampa Bay fans are fanatical about their professional sports. There are professional football, ice hockey, and baseball teams, not to mention spring training for the New York Yankees, Philadelphia Phillies, Toronto Blue Jays, and hometown Rays, pro arena football, and the gamut of University of South Florida Bulls athletics.

Tampa Bay Buccaneers

Raymond James Stadium (4201 N. Dale Mabry Hwy.) is a wonderful venue in which to see Tampa's beloved **Buccaneers** (813/350-6500, www.buccaneers.com) play football. Completed in 1998, it holds more than 66,000 fans—52,000 in general seating—but tickets sometimes sell out for the season opener and other big games. Tickets for individual games are sold in person, by phone, and online at **TicketMaster** (800/745-3000, www.ticketmaster.com) outlets, or at the Raymond James Ticket Box three hours prior to kick-off on game days. Tickets for the 16 regular-season games (September-December) are $60 general admission, and special seats start at $400. The stadium features Buccaneer Cove, a 20,000-square-foot replica of an early 1800s seaport village, complete with a 103-foot-long, 43-ton pirate ship that blasts its cannons (confetti and foam footballs) every time the Bucs score—six times for a touchdown, once for an extra point, twice for a safety or two-point conversion, and three times for a field goal.

Every New Year's Day, Raymond James also plays host to football's **Outback Bowl** (813/287-8844, kickoff 11am, $80). The game matches the third-pick team from the SEC and the third-pick team from the Big Ten Conference and is the culmination of a week-long festival in Tampa.

USF Bulls

The University of South Florida **Bulls football team** (800/462-8557, www.gousfbulls.com, $20-50), have gone from nonexistent to Division I-AA Independent to I-A to Conference USA, and into the Big East Conference in 2005. For the spectator, this means real college football is played during the fall at **Raymond James Stadium** (4201 N. Dale Mabry Hwy.). **Bulls basketball** (813/974-3002, $11-27) has also been notched up in recent years, resulting in the team

Lightning Strikes

Alligators are dangerous, but lightning is much more deadly in Florida, with about 50 people struck each year in the state. Most of them are hospitalized and recover, but there are about 10 fatalities annually. The Tampa area is the Lightning Capital of the United States (Rwanda is the lightning capital of the world), with around 25 cloud-to-ground lightning bolt blasts on each square mile annually. The temperature of a single bolt can reach 50,000°F, about three times as hot as the sun's surface.

The problem is the tropical afternoon thunderstorms each summer, about 90 of which are electrical storms. Short-lived but intense, the storms' clouds are charged like giant capacitors, the upper portion positively charged and the lower portion negatively charged. Current flows between the cloud bottom and the top, or in the case of cloud-to-ground lightning, the positively charged earth's surface. Bolts, sheets, ribbons, and, rarely, balls of lightning hit the ground.

There's not much you can do to ward off lightning except to avoid being in the wrong place at the wrong time. The summer months, June-September, have the highest number of lightning-related injuries and deaths. Usually lightning occurs during daylight hours, with the highest concentration 3pm-4pm, when the afternoon storms peak. Lightning strikes usually occur either at the beginning or end of a storm and can strike up to 10 miles from the center of the storm.

Still, 9 out of 10 people survive being struck. As long as the electrical surge is not to your brain, you are likely to be treatable. A lightning strike will often singe and burn skin or clothes, but even when the electrical surge stops a victim's heart, emergency rooms have a high success rate of restarting the ticker.

TIPS

- Stay vigilant and go inside as soon as clouds darken and thunderstorms develop.

- If the time between seeing the lightning flash and hearing the thunder is less than 30 seconds, take shelter.

- Stay away from the Gulf, pools, lakes, or other bodies of water.

- Avoid using a tree or other tall object as shelter. Lightning usually strikes the tallest object in a given area.

- Stay away from metal objects (bikes, golf carts, and fencing are bad, but a car's rubber tires render the automobile's interior a safe retreat).

- The safest place to be during an electrical storm is inside and away from windows and electrical appliances.

moving to the Big East Conference. Home games are played at the **USF Sun Dome** (4202 E. Fowler Ave.).

Tampa Bay Lightning

The 21,000-seat, $153 million **Amalie Arena** (401 Channelside Dr.) on Tampa's downtown waterfront is home to Tampa's professional ice hockey team, the **Tampa Bay Lightning** (813/301-6500, www.nhl.com, $15-349), 2004 Stanley Cup champions. The season runs October-April.

Tampa Bay Rays

Since 1998 Tampa has also been home to Major League Baseball's **Tampa Bay Rays** (888/326-7297, www.mlb.com, game times usually 2:15pm or 7:15pm, tickets $18-80), who play at **Tropicana Field** (1 Tropicana Dr., St. Petersburg). As a concession to summer temperatures and humidity, the ballpark has a dome roof, which is lit orange when the Rays win at home, and artificial turf.

There has been a great deal of dissatisfaction from Rays fans with Tropicana Field

over the years. The park is known for a heart-breakingly long list of lasts. It is the last Major League Baseball park to have a retractable roof, and the last to use artificial turf on the field instead of fan-preferred natural grass. Tropicana Field is also ranked last in stadium rankings by *USA Today* and ESPN, and the Rays games have among the lowest attendance rates. However, low attendance can't be blamed on the team's poor performance. The Rays have been to the playoffs four times in the last decade, and went to the World Series in 2008, but lost to the Phillies.

TOP EXPERIENCE

★ **SPRING TRAINING**
If you're in the area during spring training time, you can also catch the Rays at the **Charlotte Sports Park** (2300 El Jobean Rd., Port Charlotte, 941/235-5010, www.tampabay.rays.mlb.com, $10-30), their spring training home, with a 7,000-seat natural grass field.

The Grapefruit League's spring training remains a serious draw for sports fans each March. Since 1988 the **New York Yankees** have based their minor-league operation, spring training, and year-round headquarters for player development in Tampa. Modeled after the original Yankee Stadium in New York City, **George M. Steinbrenner Field** (1 Steinbrenner Dr., off N. Dale Mabry Hwy., 813/875-7753, www.gmsfield.com, $10-38) has been the Yankees' home since 1996. The complex houses a 10,000-seat stadium with 13 swanky luxury suites ($375-500), a community-use field, and a major-league practice field. A 2016 renovation included new seats, roof replacement, suite upgrades, a right-field bar, and a new outfield concourse. It's also the home of the five-time **Florida State League Champion's Tampa Yankees** (New York Yankees-Florida State League Single-A Affiliate) and the **Hillsborough Community College Hawks** baseball team.

Entertainment and Events

MUSIC, THEATER, AND CINEMA
Straz Center for the Performing Arts
Tampa's heavy hitter for performing arts is the **Straz Center for the Performing Arts** (1010 N. W. C. MacInnes Place, 1 block off Ashley St., 813/229-7827, www.strazcenter.org), a huge arts complex housing four theaters where audiences can see Opera Tampa (the resident company), the Florida Orchestra, comedies, dramas, cabaret, dance, music, alternative theater, children's theater, and an annual Broadway series. Many local arts series and events find a home at the performing arts center—Latin Nights, Patel Conservatory's Series—you name it, the curtain goes up here.

Tampa Improv
If music and drinking aren't your objective, stop into the **Improv** Comedy Theater (1600 E. 8th Ave., 813/864-4000, www.improvtampa.com) for an evening of live stand-up with mostly local and regional acts.

Mid-Florida Credit Union Amphitheater
Tampa's outdoor open-air **Mid-Florida Credit Union Amphitheater** (4802 U.S. 301 N., 813/740-2446), formerly Ford Amphitheater, 1-800-ASK-GARY Amphitheater, and Live Nation Amphitheater, is a state-of-the-art venue for 30-plus big-league music concerts a year. With huge video screens, a 7,200-square-foot stage, 9,900 reserved seats, and room for

1: the Raymond James Stadium, home of the Tampa Bay Buccaneers **2:** George M. Steinbrenner Field

10,500 more on the lawn, big space-age sound shields provide relief to neighbors. It's gorgeous, like a huge circus tent mated with the *Millennium Falcon.* There are enough restrooms and lots of tasty food options.

★ Tampa Theatre

Tampa has its share of movie multiplexes, but skip the 20-screeners in favor of two hours in the dark at the **Tampa Theatre** (711 N. Franklin St., 813/274-8981, www. tampatheatre.org, $11). Built in 1926, it's a beloved downtown landmark with an acclaimed film series, concerts, special events, and backstage tours. The motion picture palace's interior is vintage, with statues and gargoyles and intricately carved doors. Many believe that the theater is haunted by the ghost of Foster Finley, who spent 20 years as the theater's projectionist; if you feel a hand in your popcorn, it may not be your seatmate's. Some of the films shown are classics, complete with a Wurlitzer performance, and other times it's more indie; check the website. Theater concessions include excellent popcorn, sophisticated candies, and beer and wine. Interesting fact: It was the first public building in Tampa to be equipped with air-conditioning.

FESTIVALS AND EVENTS

Gasparilla Pirate Fest

The biggest party in Tampa comes late January-early February with the **Gasparilla Pirate Fest** (www.gasparillapiratefest.com), a fun century-old celebration in honor of legendary pirate José Gaspar, "last of the buccaneers," who terrorized the coastal waters of western Florida during the late 18th and early 19th centuries. The weekend festivities start with 1,000 people in pirate costume sailing into downtown on a fully rigged pirate ship, a replica of an 18th-century craft that is 165 feet long by 35 feet across the beam, with three masts standing 100 feet tall. The ship is met by a flotilla of hundreds of pleasure craft intent on "defending the city." The upshot is that pirates take over Tampa for a

while, like Mardi Gras, only with more "argh, me matey" and eye patches accompanying the beads and buried treasure. The length of Bayshore Boulevard is lined with bleachers for the occasion, musical acts sprout on stages all over town, and there's general merriment and carousing.

Guavaween

The second-biggest party is not unlike Gasparilla for its focus on wild costumes and wilder revelry. **Guavaween** (www. guavaweentampa.com, end of Oct.) is the city's Cuban-style Halloween celebration, held near Halloween. Riffing on the fact that Tampa was nicknamed the Big Guava, the celebration features the Mama Guava, who has sworn to take the "bore" out of Ybor City. Really, after the parade is over, it's just a big excuse to drink too much and wander the streets of Ybor City in preposterous attire.

Gasparilla International Film Festival

The **Gasparilla International Film Festival** (813/693-2367, www. gasparillafilmfestival.com) began in 2006 and takes place in late March at venues in and around Ybor City. Over five days, more than 40 films are screened in a variety of genres. It's spiced up with a handful of industry panel discussions, VIP parties, glamorous dinners, and celebrity sightings.

Florida State Fair

In mid-February is the **Florida State Fair** (813/740-2446, www.floridastatefair.com), a 12-day salute to the state's best in agriculture, industry, entertainment, and foods on a stick.

Florida Strawberry Festival

Also in February is a county fair, the **Florida Strawberry Festival** (813/752-9194, www. flstrawberryfestival.com), with a huge midway and lots of strawberry cook-offs. Plant City is known as the Winter Strawberry Capital of the World, and these sweet babies are delicious.

Nightlife

DOWNTOWN TAMPA

Downtown mostly caters to tourists and sports fans. It's the place to be before or after the game.

Bars and Pubs

A top choice on game day is **Hattricks** (107 S. Franklin St., 813/225-4288, 11:15am-3am daily), which caters to the ice hockey crowd. If a Lightning game is on at the same time your favorite nonhockey sports team is playing, you may be out of luck, but this is a fun spot to be before and after any sports game that is taking place. Standing room only is the norm for the after-game parties. The menu for food and beverages is lengthy and delicious, the prices are reasonable, and the atmosphere is classic brick-and-wood-paneled sports bar.

Fly Bar (1202 N. Franklin St., 813/275-5000, 4pm-2am Mon.-Fri., 5:30pm-3am Sat., 4pm-midnight Sun.) is trendier and mostly attracts the younger crowd. The taps carry smaller microbrews as well as the big names in beer. The hipster-inspired interior has colorful paintings crowding the walls and modern light fixtures, giving this artsy bar a Brooklyn vibe. The plush booths let you sink in for some tasty food on their surprisingly upscale and health-centric menu. The open-air rooftop bar is spectacular and offers some of the best sunsets downtown.

Live Music

For live music and drinks close to the Amelia Arena, go to **Ferg's Live** (490 Channelside Dr., 813/443-8403, 11am-1am Mon.-Thurs., 11am-3am Fri.-Sat., 11am-11pm Sun.). This two-level bar is conveniently located near the arena. The first level has TVs lining the walls, so most big games can be tuned in. Tables fill a large outdoor seating area, and on the second floor you can hear live bands that tend to perform rock, alt-country, blues, and pop. The kitchen serves wings, sandwiches, burgers, and bar snacks to go with cold beers and cocktails.

YBOR CITY

Ybor City is where people come out to party in Tampa. It's quieter during the week, but it's the place to go if you're looking for fun on the weekend.

Bars and Pubs

Coyote Ugly (1722 E. 7th Ave., 813/241-8459, 5pm-3am Tues.-Sat., 2pm-midnight Sun.) is often the biggest party in Ybor City, presided over by the most audacious women bartenders to ever wield a shot glass. If you have to ask what a body shot is, you're ripe for a hard life lesson. Just like in the eponymous movie, which was based on a bar in New York City, the bartenders drag the unsuspecting victim up on the bar for some raunchy drinking, dancing, and whatever. The bare-bones room is festooned with discarded brassieres from exuberant patrons. The **Green Iguana** (4029 S. West Shore Blvd., 813/837-1234, 11am-3am daily) is another bar for grown-ups: good drinks, perfectly acceptable food, and audible conversation.

James Joyce Irish Pub and Eatery (1724 E. 8th Ave., 813/247-1896, 11am-3am daily) can't decide if it's an Irish pub or a sports bar, but it does a perfect job as both. The wings, seafood, burgers, and traditional Irish food are excellent. The seven TVs make it easy to watch your game, and with more than 50 beers on tap, 30 Irish whiskeys, and a top shelf selection of scotch, they're certain to have your drink. The exquisite dark-wood interior is as classy and warm as the smooth Irish whisky.

Breweries

Confess your sins at **Coppertail Brewing Company** (2601 E. 2nd Ave., 813/247-1500, 11am-11pm Mon.-Thurs., 11am-midnight Fri.-Sat., noon-9pm Sun.) with a visit to the

Cruising into Tampa

the Port of Tampa Bay

The Port of Tampa is the fastest-growing cruise port in North America, with a passenger counts rising from 200,000 in 1998 to over a million in 2018. Newer and larger vessels steam into the downtown port all the time. It started with Carnival and Holland America cruise lines back in 1994, but these days a number of lines head out of Tampa on four- to seven-day itineraries. Tampa now homeports five vessels from four cruise lines:

- Carnival has two ships in Tampa. The *Paradise* has four- and five-day cruises to the western Caribbean. The *Miracle* offers seven-day cruises to the western Caribbean.

- Royal Caribbean International has two ships here. *Brilliance of the Seas* offers four- to seven-day cruises to the western Caribbean in the winter, and the *Majesty of the Seas* has four- to six-day cruises to Central America, the western Caribbean, the Bahamas, and Cuba.

- Holland America Lines' *Rotterdam* offers passengers 7- to 21-day itineraries of the Caribbean and Mexico.

- Norwegian Cruise Lines' *Norwegian Pearl* has 14-day cruises to Central America and the Caribbean.

The port's cruise terminals include customer-friendly information areas, superior security, full passenger amenities, and a covered on-terminal parking garage (reservations recommended, $15 per day). Valet parking ($19 per day) is also available. The port is close to the interstate highway system. For directions to the cruise terminals, call 866/938-7275.

church confessional booth just steps from the bar. The beer is sinfully good, so sample as many as you can responsibly handle. The padded benches lining the walls make this a great space for groups small and large, and the high ceilings and glass viewing wall gives you a spectacular glimpse into the beer-brewing process as you sip the results.

This is a drinking establishment that also offers a small selection of soups, salads, burgers, sandwiches, and several seafood options.

Try the beer flights at **Tampa Bay Brewing Company** (1600 E. 9th Ave., 813/247-1422, 11am-11pm Mon.-Thurs., 11am-midnight Fri.-Sat., 11am-10pm Sun.), where the food is as good as the brews (try one of their huge calzones). The outdoor bar and seating area is a great spot to people-watch at Ybor Centro. The air conditioning inside is nice on hot Tampa days.

Clubs

Club Skye (1509 E. 8th Ave., 813/516-7593, 10pm-3am Tues.-Sat., cover varies, no cover before 11pm on Sat.) is a trendy spot for late-night partying that always draws a young crowd. The club mostly features hip-hop and DJs spinning dance music. Whether you're here for College Ladies Night, International Night, or DJ nights, Skye is the party to beat in Ybor.

Gay-Friendly

The Honey Pot (1507 E. 7th Ave., 813/247-4663, 10pm-3am daily) is a hopping LGBT club in Tampa. There are themed nights, drag shows, DJs, dancers, and usually a lively crowd.

HYDE PARK

There's lots of good nightlife in this sophisticated South Tampa neighborhood, with some Irish zeal on and around Azeele.

Bars and Pubs

If you like your music—or your flirting—with a heavy brogue, head to everyone's favorite quaint Irish bar, **Dubliner Pub** (2307 W. Azeele St., 813/258-2257, 4pm-3am Tues.-Sun.). **Four Green Fields** (205 W. Platt St., 813/254-4444, 11am-3am daily) is another legendary Irish pub, with lots of regulars and lively conversation. The french-fry basket is a bargain and could feed a small nation. **MacDinton's Soho** (405 S. Howard Ave., 813/251-8999, 4pm-3am Mon.-Fri., 10am-3am Sat., 11am-3pm Sun.) is another Irish entry, with a killer black and tan, a warming Irish coffee, and a fair representation of Irish staples, from rib-sticking, mashed-potatoey shepherd's pie to corned beef and cabbage, a brunch (11am-3pm Sat.-Sun.), and a variety of burgers and sandwiches. This is the biggest

scene in Tampa, with lines around the block on weekend nights.

Irish 31 (1611 W. Swann Ave., 813/250-0031, 11am-midnight Mon.-Wed., 11am-1am Thurs., 11am-2am Fri.-Sat., 10am-midnight Sun.) opened their first pub in 2011, and quickly expanded to three locations in Tampa. The affordable drinks, traditional Irish fare, comfy pub atmosphere, nightly live music, and sports-centric theme have garnered rave reviews and loyal customers. They keep late hours and have dozens of TVs to cover a range of sporting events. Outside Hyde Park you can visit other Irish 31 locations in Westchase and at the Westshore Plaza.

Wine Lounges

In Old Hyde Park Village, **The Wine Exchange** (1609 W. Snow Ave., 813/254-9463, 11:30am-10pm Tues.-Thurs., 11:30am-11pm Fri.-Sat., 11:30am-9pm Sun.-Mon.) focuses on the vine, and the extensive wine list doesn't disappoint. A favorite spot for business lunches, this gem also pulls in the brunch crowd on Sunday. The menu is eclectic with mostly American and Italian dishes. When the weather is nice, ask to be seated outdoors.

NORTH TAMPA

With the university nearby, the bars in this area tend to cater to the beer-swilling, late-night-partying college crowd. Several top-notch breweries provide plenty of options, whether you're looking to drink day or night.

Bars and Pubs

Near the university, you'll find over 500 beers at **World of Beer** (2815 E. Fowler Ave., 813/559-1530, 11am-midnight Sun.-Tues., 11am-1am Wed.-Thurs., 11am-2am Fri.-Sat.). There is a tasty, beer-centric menu with burgers, bratwurst, and pretzels. The college crowd tends to frequent this place, but beer aficionados of any age will feel at home, and the TVs keep the place busy during game time. This reliable chain has four locations in Tampa.

Breweries

Tour the oldest brewery in the United States at the **Yuengling Brewing Company** (11111 N. 30th St., 813/972-8529, www.yuengling.com, tours 10:30am and 1pm Wed.-Sat., free). The hour-long tour takes you through the brew house, where they produce and bottle beer and offer two free nice-size samples of beer at the end. You must wear closed-toe shoes.

GREATER TAMPA
Bars and Pubs

Bahama Breeze (3045 N. Rocky Point Dr. E., 813/289-7922, roughly 11am-midnight Sun.-Thurs., 11am-2am Fri.-Sat.) is a tropical-themed singles hangout with a huge water-side deck from which you can view a great sunset. In west Tampa, the **Brick House Tavern and Tap** (1102 N. Dale Mabry Hwy., 813/350-9108, 11am-1am Mon.-Thurs., 11am-2am Fri.-Sat., 11am-midnight Sun.) gets a top nod from foodies, beer lovers, and dog lovers alike. This pet-friendly bar has games on the big screens indoors and a nice covered patio outdoors. The indoor fireplace gives the place a cozy feel. The menu has great sandwiches and delicious chicken and waffles. It's exceptionally popular for lunch and on weekends. If there's a home game on, you might find standing room only.

A memorable night on the town can only be complemented by a drink on the roof-top restaurant and bar at **Armani's** (2900 Bayport Dr., 813/207-6800, 6pm-10pm Mon.-Fri., 5:30pm-10pm Sat.), located in the Grand Hyatt Tampa Bay. The glass panel-lined patio offers a breathtaking waterfront view, and sitting around a fire on a plush couch will turn any evening into a classy, romantic affair. The drinks are expensive, but the experience is worth it.

Breweries

The **Cigar City Brewing Company** (3924 W. Spruce St., 813/348-6363, 11am-11pm Sun.-Thurs., 11am-1am Fri.-Sat., tours $8) offers delicious craft beers at the bar. They also offer tours of the brewery, with exceptional guides and a generous tasting that make it well worth the money.

Wine Lounges

Cooper's Hawk Winery and Restaurant (4110 W. Boy Scout Blvd., 813/873-9463, 11:30am-9:30pm Mon.-Thurs., 11:30am-10:30pm Fri.-Sat., 11am-9pm Sun.) is a successful chain with a great wine list (glasses $6-13, bottles $22-47). The dining room is upscale casual, and the outdoor seating will make you feel comfortable if you're not as dressed up. You can also enjoy wine-tasting in the lobby or relax at the bar.

Shopping

DOWNTOWN AND SPARKMAN WHARF

Shopping Malls and Centers

Sparkman Wharf (615 Channelside Dr., 813/223-4250), the new entertainment center on Tampa's downtown waterfront adjacent to the Florida Aquarium and the cruise terminal, is replacing popular waterfront Channelside district. The new plans include office and re-tail space, a bowling alley, an outdoor lawn with a stage for live music, and a variety of restaurants and bars. Currently you'll find a nice lawn surrounded by several excellent food trucks and a large covered bar and grill. It's the perfect spot to relax while you wait to board your cruise ship.

YBOR CITY

Shopping along **7th Avenue** in Ybor City, Tampa's Latin Quarter, will yield some interesting finds. It's a little gritty, with a few

1: Sparkman Wharf **2:** International Plaza

vintage clothing shops and a fair amount of racy lingerie.

Cigars

In addition to being a great café and bar, **King Corona Cigars Café and Bar** (1523 E. 7th Ave., 813/241-9109, www.kingcoronacigars.com, 8am-midnight Mon.-Thurs., 8am-2am Fri., 11am-11pm Sun.) sells excellent Cuban coffee, cigars, and many other things related to the smoking life.

SOUTH TAMPA AND HYDE PARK

Shopping Malls and Centers

Tampa's downtown doesn't really have a retail center. For that, you need to visit **Hyde Park Village** (744 S. Village Circle, 813/251-3500). It's not vast, but the outdoor shopping area along Hyde Park's West Swann Avenue, South Dakota Avenue, and Snow Avenue is the most appealing shopping destination in town, especially when the weather's nice. There's a large covered parking lot, free to shoppers, and a nicely landscaped plaza at the center. Pottery Barn and West Elm are among the bigger stores, with Lululemon, Brooks Brothers, Anthropologie, and Francesca's. Top restaurants include the Wine Exchange Bistro and Wine Bar, the indoor-outdoor Sinatra-addled Timpano Italian Chophouse, and a French-inspired gem called Piquant.

NORTH TAMPA

Shopping Malls and Centers

With anchor stores Neiman Marcus and Nordstrom, **International Plaza** (2223 N. Westshore Blvd., 813/342-3790, www.shopinternationalplaza.com, 10am-9pm Mon.-Sat., 11am-6pm Sun.) gets the nod for fanciest shopping. A handful of usual mall stores (J.Crew, Banana Republic, Ann Taylor) are spiffed up by their proximity to 200 other specialty shops such as Tiffany & Co., Louis Vuitton, Montblanc, Gucci, Apple, and Coach. It's the most upscale assembly of stores in any shopping center on the Gulf Coast, served by an open-air village of restaurants called

Bay Street, all minutes from the airport and downtown. During the Christmas season, the Neiman Marcus store goes all out with decorations.

Located across the street from USF, **University Mall** (2200 E. Fowler Ave., 813/971-3465) is a typical indoor shopping center with mostly familiar mall stores, a 16-screen movie theater, and a standard food court. In Wesley Chapel, **The Shops at Wiregrass** (28211 Paseo Dr., 813/994-2242, www.theshopsatwiregrass.com, 10am-9pm Mon.-Sat., noon-6pm Sun.) comprises 50 stores in a fairly upscale outdoor and indoor shopping center. The mall is anchored by JCPenney, Macy's, Dillard's, and a Barnes & Noble. You'll find plenty of other chain shops and restaurants.

For sales from leading retailers, head to **Tampa Premium Outlets** (2300 Grand Cypress Dr., Lutz, 813/938-6272, www.premiumoutlets.com, 10am-9pm Mon.-Sat., 10am-7pm Sun.), where you'll find the usual outlet mall suspects, including Gap, Under Armour, and Tommy Hilfiger. The shopping center has excellent outdoor space and several chain restaurants to keep you fueled for a full day of credit card swiping. Several upscale chains, such as Saks Fifth Avenue, Polo Ralph Lauren, and Michael Kors have outlet stores here with exceptional bargains.

About a minute from International Plaza, **Westshore Plaza** (250 Westshore Plaza, 813/286-0790) features more than 100 similarly fancy specialty shops and four major department stores, including a Macy's. It contains a 14-screen AMC Theater and restaurants like Maggiano's Little Italy, P. F. Chang's, and Mitchell's Fish Market.

GREATER TAMPA

Shopping Malls and Centers

Fairly far from where most visitors stay, **Westfield Brandon** (459 Brandon Town Center Dr., 813/661-6255) and **Westfield Citrus Park** (8021 Citrus Park Town Center Blvd., 813/926-4644) are both enjoyable malls with the full gamut of small shops and

Cigar Basics

hand-rolled cigars

Want to try a cigar but don't know the first thing about them? Tampa's a good place to begin. Even before you light up, a cigar's visual specifications can give clues to its character. The outer wrapper's color indicates a cigar's flavor. A *maduro* wrapper is a rich, deep brown, imparting a cigar with deep, strong flavors. A *claro* wrapper is a light tan and lends little additional flavor to a cigar. There are essentially six color grades. Roughly from lightest to darkest, these are *candela* (pale green), *claro, natural* (light brown), *colorado* (reddish brown), *maduro,* and *oscuro* (almost black).

Shape is another central factor in cigar selection. Among *parejos,* or straight-sided cigars, there are three basic categories. A *corona* is classically six inches long, with an open foot (the end that is lighted) and a closed head (the end that is smoked). Within this category, *Churchills* are a bit longer and thicker, *robustos* are shorter and much thicker, and a *double corona* is significantly longer. *Panetelas,* the second category, are longer and much thinner than *coronas,* and the third category, *lonsdales,* are thicker than *panetelas* and thinner and longer than *coronas.*

Figurados are the other class of cigar, which spans all of the irregularly shaped types. This includes torpedo shapes, braided *culebras,* and pyramid shapes that have a closed, pointed head and an open foot.

A cigar band is generally wrapped around the closed head of a cigar. Its original function was to minimize finger staining, not to identify brands. Nonetheless, on the band you will find the name a manufacturer has designated for a particular line of cigars—names like Partagas, Macanudo, Punch, and Montecristo. Keep in mind that after 1959, many cigar manufacturers fled Cuba to open shops elsewhere, taking their brand names with them. Thus, a brand name does not always betray a cigar's country of origin.

For neophytes lighting up for the first time, a milder cigar may ease you in. The Macanudo Hyde Park is a mild smoke, as is the Don Diego Playboy Robusto or Lonsdale. For a fuller-bodied cigar, the Punch Diademas and the Partagas Number 10 are both popular. If you're looking for a robust, ultra-full-bodied taste, you might try the Hoyo de Monterrey Double Corona. The best way to discover your own personal tastes is to stop into a tobacconist or cigar-friendly restaurant and have a chat.

Market to Market

Spend a few hours at the **Ybor City Saturday Market** (Centennial Park, 1901 N. 19th St., at 8th Ave., www.ybormarket.com, 9am-1pm Sat., free), where vendors typically sell produce, arts and crafts, sweets, cigars, and souvenirs. The prices are much lower than you'll find in the shops around Ybor, but you'll have more variety with cigars in the more popular cigar stores. Use the free parking in the city lot across from the market. Well-behaved pets are welcome.

In Thonotosassa, near Busch Gardens, the **Big Top Flea Market** (9250 E. Fowler Ave., 813/986-4004, www.bigtopfleamarket.com, 9am-4:30pm Sat.-Sun.) has more than 1,200 booths in four large buildings. Pretty much anything and everything can be found at this large flea market. You can buy tools, eat fair-style food, or even get a tattoo. It's a good way to spend a few hours on a rainy day if you love shopping and don't mind sorting through junk for a great deal.

Bearss Groves (14316 Lake Magdalene Blvd., 813/963-5125, www.bearssgroves.com, 9am-7pm daily) is the place for fresh, local produce. From oranges and watermelons to corn and collards, you'll find low prices, excellent quality, and superb customer service. They also sell fresh-squeezed juices that hit the spot on a hot Florida summer day. The fruit pies are winners as well. Food trucks are on-site if you want to pick up lunch or dinner during your visit.

anchors, mostly serving the local community. Citrus Park is a little nicer, with a 20-screen Regal Cinema.

If you want to get some great deals on name brands, you need to drive south on I-75 for 40 minutes to the **Ellenton Premium Outlets** (5461 Factory Shops Blvd., 941/723-1150). You'll find Ann Taylor, Nautica, Under Armour, Nike, and Polo Ralph Lauren—all offering deep discounts.

Food

Maybe it's Tampa residents' deep streak of loyalty, maybe their plodding constancy, but marketing geniuses have determined that Tampa is the perfect test market for new chain restaurant concepts. They are trotted out here, and if they fly, they are launched in the rest of the country. For this reason, Tampa is the home of numerous national and regional chains—Hooters, Durango Steakhouse, Beef O'Brady's, Checkers, Hops Restaurant Bar and Brewery, Shells' Seafood Restaurant, Carrabba's, and Outback Steakhouse. Outback is also the mastermind behind chains Lee Roy Selmon's, Fleming's Prime Steakhouse, Bonefish Grill, and Roy's.

You will find more Chili's, Macaroni Grills, TGI Fridays, and Bennigan's restaurants than you could possibly patronize. For this reason, only the unique, discrete, more-or-less independently owned restaurants that are the exception to the rule in Tampa are covered here.

DOWNTOWN AND SPARKMAN WHARF

Sparkman Wharf is dockside at the Port of Tampa, where all the cruise ships come in. The shopping, dining, and entertainment complex has a big movie theater with IMAX; a fun upscale bowling alley, small mostly independently owned shops, and a dozen restaurants.

American

Head first to the bowling alley-restaurant **Splitsville** (615 Channelside Dr., 813/514-2695, 4pm-1am Tues.-Fri., noon-2am Sat.-Sun., $7-18), in the new Sparkman Wharf development that replaced Channelside. It's good food, a whimsical environment, and the coolest bowling shoes ever. The decor is over-size bowling-pin columns, red velvet ropes, and 12 faultless lanes, and the food is excellent bar snacks.

Breakfast

Enjoy breakfast, lunch, or brunch near the University of Tampa in a stunning setting at **Oxford Exchange** (420 W. Kennedy Blvd., 813/253-0222, www.oxfordexchange.com, 7:30am-5:30pm Mon.-Fri., 9am-5:30pm Sat.-Sun., $10-20). Eat indoors surrounded by stylish wood-paneled walls or enjoy a meal in the glass-roofed conservatory. The exquisite architecture of this building, once a stable for the Tampa Bay Hotel, was painstakingly renovated to preserve its brick walls and wood-beamed ceilings. For breakfast, the eggs benedict is an excellent choice, and for lunch, the grilled chicken sandwich with garlic aioli on a ciabatta is a favorite.

Steak House

For a great steak, head to **Malio's Prime** (400 N. Ashley Dr., 813/223-7746, 11:30am-9:30pm Mon.-Tues., 11:30am-10pm Wed.-Thurs., 11:30am-10:30pm Fri., 5pm-10:30pm Sat., $21-37). It opened downtown in Rivergate Tower, only in name similar to a historic restaurant that Malio Iavarone ran on Dale Mabry. It has prime steaks served in a soaring-ceilinged dining room with banks of riverside windows.

YBOR CITY

The neighborhood's restaurants are spread along many blocks on **7th Avenue,** closed to cars on weekends. It gets packed on the weekend with young partiers, but the area is calmer during the week.

American

Tampa Bay Brewing Company (1600 E. 8th Ave., 813/247-1422, www.tampabaybrewingcompany.com, 11am-11pm Mon.-Thurs., 11am-midnight Fri.-Sat., 11am-10pm Sun., $7-12), on the plaza level under Muvico, anchors Centro. There's good live music, excellent proprietary brews (try the

Redeye Ale), and a fresh American bistro menu.

Asian
Samurai Blue Sushi and Sake Bar (813/242-6688, 11:30am-2pm and 5pm-11pm Sun.-Tues., 11:30am-2pm and 5pm-midnight Wed.-Thurs., 11:30am-2pm and 5pm-1am Sat.-Sun., $10-30) is another big lively joint, but this one serves sake bombers, "spontaneous combustion rolls," and other unique spins on Japanese bar staples.

Cuban-Spanish
Nearly at the end of the strip of commerce you'll find the **Columbia Restaurant** (2025 E. 7th Ave., 813/248-4961, 11am-10pm Mon.-Thurs., 11am-11pm Fri.-Sat., 11:30am-9pm Sun., $21-30), which bears the distinction of being the oldest restaurant in Florida (started in 1905) and the nation's largest Spanish-Cuban restaurant (13 rooms extending one city block). The food is authentic, and the experience is worth it. Some of these waiters have been here a lifetime, the many rooms manage to stay packed, and there are stirring flamenco shows Monday-Saturday nights.

Italian
Grab a slice of Italian heaven at **La Terrazza Restaurant** (1727 E. 7th Ave., 813/248-1326, www.laterrazzayborcity.com, 11:30am-2pm and 5:30pm-10pm Tues.-Fri., 5pm-10:30pm Sat., $15-25). The menu features traditional northern Italian favorites and an extensive wine list. Owner-chef Andrea Fenu created an unpretentious atmosphere that makes you feel as if you're dining in Italy at a quaint café.

People-watching is a popular pastime in Ybor City. For the best sidewalk seat in town, pull up a chair at ★ **Bernini** (1702 E. 7th Ave., 813/248-0099, 11:30am-10pm Mon.-Thurs., 11:30am-11pm Fri.-Sat., 11:30am-9pm Sun., $10-24). It's set in the historic Bank of Ybor City building and serves Cal-Ital cuisine—beef carpaccio and filet mignon with sweet corn puree. It attracts an older crowd than the bars and clubs around it.

TAMPA FOOD

Mexican

Centro Cantina (813/241-8588, 11am-9pm Mon., 11am-11pm Tues., 11am-1am Wed.-Thurs., 11am-1am Fri.-Sat., noon-1am Sun., $7-15) is more a drinking establishment. They have good margaritas and the usual Mexican dishes, so the draw is the rustic indoor-outdoor space and abounding colorful atmosphere. After this, regroup at the Centro Ybor movie theater across the plaza.

HYDE PARK

This is the upscale part of town, a historical residential district served by the Old Hyde Park Village of high-end shops and the long stretch of South Howard Avenue, or SoHo, with some great restaurants.

American

Not among the 35 or so restaurants along South Howard, but still considered Hyde Park, Mise en Place (442 W. Kennedy Blvd., 813/254-5373, 11:30am-2:30pm and 5:30pm-10pm Tues.-Thurs., 11:30am-2:30pm and 5:30pm-11pm Fri.-Sat., $15-32) is a romantic, intimate spot near the University of Tampa. The weekly changing menu ranges from pizza with chorizo, roast corn, chilies, and manchego to mole spice-rubbed seared tuna with purple potatoes, vanilla bean pineapple salad, and a prickly pear habanero vinaigrette. They also take great care to accommodate special diets.

Asian

Picking out just a handful along Restaurant Row is difficult. For casual dining, ★ Ciccio Water (1015 S. Howard Ave., 813/251-8406, 11:30am-9:30pm Mon., 11:30am-10pm Tues.-Thurs., 11:30am-11pm Fri., 11am-11pm Sat., 11pm-9:30pm Sun., $8-12) is a Japanese-inspired seafood joint and a late-night hangout for the neighborhood that has live music almost nightly. Water specializes in rice paper-rolled sushi (no nori) paired with punchy sauces and dynamic side dishes. A minimalist design aesthetic and a no-reservations policy cannot douse the

The Cubano

In Tampa, the Cubano is the king of sandwiches. It starts with the bread. If you've eaten anywhere in Ybor City, you've probably eaten Cuban bread. But why not go to the source? Rumor has it that La Segunda Central Bakery (2512 N. 15th St., 813/248-1531, www.lesugundabakery.com, 6:30am-5pm Mon.-Fri., 7am-3pm Sat.-Sun.) churns out up to 12,000 Cuban loaves daily.

You only need one loaf, in the form of the archetypal Cubano sandwich. The loaves themselves are about 36 inches long with a zipper-like seam down the top. The third-generation owners of La Segunda have reason to be proud of their bread's thin flaky crust and soft pillowy interior, even more so when piled high with roast pork and Genoa salami (a strictly Tampa twist), swiss cheese (some say emmentaler), sour pickles, and spicy mustard—the whole thing warmed and flattened in a special hot press. The outside is crisp, and the inside warm and a little gooey. It's perfection.

enthusiasm for vibrant combos like *unagi*, banana, and avocado.

Hoa Wah Chinese Restaurant (1713 S. Dale Mabry Hwy., 813/253-2095, 11:30am-9:30pm daily, $10-20) serves traditional Chinese, Japanese, and Vietnamese food in a stylish space with big tables perfect for large parties.

European Fusion

Haven (2208 W. Morrison Ave., 813/258-2233, 5pm-10pm Mon.-Thurs., 5pm-11pm Fri.-Sat., $18-32), affiliated with the famous Bern's, offers a more contemporary approach than the formal steak house. The kitchen turns out great world-beat small plates and charcuterie with European, Asian, and Mediterranean influences. The daily-changing selection of breads is absolutely a knockout (curry sesame flatbread, kalamata and fig loaf).

French-Vietnamese

After 15 years of being at the forefront of

Tampa's restaurant scene, B. T. Nguyen may have reached her pinnacle in **Restaurant BT** (2507 S. MacDill Ave., 813/258-1916, 5pm-10pm Tues.-Thurs., 5pm-11pm Fri.-Sat., $10-30), located at the dead center of Old Hyde Park Village. Classic Vietnamese and French dishes are innovatively presented in the stylish indoor-outdoor dining room. Trained as a sommelier, Nguyen has created an exceptional wine list and a short list of cocktails, which explains the locale's popularity as an evening gathering place.

Italian

A thin-crust pizza hotshot by day, ★ **Pane Rustica** (3225 S. MacDill Ave., 813/902-8828, 8am-5pm Tues., 8am-10pm Wed.-Sat., 8am-3pm Sun., $8-25) hosts some of the fanciest Cal-Ital dinners around Wednesday-Saturday, with full table service and a well-selected short wine list. You can still opt for one of those delicious thin-crust pizzas (maybe one with gorgonzola and sweet caramelized shallot, or perhaps ricotta salata with olive tapenade and sun-dried tomatoes), or even a laid-back burger with brie and roasted red peppers. Don't miss Kevin and Karyn Kruszewski's awesome cookies, cakes, and other house-made desserts.

Mexican

From the same company who owns Water Sushi, **Green Lemon** (915 S. Howard Ave., 813/868-5463, 11am-10pm Mon., 11am-11pm Tues.-Thurs., 11am-1am Fri., 10am-1am Sat., $8-15) is a super lively hangout for fresh Mexican fare and good margaritas.

Spanish

Not on the row, but on the more upscale waterside Bayshore, the late-night **Bullas Gastrobar** (930 S. Howard Ave., 813/773-8626, 11:30am-10pm Mon.-Wed., 11:30am-11pm Thurs., 11:30am-midnight Fri., 11am-midnight Sat., 11am-10pm Sun., $14-28) serves a variety of compact tapas dishes, cocktails, beer, and wine. The rooftop bar is an excellent late-night location, and the outdoor seating is perfect for sunny days.

Steak House

The biggest gorilla on the Tampa dining scene is on a run-down stretch of South Howard Avenue, but fans of **Bern's Steak House** (1208 S. Howard Ave., 813/251-2421, reservations recommended, 5pm-10pm Sun.-Thurs., 5pm-11pm Fri.-Sat., $18-100) are undeterred. This world-famous decades-old landmark has a wine list that could break a toe and a menu that so thoroughly explains dishes that it can sometimes seem exaggerated. Waiters go through a grueling years-long apprenticeship, resulting in staff that could, and does, quote verbatim from the offerings. What's offered is prime beef, aged and nurtured in Bern's own meat lockers. You, the customer, dictate the size, cut, cooking temperature, and many other details. After dinner, take the tour of the kitchen and wine cellar ★

Then head upstairs to ★ **The Harry Waugh Dessert Room at Bern's Steak House** (1208 S. Howard Ave., 813/251-2421, 6pm-10:30pm Sun.-Thurs., 6pm-11:30pm Fri.-Sat., $10-20). Nothing prepares you for it. People tell you, "You dine in individual hollowed-out wine casks." Someone says, "There are individual wall-mounted radios to set the mood at your table." You hear a rumor about an accordionist, maybe something about flambéing waiters. The romantic date-night possibilities of this dessert-only upstairs at Bern's (named after a wine-writing crony of Bern himself) are endless. If that's not enough, there's Chocolate-Chocolate-Chocolate, the name of the chocolate-shellacked cylinder packing chocolate cheese pie, chocolate mousse, and chocolate cheesecake into one deadly package.

DAVIS ISLANDS
American

Nestled in the charming business district of Davis Islands, opinions on the best tables at **220 East** (220 E. Davis Blvd., 813/259-1220, 11am-3pm and 5pm-10pm Mon.-Wed., 11am-4pm and 5pm-11pm Thurs., 11am-3pm and 5pm-11pm Fri., 5pm-11pm Sat., 10:30am-10pm Sun., $15-20) are divided—out front at

one of the handful on the patio, or inside at one of the deep green booths. The restaurant is busy and waitstaff is exceptionally friendly, serving fairly priced casual American, Asian, and even Cajun dishes.

NORTH TAMPA
Asian
One of the innovative Hawaiian-fusion restaurants founded by acclaimed chef Roy Yamaguchi, **Roy's** (4342 W. Boy Scout Blvd., 813/873-7697, 11am-10pm Mon.-Thurs., 11am-11pm Fri., 4pm-11pm Sat., 4pm-9pm Sun., $20-40) is an expense-account favorite in Tampa. An exceptionally good deal can be had with the three-course dinner ($35). It may start with grilled Hawaiian satay skewers, then segue to Thai lemongrass chicken with bok choy, finishing up with Roy's signature melting hot chocolate soufflé.

European
In the upscale neighborhood of Carrollwood near northwest Tampa, Andrea and Michael Reilly's little **Michael's Grill** (11720 N. Dale Mabry Hwy., 813/964-8334, 11am-9pm Mon.-Thurs., 11am-10pm Fri., 10am-10pm Sat., 9am-3pm Sun., $15-27) is an institution, as much for the warm and neighborly service as for the friendly patio and spare brasserie-style dining room. You can eat your french onion soup or penne bolognese at the bar and take in all the drama of the bustling open kitchen, but the patrons out on the patio always seems to be having more fun. The daily breakfast and Sunday brunch are a treat with items like french toast and eggs benedict.

New American
Also near Carrollwood, **Rooster and the Till** (6500 N. Florida Ave., 813/374-8940, 4pm-10pm Mon.-Thurs., 4pm-11pm Fri.-Sat., $20-40) was named number-one restaurant in Tampa by Laura Riley and the *Tampa Bay Times.* Chef Farrell Alvarez and Ty Rodriguez have a strong New American approach with an adventurous and short menu featuring tasting, small, and slightly larger plates. The James Beard and Golden Spoon winners have created excellent dinner, drink, and dessert menus that are sure to delight the true gourmet.

Peruvian
Look for **Happy Fish** (4046 N. Armenia Ave., 813/871-6953, www.happyfishtampa.com, 11:30am-8pm Mon.-Thurs., 11:30am-9pm Fri.-Sat., noon-8pm Sun., $8-15) tucked in the corner of Fiesta Plaza, a strip mall just south of St. Joseph's Children Hospital. It's a casual Peruvian food spot that has garnered high praise for its unique fusion of South American flavors. Try the delicious ceviche or *jalea con yuca,* a platter of fried fish, shrimp, and calamari topped with yuca, onions, and lemon juice. For desert, the Peruvian doughnuts drizzled with sweet syrup are the perfect complement.

Seafood
Eddie V's Prime Seafood (4400 W. Boy Scout Blvd., 813/877-7290, 4pm-11pm Mon.-Thurs., 4pm-midnight Fri.-Sat., 4pm-10pm Sun., $20-40) is a formal white-tablecloth restaurant that specializes in steaks and seafood. The food, service, and atmosphere are exceptional. Try the lobster bisque or lobster tacos to start and the steak or the red snapper for dinner. The wine list is expertly selected, and the cocktails are mixed to strong perfection. For your sweet course, don't miss the bananas foster. Live music from the baby grand piano is always tasteful, soft, and usually jazzy. This is the perfect place for a special occasion or if you want some of the best food in Tampa.

NEW TAMPA
American
New Tampa, as the name indicates, is all new. The upside is that things are clean, pristine, and hygienic; the downside is that there's no sense of history, no gritty timeworn ambience.

1: a Cubano sandwich **2:** Michael's Grill in North Tampa **3:** Spanish tile on the exterior of the Columbia Restaurant in Ybor City

For something older than a decade or so, ★ **Skipper's Smokehouse** (910 Skipper Rd., 813/971-0666, 11am-10:30pm Tues.-Fri., noon-11pm Sat., 1pm-9:30pm Sun., $7-15) has the ambience of a place 10 times its age. It's Tampa's best live music venue (blues, alt-rock, Tuvan throat singers—the gamut), with concerts held outdoors under the canopy of a huge moss-festooned live oak. It has a lively 30s-and-up bar scene and a mighty fine mojito. A ramshackle restaurant serves a wonderful blackened grouper Reuben sandwich, gator tail, and fried crawfish po'boy.

Fusion

A favorite restaurant in New Tampa—the mostly residential area northeast of downtown—is **Ciccio Cali** (17004 Palm Pointe Dr., 813/975-1222, 11am-9:30pm Mon.-Thurs., 11am-10pm Fri., 10am-10pm Sat., 10am-9pm Sun., $9-12). Most nights it teems with families devoted to this health-conscious neighborhood favorite. Ciccio Cali serves thin, crunchy New York-style pizzas topped with interesting picks like caramelized eggplant and goat cheese, as well as a wide variety of sushi, sandwiches, and Asian-inspired entrées at lunch. Ciccio Cali is owned by the same company that owns Water Sushi and Green Lemon in Hyde Park.

Greek

The **Acropolis Greek Tavern** (14947 Bruce B. Downs Blvd., 813/971-1787, 11am-midnight Sun.-Thurs., 11am-1am Fri.-Sat., $6-15) offers late hours, lively fun, and people yelling "opa" regularly.

GREATER TAMPA

Asian

About three miles south of the Hard Rock Casino is something entirely different at the **Wat Mongkolratanaram Thai Temple** (5306 Palm River Rd., 813/621-1669, www.wattampainenglish.com, 8:30am-1pm Sun., $4-10). On Sunday, the extremely ornate Buddhist Temple opens its doors for a market and brunch. You'll find a wide variety of traditional Thai foods, including spring rolls, curries, pad thai, *som dow* (Thai papaya salad), and fried bananas. The food is reasonably priced, with most entrées around $5. Grab one of the fresh fruit juices ($1) as well. Be sure to explore the temple—inside is even more impressive than the exterior. There is excellent outdoor seating with a view of the river. Parking is limited, so arrive early, as this is a very popular Sunday event in the area.

Deli

Wright's Gourmet House (1200 S. Dale Mabry Hwy., 813/253-3838, www.wrightsgourmet.com, 7am-6pm Mon.-Fri., 8am-4pm Sat., $5-12) is near the Palma Ceia Golf and Country Club in Southwest Tampa, dishing out fresh breakfast, lunch, and baked goods from the café and deli. The servings are generous and the ingredients high-quality. The Cuban, Reuben, or turkey sandwiches are excellent, and any of the cakes will make you a regular.

Brocato's Sandwich Shop (5021 E. Columbus Dr., 813/248-9977, www.brocatossandwich.com, 7:30am-5:30pm Mon.-Fri., 7:30am-4pm Sat., $6-15) is a popular lunch and breakfast spot. It gets very crowded, so make sure you have an hour for lunch if you're arriving at noon, or get here during less popular hours for a quick bite. The sandwiches are piled high with meat, and the Cubano here is one of the best. The deviled crab and stuffed potatoes are also legendary.

International Plaza

Tampa's fanciest mall, **International Plaza** (2223 N. Westshore Blvd., 813/342-3790), is also home to good restaurants. It contains **The Cheesecake Factory** (813/353-4200, 11am-11pm Mon.-Thurs., 11am-12:30am Fri., 10am-12:30am Sat., 10am-11pm Sun., $12-20), **California Pizza Kitchen** (813/353-8155, 11am-9:30pm Mon.-Sat., 11am-7pm Sun., $8-15), **Earl of Sandwich** (813/879-1762, 9am-9pm Mon.-Sat., 11am-6pm Sun., $6-12), and **The Capital Grille** (813/830-9433, 11:30am-10pm Mon.-Thurs., 11:30am-11pm

Fri.-Sat., 5pm-9pm Sun., $30-60), for when you want to splurge on a $40 dry-aged steak. The mall's Bay Street is a Caribbean-themed pedestrian promenade lined with several good restaurants.

Best bets for a drink: **Bar Louie** (813/874-1919, 11am-2am Mon.-Thurs., 11am-3am Fri., 10am-3am Sat., 10am-2am Sun., $12-20) has 40 beers on tap, cooks up excellent burgers, and offers a large variety of small plates, from pan-seared pork pot-stickers to hand-battered calamari. **The Pub Tampa Bay** (813/443-5642, 11am-midnight Mon.-Thurs., 11am-2am Fri., 10am-2am Sat., 11am-11pm Sun., $10-20) is for when you aim to go the traditional British route, with a menu and atmosphere of a favorite English pub. You'll find bangers and mash, pot roast, fish-and-chips, and other staples from across the pond on the menus, as well as burgers, sliders, and lots of bar snack plates. The drink menu is extensive, with a huge selection of beers, wines, and liquors from around the world, with a focus on European products.

Fine Dining

When you want to get a sense of Tampa's scale, distance, and scope, dig deep into your wallet and head to **Armani's** (2900 Bayport Dr., 813/207-6800, 6pm-10pm Mon.-Fri., 5:30pm-10pm Sat., $25-40) atop the Grand Hyatt Tampa Bay. It's the undisputed top special-occasion restaurant in town, partly for the view, partly for the solicitous service, and partly for the scaloppine Armani (thin-pounded veal sautéed with wild mushrooms and cognac in a truffle sauce) or the grilled duck breast stuffed with liver pâté and dried cherries in vanilla sauce. The wine list is extensive, with an emphasis on California and French wines.

Fusion

Named after a Native American princess, **Ulele** (1810 N. Highland Ave., 813/999-4952, www.ulele.com, 11am-10pm Sun.-Thurs., 11am-11pm Fri.-Sat., $20-40) blends traditional Native American food with American,

Floridian, and European cuisine. This adventurous restaurant and brewery in Tampa Heights has excellent dishes like Native Chili, a delicious combination of alligator, wild boar, venison, duck, and ground beef with beans and spices. Or try the fire-roasted chicken crusted with citrus-herb garlic and served with a cheddar jalapeño grit cake. If you'd like something more familiar, they have wonderful steak and seafood choices. Located on the Riverwalk, you have your pick between indoor and outdoor seating with excellent water views.

Italian

Another great restaurant is **Pelagia Trattoria** (4200 Jim Walter Blvd., 813/313-3235, 6:30am-10pm daily, $15-25), on the main level in the Renaissance Tampa Hotel, Bay Street. Chef Brett Gardiner serves Mediterranean-inspired dishes: Breakfast is Godiva chocolate pancakes with a white chocolate mousse; at lunch, ricotta and asparagus ravioli served in a hot truffle butter sauce; and for dinner, lamb T-bone with juniper berry sauce. It's the most beautiful hotel restaurant in Tampa and also has an express lunch menu that gets people in and out quickly.

Seafood

Oystercatchers (2900 Bayport Dr., 813/207-6815, 11:30am-2:30pm and 5:30pm-10pm Mon.-Sat., 10:30am-2pm and 6pm-9pm Sun., $18-35) is a top pick for seafood, with exceptionally fresh seafood in a beautiful and upscale but still comfortably casual waterfront setting. The outdoor dining area features romantic fire pits right on the water that can be reserved. For dinner, choose dishes like wood-grilled Gulf snapper served with tuxedo orzo and baby vegetables, or seared tuna drizzled with key lime and caper butter. The incredible water views and superb brunch make this a Tampa favorite.

In east Tampa, **Council Oak** (5223 N. Orient Rd., 813/627-7600, 5pm-10pm Sun.-Thurs., 5pm-midnight Fri.-Sat., $24-40) opened with much fanfare as part of the

Seminole Hard Rock Hotel and Casino. Smack in the center of the gaming excitement, it mainly serves seafood and steaks, all well prepared and offered by an extremely knowledgeable waitstaff.

Charley's Steakhouse and Market Fresh Fish (4444 W. Cypress St., 813/353-9706, 5pm-10pm Sun.-Thurs., 5pm-11pm Fri.-Sat., $30-44) has fat grilled steaks and California wines. Some of the selections include five pepper-crusted filet mignon with pesto, roast garlic mashed potatoes, and oak-grilled vegetables, or shrimp and scallop scampi with a side of grilled asparagus and a baked potato.

Steak House
Some of the old guard are fairly far-flung:

Shula's Steak House (Westshore Grand Hotel, 4860 W. Kennedy Blvd., 813/286-4366, 11:30am-2:30pm and 5:30am-10pm Mon.-Sat., $20-40), is in Beach Park inside the Westshore Grand, which used to be the Intercontinental. Not surprisingly, given coach Don Shula's hand in it, the white-tablecloth chop house features decor in tribute to the Miami Dolphins football team. It's the most elegant experience with football you are ever likely to have. Everything at Shula's is huge, and the steaks are well-seasoned and perfectly prepared up to 48 ounces. Even the salads are oversize. The waitstaff is exceptional, and Shula's serves exemplary mixed drinks. Some prefer Bern's or Ruth's Chris, but football fans will root for Shula's.

Accommodations

Tampa's hotel scene is stymied by one thing: Tampa has no beaches. Although it's on the water—with the active Port of Tampa and waterside residential communities like Davis and Harbour Island—there is no beach lodging. For that kind of experience, head over the bay to St. Pete or Clearwater. Tampa does have a preponderance of pleasant, fairly priced accommodations spread around the bay area, including the Latin Quarter of Ybor City, the Westshore business district, the Tampa Convention Center, and near Busch Gardens and the University of South Florida.

DOWNTOWN AND SPARKMAN WHARF
$200-300
Le Meridien Tampa (601 N. Florida Ave., 813/221-9555, www.lemeridientampa.com, $230-450) is the only four-diamond hotel in downtown Tampa. Formerly a federal courthouse, the classical building has been given a sleek modern uplift. The desk in the lobby

was once the judge's bench, and the granite columns date to 1905. On-site is Bizzou Brasserie, which serves impeccable international cuisine, as well as an ultramodern cocktail lounge, a fitness center, and a beautiful outdoor pool.

Over $300
Enjoy excellent views of Hillsborough Bay, downtown Tampa, and Davis Islands at the **Tampa Marriott Waterside Hotel & Marina** (700 S. Florida Ave., 813/221-4900, www.marriott.com, $310-400), an excellent location when taking a cruise from Tampa or exploring downtown. There is a rooftop pool, a full-service spa, a fitness center, and several restaurants and bars on-site. Rooms and suites include a balcony with excellent views. The pool area is surrounded by palm trees and includes a hot tub.

YBOR CITY
$100-200
The **Bonita Casitas de Ybor** (1813-1815 E.

5th Ave., 813/334-1857, $100-200) offers two charming private guest cottages with full kitchens and two bedrooms each.

SOUTH TAMPA, HYDE PARK, AND DAVIS ISLANDS
$100-200

The **Tahitian Inn** (601 S. Dale Mabry Hwy., 813/877-6721, www.tahitianinn.com, $95-169) is a wonderful two-story family-run motel with 60 Tahitian-themed (dark wood, tropical accessories) moderately priced rooms and 20 executive suites, a lovely pool with tiki huts and hammocks, and the Serenity Spa with massage and Tahitian hot stone treatments. There's also a lovely little on-site café with patio seating near a koi pond. The location is close to I-275 and lots of commerce.

Over $300

★ **The Epicurean Hotel, Autograph Collection** (1207 S. Howard Ave., 813/999-8700, www.epicureanhotel.com, $350-600) is a boutique hotel across the street from Bern's Steak House. The hotel has a modern style that highlights its focus on fine food and wine; there are even butcher-block countertops and wine crate-lined walls in the lobby. The excellent on-site restaurant Elevage is open for breakfast, lunch, and dinner and serves American cuisine classics. Or treat yourself at Chocolate Pi, the hotel's bakery, specializing in handmade chocolates, gourmet cakes, and exceptional teas and coffees. The hotel also offers cooking classes at the culinary theater. There is an outdoor heated pool, and Bayshore Boulevard is nearby.

NORTH TAMPA
Under $100

If you want to stay near USF or Busch Gardens and MOSI, there are a handful of reasonably priced chains. **La Quinta Inn Tampa Near Busch Gardens** (9202 N. 30th St., 813/930-6900, $70-120) is adjacent to Busch Gardens' entrance, with 144 nicely appointed rooms

with roomy baths, good lighting, large desks, and Wi-Fi. There's also a good-size pool.

$100-200

Holiday Inn Express I-75 (8310 Galbraith Rd., 877/859-5095, www.ihg.com, $170-240) is a pet-friendly hotel about three miles from Busch Gardens and the University of South Florida. Conveniently located off I-75 at exit 270, this is a perfect base for families traveling between Orlando and Tampa, or a wonderful place to stay before a cruise. A full breakfast is included, and the outdoor heated pool is a plus.

Six miles from Busch Gardens, you'll find a wonderful bargain at the **Hampton Inn & Suites Tampa North** (8210 Hidden River Pkwy., 813/903-6000, www.hamptoninn.com, $120-200). Enjoy the free breakfast and internet access. There is a large pool in the cozy courtyard and a fitness center on-site. The rooms are simple but nicely furnished. Suites offer a full kitchen with a fridge, stove, dishwasher, sink, and microwave.

$200-300

The USF hotel of choice is **Embassy Suites USF Near Busch Gardens** (3705 Spectrum Blvd., 813/977-7066, $150-300), across the road from the university. It's a tall suites-only hotel with nice rooms, spacious living rooms, private bedrooms with either a king or two double beds, and two TVs in every room. Although the rooms cost a little more, included in the price is a nice daily cooked-to-order breakfast buffet and free cocktails and snacks each evening.

Emerald Greens Condo Resort (13941 Clubhouse Dr., 813/961-9400, www.emeraldgreensresort.com, $200-300) is perfect for families or couples looking for an extended-stay option. The 50 units are each 1,200 square feet, have two bedrooms, and feature a full kitchen, separate living and dining areas, and a private balcony. The resort is on the Carrollwood Country Club property, and guests have access to the golf course, tennis courts, and pool. Daily housekeeping service and free internet are included.

GREATER TAMPA

Under $100

For a wild experience at a tame price, **Gram's Place Hostel** (3109 N. Ola Ave., 813/221-0596, www.grams-inn-tampa.com, dorm $28, private room $55-65) in Ybor City fits the bill. It's eccentric, with a different music theme (jazz, blues, rock) in each of the private suites and hostel-style bunkrooms. The private rooms are set in two cottages and share an oversize in-ground whirlpool tub, a BYOB bar in the courtyard, and a multitrack recording studio.

$100-200

Hilton Garden Inn Tampa Airport Westshore (5312 Avion Park Dr., 813/289-2700, www.hilton.com, $150-230) is an excellent choice if you want to stay close to the airport (sometimes you will hear jets taking off). The bright color scheme and updated furnishings make the rooms feel modern and cheerful. Breakfast costs extra, but it's highly recommended. The hotel is reliable, has great customer service, and is a top choice for business travelers.

The ★ **Grand Hyatt Tampa Bay** (2900 Bayport Dr., 813/874-1234, www. tampabay.grand.hyatt.com, $150-350) is a big hotel near the airport that caters mainly to corporate travelers. There are 445 deluxe guest rooms and suites, including 38 Spanish-style casita rooms and 7 casita suites in a secluded area at the south end of the property, which is set in a 35-acre wildlife preserve on the shores of Tampa Bay. The Hyatt contains two of the best restaurants in town, Armani's and Oystercatchers. The rooftop fire pit offers one of the best views of Tampa Bay and is an excellent spot to watch the sunset.

Numerous hotels cluster along Rocky Point Drive and Cypress Street, just a couple of minutes from the airport, Westshore business district, and Tampa Convention Center. These hotels have lots of business amenities and often offer significantly cheaper rates on the weekend. Of the chains, there's **DoubleTree Hotel Tampa Airport Westshore** (4500 W. Cypress St., 813/879-4800, www.doubletreetampawestshore.com, $100-300), **Courtyard by Marriott Tampa Westshore** (3805 W. Cypress St., 813/874-0555, $100-250), and the **Holiday Inn Express and Suites Rocky Point** (3025 N. Rocky Point Dr., 813/287-8585, $150-250), among many others, all with water views of the bay, pools, and other amenities.

For a more independent approach in the same location, try **Sailport Waterfront Suites** (2506 N. Rocky Point Dr., 813/281-9599, $110-230), a four-story all-suites hotel (all rooms have a queen-size sleeper sofa in the living room, convenient for families) with full-size kitchens, barbecue grills, an outdoor heated pool, a lighted tennis court, and a fishing pier.

$200-300

The **Seminole Hard Rock Hotel and Casino** (5223 Orient Rd., 813/627-7625, www.seminolehardrocktampa.com, $249-359) is the 12-story tower with a 90,000-square-foot casino—the sixth-largest casino in the world—and popular restaurants like Kuro and Council Oak. The 250 guest rooms and suites have an art deco design. The most luxurious part is the pool area, with cascading fountains and private cabanas.

Hilton Garden Inn Tampa East/ Brandon (10309 Highland Manor Dr., 813/626-6700, www.hilton.com, $220-350) is an excellent alternative to staying at the Hard Rock. They offer shuttles to and from the Hard Rock Casino while offering a quiet retreat from the gaming center. The rooms are spacious, and there is a beautiful courtyard outside. They have a billiard room, an outdoor pool, and two restaurants that serve a variety of American favorites at breakfast, lunch, and dinner.

Over $300

One of Tampa's nicest luxury hotels is the

★ **Renaissance Tampa International Plaza Hotel** (4200 Jim Walter Blvd., 813/877-9200, $339-389), near the Westshore business district at the International Plaza mall. The lavish decor is reminiscent of a Mediterranean villa. The hotel is not small, with 293 guest rooms on eight floors, but the service is personal and attentive, and it seems especially geared to repeat high-end business travelers.

Information and Services

Tampa is in the **eastern time zone.**

VISITOR INFORMATION

Tampa Bay's **Visitor Information Center** (401 E. Jackson St., 813/223-1111, www.visittampabay.com, 10am-5:30pm Mon.-Sat.) is at Sparkman Wharf at the Port of Tampa. It provides lots of brochures and information on attractions, events, and accommodations.

POLICE AND EMERGENCIES

In an emergency, dial 911 for immediate assistance. If you need police assistance in a nonemergency, visit or call the **Tampa Police Department** (411 N. Franklin St., 813/276-3200).

Tampa has several hospitals equipped with emergency rooms: If you have a medical emergency in the Hyde Park area, go to **Memorial Hospital of Tampa** (2901 Swann Ave., 813/873-6400). In Carrollwood, visit the **Florida Hospital Carrollwood** (7171 N. Dale Mabry Hwy., 813/932-2222). In the Westshore area, go to **University Community Health** (5101 E. Busch Blvd., 813/830-6236). Downtown, make your way to **Tampa General Hospital** (1 Tampa General Circle, 813/844-7000), near the causeway to Davis Islands.

the Tampa trolley

Transportation

AIR

Tampa International Airport (TPA, 4100 George J. Bean Pkwy., 813/870-8700, www.tampaairport.com) is perhaps the best mid-size airport in the country—clean, easily traversed, with good signage and efficient staff. With one of the best on-time records, it's Florida's fourth-busiest airport, just seven miles southwest of downtown Tampa. It's served by Air Canada, Alaska, American, British Airways, Cayman Airways, Copa, Delta, Edelweiss, Frontier, Icelandair, JetBlue, Lufthansa, Silver, Southwest, Spirit, Sun Country, Swift, United, WestJet, and World Atlantic.

Located on the airport premises, **Avis** (800/831-2847), **Budget** (800/527-0700), **Dollar** (800/800-4000 domestic, 800/800-6000 international), **Enterprise** (800/736-8222), **Hertz** (800/654-3131), and **Thrifty** (800/847-4389) provide rental-car service. Tampa has unbelievably good deals on rental cars from the airport—celebrate by upgrading to something stylish.

CAR

Both I-75 and I-275 travel north-south, but I-75 skirts the edge of Tampa while I-275 travels through the city and over the bay. Both connect to I-4, which travels east-west, connecting Tampa Bay to Orlando and the east coast of Florida.

Once in town, from north to south, Bearrs, Fletcher, Fowler, and Busch Boulevards are the big east-west roads. Dale Mabry and Bruce B. Downs are the biggest north-south roads. This all sounds fairly simple, but once you get downtown in Tampa, you need a map to find your way out. There are lots of one-way streets, and the highway on-ramps are difficult to find. The Busch Gardens area and University of South Florida lie between I-75 and I-275 northeast of downtown. The airport is just southwest of downtown.

BUS AND TRAIN

Taxi service from the airport to downtown is about $18. Taxis must be called rather than flagged down. Most hotels offer shuttle service to the airport and major attractions.

Greyhound (813/229-2174) has a station downtown, as does **Amtrak** (800/872-7245), operating in historic Tampa Union Station (601 N. Nebraska Ave.) with north-south trains and links to nationwide rail travel.

Within the city, **Hillsborough Area Regional Transit Authority** (813/623-5835, www.gohart.org, day pass $4) provides city bus service on 26 routes, nine trolleys, and eight electric streetcars. The In Town Trolley runs north-south through downtown and connects to the **TECO Line Streetcar System,** which runs from downtown to the Channel District and Port as well as Ybor City. Still, Tampa is so spread out that it's not easy to be without a car.

St. Petersburg and Pinellas County

In some ways, Henry Ford's affordable $400 Model T foreshadowed the real estate boom in St. Petersburg in the early 1920s. It was the beginning of road-tripping—folks hopping in the car in search of sun, sand, and fun. They found the peninsula that hangs down Florida's west side like a thumb, the east side of it nestled against placid Old Tampa Bay, its west side flanked by sandy beaches and the Gulf of Mexico. People bought up land, building big resort hotels, affordable motels, and homes.

Today, St. Petersburg is Florida's fourth-largest city, the anchor of Pinellas County. Combined with neighboring Tampa, it's the largest urban area in the state. It has had another boom period in recent years, an influx of tech businesses drawing younger families and driving

Highlights

Look for ★ to find recommended sights, activities, dining, and lodging.

★ **Salvador Dalí Museum:** The famous Spanish surrealist is honored in a sleek museum of his work and the work of those inspired by him (page 195).

★ **St. Pete Beach:** Watch the sunset or search for shells along this white sandy shore, lined with hotels and restaurants (page 202).

★ **Clearwater Beach:** The whole family will enjoy the evening fairs that take place at this beautiful beach (page 202).

★ **Fort De Soto Park:** Beyond the site of a fort built during the Spanish-American War, this park features 1,136 acres of pristine coastal environment to explore (page 202).

★ **Honeymoon Island and Caladesi Island Beaches:** Why settle for just one beach when you can opt for a pair of white-sand barrier islands (page 204)?

★ **Sunken Gardens:** This beloved garden has been restored to its former glory (page 205).

★ **Sunshine Skyway Fishing Piers:** A local bridge has been repurposed as the world's longest fishing pier, taking advantage of a tremendous concentration of sport fish lurking in the deep waters below (page 209).

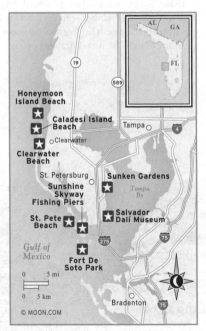

down the median age. The city's downtown—on the bay, not the Gulf—has seen lots of growth, from pricey condos to the Sundial shopping complex.

St. Pete Beach is not just the shortened name for St. Petersburg Beach. St. Petersburg is the big city adjacent to Old Tampa Bay, which looks out across at the big city of Tampa. St. Pete Beach, on the other hand, is an autonomous barrier-island town to the south and west of St. Petersburg. St. Pete Beach stretches seven miles from Pass-a-Grille on the south to Blind Pass on the north, before Treasure Island. The city of Clearwater is on the mainland, but Clearwater Beach is on a barrier island connected by Memorial Causeway.

The Gulf beaches are 20 minutes from downtown St. Petersburg across the peninsula. More than 20 little towns dot the coastline in Pinellas County, St. Pete Beach and Clearwater Beach being perhaps the favorites for family vacations. Clearwater Beach offers a wide inviting shore, serious beach volleyball, and lots of nightlife and casual seafood restaurants. The Jolley Trolley whisks visitors from their hotel through town to the beachside Pier 60, something like the center of town.

Clearwater and St. Pete Beaches aren't the only strands that draw accolades. Caladesi Island State Park, accessible only by boat to the north of Clearwater Beach, is often rated one of the top 10 beaches in the country, as is Honeymoon Island.

PLANNING YOUR TIME

Pinellas County is a peninsula, with Tampa Bay to the east and the Gulf of Mexico to the west. Its location, adjacent to Tampa but with the benefit of long and wonderful beaches, makes it an ideal base for a lengthy Gulf Coast stay, especially for families. Even Disney World is a convenient 90 minutes to the east. The sights and attractions are more compelling on the Tampa side of the bay

(Busch Gardens, lots of professional sports), and these are easily accessed by either the Howard Frankland Bridge (I-275) or the Courtney Campbell Causeway (Hwy. 60). In high-season traffic, the drive can be 45 minutes. The best way to explore the area is by car, especially if you want to drive the length of the barrier islands. The area is served by **Tampa International Airport** (TPA, 4100 George J. Bean Pkwy., 813/870-8700) and **St. Petersburg-Clearwater International Airport** (PIE, 14700 Terminal Blvd., Clearwater, 727/453-7800).

Where you stay depends on your priorities. The city of St. Petersburg lies on the bay side of the peninsula and has more history, more sense of place and sophistication than the beach towns along the Gulf side. There are romantic bed-and-breakfasts, fine restaurants, and cultural attractions. Clearwater Beach and St. Pete Beach on the Gulf side have the densest concentrations of beachside accommodations—in Clearwater this often means tall resort hotels and condos right on the beach; in St. Pete Beach it's low-rise motels that date back a few decades. The communities between these two—Belleair and Belleair Beach; Indian Rocks Beach and Indian Shores; Redington Shores, North Redington Beach, and Redington Beach; Madeira Beach; and Treasure Island—are residential but with pockets of beachside hotels, motels, and rentals. The whole Gulf side is composed of a series of tiny barrier islands connected to the mainland by causeways—it may not be totally clear to you when driving, but spend a little time with the map so you know whether you're looking at boats bobbing on the Intracoastal Waterway, Boca Ciega Bay, Clearwater Harbor, or the Gulf.

The peak season runs November-May, more spread out than at other Gulf Coast beach spots because U.S. families on spring break come in March-April, and lots of European travelers fill in the time around

---

St. Petersburg and Pinellas County

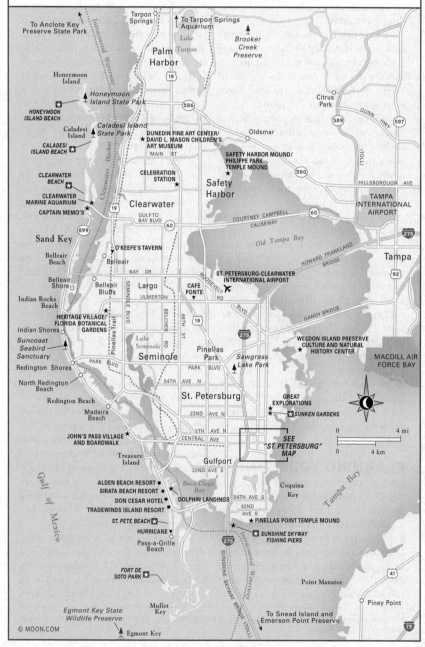

© MOON.COM

that. In summer the waters here are so warm as to be slightly off-putting. September-October are great times to visit. In October, added enticements include the beloved annual **Clearwater Jazz Holiday** (727/461-5200, www.clearwaterjazz.com) during the third week of the month, with four days of free world-class jazz in Coachman Park. There's also the local **Stone Crab Festival** (www.visitstpeteclearwater.com) at the same time.

The best camping is at Fort De Soto Park, and the best beaches in the area are at Clearwater Beach, Fort De Soto Park, Honeymoon Island and Caladesi Island, St. Pete Beach, Madeira Beach, Sand Key County Park, and Egmont Key State Wildlife Preserve.

Sights

DOWNTOWN ST. PETERSBURG

★ Salvador Dalí Museum

Perhaps the most popular art museum in Pinellas County is the **Salvador Dalí Museum** (1 Dali Blvd., 727/823-3767, www.thedali.org, 10am-5:30pm Fri.-Wed., 10am-8pm Thurs., $24 adults, $22 seniors, military, police, firefighters, and educators with ID, $17 students and ages 13-17, $10 ages 6-12, free under age 6), the world's most comprehensive collection of permanent works by the famous Spanish surrealist master, with other exhibits relating to Dalí. Architect Yann Weymouth designed an awe-inspiring structure described as a "building that combines the rational with the fantastical: a simple rectangle with 18-inch-thick hurricane-proof walls out of which erupts a large free-form geodesic glass bubble known as the enigma." The impressive helical staircase inside the building recalls Dalí's own obsession with spirals and the double helix shape of the DNA molecule. The new Avante Garden outside the building extends this theme and provides a calming space to explore the relationship between math and nature. The new museum has quickly become nearly as popular as the collection housed inside. AOL Travel News listed the museum as one of the top 20 buildings to see in your lifetime, and the Florida Association of the American Institute of Architects named it as the top museum design in the state.

Dalí himself is as recognizable as his "paranoiac-critical" paintings. Maybe only Van Gogh in his post-ear incident self-portrait is more reliably identified than Dalí, with his long waxed mustache and extreme arched eyebrows. Upon moving to the United States in the 1940s, Dalí made himself the lovable eccentric who introduced the average American to surrealism—and the average American really liked it.

The Salvador Dalí Museum is a dense concentration of his surrealist works, what he described as a "spontaneous method of irrational knowledge based on the critical and systematic objectivation of delirious associations and interpretations." Even if you don't care for what you have seen of his work in books and prints, it is an incredible experience to view the original works in their larger-than-life sizes. And if you have never experienced his works at all, the museum is almost sure to make you a fan.

Museum of Fine Arts

The **Museum of Fine Arts** (255 Beach Dr. NE, 727/896-2667, www.mfastpete.org, 10am-5pm Mon.-Wed. and Fri.-Sat., 10am-8pm Thurs., noon-5pm Sun., $20 adults, $15 seniors and military, $15 Florida teachers and students, $10 ages 7-17, free under age 7) features works by such noted artists as Renoir, Léger, Pissarro, Matisse, Fabergé, Chuck Close, and James Rosenquist. Right on the waterfront adjacent to Straub Park, the museum contains a full range of art from antiquity to the present day. The collection of 4,000 objects includes significant works by

St. Petersburg

To Ruth Eckerd Hall

To Boyd Hill
Nature Preserve

0   200 yds

0   200 m

HASLAM'S
BOOK STORE

TROPICANA FIELD

GREEN BENCH
BREWING COMPANY

DOWNTOWN
ST. PETERSBURG

THE MOREAN
ARTS CENTER

ST. PETERSBURG
BRASSERIE

FLORIDA
HOLOCAUST
MUSEUM

AMERICAN
STAGE

BAYWALK

Williams
Park

THE COLISEUM

THE MANSION INN

Round Park

North
Park

JANNUS
LANDING

CAFÉ ALMA

RED MESA
CANTINA

MORNING MARKET

SATURDAY

PROGRESS
ENERGY PARK

AL LANG
FIELD

MAHAFFEY
THEATER

DELMAR TER S

BEACH DR

PARKSHORE
GRILL

THE VERANDA B&B

Strand Park

SALVADOR DALÍ
MUSEUM

Marina

ALBERT WHITTED
AIRPORT

MUSEUM OF
FINE ARTS

RENAISSANCE VINOY
RESORT AND GOLF CLUB

ST. PETERSBURG
MUSEUM OF HISTORY

THE PIER

St. Petersburg

To SUNKEN GARDENS
and Great Explorations

North
Shore
Park

T a m p a

B a y

© MOON.COM

Cézanne, Monet, Gauguin, Renoir, Rodin, and O'Keeffe. Its permanent collection's strength is 17th- and 18th-century European art, and the museum has a lovely garden as well.

St. Petersburg Museum of History

St. Petersburg Museum of History (335 2nd Ave. NE, 727/894-1052, www.spmoh. org, 10am-5pm Mon.-Sat., noon-5pm Sun., $15 adults, $12 seniors, $9 military, veterans, students, teachers, and ages 7-17, free under age 7) is one of the oldest historical museums in the state, with family-friendly displays and exhibits depicting St. Petersburg's past. A local history exhibit contains a Native American dugout canoe, an exact replica of the world's first scheduled commercial airliner (it flew out of St. Petersburg), and lots of other interesting exhibits.

Florida Holocaust Museum

The **Florida Holocaust Museum** (55 5th St. S., 727/820-0100, www.flholocaustmuseum. org, 10am-5pm daily, $16 adults, $14 seniors, $10 students, $8 ages 7-18, free for active military, USF students, and under age 7) is the third largest of its kind in the United States. Part of the museum is devoted to the memory of the millions of victims of the Holocaust, and it also showcases loosely linked exhibits, such as the work of Czech artist Charles Pachner (who lost his whole family during the war) or the mixed-media paintings, sculptures, and installations of contemporary French artist Marc Ash.

The Morean Arts Center

The arts are booming in St. Petersburg, especially visual arts. Opened in 2010, the 5,000 square feet of gallery space at the **Chihuly Collection at the Morean Arts Center** (719 Central Ave., 727/822-7872, 10am-5pm Mon.-Sat., noon-5pm Sun., $20) is a beautiful showcase for the Seattle glassblower's eccentric work. The center is divided into six small galleries, plus classroom space for ceramics, painting, drawing, digital imaging, photography, printmaking, jewelry making, metalworking, and sculpture classes.

Great Explorations

After spending time at Sunken Gardens, give the kids their due next door at **Great Explorations** (1925 4th St. N., 727/821-8992, www.greatex.org, 10am-4:30pm Mon.-Sat., noon-4:30pm Sun., $10 adults, $9 over age 54, free under age 1). The hands-on science center has lots of slick educational exhibits on things like the architecture, health, or the ecosystem of the ocean. Many of the exhibits are best appreciated by kids up to age 11. If your family enjoys hands-on science museums, head over to Tampa's MOSI for a bigger dose.

The St. Petersburg Pier

As of 2018, **The Pier** (800 2nd Ave. NE, 727/895-7437) is undergoing a massive renovation that will bring more waterfront commercial space and extend the park along the shoreline. When it's finished, you'll be able to rent bikes, grab a rental rod and reel and fish off the end, visit the little aquarium, dine in the family-friendly food court, launch kayaks, or browse the complex's many shops. During renovation, you can still depart from the marina on a sightseeing boat charter, or see a flick at the nearby 20-screen movie theater.

ST. PETE BEACH AND GULFPORT
Dolphin Landings

Farther south, **Dolphin Landings** (4737 Gulf Blvd., St. Pete Beach, 727/360-7411, www. dolphinlandings.com, $30-50), behind the Dolphin Village Shopping Center, conducts two-hour dolphin-watch and sunset cruises and longer three- to four-hour trips to Shell Key and Egmont Key, two undeveloped barrier islands. The scheduled trips and private charters are conducted on one of 40 locally owned sailboats, pontoon boats, and deep-sea fishing yachts.

CLEARWATER, CLEARWATER BEACH, AND DUNEDIN

Clearwater Marine Aquarium

Just over the bay in Tampa, the Florida Aquarium usually gets most of the visitors. **Clearwater Marine Aquarium** (249 Windward Passage, Clearwater, 727/441-1790, www.seewinter.com, 10am-6pm daily, $25 adults, $23 seniors, $20 ages 3-12) is a smaller, more modest working research facility and home to rescued and recuperating dolphins, whales, and otters, among other marine mammals, including Winter, the dolphin that lost her tail and was made famous in the Disney movie *Dolphin Tale*. For the visitor, the thrust is education, with hourly animal care and training presentations and exhibits on animal rescue, rehabilitation, and release—and how the public can help to protect and conserve endangered marinelife. The aquarium offers on-site feeding and care programs for interested visitors and operates a daily 90-minute **Sea Life Safari** (25 Causeway Blvd., Slip 58, Clearwater Beach, 727/462-2628, $26 adults, $23 seniors, $17 ages 3-12, free under age 3) that takes visitors around the Clearwater estuary and Intracoastal Waterway with commentary by a marine biologist.

Captain Memo's Original Pirate Cruise

Bilgewater Bill, Mad Dog Mike, Gangplank Gary, and the other pirates will greet you with an "argh, me matey" on the deck of **Captain Memo's Original Pirate Cruise** (25 Causeway Blvd., Dock 3, Clearwater Beach, 727/446-2587, www.captainmemo.com, 10am, 2pm, and sunset daily, $36 adults, $33 seniors, $31 ages 13-17, $28 ages 3-12, $11 under age 3), a two-hour pirate cruise on a fancy bright-red pirate ship.

Celebration Station

If you're looking for something a little more exciting, **Celebration Station** (24546 U.S. 19 N., Clearwater, 727/791-1799, www.celebrationstation.com, 11am-9pm Sun.-Thurs., 11am-11pm Fri., 10am-11pm Sat., prices vary by activity) brings you go-karts, bumper boats, games, miniature golf, batting cages, laser tag, and pizza.

GREATER PINELLAS COUNTY

Beach Art Center

Beach Art Center (1515 Bay Palm Blvd., Indian Rocks Beach, 727/596-4331, 8:45am-4pm Mon.-Fri., 10am-2 Sat.) is another sweet nonprofit arts center with classes for locals in fine arts and crafts. It also has two small galleries set up in the old American Legion Hall.

Dunedin Fine Art Center & Children's Art Museum

The **Dunedin Fine Art Center & Children's Art Museum** (1143 Michigan Blvd., Dunedin, 727/298-3322, www.dfac.org, 10am-5pm Mon.-Fri., 10am-2pm Sat., 1pm-4pm Sun., admission varies) has four galleries, studio classrooms, a children's museum, the Palm Cafe, and a gallery gift shop. The exhibits are often the work of students.

Heritage Village

Beyond these, history buffs can visit the restored homes and buildings of the **Heritage Village** (11909 125th St. N., Largo, 727/582-2123, www.pinellascounty.org, 10am-4pm Wed.-Sat., 1pm-4pm Sun., free). It's a living history museum with people in period costume spinning, weaving, and acting out other period activities. Most of the 25 structures date to the late 19th century.

Florida Botanical Gardens

If you go to Heritage Village, make a day of it and visit the **Florida Botanical Gardens** (12520 Ulmerton Rd., Largo, 727/582-2100, www.flbg.org, 7am-5pm daily, garden free), where you can take a tour through the gardens (1.5 hours, reservations required, $20 pp) led by a local master gardener. You walk 1.5 miles and learn all about Florida gardening. The

1: Salvador Dalí Museum 2: a paved path through the Florida Botanical Gardens 3: Clearwater Marine Aquarium 4: John's Pass Village & Boardwalk

approaches can be vastly different—there's a rose garden, a beach garden, a tropical courtyard, a topiary garden, a bromeliad garden, and more. On a nice day, it's a wonderful spot. Call ahead for tour times and reservations.

Tarpon Springs Aquarium

More like a really big pet store, the **Tarpon Springs Aquarium** (850 Dodecanese Blvd., Tarpon Springs, 727/938-5378, www.tarponspringsaquarium.com, 10am-5pm Mon.-Sat., noon-5pm Sun., $7.75 adults, $7 seniors, $5.75 ages 3-11, free under age 3) has a 120,000-gallon main tank aquarium with more than 30 species of fish, including nurse sharks, bonnet head sharks, snook, tarpon, and protected goliath grouper. The best time to visit is feeding times for sharks (11:30am, 1pm, 2:30pm, and 4pm daily) and alligators (12:30pm and 3:30pm daily).

Safety Harbor Mound

Pinellas County's rich Native American heritage is not very noticeable today—but there are a couple of sites that command quite a bit of enthusiasm among history buffs. One is a platform mound in a beautiful country park called both the **Safety Harbor Mound** and the **Philippe Park Temple Mound** (2525 Philippe Pkwy., Safety Harbor, 727/582-2100, 7am-sunset daily, free). The mound is behind shelter number 2 and is described with interpretive markers. The large mound complex is believed to be the village of Tocobaga, for which the Tocobaga people are named. It is said that in 1567 Pedro Menéndez de Avilés, the founder of St. Augustine, visited this Tocobaga village. For a little more insight, two miles south of Philippe Park is the **Safety Harbor Museum and Cultural Center** (329 S. Bayshore Dr., 727/724-1562, 11am-4pm Tues.-Fri., 10am-2pm Sat., free), which contains artifacts from the Weedon Island, Safety Harbor, and Mississippian periods.

Pinellas Point Temple Mound

Seeing more Tocobaga ruins requires only a short drive to the **Pinellas Point Temple Mound** (1800 Mound Place St., 8am-sunset daily, free). The large flat mound, topped by a comfy bench, is all that remains of a sizable village. To get here, head east on 62nd Avenue South and turn south onto 20th Street, which ends at the mound.

John's Pass Village & Boardwalk

In a similar vein, **John's Pass Village & Boardwalk** (12901 Gulf Blvd. E., between Madeira Beach and Treasure Island, 727/423-7824, www.boattoursjohnspass.com) offers a **Pirate Ship at John's Pass cruise** (11am, 2pm, and sunset daily, $39 adults, $33 seniors, $29 ages 2-20, $10 under age 2) on a fully outfitted pirate ship. You'll engage in water pistol battles and treasure hunts and listen to pirate stories.

John's Pass Village is home to a large commercial and charter fishing fleet, as well as art galleries, restaurants, and boutiques along a waterfront boardwalk. Families also enjoy the dolphin tours out of John's Pass and into scenic Boca Ciega Bay. A couple of companies offer these; **Hubbard's Sea Adventures dolphin tours** (departs from John's Pass boardwalk, 727/398-6577, www.hubbardsmarina.com, 1pm, 3pm, and 5pm daily spring-summer, 1pm and 3pm daily fall, $20 adults, $10 ages 2-11, free under age 2) brings you face-to-face with the bay's abundance of wildlife.

David L. Mason Children's Art Museum

Artistically inclined kids might enjoy visiting Dunedin Fine Art Center, which contains the **David L. Mason Children's Art Museum** (1143 Michigan Blvd., Dunedin, 727/298-3322, www.dfac.org, 10am-5pm Mon.-Fri., 10am-2pm Sat., 1pm-4pm Sun., $4 adults, $3 seniors, free under age 3), a gallery space for children. This smaller part of the museum provides hands-on activities that assist families in understanding and appreciating the work of Florida artists exhibited in the galleries. Even if you spend your time in the art center and not the children's museum, the scale is such that it's not intimidating or boring for kids.

Soaking Up Greek Culture

Tarpon Springs, a coastal town 15 miles north of Clearwater, has a storied past. John Corcoris, a sponge diver from Greece, brought his capabilities along with his sponge-diving equipment (a rubber suit and a heavy copper helmet) to Tarpon Springs around 1900. Soon he persuaded friends and family, sponge divers all, to relocate from Hydra and Aegena, Greece, to this little Florida backwater. A booming town of Greek restaurants, Greek Orthodox churches, and Greek festivals was born, centering on the sponge industry. Tarpon Springs was the largest U.S. sponge-diving port in the 1930s. The town is still more than one-third Greek, with a nice Old Florida charm and several fine restaurants. Sponges are still everywhere, but most of them are now imported from more sponge-rich lands.

sponges for sale in Tarpon Springs

Take an afternoon to see **Spongeorama** (510 Dodecanese Blvd., 727/943-2164, 10am-6pm daily, free), an attraction that has displays of sponge divers and shows an interesting movie called *Men and the Sea*. Visit the sponge docks, shop a little, and have dinner. If you're still angling for more sponge action, the **St. Nicholas Boat Line** (693 Dodecanese Blvd., 727/942-6425, $6 adults, $2 ages 6-12, free under age 6) offers a fun 30-minute narrated boat cruise through the sponge docks, with its own sponge-diving demonstration. Out on the main drag, Dodecanese Boulevard, there are seven blocks of shops and restaurants. Before you settle on a place to eat, stop into nearby **St. Nicholas Church** (36 N. Pinellas Ave., 727/937-3540), made of 60 tons of Greek marble. The church is a copy of the Byzantine Revival St. Sophia in Constantinople, with beautiful Czech chandeliers and stained glass.

If the weather's nice, stroll along one of the paths in nearby **Anclote River Park** (1119 Baileys Bluff Rd., Holiday, 727/938-2598, dawn-dusk daily, free). The park boasts an easy two-mile round-trip trail, as well as fishing access, a boat ramp, a playground for the kids, a swimming beach, and picnic facilities. It's also a notable destination for birders—favored for its resident reddish egrets and osprey nests. It's actually part of a cluster of parks on the Great Florida Birding Trail, along with the nearby **Key Vista Nature Park** (2700 Baileys Bluff Rd., Holiday, 727/938-2598, dawn-dusk daily, $2 parking), which has even more diverse natural habitats, from fresh- and saltwater marshes to pine uplands and tidal flats, all the better for observing species like loons and migratory warblers.

Everyone has a different favorite Greek restaurant here. One favorite is **Hellas Restaurant and Bakery** (785 Dodecanese Blvd., 727/943-2400, 11am-10pm Sun.-Thurs., 11am-11pm Fri.-Sat., $10-20), a lively spot with a full bar and a wonderful Greek bakery attached. The best entrée is its slowly braised tomatoey lamb shanks. There are addictive garlic shrimp, gyros in warm Greek pita, and a delicious Greek salad. Others swear by **Mykonos** (628 Dodecanese Blvd., 727/934-4306, 11:30am-10pm daily, $10-20) for the lamb chops, Greek meatloaf, and the slightly more upscale atmosphere. Still, **Mama's** (735 Dodecanese Blvd., 727/944-2888, 11am-10pm daily, $7-14) often gets the nod for casual family-friendly booths and delicious but messy chicken souvlaki sandwiches.

For more information about Tarpon Springs, contact the **Tarpon Springs Cultural Center** (101 Pinellas Ave., 727/942-5605, www.tarponarts.com) or the **Chamber of Commerce** (1 N. Pinellas Ave., Suite B, 727/937-6109, www.tarponspringschamber.com).

Beaches

The beaches of Clearwater and St. Pete are textbook stretches of white sand and clear warm Gulf water, with lots of comfy beachside hotels and waterside amenities for families. The area is home to a couple of world-class beach destinations that often make Dr. Stephen Leatherman's ("Dr. Beach" ranks the nation's beaches) annual top 10 list.

★ St. Pete Beach

St. Pete Beach has a lot of low-rise pastel motels and its fair share of high-rise hotel towers. For some reason you'll run into a lot of European travelers here; it has a livelier vibe than many Gulf Coast beaches, but not quite the spring break magnitude of Panama City Beach and other popular party spots. It is also a popular destination for families, and the resorts and hotels in the area commonly provide great children's amenities and entertainment to keep them occupied and having a good time. The beach is long and wide, mostly as a result of sand restoration projects, with plenty of room to spread out and find a private patch of sand on the Gulf. There are concessions, picnic tables, lots of parking, showers, and restrooms.

★ Clearwater Beach

An urban beach, **Clearwater Beach** (west on Hwy. 60), the only Pinellas County beach with year-round lifeguards (9:30am-4:30pm daily), is a long wide stretch offering showers, restrooms, concessions, cabanas, umbrella rentals, volleyball, and metered parking. **Pier 60**, where the beach meets the causeway, is the locus of lots of local revelry and activity—during the day it's a heavily trafficked fishing pier, while at night the focus is **Sunsets at Pier 60**, a festival that runs daily two hours before sunset to two hours past sunset, with crafts, magicians, and musicians vying for your attention with the showy sunset display over the Gulf of Mexico. They also show movies on an outdoor screen on Sunday-Monday nights (movies start at dusk, Aug.-Oct.) in the summer. Pier 60 contains a covered playground for the little ones, who will also like catching the bright-red **Jolley Trolley** (727/445-1200, www.clearwaterjolleytrolley.com, $2.25 per ride, day pass $5, free under age 6) from Clearwater Beach back to your hotel, downtown, or Sand Key.

Clearwater Beach has a few rules: No alcohol on the beach. Swim within the "safe bathing limit" area, extending 300 feet west of the high water line and clearly marked by buoys or pilings. Personal watercraft and boats are not allowed within this area.

★ Fort De Soto Park

South of St. Petersburg, **Fort De Soto Park** (3500 Pinellas Bayway S., Tierra Verde, 727/582-2267, www.pinellascounty.org, sunrise-sunset daily, parking $5 per vehicle, free for pedestrians and bicyclists) is 1,136 unspoiled acres with seven miles of beaches, two fishing piers, picnic and camping areas, a small history museum, and a 2,000-foot barrier-free nature trail for guests with disabilities set on five little interconnected islands. The fort itself is in the southwest corner of Mullet Key, and there's a toll ($0.85) on the bridges leading into the park. The islands were once inhabited by the Tocobaga people and visited by Spanish explorers. It was surveyed by Robert E. Lee before the Civil War, and during the war Union troops had a detachment on both Egmont and Mullet Keys. The fort was built in 1898 to protect Tampa Bay during the Spanish-American War and is listed on the National Register of Historic Places. During World War II, the island was used for bombing practice by the pilot who dropped the bomb on Hiroshima.

1: St. Pete Beach 2: Caladesi Island Beach

Exploring the old fort is part of what makes this experience special, drawing more than 2.7 million visitors annually. After checking out the four 12-inch seacoast rifled mortars (the only ones of their kind in the United States), head over to one of the two swim centers, the better of which is the North Beach Swim Center (it has concessions). At the beach you're likely to see gulls, ibis, and ospreys, as well as beach sunflowers and beach morning glories peeking out from the sea oats. Fishing enthusiasts can choose between the 500-foot-long pier on the Tampa Bay side or the 1,000-foot-long pier on the Gulf side. Each has a food and bait concession.

Once in the park, take a right at the stop sign, go one mile, and on the right look for **United Park Services** (3500 Pinellas Bayway S., Tierra Verde, 727/864-1376, www. unitedparkservices.com, 10am-5pm daily, last rental 3:30pm). It issues maps of the area and rents out single kayaks ($23 for 1 hour, $29 for 2 hours) and canoes ($30 for 1 hour, $40 for 2 hours). Bicycle rentals ($8 per hour) are available inside the park. Numbered signs along the shore mark a 2.25-mile kayak trail through Mullet Key Bayou.

Fort De Soto Park has the best **camping** ($33-40 tent sites, $40-46 RV sites) in the area, with campsites right on the Gulf. It's a popular campground, so make reservations as far in advance as possible. Reservations can be made online or in person. There are a handful of walk-in campsites available, but they are in high demand. All sites have water and electrical hookups, and there are modern restrooms, dump stations, a camp store, washers and dryers, and grills. Primitive campsites are available at the Shell Key Preserve area of the park. Permits to camp at this primitive area are free and must be obtained from the park office in person. Pets are allowed in Area 2, and some of the spots are directly on the water. Be advised that the resident raccoons are more skillful than most, able to pick cooler locks and unwrap lunch meat with ease.

★ Honeymoon Island and Caladesi Island Beaches

Honeymoon Island and Caladesi Island are a double whammy, perfectly suited to visiting back-to-back. In fact, the two islands were once part of a single larger barrier island, split in half during a savage hurricane in 1921. Together, they offer 1,000 acres of mostly undeveloped land, not too changed from how it looked when Spanish explorers surveyed the coast in the mid-1500s.

After a huge beach replenishment project in 2007, **Honeymoon Island** (1 Causeway Blvd., west end of Hwy. 586, Dunedin, 727/469-5942, 8am-sunset daily, $8 per car for up to 8 people, $4 per car single driver, $2 pedestrians and bicyclists) offers visitors all kinds of fun activities, but especially good is the fishing—you're likely to catch flounder, snook, trout, redfish, snapper, whiting, sheepshead, and, occasionally, tarpon. The island is home to 208 species of plants and a wealth of shore and wading birds, including a few endangered bird species. There is also a popular pet beach worth visiting if you're traveling with your pet.

Directly to the south of Honeymoon and accessible only by boat, **Caladesi** (727/469-5918, hourly ferry service 8am-sunset daily from Honeymoon, $14 adults, $7 ages 6-12, free under age 5) is the wilder of the two islands. There's the state park marina and swim beach near where the ferry drops you, but the rest of the island remains undeveloped. The Gulf side of the island has three miles of white-sand beach, which always makes the top rankings for beaches; the Tampa Bay side has a mangrove shoreline and sea grass flats. So, the Gulf side is for swimming and beach lolling, and the bay side is for birding and wildlife-watching.

If you're a strong kayaker or sailor, you might take advantage of the kayak and sailboat rentals on the causeway near Honeymoon Island. Once on Caladesi, there's a 3.5-mile canoe trail starting and ending at the south end of the marina that leads paddlers through mangrove canals and tunnels and along sea grass flats on the bay side of the island.

Two cautions about Caladesi: Don't miss the last ferry, or you'll be stuck. And if you brought a dog over to the dog beach at Honeymoon, Caladesi doesn't allow pets on the ferry. If you go by private boat, pets are allowed on a leash.

OTHER BEACHES

There are several good beaches along **Sand Key,** which contains eight communities between John's Pass and Clearwater Pass. **John's Pass Beach,** at the southern end of Sand Key, and north for a couple of miles in **Madeira Beach** have beautiful sand and good fishing. Going north, the beaches in **Redington Beach** have limited public access but are pretty. Still farther north, **Indian Rocks Beach** has good public access and a party vibe, with lively beach bars. Bypass the beaches in **Belleair,** as access and amenities are limited, in favor of an afternoon at **Sand Key County Park** (north end of Gulf Blvd. at Clearwater Pass, 727/588-4852, parking $5 per vehicle), which has lifeguards, playgrounds, cabana rentals, and lots of wide white-sand beach.

Sports and Recreation

GARDENS AND PARKS
★ Sunken Gardens

The four-acre 100-year-old **Sunken Gardens** (1825 4th St. N., St. Petersburg, 727/551-3102, www.stpete.org, 10am-4:30pm Mon.-Sat., noon-4:30pm Sun., $10 adults, $8 seniors, $4 ages 2-11) was saved by the city of St. Petersburg in 1999. There are 50,000 tropical plants and flowers, demonstration gardens, a 200-year-old oak tree, cascading waterfalls, and flamingos. More than a garden, it's St. Petersburg's most beloved Old Florida attraction. In 1903, a plumber named George Turner Sr. bought the property, which contained a large sinkhole and a shallow lake. He drained the lake and sold the tropical fruit he grew here at a roadside stand, but visitors liked walking through the tranquil greenery so much that he started charging admission. By 1935 the garden was officially Turner's Sunken Gardens (because of the former lake and sinkhole, the whole thing sits low in a basin), attracting 300,000 visitors per year. It was followed by some other attractions: the World's Largest Gift Shop and the King of Kings Wax Museum.

As is common for these kinds of Florida attractions, business fell off as more upscale venues became popular. The city also restored the gift shop and wax museum space to its former glory; the children's museum **Great Explorations** (1925 4th St. N., 727/821-8992, www.greatex.org, 10am-4:30pm Mon.-Sat., noon-4:30pm Sun., $10, $9 seniors, free under age 2) is housed here. If you're only able to visit one attraction, make it Sunken Gardens. It is beautiful and a slice of local history—a must if you can tear yourself away from the beach.

Brooker Creek Preserve

For an outdoors experience, drive up to **Brooker Creek Preserve** (3940 Keystone Rd., Tarpon Springs, 727/453-6800, www. brookercreekpreserve.org, trail sunrise-sunset daily), an 8,700-acre wilderness in the northern section of the county near Tarpon Springs. Currently its environmental education center offers four miles of self-guided hiking trails at the southern end of Lora Lane off Keystone Road, about 0.5 miles east of East Lake Road. The preserve also offers guided hikes every Saturday (reservation required by phone or online) and hosts the annual **Music Jamboree** in early April, a multi-genre

acoustic jam session where musicians are encouraged to bring their instruments and join the fun.

Weedon Island Preserve Cultural and Natural History Center

Extending along the west side of Tampa Bay in Pinellas County, **Weedon Island Preserve Cultural and Natural History Center** (1800 Weedon Island Dr., St. Petersburg, 727/453-6500, www.weedonislandpreserve. org, preserve 7am-sunset daily, cultural center 9am-4pm Thurs.-Sat., 11am-4pm Sun., free) is hard to classify. The low-lying islands in north St. Petersburg were home to Timucua and Manasota people as long as 10,000 years ago. The largest estuarine preserve in the county, it is also home to a large shell midden and burial mound complex. Visitors to the cultural center can see artifacts excavated from the site by the Smithsonian in the 1920s in exhibits designed collaboratively by anthropologists, historians, and Native Americans. The park has a four-mile canoe trail loop, a boardwalk and observation tower, three gentle miles of hiking trails, a fishing pier (snook, redfish, spotted trout), and waterfront picnic facilities. Guided nature hikes (9am-11am Sat., free) are offered.

Egmont Key State Park

Accessible only by ferry or private boat, at the mouth of Tampa Bay, **Egmont Key State Park** (4905 34th St., St. Petersburg, 727/893-2627, www.floridastateparks.org, 8am-sunset daily, free) makes a great day trip. There are few facilities on the island, which is wilderness except for the ruins of historic **Fort Dade** and brick paths that remain from when it was an active community with 300 residents. See the 150-year-old working lighthouse, constructed in 1858 to "withstand any storm" after a first one was ravaged by hurricanes in 1848 and 1852, as well as gun batteries built in 1898, a pretty stretch of beach, and lots of gopher tortoises and hummingbirds. There is no camping on Egmont Key.

Snead Island

Owned by the state of Florida and maintained by the Manatee County Conservation Lands Management team, **Snead Island** (941/776-2295, 8am-sunset daily, free) is just east of Egmont Key and another good opportunity to get out into the wilderness of this area—15 miles of it bordering shoreline along the Gulf and the lovely Manatee River. The park is favored by hikers because of its variety of trails and loops, with occasional boardwalks hugging the waterways. To get here, take U.S. 41 to Palmetto, turn right onto 10th Street West, and follow signs to the island.

Emerson Point Preserve

The west end of Snead Island is home to **Emerson Point Preserve** (5801 17th St. W., Palmetto, 941/721-6885, 8am-sunset daily, free), worth tacking on to your adventure—the park's 195 acres of salt marshes, beaches, mangrove swamp, lagoons, grass flats, hardwood hammocks, and semi-upland wooded areas are viewable from a well-maintained eight-foot-wide shell path, as well as more rustic walking and biking paths. Manatee County has poured money into this park in recent years such that master gardeners convene here regularly for guided walking tours of the varied plant and animal life. Call for the tour schedule.

Of special note to Native American history buffs, Emerson Point Park is home to the **Portavant Temple Mound** (east end of 17th St. W., Snead Island), an impressive mound complex. Walkways and boardwalks take you over and around a huge 150-foot flat-top temple mound and several horseshoe-shaped shell middens. Interpretive markers describe the site.

1: a great blue heron at Boyd Hill Nature Preserve 2: tropical plants and trees near a Chinese sculpture at the Sunken Gardens 3: biking on the Pinellas Trail

Anclote Key Preserve State Park

Anclote Key Preserve State Park (1 Causeway Blvd., Dunedin, 727/469-5943, 8am-sunset daily, free) is a similar island preserve accessible by boat, but Anclote Key offers primitive camping and is pet-friendly. During nesting season, rangers ask people with pets to keep the animals on the southeast end, as protected nesting birds take up residence in the north.

BIKING AND RUNNING

The best way to get oriented in the Tampa Bay area is to take a bike ride. **Northeast Cycles** (1114 4th St., St. Petersburg, 727/898-2453, $20 per day, road bikes $50 per day) will rent you bikes and a rack ($10) so you can load them up and take them wherever you like, as will two locations of **Chainwheel Drive** (1770 Drew St., Clearwater, 727/441-2444, 10am-7pm Mon.-Fri., 10am-5pm Sat., 11am-5pm Sun.; Palm Lake Plaza, 32796 U.S. 19 N., Palm Harbor, 727/786-3883, 10am-7pm Mon.-Fri., 10am-5pm Sat.; hybrid $35 full-day, road bike $42 full-day).

A popular bike trail is the 34-mile-long **Pinellas Trail** (727/464-8400), one of the longest linear parks in the southeastern United States, running essentially from St. Petersburg up to the sponge docks of Tarpon Springs. A rails-to-trails conversion, the original rail track was home to the first Orange Belt Railroad train in 1888 and is now a well-maintained 15-foot-wide trail through parks and coastal areas for cyclists, in-line skaters, and joggers. There is a free guide to the Pinellas Trail available at the trail office, area libraries, and the Pinellas County Courthouse information desk; it can also be downloaded (www.pinellascounty.org). It lists rest stops, service stations, restaurants, pay phones, bike shops, and park areas along the trail.

It is not recommended to visit the trail after dark, especially the section that runs through the southern part of St. Petersburg, where there has been a significant uptick in robberies and crime in the past two years. Officials have increased their patrols of the trail, and the city even installed cameras along certain sections of the trail where crime has been an issue.

BIRDING

Every October, Pinellas County hosts the annual **Florida Birding and Nature Festival** (www.floridabirdingandnaturefestival.org), to which more than 3,000 avid birders flock every year. They come to hear a dynamic array of speakers and attend seminars, but mostly they come to tramp around on field trips to some of the region's top birding and wildlife areas. Some of the state's rarer bird species, like the reddish egret, little burrowing owls, and the Florida scrub jay, the only bird species unique to Florida, can be seen.

If you're an avid birder or would like to learn more about birds, go to the **Great Florida Birding Trail** website (www.floridabirdingtrail.com) for the West Section guide to the birding trail, which lists 117 sites in 21 counties. Many important birding sites are in Pinellas County.

Brooker Creek Preserve and **East Beach** at Fort De Soto Park are both wonderful for birding. **Shell Key** (southern end of Pass-a-Grille channel, just west of Tierra Verde), an undeveloped 180-acre barrier island only accessible by shuttle or charter boat, is an important place for wintering and nesting seabirds and shorebirds, with more than 100 species sighted. **Boyd Hill Nature Preserve** (1101 Country Club Way S., St. Petersburg, 727/893-7326, 9am-7pm Tues.-Fri., 7am-7pm Sat., 9am-7pm Sun., $3 adults, $1.50 ages 3-16, free under age 3) is 245 acres of pristine Florida wilderness with five distinct ecosystems—hardwood hammocks, sand pine scrub, pine flatwoods, willow marsh, and the Lake Maggiore shoreline. This may be my favorite, as it is incredibly convenient, just minutes from downtown, but it feels far from the crowds. Precious green space in an urban landscape, it is an important stopover on the Atlantic Flyway—165 bird species have been observed

Smokin'

Here's a tricky scenario. You're on a great Gulf Coast vacation, the weather's perfect, you're feeling relaxed, so you decide to do a little charter fishing. You're out on the boat, you feel a yank, and there's a 40-pound greater amberjack on your line. You work for a while and haul in a couple more of those and a whole mess of 20-inch Spanish mackerel. What a great day. My question: Now what? Are you going to take that fish cooler back to the Radisson and stink up the joint?

Here's what to do: Go to **Ted Peters Famous Smoked Fish** (1350 Pasadena Ave., South Pasadena, 727/381-7931, www.tedpetersfish.com, 11:30am-7:30pm Wed.-Mon., $10-23, cash only) and they'll smoke them for you for $1.50 per pound. They can even make kingfish taste good, and that's saying something. They fillet them, throw them over a smoldering red oak fire in the smokehouse, then package them up for you to take. Smoked fish keeps 4-5 days in the fridge.

If you don't have fish to smoke, still go to Ted Peters. An institution for more than 50 years and prized for its laid-back style and inviting picnic tables, the main attraction is smoked fish—try the smoked fish spread with saltines, and the salmon and mullet. Ted Peters also produces some legendary cheeseburgers and potato salad (no fries here). This beer-drinking establishment gets busy in high season and closes early.

here. You can camp at Boyd, and there's a small educational center with exhibits on the five ecosystems.

Another spot on the Great Florida Birding Trail, also lauded by the National Audubon Society, is **Sawgrass Lake Park** (7400 25th St. N., Pinellas Park, 727/582-2100, 7am-sunset daily, free), immediately west of I-275. Thousands of birds migrate through the park during the fall and spring. A one-mile elevated boardwalk winds through a maple swamp and oak hammock. There's an observation tower with views of the park's swamps, canals, and lake, where you're likely to see wood storks, herons, egrets, and ibis in addition to gators and turtles. The park has naturalist-led nature tours and field trips, and its Anderson Environmental Center contains a large freshwater aquarium and exhibits on the area. Note that during the wet months, the park can get flooded.

If you find an injured bird in your wandering, call **Suncoast Seabird Sanctuary** (18328 Gulf Blvd., Indian Shores, 727/391-6211, 8am-4pm daily), one of the country's largest nonprofit wild bird hospitals. With a hospital facility, the sanctuary rescues and releases hundreds of birds each year into the wild. Visitors can call ahead and schedule a tour of the sanctuary.

FISHING
★ Sunshine Skyway Fishing Piers

It must have been a sight to see. In 1980 the largest bridge demolition in Florida history brought down the 1954 Sunshine Skyway Bridge, a 15-mile crossing from St. Petersburg to Bradenton. From a long causeway on both sides, the steel bridge had a steep cantilever truss, 750 feet wide and 150 feet above the water.

It wasn't enough clearance: At least five freighters or barges hit the bridge, most with minor damage, but during a violent storm in 1980, when visibility was nil, the empty phosphate freighter *Summit Venture* slammed into the south pier of the southbound span and knocked 1,261 feet out of the center span, the cantilever, and part of the roadway into Tampa Bay. Thirty-five people on the bridge at the time died, most of them in a Greyhound bus headed for Miami. The only survivor was in a truck that landed by chance on the deck of the *Summit Venture*. One of the worst bridge disasters in history, it prompted the design, funding, and building of a new **Sunshine Skyway Bridge,** the world's longest cable-stayed bridge, with a main span of 1,200 feet and vertical clearance of 193 feet. The four-mile bridge opened in 1987, equipped with a bridge protection system involving 36 large concrete bumpers (oddly called dolphins) built to withstand impact from tankers up to 87,000 tons traveling at 10 knots.

So, you probably think I'm leading up to saying, "It's a gorgeous bridge, a real local landmark; you must drive over this thing." True, but it's only part of the story. During the demolition of the old bridge spans, portions of it were preserved as fishing piers, and the rubble was piled alongside to form fish-friendly artificial reefs. Since the original bridge was built, fishers have been bragging about the variety they catch: shark, tarpon, goliath grouper, kingfish, Spanish mackerel, and sea bass. Usually you have to be in a boat to find water deep enough for many of these species. Anglers have caught 1,000-pound tiger sharks from the bridge, traffic honking behind them. And now, with the artificial reefs adding extra enticement to the fish, the Sunshine Skyway Fishing Piers are prime fishing spots.

The 0.75-mile-long **North Pier** (727/865-0668) and the 1.5-mile-long **South Pier** (941/729-0117) together are said to be the world's longest fishing pier. You can drive onto the pier and park next to your fishing spot, parallel parking on the left lane, with room for cars to pass and walkways on either side of the span. There are restrooms on both piers, and bait shops sell live and frozen bait, tackle, drinks, and snacks. They also rent rods. The North Pier has a large picnic area next to the bait shop.

To get here, head south on I-275 toward Bradenton. The North Pier ($4 per vehicle plus $4 pp, $2 ages 6-12, free under age 6) is about one mile past the toll gate ($1.25). To reach the South Pier, continue over the bridge and follow the signs. You don't need a fishing license to fish off the piers. So drive over the new bridge, but, more importantly, wet a line on the remnants of the old one.

SAILING

For sailing charters, head to St. Pete Beach or Clearwater Beach for the most variety and availability.

Families won't want to miss the opportunity to board the **Pirate Ship at John's Pass** (140 Boardwalk Place W., 727/423-7824, www.boattoursjohnspass.com, $33 over age 64, $39 ages 21-64, $29 ages 2-20, $10 under age 2), a recreated pirate ship that departs from the John's Pass Village and Boardwalk on Madeira Beach. The crew dresses up as pirates and will fill your ear with all the "aye, mateys" and "batten down the hatches" you can handle.

The same company also offers 1.5-hour dolphin tours aboard the **Dolphin Quest** (727/392-7090, noon, 2pm, 4pm, and 6pm daily, $24.50 adults, $22.50 seniors, $19.50 ages 2-20, free under age 2), which departs at the same dock as the Pirate Ship. You're guaranteed to see dolphins, and the onboard narrators will teach you all about Boca Ciega Bay. There are restrooms onboard, and the seats are cushioned. Snacks and drinks are available throughout the cruise.

Adults will enjoy boarding a sailboat for a sightseeing cruise with **Dolphin Landings Charter Boat Center** (4737 Gulf Blvd., 727/367-7411, St. Pete Beach, www.dolphinlandings.com, $40 adults, $30 children, free under age 2). They offer two-hour sailing trips that look for dolphins. The sunset sail is particularly enjoyable. Bring your own alcoholic drinks, and free soda and bottled water are provided. It's hard to come up with a better way to spend a few hours on St. Pete Beach.

SPECTATOR SPORTS
Baseball

Tropicana Field (1 Tropicana Dr., St. Petersburg, 727/825-3250) is currently home to the Tampa Bay Rays professional baseball team (game time usually 2:15pm or 7:15pm, $5-32). As a concession to summer temperatures and humidity, the ballpark has a domed roof (lit orange when the Rays win at home) and artificial turf. Out of season, Tropicana Field hosts other athletic events, conventions, trade shows, and concerts, with a seating capacity of 43,773.

Each spring for spring training, the Rays relocate to grass-surfaced **Charlotte County**

Sports Park, with 7,000 seats, a couple of hours south in Port Charlotte. Other spring training action is closer: Spring training games run all month in March, and tickets usually go on sale January 15. The Philadelphia Phillies have been training at Spectrum Field (601 Old Coachman Rd., Clearwater, 727/762-4457, game time usually 1:05pm or 7:05pm, $15-32) in Clearwater since 1948. It's a great venue, with a tiki-hut pavilion in left field, a kids play area, group picnic areas, party suites, and club seats. The Toronto Blue Jays also have spring training in the area at Dunedin Stadium (373 Douglas Ave., Dunedin, 727/733-9302, game time usually 1:05pm, $13-24). Built in 1990, it's a smaller ballpark in a residential area; you end up paying as much for parking as for your ticket. There are upper and lower sections, and the upper section has a slight overhang, which can be cooling during warm day games.

Entertainment and Events

MUSIC

A couple of big venues host a range of performances. Ruth Eckerd Hall (1111 McMullen Booth Rd. N., Clearwater, 727/791-7400, www.rutheckerdhall.com) is the locus for much of the area's lively arts activity. The 2,200-seat space was designed by the Frank Lloyd Wright Foundation 25 years ago, and the space still looks fresh; acoustically, it had a recent overhaul, and the sound is full and lush. It's home to the top regional Florida Orchestra (727/892-3331, www.floridaorchestra.org), performing 130 concerts annually here, at the Mahaffey Theater, and elsewhere. Ruth Eckerd also hosts pop acts, visiting theater, and other performing arts. Its educational wing, the Marcia P. Hoffman School of the Arts, features the 182-seat Murray Studio Theatre, three studio classrooms, four private teaching studios, a dance studio, and an arts resource library.

The Mahaffey Theater at the Duke Energy Center for the Performing Arts (400 1st St. S., St. Petersburg, 727/892-5798, www.themahaffey.com) changed in 2004 when the Bayfront Center Arena was demolished. A renovation project doubled the lobby size and expanded capacity and versatility. The signature component is a three-story glass-curtain wall and glass-enclosed atrium that overlooks the city's beautiful downtown waterfront. The lovely theater hosts performances of the Florida Orchestra, jazz, ballet, opera, the circus, and contemporary performers. The Mahaffey is on the waterfront, within walking distance of shopping, fine restaurants, and many downtown museums.

A smaller venue for rock and contemporary acts, Jannus Live (200 1st Ave. N., St. Petersburg, 727/565-0550, www.jannuslive.com) is said to be the oldest outdoor concert venue in Florida. From jam bands like the Allman Brothers to Grizfolk and Lucinda Williams, it all sounds great from a spot in the outdoor courtyard. It's bigger than a nightclub, with bigger acts, but there's still a cool club vibe and usually a 30s-and-up crowd.

The historic Coliseum (535 4th Ave. N., 727/892-5202, $5 parking on the left) was built in 1924 and purchased by the city of St. Petersburg in 1989. It has updated the beautiful space and reopened it as a multiuse facility, hosting a variety of events such as Florida Orchestra pops concerts, the Toronto All Star Big Band, and an exotic bird show.

THEATER

At the top of the dramatic arts heap in Pinellas County, American Stage Theatre Company at the Raymond James Theatre (163 3rd St. N., St. Petersburg, 727/823-7529, www.americanstage.org, curtain usually 7:30pm Tues.-Thurs., 8pm Fri.-Sat., 3pm

Sat.-Sun., $22-35) is Tampa Bay's oldest professional theater, with a six-play season on the main stage plus children's theater, educational outreach, and the annual Shakespeare in the Park festival.

In its 41st year in 2019, American Stage is now performing in a brand-new state-of-the-art building in the heart of downtown St. Petersburg, facing Williams Park, only four blocks from the original location. The theater has expanded its audience capacity to 182 and added two large lobbies. There is free parking at the nearby Synovis Bank during performances.

For local community theater, several companies are worth checking out, all with reasonable ticket prices. Throughout its 83 years as Florida's oldest continuously operating community theater, **St. Petersburg City Theatre** (4025 31st St. S., St. Petersburg, 727/866-1973, www.spcitytheatre.org, curtain 8pm, 2pm Sun., $15-22) has presented up to six community productions per season— musicals, comedies, and dramas, usually crowd-pleasers like *Noises Off* or Neil Simon's *Brighton Beach Memoirs*. **Francis Wilson Playhouse** (302 Seminole St., Clearwater, 727/446-1360, www.franciswilsonplayhouse. org, curtain 8pm, 2pm Sun., $26 adults, $15 children and students) is another venerable community playhouse dating to 1930. The intimate 182-seat theater showcases eight comedies and musicals per season and a family-oriented program in December.

In the little town of Gulfport on Boca Ciega Bay, the **Catherine Hickman Theater** (5501 27th Ave. S., 727/893-1070) hosts Gulfport Community Players community theater productions and Pinellas Park Civic Orchestra concerts.

FESTIVALS AND EVENTS

In late April, the **Mainsail Art Festival** (www.mainsailart.org) draws over 100,000 visitors to Vinoy Park. More than 250 fine artists display their work and compete for cash prizes, and visitors can peruse or purchase some of the best contemporary art in the country. *Sunshine Artist Magazine* ranked it in the top 100 fine-art festivals in the country.

In mid-October, music lovers can shake a tail feather at the **Clearwater Jazz Holiday** (www.clearwaterjazz.com). While the festival focuses on jazz artists new and old, the lineup regularly contains pop and dance groups. In recent years, the Jazz Holiday has hosted acts such as UB40, Kool and the Gang, Grace Potter, Sheryl Crow, and the Preservation Hall Jazz Band, straight out of New Orleans. A wide variety of food and drink vendors also congregate downtown at the waterfront Coachman Park.

In April, a bit north of Clearwater, visit Scotland in spirit at the **Dunedin Highland Games and Festival** (www. dunedinhighlandgames.com). You can watch Scottish athletes compete in traditional Highland games, such as tipping the caber and shot put, or listen to traditional Scottish musicians compete for prizes.

Nightlife

DOWNTOWN ST. PETERSBURG
Bars and Pubs

For something fun and memorable, hop aboard the **PedalPub St. Pete** (1975 3rd Ave. S., 727/581-3388, www.pedalpubstpete. com, $33 pp Sun.-Thurs., $39 pp Fri.-Sat.), a 2-hour tour through the city on a 16-person bicycle. The party bike pedals to three local breweries. Patrons can choose from a list of routes and stops that include Pinellas Ale Works, Green Bench, and Ferg's. It's a

1: the historic Coliseum **2:** Vinoy Park

rollicking good time, and you'll get some light exercise while you wheel around with brews and cocktails in hand.

Two blocks north of Tropicana Field, you can buy a locally crafted beer before or after the baseball game at **Green Bench Brewing Company** (1133 Baum Ave. N., 727/800-7836, www.greenbenchbrewing.com, noon-10pm Tues.-Thurs., noon-midnight Fri.-Sat., noon-10pm Sun., $5-10). The brewery makes IPAs, ales, stouts, and a good wheat beer, Skyway Wheat. The most popular is the Green Bench IPA, with a citrus flavor and a dry, bitter finish. Check the website for regular live music.

Four blocks east of Green Bench Brewery, the **St. Pete Brewing Company** (544 1st Ave. N., 727/623-4837, www.stpetebrewingcompany.com, 2pm-10pm Mon.-Thurs., noon-midnight Fri., 11am-midnight Sat., noon-10pm Sun., $5-10) has nearly a dozen brews and serves a variety of bar snacks, salads, and pizzas. Well-behaved dogs are welcome in the bar, but you may find it hard to keep your pooch from begging if you order the pint of bacon ($7). They offer beer flights to taste a sampling of the excellent suds prepared by their brewmaster, John McCracken.

Live Music

For a night of live music, put on your dancing shoes and head to **Jannus Live** (200 1st Ave. N. St., 727/565-0550, www.jannuslive.com). The outdoor venue is nestled in a courtyard near the corner of 1st Avenue and 2nd Street North near Williams Park. Focusing on rock, blues, and reggae, the venue has hosted acts like the Red Hot Chili Peppers, Pearl Jam, Cheap Trick, and Ted Nugent. All shows are all-ages and take place rain or shine. There are several full-service bars that surround the venue, and you can satisfy your munchies with Joey Brooklyn's Pizza. There are only a few benches for sitting, so be prepared to stand and walk around.

ST. PETE BEACH
Bars and Pubs

One of the most fun and casual beachside bars is **Bongo's Beach Bar and Grill** (5250 Gulf Blvd., 727/360-1811, www.grandplazaflorida. com, 11am-3am daily). Put your toes in the sand and enjoy the waterfront view as you sip tropical drinks at this tiki-style paradise. It's an excellent spot to watch the sunset, and there is live music nearly every night. The menu is hearty burgers, sandwiches, tacos, and seafood, and there are multiple TVs playing sports. Located at the Grand Plaza Hotel, the place is open to nonguests and is a local favorite.

Also in the Grand Plaza Resort, the **Level 11 Rooftop** (5250 Gulf Blvd., 727/360-1811, www.grandplazaflorida.com, 3pm-1am daily) has 360-degree views of beautiful St. Pete Beach and is located just steps away. After spending the day in the sun, enjoy the sunset with a cocktail and some light bites on the outdoor deck. The cheese board is excellent, and the seating is exceptionally comfortable.

In the "dive bar" category, **The Drunken Clam** (46 46th Ave., 727/360-1800, www. drunkenclambar.com, 10am-2am daily) is a small no-frills sports bar. It's a wonderfully kitschy spot to watch a game on the beach or hang out until the wee hours with a lively mix of locals and tourists. They have live music many nights a week, and their affordably priced menu features wings, nachos, steamed shrimp, and good burgers. Reasonably priced domestic pitchers ($8.50) and well drinks ($3) make it one of the cheapest spots to drink on this stretch of the coast.

Jimmy B's Beach Bar (6200 Gulf Blvd., 727/367-1902, www.beachcomberflorida. com, 11am-3am daily) is a casual bar just steps from the beach at the Beachcomber Beach Resort. The low-rise bar is nestled between two pools at the resort and has spectacular waterfront views. There is live music day and night featuring beach music, like reggae, yacht rock, and Jimmy Buffett-style songs. To continue the Key West vibe, order coconut shrimp or a slice of key lime pie from the extensive menu with American, Mexican, and Caribbean choices.

CLEARWATER BEACH
Bars and Pubs

Hooters (381 Mandalay Ave., 727/443-7263, www.originalhooters.com, 11am-10pm daily) is exactly what you would expect: cold beer, hot wings, and waitresses wearing short orange shorts. They call it a family restaurant, but use your own judgment. The bar is mostly open-air and located near the end of the main pier, giving it great ocean views. It's an incredibly popular place with a lively scene most nights. Wings are king on this menu, but you'll also find burgers, salads, and other American bar regulars. They have daily drink specials, and you can get buckets of five Coronas ($15) every day.

At the south end of Mandalay Park,

Frenchy's Rockaway Grill (7 Rockaway St., 727/446-4844, www.frenchysonline.com, 11am-midnight Sun.-Thurs., 11am-1am Fri.-Sat.) is a beachfront bar with a sprawling deck and excellent sunset views. The drinks are tropical and fruity, and the menu leans toward seafood. Try the she crab soup and the grouper Santorini for lunch or dinner. The margarita and rum runners are good drink choices. There's live music nightly, and inside you'll find pool tables and indoor seating.

The drinks are pricier at the **Pier House 60 Rooftop Bar** (101 Coronado Dr., 855/859-2952, www.pierhouse60.com, noon-midnight daily), but the incredible views make them worth the price. It's a small, intimate place that feels equally suitable for a break from the beach or a romantic glass of wine. It gets packed in the evening on weekends and can become standing room only.

Shopping

DOWNTOWN ST. PETERSBURG
Art

The Morean Art Center (719 Central Ave., 727/822-7872, www.moreanartscenter.org, 10am-5pm Mon.-Sat., noon-5pm Sun., $20 adults, $18 seniors, $13 students, free under age 6) houses an incredible glass art collection by the world-renowned artist Dale Chihuly. If you don't recognize his name, you'd still recognize his work. His signature pieces are large chandelier-like sculptures with twisted strands of glass that resemble something close to a colorful mass of jellyfish tentacles. A whimsical 20-foot sculpture was produced by Chihuly specifically for the entrance to the gallery. Included in admission is access to a separate glass art gallery and shop that features the work of over 40 local artists, as well as access to live

glassblowing demonstrations at the glass art studio.

For more glass art, visit the gallery and shop at **The Duncan McClellan Gallery** (2342 Emerson Ave. S., www.dmglass.com, 855/436-4527, 10am-5pm Mon.-Sat.), west of downtown St. Petersburg in the Art Warehouse district. The 7,800-square-foot warehouse has been transformed from a former fish-packing plant into an impressively beautiful gallery housing the works of over 60 artists, a glass art workshop, and an on-site shop that gives you the opportunity to purchase one of their glass creations. Check the calendar and visit while there is a glass blowing demonstration happening in the workshop.

Books and Music

Florida's largest new and used bookstore

Market to Market

ST. PETE BEACH

The **Corey Avenue Sunday Market** (Corey Ave. between Boca Ciega Ave. and Gulf Blvd., www.coreyave.com, 10am-2pm Sun. Oct.-May) is a favorite open-air farmers market, featuring local vendors selling fresh produce, plants, home-baked goods, crafts, art, and a variety of ready-to-eat food. During the market hours, the surrounding shops, galleries, and restaurants are also open for business. This is a great stop to pick up a lunch and more on your way to the beach on Sunday morning.

CLEARWATER

The **Downtown Clearwater Farmer's Market** (612 Cleveland St., 10am-2pm Sat. year-round) happens every Saturday in the 500-600 blocks of Cleveland Street downtown. Vendors sell produce, food, jewelry, soaps, clothes, vintage items, flowers, and more in a relaxing open-air setting. From the market you can head to Coachman Park and enjoy the marina and waterfront walk.

DOWNTOWN ST. PETERSBURG

The **Locale Market** (179 2nd Ave. N., 727/523-6300, www.localegourmetmarket.com, 8am-9pm Sun.-Thurs., 8am-10pm Fri.-Sat., $6-17) is a gourmet market and café that sells a wide variety of high-end cheeses, meats, coffees, wine, beer, and raw foods. In the café, choose from a huge menu, with burgers, pizza, sushi, and a variety of sweets. All of the ingredients are high-quality and hand-selected by the resident chefs and owners. It's a foodie's paradise. I suggest wrapping your hands around a thick burger that has local dry-aged beef, double smoked bacon, grilled mushrooms and onions, and gooey gouda. There's also a large selection of organic, vegetarian, and generally healthy options.

If you love fresh food, visit the **Saturday Morning Market** (101 1st St. SE, 727/455-4921, www.saturdaymorningmarket.com, 9am-2pm Sat.), located downtown in the Al Lang Field parking lot. The delightful open-air market has delicious fresh fruits and vegetables as well as food trucks and stands serving a wide variety of food from around the globe. The market includes craft booths, artists, and live music. It's a fun family atmosphere and a great way to spend a few hours on Saturday morning.

---

merits a couple of hours of browsing, especially if the weather is inclement (a rarity). The independent **Haslam's Book Store** (2025 Central Ave., St. Petersburg, 727/822-8616, www.haslams.com, 10am-6:30pm Mon.-Sat., noon-5pm Sun.) is now owned by the third generation of the same family and has more than 300,000 volumes. The store has a large number of rare books, and they seem to be really into science fiction.

Shopping Malls and Centers

Sundial St. Pete (153 2nd Ave. N., 727/800-3201, www.sundialstpete.com, 10am-9pm Mon.-Sat., noon-8pm Sun.) is a shopping center near South Straub Park. It features a gourmet market, a movie theater, a day spa, and a variety of retail and health-and-wellness stores.

Tyrone Square Mall (6901 22nd Ave. N., 727/347-3889, 10am-9pm Mon.-Sat., 11am-7pm Sun.), in West St. Petersburg near Azalea park, is a typical indoor mall experience with more than 170 restaurants and shops, including Macy's, Dillard's, JCPenney, and Old Navy.

ST. PETE BEACH
Shopping Malls and Centers

North of St. Pete Beach on Madeira Beach, **John's Pass Village** features more than 100 retailers, restaurants, and attractions. Most of the shops sell beachy souvenirs, clothes and accessories, and surf gear.

Food

Pinellas County is awash in restaurants, most of them fun and casual, many of them worthy of recommendation. Because the area is densely populated and traffic can get congested during high season, you're more likely to grab a bite near where you're staying or near the beach from which you're departing. There are, however, places that are worth a drive in traffic—what restaurateurs call "destination restaurants."

DOWNTOWN ST. PETERSBURG

Remember that downtown St. Petersburg is on the east side of the peninsula, not on the Gulf but on Old Tampa Bay. There are several wonderful picks here—definitely the densest concentration of fine dining in Pinellas County.

American

For a simple burger, go to **El Cap** (3500 4th St. N., 727/521-1314, 11am-11pm daily, $4-7).

Italian

Mazzaro's Italian Market (2909 22nd Ave. N., 727/321-2400, 9am-6pm Mon.-Fri., 9am-2:30pm Sat., $8-16) comprises a store and a deli-market housed in two separate buildings. The store sells a variety of housewares and Italian-themed decor, and the deli serves hot or cold Italian sandwiches on the outdoor patio. Indoors the large market sells fresh-roasted coffees, meats, cheeses, handmade pastas, pastries, gelato, gourmet imports, seafood, wine, and beer, most of which are sourced from Italy. It's a wonderfully authentic Mediterranean environment. If you love Italian food and culture, this is a must-stop.

Mexican

For some excellent Mexican food, try **Red Mesa Cantina** (128 3rd St. S., 727/896-8226, 11am-midnight Sun.-Wed., 11am-2am Thurs.-Sat., $10-20), which offers a hip menu of regional Mexican and ceviche.

Seafood

Near the pier, you can sit outside on the patio and enjoy the waterfront views beyond North Straub Park at **400 Beach Seafood and Tap House** (400 Beach Dr. NE., 727/896-2400, www.400beachseafood.com, 11am-10pm Mon.-Thurs., 11am-11pm Fri.-Sat., 10am-10pm Sun., $17-28). The fare is casual American with great steak and seafood options, and the beer and wine menu are extensive. There is nice outdoor seating and a beautiful dining room indoors with large floor-to-ceiling arched windows. The brunch buffet (10am-3pm Sun., $25) is very popular, offering a wide range of pastries, breakfast items, seafood, and meat.

The **Parkshore Grill** (300 Beach Dr. NE, 727/896-9463, 11am-10pm Mon.-Thurs., 11am-11pm Fri.-Sat., 10am-10pm Sun., $25-45), has a wonderful outside patio within sight of the Museum of Fine Arts. The menu leans to smart spins on contemporary American cuisine, with spice-seared tuna and roasted organic salmon fillet. The restaurant has received numerous accolades in recent years, the most remarkable being two Golden Spoon Awards in 2012 and 2013.

ST. PETE BEACH

Breakfast

Try the orange-pecan french toast or the creamed chipped beef on toast for breakfast at **Skyway Jack's Restaurant** (2795 34th St. S., 727/867-1907, 5am-3pm daily, $5-10). It's a local classic that once moved because it was on the approach to the Sunshine Skyway Bridge and got pushed out to make room for more lanes. Stick with regular breakfast food or the smoked mullet and you won't be disappointed.

Italian

Located in the Tradewinds Island Grand Resort, the **Palm Court Italian Grill** (5500 Gulf Blvd., 727/363-2358, www.tradewindsresort.com, 11:30am-2pm and 5pm-10pm Mon.-Sat., 11am-2pm Sun., $20-35) serves traditional Italian fare in a beautiful Mediterranean environment. The outdoor courtyard is better for more casual dining, while indoors you'll find an environment more suited to special occasions. The menu is traditional Italian with a variety of seafood, beef, chicken, pasta, and vegetarian options. Try the angel-hair pasta with Gulf shrimp or the lobster tortellini for the main course. On Sunday, there's an excellent brunch with eggs benedict, fresh shrimp, salad, fruits, desserts, and complimentary Bellinis and mimosas.

Seafood

If you can go to just one place in St. Pete Beach, get the blackened grouper sandwich at ★ **The Hurricane** (Pass-a-Grille Beach, 809 Gulf Way, 727/360-9558, 7am-10pm Sun.-Thurs., 7am-11pm Fri.-Sat., $8-24). I don't care if the place seems a little touristy; give me a grouper fillet, add some tomato and lettuce on a bread roll, and that's as good as it gets in

Pinellas County. There's a nice bar adjacent to the restaurant and a rooftop sundeck up top for watching the sunset.

The Grand Plaza Hotel has several excellent dining choices, including **Level 11** (5250 Gulf Blvd., www.grandplazaflorida.com, 727/360-1811, 3pm-2am daily, $8-15) on the rooftop of the hotel. Enjoy excellent views of the beach from plush love seats and chairs. This place is great for drinks and sharing small plates with a group. The menu is diverse, with options like seared sea scallops, kebabs, crab-stuffed shrimp, and barbecue sliders. Try the fig and filet plate, which has pieces of seared filet mignon, prosciutto, and figs. For dessert, the key lime pie or chocolate cake with keokee coffee (brandy, Kahlua, and dark crème de cacao) are good bets.

Also in the Grand Plaza Hotel, **Spinners Rooftop Revolving Bistro and Lounge** (5250 Gulf Blvd., www.grandplazaflorida.com, 727/360-1811, 11am-11pm daily, $25-40) is a fine-dining restaurant with floor-to-ceiling windows looking out onto the beautiful coastline. The entire restaurant rotates so that diners can see the view from all sides. It takes about 1.5 hours to complete a full rotation, so take this into consideration when you're choosing your table. The lunch

The Hurricane restaurant on St. Pete Beach

menu offers salads, wraps, tacos, burgers, sandwiches and a small number of entrées like grilled salmon and chicken pasta. The dinner menu features a wide selection of mostly steak and seafood entrées with a few chicken dishes. Try the steak and shrimp or the mahimahi. The prices are a bit high, but the food is excellent, and the views and experience are worth it.

GULFPORT
American
Like the sound of candied bacon? Try **Little Tommie's Tiki** (5519 Shore Blvd. S., 727/498-8826, 11am-midnight daily, $7-12). The tiki bar has water views and indoor and outdoor seating. It's a great place to go for an ultra-casual experience where you can get a drink and watch the sunset. The menu features bar staples like fish tacos, wings, and nachos; the fried pickles and salmon burger are good choices too. There is a nice selection of brews on tap, several of them local crafts. If you're traveling by boat, you can dock at the marina near the Gulfport Casino.

French and Vietnamese
Gulfport has exploded on the dining scene in the past few years, with worthwhile restaurants lining several blocks. A local favorite is **Alesia Restaurant** (7204 Central Ave., 727/345-9701, 11:30am-2:30pm and 5:30pm-9pm Tues.-Fri., 10am-2:30pm and 5:30pm-9pm Sat., $16-24), which serves up an interesting mix of French and Vietnamese cuisine. It's definitely strange to see ratatouille and Vietnamese *pho* on the same menu, but the food is so good that the bizarre concept works well.

Italian
A local favorite for Italian food is **Pia's Trattoria** (3054 Beach Blvd. S., 727/327-2190, 4pm-9pm Mon., 11am-9pm Tues.-Thurs., 11am-10pm Fri.-Sat., 11am-9pm Sun., $8-20). Try the chicken piccata cooked in a wonderful caper and butter sauce. The lasagna is a lunch specialty and is highly recommended. If the

weather is nice, don't miss the charming outdoor patio area.

Southern
One block northeast of Little Tommie's Tiki, **Stella's** (3119 Beach Blvd. S., 727/498-8950, www.stellasingulfport.com, 7am-2pm daily, $6-10) serves a fantastic breakfast, lunch, and brunch any time it's open. It has a casual diner-style setting with nostalgic pictures from around Gulfport on the walls. The outdoor seating area is shaded and a nice spot for people-watching. The breakfast fare is classic Southern, like shrimp and grits, with a few European options like quiche. The fried green tomato benedict is delicious. For lunch, it's exceptional for sandwiches and burgers. Stella's is dog-friendly—they give a free dog treat to every pooch that visits, and there is even a dog menu. Like Tommie's, Stella's is within walking distance if you are traveling by boat and would like to dock at the marina near the Casino.

Vegetarian
For a healthy lunch, look no farther than **Golden Dinosaurs Vegan Deli** (2930 Beach Blvd. S., 727/873-6901, www.mangiagourmet. com, 10am-3pm Mon.-Tues., 10am-9pm Thurs.-Sat., 10am-7pm Sun., lunch $6-10), in the former home of Mangia Gourmet. It's a 100-percent vegan deli and bakery that also serves salads, coffee, wine, beer, and kombucha, a fermented green or black tea. Most items are made from scratch, and the outdoor seating is shaded and comfortable. Look for the little pink-and-white building two blocks south of the Gulfport Public Library.

CLEARWATER
American
The **Beach Shanty Café** (397 Mandalay Ave., 727/443-1616, 7am-4pm daily, $4-8) serves remarkably cheap and tasty breakfast featuring classic American staples. They offer breakfast all day, and that's all they offer. The café is sandwiched between two larger buildings right on the main strip of Mandalay Avenue, so don't blink or you may miss it. The

interior is much larger than you would expect from the small storefront, and there's a good amount of seating.

Clearwater has a fairly dense concentration of good restaurants. But really, you owe it to yourself to go to the original **Hooters** (2800 Gulf to Bay Blvd., 727/797-4008, www.originalhooters.com, 11am-11pm Sun.-Thurs., 11am-midnight Fri.-Sat., $8-20) for some good chicken wings. The original sports-oriented joint has spawned an international empire. It's a family restaurant, really—it's just that the waitresses are wearing flesh-colored pantyhose under orange nylon short-shorts. Use your own judgement.

Breakfast

Lenny's Restaurant (21220 U.S. 19 N., 727/799-0402, 6am-3pm daily, $5-12) is the hands-down winner for breakfast, with Jewish staple blintzes, knishes, and latkes.

Cuban-Spanish

For an upscale Cuban-Spanish lunch or dinner, head to the **Columbia** (1241 Gulf Blvd., 727/596-8400, www.columbiarestaurant.com, 11:30am-10pm daily, $20-35), which started in Ybor City and now has six locations in Florida. The menu has an excellent Cubano sandwich and *mojo* chicken, as well as great mojitos and sangria. The menu is remarkably large, with plenty of seafood, beef, and chicken dishes, many of them with traditional Spanish preparations. The wine list is excellent, and the *café con leche* is perfection. The dining room is exceptionally elegant, with white tablecloths, large windows that bring in the bright sunlight, exposed dark-wood beams, and tropical plants all around.

Irish

Evening partying is found all around, in tiki huts and outdoor decks along the Gulf beaches. One bar is worth mentioning: ★ **O'Keefe's Tavern and Grill** (1219 S. Fort Harrison Ave., 727/442-9034, 11am-11pm daily, $7-14), the bar to beat for St. Patrick's Day. The Irish pub's history goes back to the

1960s when it was O'Keefe's Tap Room. A white brick exterior gives way to a comfortable series of rooms decked out with lots of green accents and Irishobilia. The brogue-required bartenders are fast and furious with the beers (there are more than 100 offerings), and the all-ages crowd is unified by their affection for the place. Once known for its "seven-course Irish dinner" (that's six beers and a potato), O'Keefe actually serves good food.

Seafood

By the way, a cooter is a red-bellied turtle that was historically serious eats for early Floridians. That's why **Cooters Restaurant and Bar** (423 Poinsettia Ave., 727/462-2668, www.cooters.com, 11am-11pm Sun.-Thurs., 11am-midnight Fri.-Sat., $9-20) bears that name. It's a fun place with good steamed crab legs and fried grouper.

DUNEDIN
American

On the bike path that runs through the center of town, **Café Alfresco** (344 Main St., 727/736-4299, www.cafealfresco.com, 11am-9pm Mon.-Thurs., 9am-10pm Fri.-Sat., 9am-9pm Sun., $12-20) is a perfect stop during a long walk or peddle. They serve a broad range of American, Asian, Italian, and seafood selections for lunch and dinner. With options that include gumbo, egg rolls, meatloaf, chicken curry, and Hawaiian salad, there's really something for everyone, and the food is wonderful. They have a popular brunch Friday-Sunday. The best seating, true to the café's name, is outdoors on the large and covered patio.

Grab a bite and a brew at **Dunedin Brewery** (937 Douglas Ave., 727/736-0606, www.dunedinbrewery.com, 11am-11pm Sun.-Tues., 11am-1am Wed.-Thurs., 11am-2am Fri.-Sat., $7-10), a local microbrewery with a large list of original crafts. The most popular drink is the apricot peach ale. Enjoy a casual lunch or dinner with a menu that features salads, wraps, tacos, burritos, burgers, and sandwiches. Live music happens on most weekends and sometimes on Thursday. Happy hour is 4pm-7pm daily.

Just as family-friendly, **Kelly's Restaurant** (319 Main St., 727/736-5284, 8am-10pm Sun.-Thurs., 8am-11pm Fri.-Sat., $8-20) has a comfort food menu that leaves no stone unturned, from baby back ribs to butternut squash ravioli. It's a kids kind of joint: friendly and accommodating.

Asian

In Dunedin since 1993, **Ivory Chinese Bistro** (2192 Main St., 727/734-3998, 11am-9:30pm Mon.-Thurs., 11am-10pm Fri.-Sat., $8-25) has slowly accrued a wall's worth of accolades and "best of" awards along with its devoted clientele. Crisp linens and Chinese floral prints make the place feel more formal, but the menu reads like a greatest-hits list of Cantonese American dishes. That means hot and sour soup, juicy pork spareribs, sweet-tangy orange beef, and pan-fried *chow fun* noodles.

Mexican

Downtown Dunedin has been reinvigorated with restaurants and cafés in recent years. For casual Mexican, go to **Casa Tina** (365 Main St., 727/734-9226, 11am-10pm Sun.-Thurs., 11am-11pm Fri.-Sat., $7-15). It's lively, with an eye-catching color scheme, and the food is a little less heavy than many local Mexican joints—that said, try the wild mushroom quesadilla.

Seafood

A fun place to casually dine in Pinellas County is **Bon Appétit** (148 Marina Plaza, 727/733-2151, 11:30am-9pm Sun.-Thurs., 11:30am-10pm Fri.-Sat., $12-35). It's in the Best Western Yacht Harbor Inn and Suites, and the seafood-heavy menu includes grilled sea scallops with a mango chutney or the season's freshest stone crabs with only a squeeze of lemon and butter. Dine at the **Marine Café** adjacent to the restaurant to watch the dolphins play as the sun sets on the water without breaking the bank. It's a different menu from the fancier Bon Appétit, but a single sheet of signature dishes from the main restaurant is available outside.

GREATER PINELLAS COUNTY

Fine Dining

In keeping with the glitz of the historic Vinoy, its restaurant, **Marchand's Grill** (Vinoy Renaissance Resort, 501 5th Ave. NE, St. Petersburg, 727/824-8072, 6:30am-2:30pm and 5pm-10pm Mon.-Sat., 9am-2pm and 5pm-10pm Sun., $18-35), features the central Vinoy Bar with velvet armchairs around the tables. A small wine cellar provides an intimate dining space for four. The kitchen has a seafood focus, but dishes reflect a Mediterranean approach. If you want to pull out all the stops at the Vinoy, **Fred's Steakhouse** is even more of a splurge, but you have to be a member or a resort guest to enjoy it.

The ★ **Cafe Ponte** (13505 Icot Blvd., Clearwater, 727/538-5768, www.cafeponte.com, 11:30am-2pm and 5:30pm-9pm Mon.-Thurs., 11:30am-2pm and 5:30pm-10pm Fri., 5:30pm-10pm Sat., $12-32) features chef Christopher Ponte, who trained at Taillevent in Paris and studied at Johnson & Wales and the Cordon Bleu. His upscale restaurant in the Icot Center is located in a strip mall; the setting may confound would-be diners, but a single meal will set them straight. The kitchen prepares offerings such as a rich mushroom soup with a spoon of truffle cream and a potato-crusted sea bass.

Maritana Grille at the Don CeSar (3400 Gulf Blvd., St. Pete Beach, 727/360-1882, www.loewshotels.com, 5:30pm-10pm daily, $18-40) has a great chef's table for groups up to eight, at which executive chef Kenny Hunsberger is put through his Floribbean-cuisine paces, from pan-seared scallops served with purple potatoes to grilled filet mignon with truffled mashed potatoes and candied shallots. The restaurant's interior is incredible, with the patrons surrounded by 1,500 gallons of saltwater aquariums and indigenous Florida fish.

Seafood

If you're a fan of Jimmy Buffett, check out the restaurant owned by his sister—**Lulu's Oyster Bar and Tap House** (500 1st St., Indian Rocks Beach, 727/333-7944, www.lulusoysterbar.com, 11am-10pm daily, $6-12). The prices are low and the atmosphere is bright, tropical, and whimsical with a classic Old Florida diner feel. The menu is mostly seafood, steak, tacos, and burgers with a few Southern favorites like fried chicken. The seafood is fresh and the shrimp and oysters are prepared blackened, grilled, fried, or beer battered.

Seabreeze Island Grill (17855 Gulf Blvd., 727/498-8688, 11am-10pm Sun.-Thurs., 11am-midnight Fri.-Sat., $9-21) offers great water views from every seat indoors and on the wraparound deck outside. The atmosphere is upbeat and beachy. The menu features burgers, tacos, steaks, and lots and lots of seafood prepared in a Key West and Caribbean style. Try the coconut shrimp, crab cakes, rum-pineapple chicken, lobster mac and cheese, or the grouper tacos. It's also a good place just to grab a cold beer or a tropical cocktail and enjoy the sunset.

Crabby Bill's (401 Gulf Blvd., Indian Rocks Beach, 727/595-4825, www.crabbybillsirb.com, 7am-2am daily, $8-22) is a family-owned regional chain that has made a name for itself with family-style seating, group singing, seafood cookery, and flowing beverages.

Salt Rock Grill (19325 Gulf Blvd., Indian Shores, 727/593-7625, www.saltrockgrill.com, 4pm-10pm Mon.-Thurs., 4pm-11pm Fri.-Sat., noon-10pm Sun., $15-30) is fairly mobbed every night. The menu has enticing seafood, like pan-seared scallops and mussels in white wine sauce, as well as expertly prepared steaks aged in-house and grilled over a super-hot natural oak and citrus wood pit fire. It's more formal than most beachside spots around here, and the locals love it.

Accommodations

DOWNTOWN ST. PETERSBURG
$100-200

Especially for romance seekers, The **Mansion Inn** (105 5th Ave. NE, 727/289-2121, www.mymansioninn.com, $130-230) has 12 rooms in two Craftsman-style houses, one of which is thought to have been built 1901-1904 by St. Petersburg's first mayor, David Mofett. A courtyard between the houses is perfect for a little reading or downtime. The pool on the property is a plus.

The boutique **Hollander Hotel** (421 4th Ave. N., 727/873-7900, www.hollanderhotel.com, $150-200) is in an excellent location downtown. There are queen and king rooms with a balcony option and king and queen suites with a sleeper sofa and an optional full kitchen. The heated pool area is beautiful and full of comfy loungers, chairs, and cabanas.

There's a small and stylish bar, a coffee shop, a bakery, and a wonderful restaurant on-site.

Find a bit of boutique charm at the **Inn on Third** (342 3rd Ave. N., 727/894-3248, www.theinnonthird.com, $90-150). This small hotel, in the heart of downtown, has traditional and stylish decor. The downtown trolley stops right outside the front door, so you'll have convenient access to all of downtown. Many of the rooms have four-poster beds and antique furnishings, and there is a delicious complimentary breakfast in the morning. This cute inn is a top choice for budget travelers.

Over $300

★ **The Vinoy Renaissance Resort & Golf Club** (501 5th Ave. NE, 727/894-1000, www.

1: TradeWinds Island Resorts 2: The Vinoy Renaissance Resort & Golf Club

renaissancehotels.com, $250-600) was built by Pennsylvania oilman Aymer Vinoy Laughner in 1925. At $3.5 million, the Mediterranean Revival-style hotel was the largest construction project in Florida's history. Painstakingly restored in 1992 at a cost of $93 million, the resort is incredible, with 360 guest rooms and 15 suites, many with views of the marina. The hotel also has a spa, a lovely pool, five restaurants, tennis courts, and an 18-hole golf course designed by Ron Garl. It hosts its own marina and is listed on the National Register of Historic Places.

ST. PETE BEACH
$100-200

The best value on the beach is **Gulf Tides Inn** (600 68th Ave., 727/367-2979, www.gulftidesinn.com, studios $89, $650 weekly, $2,350 monthly, apartments $109, $650 weekly, $2,350 monthly). This small motel has 10 units, either one-bedrooms or studios. All rooms are equipped with a full kitchen. There's nothing fancy about the place, but it has an Old Florida charm that gives it a retro feel. The inn is on a quiet street, and there's a heated pool.

For families, the **TradeWinds Island Resorts** (5500 Gulf Blvd., 727/367-6461, www.tradewindsresort.com) is the way to go, with a variety of lodging at the **TradeWinds Island Grand** ($150-450) and the new **Guy Harvey Outpost** ($125-200), formerly the Sandpiper Hotel and Suites. Whichever one you choose includes playtime privileges at the other. The Island Grand is the fancier, a four-diamond property with soaring palms and a grand lobby. The whole complex offers multiple pools, a dozen places to eat and drink, multiple fitness centers, tennis courts, a pedal-boat canal, and a wide private beach. Right out back you can rent fishing or snorkeling equipment and try parasailing, waterskiing, and water scooters. The tremendous kids program, KONK (Kids Only, No Kidding!), has seasonal programs. For adults there is lively nightlife at the many bars and restaurants and an on-site Beef O'Brady's Sports Bar.

★ **Sirata Beach Resort** (5300 Gulf Blvd., 727/363-5100, www.sirata.com, $140-350) used to be connected to the TradeWinds but is now a family-run hotel with a range of kids programs and activities. It's the kind of place that locals take the family for a weekend of R&R. Of the 382 rooms, 170 are one-bedroom suites, and most have excellent views of the Gulf. The kid-friendly suites have bunk beds and entertainment centers that include video game consoles. Suites with jetted tubs are available. Enjoy the three beachfront pools and two hot tubs, as well as a relaxing beachside fire pit area.

Nearby, the ★ **Alden Beach Resort** (5900 Gulf Blvd., 727/360-7081, www.aldenbeachresort.com, $125-250), a beach resort with 149 suites, is especially favored by kids. It has tennis, volleyball, two heated pools (it's a little far from the beach, so the walk takes time for little ones), a hot tub, and an arcade. Rooms on the pool side are significantly cheaper than on the Gulf side. Consider staying in a one-bedroom suite with a kitchenette and water views.

The **Coconut Inn** (113 11th Ave., 941/367-1305, www.pagbeachinns.com, $155-365, $1,000-2,200 weekly) is a charming non-chain option on the southern end of Pass-a-Grille Beach, just a short walk from the beach. There's a small heated pool and bikes to use. Some of the rooms are small, so ask about room size. Many of the rooms on the second floor have nice balconies that overlook the pool, but they're pricier.

$200-300

Inn on the Beach (1401 Gulf Way, 727/240-2614, www.innonbeach.com, $200-450) is a charming and beautiful Florida seaside inn. In addition to the rooms and suites at the inn, you can rent a one- or two-bedroom cottage with a patio, a full kitchen, and a living room. The rooms and cottages are bright and airy, painted in white with stylish accents. The inn surrounds a palm tree-filled courtyard, and the beach is just steps away across the road.

Over $300

For something more upscale, the huge, unmistakably pink **Don CeSar Hotel** (3400 Gulf Blvd., 727/360-1881, www.doncesar.com, $250-550) is a landmark in St. Pete. Originally opened in 1928, the property was commandeered during World War II and eventually abandoned. These days, it's a Loews hotel, with 340 lovely rooms, fishing, golfing, tennis, and the soothing Beach Club & Spa. Even if you don't stay here, take the tour and visit its old-fashioned ice cream parlor.

CLEARWATER
$100-200

In the heart of Clearwater Beach, **Frenchy's Oasis Motel** (423 East Shore Dr., 727/446-6835, www.frenchysoasismotel.com, $139-199, $805-1,095 weekly) is a boutique motel with a mid-century Florida vibe. There are 15 one- or two-bedroom units, each with a full kitchen. It's a short walk to the beach, and there are excellent restaurants, shops, and nightlife nearby. The best rooms, on the second floor at the back of the motel, have elevated views of the bay.

An excellent value for visits a week or more, the **East Shore Resort** (473 E. Shore Dr., 727/442-3636, www.eastshoreresort.com, $735-1,500 weekly, $2,500-4,600 monthly) is located on Clearwater Bay. The beach is a five-minute walk. There are 11 one- and two-bedroom units with full kitchens and private porches. There's a heated pool, bikes, and fishing gear to use on their pier. Boats up to 65 feet can dock at the marina for an additional fee.

Over $300

For beachfront resort-style accommodations, stay at the **Hyatt Regency Clearwater Beach** (301 South Gulfview Blvd., 727/373-1234, www.hyatt.com, $400-1,300). The rooms are spacious, ranging 600 to 1,100 square feet, and the balconies offer stunning views of the Gulf. All rooms have full kitchens. The pool area is surrounded by fountains and tropical plants and features an elevated view of the Gulf. There's a poolside bar, a spa, a fitness center, and three on-site restaurants.

One of the newest resorts on Clearwater Beach, the **Sandpearl Resort** (500 Mandalay Ave., Clearwater, 727/441-2425, www.sandpearl.com, $250-700) is a 253-room hotel with a full-service spa, upscale dining, 117 condominium units, and 700 feet of Gulf of Mexico beachfront. Rooms have an open airy feel with balconies, high ceilings, and upscale furnishings. The best views are from some of the 50 one- and two-bedroom suites on the top two floors of the resort.

GREATER PINELLAS COUNTY
$100-200

The **Safety Harbor Resort and Spa** (105 N. Bayshore Dr., 727/726-1161, www.safetyharborspa.com, $95-300) claims to contain the Fountain of Youth at the 50,000-square-foot spa and tennis academy. The waters fill three pools and are used in spa treatments. The resort is also home to a tennis academy, a fine-dining restaurant, and an upscale salon. The 174 guest rooms and suites are spacious and offer nice views of Tampa Bay.

Near the airport, the **Hilton Saint Petersburg Carillon Park** (950 Lake Carillon Dr., 727/540-0050, www.hilton.com, $140-220) is 10 minutes' drive to downtown. The boardwalk around Lake Carillon is a wonderful spot for a stroll. The heated outdoor infinity pool is a nice bonus. The beautiful dining room at Luna serves a classic breakfast menu that includes a buffet ($15). For lunch and dinner there are yummy American and Italian entrées.

$200-300

For golfers, **Innisbrook Golf and Spa Resort** (36750 U.S. 19 N., Palm Harbor, 727/942-2000, www.innisbrookgolfresort.com, $120-550) is a 900-acre property just north of Clearwater. It has four top-ranked golf courses, 11 tennis courts, six swimming pools, a children's recreation center, several restaurants, and 60 acres with jogging and cycling trails. All rooms are suites with kitchens. Its Copperhead Golf Course stretches more than 7,300 yards and is home to the PGA Tour's PODS Championship.

VACATION RENTALS

Most of the vacation rentals are found around St. Pete Beach and Clearwater, with the offerings getting thinner the farther you venture away from those two main centers of action. Most rentals in this area are condos that range from the modest to the luxurious, but private homes are available in lesser numbers. Expect to pay $150 to $300 per night, $800 to $2,000 per week. Homes generally cost about 20 percent more. Contact **Florida Beach Rentals** (516 Mandalay Ave., Clearwater, 727/288-2020, www.florida-beachrentals.com), which has extensive offerings throughout the region. For Clearwater rentals, contact **Beach Time Rentals** (800/691-8183, www.beachtimerentals.com).

Information and Services

Clearwater and St. Petersburg are in the **eastern time zone.**

VISITOR INFORMATION

St. Petersburg Area Chamber of Commerce (100 2nd Ave. N., Suite 150, 727/821-4069, www.stpete.com, 8am-5pm Mon.-Fri.) has a decent walk-in site with brochures and maps.

POLICE AND EMERGENCIES

In an emergency, dial 911. For a nonemergency police request, contact the **St. Petersburg Police Department** (1300 1st Ave. N., 727/893-7780).

If you need medical assistance, the area has several large hospitals with good emergency care: **St. Petersburg General Hospital** (6500 38th Ave. N., St. Petersburg, 727/384-1414) and **St. Anthony's Hospital** (1200 7th Ave. N., St. Petersburg, 727/825-1100) in the south of the county, and **Largo Medical Center** (201 14th St. SW, Largo, 727/588-0700) in northern Pinellas County.

Transportation

AIR

The area is served by two midsize, easily traversed airports. **Tampa International Airport** (TPA, 4100 George J. Bean Pkwy., 813/870-8700, www.tampaairport.com) is located just over the bridge and causeway from St. Petersburg and Clearwater and about 30 to 45 minutes from beachfront accommodations. It is served by Air Transat, Air Canada, Alaska, American, British Airways, Cayman Airways, Copa, Delta, Edelweiss Air, Frontier, Icelandair, JetBlue, Lufthansa, Silver, Southwest, Spirit, Sun Country, Swift Air, United, WestJet, and World Atlantic.

You'll probably fly in and out of Tampa, unless you're coming from Canada, but there's also **St. Petersburg-Clearwater International Airport** (PIE, 14700 Terminal Blvd., Clearwater, 727/453-7800), served by Allegiant, Sun Country, Sunwing, and Flair Airlines.

Alamo (800/327-9633), **Avis** (800/831-2847), **Budget** (800/527-0700), **Dollar** (800/800-4000 domestic, 800/800-6000 international), and **National** (800/227-7368) provide rental cars from both airports.

CAR

Pinellas County is easily accessible from major interstate highways along the Midwest (I-75) and Northeast (I-95) corridors, as well as from Orlando (I-4). I-275 serves the western portions of the area, including downtown Tampa, St. Petersburg, and Bradenton. It starts in the south at I-75 in Bradenton and runs through St. Petersburg and Tampa, connected by two major bridges, the Sunshine Skyway in the south and Howard Frankland to the north, before reuniting with I-75 at Lutz. I-75, by contrast, skirts both cities and acts as a bypass to southwest Florida and the Gulf Coast.

Once in Pinellas County, Clearwater is in the north along the Gulf, St. Petersburg is in the south along the bay. To reach St. Petersburg from Clearwater, head south on U.S. 19A, a slow, densely trafficked mess. Farther east, the regular U.S. 19 cuts down through the center of the peninsula to St. Petersburg.

In St. Petersburg, streets are set up in a grid pattern, with avenues running east-west and streets running north-south. Central Avenue divides north and south St. Petersburg, with the numbered avenues on either side—it's tricky, though, as to the left of Central there's 1st Avenue North, to the right it's 1st Avenue South. There are some sections of town that are all one-way streets, so you may make a lot of turns while driving.

From St. Pete Beach all the way up through Clearwater, all you need to know is that Gulf Boulevard (Hwy. 699) runs up the coast and through each little town. The city of Clearwater is on the mainland, but Clearwater Beach is on a barrier island connected by Memorial Causeway.

BUS AND TRAIN

Amtrak (800/872-7245, www.amtrak.com) offers train service in nearby Tampa. Some trains even allow you to bring your car with you. **Greyhound** (727/898-1496, www.greyhound.com) provides regular bus service to St. Petersburg (180 9th St. N., 727/898-1496). If you stay in Clearwater, it's easy to ditch your rental car and use the **Jolley Trolley** (727/445-1200, www.clearwaterjolleytrolley.com, $2.25 per ride, day pass $5) or the **Suncoast Beach Trolley** (727/540-1900, $2.25 per ride, day pass $5, $2.50 seniors, students, disabled, and children) to get around. **Pinellas Suncoast Transit Authority** (727/540-1800, $2.25 per ride, day pass $5, $2.50 seniors, students, disabled, and children) also has a fairly extensive busing system around the city.

The Nature Coast

The Nature Coast, known as "Mother Nature's

theme park," is the rebuttal to Orlando's Disney World. To fish, explore the outdoors, or just relax in a laid-back coastal town, the Nature Coast doesn't disappoint. Nothing here is marketed, packaged, or sanitized. It's rural, with the majority of the area set aside as parkland, preserves, reserves, and animal refuges.

In the weathered fishing villages along the coast and the quaint little inland towns, you'll see a spiffy fishing boat in every driveway. Residents stay for the affordable living, for the area's easy live-and-let-live tolerance, for the unhurried pace, and—for many, the most important reason—the fish. Visitors come to see manatees, black bears, and wading birds; to catch fish; and to dive, kayak, or simply

Highlights

Look for ★ to find recommended sights, activities, dining, and lodging.

★ **Ellie Schiller Homosassa Springs Wildlife State Park:** Find out why *Scuba Diving* magazine awards this area the Best Place to See Large Animals—the manatee is the goliath in question. See it up close in the underwater "fishbowl" at this wildlife park (page 233).

★ **Nature Coast Canoe and Kayak Trail:** See this area as the Native Americans and early Spanish explorers did, from the seat of a canoe or a kayak along the backwaters of this 20-mile paddling trail (page 237).

★ **Dock Street:** Enjoy the shops, galleries, and restaurants along the wooden boardwalk, then join the pelicans on the pier to watch the sunset (page 243).

★ **Cedar Key Scrub State Reserve:** Walk this rare ecosystem to catch a glimpse of the threatened Florida scrub jay and endangered burrowing owls (page 245).

★ **Offshore Fishing:** With 62 miles of Gulf Coast, 106 miles of rivers, and 19,111 acres of lakes—in Citrus County alone—you'll find lots of trophy fish in these waters, including tarpon, redfish, and bass (page 251).

contemplate the area's wealth of waterways. There are no white-sand beaches crowded with bikini-clad college kids, no swanky nightclubs with throbbing VIP rooms. From north of Clearwater all the way to the Big Bend, where the Florida peninsula tucks west into the Panhandle, there are precious few multiplexes, museums, or cultural attractions.

Bring the fishing rods, bikes, and kayaks. Weeki Wachee, the southernmost town on the Nature Coast, is known for its manatees, paddling, and mermaids. Farther north, launch a boat, canoe, or kayak into the Chassahowitzka and Homosassa Rivers for access to spring-fed tributaries frequented by manatees. The fishing in these rivers is always outstanding. Cedar Key and Steinhatchee on the north end of the Nature Coast are small fishing villages known for their scallops, clams, and fish. Cedar Key is the larger of the two, with a historic downtown that might keep you interested for a day or two. However, it's not the towns themselves that matter most in this angler's paradise, because that's only where you're going to sleep. The rest of the time you'll be out on the water with a paddle or fishing rod in hand and a smile on your face.

PLANNING YOUR TIME

The Nature Coast has 700 square miles of scenic driving. The area is west of I-75 and accessible by north-south U.S. 19, the main highway through the area. From south of Spring Hill, the long corridor runs through small towns with a high number of boat dealers, fishing guides, and bait shops. North of Crystal River, U.S. 19 gets rural, with only the occasional mailbox and long driveway leading back to someone's private slice of heaven. Along the way you'll see ospreys hunting overhead and cross an incredible number of waterways worth exploring. When you are traveling in this area, it is highly recommended to have a boat in tow or a canoe strapped to the roof of the car. It is one thing to see these amazing

rivers, creeks, and bays from the shore, but the experience of getting into a boat and exploring them in depth is not to be missed. This is also the best way to fish.

Weeki Wachee Springs, Homosassa, and **Crystal River** are directly along U.S. 19. To get to any of the little towns perched along the Gulf's edge—**Yankeetown, Cedar Key, Suwannee,** and **Steinhatchee,** from south to north—you have to drive west on rural two-lane roads. None of these can be reached one from the other, except by boat or by driving back east, rejoining U.S. 19, and then more driving.

Weeki Wachee Springs is well worth a day trip, especially for families, either as an add-on to seeing Tarpon Springs farther south, or as an addition to a trip to elsewhere on the Nature Coast. Since manatee-viewing is best early in the morning, and fishing trips often disembark early as well, it makes sense to stay over a night in Crystal River or Homosassa. Cedar Key and Steinhatchee, partly because they're harder to get to and partly because they're so charming, are each worth a couple of days of exploration.

Most of the Nature Coast is accessible by car or boat only. There is no public transportation besides two southbound and two northbound Greyhound buses that stop daily in Crystal River and Chiefland—but once you've arrived, you still need a car to get around. Driving in Florida during the summer months can be especially challenging, with periods of heat and humidity and tremendous thunderstorms almost every afternoon. It pays to have your car equipped with a first-aid kit, jumper cables, flashlight with new batteries, a jack, and a cell phone (although cell phone service can be spotty in the more rural communities).

If you happen to be piloting your own small plane, Cedar Key has a single 2,300-foot hard-surfaced runway, but this is uncontrolled airspace. The closest commercial airports are **Gainesville Regional Airport** (GNV, 3880

Previous: kayaking on the Nature Coast; snorkeling on the Crystal River; Steinhatchee Landing Resort

The Nature Coast

NE 39th St., 352/373-0249), approximately one hour away, with flights by American Airlines and Delta, and also one hour away, **Tallahassee International Airport** (TLH, 3300 Capital Circle SW, 850/891-7800), seven miles north of Tallahassee, with flights by American Airlines, Delta, and Silver Airways. **Orlando International Airport** (MCO, 1 Jeff Fuqua Blvd., 407/825-2001) and **Tampa International Airport** (TPA, 4100 George J. Bean Pkwy., 813/870-8700, www.tampaairport.com) are both 1.5 hours by car, and both offer many more commercial flights.

Alamo (800/327-9633), **Avis** (800/831-2847), **Budget** (800/527-0700), **Dollar** (800/800-4000 domestic, 800/800-6000 international), and **National** (800/227-7368) all provide rental cars from these airports.

Weeki Wachee to Crystal River

Florida is home to 700 freshwater springs, 33 of them first magnitude, meaning they discharge at least 100 cubic feet of water per second. Several of these first-magnitude springs are along the Nature Coast, and they are a huge draw for swimmers, divers, and paddlers. One of the most popular is Weeki Wachee Springs, where you'll find an underwater mermaid show that's the kind of Old Florida attraction that makes people misty-eyed about the good old days. After nearly faltering, Weeki Wachee was added to the state park system in 2008. Let's hope that saves those mermaids well into the future.

Farther north, manatees are a main attraction. Local cynics refer to these gentle mammals as "cash cows," and indeed the sea cows bring in a sizable revenue stream to the little towns of Homosassa and Crystal River. Upward of 400 West Indian manatees make this their winter home, drawn by the warm waters of the seven spring-driven rivers that meet here at the Gulf of Mexico. Were it not

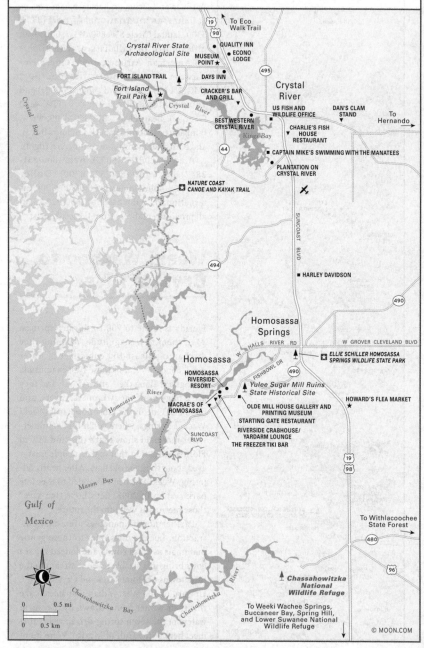

Homosassa to Crystal River

To Eco Walk Trail

19
98

Crystal River State Archaeological Site

QUALITY INN
ECONO LODGE
MUSEUM POINT ★
DAYS INN

495

Crystal River

FORT ISLAND TRAIL

Fort Island Trail Park ★

Crystal River

CRACKER'S BAR AND GRILL

US FISH AND WILDLIFE OFFICE

DAN'S CLAM STAND

To Hernando

Crystal Bay

BEST WESTERN CRYSTAL RIVER

Kings Bay

CHARLIE'S FISH HOUSE RESTAURANT

44

CAPTAIN MIKE'S SWIMMING WITH THE MANATEES

PLANTATION ON CRYSTAL RIVER

NATURE COAST CANOE AND KAYAK TRAIL

SUNCOAST BLVD

494

HARLEY DAVIDSON

490

Homosassa Springs

W HALLS RIVER RD

W GROVER CLEVELAND BLVD

ELLIE SCHILLER HOMOSASSA SPRINGS WILDLIFE STATE PARK

Homosassa

River

FISHBOWL DR

490

HOMOSASSA RIVERSIDE RESORT

Yulee Sugar Mill Ruins State Historical Site

HOWARD'S FLEA MARKET ★

Homosassa River

MACRAE'S OF HOMOSASSA

OLDE MILL HOUSE GALLERY AND PRINTING MUSEUM

STARTING GATE RESTAURANT

SUNCOAST BLVD

RIVERSIDE CRABHOUSE/ YARDARM LOUNGE

THE FREEZER TIKI BAR

19
98

Mason Bay

Gulf of Mexico

To Withlacoochee State Forest

480

96

0   0.5 mi

0   0.5 km

Chassahowitzka Bay

Chassahowitzka River

Chassahowitzka National Wildlife Refuge

To Weeki Wachee Springs, Buccaneer Bay, Spring Hill, and Lower Suwanee National Wildlife Refuge

© MOON.COM

for the manatees, both towns would still be on the map as fishing destinations. The area's anglers and manatee advocates make uneasy bedfellows, however: Many anglers feel that overzealous Save the Manatee legislation has put unnecessary restrictions on boating here.

Older than Crystal River, Homosassa has more charm and the greater reputation as a fishing draw. This rural area has developed a mighty reputation among sporting enthusiasts, who are drawn to the region for the beautiful rivers, unmanicured wilderness, paddling, diving, and fishing.

SIGHTS

★ Ellie Schiller Homosassa Springs Wildlife State Park

Manatees, so famous in these parts, can weigh up to 2,000 pounds and are often seen feasting on algae and barnacles. You'll catch sight of them most often during cooler months, December-March, in the Suwannee River or at Manatee or Fanning Springs State Parks. From boat or shore, look for swirly "footprints" on the water's surface or torpedo-like shapes ambling across the shallow bottom. If you want a guaranteed viewing, stop into **Ellie Schiller Homosassa Springs Wildlife State Park** (4150 S. Suncoast Blvd., Homosassa, 352/628-5343, 9am-5:30pm daily, $13 adults, $5 ages 6-12), where you can see these marine mammals several ways. Visitors are loaded onto pontoon boats and shuttled through the canopied headwaters of the Homosassa River to a refuge for injured manatees and other animals. Alternatively, at 11:30am, 1:30pm, and 3:30pm daily, a manatee program allows you to watch guides wade out to feed stubby carrots to a slow-moving swarm of these creatures, many etched with outboard motor scars from run-ins with boats. Afterward you can walk down to the glass-fronted Fishbowl Underwater Observatory and see eye-to-eye with the gentle giants and the park's other indigenous aquatic creatures. Mysteriously, the park hosts a hippo named Lu—a washed-up animal actor—that former governor Lawton Chiles declared an honorary Florida citizen.

Yulee Sugar Mill Ruins and Vicinity

David Levy Yulee brought the railroad to Cedar Key in 1860 and put Cedar Key on the map. He was the state's first U.S. senator in 1845, and by 1851 his mill on the Homosassa River employed more than 1,000 people, producing sugar, syrup, and molasses. Yulee was imprisoned briefly for siding with the Confederacy during the Civil War, and his mill was permanently closed. Now the **Yulee Sugar Mill Ruins State Historical Site** (352/795-3817, 8am-sunset daily, free) is hardly more than a huge stone chimney and the bones of a partially restored 40-foot-long structure that houses steam boilers, crushing machinery, and large cooking kettles. Visitors walk on a short path through the six-acre site with interpretive plaques, and there is a small nearby picnic area with grills. To reach the site, take U.S. 19 to the town of Homosassa Springs, then turn west onto County Road 490 (Yulee Dr.). Proceed 2.5 miles to the park.

If the Yulee Sugar Mill doesn't sound like enough to make you detour from U.S. 19, right down the block is a nice museum-café called the **Olde Mill House Gallery & Printing Museum** (10466 W. Yulee Dr., 352/628-1081, 10am-3pm Tues.-Sat., tours by appointment, free). Presided over by Jim Anderson, the little museum explores the history of printing, focusing on the letterpress era. The café sells tasty authentic Cubano sandwiches and black beans and rice. For even more return on your mileage investment, continue west on County Road 490 a short distance to **Historic Old Homosassa,** a collection of craft and gift shops, restaurants, and one of the oldest residential communities on Florida's Gulf Coast.

Crystal River State Archaeological Site

In 200 BC, this was a happening spot. Florida's Native Americans came from all over to bury their dead and to participate in ceremonies and trade activities. Archaeologists estimate that, for 1,600 years, roughly 7,500 people visited these 14 acres every year. Today, **Crystal**

Mermaid Tales

The job requirements are tough: a winning smile, powerful athleticism, and a great body. Now add to that the ability to hold one's breath for 2.5 minutes. Florida is home to a variety of rare aquatic creatures, but perhaps none as singular as the 20 mermaids and mermen who swim through their daily choreographed show at Weeki Wachee Springs (6131 Commercial Way, Spring Hill, 352/592-5656, 9am-5:30pm daily, $13 adults, $8 ages 6-12, includes admission to Buccaneer Bay). Weeki Wachee is open year-round, but Buccaneer Bay is closed during the winter months, September-mid-March.

the mermaid show at Weeki Wachee Springs

More than 170 million gallons of 72°F water pour dramatically into the Weeki Wachee River daily. In 1947, former U.S. Navy frogman Newton Perry made the springs more attractive by adding a school of beautiful mermaids. He taught a group of powerful swimmers to breathe through submerged air hoses supplied by an air compressor, resulting in a remarkable 30- to 45-minute underwater extravaganza. Conceived in the heyday of MGM's trademark aquatic musical spectaculars starring Esther Williams, the show at Weeki Wachee Springs is a family affair. These bathing beauties perform in a show that usually draws from past Disney movies such as, unsurprisingly, *The Little Mermaid* and *Pocahontas*.

The audience sits in a small underground amphitheater in front of a four-inch-thick plate-glass window, behind which the blue waters of the springs teem with fish, turtles, eels, and women in oversize shimmering tails who twirl, undulate, and lip synch on cue. Many of the mermaids have been with the show for decades, which can be ascertained with a look through photos and memorabilia in the small Mermaid Museum (a wall of fame includes early sea nymphs cavorting with Elvis and Don Knotts), opened to commemorate the show's 50th anniversary in 1997. For a truly wonderful record of the attraction's history, pick up a copy of Lu Vickers's *Weeki Wachee, City of Mermaids: A History of One of Florida's Oldest Roadside Attractions*, if only for the historic pictures.

After getting your picture taken with a mermaid, it's off to the rest of the 200-acre family entertainment park, Florida's only natural spring water park. This includes a flume ride at Buccaneer Bay, a low-key Birds of Prey show, a petting zoo, and a jungle river cruise.

River State Archaeological Site (3400 N. Museum Point, Crystal River, 352/795-3817, park 8am-sunset daily, visitors center 9am-5pm daily, $3 per vehicle) is still hosting visitors to the banks of the Crystal River. They come to see the six mounds built by what are now referred to prosaically as the pre-Columbian mound builders. After viewing an eight-minute interpretive video and seeing the small museum's exhibit chronicling the archaeological excavations begun in 1903, you'll be better equipped to walk a paved 0.5-mile loop and marvel at the mounds, studded with shells, bones, jewelry, and pottery from early civilizations. The park also has an interesting dugout canoe exhibit and a Sifting for Technology interactive exhibit. With the latter, there are biweekly programs for the general public in which participants use sifting screens and other archaeological tools to recover artifacts from the spoils of a dredged boat slip.

1: a manatee in its winter home in the Crystal River-Homosassa area. **2:** Yulee Sugar Mill Ruins State Historical Site

1

2

Fishing for the Silver King

Any fly fisher will tell you that Homosassa is the place to catch tarpon, "the silver king." This little Old Florida town is where the big tarpon congregate, for reasons unknown. The current world record—202.8 pounds—was caught right here. But you won't find annual tarpon tournaments broadcast on ESPN. It's a low-key endeavor, with patience often yielding nothing but sunburn. On any given day, you'll see the river dotted with 25 or 30 flat boats navigated with push poles in a hushed silence of profound concentration, everyone waiting to see one roll along the surface in water depths of 5-25 feet. People come from all over the world to the Nature Coast to sight-fish for these behemoths before releasing them gently into the warm, clear water.

fishing on the Nature Coast

Regulations changed in 2013, and now only hook and line is allowed for tarpon fishing. Several other new rules have been adopted; keep up to date at the **Florida Fish and Wildlife website** (www.myfwc.com). Tarpon begin to run the last weeks of April and fade out in July. What many consider the Super Bowl of fishing, tarpon fishing requires a special $50 tag to keep one, along with some serious know-how. The initial jumps and runs of that hooked fish are very exciting.

If you want to try your hand at chasing giant tarpon on the Gulf or in the backwaters from Homosassa to Cedar Key, try **Captain Rick LeFiles** (Osprey Guide Services, 6115 Riverside Dr., Yankeetown, 352/400-0133, $350 for a day of inshore fishing for reds and trout, $450 for tarpon) or fourth-generation Homosassa **Captain William Toney** (352/422-4141, www.homosassainshorefishing.com, half-day $350, full-day $450 for 1-2 people, $50 each additional person).

SPORTS AND RECREATION

Buccaneer Bay

If you've been entranced by the lip-synching mermaids of Weeki Wachee Springs, you'll be inspired to try some of your own aquatic tricks at the adjacent **Buccaneer Bay Waterpark** (6131 Commercial Way, Spring Hill, 352/592-5656, 9am-5pm Sat.-Sun. mid-Mar.-May and mid-Aug.-Sept., 9am-5pm daily June-mid-Aug., $13 adults, $8 ages 6-12, free under age 6). The admission cost covers both the water park and Weeki Wachee Springs State Park. Pure cold springwater laps against a tiny white-sand beach while families zoom down the flume rides and waterslides or hang out on the floating dock. It's a safe place to let kids roam free (lots of strict eagle-eyed lifeguards make sure of that), and when they're exhausted, you can trot off to the riverboat cruise, petting zoo, and sweet animal show. Weeki Wachee Springs also hosts two-day **mermaid camps** (352/592-5656, ext. 30, $300), in which kids are taught the finer points of mermaidhood.

When you're ready to get away from the crowds, head for the rear of the water park parking lot and follow the arrows for **Paddling Adventures** (352/597-8484, $35 single-seat kayak, $40 two-seat kayak or canoe). It takes about three hours to paddle this serene stretch of the Weeki Wachee River, and when you've finished, they'll pick you up and bring you back upstream by van. Bring lunch or a beverage: There are spots along the river where you can hop out on a sandy beach, swim, and relax.

Golf

Golfers will be tempted to sneak away while their families visit Weeki Wachee Springs. The big kahuna of courses in these parts is the famous Tom Fazio-built **World Woods** (17590 Ponce de Leon Blvd., Brooksville, 352/796-5500, www.worldwoods.com, greens fees $35-120), just minutes away in Brooksville. It's a 45-hole complex with challenges for every golfer. Begin the day warming up on one of the hugest driving ranges you've ever laid eyes on (23 acres). From there you can bone up on the nine-hole short course featuring seven par 3's and two par 4's, and then attempt either the 18-hole Pine Barrens, modeled after the great Pine Valley, or the stately and refined Rolling Oaks parkland course, an homage to Augusta National.

Swimming with the Manatees

The West Indian manatee is listed as an endangered species, but the population has rebounded tremendously in the past few years in this area. Manatee season is mid-October-March, but you'll spot them all year long. Kings Bay in Crystal River has the densest concentration, but the Blue Waters area of the Homosassa River is less trafficked by boats and thus quieter. You can swim with these gentle mammals from the distance that suits you (up close, their size is unsettling—just remember they are herbivores, with blunt teeth so far back in their heads that you could, were it legal, safely hand-feed them). **Manatee Tour & Dive** (267 NW 3rd St., Crystal River, 352/795-1333, www.manateetouranddive.com, tour $45-55, gear $20-30) offers two-hour manatee swim and snorkeling trips suitable for the whole family in the waters of Crystal River, and scuba trips in Crystal Springs and Kings Spring, an underwater cavern praised for its excellent visibility, size, and potential for underwater photography (thousands of saltwater fish congregate at the cavern's two exits).

Captain Mike's Swimming with the Manatees (1610 SE Paradise Circle, 352/571-1888, www.swimmingwiththemanatees.com, $20-99) has a similar range of guided ecotourism escapades in Homosassa. If a manatee swim and snorkel tour doesn't sound like a good way to take to the waters, you can try your hand at scalloping (July-Sept. 25), or just enjoy a boat ride to follow the river out to the Gulf of Mexico.

Canoeing, Kayaking, and Boating

During the warm months, when manatees are a scarce elsewhere in Crystal River and Homosassa, head to **Chassahowitzka National Wildlife Refuge** (1502 Southeast Kings Bay, 352/563-2088, 8am-sunset daily, free), south of Homosassa, accessible from County Road 480 off U.S. 19, where they seem to congregate. During the colder months, you're likely to spot endangered whooping cranes that make this their winter home. There are no walking trails at the refuge, but there is a small visitors center that will quickly connect you with a commercial boat tour or rental. The 30,500 acres of saltwater bays, estuaries, and brackish marshes are home to nearly 250 species of birds, 50 species of reptiles and amphibians, and at least 25 species of mammals. You can't camp here, but several miles east of the refuge is **Chassahowitzka River Campground** (8600 W. Miss Maggie Rd., 352/382-2200, www.chassahowitzkaflorida.com, $23), which has a nice canoe and boat launch of its own, as well as tent and RV camping. The sites are spacious, and the campground gives you excellent access to fishing and paddling the river.

★ NATURE COAST CANOE AND KAYAK TRAIL

This trail is 17 miles long, beginning in the north on the Salt River, about one mile west of the town of Crystal River, near the Marine Science Station on Highway 44. Follow the markers on the Salt River south to the Homosassa River. From here, the trail goes

east on the Homosassa River a few hundred feet to a little stretch of water called Battle Creek, and then it jags to the south through Seven Cabbage Cut to the mouth of the Chassahowitzka River. The calm, protected waters of this estuarine ecosystem, part of the Great Florida Birding Trail, are home to ospreys, cormorants, wood storks, and loads of other wading birds.

For paddling tours, go to **Aardvark's Florida Kayak Company** (707 N. Citrus Ave., Crystal River, 352/795-5650, www.floridakayakcompany.com, $50-185, Wed.-Sun. or by appointment). For kayak rentals, **Crystal River Kayak Company and Dive Center** (1422 SE U.S. 19, Crystal River, 352/795-2255, www.crystalriverkayakcompany.com, $25-65) offers kayak or canoe rental, as well as excellent tours on Crystal River, Bennet's Creek, and Kings Bay.

Birding

The area's salt marshes, hammocks, uplands, forest and prairie, freshwater marshes, swamps, lakes, and rivers provide a variety of habitats, which in turn draw a variety of birds. Hundreds of bird species call this area home, and birders can observe them boating along waterways, driving trails, and walking trails all over Citrus County. Roseate spoonbills, great blue herons, ibis, and other wading birds; ospreys, bald eagles, and other birds of prey; shorebirds, wetland birds, and beach birds are all on view. March-May is a good time to see colorful mating plumage. One of the largest undeveloped river delta-estuarine systems in the United States, the **Lower Suwannee National Wildlife Refuge** (County Rd. 347, 16 miles west of U.S. 19, 352/493-0238) was established in 1979 in an effort to protect and maintain a rare ecosystem. The park is bisected by the Suwannee River, its tributary creeks fringed with majestic cypress (this part is best seen from the one-mile River Trail). Be sure to visit the upland area dotted with scrub oak and pine, and then explore some of the 26-mile stretch of tidal marshes along the Gulf.

Birders also gravitate to the **Withlacoochee Bay Trail** (Sunset Parkway Rd., east from U.S. 19, 352/236-7143), a five-mile walking trail from Felburn Park Trailhead to the Gulf. The child-friendly, two-mile loop **Eco Walk Trail** (5990 N. Tallahassee Rd., 352/563-0450) can be reached by taking U.S. 19 north to just before Seven Rivers Regional Medical Center, then turning left onto Curtis Tool Road for the Eco Walk Trailhead, which is at the intersection of Curtis Tool and Tallahassee Road. **Fort Island Trail** (Fort Island Trail, 5 miles west of U.S. 19) is a flat, paved, nine-mile trail that ends at Fort Island Trail Beach. All of these parks are open 8am-sunset, and admission is free.

Motorcycling

If you need a break from all that outdoor activity, hop on a hog and play *Easy Rider* at the **Harley-Davidson Shop of Crystal River** (1785 S. Suncoast Blvd., 352/563-9900, 9am-6pm Mon.-Fri., 10am-4pm Sun.).

FESTIVALS AND EVENTS

The average annual temperature along the Nature Coast is 70°F, with an average of 294 days of sunshine. That means it's pretty all year, but you might want to schedule a visit to correspond to one of the local festivals.

In January, Crystal River hosts the three-day **Florida Manatee Festival** (Citrus County Chamber of Commerce, 352/795-3149) with free manatee-sightseeing boat tours, crafts, food, and entertainment. The **Cedar Key Arts Festival** (www.cedarkeyartsfestival.com) in April is known as a hot place to find new talent. It's a big, fun arts show with lots of crafts for sale.

The Homosassa River is home to a number of fishing tournaments worth watching: The annual Homosassa **Cobia Tournament**

1: canoes beside Manatee Springs **2:** pelicans at a dock **3:** Crystal River

(MacRae's Bait and Tackle, 352/628-2602) is in mid-June, and the famous **Southern Redfish Tour** (www.redfishtour.com) comes a few weeks later in July. Cedar Key has a Fourth of July **Cedar Key Old Florida Clamfest** (352/543-5600, www.cedarkey.org) with live music, clam hunts, clam-shucking demonstrations, clam bag races, and so forth.

The third weekend in October, the **Cedar Key Seafood Festival** (352/477-1276, www.cedarkey.org) draws 30,000 people for two days of seafood gluttony (book a room far in advance). On the second weekend in November, the **Homosassa Arts, Crafts, and Seafood Festival** (www.homosassaseafoodfestival.com) whips up chowders and soft-shell crabs for the masses.

SHOPPING

Heavy shoppers will find meager retail options on the Nature Coast. The **Crystal River Mall** (1801 NW U.S. 19, 352/795-2585) has stores such as GNC, the Georgia Meyer Bookstore, and Crystal Rover Mini Putt Putt, and **Cedar Key's Dock Street** is host to the kinds of shell-themed giftware and handicrafts stores found in many little seaside towns.

For a real local bit of excitement, sift through the 300 or so booths at **Howard's Flea Market** (6373 S. Suncoast Blvd., Homosassa Springs, 352/628-3532, 7am-3pm Sat.-Sun.). To safeguard against rain and muggy weather, the market is enclosed, with vendors selling leather goods, antiques, tools, fishing gear, and even pets. A bird aviary and food vendors (good barbecue and excellent old-fashioned root beer) make it fun for the whole family.

FOOD
Weeki Wachee
The town of Spring Hill, where Weeki Wachee Springs is found, has a couple of fun family-friendly places to refuel after a grueling day at the water park. **Richie Cheesesteak** (6191 Deltona Blvd., 352/600-7999, 10am-9pm Mon.-Thurs., 10am-10pm Fri.-Sat.,

$6-10) is the go-to place for lunch sandwiches, hamburgers, and cheesesteaks, of course. **Greek City Cafe** (3125 Commercial Way, 352/683-6606, 11am-9pm daily, $7-10) is a favorite for healthy lunches and dinners of Mediterranean-style salads, pizzas, wraps, and rice bowls.

For something a little nicer, **La Bella Napoli Italian Restaurant** (7390 Shoal Line Blvd., 352/556-5274, 3pm-9pm Tues.-Sun., $12-25) serves up the best Italian food in town. The homemade meatballs, cannoli, and bread rolls are a favorite. The refined atmosphere is fitting for a romantic dinner.

Homosassa
Dan's Clam Stand (7364 W. Grover Cleveland Blvd., 352/628-9588, 11am-8pm Tues.-Sat., $8-15) is no-frills but makes a mean clam chowder, a serviceable lobster roll, and a fine fried grouper sandwich. If you don't love seafood, the buffalo wings are hot and tasty. And **The Starting Gate Restaurant** (10605 W. Yulee Dr., 352/503-2076, 6:30am-noon Fri.-Sun., $8-10) is the place to try the local breakfast: fried cornmeal-crusted mullet with cheese grits.

For nightlife in Homosassa, locals go to **The Freezer Tiki Bar** (5590 S. Boulevard Dr., 352/628-2452, 11:30am-9pm Sun.-Thurs., 11:30am-10pm Sat.-Sun.), attempt a little karaoke at the **Dunbar's Old Mill Tavern** (10465 W. Yulee Dr., 352/628-2669), or have a leisurely riverside beer at **The Shed at MacRae's** (5300 S. Cherokee Way, 352/628-2602).

Locals were dismayed when the memorable **Riverside Crab House** (5297 S. Cherokee Way, 352/621-5080, 11am-9pm Mon.-Thurs., 11am-10pm Fri., 11am-10pm Sat.-Sun., $9-30) was damaged by a hurricane. Thankfully rebuilding is underway. This relaxed and casual joint, specializing in two-foot platters heaped with sweet corn, hush puppies, scallops, soft-shell crab, steamed blue crab, clams, and catfish, is worth a visit. The attached Yardarm Lounge and the outdoor Monkey Bar tiki lounge are great places to spy on the four mostly tame monkeys who live on a tiny island a stone's throw away.

Crystal River

In Crystal River, people tend to send visitors to **Charlie's Fish House Restaurant** (244 NW U.S. 19, 352/795-3949, 11am-9pm daily, $9-16) for the views of the river and the simply prepared local fish, as well as oysters and stone crab claws (you eat only the claws because anglers haul them up, yank off one claw, and throw them back to grow another). The restaurant has a substantial boat dock for waterborne diners.

Cracker's Bar and Grill (502 NW 6th St., 352/795-3999, 11am-10pm daily, $6-13), just up the block, is a local hangout with a commitment to big portions and providing something for everyone. The menu is vast, with burgers, nachos, and such alongside sautéed scallops and shrimp. Live entertainment has things hopping in the tiki bar and on the deck on the weekend, with karaoke many nights. Tie your boat up to one of the restaurant's 14 slips, or hop on the restaurant's water taxi and see some of Kings Bay.

For nightlife, the young folks gather at **Castaway's Bar and Grill** (5430 N. Suncoast Blvd., 352/795-3653, 7:30am-2am daily).

ACCOMMODATIONS

People are drawn to the Nature Coast for a raw view of the natural world. They come with rods and reels, their boats topped with gas and canoes packed to the brim with stocked coolers and camping gear. As a result, this swath of Florida has RV parks, campgrounds, and fish camps that run from rough wooden cabins to affordable simple motels. In the small towns that dot U.S. 19 or the little roads west to the Gulf, you can bet on finding a clean room in a casual independently owned motel, where the amenities are whatever is happening out on the river, bay, or spring.

It in addition, the area provides opportunities to stay on a houseboat. Go "way down upon the Suwannee River" with a 44-foot houseboat rented from **Gateway Marina & Houseboats** (90 SE County Rd. 349, Suwannee, 352/542-7349, www.suwanneehouseboats.com, $599-899 for 2 days, 1,799 per week). Houseboats sleep up to eight and are equipped with showers, toilets, linens, full kitchens, and cookware. The owners take renters on a warm-up cruise to teach them the basics, and then you're on your own with 70 miles of river, countless springs, and an up-close view of the area's wildlife. It's a great way to pretend you're Huckleberry Finn.

Under $100

For RV travelers, there are 398 picturesque sites on 80 acres at **Rock Crusher Canyon RV Resort** (275 S. Rock Crusher Rd., Crystal River, 352/564-9350, www.sunrvresorts.com, $45). It contains a 7,000-seat outdoor amphitheater that has welcomed Willie Nelson, Three Dog Night, and Joan Jett, as well as some humongous RV rallies. Also in Crystal River, with lakeside and canal-side spots that include your own boat dock space, **Crystal Isles Resort** (11419 W. Fort Island Trail, Crystal River, 352/795-3774, $45-75) is a 30-acre RV resort not far from the Fort Island Trail Beach. For inexpensive and pleasant waterside accommodations in Cedar Key, try **Sunset Isle RV Park/Motel** (11850 Hwy. 24, 352/543-5375, www.cedarkeyrv.com, RV campsites from $43, motel rooms from $75).

In Crystal River are many of the inexpensive chains, such as **Best Western Crystal River Resort** (614 NW U.S. 19, Crystal River, 352/795-3171, $80-120), with its own marina and excellent fish and dive shop; **Quality Inn** (4486 N. Suncoast Blvd., Crystal River, 352/563-1500, $60-90); **Days Inn** (2380 NW U.S. 19, Crystal River, 352/795-2111, $55-90); and **Econo Lodge** (2575 NW U.S. 19, Crystal River, 352/795-9447, $55-85). Most cater to visiting anglers with rates around $75, many without amenities beyond a computer in the lobby to check email. For a more authentic experience, spend a little more and head for one of the independently owned places.

The area right around Weeki Wachee Springs has a lot of suburban sprawl, so it isn't the best vacation spot on the Nature Coast, but if you really want to be near this particular spring, the **Quality Inn Weeki Wachee** (9373 Cortez Blvd., 352/596-9000, $80-99) is the best bet, across the street from the spring and its water park, with 116 rooms in a nice two-story building.

$100-200

Homosassa Riverside Resort (5297 S. Cherokee Way, Homosassa, 352/628-2474, www.riversideresorts.com, $65-210) is the oldest resort along the Homosassa River. Many rooms have full kitchens, and the on-site restaurant and lounge are definitely worth a visit. Arrange a manatee awareness tour, kayak and canoe rentals, airboat rides, and other adventures here.

Presided over by Gator MacRae, **MacRae's of Homosassa** (5300 S. Cherokee Way, Homosassa, 352/628-2602, www.macraesofhomosassa.com, $100-150) is the rustic anglers' pick, with a series of log cabin-like squat structures and old-fashioned rockers on the front porches. There are 12 guest rooms and 10 suites with kitchens, and laundry facilities on the premises. Its riverside marina offers boat rentals, a bait shop, and fishing charters.

Also in the "something different" category, **Nature's Resort Campground and Marina** (10359 W. Halls River Rd., Homosassa Springs, 352/628-9544, www.naturesresortfla.com, $120 cabins, $48-58 RV and tent sites) has cabins; several hundred RV campsites; tent camping; canoe, kayak, and pontoon boat rentals; a marina; a country store; hiking trails; a pool; a restaurant; and a marina bar on 97 lush acres along the Halls River. There's a band shell that hosts country and gospel acts when the weather accommodates.

Nice and romantic, **Pine Lodge Country Inn** (649 Hwy. 40 W./Follow That Dream Pkwy., Inglis, 352/447-7463, www.pinelodgefl.com, $110-160) is a bed-and-breakfast with four rooms, built in the 1940s in the natural settings of Inglis. At the Levy County-Citrus County line, it's along the picturesque Withlacoochee River.

The **Izaak Walton Lodge** (6301 Riverside Dr., Yankeetown, 352/447-4899, www.izaakwaltonlodge.com, call for rates) is one of the few reasons to get off U.S. 19 and amble down Highway 40 to Yankeetown. The small inn has a serene setting on the banks of the Withlacoochee River, with dock space where you can tie up your boat. The onsite restaurant, The Riverside Inn, includes a dining room and bar on the first floor and a multitiered dining terrace. The menu has excellent local seafood choices such as oysters Rockefeller and fried gator nuggets along with entrées like New York strip and lobster.

$200-300

The Nature Coast doesn't offer the abundance of golfing opportunities available elsewhere in Florida. If you're jonesing to tee off, the **Plantation on Crystal River** (9301 W. Fort Island Trail, Crystal River, 352/795-4211, www.plantationoncrystalriver.com, $140-325, including greens fees) boasts an 18-hole par-72 championship course and a 9-hole executive course for training and practice, in addition to manatee snorkeling tours, guided scuba diving, and 145 guest rooms (with 12 golf villas and six condos). Given all the amenities and glitz, room rates are reasonable.

TRANSPORTATION

From south to north, Spring Hill (the town of Weeki Wachee Springs), Homosassa, and Crystal River are lined up adjacent to each other along U.S. 19. The 27-mile drive from Spring Hill to Homosassa takes 40 minutes. From Homosassa to Crystal River, the 10-mile drive takes 20 minutes. Two northbound Greyhound buses stop daily in Crystal River, but once you arrive, you still need a car to get around.

Cedar Key

They say in Cedar Key it takes two hours to watch *60 Minutes*. There's only one road in and out of town; there's no movie theater, no Starbucks, and no fast food. In fact, there's no fast anything.

Today, the constellation of tiny islands that juts three miles out into the Gulf of Mexico is inhabited by fewer than 900 year-round residents. Florida's 1995 net ban ended the bustle of commercial fishing fleets. What that leaves are an abundance of birds, fish, and other wildlife; beautiful sunsets; and a profusion of dappled creeks and rivers that flow into the warm Gulf. Recently Cedar Key has become home to a substantial resident artist community, which has brought color to the town. It hasn't lost its casual rough edge, though. It is still the kind of place where the only locals who seem impatient are the pelicans on the Dock Street pier, hoping to steal some angler's unguarded bait stash.

SIGHTS

Southern Cross Sea Farms

You could call Cedar Key "Clamelot": Clamming is a backbreaking, difficult business that requires the salty seadog's perseverance and grit combined with a huge amount of scientific knowledge. The town is the nation's number-one producer of farm-raised littlenecks, available year-round. If you want to learn more, sweet-talk your way into **Southern Cross Sea Farms** (12170 Hwy. 24, Cedar Key, 352/543-5980, www.clambiz.com, 8am-4pm Mon.-Fri., 9am-2pm Sat.-Sun.). They don't give official tours, but if you show an interest, they'll walk you through the process, from the saltwater larva tanks thick with silt (which, under a microscope, hosts millions of perfect clams, each 60 microns in size) to the clam nursery and out to the clam bags sunk in the Gulf, where the bivalves spend 18 months maturing. Interesting clam tidbit: All are born male; at maturity 50 percent become female.

★ Dock Street

Cedar Key is lean on attractions, but that's part of the attraction. Cedar Key is made up of a series of small barrier islands, but the commercial and residential parts of town are clustered on Way Key, where the place to be is Dock Street. The fishing pier is the center of the action, where anglers, pelicans, and onlookers enjoy the sunset over the wide wooden boardwalk. On the weekend live music wafts out from Seabreeze-Big Deck Raw Bar or Steamers, along with the aroma of just-caught seafood. The few blocks of Dock Street on either side of the pier are crowded with gift shops, galleries, restaurants, and bars—a rewarding stroll at any time of day.

Cedar Key Museums

St. Clair Whitman invented tools for the Standard Manufacturing Company in the early 1900s, and he was a persistent collector of antique glassware, old bottles, photographs of Cedar Key, and an incredible number of seashells. The **Cedar Key Museum State Park** (12231 SW 166 Court, 352/543-5350, 10am-5pm Thurs.-Mon., $2), in Whitman's house, restored as it was in its 1920s heyday, displays all his collections. More than just a sweet little museum to see his treasures, exhibits provide insight into the Timucua people who once inhabited this stretch of coast as well as Cedar Key's 19th-century history as a center for manufacturing pencils and fiber brooms and brushes. Docent-led tours are offered 1pm-4pm. Save this for an afternoon when the weather is gloomy or the fish aren't biting.

There are more opportunities to explore Cedar Key history at the **Cedar Key Historical Museum** (609 2nd St., 352/543-5549, 1pm-4pm Sun.-Fri., 11am-5pm Sat., $1 adults, $0.50 children) downtown. Housed in one room of a former private residence built circa 1871, the museum tells the story

Cedar Key

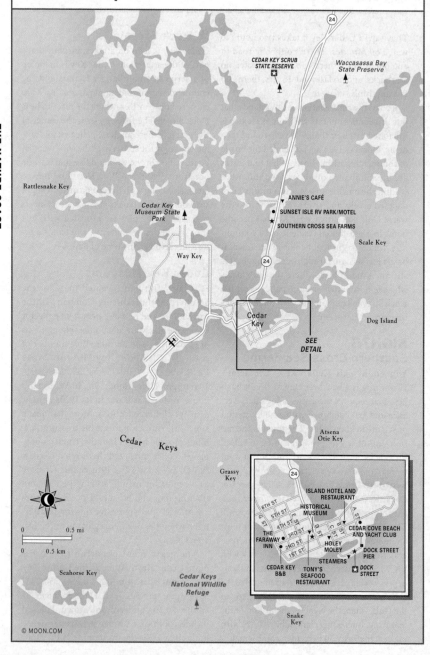

CEDAR KEY SCRUB
STATE RESERVE

Waccasassa Bay
State Preserve

24

Rattlesnake Key

Cedar Key
Museum State
Park

ANNIE'S CAFÉ

SUNSET ISLE RV PARK/MOTEL

SOUTHERN CROSS SEA FARMS

Scale Key

Way Key

24

Dog Island

Cedar
Key

SEE
DETAIL

Atsena
Otie Key

Cedar   Keys

Grassy
Key

24

ISLAND HOTEL AND
RESTAURANT

6TH ST
5TH ST
4TH ST
3RD ST
2ND ST
1ST ST

G ST
F ST
E ST
D ST

HISTORICAL
MUSEUM

C ST
B ST
A ST

CEDAR COVE BEACH
AND YACHT CLUB

THE
FARAWAY
INN

HOLEY
MOLEY

DOCK
STREET
PIER

CEDAR KEY
B&B

TONY'S
SEAFOOD
RESTAURANT

STEAMERS

DOCK
STREET

Seahorse Key

Cedar Keys
National Wildlife
Refuge

Snake
Key

0   0.5 mi

0   0.5 km

© MOON.COM

of Cedar Key through historic photos and an idiosyncratic assortment of memorabilia, as well as displays of Native American artifacts, minerals, and woodworking tools. It's worth checking out, especially if one of the guides is available to talk about the local lumber, pencil, and fishing industries. Although it's a little pricey ($4.50), the brochure for a self-guided historical walking tour of downtown is a great short course on the area.

SPORTS AND RECREATION
★ Cedar Key Scrub State Reserve

See some scrub before it vanishes. Scrub is an austere local plant community characterized by the dominance of shrubs, unlike forests, which are dominated by trees, and prairies by grasses. It is one of the fastest disappearing habitats in Florida. In the wet months, rainwater and wind rush through, cutting channels in the loose soil; when it's dry, fires sweep in and burn the scrub to the ground, after which the shrubs grow again. Extremely hot in summer, the arid sandy terrain is home to the Florida scrub jay and other hardy fauna. **Cedar Key Scrub State Reserve** (Hwy. 24, 6 miles northeast of Cedar Key, 352/543-5567, 8am-sunset daily, free) consists of 12 miles of beautiful marked walking trails. It's dramatic in a quiet way. Pets are welcome on a leash.

Fishing

Cedar Key has lots of ways to make you feel "reel" talented. Freshwater anglers can wet a line in the 3,657-acre **Lake Rousseau/ Withlacoochee River** area to bag bluegill, redear sunfish, catfish, black crappie, or largemouth bass. For saltwater fishing, the waters of **Cedar Keys National Wildlife Refuge** and the **Lower Suwannee National Wildlife Refuge** teem with spotted sea trout, redfish, and sheepshead. And **Waccasassa Bay Preserve State Park** provides both freshwater and saltwater fishing opportunities.

Canoeing, Kayaking, and Boating

Designated a refuge by President Hoover way back in 1929, the **Cedar Keys National Wildlife Refuge** (at the end of Hwy. 24, most islands accessible only by boat, 352/493-0238) encompasses 800 acres and 13 barrier islands in the Gulf of Mexico. The refuge is home to as many as 200,000 birds, making it a hot spot for bird-watchers. To protect the area's wildlife and fragile ecosystems, the refuge is accessible only by boat (time your trip for high tide, otherwise the shallow mud and grass flats can slow your progress), and all of the islands' interiors are closed to the public except Atsena Otie Key, the easiest island to access. You can paddle out from Cedar Key and collect shells, identify birds, picnic, and take pictures year-round. It's worth the effort—egrets, white ibis, cormorants, herons, pelicans, and anhingas make it a genuine avian convention.

Part of Seahorse Key, including the lighthouse, is leased by the University of Florida as a marine research laboratory and classroom. A few days each year, the refuge and university host an open house where the public is invited to visit the lighthouse. Contact the University of Florida Nature Coast Biological Station (www.ncbs.ifas.ufl.edu/openhouse, 352/325-6078) for information on the Seahorse Lighthouse open house dates. A giant kidney-shaped sand dune, Seahorse Key rises to 52 feet, the highest point on the state's west coast. It was a military hospital and detention center for captured Native Americans during the Seminole Wars, with a decommissioned lighthouse that was built in 1855. Visitors, when they are allowed, are asked to pack out anything they take onto the islands and to refrain from removing anything from the island.

Cedar Key Boat Rentals and Island Tours (8070 A St., east end of Dock St., 352/231-4435, 9am-6pm daily, $25 adults, $15 children) can help access the islands. From the **city marina** (352/949-0200) you can also rent pontoon boats, skiffs, kayaks, and canoes. You can also rent canoes and kayaks from **Kayak Cedar Keys** (Cedar Key Beach and

Park, 1st St. and A St., 352/543-9447, www. kayakcedarkeys.com, $25-45), across from the Gulf Kart Company, next to the marina.

If you don't want to go out on your own, **Brack Barker's Wild Florida Adventures** (Williston, 352/215-4396) leads kayak tours from Shell Mound near Cedar Key to the estuaries and coastal islands of the Lower Suwannee National Wildlife Refuge, out to Atsena Otie, exploring the coastal marshes of Steinhatchee, and along the Waccasassa River.

Adjacent to Cedar Key Scrub State Reserve, the **Waccasassa Bay Preserve State Park** (352/543-5567, 8am-sunset daily, free) is also accessible only by boat. Boats can be launched from Highway 40 in Yankeetown, County Rd. 326 in Gulf Hammock, and from Cedar Key. This 32,777-acre coastal wilderness area consists of salt marsh scattered with wooded islands, themselves striated with more than 100 tidal creeks that flow into the estuary. Once here, visitors enjoy fresh- and saltwater fishing, canoeing, primitive camping, and checking out the local population of bald eagles, black bears, and manatees.

Biking

At the turn of the 20th century, steamships won out over the railroad as preferred freight and passenger carriers in this area. As in so many parts of the country, this left miles of abandoned track, which have slowly been repurposed to meet the needs of outdoor enthusiasts. The 32-mile paved **Nature Coast Trail State Park** (U.S. 19, just south of downtown Chiefland, 352/535-5181, 8am-sunset daily, free) links several wildlife and recreation areas, including **Fanning Springs State Park** and **Andrews Wildlife Management Area.** The various trails wind along the Suwannee River, ranging in length from 4.3 miles up to 10 miles, with trailheads in the downtowns of five communities, including Cross City (along U.S. 98), Old Town (adjacent

to the Old Town Fire Station), Fanning Springs (near the Agricultural Inspection Station), Trenton (2 blocks off Main St. at the railroad depot), and Chiefland (near the railroad depot, 2 blocks beyond downtown). This makes it easy to enjoy a ride and finish up with lunch or dinner in one of these sweet inland towns.

Bikes can be rented at **Suncoast Bicycles** (322 N. Pine Ave., Inverness, 352/637-5757, www.suncoastbicycles.com, $15-80). There are also group rides that leave from the store most days, and the store's website contains great local cycling routes. Right downtown in Cedar Key, across from City Park, the **Gulf Kart Company** (A St. at 1st St., 352/543-5090, www.gulfkart.com) rents golf carts that seat 2-6 people ($60 for 2 people full-day, $75 for 4, $100 for 6, $35 for 4 hours for 2 people, $45 for 4), a fun way to move around the island.

FOOD

Cedar Key has a handful of great restaurants, especially when it comes to fresh seafood. **Annie's Café** (Hwy. 24, just over the causeway, 352/543-6141, 6:30am-3:30pm Thurs.-Tues., $4-8) is a local favorite for birdwatching over breakfasts of mullet, grits, sliced tomato, and a freshly made steaming biscuit. Built in 1859, the **Island Hotel and Restaurant** (373 2nd St., 352/543-5111, 5pm-9pm Tues.-Sun., $15-25) is purportedly haunted by 13 ghosts, particularly during grisly weather. Even if you don't believe the story of the restless spirit of a murdered former owner, you'll enjoy the hearts of palm salad, the crab bisque, or just a stop at the friendly bar.

For more upscale waterside dining, head to the **Island Room Restaurant at Cedar Cove** (192 E. 2nd St., 352/543-6520, www. islandroom.com, 5pm-9pm Mon.-Sat., 9am-2pm Sun., $14-28) for Chef Peter Stefani's house-grown veggies and greens or bread pudding with bourbon sauce. After dinner, if you're not quite ready to turn in, head over to Dock Street for a drink with the locals at **Steamers** (420 Dock St., 352/543-5142,

THE NATURE COAST

CEDAR KEY

1: a nine-banded armadillo at Cedar Key Scrub State Reserve **2:** Cedar Key Bed and Breakfast **3:** Dock Street waterfront

Catch of the Day

Before you head out for a day on the water to hook your catch, make sure you're aware of the legal limits and size restrictions of the species you may reel in. Here's a list of the most common and popular fish species, restrictions, and other details.

AMBERJACK, GREATER

When: Caught year-round, this Atlantic species is often bagged way offshore.
Limit: 1 fish per person, minimum size 34 inches to the fork of the tail
Fun Factor: They're a big, strong fish, offering a wonderful pull and feisty runs to the bottom.

COBIA

When: They have a spring run and a late-fall run, but are generally caught in spring.
Limit: 1 fish per person or 6 fish per vessel (whichever is less), 33-inch minimum
Fun Factor: Exceptional pullers, they will readily bite. They prefer to hang out near structures like pilings or channel markers.

FLOUNDER

When: Caught year-round
Limit: 10 fish per person, 12-inch minimum
Fun Factor: A smaller species than the Atlantic version (often under 10 inches), they are excellent table fare, but cleaning them is tricky.

GROUPER (BLACK OR GAG)

When: July 1-December 3 for most areas, but they swim way out in the summer. They move inshore fall and winter, in as little as 6 feet of water.
Limit: 2 gag per person (all other grouper species 4 total per day), 22-inch minimum (red, yellowfin, and yellowmouth species have a 20-inch minimum; scamp have a 16-inch minimum in Gulf waters; there is no size minimum for rock hind and red hind species).
Fun Factor: People love their fight and flavor so much that the big ones are mostly fished out. You'll find lots under 22 inches.

JACK CREVALLE

When: Caught year-round, they school in the summer months.
Limit: No limits
Fun Factor: The thuggish brute that hangs out in the dark alley, it's the toughest fighting fish in the Gulf. No good to eat.

KINGFISH

When: Caught year-round, but better in late winter
Limit: No limits
Fun Factor: With lots of fight, they are beautiful, long, silvery fish that taste terrible. They tend to hunt in schools.

MANGROVE SNAPPER

When: Caught year-round
Limit: 10 fish per person, 10-inch minimum
Fun Factor: One of the smaller snappers, it rarely exceeds five pounds. Find them around docks and piers. Watch out—they bite. Also called gray or mango snapper.

MULLET

When: Caught year-round
Limit: 50 per person, no size limit
Fun Factor: This fish jumps out of the water frequently and prefers vegetation; cast net or use cane poles and dough balls of white bread.

REDFISH

When: Caught year-round
Limit: 1 fish per person, 18-inch minimum, 27-inch maximum
Fun Factor: The bread-and-butter fish in this area, they are delicious table fare and good fighters. They have become the new inshore and shallow water tournament fish of choice. Also called red drum.

SEABASS, BLACK

When: Caught year-round
Limit: 100 pounds per person in the Gulf, 5 fish per person in the Atlantic; 10-inch minimum in the Gulf, 13-inch minimum in the Atlantic
Fun Factor: Extremely small in this area, they are generally too small to keep. More an offshore and Atlantic species.

SHEEPSHEAD

When: Caught year-round, but easier to get in winter
Limit: 15 fish per person, 12-inch minimum
Fun Factor: With jailhouse stripes, it's not surprising they're bait thieves. They hang out near barnacle-crusted structures. Good table fare but a little on the bony side.

SPANISH MACKEREL

When: Caught spring-fall
Limit: 15 per person, 12-inch minimum
Fun Factor: Caught on light tackle, they are generally under five pounds, travel in large schools, and are easy to catch. Most locals smoke them.

SPOTTED SEA TROUT

When: Caught year-round, season closed November-December in southern areas, February in northwest areas
Limit: Between 4 and 6 fish per person depending on the location, 15-inch minimum, 20-inch maximum; you can keep one over 20 inches per day
Fun Factor: One of the most abundant fish in the area, they like the grass flats. The commercial netting ban has increased their numbers.

TARPON

When: Caught April-June
Limit: Catch-and-release only
Fun Factor: A protected species, they can only be caught and released using line and hook, and require a $50 tag to fish for them. They are the most explosive of inshore species.

11am-9pm Mon.-Thurs., 11am-10pm Fri.-Sat., 11am-8pm Sun.) or **Tony's Seafood Restaurant** (597 2nd St., 352/543-0022, 11am-8pm Sun.-Thurs., 11am-9pm Fri.-Sat., $20-35). They serve a variety of seafood and incredible clam chowder which is so good it's worth stopping in for just a small bowl. Also on the menu are seafood platters, clams, oysters, fish, shrimp, salads, burgers, and po'boy sandwiches.

Owned by Peter Stefani of the Island Room, **Dock Street Depot** (490 Dock St., 352/543-0202, 11am-10pm daily, $8-15) serves great seafood jambalaya and shrimp Creole along with a menu of other seafood, fried or broiled.

ACCOMMODATIONS

★ **The Faraway Inn** (847 3rd St., 352/792-0933, www.farawayinn.com, $90-170) is set within a quiet, attractive residential area away from traffic and nightlife, but within a five-minute walk past Victorian and traditional Cracker homes to restaurants, convenience stores, shops, boat launches, the public beach, and the city dock. Built in the early 1950s on the original site of the 19th-century Eagle Pencil Company Cedar Mill, the inn has little freestanding efficiencies and cottages as well as more motel-like accommodations. It's pet-friendly too.

Cedar Cove (192 2nd St., 352/543-5332, www.cedarcovehotel.com, $119-129) has more upscale amenities than most properties in this area. All rooms are fully equipped efficiencies with private balconies and access to a heated pool and an extensive fitness facility. A stop on the town's historical district walking tour, the **Cedar Key Bed and Breakfast** (810 3rd St., 352/543-9000, www.cedarkeybedandbreakfast.com, $105-225) was built in 1880 as a home for Eagle Pencil Company employees. Today it's a comfortable six-room inn with a nice breakfast.

TRANSPORTATION

To get to Cedar Key, take U.S. 19, then head 23 miles southwest on Highway 24, the only road in and out of town. Much of Highway 24 is a quite rural two-lane highway until you cross the causeway into town. Cedar Key is 55 miles north of Crystal River, one hour's drive.

If you happen to be piloting your own small plane, Cedar Key has a single 2,300-foot hard-surfaced runway, but this is uncontrolled airspace.

Steinhatchee

If you're really looking to get out into the wilderness of this region, you can get deeper into the backcountry in Steinhatchee (STEEN-hatchee, pop. 1,500). The fishing and hunting are incredible, with trout, redfish, and wild game. The mouth of the Steinhatchee River, called Deadman's Bay, was home to thousands of Native Americans who came for the exceptional fishing and beautiful environment. Hunters and fisherfolk have been following suit since the mid-1800s. In recent years Steinhatchee's appeal has broadened, thanks in large measure to a Georgia entrepreneur named Dean Fowler.

Fowler's place, Steinhatchee Landing Resort, has drawn accolades from an array of travel magazines in recent years. This hasn't accelerated things—in fact, at his place the posted speed limit is 9 mph. Why, you ask? "If it was 10, no one would pay it any mind," says Fowler.

The Steinhatchee River—along with the Suwannee, Wacissa, Econfina, Fenholloway, and St. Marks Rivers—empty their rich contents here into the Apalachee Bay of the Gulf of Mexico. The shallow bay's gentle, gradual slope and fertile grass flats have made it a world-class fishing destination and a summer scalloping hot spot. It's a place where "live bait and cold beer" sound like two of the central ingredients to happiness.

BEACHES

Of all the hundreds of miles of Florida's Gulf Coast, the Nature Coast offers the most limited beach access, and much of it is unsuitable for swimming. Tiny barrier islands and shallow grassy flats protect the coast from Gulf winds and surf but also preclude the soft white sand of elsewhere on the Gulf Coast. If you want to make a day of it, the best bet is Keaton Beach, a neat little beach town 17 miles north of Steinhatchee. Families and fisherfolk are drawn to the wide natural public beach, the 700-foot fishing pier, and the large boat ramp. The trick is getting here: Follow U.S. 19 north through Cross City, go 11 miles, and turn left onto County Road 358. At the flashing light, stay to the right, and once you go through Jena, turn right. Go over the bridge, turn left at the stop sign, and at next stop sign turn right. Go another 17 miles and turn left at the stop sign.

Beyond that, Cedar Key has private beaches, but public access is limited to the downtown city park next to a colorful kids' playground on 2nd Street. The bay here is shallow and muddy, due to the outflow of numerous creeks and rivers, and the sand is rocky and hard on bare feet. A better bet is to head out to Fort Island Trail Beach (Fort Island Trail, 10 miles west of U.S. 19, daylight-9:30pm daily). This Gulf-side beach is about 1,000 feet long, with a new fishing pier, concessions, and picnic facilities. A lifeguard is on duty Memorial Day-Labor Day.

SPORTS AND RECREATION

Scalloping

July 1-September 10, the scalloping season brings thousands of visitors to the little town of Steinhatchee. You need a recreational saltwater fishing license (888/347-4356, www.myfwc.com, 3-day license $17 non-Florida residents, annual license $17 Florida residents) before you can wade out into the grassy shallows to scoop up the sweet bay bivalves. Each harvester is limited to two gallons of whole scallops or one pint of shucked meat per day. Pack a snorkel, swim shoes, and a mesh bag for your catch.

★ Offshore Fishing

Folks visiting this area most often spend their time, and considerable money, on half-day or full-day charters out into the Gulf in search of amberjack, kingfish (not the best tasting, but a beautiful sport fish), redfish, cobia, and grouper. Black grouper limits are five per person per day, and they must be at least 22 inches long. Big Bend Charters (877/852-3474) takes groups of up to six far out on offshore ($1,200) or inshore ($500) trips, or a "thrill" fishing trip that targets a range of species ($1,400).

Closer in, spotted sea trout, catfish, and redfish can be coaxed out of the grass flats of Deadman's Bay or the slow-moving Steinhatchee River. Kingfish travel through Steinhatchee spring and fall to stay in the perfect water temperature (72°F), and the town is a legendary trout and redfish fishery in the wintertime when the fish move up into the river. Freshwater fishing can be accomplished dockside or from a rented canoe, but it's more fun in a shallow-draft boat with a motor: Get a 24-foot deck boat with a 200-horsepower Yamaha motor with a bimini (half-day $150 plus fuel) at the River Haven Marina (1110 Riverside Dr. SE, 352/498-0709, www.riverhavenmarine.com). First-timers should hire a guide (it's an eminent place to learn saltwater fly-fishing techniques), but if you're striking out on your own, head to one of the local marinas (Sea Hag, River Haven, or Gulf Stream) and listen carefully to find out about the latest hot spots and irresistible baits. Tip: Wear sunglasses with polarized lenses so you can see into the water more effectively.

Diving

Rodale's *Scuba Diving* magazine is always heaping kudos on the Nature Coast, and scuba devotees come from all over to try cave and freshwater diving in the crystal-clear water. Many of the spots are north and east of Steinhatchee and Cedar Key.

Along the Santa Fe River in High Springs, **Ginnie Springs** (Hwy. 47, northeast of U.S. 19, 386/454-7188, www.ginniespringsoutdoors.com, $14 adults, $4 ages 6-12, free under age 6) may be one of the most popular freshwater dive sites in the world, a place Jacques Cousteau once characterized as "visibility forever." Certified cave divers will also have heard of its Devil's Eye/Ear cave system. If you're diving for the first time, Ginnie Springs is perfect—no waves or breaking surf and no boats to contend with. There's also a noncertification guided Discover Scuba Diving program ($99 pp).

There are also two first-magnitude springs, 10 minutes from each other and 30 minutes northeast from Cedar Key. **Manatee Springs State Park** (Hwy. 320, west of Chiefland, 352/493-6072), in a 2,075-acre park, has springs that produce 117 million gallons of clear blue water daily, a haven for manatees, fish, wading birds, scuba divers, and swimmers alike. There are two spots for excellent cavern and cave diving, Manatee Springs State Park and Catfish Hotel Sink. You can camp, fish, boat, and hike in the park as well, but for a quick day trip, the boardwalk through cypress swamp to the Suwannee River is a must-see. At **Fanning Springs State Park** (18020 U.S. 19, Fanning Springs, 352/463-3420), the springs release 50 million gallons of water a day, and swimmers and snorkelers explore the 20-foot-deep spring basin fed by two springs, Big Fanning and Little Fanning. Fanning Springs also has a cool boardwalk to the river, a nature trail, volleyball, and picnic facilities.

And a little farther away in the town of Williston are two diving draws: Visitors to **Devil's Den Resort & Springs** (5390 NE 180th Ave., 352/528-3344, www.devilsden.com, admission $15-20, snorkel gear rental $10, diving $38, dive gear rental $40) descend wooden steps through a rock tunnel to a floating dock, and then the dive begins about 40 feet down with swim-throughs, nooks, and crannies to explore. One of the safest cavern dives in the state is the nearby **Blue Grotto** (3852 NE 172nd Court, 352/528-5770, www.divebluegrotto.com, dive fee $40), a limestone sink with heavy-duty guidelines and platforms down to 100-foot depths.

Farther south, if you want to get a sense for the history of the Suwannee River steamboat era, you can dive to see the **City of Hawkinsville Underwater Archaeological Preserve** (western bank of the Suwannee River, Old Town, accessible only by boat, 850/245-6444). Built in 1896 for the Hawkinsville Deep Water Boat Lines, the steamboat was used on the Suwannee River for the booming lumber industry before it ceased operation in 1922. Today, divers can explore the intact 141-foot hull of the sunken steamer, swimming along the long deck of the vessel to the stern paddlewheel alongside the area's more intrepid fish.

For diving equipment and services, options are plentiful. **American Pro Diving Center** (821 SE U.S. 19, Crystal River, 352/563-0041), **Bird's Underwater** (320 NW U.S. 19, Crystal River, 352/563-2763, www.birdsunderwater.com), and **Steve's Scuba & Snorkeling** (669 NE U.S. 19, Crystal River, 352/795-1551) all have good reputations in the area.

FOOD

The dining scene is dominated by **Fiddler's Restaurant** (1306 Riverside Dr., 352/498-7427, www.fiddlersrestaurant.com, 4pm-10pm Mon.-Fri., 6am-10pm Sat.-Sun., $10-20), a sprawling lively spot populated by men swapping big fish stories and tucking into fried grouper (you can bring your own cleaned catch and have them cook it up). **Roy's** (100 1st Ave. SW, 352/498-5000, www.roys-restaurant.com, 11am-9pm daily, $13-16), a longtime local favorite, doesn't serve any booze but has an exhaustive salad bar, fried seafood, and fat burgers that keep people happy. **Kathi's Krab Shack** (202 15th St., 352/498-0605, 6am-8pm Wed. and Sun., 6am-9pm Thurs., 6am-10pm Fri.-Sat., $7-20)

1: Fort Island Trail Beach **2:** cottages at Steinhatchee Landing Resort **3:** Manatee Springs State Park **4:** a pier on the Steinhatchee River

offers a familiar range of American options including omelets and pancakes at breakfast, sandwiches and seafood plates for lunch, and excellent seafood dinner selections.

ACCOMMODATIONS

★ **Steinhatchee Landing Resort** (228 NE Hwy. 51, 352/498-0696, www.steinhatcheelanding.com, $140-500) is as upscale as it gets along the Nature Coast. Its 35 acres are dotted with dozens of individual one- to three-bedroom Victorian and Florida Cracker cottages, most equipped with French country furniture and oversize spa tubs. There's a new swimming pool and patio area, and it accepts pets up to 28 pounds.

The same folks own the nearby 17-room budget-friendly **Steinhatchee River Inn** (1111 Riverside Dr., 352/498-4049, www.steinhatcheeriverinn.net, $79-129), where the rates change seasonally.

TRANSPORTATION

Steinhatchee is 33 miles north of Cedar Key on U.S. 19, and then 12 miles west on Highway 51.

Information and Services

The Nature Coast is in the **eastern time zone.**

VISITOR INFORMATION

Citrus County Chamber of Commerce (915 N. Suncoast Blvd., Crystal River, 352/795-3149, 9am-5pm Mon.-Fri.), stocks racks of local brochures and pamphlets. **Cedar Key Chamber of Commerce** (450 2nd St., 352/543-5600, 10am-4pm Mon.-Sat.), right down the block from the city hall and library, has limited hours and limited offerings.

For other visitor information and maps of the area, contact **Florida's Pure Water Wilderness** (352/463-3467, www.purewaterwilderness.com). Birders will want to check out the award-winning website www.citruscountyaudubon.org, which catalogs birding opportunities on virtually every trail in the area.

POLICE AND EMERGENCIES

The **Crystal River Police Department** (123 NW U.S. 19, 352/795-4241), the largest along the Nature Coast, is in back of city hall. In the event of a medical emergency, **Bayfront Health Seven Rivers** (6201 N. Suncoast Blvd., Crystal River, 352/795-6560) has emergency services, as does **Nature Coast Regional Hospital** (125 SW 7th St., Williston, 352/528-2801). For anything major, head to **North Florida Regional Medical Center** in Gainesville.

FISHING LICENSES

If you haven't planned ahead, fishing licenses can be purchased on the fly in Crystal River at the **Ace Hardware** (999 NE 5th St., 352/228-4583), and in Homosassa at **Walmart** (6885 S. Suncoast Blvd., 352/628-4161).

The Forgotten Coast

Despite its name, the area between Panama

City and St. Marks is one of the most memorable regions on the Gulf Coast. The Forgotten Coast is best known for its protected lands (87 percent of the region is national or state park land), top-rated and less-crowded beaches, tasty oysters, affordable cost of living, and pristine waters. Apalachicola Bay is one of the most productive in the United States, providing 90 percent of the oysters consumed in Florida and supports extensive shrimping, crabbing, and commercial fishing. The Apalachicola watershed has the greatest number of freshwater fish species in Florida and the highest density and diversity of amphibian species in North America.

In the early 1800s, the town of Apalachicola was founded by cotton

Highlights

Look for ★ to find recommended sights, activities, dining, and lodging.

© MOON.COM

★ **Self-Guided Historic Walking Tour:** Go back in time to an era of grace and charm with a leisurely stroll in downtown Apalachicola. More than 200 of the buildings downtown are on the National Register of Historic Places (page 262).

★ **St. Joseph Peninsula State Park:** This 2,500-acre park keeps showing up on Dr. Beach's top-10 list due to its superior sand, surf, shells, and weather (page 263).

★ **Florida Seafood Festival:** You'll gain a robust appreciation for Apalachicola's beloved eastern oysters in November at this annual festival (page 268).

★ **Tupelo Honey:** Stop by one of the few operating tupelo honey apiaries in the world and sample the esteemed sweet treat (page 268).

★ **St. George Island State Park:** A nighttime beach walk on St. George reveals one of the darkest night skies in the United States (telescope optional). You may also see baby loggerhead turtles flapping their way back out to sea under a luminous moon (page 275).

★ **Biking St. George Island:** Start from the western side of the island, stop in town for a cool ice cream cone, and then continue along the roadside path until you reach the state park at the island's eastern end (page 277).

★ **Apalachicola Reserve Nature Center:** Learn more about fertile Apalachicola Bay's flora and fauna and check out aquariums of local fish and turtles (page 281).

★ **Big Bend Saltwater Paddling Trail:** Extending 60 miles along the Gulf Coast, this area is home to many bird species as well as a meandering 105-mile mapped kayak and canoe trail (page 287).

★ **Wakulla Springs State Park:** What do *Airport '77* and *Tarzan's Secret Treasure* have in common? They were both filmed in the lush wilderness surrounding these crystal-clear springs, which pump 600,000 gallons of water per minute (page 287).

and lumber magnates to provide an accessible port for the South's cotton plantations. Cotton warehouses were quickly erected, making it the third-largest cotton port on the Gulf Coast. More overlooked than forgotten, this region was disregarded by tourists for the greater part of the 1900s due to its unpalatable mix of industrial development and lack of infrastructure across large spans of wilderness.

The Forgotten Coast doesn't offer everything to everyone: There are no amusement parks, few malls, even fewer fast-food restaurants. Yet this is precisely the appeal for visitors who seek a more natural and adventurous Florida experience. The region reaches back to Florida's past, a time before most of the landscape became resorts and vacation homes seemingly overnight.

Where you set up your base is a matter of preference. The historic port of Apalachicola is known for its restored Georgian and Victorian homes, cotton warehouses converted into antiques shops, and mouthwatering seafood restaurants. St. George Island is an unparalleled barrier island retreat, with hundreds of beachfront rentals ranging in size and price. And Eastpoint on the mainland or St. Joseph Peninsula is where to go if you're here to fish, camp, paddle, boat, or otherwise explore the unforgettable outdoor adventures of the Forgotten Coast.

PLANNING YOUR TIME

The Forgotten Coast is roughly bounded on the west by Mexico Beach and on the east by St. Marks. From west to east, it includes the communities of St. Joe Beach and Port St. Joe, Simmons Bayou, Cape San Blas, Indian Pass, Apalachicola, St. George Island, Eastpoint, Carrabelle, Ochlockonee Bay, and Panacea. The communities worthy of most of your attention are Apalachicola and St. George Island. (Apalachicola will hold your interest for a minimum of a weekend, and St. George Island rentals, at least during high season, are

mostly by the full week.) For tent camping, RV camping, and paddling, St. Joseph Peninsula State Park's Shady Pine campground is on the Gulf of Mexico and is one of the best on the Gulf Coast. Eastpoint, Carrabelle, and Apalachicola are the main hot spots for fishing guides and services in the surrounding bays, rivers, and offshore in the Gulf.

A slower pace suits the area. The beaches of St. George Island, Cape San Blas, St. Vincent Island, and St. Joseph Peninsula State Park often make people's lists of top beaches in the United States. There are lighthouses, dunes towering 30 feet high anchored by sea oats and magnolia trees, miles of white sand dotted with perfect sand dollars, and hardly another person in sight.

High season is different from the rest of coastal Florida. It stays cooler than elsewhere on the Gulf, making it a little chilly in the winter and more than tolerable in the summer. Summer is the peak, with rental prices jumping substantially on beach houses on St. George and hotel rooms in Apalachicola. Many beach houses book as far as a year in advance for summer. If you are more impulsive, try off-peak times to get a room on the fly. Spring and fall are gorgeous on this stretch of the coast, especially for camping and paddling trips, but watch out: Easter week tends to be a difficult time to get a reservation.

Transportation

To reach the Forgotten Coast by car, there are several routes worth considering. From the north, if your aim is to minimize back roads, take I-75 south to Tifton, then U.S. 319 to Tallahassee, then U.S. 98 to the St. George Island Bridge at Eastpoint, or continue west to Apalachicola. If you're coming west from, say, Orlando, find your way to I-75 heading north; exit on U.S. 441 west at Alachua, just before Lake City, quickly changing to U.S. 27, which intersects with U.S. 98 near Perry.

By boat, on the Gulf Intracoastal Waterway

The Forgotten Coast

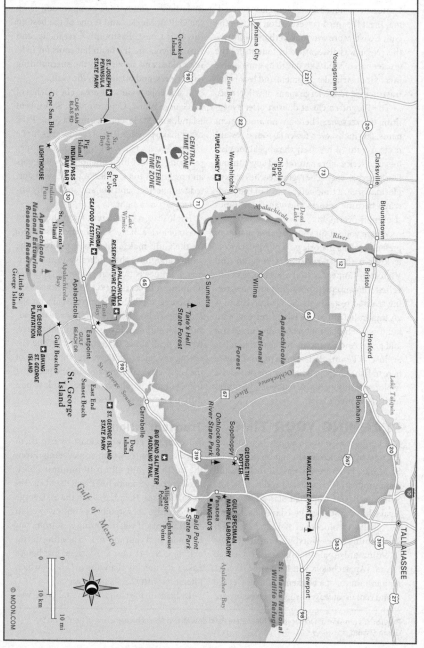

© MOON.COM

from Florida's west coast, enter at St. George Sound through East Pass, between Dog Island and St. George Island, or through Bob Sikes Cut (pretty shallow). From the west, take the Intracoastal Waterway through East Bay from Panama City, then on past White City. Continue east through Wimico to the Jackson River, which leads to the Apalachicola River. Follow markers past the Railroad Bridge to Apalachicola.

If you're piloting your own small plane, **Apalachicola Regional Airport** (8 Airport Rd., Apalachicola, 850/290-8282) is a former military base that served B-17s in World War II, with three concrete runways and fuel available. The closest commercial airports are **Tallahassee International Airport** (TLH, 3300 Capital Circle SW, Tallahassee, 850/891-7800) with flights on Delta, American Airlines, and Silver Airways; and **Northwest Florida Beaches International Airport** (ECP, 6300 West Bay Pkwy., Panama City, 850/763-6751), 60 miles west, with flights

on American, Delta, United, and Southwest. **Alamo** (877/222-9075), **Avis** (800/230-4898), **Budget** (800/527-0700), **Dollar** (800/800-3665 domestic, 800/800-6000 international), and **National** (800/367-6767) provide rental cars from these airports.

Once you're in the region, the best way to explore is by car, as there are no buses or trains. U.S. 98 is sometimes slow and congested, but it is a picturesque roadway that stretches 300 miles along the northwest Florida coast. An easy way to explore the Apalachicola River Basin and Apalachicola National Forest is to take Highway 12, also known as the Apalachee Savannas National Scenic Byway. It begins in Bristol, Florida, and winds alongside the Apalachicola River for most of the way before veering into the heart of the national forest. Driving south from Alabama and Georgia, you can make time along east-west I-10, about 65 miles to the north, but eventually you have to hook up with U.S. 98 and slow down.

Port St. Joe

As you drive toward Apalachicola on U.S. 98, consider making a stop in Port St. Joe. The once sleepy coastal town of 3,000 has experienced a renaissance in recent years. Sure, we all used to drive right through the former port on St. Joseph Bay, but these days it's worth spending an evening or two exploring new restaurants and shops in the historic downtown district, and perhaps booking a fishing charter or renting kayaks to explore the beautiful surrounding bay and waterways.

SIGHTS AND RECREATION

A good place to start exploring is at the **Port St. Joe Marina** (340 Marina Dr., 850/227-9393, www.psjmarina.com), one of the main gateways to the open water of the Gulf in the area. Sailing into Port St. Joe, you'll find 109 wet slips, a gift shop, and a spacious bathhouse

facility with laundry machines. Both landlubbers and salty sailors can get a break from the hardtack and sit down for a delicious meal at Dockside Seafood and Rawbar. Whether you eat at Dockside or not, the marina is an excellent place to watch the sunset.

Several fishing charters board at the Port St. Joe Marina, including the popular **Break-A-Way Charters** (850/340-1188, www.break-a-waycharters.com, $100 per hour for up to 6 people). Father-son duo captains Bobby and Wade Guilford offer inshore and offshore fishing trips, bottom fishing, trolling, tarpon trips, diving and scalloping trips, and sightseeing cruises. For diving trips they use a hookah rig system, which allows visitors to dive without a tank, and here's the best part—no special certification is needed.

More independent-minded anglers may want to rent a boat on their own. **Seahorse**

Water Safaris (340 Marina Dr., Port St. Joe, 850/227-1099, www.seahorsewatersafaris. com, $229-309 half-day plus fuel cost) rents three sizes of pontoon boats holding 6-10 people to take out on St. Joseph Bay.

To take an ecotour, snorkel trip, or sunset cruise with an experienced captain with a master's degree in marine biology, call Captain Charlene Burke at **Seahorse Water Safari** (340 Marina Dr., 850/227-1099, www. seahorsewatersafaris.com, $24-44). She'll take you out on the *Island Princess* for a snorkel tour around St. Joseph Bay or to search for wildlife and listen to the knowledgeable captain tell you all about the natural history and beautiful scenery that you'll see on one of her sightseeing ecotours, which can also be booked as a sunset cruise.

If you'd rather keep your feet on dry land, explore the waterfront trails and other fun stuff at **Frank Pate Park** (502 Monument Ave.), connected to the Port St. Joe Marina by the 0.7-mile Bay Walk Trail that leads to a pirate-themed playground, a boat launch, and a picturesque fishing pier with a nice viewing pavilion. From the park, you can take the short Pelican Run Trail to the historic downtown area of Port St. Joe, only 0.2 miles north of Frank Pate Park. After passing downtown, you can continue on the 0.75-mile Sandpiper Run Greenway that connects 10th Street Forrest Park and Buck Griffin Lake, a nice way to explore Port St. Joe on foot.

For the best beaches in the area, head north to one of the public access points near Mexico Beach, or drive south to Cape San Blas, St. Joseph Peninsula, or St. George Island.

FESTIVALS AND EVENTS

The first weekend in October, make sure to spend some time cracking shells and dancing at the **Florida Scallop and Music Festival** (outside The Haughty Heron, 117 Sailor's Cove Dr., Port St. Joe, 850/229-3463, www. scallopfest.org, $10 per day). It's the largest annual festival in Gulf County, and the celebration is all about the scallop. The gates open at 5pm Friday and 10am Saturday, and the headlining musical act takes the stage at 9pm. While vendors serve up the tasty saltwater clam prepared every way imaginable, the crowd dances the night away to music that can be heard clear across St. Joseph Bay.

FOOD

Dockside Seafood and Rawbar (340 Marina Dr., 850/229-5200, www.dockside-seafoodandrawbar.com, 11am-9pm Sun.-Thurs., 11am-10pm Fri.-Sat., $12-25) is on the Port St. Joe Marina. As the name implies, they feature seafood dishes, a variety of sandwiches, and raw oysters. The views of the marina are wonderful, and you can watch the charter boats sail in after a day of fishing and then gawk as they lay their catch on the docks.

While you're downtown, grab a pizza pie at **Joe Mama's Wood Fired Pizzas** (406 Reid Ave., 850/229-6262, 4:30pm-9pm Tues.-Sat., $7-15). They've kept the menu simple and offer salads, a wide variety of pizza, and a few starters like baked focaccia and grilled bruschetta. For dessert are two excellent options: a delicious cheesecake or something called a pot of chocolate, which is exactly what it sounds like and will make you wish you could take a pot of it home.

Another downtown favorite is **Provisions** (222 Reid Ave., 850/229-9200, 11am-9pm Mon.-Wed., 11am-10pm Thurs.-Sat., $7-15), with a variety of international entrées, from Southern comfort food to Italian pasta dishes and Asian-inspired noodle plates. The connecting factor is that all the food is delicious, no matter if you order the prime rib sandwich, the Thai stir-fry with peanut sauce, or the shrimp carbonara.

For something ultra-casual, stop by the **No Name Cafe** (325 Reid Ave., 850/229-1999, 11:30am-2:30pm Tues.-Fri., $6-10). They serve a small selection of hot and cold sandwiches, soups, and some mighty tasty pastries, cookies, and coffees. Avid readers will love browsing their selection of used and new books.

Get your taco and margarita fix at **Pepper's Mexican Grill** (224 Reid Ave., 850/229-8540, 11am-10pm Mon.-Thurs.,

11am-11pm Fri.-Sat., 11am-9pm Sun., $8-12). The atmosphere is fun and bright, as you would expect from the hippest Mexican joint in town. The cold margaritas and tasty sizzling fajitas may also get you in a festive mood.

ACCOMMODATIONS

There are several small motels along U.S. 98, but the best place to stay in town is the **Port Inn** (501 Monument Ave., 850/229-7678, www.portinnfl.com, $130-190). The historic two-story inn, built in 1909, has 21 rooms, 10 of them with a view of the bay. In the morning, eat breakfast in the dining room downstairs. At night, enjoy drinks at the Thirsty Goat, a cozy lounge that's a popular spot to watch the sunset.

A few miles south along U.S. 98, **Mainstay Suites** (3951 E. U.S. 98, 855/849-1513, $100-160) is more of a bargain. It will get you closer to the beaches, but keep you near enough town to enjoy the restaurants and shopping. Rooms have full kitchens that include a large fridge, nice if you want to cut down on dining costs. The hotel is clean and pet-friendly, and has spacious rooms and continental breakfast every morning.

GETTING THERE

From Apalachicola, drive west on U.S. 98 to reach Port St. Joe. This 23-mile route takes 30 minutes in normal traffic. From Panama City, drive east on U.S. 98 for 36 miles, which takes an hour in normal traffic.

Apalachicola

Say it with me: a-pa-LATCH-ee-CO-la. The locals shorten it to Apalach, and more so than many places along the Gulf Coast of Florida, they have strong Southern accents. The population is roughly 3,000, but Apalachicola has the cultural opportunities of a much larger city and a coastal Southern charm only found in smaller Gulf-front communities. Find Georgian and Victorian homes along wide avenues shaded by moss-covered live oaks, and civic pride that reflects the area's long and rich history.

You can't hold Apalachicola down. Even though the city has been pummeled by hurricanes and the BP oil spill in 2010, it continues to prove its resilience. The downtown historic district has been transformed from a crusty dilapidated fishing town to a picturesque waterfront destination with a wide variety of shops and restaurants. This is a wonderful place to spend a day or two exploring the historic homes, enjoying the bountiful seafood brought in daily aboard the local fishing fleet, and searching through the plentiful antiques and maritime-themed boutiques. The hub of activity is along Market and Water Streets, which border the Apalachicola River, and this is where your visit to Apalachicola should begin, preferably tucked into a plate of oysters and shrimp while you stare out into the Gulf of Mexico.

Locals will tell you that the oysters bring most people to Apalachicola. The plentiful mollusks are believed to have attracted the first Native American inhabitants, as evidenced by the ancient oyster shell mounds they left behind throughout the region. Today Apalachicola is the hub of an oyster industry that provides 90 percent of the oysters consumed in Florida and 10 percent of the oysters consumed in the United States. While you're in town, consider hiring a local guide to take you oyster harvesting in Apalachicola Bay. Shuck the oyster on the bow of the boat. Throw it raw right on a cracker with a little horseradish, cocktail sauce, and a squeeze of fresh lemon juice and enjoy a culinary history dating back thousands of years. At the very least, buy some raw oysters at one of the restaurants that serve the popular seafood item. A raw oyster is a lot like the Forgotten Coast; it's not for everyone. But whether you love it or

Apalachicola

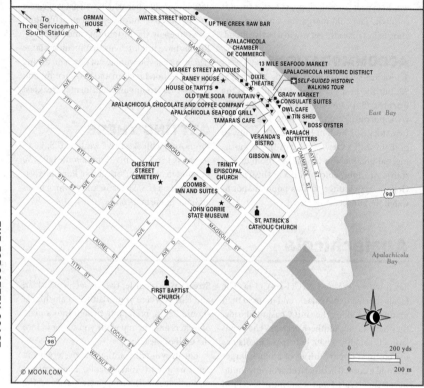

To Three Servicemen South Statue

ORMAN HOUSE ★

WATER STREET HOTEL

UP THE CREEK RAW BAR

4TH ST

MARKET ST

AVE J

AVE H

6TH ST

7TH ST

APALACHICOLA CHAMBER OF COMMERCE

13 MILE SEAFOOD MARKET

APALACHICOLA HISTORIC DISTRICT

★ SELF-GUIDED HISTORIC WALKING TOUR

MARKET STREET ANTIQUES

RANEY HOUSE ★

DIXIE THEATRE

HOUSE OF TARTTS ●

OLD TIME SODA FOUNTAIN

GRADY MARKET

★ CONSULATE SUITES

APALACHICOLA CHOCOLATE AND COFFEE COMPANY

APALACHICOLA SEAFOOD GRILL

OWL CAFE

TIN SHED

TAMARA'S CAFE

BOSS OYSTER

East Bay

5TH ST

VERANDA'S BISTRO

APALACH OUTFITTERS

BROAD ST

GIBSON INN ●

8TH ST

AVE G

9TH ST

CHESTNUT STREET CEMETERY ★

TRINITY EPISCOPAL CHURCH

WATER ST

COMMERCE ST

COOMBS INN AND SUITES

6TH ST

AVE F

JOHN GORRIE STATE MUSEUM

MAGNOLIA ST

ST. PATRICK'S CATHOLIC CHURCH

98

AVE E

LAUREL ST

AVE D

11TH ST

Apalachicola Bay

FIRST BAPTIST CHURCH

AVE C

LOCUST ST

AVE B

BAY ST

98

WALNUT ST

© MOON.COM

0   200 yds

0   200 m

vow to never try it again, it's a Southern treat that you won't soon forget.

SIGHTS
★ Self-Guided Historic Walking Tour

Stop in at the **Apalachicola Chamber of Commerce** (122 Commerce St., 850/653-9419, www.apalachicolabay.org, 9am-5pm Mon.-Fri., 11am-4pm Sat.) for a copy of the self-guided historic walking tour map. More than 200 of the regal old homes in Apalachicola are listed on the National Register of Historic Places. Not all of them are in mint condition, but an hour or two of walking, gawking, and reading the brochure is a great way to get to know the downtown area.

There are a handful of historic little churches: **Trinity Episcopal Church** (79 6th St., 850/653-9550) dates all the way back to when Andrew Jackson was president and Florida was still a territory. It was actually built of white pine in New York and shipped down to Apalachicola—the white Greek Revival building is the sixth-oldest church in Florida and the second-oldest still holding services. Not far away are the **First Baptist Church** (46 9th St., 850/653-9540), originally built on the corner of 6th Street and Avenue H, and the Romanesque **St. Patrick's Catholic Church** (27 6th St., 850/653-9543), built in 1929, although the congregation dates to 1845; the first structure was destroyed in a big fire that consumed 70 downtown buildings in 1846.

The historic homes are even more

compelling, several of them tourable. Each May there is a fling-open-the-doors tour of historic homes (guided tour $25). Contact the Apalachicola Bay Chamber of Commerce for information and to purchase tickets (www.apalachicolabay.org, 850/653-9419). As part of a Florida state park, the **Orman House** (177 5th St., 850/653-1209, 9am-5pm Thurs.-Mon., $2), the original 1838 home of cotton merchant Thomas Orman, is open to the public. There is an hour-long narrated tour of the Federal and Greek Revival two-story house, the wood for which was cut and measured near Syracuse, New York, and shipped to Apalachicola by sailboat around the Florida Keys. The majestic columned **Raney House** (128 Market St., 850/653-1700, 1pm-4pm Sun.-Thurs., 10am-4pm Fri.-Sat., free), the home of David Greenway Raney and family, dates to the same year. The interior is now a small museum run by the Apalachicola Area Historical Society.

Chestnut Street Cemetery

Dating before 1831, historic **Chestnut Street Cemetery** (U.S. 98 between 6th St. and 8th St.) houses the remains of many Confederate soldiers, the world-famous botanist Dr. Alvin Wentworth Chapman, and many victims of yellow fever. The broad range of surnames speaks to the town's early diversity (Spanish and French settlers, shipwreck victims). To some spooky, to others just peaceful, the little urban cemetery contains beautifully carved funerary art tucked in the dappled shadows cast by gnarled old live oaks shrouded with Spanish moss.

Dixie Theatre

If you're looking to determine whether Apalachicola is on the wax or wane, the **Dixie Theatre** (21 Ave. E., 850/653-3200, performances usually 8pm Fri.-Sat., 3pm Wed. and Sun., $15-25) is a pretty optimistic sign. Built in 1912, it was the county's locus of cultural activity—stage performances, then silent pictures, then the talkies—for decades. It foundered in the late 1960s, but recent boosters

have gotten it back up and running. The original building's decrepitude led to some ingenious restoration and re-creation. In 1998 the building was completed, with a facade that looks much like it did in 1912, and the original ticket booth painstakingly restored. There's now a winter repertory theater season, and it shows the occasional ragtime piano show or big-town gala.

BEACHES

★ St. Joseph Peninsula State Park

St. Joseph Peninsula State Park (8899 Cape San Blas Rd., Port St. Joe, 850/227-1327) was closed at press time due to damage from 2018's Hurricane Michael; check with the park to make sure it has reopened. Dr. Beach, a man named Stephen Leatherman, conducts an annual ranking of American beaches, and this is one that keeps showing up on his top 10 list. Projecting seven miles out into the Gulf, this barrier peninsula is reachable from the mainland across Apalachicola Bay and via Cape San Blas. Sand blows up across the beach and lodges in sea oats to produce exceptionally tall 30-foot dunes, the water is a sparkling aquamarine and hovers around 84°F in summer, the surf is gentle, and the 2,500-acre beach park is never crowded. Here's what Dr. Beach has to say about the local sand:

> The sand is nearly pure quartz crystal. While most noncarbonated (noncoral) beaches are composed of 15 to 20 different types of sand, the Panhandle beaches are like a bar of Ivory soap—99.44 percent pure. What we find on the Panhandle beaches today is quartz sand crystal at its terminal size, meaning that all the grains are nearly the same size (well sorted in geologic terms).

It's not all beach, though: The park includes a large expanse of heavy pine forest that is home to bobcats, deer, raccoons, and rattlesnakes, as well as bald eagles, ospreys, and peregrine falcons. In the fall hawks and monarch butterflies pause on their migration along the Yucatan Express to Mexico. And

in July-August, visitors search the bayside for sweet scallops.

There are no hotels in the park. Eight loft-style furnished cabins on the bay side of the park accommodate 5-7 people ($100) and 119 campsites ($24) with water and electricity available in two areas: Gulf Breeze sites are more open and thus better for RVs and big cars, and the Shady Pines area is more secluded and shaded. You can also camp at primitive sites on the peninsula ($4 pp), but reservations are a must. A trail winds across the peninsula, and backpackers can hike to designated camp areas and also camp on the beach. Fires are permitted in some areas, and the primitive campsites are great for overnight paddling and boating trips in the area. A marina with a boat ramp ($5 per day) is near the park entrance. Use of the ramp is free for overnight guests, who are permitted to leave their boats moored at the marina.

On your way to the park, visit the **Cape San Blas Lighthouse** (200 Miss Zola's Dr., Port St. Joe, 11am-5pm Wed.-Sat., $5 to climb the lighthouse). The picturesque iron tower was built on the site of two former brick lighthouses that were removed due to beach erosion. In 2014, thanks to the tireless campaigning of local lighthouse preservationists, the lighthouse and the light-keeper's historic home and facilities were moved inland to Port St. Joe, where they will be preserved and protected from erosion.

SPORTS AND RECREATION
Barrier Islands

The Forgotten Coast's barrier islands serve to separate Apalachicola Bay from the Gulf of Mexico, acting as shock absorbers to protect the mainland from winds, storms, and waves. These little islands are also fabulous places to relax and explore.

Birding, shelling, surf fishing, beach

relaxation are on offer on **Dog Island,** east of St. George Island and accessible only by water taxi from Carrabelle or by private watercraft. It's known as a refuge for loggerhead and leatherback turtles, and only a handful of people live on the island. There's no formal lodging since the Pelican Inn closed after being damaged in 2018's Hurricane Michael, but several residents rent rooms and houses on websites like Airbnb and VRBO. However, be advised—there are no stores, no restaurants, and no other amenities on the island, so you have to bring everything you need with you. Hire a boat to take you to the island ($100-175 round-trip).

St. George Island used to be 28 miles long. In 1954 the U.S. Army Corps of Engineers carved out an artificial channel to create two separate barrier islands to make it easier for the shrimpers to get out to the Gulf. The larger is still St. George Island, and the smaller boomerang-shaped island is known locally as **Little St. George Island** and more formally as **Cape St. George State Reserve.**

Little St. George can be reached only by private boat—a worthwhile excursion. The nine-mile-long island is part of the Apalachicola National Estuarine Research Reserve, protecting it from development. It's remote, wild, and populated only by an idiosyncratic assortment of creatures. Originally for waterfowl, the reserve's aim has broadened to protect the bald eagles that nest in pines along the island's freshwater marshes; loggerhead sea turtles that nest on the white-sand beaches; visiting wood storks; and indigo snakes that burrow in the dunes.

Little St. George is open for swimming, fishing, birding, and hiking. Primitive camping (850/670-7700) is permitted at designated sites at West Pass and Sike's Cut, at either end of the island with advance reservations. Fires are permitted at the campsites, but no live wood can be cut.

You have to book your own shuttle to get to **St. Vincent Island,** to the west of Little St. George. **Captain Joey Romanelli**

1: downtown Apalachicola 2: the historic Dixie Theatre 3: the High Bluff Coastal Trail trailhead in Apalachicola National Forest 4: a houseboat in Apalachicola

(850/229-1065, round-trip $10 adults, $7 under age 10) will take you out on his 27-foot pontoon boat, departing from the end of Indian Pass Road. The whole island constitutes the **St. Vincent National Wildlife Refuge,** with 12,358 acres of dunes and woods.

In 1990 the island became a haven for endangered red wolves. These solitary animals once roamed the Southeast, but habitat loss reduced their numbers to just 100, confined to a small area of coastal Louisiana and Texas. Bigger than a coyote and smaller than a gray wolf, they now populate St. Vincent, and when pups are weaned, they are taken to reintroduction facilities around the country.

Before becoming a refuge, the island was a private hunting and fishing preserve. Previous exotic-minded owners introduced a Southeast Asian elk species called sambar deer to the island, and they can still be spotted. They weigh up to 600 pounds, while the native white-tailed deer weigh about 100 pounds. There are native whitetails here too, and other species, including lots of rattlers, so beware. Bring a bike with you on the shuttle ($10) or just hike the trails and beaches.

Fishing

Apalachicola Bay, the Apalachicola River, and the Gulf of Mexico each provide stellar fishing experiences for the rookie or serious angler. There are dozens of charter providers in the area, but a handful come up in locals' recommendations: **Captain Charlie's Charters** (850/653-6482, www.captcharlescharters. com, bay fishing $400-500, near-shore fishing $650-850) leads bay and near-shore fishing groups, sightseeing and shelling expeditions, oystering adventures, and, in season, tarpon trips; **Backwater Guide Service** (850/899-0063, www.backwaterguideservice. com, $400-500) takes people bass fishing or fly-fishing on the river and in the bay on a 21-foot boat and offers sightseeing trips on the Apalachicola River, shelling trips to the barrier islands, and dolphin-watching tours; and the **Robinson Brothers Guide Service** (850/653-8896, $400-1,500) gets the nod for flats fishing (in shallow water, where anglers stand on the bow of a boat with their fly rod or spinning rod) as well as bay and offshore fishing with live bait in a bigger boat and deeper water. Tommy and Chris Robinson's knowledge of the area is impressive.

Diving

Scuba enthusiasts have a few excellent options in the area, including some nice artificial reef diving and clam-covered rock ledges in St. Joe, but the most celebrated wreck dive can be found 105 feet down, 20 miles south of Cape San Blas. Undulating with packs of curious amberjack, barracuda, snapper, and rays, the British oil tanker *Empire Mica,* built in 1941, lies in disarray on the floor of the Gulf. En route from Houston to England on June 29, 1942, two German submarine torpedoes ignited the 12,000 tons of oil it was carrying. The ship went down in a series of fiery explosions, killing 33 men on board. Today the bow section of the 479-foot-long ship is intact, as are 60-80 feet of deck, the metal getting lacy and thin. **Daly's Dock and Dive Center** (Port St. Joe, 850/229-6330, $165 includes air, weights, drinks, and snacks) provides wonderful all-day trips to the SS *Vamar,* one of Florida's Underwater Archaeological Preserves. **Seahorse Water Safaris** (850/227-1099) offers diving trips and guided snorkel tours ($44, includes gear rental).

Forests

The story goes that a man named Cebe Tate once entered a vast swamp in search of a Florida panther that was killing his livestock. Gone for seven days and nights, when Tate emerged with his trusty hunting dog, shaken and thirsty, he announced, "My name is Cebe Tate, and I just came from Hell!" That's how **Tate's Hell State Forest** (access from U.S. 98, County Rd. 67, or Hwy. 65, 850/697-3734, free, camping $10) got its ominous name. It's 185,000 acres between the Apalachicola and Ochlockonee Rivers, much of it suitable for hiking and biking. There's an observation

Ice, Ice, Baby

Ice cube museum. Hmm. Are you imagining a cold room containing, maybe, a piece of the iceberg that sank the *Titanic*, a cube from Dean Martin's final cocktail, or the original "fly-in-the-ice cube" novelty gag? Apalachicola luminary **John Gorrie** is known in the history books as the father of air-conditioning and ice manufacturing, recipient of the first patent for mechanical refrigeration in 1851. A charming museum in a little historic home tells the Gorrie story.

By the time the young doctor arrived in town in 1833, Apalachicola was bustling as the third-largest port on the Gulf, shipping cotton to Europe and New England. During his time in town, Gorrie served as mayor, postmaster, city council member, bank director, and founder of Trinity Church. But all that civic-mindedness pales when compared to his medical work. Yellow fever was a menace in those years, and no one had linked the terrifying sickness to the swarms of mosquitoes that plagued these swampy, humid, low-lying floodplains. In addition to chills, headache, muscle aches, vomiting, and backache, the onset of the illness was marked by high fever. Gorrie posited that bringing the fever down was essential to prevent the shock, bleeding, and kidney and liver failure that often led to death.

As cold temperatures were hard to come by in these parts, he set about making some. His idea is used in today's refrigeration: Cooling can be achieved through the rapid expansion of gases. He built a machine with two pumps that condensed and then rarefied air. It cooled the air, but the machine kept clogging with ice cubes. Unfortunately, Gorrie died before he was able to market his ingenious apparatus, but his contributions to our everyday lives can be seen and appreciated in so many ways, especially when you're visiting the Florida Gulf Coast in the middle of summer.

The **John Gorrie State Museum** (46 6th St., Apalachicola, 850/653-9347, 9am-5pm Thurs.-Mon., $2, free under age 5) contains a replica of Gorrie's ice machine, built from his specs. There are also wonderful exhibits on the history of the area, from its days as a cotton port to sponge diving and oyster harvesting. The museum interpreters are a wealth of knowledge and are willing to expound at length on Apalachicola lore.

tower at the **Ralph G. Kendrick Boardwalk,** from which visitors can look out over a dense stand of rare dwarf, or hatrack, cypress, many of them 150 years old and only 15 feet tall. A number of endangered or threatened species call Hell home, including the bald eagle, red-cockaded woodpecker, gopher tortoise, and Florida black bear.

The forest contains 35 miles of rivers, streams, and creeks available for canoeing, boating, fishing (boat launch at Cash Creek and other sites), and primitive camping. The **High Bluff Coastal Trail** is a wonderful hiking path that's part of the Florida Division of Forestry's Trailwalker Program. Its trailhead is on U.S. 98, four miles west of Carrabelle.

To the north, abutting Tate's Hell State Forest, is **Apalachicola National Forest** (850/643-2282, www.fs.usda.gov), the largest national forest in Florida, spanning 632,890 acres. Destroyed at the turn of the

20th century by the timber and turpentine industries, since 1936 it has been allowed to grow, and now has the largest red-cockaded woodpecker population in the world. Much of the forest is difficult to get to, but there are a few day hikes that are easily accessible: the 4.5-mile **Wright Lake Trail,** the 6-mile **Trail of Lakes,** and the 5.4-mile **Leon Sinks Geological Area Trail.** Mountain bikers will head to the **Munson Hills Off-Road Bicycle Trail,** in the eastern part of the forest, and the 16-mile paved **St. Marks Trail,** which is part of a rails-to-trails program that passes through the forest and terminates in the town of St. Marks. For serious backpackers and remoter hiking, there's also a 68.7-mile section of the **Florida Trail** running through the forest that's a designated part of the Florida Statewide Greenways and Trails System. For a trail map and more information, visit www.florida-trail.org.

FESTIVALS AND EVENTS

★ Florida Seafood Festival

Apalachicola and surrounding towns are the undisputed eastern oyster capital of the world. The oyster industry began in the late 19th century, and by 1896 there were three oyster-canning factories shipping something 50,000 cans daily, the first time canning was attempted in Florida. In 2011 the Apalachicola oyster industry harvested 2.3 million pounds of oysters, worth an estimated $6.4 million.

Naturally, oysters provide the foundation for the area's biggest annual party. The Florida Seafood Festival (850/653-4720, www.floridaseafoodfestival.com) is actually the oldest maritime festival in the state, drawing thousands during the first weekend in November. There are oyster-shucking and eating contests, parades, arts and crafts, musical entertainment, and a foot race—but the big draw is pot upon pot of just-caught seafood in a multitude of preparations.

Big Bend Saltwater Classic

The other big annual draw is the Big Bend Saltwater Classic (850/697-9831) fishing tournament in Carrabelle in June, an opportunity to see more than 700 serious anglers competing for big prizes in a weekend event that benefits the Organization for Artificial Reefs.

SHOPPING

The nine square blocks of downtown Apalachicola offer plenty of options for shopping. Retailers are spread among repurposed brick and tin cotton warehouses and early 1900s cottages. Located across from the docks, the Grady Market (76 Water St., 850/653-4099, 10am-5:30pm Mon.-Sat.) is a local pride and joy, a 19th-century ship's chandlery made over to house a dozen boutiques and galleries, including that of black-and-white photographer Richard Bickel. A block from there is a more eccentric spot called the Tin Shed (170 Water St., 850/653-3635, 10am-5:30pm daily), specializing in antique nautical items like Japanese fishing floats, captains' telescopes, compasses, and ships' bells.

Market St. Antiques (115 Market St., 850/653-1006, 10am-5pm Thurs.-Mon., noon-5pm Sun.) is a reasonably priced shop offering antiques and reproduction pieces, a small assortment of children's clothing, gifts, lamps, folk art, and marine-themed interior accessories.

For crystal jewelry, lotions, gowns, wraps, and accessories, head to Riverlily (78 Commerce St., 850/653-2600, 10am-5:30pm Mon.-Sat.). Nearby, The Oystercatcher (79 Market St., 850/653-1616, 10am-6pm Mon.-Sat., 1pm-4pm Sun.) is a funky boutique chock-full of denim, dresses, swimwear, and jewelry. Also an interesting spot, Petunia (14 Ave. D, 850/653-9144, 10am-5:30pm Mon.-Sat., 11am-4pm Sun.) has a small collection of gifts and apparel for pets and their people.

For a large selection of rods, reels, fly-fishing tackle, and camping gear, head over to Apalach Outfitters (32 Ave. D, 850/653-3474, 10:30am-6pm Mon.-Sat., 10:30am-5pm Sun. summer), with a full line of outdoor clothing and footwear with brands like North Face, Patagonia, and Prana. A couple of doors down is Apalachicola Chocolate and Coffee Company (75 Market St., 850/653-1025), for delicious handmade chocolates and homemade gelato.

★ Tupelo Honey

Just what was Van Morrison singing about in that song, anyway? He was comparing his sweetie to a rare honey, said by connoisseurs to be among the world's finest. Prized for its flavor and for the fact that it never granulates, tupelo honey is produced by bees that cavort in the tupelo gum trees that grow along the Apalachicola River. Harvested for two weeks in late April, tupelo honey was featured in the Peter Fonda movie *Ulee's Gold*.

The locus of tupelo production is in

1: Apalach Outfitters 2: tasty shrimp at Up the Creek Raw Bar 3: a variety of shops and restaurants along Apalachicola's historic waterfront

Wewahitchka, the only place in the world the honey is produced commercially. The process starts when bees are placed on elevated platforms along the river's edge. The bees swarm the tupelo blossom-laden swamps and return with their treasure. The resulting honey is a pale amber color with a slight greenish cast, its flavor delicate and distinctive. Because it costs more to produce, tupelo is more expensive than many other honeys. But this is the good stuff. The ongoing colony collapse disorder crisis, combined with Georgia's water shortage that results in less freshwater in Florida, means tupelo honey may be an endangered commodity; get it while you can.

Every spring at Lake Alice Park in Wewahitchka, folks gather to celebrate the apian masterpiece. For years the **Tupelo Honey Festival** (850/832-7006, www.tupelo-honeyfestival.com) took place in April during the pollinating time, but in recent years it's been moved to the third weekend in May to coincide with when the keepers scoop the honey from the hives. There's entertainment, arts and crafts, kids activities, and a whole lot of things containing tupelo honey, from lotions to snacks.

To take it home with you, many shops in the area stock it. Check on availability with **L.L. Lanier & Son's Tupelo Honey** (850/639-2371, www.lltupelohoney.com), or stop by the extremely friendly **Smiley Honey** (163 Bozeman Circle, Wewahitchka, 850/639-5672, www.smileyhoney.com) to buy a bottle from Donald Smiley's front porch.

FOOD
Oyster Bars
★ **Boss Oyster** (125 Water St., 850/653-9364, 11:30am-9pm daily, $10-25) seems to be the oyster palace to beat (tagline: Oysters All Ways 'n' Oysters Always). Topped with the sensible (a squeeze of lemon and a dash of Tabasco) and the nearly obscene (a broiled oyster stacked with bacon, jalapeños, colby, and a splash of hot sauce), the local oysters are briny bliss. A lively family-oriented crowd, nightly drink specials, and a casual

Apalachicola River-side setting keep it full. Try the heads-on shrimp; roll up your sleeves and don't be fussy. If you advocate topping an oyster with something out of the ordinary, tell the staff and they just might name a dish after you.

Other staunch adherents of the slippery bivalves are at **Papa Joe's Oyster Bar and Grill** (Scipio Creek Marina, 45 Ave. B, 850/653-1189, 11:30am-9pm Mon.-Thurs., 11:30am-10pm Fri.-Sat., $6-20), another waterside seafood-and-steak joint with a serious emphasis on local oysters, raw or broiled.

About 17 miles west of Apalachicola, the absolute must-eat destination is the ★ **Indian Pass Raw Bar** (8391 County Rd. C-30A, Indian Pass, 850/227-1670, noon-9pm Tues.-Sun., $5-10). It is always a party in this roadside shack (recently spruced up somewhat), every vinyl stool filled with someone vigilantly watching as the oyster shucker works his or her magic at the end of the bar. Raw on the half shell is best, but the garlic butter and parmesan-baked version is a delicious spin on these briny beauties. Grab your own drink from the cooler and be sure to order the key lime pie.

Rustic and casual **Up the Creek Raw Bar** (313 Water St., 850/653-2525, noon-9pm daily, $5-10) has become one of the most popular waterfront restaurants in Apalachicola. The large deck overlooking the bay and river is a relaxing spot to watch fishing boats come ashore. They serve oysters raw, steamed, and with toppings that feature regional ingredients, like oysters served "Southern fella" style, topped with collard greens, parmesan, and bacon. The menu includes Southern seafood classics but also features a variety of healthy, creative fusion choices. Try the blackened shrimp basket with sweet potato fries if you're in the mood for seafood.

Fish Markets
If you're renting a house in the area or staying at a hotel with a kitchenette, consider buying fresh seafood from the local fish market and cooking it yourself. You'll find the best

Eastern Oysters

Franklin County has historically harvested 90 percent of the state's oysters and around 10 percent of the nation's. However, times have changed—oyster harvesting is nearly nonexistent in Apalachicola Bay. Most of the oysters these days come from hatcheries and from Texas. More than 1,000 people in the county used to make their living in the oyster business.

The oyster beds in Apalachicola suffered human and natural impacts. A long-running drought in Georgia has been exacerbated by the growing urban population of the city, and the 2010 BP oil spill may have impacted oyster health and reproduction. As the amount of fresh water that flows down the Apalachicola River keeps dwindling, the saltwater from the gulf continues to encroach on the upriver estuaries, where all that tasty Gulf seafood spawns. Let's hope this industry can bounce back—not just for the money, but for the health of the bay ecosystem.

Found around the Gulf of Mexico and up the eastern seaboard to Canada, eastern oysters historically flourished in the bay, which encompasses the waters of St. George Sound and St. Vincent Sound, renewed constantly by the nutrient-rich freshwater of Apalachicola River. The balance of fresh- and saltwater seemed to act as a growth serum. Oysters grew fast and sweet, reaching marketable size in less than two years (in colder climates it can take as long as six years). The 210-square-mile estuary was shallow, 6-9 feet deep at low tide, with oyster harvesters skimming along in small boats to scoop up their mussels from the bottom with long-handled tongs.

Local oysters are still carefully monitored. The Department of Health Services, the EPA, and other agencies test for water purity and natural threats such as red tide. The Department of Agriculture and Consumer Services has sponsored extensive efforts to restock oyster shell in the bay to create new oyster bars, and even to "plant" more than 100,000 bushels of adult and juvenile oysters on public oyster reefs in the bay. These transplanted oysters are taken from waters where harvesting is not allowed or where growth is poor and relocated to approved waters where conditions are more favorable for oysters to healthfully grow to market size. The ultimate aim: increasing oyster production and quality.

Although oysters can be dangerous if you have health issues, oysters are good for you. A dozen is about 110 calories and rich in iron, copper, and iodine and high in calcium and vitamin A. Around here they are sold by the dozen, half bushel, peck, or bushel, graded according to size: The largest marketed are "selects" and the average are "standards." Look for oysters that close tightly when handled. They'll live in a cold fridge for more than a week (cover them loosely with a damp cloth, never in an airtight container). If you buy them already shucked, use them right away and don't freeze them.

While you're in Apalachicola, try them on the half shell. If you aren't in the mood to challenge fate by eating them raw, they are a treat eaten fried, baked, steamed, or broiled—that's paradise on the Forgotten Coast.

selection and service at **13 Mile Seafood Market** (227 Water St., 850/653-1399, 10am-6pm Mon.-Sat.) in downtown Apalachicola. They specialize in oysters and shrimp, but you can also pick up fresh grouper, sushi-grade tuna, mullet, flounder, crabs, and a nice selection of dips and smoked fish. Call ahead for big orders of steamed shrimp, or just stop in and pick up a delicious to-go box of steamed shrimp, corn, and potatoes for lunch. While they may have the only retail storefront in town, you're likely to find better prices at a small roadside stand, which are often operated by the fishing boat owners who are trying to make better profits by selling directly to consumers. Look for large coolers strapped down in the back of pickups for the chance to reel in the best seafood prices in the region, as well as the greatest opportunity to support local fishermen and women.

Lunch

Apalachicola Seafood Grill (100 Market St., 850/653-9510, 11am-9pm Mon.-Sat., $8-15) is the oldest seafood restaurant in town, and usually the first stop for many visitors.

They've been open since 1903 and serve a wonderful fried fish sandwich—"largest in the world," although that may be hyperbole. You'll find them under the town's only traffic light, and they offer a large selection of seafood and American diner food.

The **Owl Café** (15 Ave. D, 850/653-9888, 11am-3pm and 5:30pm-10pm Mon.-Sat., brunch 10:30am-3pm Sun., $10-25), a long-time lunch favorite, features black-and-white photos by local photographer Richard Bickel on the walls (if you like his work, local shops carry his book *Apalachicola River: An American Treasure*), pretty wood floors, a second floor, and an adjacent wine room. The high-ceilinged clapboard building is a replica of the original, lost to fire in 1911. Seafood is the strong suit, from the black grouper with garlic, capers, and artichokes to seafood pastas. The chicken Caesar salad is not to be missed, and the wine list merits some perusal.

The **Old Time Soda Fountain** (93 Market St., 850/653-2606, 10am-5pm Mon.-Sat., $4-9) will satisfy your hankering for malts, floats, ice-cream sodas, and diner-style sandwiches. It's a 1950s-style stools-at-the-counter relic that was once the town's drugstore. If you need a strong cup of organic Venezuelan coffee, a healthy sandwich, a wonderful salad, or a tasty pastry with a side of Wi-Fi, head to **Café Con Leche** (234 Water St., 850/653-2233, 8am-2pm daily, $7-10), located in the Grady Market building and serving breakfast and lunch.

Fine Dining

Boss Oyster's sister restaurant, **Caroline's Dining on the River** (123 Water St., 850/653-8139, 7am-3pm daily, $16-24) combines a fine-dining atmosphere with a creative American seafood menu. Presided over by Caroline Maddren, it's in the Apalachicola River Inn and the place to luxuriate in a lengthy Sunday brunch (opt for the oyster cakes or zingy shrimp Creole heaped over buttermilk biscuits). As with most places around here, the oysters and fresh finfish get the nod, and you can watch the shrimp and fish boats tooling by outside with the day's catch.

Latin

While seafood—oysters in particular—dominates this area, a few restaurants give their marine creatures a little twist. ★ **Tamara's Café** (71 Market St., 850/653-4111, 11am-10pm Mon.-Sat., $12-20) is where local seafood gets Caribbean and South American inflections, such as paella or a pecan-crusted grouper with a creamy jalapeño sauce, everything served with black beans and rice. Wednesday nights are the best times to take a group—it's tapas night, with classics like shrimp sautéed with lots of garlic and a Spanish tortilla, and all the little dishes are affordable.

ACCOMMODATIONS
Under $100

Pretty much nothing in Apalachicola runs under $50, but two places, right next to each other in a convenient location, have rates around $85-130: The **Best Western Apalach Inn** (249 U.S. 98 W., 850/653-9131) has complimentary hot breakfast, an outdoor pool, and children 17 under stay free. The **Apalachicola Bay Inn** (240 U.S. 98 W., 850/653-9435, www.apalachicolabayinn.com) has an outdoor pool and can help you schedule fishing charters and boat tours.

$100-200

The **Gibson Inn** (51 Ave. C, 850/653-2191, www.gibsoninn.com, $120-270), on the National Register of Historic Places, has the dignity of wide wraparound porches, four-poster beds, antiques, and slowly revolving ceiling fans. This gracious tin-roofed Victorian right downtown, built in 1907 as a hotel, contains 30 rooms, each different. It's well-suited for romance-seekers and history buffs, and the inn allows pets in certain rooms.

In a similarly Victorian vein, but even

1: The Gibson Inn 2: the Coombs Inn and Suites

more spruce, the sunny yellow **Coombs Inn and Suites** (80 6th St., 850/653-9199, www.coombsinnandsuites.com, $125-275), built in 1905, is a three-story mansion with high ceilings, an ornate oak staircase, nine wide fireplaces, and a slew of historical photos. Guests in the 20 antique-bedecked rooms enjoy a pleasant breakfast, weekend evening wine receptions, and use of the inn's bikes, umbrellas, and beach chairs.

The **House of Tartts** (50 Ave. F, 850/653-4687, $120-135) is a restored guesthouse with three private rooms. A second-story carriage house ($215) includes two bedrooms, two baths, and kitchen.

The **Water Street Hotel & Marina** (329 Water St., 850/653-3700, www.waterstreethotel.com, $169-225) opened in 2007 with 30 suites and a 20-slip marina (a floating dock serving boats up to 55 feet), just blocks from the center of downtown Apalachicola. Despite a turn-of-the-20th-century vibe, it still boasts contemporary amenities such as wireless internet and has enough space to make it family-friendly.

For a little more privacy, the **Raney Guest Cottage** (46 Ave. F, 850/653-9749, $175) is a historic house that dates back to 1835, one of the oldest buildings in Apalachicola. Sit on a rocker on the wraparound porch or walk the block into town (two blocks to the river). It's charming,

and the house is all yours, with two cozy bedrooms, two baths, a dining room, a kitchen, a screened back porch, two gas-burning fireplaces, a washer and dryer, and a grill.

$200-300

Guests at the **Consulate Suites** (76 Water St., 850/635-1515, www.consulatesuites.com, $140-305) can pretend they're visiting dignitaries. Prior to the Civil War, the French consulate was located on the second floor. The property has been renovated and transformed into a shopping attraction of boutiques. Above it are four apartment-size luxury suites with 11-foot tin ceilings. Three of the four suites overlook the river, and all have balconies and sleep four people.

TRANSPORTATION

From Tallahassee, follow South Monroe Street to U.S. 61. Veer to the right onto U.S. 61 and follow it for 4.2 miles. After U.S. 61 turns into U.S. 319, follow U.S. 319 for 72 miles until you reach Apalachicola. The 76-mile drive takes 1.5 hours in normal traffic.

If you're piloting your own small plane, **Apalachicola Regional Airport** (8 Airport Rd., Apalachicola, 850/290-8282) is a former military base that served B-17s in World War II, with three concrete runways and fuel available.

St. George Island

East of St. Vincent Island, St. George Island shelters Apalachicola Bay and St. George Sound, both productive bodies of water for commercial fishing and sportfishing. A 4.1-mile bridge connects the island to the mainland fishing village of Eastpoint. The eastern end of the island is the 1,900-acre St. George Island State Park, which contains some of the most pristine and underpopulated white-sand beaches in Florida, as well as first-class fishing. St. George has got it all, and only a lucky few seem to know about it.

For much of its 5,000 years, the island has been inhabited mostly by birds, reptiles, and a few small mammals. Humans arrived in the early 1900s to harvest the sap from the island's slash pines, used to make turpentine. The island's dunes were used for training exercises during World War II, but it's been underutilized since then.

In 1970, a Tallahassee real estate developer bought up much of the island, then sold Little St. George and the east end, now the state park, to the state of Florida. His company started selling five- and eight-acre tracts. Growth was quick in what is now the Plantation area, but strict environmental rules keep the sight lines low and the water views spectacular. There are still only 1,000 year-round residents, but thousands flock to the island for luxurious beachfront house and condo rentals during the summer months.

SPORTS AND RECREATION
★ St. George Island State Park

Officially the **Dr. Julian G. Bruce St. George Island State Park** (1900 E. Gulf Beach Dr., 850/927-2111, 8am-dusk daily, $6 per vehicle), the park was closed at press time due to damage from 2018's Hurricane Michael; check with the park to make sure it has reopened. Most locals call it the state park. The land was acquired in 1963, and the completed facilities opened in 1980. Imagine 1,900 acres of windswept sea oat-fringed dunes, gorgeous enough and underpopulated enough to make most lists of best beaches in the United States. The whole east end of the island is state park land, so officially it's the longest state park beach in Florida—nine miles of white sand.

The water is warm, shallow, and usually calm enough for hours of swimming. (Sorry, surfers, they don't call it the pond of Mexico for nothing.) The beaches seem to be stocked with perfect shells, and the abundant fish are often biting. Along the beach you'll see starfish and sand dollars, jellyfish, loggerhead sea turtle nests during summer, and hardly another person. When you get tired of the perfect white sand, there are nature trails through the pine flatwood forest and live oak hammocks.

The park has no lifeguards or concessions, so bring your own picnic provisions and toys. There are, however, six sets of rustic wood-beamed pavilions with sheltered picnic tables, water fountains, outside showers, and restrooms. It is illegal to walk through the sea oats along the high sand dunes—walk

from the parking area out to the beach only along the weathered wooden boardwalks. Be on the lookout for the burrowing ghost crab, its semitransparent carapace and huge eyes making it a wild sight (they can also run up to 10 mph). In the woods you might glimpse raccoons, snakes, and diamondback terrapins.

Anglers most often catch whiting, but you'll see them reeling in flounder, redfish, pompano, sea trout, and Spanish mackerel as well. (A saltwater fishing license is required.) Birders, on the other hand, train their sights on ospreys, eagles, snowy plover, least terns, black skimmers, and willets.

RV and tent camping is permitted in the 60 pine-shaded campsites ($24) in the forests on the bay side, set behind the dunes. The campground features a dump station, flush toilets, and nature trails. The maximum stay is 14 nights; there are sites to camp with pets. There are also primitive campsites at Gap Point, a hike in along a 2.5-mile trail that meanders from the bay through the pine flatwood forest. As with all Florida state parks, reserve campsites at www.reserveamerica.com. Boat ramps are located at the Youth Camp Area and East Slough, and kayaks are available for daily rental.

Loggerhead Turtles

St. George Island is said to have one of the darkest night skies in the continental United States, making it a favorable place for stargazing. While this is a byproduct of low population density, some of it is by design: Franklin County adopted the Lighting Ordinance for Marine Turtle Protection in 1998, which restricts house lights, streetlights, and even flashlight use on the island.

Florida beaches are home to 90 percent of the loggerhead sea turtle nests in the southeastern United States, the largest population in the western hemisphere and one of the two largest in the world. St. George Island provides habitat for loggerhead, green, and leatherback turtles. Every year, starting around May 1, would-be mother loggerheads travel tremendous distances to come ashore here to

nest (scientists think they return to the beach on which they were born). It's been shown that lights on and around beach homes can distract the mothers from their task and disorient the hatchlings enough to send them crawling inland instead of toward the sea, making them easy snacks for their many predators.

Currently, all seven sea turtle species are listed as either threatened or endangered. But finally there is some good news: Since 2009, the number of turtle nests has increased every year. Nest numbers spiked in 2012 for all five species that swim in the Gulf of Mexico and nest along the Florida Gulf Coast. There were five times the number of loggerhead nests recorded in 2012 compared to 2009. Conservation efforts are still vital for this species, and it is important for visitors to help keep these species safe. If you've rented a beach house, keep outdoor house lights off as much as possible and pull your shades at night to minimize window light pollution on the beaches. Beyond that, call **Apalachicola Riverkeeper** (850/653-8936) to report disoriented hatchlings or injured or stranded turtles.

If your visit to St. George Island coincides with nesting season (May-Oct.), you can take a night beach walk in the hopes of glimpsing mother sea turtles crawling ashore—they leave a distinctive filigreed track in the sand—or the hatchlings clumsily flapping their way back out to sea. A single female loggerhead builds as many as three or four nests in a single season, laying about a hundred eggs in each one—it's quite a sight to see the little guys struggling to meet the sea, but resist the impulse to take flash photographs. You can volunteer with St. George Island Volunteer Turtlers to find, mark, and protect turtle nests incubating in the warm sand. Call the **Apalachicola National Estuarine Research Reserve** (850/670-7721) to ask about volunteer efforts.

1: St. George Island State Park 2: The Beach Pit, a favorite for breakfast and barbecue on St. George Island 3: Doug's Fresh Seafood Market 4: kayaks on St. George Island Beach

★ Biking St. George Island

If you enjoy a nice bike ride, you'll probably love St. George Island, which has excellent bike accessibility and a remarkable number of paved bike paths. All the way from the Plantation side (west end) to the state park at the east end, there are straight flat roadside paths for bicyclists, and miles of off-roading possibilities as well. Bikes can be rented from **Island Adventures** (105 E. Gulf Beach Dr., 850/927-3655, $15 per day, $45 per week). If you'd rather rent a golf cart, visit **Jolly Roger Beach Shop** (139 West Gorrie Dr., 850/927-2999, $195 per day). To ride in style, rent their limo golf cart ($44 per hour, $225 per day, $595 per week). They also rent surfboards ($45 per day), kayaks ($60 per day), and a long list of beach gear.

Birding

The shores and inland areas of St. George Island are rife with birding possibilities. In the sheltered harbor of Eastpoint, loons, gulls, and waterfowl host a number of vagrant bird species in the fall. From the bridge linking Eastpoint with St. George Island, you'll see the nests of large colonies of least terns and black skimmers April-July. As its name implies, the least tern is the smallest of the terns, weighing about one ounce. Don't confuse them with the medium-size gull-billed terns, with their heavy black bills and short forked tails, that also occasionally hang out here.

Florida birders also boast of the area's abundance of Sprague's pipit in the late fall. These are hard to see, usually choosing to hang out in fields of short grass. In the winter it's not uncommon to see the common goldeneye in nearby water.

Walking the shores of St. George Island, you'll view American oystercatchers, spotted sandpipers, ruddy turnstones, willets, sanderlings, several kinds of plover, and loads of other shorebirds. Driving down the island's many wooded dirt roads yields a wealth of sightings in the spring and fall—bald eagles nest here, and in the fall you're likely to see sharp-shinned hawks, peregrine falcons, northern harriers, and American kestrels.

In the early spring, the youth campsite's oak hammock at St. George Island State Park is a good place to spot newly arrived migratory birds, possibly something as rare as a Connecticut warbler. If you go to the end of the park's paved road and walk out to the beach, you may find some snowy plover. In winter, northern gannets are sometimes spotted in the park or in offshore waters.

One of the best ways to view many of the island's 200 species of birds is to arrange a bird-focused kayak trip with the guides at **Journeys of St. George Island** (850/927-3259, www.sgislandjourneys.com, $50 pp). They'll take you on a relaxing paddle on the back side of St. George Island and identify the marine and birdlife while you explore one of the finest stretches of the Forgotten Coast.

Guided Tours

Journeys of St. George Island (850/927-3259, www.sgislandjourneys.com) also offers a large variety of family ecotours and kids-only trips, including dolphin-watching, shark fishing adventures, fly-fishing excursions, and bait-fishing trips both in the bay and offshore. The ecotours, fishing trips, guided paddling trips, and boat cruises range $30-450. The kayak tours on the Apalachicola River (3 hours, $50, $30 children) are a great deal.

SHOPPING

St. George isn't famous for its shopping beyond a couple of gas stations, a handful of beach supply shops, and a plethora of ice-cream stands, most with prices that reflect isolation inflation. **Island Outfitters** (235 E. Gulf Beach Dr., 850/927-2604, 10am-5pm daily), has resort wear and bathing suits along with saltwater fishing tackle, rods, reels, and other beach accessories. Island Outfitters offers inshore fishing charters for up to four people (5 hours, $400) in the bay and along the Apalachicola River. **Sometimes It's Hotter Seasoning Company** (37 E. Pine Ave., 850/927-5039, 10am-6pm daily) is a unique local institution and a nice place to pick up dried herbs and spicy sauces for grilling, blackening, and boiling seafood and meats.

If you arrived on-island without your beach essentials, the nearby **St. George Island Beach Chair Rentals** (137 E. Pine St., 850/670-4536, 9am-7pm daily) rents beach chairs ($5 per day), beach umbrellas ($20 per day), kayaks (2-seater $15 per hour), surfboards ($10 per day, $60 per week), Hobie catamarans ($40 per hour, $140 per half-day), and other beach necessities. They offer free delivery to any St. George Island rental unit.

FOOD

The majority of the island is given over to beach houses, many with impressive kitchens overlooking the bay or Gulf. Most vacationers come prepared to dine in. Grocery stores include a **Piggly Wiggly** (130 U.S. 98, 850/927-2808) and an **IGA** (425 U.S. 98, 850/653-9695) in Apalachicola. Beyond that, definitely patronize some of the local seafood retailers. On the island, look for **Doug's Fresh Seafood Market** (Gulf Beach Dr. W. and W. Chili Dr.). He parks his food truck next to the lighthouse, and he's got excellent shrimp, crabs, scallops, oysters, grouper, amberjack, and mahimahi, all at great prices.

Seafood

Restaurants on the island are more casual than those in Apalachicola, but that's fitting. On the beach side (the Gulf side, as opposed to the bay side of this long strip of an island), people gravitate toward the **Blue Parrot Oceanfront Café** (68 W. Gorrie Dr., 850/927-2987, 11am-10pm daily, $9-25), to relax on the wide deck or sidle up to the tiki bar, enjoying beer and cocktails over an excellent po'boy sandwich or burger. Opt for the local seafood (grouper and oysters) over the imports (conch fritters and Alaskan crab, for crying out loud) and you'll navigate the menu just fine.

In June the Blue Parrot often holds the annual **mullet toss.** They build a mullet-tossing range, and you pay a small fee to try your hand at flinging these slippery raw fish as far as you can. Underhanded, overhanded, football-style—there are several competition divisions: men, women, children, and free-form (in which you build a mechanical device to catapult your fish to victory).

On the bay side, **Paddy's Raw Bar** (240 3rd St., 850/927-2299, 11am-midnight daily, $10-20) offers up cold beer, oysters, peel-and-eat shrimp, sandwiches, salads, gumbo, and a variety of seafood platters, with live music on most weekends.

American

The Beach Pit (49 W. Pine Ave., 850/799-1020, 7:30am-8:30pm daily, $6-20) is one of the few options for standard American breakfast or a barbecue lunch. The food and the atmosphere aren't anything exceptional, but the prices are good and there are a few healthy options. Imagine a place with checkered tablecloths that serves biscuits and gravy and other heavy American-style selections at breakfast, as well as lunches of ribs and other barbecue delights that are smothered in sweet sauce and come with picnic-style sides. The dinner menu has steaks and a variety of seafood.

Mexican

For budget travelers who want something fast, visit **St. George Cantina** (37 E. Pine Ave., 850/927-2222, 11am-8pm Tues.-Thurs., 11am-9pm Fri.-Sat., noon-8pm Sun., $6-12), with a variety of Mexican classics like tacos, quesadillas, and nachos as well as vegetarian options and several American items like chicken wings and hot dogs. Tuesday-Thursday they offer specials on tacos.

Pizza and Ice Cream

BJ's Pizza & Subs (105 W. Gulf Beach Dr., 850/927-2805, 11am-10pm daily, $7-20) tosses good pizzas (also offered by the slice) and has a raucous game room in which to rapidly lose a pocketful of quarters. **Aunt Ebby's Island Deli & Ice Cream** (147 E. Gulf Beach Dr., 850/927-3229, 11am-5pm daily Mar.-Sept.) is

the place to stop for a frozen treat after a long hot day at the beach.

Drinks

Harry A's (28 W. Bayshore Dr., 850/927-3400, 11am-midnight Sun.-Thurs., 11am-2am Fri.-Sat.) is just about the oldest building on the island, with the kind of wide, inviting front porch that's more and more difficult to leave after each successive beer. The tavern where locals meet visitors over a pint and some hot wings, Harry's A's brings in musical entertainment most nights and serves up straightforward bar fare like pizza, tacos, and fried seafood.

ACCOMMODATIONS

On St. George Island, hotel or inn accommodations are only sensible if you are staying for less than two days and are traveling alone or as a couple. Families tend to rent one of 800 beach cottages or houses on the island, most offered by the week (and by the weekend off-season). Some of these houses are remarkably large, with more than 10 bedrooms, and provide a wonderful opportunity to convene several generations of your family. Pets are often allowed, and many homes have private pools, game rooms, and tremendous kitchens for preparing the daily catch.

Hotels

Affordable and geared toward families, the **Buccaneer Inn** (160 W. Gorrie Dr., 850/927-2585, www.buccinn.com, $85-220) is a 1960s-style low-rise beachfront motel. Rooms are clean and no-nonsense, with a lot of pale pastel coverlets and serviceable kitchenettes, and there's a courtyard swimming pool and a Gulf-side tiki hut.

A little fancier, the **St. George Inn** (135 Franklin Blvd., 850/827-5740, www.stgeorge-inn.com, $120-195) is two blocks from the beach, with clean, modest rooms. The sprawling house, with wraparound porches affording Gulf and bay views, has recently been remodeled to include a few two-room suites and a conference room.

Vacation Rentals

★ **Resort Vacation Properties** (850/927-2322, www.resortvacationproperties.com) handles many of the upscale rental houses, with detailed descriptions and photos of properties on the website. They deal with properties all over the island but seem to have a special lock on the large houses in the Plantation, the private community on the western end of the island. Other agents that traffic in properties all over the island include **Collins Vacation Rentals** (850/927-2900, www.collinsvacationrentals.com) and **Suncoast Realty** (800/341-2021, www.uncommonflorida.com). Beyond picking your price range (they go from $1,000 per week up to over $5,000 for more luxurious homes), other factors to consider include whether to be on the Gulf or bay side, how close to town you want to be, and the kind of neighborhood in which you feel most comfortable.

ST. GEORGE PLANTATION

This is a gated community stretching from the Gulf to the bay on the island's west end, with slow winding roads and lots of speed bumps to keep the pace leisurely. Homes are all distinctive in terms of architecture, amenities (many with spa or pool), and decor, but the general vibe is luxury. It's mostly large three-story homes that sleep eight or more. Something to consider here is that the farther toward the west end of the island you settle, the longer the drive is to get a gallon of milk back in town. Within the Plantation is an even more exclusive and secluded area called The Bluffs. It's two quiet cul-de-sacs of luxury homes, each with spectacular views of the Gulf and Apalachicola Bay beyond towering 25-foot dunes.

GULF BEACHES AND EAST END

The four miles in the center of the island are called the Gulf Beaches area. In this, the first populated area on the island, the architectural styles are all over the map, from little Cracker cottages to huge windswept wooden structures on stilts decked out with widow's walks. Not as fancy as those at the Plantation, the homes have the benefit of being a quick bike ride into town for ice cream. Going east, the two miles before you get to the state park are called, not surprisingly, East End. This is less densely populated, with comfortable-looking houses widely spaced, mostly up on high stilts, with great beach access. In the East End area, there are also town houses in a community called 300 Ocean Mile. It is close to the state park, and rentals, while not so fancy, are affordable (around $800 per week, $400 for 3 nights spring and fall, $625 per week winter).

SUNSET BEACH

This community on the Gulf is densely packed with Spanish tile-and-stucco villas and has a decidedly Mediterranean vibe. It has a pool and tennis courts and provides easy access to the state park, which makes it a great choice for birders, anglers, and anyone interested in exploring the park's miles of undeveloped beaches. There are a wide range of options for renters, including homes, condos, and duplexes.

Camping

St. George Island State Park (1900 E. Gulf Beach Dr., 850/927-2111, $24 per day) has 60 campsites with electric and water hookups for RV and tent camping. Reserve far in advance with **ReserveAmerica** (800/326-3521, www.reserveamerica.com). Primitive campsites are available at Gap Point, a 2.5-mile backpacking hike-in site, which can be reserved by calling the park office. There is tents-only youth-group camping for organized groups of 6-25 campers.

TRANSPORTATION

From Apalachicola, drive east on U.S. 98 (South Bayshore Dr.) for 12 miles. Turn right to stay on South Bayshore Drive and continue for 1 mile. Veer right onto Highway 300 and continue for 4.8 miles until you reach St. George Island. The 12-mile drive takes 20 minutes in normal traffic.

Eastpoint and Carrabelle

In spite of the challenges facing Franklin County's oyster industry, the town of Eastpoint, traditionally populated by career oysterers, has managed to maintain its gruff fishing-village beauty. Stop along the roadside waterfront to watch the remaining "housemen" at the wholesale seafood houses manhandle oysters, shrimp, and finfish, brusquely sorting and packing the catch into boxes or bags. It's a year-round venture, with the dwindling oyster harvest rotated seasonally from oyster beds in St. George Sound and environs. Virtually the whole length of Eastpoint's commercial district is perfumed with the briny waft of seafood docks and the sounds of WOYS FM, Oyster Radio, out of Apalachicola, competing with the boisterous calls of fishermen and women getting off work for the day.

Visit soon, because all signs point to significant cultural changes in the future. Eastpoint has never had the amenities to make it a big tourist draw, just a few restaurants, rustic bars, and lots of seafood. But like the rest of the Florida Gulf Coast, it is likely to be developed as soon as the rest of the surrounding shoreline is maxed out with condos, resorts, and beach house rentals.

Carrabelle, 16.5 miles east of Eastpoint, is still an active fishing town with shrimpers and finfishers unloading their daily catch. For just this reason, it's been the filming location for a couple of Victor Nuñez movies, including *Ulee's Gold* starring Peter Fonda and *Coastlines* with Josh Brolin.

EASTPOINT
Apalachicola National Estuarine Research Reserve

Apalachicola Bay is one of the most productive estuarine systems in the northern hemisphere (an estuary is where a river meets the sea, where freshwater meets saltwater). You might get a sense for this while touring the **Apalachicola National Estuarine Research Reserve** and its Nature Center. The reserve houses 1,162 subspecies of plants, 308 species of birds, 186 species of fish, and 57 species of mammals. Much of it is inaccessible unless you have a boat, and stomping around in some parts is discouraged.

★ APALACHICOLA RESERVE NATURE CENTER

The **Nature Center** (108 Island Dr., Eastpoint, 850/670-7700, 9am-4pm Tues.-Sat., free) is on Apalachicola Bay at the foot of the St. George Island Bridge in Eastpoint, and it's an excellent outing for the whole family. The 4,800-square-foot visitors center offers educational exhibits as well as aquariums of local fish and turtles, surrounded by a bayfront park complete with picnic pavilions and an outdoor amphitheater. You're likely to see dolphins, crabs, turtles, snakes, a variety of fish, ospreys, and eagles during a stroll around the visitors center and the surrounding Apalachicola Bay shore park.

ESTUARY TOUR

A remarkable way to explore the estuary is with **Apalach Tours** (850/899-5000, www.apalachtours.com, $40 pp). The guides take you on an hour-long tour that explores the estuary while you wander upriver, through the marsh, and into the swamps.

For something a little more exciting, head out on an airboat and travel up to 40 mph through the estuary with **Apalachicola Airboat Adventures** (850/653-5746, www.apalachicolaairboatadventures.com, $35 pp). They offer tours of one hour and more, with the longer ones exploring the interior of the St. Vincent Wildlife Preserve. They can get to spots only airboats can get to, and you can take home a video of your adventure for an extra fee. The more adventurous should consider their stellar one-hour nighttime airboat

excursions, where you'll see the stars twinkling above as you race through the wetlands spotting alligators, raccoons, flying fish, and all sorts of other skittish nocturnal creatures.

CARRABELLE

There are still fewer than 1,200 residents in Carrabelle, and the downtown has never been gentrified or prettied up for the tourists. It seems that terms like *rustic, quaint,* and even *crusty* were invented for places like this. The town has historically had the world's smallest **police station** (a phone booth), but the force now works outside of that Superman-esque environment. The town had its five minutes of fame when the phone booth police station was featured on the *Tonight Show with Johnny Carson* and *The Today Show.*

It doesn't take long to explore all the police station has to offer, so after you're done, visit the State Forestry Division's **Carrabelle Fire Tower** (9am-sunset, free) on the east side of town, which has great views of the area, or the **Camp Gordon Johnston World War II Museum** (1001 Gray Ave., 850/697-8575, 11am-5pm Tues.-Sat., free) that pays tribute to the amphibious soldiers who trained here and served in World War II, Korea, and Vietnam. Camp Gordon Johnston actually covered 165,000 acres along the Big Bend, with 36 miles along the shores of the Gulf of Mexico. The area was left in its natural state for training purposes, where thousands of soldiers learned to land the craft that would be used on the beaches of Normandy on D-Day.

Carrabelle also boasts the **Crooked River Lighthouse** (1975 W. U.S. 98), a rickety 103-foot iron tower built in 1985 to replace the lighthouse on Dog Island that was destroyed by a hurricane in 1873. In 2007 the Carrabelle Lighthouse Association restored and relit the structure. **Carrabelle Beach,** just west of town, is a popular spot for picnickers and beachcombers.

1: the Apalachicola National Estuarine Research Reserve's Nature Center **2:** Crooked River Lighthouse **3:** the Carrabelle waterfront

FOOD
Eastpoint

There are plenty of seafood markets in Eastpoint around the 300-500 blocks of U.S. 98: **Lynn's Quality Oysters** (402 U.S. 98, 850/670-8796), **Fred's Central Seafood** (322 Patton St., 850/670-8381), and **Barber Seafood** (510 U.S. 98, 850/670-8830) are top choices.

Carrabelle

Harry's in Carrabelle (306 Marine St., Carrabelle, 850/697-9982, 10am-midnight Sun.-Thurs., 10am-2am Fri.-Sat.), just behind the Georgian Motel, opens bright and early to serve the fisherfolk heading into the Gulf. It's mostly a drinking establishment. For food in Carrabelle, head for the ribs at **Hog Wild BBQ** (1593 U.S. 98 E., 850/697-2776, 11am-8pm Mon., 11am-8pm Thurs., 11am-9pm Fri.-Sat., 11am-3pm Sun., $6-12). They also have a popular all-you-can-eat breakfast buffet ($8 adults, $4 under age 12) with unbeatable prices.

ACCOMMODATIONS
Eastpoint

The only lodging in Eastpoint is the **Sportsman Lodge Motel & Marina** (99 N. Bayshore Dr., 850/670-8423, $72-95), a rustic fish camp-style motel and marina overlooking the East Bay. It's wooded, and amenities include kitchenettes, a boat dock, a ramp, and easy access to fishing guides and charters. It has an Old Florida vibe and is an option for budget travelers, but it may not be well suited for families or those looking for quiet and well-maintained rooms. Even if you aim to explore the oyster-fishing charms of Eastpoint, you have a much greater range of hotel options in nearby Apalachicola, and you will find higher quality rooms at the **Buccaneer Inn** (160 W. Gorrie Dr., 850/927-2585, www.buccinn.com, $85-220) just over the bridge on St. George Island.

Campers can stay at the **Coastline RV Resort** (957 U.S. 98, 850/799-1016, $32-60, $197-360 per week, $410-650 per month) and enjoy their well-maintained waterfront sites 3.4 miles east of Eastpoint. Features include a fishing pier, a pool, a bathhouse, and a gift shop. You can rough it in luxury with access to their full kitchen, Wi-Fi, game room, and a small gym. Primitive campsites are available for tent campers ($20, $120 per week), and the entire resort is pet-friendly.

Carrabelle

If you're exploring the Intracoastal Waterway in your own boat, or if you just enjoy being close to marina and sailing culture, stay at **Moorings of Carrabelle** (1000 U.S. 98, 850/697-2800, hotel rooms $89, slips $1.50 per foot per night) located on the Carrabelle River. They offer single hotel rooms, one- and two-bedroom condos, as well as nightly, weekly, and monthly slip rates. They have a full-service marina, and the marina store stocks bait, tackle, and boat supplies.

For something more historic and charming, stay at **The Old Carrabelle Hotel** (201 Tallahassee St., 850/528-3983, www.old-carrabellehotel.com, $97-127). Opened in 2002, owners Kathy and Skip Frink revived the beautiful house that was built in the 1800s. Four guest rooms each have unique and tasteful decor, or rent the detached cottage ($400-450 for 3 nights, $600-800 per week) with three bedrooms, two baths, a full kitchen, a living room, and an excellent screened porch.

TRANSPORTATION

To reach Eastpoint from Apalachicola, drive east on U.S. 98 for six miles, a 10-minute trip in normal traffic.

Apalachee Bay

The colorful little towns of **Panacea** and **Sopchoppy** are both in Wakulla County, south of Tallahassee between Carrabelle and Crawfordville, along U.S. 98 near Apalachee Bay and the Gulf of Mexico, and tucked between Apalachicola National Forest and the St. Marks Wildlife Refuge. Sopchoppy is the nearest town to Alligator Point, and between those two towns is a strange prevalence of white squirrels. There are many lyrical myths about how and why these creatures got here. A great many monarch butterflies also appear here in September-October on their migration to Mexico. During fall, the beaches can be dotted with these beautiful butterflies. Panacea was developed as a tourist resort more than 100 years ago by residents looking to market the incredible local springs. These days it's a sweet town of about 1,000 people, with seafood shops along the main street.

A bigger draw than the towns are the many parks in the area that bring outdoors enthusiasts from around the world. The birding here is exceptional, so pack binoculars. There are also plenty of opportunities to paddle, hike, and camp in diverse landscapes. The most popular parks are Ochlockonee River State Park and Wakulla Springs State Park, due to their developed campgrounds and amenities like hot showers and RV hookups. On the wilder side, consider exploring the less-visited St. Marks National Wildlife Refuge or paddling around in the Big Bend Wildlife Management Area.

SIGHTS
Gulf Specimen Marine Laboratory

Visit Anne and Jack Rudloe's **Gulf Specimen Marine Laboratory** (222 Clark Dr., Panacea, 850/984-5297, 9am-5pm Mon.-Fri., 10am-5pm Sat., 10am-5pm Sun., $10 adults, $9 seniors, $8 ages 3-11). Both Rudloes are marine biologists and authors of well-known books on Florida natural history and marinelife. The nonprofit environmental center and aquarium enable visitors to see green shrimp, scarlet sponges, comb jellyfish, and other local marinelife in a sea-grass meadow or on a limestone outcrop in a collection of seawater tanks and aquariums. It's a "small is beautiful" approach to aquatic creatures.

There's a grassy landing strip in Panacea, where a few enterprising pilots take small charters. Show up and ask around and you might find a pilot to zip you over to Dog Island for the day.

George the Potter

George the Potter (110 Suncat Ridge, 850/962-9311) is a beloved local attraction, with a studio down a dirt road, south off U.S. 319, just east of Sopchoppy. Look for his sign. He makes lovely bowls and mugs, and has a savvy self-promoting bumper sticker that says "Been to Sopchoppy met the potter."

SPORTS AND RECREATION

Ochlockonee River State Park

Near Sopchoppy, on the northern border of Franklin County, you'll find **Ochlockonee River State Park** (429 State Park Rd., Sopchoppy, 850/962-2771, 8am-sunset daily, $4 per vehicle, boat launch $4). An extensive network of hiking and biking trails allow visitors to explore the pine flatwoods and oak thickets that border the Ochlockonee River. Bikes ($10 per day) are available for rent at the park office. Anglers, boaters, and paddlers can access the brackish water Ochlockonee River and the freshwater Dead River from several boat ramps in the park. Thirty campsites ($18) with electrical hookups are nestled in a beautiful oak forest and provide overnight campers with plenty of shade and access to hot showers in the bathhouse. A swimming area is along the Dead River, and birders should bring their binoculars for viewing the healthy population of red-cockaded woodpeckers and ospreys found in the park.

Bald Point State Park

Another popular destination for birding and wildlife-viewing is **Bald Point State Park** (146 Box Cut Rd., off Alligator Dr., 850/349-9146, 8am-sunset daily, $4 per vehicle, $2 pedestrians and bicyclists), located on Alligator Point, where Ochlockonee Bay meets Apalachee Bay. The park has two beaches, Sunrise and North End, which provide excellent habitat for coastal birds and nesting sea turtles, with picnic pavilions at Sunrise Beach. Paddlers can enjoy exploring the coast or venture into the interior of the park by launching a kayak at the boat ramp on the brackish water Tucker Lake, which feeds into Chaires Creek. Surf fishing is permitted at the beaches, and fishing is allowed by kayak or canoe in Tucker Lake and at the bridge over Chaires Creek on Range Road. This is an excellent spot to catch blue crabs, mullet, sea trout, redfish, flounder, and sheepshead. No camping is allowed in the park, but hiking is available along more than 18 miles of trails. To view wildlife and birds, head to the observation deck and boardwalk that overlooks the marsh near North End beach.

St. Marks National Wildlife Refuge

St. Marks National Wildlife Refuge (1255 Lighthouse Rd., St. Marks, 850/925-6121, sunrise-sunset daily, $5 per vehicle) is one of the oldest refuges in the National Wildlife Refuge System, established in 1931 with 68,000 acres of protected coastal land. The coastal marshes, islands, tidal creeks, and estuaries of seven north Florida rivers can be explored by boat or by foot. Stop in first at the **visitors center** (8am-4pm Mon.-Fri., 10am-5pm Sat.-Sun.) to get an overview of what there is to do and see in the park.

The refuge has 75 miles of trails, including a 50-mile segment of the Florida National Scenic Trail, but there are wonderful short walking trails as well: the Plum Orchard Pond Trail (0.3 miles), Headquarters Pond Trail (0.25 miles), and Lighthouse Levee Trail (0.5 miles—the St. Marks Lighthouse is still in use today), and the Mounds Interpretive Trail (1 mile), which offers a diversity of habitats for bird-watching and wildlife-viewing. Hiking here is less pleasant in the summer months,

when you might opt to explore via a driving tour with the air-conditioning on.

The park is a magnet for birders, who come for the myriad wading birds as well as the ospreys, red-cockaded woodpeckers, kestrels, red-shouldered hawks, and bald eagles. The refuge is open to fishing year-round and hunting in season. There are restrooms at the visitors center, Mounds Trail, and Otter Lake Recreation Area, and picnic facilities are next to Mounds Trail and at Otter Lake.

★ Big Bend Saltwater Paddling Trail

Birders enthuse about the **Big Bend Wildlife Management Area's Hickory Mound Impoundment** (850/488-5520). From Tallahassee, take U.S. 98 east, turn right on Cow Creek Grade, and go six miles to the check station. The list of birds here includes waders, ospreys, swallow-tailed and Mississippi kites, bald eagles, buffleheads, gadwalls, and American wigeons. This area is just one of the five, along with Spring Creek, Tide Swamp, Jena, and Snipe Island, that make up the Big Bend Wildlife Management Area, extending 60 miles along the Gulf Coast, with Tallahassee 40 miles north of the northernmost part. All of it is gorgeous wilderness to explore by bike, horseback, foot, or—the best way—kayak. The 105-mile **Big Bend Saltwater Paddling Trail** (Sept.-June) has a 40-page paddling guide (www.myfwc.com, $15) that details seven designated primitive campsites exclusively for trail users, spaced 10-14 miles apart (permits required).

Canoes and kayaks can be rented in Tallahassee at **The Wilderness Way** (3152 Shadeville Rd., 850/877-7200, www.thewildernessway.net, single kayaks or canoes $45 per day, $225 per week, tandem kayaks or canoes $55 per day, $275 per week), which also leads nature-based canoe and kayak tours around the Panhandle.

1: Ochlockonee River State Park 2: historic Sopchoppy train depot

★ Wakulla Springs State Park

A must-see at **Wakulla Springs State Park** (465 Wakulla Park Dr., Wakulla Springs, 850/561-7276, 8am-sunset daily, $6 per vehicle) is the 30-minute narrated glass-bottom boat tour ($8 adults, $5 under age 12), offered only when the water is clear, providing a glimpse into the crystalline 125-foot depths and a window into north Florida's past. A high-jumping fish named Henry is involved. The park offers a 60-minute riverboat tour that takes a different route, but opt for the glass-bottom boat if it's running.

Wakulla Springs are said to be the world's largest and deepest freshwater springs, in which the water temperature remains a constant 70°F. Just 15 miles south of Tallahassee, the springs have been the site of lots of Hollywood filming because of their wild jungle feel. They were a tourist attraction long before Johnny Weissmuller starred as Tarzan or Ricou Browning donned the rubber suit for the 1954 film *Creature from the Black Lagoon*. As a teenager Browning was a lifeguard at Wakulla Springs and put on underwater shows for the glass-bottom boat tours that still run today.

In the past few years, Wakulla has become home to numerous manatees that remain in park waters year-round. The park contains a wonderful six-mile nature trail, picnic facilities, swimming (only in designated areas, as it's gator country), and the stately **Wakulla Lodge** (850/421-2000, $95-150).

Flowing from Wakulla Springs nine miles to the St. Marks River is the crystal-clear **Wakulla River.** Along the Spanish moss-trimmed cypress lining the river's banks is abundant wildlife: manatees, otters, eagles, and numerous waterfowl. Several boat ramps provide access to the river, a perfect day's paddle by kayak or canoe. **TNT Hideaway** (6527 Coastal Hwy., Crawfordville, 850/925-6412, 9am-5pm daily) is a small family-owned business with 20 canoes (2-person $40, 3-person $45 for 4 hours) and 20 kayaks (single $35, double $45 for 4 hours), offering guided tours on the Wakulla River as well as off-the-beaten-path tours to St. Marks Lighthouse and National Wildlife Refuge, Spring Creek, the Aucilla River, the Sopchoppy River, and the Ochlockonee River. To spot manatees, the weekly *Wakulla News* carries a manatee-watch section that gives the specifics of recent sightings.

FESTIVALS AND EVENTS

The first weekend in May draws 20,000 people to Panacea for the **Blue Crab Festival.** At night in summer, the thing to do in these parts is to go swimming in the Gulf when the water's **bioluminescence** lends an eerie shimmer to the dark water. Totally safe (the chemical-based light is produced by a multitude of marine organisms), the gleam seems to echo the stars in the Panacea or Sopchoppy night sky.

In Sopchoppy, the biggest industry is raising worms. Worm grunters pierce loose soil with a wooden stake called a stob. Once the stob is driven into the soil, it gets rubbed with a flat piece of metal called the bat. The vibrations in the ground drive the big earthworms up, where they are scooped, packaged, and sold for bait. If you want to see how it's done, there's an unbelievable nine-minute movie about it on YouTube. This is such a compelling calling that the town of about 500 holds a well-attended **Worm Gruntin' Festival** each April. The second-biggest festival comes in June with the **June Jam** of mostly local musicians performing in the square.

FOOD

For dinner in Panacea, the obvious choice is **Angelo's and Son's Seafood Restaurant** (U.S. 98, east side of the bridge, 850/984-5168, 4:30pm-9pm Thurs., 4:30pm-10pm Fri.-Sat., 11am-9pm Sun., $12-22), on pilings over Ochlockonee Bay. Destroyed in the storm surge from 2005's Hurricane Dennis, it's back in a sturdier structure, with just-caught fish and great views. **Posey's Beyond the Bay** (1506 Coastal Hwy., 850/984-5799, 11am-9pm Tues.-Thurs., 11am-10pm Fri.-Sat., 11am-9pm

Sun., $11-25) is for topless oysters or smoked mullet, or enjoy the restorative comforts at the **Coastal Restaurant** (1305 Coastal Hwy., 850/984-2933, 6am-8pm Thurs.-Mon., $7-15).

Also in Panacea, **Angelo's** (5 Mashers Sand Rd., 850/984-5168, 4:30pm-9pm Thurs., 4:30pm-10pm Fri.-Sat., 11am-9pm Sun., $12-22) is a long-standing and justifiably famous purveyor of the local blue crabmeat (try the seafood cakes). There are waterside tables, a wide wraparound porch, and friendly locals.

For great burgers, sandwiches, and the best pizza in Sopchoppy, head to **Sopchoppy Pizza Company** (106 Municipal Ave., 850/962-1155, 5pm-8pm Wed., 5pm-9pm Thurs.-Fri., 11:30am-9pm Sat., $10-20), in the historic district. Look for the carved gorilla out front.

ACCOMMODATIONS

The **Magnuson Hotel Wildwood Inn** (3896 Coastal U.S. 98, Wakulla, 850/926-4455, $90-150) is a nature and golf resort that's a Certified Green Lodge with an 18-hole golf course, 71 rooms and suites, a fitness center, a pool, and an indoor and outdoor meeting space that can accommodate up to 200, all near the St. Marks National Wildlife Refuge, the Apalachicola National Forest, and Wakulla Springs State Park.

The stately **Wakulla Lodge** (850/421-2000, $95-150) in Wakulla Springs State Park was built in 1937, with 27 individually decorated rooms that have antiques and period furniture. If you try the Ball Room Restaurant, order the excellent navy bean soup or fried chicken. During the slow season (Sept.-Feb.), rates drop and good specials are offered, like the dinner and a boat tour for two plus a night at the lodge ($99).

After a day at Wakulla Springs or along the Wakulla River, bunk down at the **Sweet Magnolia Inn** (803 Port Leon Dr., St. Marks, 850/925-7670, $149-219) or one of the area's campgrounds: **Ochlockonee River State Park** (429 State Park Rd., U.S. 319, 4 miles south of Sopchoppy, 850/962-2771, $18) or

Holiday Campground (14 Coastal Hwy., Ochlockonee Bay, 850/984-5757, around $30). You can also camp in Sopchoppy at the Myron B. Hodge City Park (Sheldon St. and Park Ave., 850/962-4611, $15).

TRANSPORTATION

To reach Sopchoppy from Apalachicola, drive east on U.S. 98 for 32.4 miles, then veer left onto U.S. 319 and follow it for 10.5 miles until you reach Sopchoppy. The 43-mile drive takes 55 minutes in normal traffic. To reach Panacea from Sopchoppy, drive north on U.S. 319 for 6.3 miles, then turn left onto U.S. 98 and follow it for 3.7 miles. The 11-mile drive takes 15 minutes in normal traffic. To reach Panacea from Apalachicola, drive east on U.S. 98. The 47.8-mile drive takes 55 minutes in normal traffic.

Information and Services

The Forgotten Coast is in the **eastern time zone.**

VISITOR INFORMATION

Anita Grove at the **Apalachicola Chamber of Commerce** (122 Commerce St., 850/653-9419, www.apalachicolabay.org, 9am-5pm Mon.-Fri., 11am-4pm Sat.) is also a tremendous resource. Be sure to pick up the historic walking tour brochure.

POLICE AND EMERGENCIES

In an emergency, dial 911. For nonemergencies, there's the **Apalachicola Police Department** (127 Ave. E, 850/653-9755), the **Franklin County Sheriff's Department** (270 Hwy. 65, Eastpoint, 850/670-8500), and the **Carrabelle Police Department** (1001 Gray Ave., 850/697-3691), which until recently was the smallest in the United States, located inside the phone booth in town.

If you find yourself in need of a doctor, try the **Eastpoint Medical Center** (35 Island Dr., Eastpoint, 850/670-8585, 8am-noon and 1pm-5pm Mon.-Fri., no emergency services), **George E. Weems Memorial Hospital** (135 Ave. G, Apalachicola, 850/653-8853), and **Weems East Medical Center** (110 NE 5th St., Carrabelle, 850/697-2345).

For pharmacy needs, try **Buy Rite Drugs** (45 Ave. D, Apalachicola, 850/653-8825) or **CVS** (139 Ave. E, Apalachicola, 850/653-8737). Pet emergencies are best handled at **Apalachicola Bay Animal Clinic** (187 U.S. 98, Eastpoint, 850/670-8306).

FISHING LICENSES

Fishing licenses are sold in the **County Tax Collector's Office** (33 Ave. B, 850/653-9323) or most places that hunting and fishing gear and bait are sold. It is free for Florida residents to obtain a saltwater license to fish from the shore or structures, but you still need to have a license. An annual saltwater license for Florida residents to fish from a boat is $17 and $32 for annual saltwater and freshwater combo. Saltwater annual license for nonresidents is $47; a nonresident three-day saltwater license is $17, and a seven-day saltwater license is $30.

Panama City Beach and the Emerald Coast

Unified by their eye-catching emerald water,

the beaches of northwest Florida, from Pensacola to South Walton and Panama City, offer miles of unspoiled natural beauty. Some say the emerald color of the water in this area is the result of blue-green algae. Not true—it's just very clear water, layered over reflective white sand in the shallows that produces the green color—the deeper the water, the bluer it gets.

Each of the destinations in this region has its own distinct draws and dramatically different character. Panama City Beach is the biggest draw along the Gulf Coast of Florida for college spring breakers. It's about crowds of people partying and enjoying themselves at the beautiful beaches, miniature golf courses, and souvenir shops. It's bustling

Highlights

Look for ★ to find recommended sights, activities, dining, and lodging.

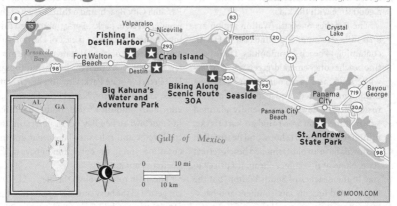

★ **St. Andrews State Park:** This state park in Panama City, at one point named "the world's best beach" by *Travel Magazine*, offers miles of Gulf-side beach as well as a broad inviting Grand Lagoon and a 700-acre offshore barrier strip called Shell Island (page 299).

★ **Big Kahuna's Water and Adventure Park:** If the beach isn't enough to fully occupy the family, head for these 25 acres of waterslides, flumes, tubing, lagoons, and wave pools (page 311).

★ **Crab Island:** People congregate daily at this partially submerged island for some fun in the sun. Rent a watercraft and join the party (page 312).

★ **Fishing in Destin Harbor:** With cobia, sailfish, and wahoo, Destin is a serious fishing destination. Arrange a charter to find out why Destin is often called the "World's Luckiest Fishing Village" (page 313).

★ **Seaside:** Spend a day exploring this picturesque town with excellent boutique shops and restaurants, beautiful beaches, and first-class rental properties (page 321).

★ **Biking Along Scenic Highway 30A:** Explore the Beaches of South Walton in your own time with a bike ride along the 19-mile paved path that follows Scenic Highway 30A (page 324).

with personal watercraft and parasailers, bikinis, restaurants heavily reliant on deep fryers, and partiers cruising the strip with their car windows down.

The Destin and Fort Walton Beach area is in the westernmost part, closest to Pensacola Beach. The fishing village of Destin has seen enormous growth as tourism has taken off, with lots of new construction, attractions, and restaurants to lure ever more people. With one of the best locations for fishing on the Gulf Coast, Destin is only 30 miles inland from the 100-Fathom Curve where the best deep-sea fishing for tuna, wahoo, blue marlin, and much more is found. It has been developed at a fast pace, but most of the beachfront is still low-rise. Folks visit Destin, Fort Walton Beach, and Okaloosa Island to go fishing, splash in the emerald-green water, and have a good time with the kids.

The Beaches of South Walton region are a 26-mile stretch of shoreline east of Destin containing 14 beach communities. These pristine beaches offer emerald-green water, sugar-white sand, and rare coastal dune lakes—a unique and varied landscape with private residences in newish ecofriendly planned communities. You won't find go-kart tracks, minimarts, or T-shirt shops, and nearly all of the towns have an old-fashioned beach-retreat style. None of this comes cheap: It's pricey to stay in the Beaches of South Walton, but the understated upscale environment and back-to-basics feel are memorable.

PLANNING YOUR TIME

The Emerald Coast region stretches 56 miles from Destin in the west to Panama City in the east. The best way to explore the area is by car along several primary feeders: U.S. 98, U.S. 331, Highway 85, and I-10. If you have the luxury of owning a boat, explore the Emerald Coast from the water and rent bikes to explore each of the towns.

There is a huge diversity of attractions

and a range of accommodations along this stretch of coast. But where to stay? Anglers: Go to Destin or Fort Walton Beach. For upscale leisure with coastal beauty: Visit the Beaches of South Walton. Spring breakers: Get to Panama City Beach, and remember to have a designated driver. Panama City Beach is worth two days of intensive revelry, three if you have a long attention span.

High season along the Panhandle is summer, with rates dropping precipitously in the fall-winter. Spring break is a brief flurry in March-April, densest in Panama City Beach. Many of the rentals along the 14 communities of the Beaches of South Walton have a minimum stay, some as long as a week during high season. The area could occupy you for that long, with a day trip to Pensacola, another day trip to visit the amusements in Panama City Beach, and a third to one of the wonderful state parks. For camping and hiking, the area to explore is east of Destin, with a whole string of coastal state parks within a few miles of each other, the best being Topsail Hill Preserve State Park, Grayton Beach State Park, and Henderson State Park. There is an enormous amount of remarkable paddling in Choctawhatchee Bay north of Destin, the freshwater and saltwater lakes that dot the coastline, and in the collection of bays to the north of Panama City.

The main road through the area is U.S. 98, congested in the busy summer-spring months. Don't miss a drive along Highway 30A, which runs south from U.S. 98 through the smaller upscale communities of Seaside, Blue Mountain Beach, WaterColor, and Rosemary Beach, among other picturesque towns along this delightful stretch of coast. Rent a bike and pedal the extensive bike path along Highway 30A. Spring to early fall, accommodations along Highway 30A tend to book farther in advance, with the most popular being the cottages at Seaside. Make plans as early as

---

Previous: miniature golf in Panama City; fishing boat in Destin Harbor; bike rental shops along Scenic Highway 30A.

Panama City Beach and the Emerald Coast

Blackwater River State Forest

Gulf Islands National Seashore

Pensacola Bay

To Pensacola

Milton

Navarre Beach

EGLIN AIR FORCE BASE

Crestview

Fort Walton Beach

FISHING IN DESTIN HARBOR

Valparaiso

Niceville

BIG KAHUNA'S WATER AND ADVENTURE PARK

Destin

Fred Gannon Rocky Bayou State Park

CRAB ISLAND

Choctawhatchee Bay

Topsail Hill Preserve State Park

Dune Allen Beach

Santa Rosa Beach

Grayton Beach

SEASIDE

Point Washington

Eden Gardens State Park

DeFuniak Springs

Gordon

Seagrove Beach

RUSSELL-FIELDS PIER

Camp Helen State Park

BIKING ALONG SCENIC ROUTE 30A

Freeport

Redbay

Prosperity

Panama City Beach

Rick Seizer Park

Schooner's Beach

ST. ANDREWS STATE PARK

Shell Island

NORTHWEST FLORIDA BEACHES INT'L AIRPORT

Panama City

West Bay

Crystal Lake

Chipley

Gulf of Mexico

St. Andrews Bay

North Bay

Falling Waters State Park

CENTRAL TIME ZONE

EASTERN TIME ZONE

Callaway

East Bay

Bayou George

Fountain

Florida Caverns State Park

Marianna

St. Joseph Bay

Port St. Joe

To Wewahitchka

To Tallahassee

Choctawhatchee River

© MOON.COM

0 10 km
0 10 mi

possible for high season. In the winter you can often find exceptional rates on upscale rooms.

The nearest airports to Destin and Fort Walton Beach are the **Destin-Fort Walton Beach Airport** (VPS, 1701 Hwy. 85 N., 850/651-7160), on Eglin Air Force Base, a small airport with flights on Delta, American, United, and Allegiant, and the **Northwest Florida Beaches International Airport** (ECP, 6300 West Bay Pkwy., Panama City, 850/763-6751), the first international airport built in the United States in a decade and served by Delta, American, Southwest, and United. A 50-minute drive west, **Pensacola International Airport** (PNS, 2430 Airport Blvd., Pensacola, 850/436-5000, www.flypensacola.com) is the biggest airport in northwest Florida.

As of this writing, the **Amtrak** (800/872-7245) *Sunset Limited* service was not operating due to the damage 2005's Hurricane Katrina caused to the tracks in New Orleans. You will need your own vehicle to get around locally.

Panama City Beach

Panama City Beach gets billed as the number-one spring break beach in the country, annually attracting 300,000 young people ready to throw down for spring break, with a ton of attractions to keep them entertained. With the same green water and white sand found elsewhere on the Emerald Coast, these beaches are more action-oriented, with volleyball, Frisbee, skim boarding, Jet Skiing, and parasailing. Although the beach is wide, with a lengthy expanse of shallows, there are hundreds of natural and artificial reefs offshore—Panama City Beach ranks with Key Largo for the best diving in the country. The fishing is also good, with mackerel, flounder, redfish, and other game fish in the clear waters.

At the east end of the city, St. Andrews State Park is one of the most popular outdoor recreation spots in Florida, with verdant woods, sea oat-fringed sand dunes, fresh- and saltwater marshes, a lagoon swimming area, fishing jetties, hiking trails, 2.5 miles of beach, and two campgrounds. From here, take the pedestrian ferry to Shell Island, an undisturbed 700-acre barrier island just across from the mainland, for sunning, shelling, birding, or watching the sunset. Along with the beaches, the area is known for attractions like miniature golf, waterslide parks, go-kart tracks, and a marine park.

PCB is packed in March-April and summer, when tourists from Georgia and Alabama flock here. But in May and early fall in is an entertaining beachside playground with loads of modestly priced accommodations. At these times that you can understand why the area has been a popular beach vacation spot for more than 40 years.

SIGHTS
Gulf World
The best family attraction is **Gulf World** (15412 Front Beach Rd., 850/234-5271, 9am-7pm daily Mar.-Aug., 10am-3pm daily Sept.-Feb., $30 adults, $22 seniors, $20 ages 5-11, free under age 5), with a state-of-the-art dolphin habitat, a new bird theater, and enclosed tropical gardens. The marine mammal park opened in 1969 with animal shows and displays. It has a facility to rehabilitate stranded or injured marine animals from all over the Panhandle. As with so many of Florida's aquariums and water parks, there is a swim-with-the-dolphins option ($99-189 pp), a trainer-for-a-day program, and a slumber-party option.

Coconut Creek Family Fun Park
Coconut Creek Family Fun Park (9807 Front Beach Rd., 850/234-2625, www.coconutcreekfun.com, 10am-10:30pm

Panama City Beach

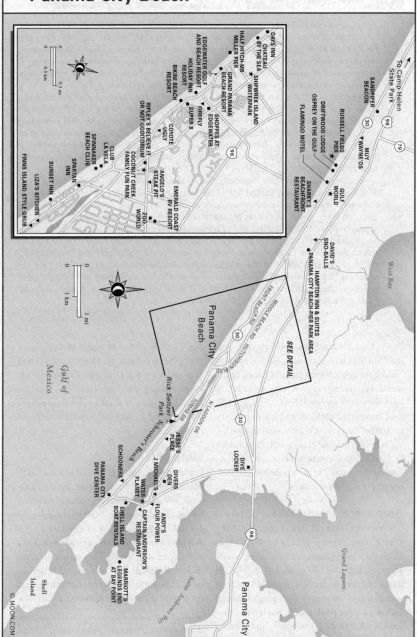

0
0.3 mi
0.5 km

0
1 mi
1 km

To Camp Helen State Park

SANDPIPER BEACON

RUSSELL FIELDS PIER

DRIFTWOOD LODGE
OSPREY ON THE GULF
FLAMINGO MOTEL

MU'Y WAYNE'OS

SHARKY'S BEACHFRONT RESTAURANT

GULF WORLD

DAVID'S SNO-BALLS
PANAMA CITY BEACH-PIER PARK AREA
HAMPTON INN & SUITES

West Bay

DAYS INN
CHATEAU BY THE SEA
SHIPWREK ISLAND WATERPARK
HALF HITCH-MB
MILLER PIER
EDGEWATER GOLF AND BEACH RESORT
GRAND PANAMA BEACH RESORT
HOLIDAY INN RESORT
BIKINI BEACH RESORT
SHOPPES AT EDGEWATER
FIREFLY
SUPER 8
RIPLEY'S BELIEVE IT OR NOT ODDITORIUM
COYOTE UGLY
ANGELO'S STEAK PIT
CLUB LA VELA
SPINNAKER BEACH CLUB
COCONUT CREEK FAMILY FUN PARK
EMERALD COAST RV RESORT
ZOO WORLD
SPARTAN INN
SUNSET INN
FINNS ISLAND STYLE GRUB
LIZA'S KITCHEN

Panama City Beach

FRONT BEACH RD.
MIDDLE BEACH RD.
HUTCHISON BLVD.

SEE DETAIL

Rick Seltzer Park

Schooner's Beach

N LAGOON DR
TOMS DR

JESSE'S PLACE

DIVERS DEN

DIVE LOCKER

J MICHAEL'S

WATER PLANET

ANDY'S FLOUR POWER

CAPTAIN ANDERSON'S RESTAURANT

PANAMA CITY DIVE CENTER

SCHOONERS

SHELL ISLAND BOAT RENTALS

MARRIOTT'S LEGENDS END AT BAY POINT

Gulf of Mexico

Shell Island

Saint Andrews Bay

Grand Lagoon

Panama City

© MOON.COM

Escape from Spring Break

If you find yourself in Panama City during Spring Break but don't want to party, head west to the more family-centric and upscale communities along Highway 30A. **Seaside, Watercolor,** and **Rosemary Beach** cater to the adult crowd, but expect to pay a high cost for all the luxuries and upscale lodging in these picture-perfect beachfront getaways. If you're already staying in Panama City, these communities make excellent day trips a short drive west, but far enough away that you won't hear the thumping bass of the Panama City party crowd.

For a quiet stretch of beach, consider **Grayton Beach State Park,** close to the restaurants, shops, and activities along Highway 30A, or **Topsail Hill Dunes State Park,** even farther west near Seaside, offering more solitude and several miles of beautiful beaches and rolling dunes. South of Panama City, **St. Andrews State Park** is a good choice, but because of its proximity to the city, you may find a few spring break stragglers looking for a quiet place to party. If you don't want to take the chances with crowds, head past Miramar Beach to **Henderson Beach State Park.**

For hiking trails, camping, and paddling slow-water streams, **Pine Log State Forest** to the northwest, **Camp Helen State Park** to the west, and **Point Washington State Forest** to the west of Panama City are excellent quiet, natural areas to explore. For a day of adventure, gallop on the horse trails with a day of horseback riding with **Sunshine Riding Trails** (2273 Rolling Pines Rd., Chipley, 850/773-1900, 8am-9pm Mon.-Sat., 8am-9pm Sun., $45 for 1 hour, $60 for 2 hours, $85 for 3 hours, $110 for 4 hours), which also runs overnight horse camping trips. To stay on the water, take a day excursion with **Ashley Gorman Shell Island Cruises** (5701 U.S. 98, east end of Hathaway Bridge, 850/785-4878, www.shellislandcruises.com, $34 adults, $12 under age 13, free under age 3). He'll motor you around St. Andrew Bay and stop by Shell Island, where you can walk the quiet beach and hunt for shells. He also offers a sunset dolphin-watching cruise on his beautiful double-decker tour boat.

Sun.-Thurs., 10am-11pm Fri.-Sat., $24, golf only $13.50, Gran Maze only $13.50) has two miniature golf courses in an African safari motif. The recently rebuilt maze is the better part, the size of a football field, where you will find disoriented children and lots of military personnel using their professional navigation skills to find the four checkpoints (Fiji, Tahiti, Samoa, and Bali) essential to successfully navigating the maze. There's no shame in crawling under to get out of here.

Shipwreck Island Waterpark

Shipwreck Island Waterpark (12201 Hutchinson Blvd., 850/234-3333, www. shipwreckisland.com, 10:30am-5pm daily summer, $36 over 50 inches tall, $30 under 50 inches, free under 35 inches, $25 seniors) is the kind of water park with long slides and flumes, a wave pool, kiddie pools—in other words, what to do if the beach isn't holding the kids' interest for another warm summer day. There is a 48-inch height restriction on two of the more exciting rides (the Rapid River Run and Tree Top Drop), and you're not allowed to bring food from outside or flotation devices, goggles, or masks. Little ones not yet potty-trained are required to wear waterproof swim diapers.

Water Planet

For close encounters of the fin kind, visit **Water Planet** (5709 N. Lagoon Dr., 850/230-6030, www.waterplanetusa.com, 4-hour tour $98 pp, 3-day program $430 pp, 1-week program $750 pp), where you can swim with dolphins in their natural environment. They offer swim sessions for kids and adults and therapy sessions for children with special needs. It's an incredible opportunity to get close to these amazing aquatic mammals. The

1: aerial view of Panama City Beach during Spring Break **2:** the Skywheel at Panama City Beach

dolphin experience includes a boat ride across the St. Andrews Bay, the dolphin encounter, shelling on Shell Island, and exploring boat wrecks in the area. The dolphins are encountered in the wild in the bay or surrounding waters.

Other Sights

Need more to do? There's a **Ripley's Believe It or Not! Museum** (9907 Front Beach Rd., 850/230-6113, 10am-6pm Sun.-Thurs., 10am-8pm Fri.-Sat., $18 adults, $14 ages 6-12) with all the requisite shrunken heads and scale models of the *Lusitania* made out of ear wax. OK, I made that one up. Nearby you'll find **Zoo World Zoological and Botanical Park** (9008 Front Beach Rd., 850/230-1243, 9:30am-4pm daily, $17 adults, $16 ages 65 and over, $14 ages 2-12), a small pleasant zoo. The best part is the interspecies interaction between Tonda the orangutan and T. K. the tabby cat. Little kids will enjoy **Sea Dragon Pirate Cruise** (departs from 5325 N. Lagoon Dr., 850/234-7400, $27 adults, $23 ages 60 and over, $19 under age 15, reservations recommended), a cruise with Captain Phil on a totally kitted-out pirate ship, heavy on the "argh." **Museum of Man in the Sea** (17314 Panama City Beach Pkwy., 850/235-4101, 10am-5pm Wed.-Sat., $7 adults, $5.50 seniors, $7 ages 6-17, free under age 6) is a small but interesting museum that delves into the history of deep-sea diving and ocean exploration. **Skywheel** (15700 L. C. Hilton Jr Dr., 850/888-0020, www.skywheelpcb.com, 11am-8pm daily, $15 adults, $10 children) is the huge Ferris wheel near the M. B. Miller pier. It gives you an exciting ride and an incredible aerial view of the beach.

BEACHES

With more than 27 miles of beaches and countless beach access points in the Panama City Beach area, it's hard to make a list of the top stretches of coast. Paradise can be found on any beach when you have a sunny day, waves rolling on shore, and good company. If you're not staying at a beachfront hotel, all you

have to do is drive down Front Beach Road and park at one of the many parking lots with beach access.

At the peak of summer, on holidays, and during spring break, it's nearly impossible to get away from the thousands of people that gather on at the beaches around Panama City. During these times, your best bet to find solitude is out at Camp Helen State Park, St. Andrews State Park, or by taking a ferry or your own boat to Shell Island.

Schooner's Beach

The hub of beach activity during spring break is **Schooner's Beach** (5121 Gulf Dr., 850/235-3555), behind Schooner's Beach Club, or the beach behind **Club La Vela** (8813 Thomas Dr., 850/234-3866), where you can find the college crowd drinking, playing beach volleyball, and generally partying hard.

Camp Helen State Park

For much quieter beaches where you can hear the surf and the sand between your toes instead of loud music, park your beach chair at **Camp Helen State Park** (23937 Panama City Beach Pkwy., 850/233-5059, 8am-sunset daily, $4 per vehicle, $2 pedestrians and bicyclists). It's a 0.5-mile walk to the beach, worth it to get to this secluded gem located just over the Phillips Inlet Bridge on the western side of Panama City Beach. Enjoy a hike here on the Oak Canopy Trail through a mix of wetland and maritime forest, or fish in the saltwater of the Gulf or the freshwater of Lake Powell.

Rick Seltzer Park

Rick Seltzer Park (7419 Thomas Dr., sunrise-sunset, free) is another less-visited beach on the east end of Panama City Beach, known as one of the best spots for collecting shells and getting away from the crowds. Eat here at Jesse's Place and then catch some rays on this quiet stretch of sand.

Shell Island

Shell Island (between the Gulf and St. Andrews Bay, near St. Andrews State Park) is actually a peninsula. Nearly seven miles long, it's only accessible by boat, and it's a great place for shelling. During spring break, it can get crowded with boats anchoring offshore and pulling up on the beaches. If you don't own a boat, take the **Shell Island Shuttle** (4607 Thomas Dr., 850/608-0623, every 30 minutes 10am-4pm daily summer, call for times spring and fall, closed winter, $20 adults, $11 under age 13). They also rent snorkel gear and pontoon boats by the half and full day if you want to go on your own.

Russell-Fields Pier

To fish or go where the crowds hang out, plant your umbrella in the sand at **Russell-Fields Pier** (16101 Front Beach Rd., 850/233-5080, $3 to walk, $7 to fish, free under age 7). Crowds gather during the spring-summer high season. Known as the City Pier and Beach, it was built in 2009 and extends 1,500 feet into the Gulf. Try your luck at reeling in a cobia, mackerel, redfish, pompano, flounder, and other types of fish. A small shop at the foot of the pier sells snacks, drinks, and bait and rents rods, tackle, and other fishing gear. This is the best place for families to swim, since this is the only Panama City beach that has lifeguards (10am-6pm daily Apr.-Sept.). Built around the same time, the **M. B. Miller Pier** (12213 Front Beach Rd., 850/236-3035, $3 to walk, $6 to fish, free under age 7) is farther east. Nearly identical to the Russell-Fields Pier, it is a great spot to catch the sunset, people-watch, or wet your fishing line.

SPORTS AND RECREATION
★ St. Andrews State Park
St. Andrews State Park (4607 State Park Lane, Panama City, 850/708-5140, 8am-sunset daily, $4 single driver, $8 per vehicle with 2-8 people, $2 pedestrians or bicyclists, camping $28) has rolling white-sand dunes separated by low swales of pinewoods or marshes. In 2018 the campground was closed due to the impacts from Hurricane Michael, but the park was open for day use. Check with the park for an update on closures. There are 2.5 miles of beach, with two different parking lots. Rent bicycles during the summer at the park and explore the trails. There's a double-sided concrete boat launch for watercraft, or take a boat tour to Shell Island (spring-summer, tickets at the park concession). They rent canoes at the boat ramp to paddle around Grand Lagoon or across the boat channel to Shell Island.

There are two fishing piers and jetties to catch Spanish mackerel, redfish, flounder, sea trout, bonito, cobia, and bluefish. The concession in the park sell bait and fishing licenses along with beachside necessities. For hikers, the Heron Pond Trail (starting at a reconstructed Cracker turpentine still) and Gator Lake Trail (yep, you'll see gators) are both easy and well-marked. There are 176 campsites in the park or on the barrier Shell Island.

Diving and Snorkeling
Panama City Beach was dubbed the "Shipwreck Capital of the South" by *Skin Diver* magazine. This part of the warm Gulf of Mexico is also an excellent breeding ground for all types of sealife. You'll see sea turtles, manta rays, puffer fish, sand dollars, blue marlin, horseshoe crabs, small coral, colorful sponges, and lots of others.

Of the "natural" wrecks in this area, you can investigate a 441-foot **World War II Liberty ship,** a 220-foot tug called *The Chippewa,* a 160-foot coastal freighter called the **SS Tarpon,** the 100-foot tug *Chickasaw,* another tug called *The Grey Ghost,* and the Gulf's most famous wreck, the 465-foot *Empire Mica.* A bunch of other artificial reef projects have sunk bridge spans, barges, and the "City of Atlantis." Many of these dive sites are at depths of 80-100 feet and are just a few miles offshore; the best time for diving is April-September.

Experts say that the top five dives are the **USS Strength,** a naval mine sweeper; the *Blackbart,* a supply vessel; another supply vessel called the *B. J. Putnam;* the *Accokeek,* a 295-foot Navy tug boat; and a huge aluminum hovercraft in 100 feet of water. To

rent diving equipment, **Dive Locker** (106 Thomas Dr., 850/230-8006), **Diver's Den** (3120 Thomas Dr., 850/234-8717), and the **Panama City Dive Center** (4823 Thomas Dr., 850/235-3390) can help you out.

Snorkelers will have a better time around the **St. Andrews Jetties,** an area with no boat traffic. Nineteen feet under the surface is an old tar barge ideal for underwater exploration. To snorkel with a guide, **Island Time** (Treasure Island Marina, 3605 Thomas Dr., 850/234-7377, $40 adults, $30 ages 3-12, $10 under age 3) offers three-hour catamaran excursions, with wet suits available, and **Captain Ashley Gorman Shell Island Cruises** (5701 U.S. 98, east end of Hathaway Bridge, 850/785-4878, www.shellislandcruises.com, $34 adults, $12 under age 13, free under age 3) does swim and snorkeling tours for the whole family.

Horseback Riding

Ride to your heart's content at **Sunshine Riding Trails** (2273 Rolling Pines Rd., Chipley, 850/773-1900, 8am-9pm Mon.-Sat., 8am-9pm Sun., $45 for 1 hour, $60 for 2 hours, $85 for 3 hours, $110 for 4 hours). Their Tennessee walking horses are friendly and easy to ride on 10,000 acres of rolling hills and forests. The facility is 30 miles north of Panama City Beach, but the drive is pleasant and scenic. Get away from the crowds for a few hours and live your dream of being a cowboy or cowgirl in the wild west Panhandle of Florida. They also offer incredible overnight horseback camping trips (1 night $250 pp, 2 nights $450 pp). They include all the camping gear, breakfast, lunch, and dinner, and you get 12 hours of horseback riding. Sit around the campfire at night and trot through the forest atop your trusty steed on this outdoor adventure of a lifetime.

Recreation Areas

All the other parks around here get

1: M. B. Miller Pier **2:** deer roaming at St. Andrews State Park

overshadowed by St. Andrews, which is a shame. **Pine Log State Forest** (5583A Longleaf Rd., Ebro, 850/535-2888) is a favorite local spot for picnicking, hiking, off-road bicycling, horseback riding, fishing, and hunting. There are 23 miles of hiking trails winding through the forest. Nearby **Point Washington State Forest** (5865 U.S. 98 E., Santa Rosa Beach, 850/267-8325) is less developed but has 19 miles of trails for mountain biking, birding, and hunting.

Hike, bike, spot birds, or look for wildlife at the **Conservation Park** (100 Conservation Dr., Panama City Beach, 850/233-5045, sunrise-sunset daily, free). It's pet-friendly, so you can walk one of the 12 trails with your four-legged friend. Leashes are required. Trail lengths vary from 0.6 miles to 11 miles, and the headquarters has restrooms, maps, and water fountains. The trails and boardwalks are exceptionally well maintained, and benches and picnic areas along the way provide rest on your outdoor adventure.

The whole area has benefited from the completion of a U.S Army Corps of Engineers beach replenishment project, Florida's longest continuous beach construction. The project elevated and widened a 16.5-mile stretch of beach by an average of 30 feet with something like a billion cubic yards of new white sand. Besides beautifying the shoreline, the sand provides critical storm protection.

NIGHTLIFE
Bars

Schooner's (5121 Gulf Dr., 850/235-3555, 11am-close Mon.-Fri., 10am-close Sat.-Sun.) is a favorite spring break hangout, with live bands on the large deck and spectacular views toward nearby St. Andrews State Park. They serve ordinary American pub grub like burgers and sandwiches, but most people come for the libations and party atmosphere. This is a great place to catch sunset.

Coyote Ugly Saloon (10512 Front Beach Rd., 850/236-5965, 5pm-4am daily) is a rowdy western-themed bar made famous by the movie of the same name. There are bras hanging on the rafters, and the waitresses are scantily clad, dressed as Annie Oakley in booty shorts. Live out your fantasy of taking body shots and dancing on the bar. Once you get nice and sauced, try riding the mechanical bull.

For something authentic to the local beach culture, wear your bikini or board shorts to the **Sandpiper Tiki Bar** (17403 Front Beach Rd., 850/234-2154, 10am-4am daily), an open-air poolside bar that's a Gulf Coast gem, hidden behind the Sandpiper Beacon Beach Resort. Live music during the summer features many of the area's top reggae bands. Watch the game on the numerous TVs or dance to the band, and then walk a few feet to the beach for swimming and great views. This small casual place gets busy during the summer and spring break, but feeling the beach breeze while you dance to Bob Marley is hard to beat. This is the perfect spot if you want to avoid the intense club scene.

Clubs

Club La Vela (8813 Thomas Dr., 850/234-3866, 11am-4am daily summer, cover varies) calls itself the largest nightclub in America, and it is certainly the heart of nightlife activity during spring break in Panama City Beach. Made world famous by the MTV spring break specials hosted here, the club has 11 rooms, 48 bar stations, and can hold more than 6,000 people, which it regularly does during the summer and when it hosts national music acts on its numerous stages. The place is one big party, with the most fun in and around the massive pool.

You can continue the party right next door at **Spinnaker Beach Club** (8795 Thomas Dr., 850/234-7882, 11am-4am daily), where you can also get a decent seafood platter and burger at their Paradise Grill. The menu has a mix of mostly seafood, Mexican, and New Orleans-style food. After the restaurant closes, the party ramps up at the connected club with two rooms: a dance room with a DJ and a rock room with a large stage and live bands.

Tootsie's Orchid Lounge (700 S. Pier Park Dr., 850/236-3459, 11am-2:30am daily, under 21 after 8pm only if accompanied by an adult, food 11am-11pm daily, music 2pm-2:30am daily summer) first opened in Nashville and brought their country-themed party to the beach in 2008. The club was immediately a huge success, thanks to their focus on quality live music and their excellent location in Pier Park. It's a honky-tonk party with a live country band taking requests and a menu full of bar food to replenish the calories you'll burn while line dancing.

SHOPPING
Pier Park

Shopping, dining, and entertainment are all within easy reach at **Pier Park**, a 900,000-square-foot retail and entertainment complex on 93 acres in the heart of downtown across from the City Pier. Target, Panera Bread, The Grand 16-Plex Theatres, and Longhorn Steakhouse are joined by a 125,000-square-foot Dillard's, JCPenney, and Jimmy Buffett's Margaritaville restaurant and nightclub, with smaller stores including Ron Jon Surf Shop, Starbucks, Victoria's Secret, Bath & Body Works, and more. Its open-air eateries take best advantage of gorgeous Gulf views.

Little pockets of shops, mostly of the sunglasses-and-suntan lotion variety, are all over. You may need to stock up on bathing suits at **Beach Scene Superstore** (10059 Hutchinson Blvd., 850/233-1662), which has something like 25,000 suits to try on. If you feel the need for more extensive browsing, the **Shoppes at Edgewater** (477 Richard Jackson Blvd., 850/249-6100) complex has a number of nice shops. Also, the Edgewater Movie Theater and Rock-It Lanes Family Entertainment Center are adjacent to the shopping center.

Spas

The spa industry is the fourth-largest leisure industry in the United States, something Panama City Beach has jumped on in recent years. The most upscale might be the 12,025-square-foot **Serenity at Bay Point** (4114 Jan Cooley Dr., 850/236-6028), but there's also the **Spa at Majestic Beach Resort** (10901 Front Beach Rd., 866/494-3364), and the **Spa at the Edgewater Beach and Golf Resort** (11212 Front Beach Rd., 855/874-8686).

FOOD
Breakfast

For breakfast, try **Andy's Flour Power** (3123 Thomas Dr., 850/230-0014, 7am-2pm Mon.-Sat., 8am-2pm Sun., $6-10). Order their exceptional french toast covered in strawberries, an omelet, or a delicious pastry. They have a nice variety of traditional American and healthier European options, and the menu is full of vegetables and fruit, which can be hard to find at a breakfast spot in the South. The lunch menu features sandwiches and salads, including a great Reuben. The club sandwich and caesar salad are also favorites. The atmosphere is colorful and fun, making this a great place to sip your morning coffee.

Near St. Andrews State Park, **Jesse's Place** (7008 Thomas Dr., 850/708-1356, 8am-2pm Tues.-Sat., $5-10) is a small breakfast and lunch café with healthy options. They serve a mix of home-cooking, soul food, and vegetarian dishes. The breakfast is wonderful and affordable. At lunch you can pick one meat, like meat loaf or fried pork chops, and three choices from their veggie-heavy sides for around $8, and that includes cornbread or a roll. The food is delicious and the service is friendly. Grab a glass of sweet iced tea and all you'll need is a rocking chair and a front porch to call yourself an honorary Southerner.

Casual

In Panama City Beach you mostly get fried seafood, wings, pizza, and burgers, as expected from a location supported by college students. Yet there are some great restaurants for all tastes. One option is to keep it simple at chains like Bonefish Grill, Carrabba's Italian Grill, or Ruth's Chris Steakhouse.

For great cheeseburgers and milkshakes, go to **Gulf Coast Burger Company** (10031 Hutchison Blvd., 850/775-1312, 11am-10pm daily, $8-12). It also serves beer to go with those tasty burgers. **Sharky's Beachfront Seafood Restaurant** (15201 Front Beach Rd., 850/235-2420, 11am-10pm daily, $15-27) is a long-standing favorite for a good sunset, fine live entertainment in the world's largest tiki hut, and seafood-centric food.

Do you know what it means to miss New Orleans? Head to **David's Sno-Balls** (13913 Panama City Beach Pkwy., 850/236-1998, 11am-8pm Mon., 9am-8pm Tues.-Sat., noon-8pm Sun., $3-8) and grab a muffuletta, a tray of sugar-dusted beignets, a po'boy shrimp sandwich, or a classic shaved ice. On Monday they have red beans and rice. For sides, grab a bag of Zapp's spicy Cajun potato chips and a Barq's root beer in a glass bottle to make you feel like you're back in The Big Easy. This small eatery is packed on the weekends. They don't have the walk-up window like most sno-ball spots on the Gulf Coast, but you can go inside on a hot summer day to enjoy the air-conditioning. The bright, clean café has several tables and wrought-iron chairs that give it a decidedly New Orleans atmosphere.

Muy Wayne O's (303 S. Arnold Rd., 850/249-6830, 11am-8pm Tues.-Fri., 9am-9pm Sat., 9am-8pm Sun., $7-12) serves Tex-Mex food and margaritas to the tourist crowd. The specialty is a smoked briquette burrito that will keep your mouth watering for days. The place has become a must-stop for those staying or passing through Panama City Beach. The festive atmosphere typical of Mexican restaurants keeps spirits high, and the thin, crunchy chips and spicy salsa help this south-of-the-border fusion spot stand out from the crowd.

Liza's Kitchen (7328 Thomas Dr., 850/233-9000, 10am-3pm Mon.-Tues., 8am-3pm Wed.-Fri., 8am-2pm Sat.-Sun., $5-9) is a small café on the eastern end of the beach near the Sunset Inn. The large menu includes hot and cold selections such as the Hippie Chick sandwich with chicken, goat cheese, spinach, red peppers, and spicy mayo on focaccia. Any sandwich can be ordered as a wrap or a salad, and you can build your own salad or sandwich from a long list of ingredients. Weekend brunch includes traditional items like eggs benedict along with unique plates like Eggs Liza, poached eggs with roast beef and pimento cheese on focaccia bread served with scallion hollandaise.

Finn's Island Style Grub (7220 Thomas Dr., 850/249-3466, 8am-3pm daily, $6-12) is a popular food truck across the road from Rick Seltzer Park. Their specialty is fish tacos, and they also offer a variety of Mexican favorites like nachos, tacos, and quesadillas. The fresh ceviche is spectacular, and the mahimahi quesadillas will bring you back to this little food cart on the beach time and again during your stay.

J' Michaels (3210 Thomas Dr., 850/233-2055, 11am-10pm daily, $8-15) is dockside of Grand Lagoon and the place to go for comfort food like red beans and rice. It's casual, with license plates and dollar bills all over the walls. They have an extensive seafood menu that includes oysters prepared all sorts of ways, and you can sit at the bar and watch them shuck the raw oysters right before you eat them.

Fine Dining

Firefly (535 Richard Jackson Blvd., 850/249-3359, 5pm-close daily, $15-25) is the place to go for a romantic, or just generally fancy, seafood dinner. The she crab soup, crab cakes, and sesame-crusted tuna over a cucumber and radish salad are top picks. The wine list is extensive, but pricey for the area, so if you're on a tight budget, pick up drinks somewhere else before and after the fine meal.

More upscale, **Angelo's Steak Pit** (9527 Front Beach Rd., 850/234-2531, 5pm-10pm daily spring-fall, $14-26) always gets the nod for fat steaks grilled over aromatic hickory. It's been here since 1958, and the resident 20,000-pound steer, Big Gus, is practically a local celebrity.

Captain Anderson's Restaurant (5550 N. Lagoon Dr., 850/234-2225, 4:30pm-9pm Mon.-Sat., $12-35) is another serious locals' establishment, focusing on seafood. It's a waterfront favorite that's been here for years—go for the heads-on shrimp or the open-hearth whole fish.

ACCOMMODATIONS

It seems that all of Panama City Beach has been under construction in the past few years, with condos, resorts, hotels, townhomes, and villas transforming the destination. Hurricane Michael hit the area hard in 2018, devastating this stretch of coast and shifting construction to rebuilding from the catastrophic storm. The amount of lodging available in recent years has grown to an all-time high of more than 30,000 rooms. Due to the surplus of rooms in the off-season during the fall and winter months, you can find some of the best deals on the Gulf Coast in Panama City Beach.

Under $100

The **Sandpiper Beacon** (17403 Front Beach Rd., 850/234-2154, $59-119) is a comfortable, family-friendly place with lots of on-site amenities for the rates. It has 1,000 feet of beachfront, with parasailing, personal watercraft, and the Big Banana Ride right out the back door. There are three pools (one indoors), a lazy river ride, and twin waterslides, a game room, a restaurant, a children's playground, and a tiki bar. There are family units, with some sleeping up to 10 people.

Super 8 Panama City Beach (207 U.S. 231, between Hwy. 77 and U.S. 98, 850/257-7153, $50-90) is a no-frills base close to the beach. It has clean rooms and basic amenities, but get this: During March-April a deposit of $200 is required, and you have to wear wristbands to prove you're actually staying here and aren't just crashing the joint.

Driftwood Lodge (15811 Front Beach Rd., 850/234-6601, $90-150) is a two-story

---

1: Captain Anderson's Restaurant on the waterfront **2:** a shrimp po'boy at David's Sno-Balls **3:** Chateau by the Sea, popular with spring breakers

motel with Old Florida charm. They have regular rooms, efficiencies with kitchens, and a suite with a private sundeck. Off-season rates are exceptional, so visit during the winter for a low-priced stay just feet from the beach. The heated pool, sunroom, and beach volleyball courts make this a great choice for families on a budget.

Spartan Inn (8614 Surf Dr., 850/234-8482, $69-125) is a great choice if you're doing a lot of cooking during your vacation. With kitchens in every spacious room, this unassuming low-rise motel is not Spartan at all. It's been popular with families since 1984 and features a large pool that's usually filled with kids. It's not beachfront, but it can be a good choice and often a bargain when other properties are full.

$100-200

Flamingo Motel (15525 Front Beach Rd., 850/234-2232, $59-199) is across the street from Gulf World and a short walk from Pier Park shopping center. It's popular with families. The property is divided into a seven-story tower and a three-story building with a lush tropical garden courtyard. Parking is free, and they don't charge for extra people. The winter monthly rates ($450-1,090) are low if you want to stay long term.

Sunset Inn (8109 Surf Dr., 850/234-7370, $55-275) opened in 1981, and even though they're right down the street from Club La Vela, they're one of the more popular places to stay for families with young children, especially if you're looking for a bargain. The low-rise inn features a heated pool, balconies with Gulf views, a large deck with grills, and several rooms with kitchens. Queen sleepers are available in suites.

Chateau by the Sea (12525 Front Beach Rd., 888/627-0625, $100-200) is a favorite among young people, with 150 Gulf-view rooms 500 feet from the sand. It's right at the center of all the Miracle Strip excitement, with restaurants, attractions, shopping, and nightlife within walking distance. If you're under 25, they make you pay an extra $100 deposit until you pass checkout inspection.

Days Inn (12818 Front Beach Rd., 850/588-1587, $115-180) is hopping, with 188 Gulf-front rooms and suites with private balconies. Room decor is tropical and breezy, but you'll spend most of your time outside at the seven-story volcano mountain waterfall. It's in the huge pool situated between the Days Inn and Ramada Limited. It's a scene out there, with athletic young people sipping tropical drinks and relaxing in the whirlpool.

Osprey on the Gulf (15801 Front Beach Rd., 850/234-0303, $140-250) has 650 feet of beachfront, a heated pool and hot tub, Gulf-front balconies, and efficiency rooms with kitchens. Kids love the family-centric activities that the hotel plans. The rooms are clean, the view from the balconies is spectacular, and the price is a decent value for the amenities and location.

Bikini Beach Resort (11001 Front Beach Rd., 850/234-3392, $139-200) is a beachfront property located about 1.3-miles from Shipwreck Island Waterpark. The clean and fashionable interiors feature modern but tropical decor, and bright color schemes keep the rooms upbeat and fun. Dave's tiki bar by the pool makes this property a top choice for spring breakers and the younger party crowd. If you want to do a little of your own cooking, some rooms have kitchens.

$200-300

The upscale ★ **Grand Panama Beach Resort** (11800 and 11807 Front Beach Rd., 850/249-1244, www.grandpanamabeachresort.com, $149 and up) is a 35-acre resort with a 240-foot stretch of beach. The property features 299 units in two beachfront towers, two pools and spas, a fitness center, two tiki bars, a playground, a game room, and a jogging and bicycle path around the perimeter of the property. Besides its own on-site concert venue, the resort is also home to the Village of Grand Panama, a 55,000-square-foot retail center with an array of shops, services, and restaurants, including a spa and salon, a wine shop, and several clothing boutiques. Guests have access to the Sterling Club at Bay Point, featuring the Nicklaus-designed golf course, the Serenity Spa at Bay Point, tennis, dining, and a watersports marina.

Hampton Inn and Suites (13505 Panama City Beach Pkwy., 850/230-9080, $150-230) is about three miles north from Pier Park. The 95 spacious rooms have elegant furnishings, exceptionally comfy beds, and a large workstation. It's a classic hotel equipped for business travelers and families. The splash fountain and outdoor pool are fun for the kids, and the free hot breakfast will save time and money in the morning.

A top pick for families is the ★ **Holiday Inn Resort** (11127 Front Beach Rd., 850/234-1111, $200-350), a modern hotel right on the Gulf. The lagoon-style pool is a tropical oasis of palm trees, picnic tables, and a large splash playground for kids. Choose from beachfront family rooms with a double bed and two sets of bunk beds, suites with a double and two singles in a portioned off area, rooms with two queens, and suites with kings. Each room has a full-size fridge, ice maker, and microwave. There's a variety of on-site dining. The spot for cocktails is on the third floor at The Sunset Lounge. There's a store with snacks and beach accessories on the ground floor, a fully equipped and modern fitness center, and a Gulf-front spa.

Edgewater Beach and Golf Resort (11212 Front Beach Rd., 855/512-3843, $81-516) is worth the splurge; it's Panama City Beach's premier resort and family-friendly, with a great location on the beach, across the street from Cinema 10 Theaters, Rock-It Lanes, miniature golf, and the Shoppes at Edgewater. On-site are two restaurants, two bars, 11 heated outdoor pools, an executive 9-hole golf course, and the 27-hole Hombre Golf Club championship course just minutes away.

Over $300

An excellent place that's a bit removed from the fray is the **Marriott's Legends Edge at Bay Point** (4000 Marriott Dr., 850/236-4200, $250-400). Each villa has a fully equipped kitchen, spacious living and dining areas, and well-appointed bedrooms. It's situated in the midst of the Club Meadows and Lagoons Legends golf courses. The Gulf of Mexico is 10 minutes away, and the Grand Lagoon of St. Andrews Bay is within walking distance.

Camping

You can park your RV a mile from the beach at **Emerald Coast RV Resort** (1957 Allison Ave., 844/377-9074, www.rvresort.com, $69-225, weekly and monthly rates available). They have 150 sites on 10 acres of expertly maintained grounds, and they are one of the few RV facilities to receive *Trailer Life*'s highest rating. A saltwater pool with a waterfall and several ponds are centerpieces of the park, and the newly added volleyball and basketball courts are nice additions for families and active campers. The on-site dog run, pet baths, and pet-friendly policies will keep your dog's tail wagging.

TRANSPORTATION

Panama City Beach is on a barrier island. Note that Panama City Beach and Panama City are two separate cities and their names should not be used interchangeably. The Hathaway Bridge crosses St. Andrews Bay and connects the two. U.S. 98 splits at Panama City Beach and becomes U.S. 98 in the north (also called Panama City Beach Pkwy.) and U.S. 98A along the beach (also called Front Beach Rd.).

The **Northwest Florida Beaches International Airport** (ECP, 6300 West Bay Pkwy., Panama City, 850/763-6751), the first international airport built in the United States in a decade, is served by Delta, American, Southwest, and United. **Greyhound** (800/231-2222) has a bus station in Panama City (917 Harrison Ave., 850/785-6111), but public transportation won't get you to most places along the Emerald Coast, unless you're just hanging out on the beach in Panama City Beach.

Fort Walton Beach and Destin

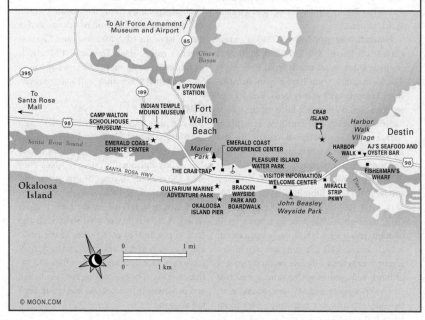

Fort Walton Beach and Destin

Spanish explorer Pánfilo de Narváez landed along the Emerald Coast in 1628 in search of water. The Creek people chased him and his men back to the boat, thirst unquenched. There's no telling why up until about 50 years ago a wide swath of the Emerald Coast, from Destin to Panama City, was unsettled sand dunes and quiet green water; most of the development dates back only a few decades.

Not so of Destin and Fort Walton Beach. In 1830, New England seafarer Leonard Destin fell for the place, the first settler in the area among several local Native American communities. He lured other New England fishermen with big fish stories, and by 1845 there were 100 residents, all employed in the fishing business. Fort Walton Beach was a Civil War campsite, its location chosen because of its protection from the Gulf by the Santa Rosa Sound and Okaloosa Island.

During Prohibition, "entrepreneurs" like Al Capone came down to the area to hide out. Mobsters being mobsters, the area was soon dotted with hopping casinos filled with shady characters evading the law up north. The casinos and mobsters are gone, but what's left is a beloved fishing destination that boasts five saltwater world records. It looks the part: Destin and Fort Walton Beach were the shooting location for *Jaws II,* both admirably portraying charming seaside resort towns.

SIGHTS
Museums

Near Eglin Air Force Base's main gate, the **Air Force Armament Museum** (Hwy. 85 and Hwy. 189, 850/822-4062, 9:30am-4:30pm

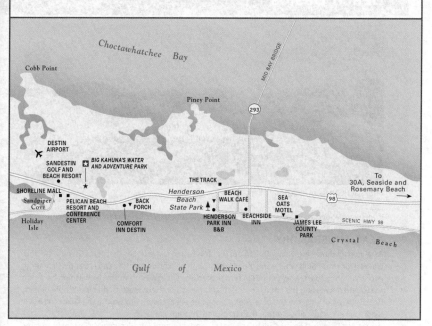

Mon.-Sat., free), seven miles north of Fort Walton Beach, is the only facility in the United States dedicated to the display of air force armament. You'll see thousands of weapons, an educational film called *Arming the Air Force*, and photography exhibits in addition to 25 cool reconnaissance planes, fighters, and bombers. There's a B-17 Flying Fortress, an F-4 Phantom II jet, and an SR-71 Blackbird Spy Plane. The museum spans four wars in its scope—World War II, Korea, Vietnam, and Persian Gulf. Kids love the fighter cockpit simulator.

The Fort Walton Beach community has a rich Native American past, having been settled by a number of prehistoric tribes as far back as 12,000 BC. The **Indian Temple Mound Museum and Park** (139 Miracle Strip Pkwy. SE, Fort Walton Beach, 850/833-9595, noon-4:30pm Mon.-Fri., 10am-4:30 Sat., $5 adults, $4.50 seniors and military, $3 ages 4-17, free under age 4) provides a look at the area's Native American history,

with a thoughtfully assembled collection of Southeastern Native American ceramic artifacts and a mound temple that dates to AD 1400 that served as a religious and civic center.

It was the first schoolhouse constructed for the children of Camp Walton, later to be known as Fort Walton Beach. **Camp Walton Schoolhouse Museum** (127 Miracle Strip Pkwy. SE, Fort Walton Beach, 850/833-9595, noon-3pm Mon.-Sat., $5 adults, $4.50 seniors, $3 ages 4-17, free under age 4) was built of native pine and oak, and when it opened in 1912, there were 15 students and one teacher. It was restored in the early 1970s and opened as an educational museum in 1976. These days, it's mostly for the benefit of local school groups, but it still makes a sweet nostalgic look at a past most of us never knew.

Family-Friendly Attractions

A good example of the compelling science museums for kids that seem to be popping up in every town these days is the **Emerald**

Beach Basics

dunes at Henderson Beach State Park

If you want your day at the beach to be, well, a day at the beach, keep a few things in mind.

BEACH HUSBANDRY

Bare coastal dunes are vulnerable to destruction by the same forces that form them: wind and waves. Dunes are built when sand blows up through beachside plantlife and is trapped, creating ever-taller mounds. These mounds in turn protect the shore during storms by washing back out to sea and decreasing the energy of the storm waves. For these reasons, do not trample or pick beachside plants like the sea oats. Along public beach accesses, always use the **boardwalks and raised walkways** rather than tramping through the sand.

Sea turtles nest on the Gulf beaches of Okaloosa County April-November. Recent hurricane seasons have wrought havoc on these already endangered species. It's illegal to disturb a nest or harm a turtle in any way. Never crowd around a turtle nest, don't impede a turtle's progress toward the water, and don't shine lights on the beaches at night.

This area's beaches are all **clothing-required.** Navarre Beach used to have a lot of nude sunbathers, but federal agents have cracked down on the depravity and lawlessness of lying nude on a beach towel. Also, beaches in this area **prohibit pets,** and that goes double for nude pets. If you see animals on the beach, they probably belong to residents who have gotten special beach pet permits, available only to locals.

BEACH SAFETY

Jellyfish are common to Gulf beaches. They aren't the big Portuguese man-of-war type, but the local species' sting can be fierce. Shuffle your feet in the water to alert nearby jellyfish to your presence. In the event that you do get stung, experts say ammonia poured on the sting relieves the pain, as does meat tenderizer and toothpaste.

Rip currents occur in any type of weather. If caught in a rip current, swim parallel to the shore until the current weakens and you can swim in.

And although shark attacks in these waters are infrequent, there are ways to minimize your chances of a **shark encounter.** You're more vulnerable if you're swimming alone, and if you swim far from shore. Sharks are most active at dusk, when they have a competitive sensory advantage. They tend to hang out in areas between sandbars or steep drop-offs—use caution when swimming in these areas. Sharks smell blood—if you have a wound or if nearby fisherfolk are cleaning fish or throwing out bait, think about postponing a swim. And remove shiny jewelry before you go in—its reflective glinting looks like the sheen of fish scales to a hungry predator.

Use **sunscreen,** and lots of it. Experts say that an average-size person should use about two tablespoons per application.

Coast Science Center (31 SW Memorial Pkwy., Fort Walton Beach, 850/664-1261, www.ecscience.org, 10am-4pm Wed.-Sat., $10 adults, $8 seniors, $8 ages 3-17, free under age 3), with an interesting section devoted to color and light. Fly and land a model airplane in a mini air tunnel or explore robots in the robotics section. There's a nature part to the museum with tarantulas, giant millipedes, and a variety of birds, snakes, amphibians, and reptiles.

Opened in 1955, **Gulfarium Marine Adventure Park** (1010 Miracle Strip Pkwy., Fort Walton Beach, 850/243-9046, 9am-4:30pm daily, $24 adults, $23 seniors, $16 ages 3-12, free under age 3) was one of the country's original marine parks. Like a mini Sea World, it hosts Atlantic bottlenose dolphins, California sea lions, Peruvian penguins, Kemp's ridley turtles, and lots of Gulf-focused educational marine exhibits. There are great dolphin shows with high jumps and soccer games, and a sweet sea lion show (they're not bad Frisbee players, considering the lack of opposable thumbs and all). For a fairly hefty fee ($169), guests can also have one-on-one interactions with the dolphins. The Gulfarium also sponsors the Dolphin Project, which focuses on interaction between dolphins and children with disabilities (like autism). Florida residents get discounts on ticket prices.

★ **BIG KAHUNA'S WATER AND ADVENTURE PARK**

Even adults get a little wide-eyed when they begin describing **Big Kahuna's Water and Adventure Park** (1007 U.S. 98 E., Destin, 850/837-8319, www.bigkahunas.com, 10am-6pm daily summer, adventure park only Sat.-Sun. winter, $46 over 48 inches, $36 under 48 inches, $36 seniors, free under age 3, season passes $50), with more than 40 water attractions and an adventure park spread over 25 acres. Wind through caves and waterfalls (the Tiagra Falls pumps 30,000 gallons of water per minute over 250 feet of mountain granite rock). There are three rivers, speed slides, body flumes, white-water tubing, leisurely lagoons, two wave pools, four children's areas with kid-size slides and variable-depth pools, and other exciting wet-and-wild attractions for all ages. Once you dry off, visit the attached Adventure Park attractions (be aware, it's a steep separate ticket price: $15 per ride or a combo pass for $28). There are 54 holes of miniature golf ($7 adults, $5 children), a bunch of other rides, and an arcade.

BEACHES

There are 24 miles of beach—the sand a shockingly fine white quartz that made its way down 130 miles of the Appalachian River—and the water is a brilliant jewel green. Nearly 60 percent of the beach here is preserved in five beachfront parks with 12 beach access ways along the Destin, Fort Walton Beach, and Okaloosa Island shoreline.

One of the best is the 208-acre **Henderson Beach State Park** (17000 Emerald Coast Pkwy., 850/837-7550, camping 800/326-3521, www.reserveamerica.com, 8am-sunset daily, $4 per vehicle single occupant, $6 per vehicle up to 8 passengers, $2 pedestrians or cyclists, camping $30), east of Destin on U.S. 98, with 6,000 feet of shoreline. There's urban sprawl to the west in Destin; the beach's entrance is across the street from a Walmart Supercenter. Once on the coastal dunes, you'd never know it—sea oats anchor the soft sand while the ocean's salt spray and wind cause the rosemary, magnolias, and scrub oak to grow low and horizontal, their limbs bent shoreward. During fall the beach is dotted with colorful blanket flower and beach morning glory carpeting the clean sand.

At Henderson you can swim, surf-fish, picnic, bike, in-line skate, walk the 0.75-mile nature trail, or camp (the campground has 60 full-facility campsites for tents or RVs). Colored flags indicate the wave and swimming conditions—the red flag means "knee deep is too deep," as there is high potential for rip currents to form, and the double red flag means the water is closed for swimming.

James Lee County Park (3510 Scenic U.S. 98, Destin, dawn to dusk daily, free parking) is a good beach at the Walton-Okaloosa County line. This park has three pavilions, 41 picnic tables, nine dune walkovers, a playground, restrooms with changing rooms, and 166 parking spaces. It's a popular beach for families, with the water shallow and clear and the Crab Trap restaurant in the middle of the beach's parking lot.

Okaloosa Island has a series of contiguous beaches—first, **John Beasley Wayside Park** (U.S. 98, Okaloosa Island, 1.2 miles east of Fort Walton Beach, 850/689-5790) is on the bay side of the barrier island just yards from the Okaloosa Boardwalk, an entertainment complex with clubs and restaurants. John Beasley has restrooms, picnic tables, showers, changing rooms, vending machines, and lifeguards. It has fishing for trout and reds, snorkeling activity, and even a little surfing. The same can be said of the adjacent **Brackin Wayside Park and Boardwalk** (U.S. 98, Okaloosa Island, 1 mile east of Fort Walton Beach, 850/651-7131), which has several pavilions, 41 picnic tables, restrooms with changing rooms, a children's playground, dune walkovers to the beach, lots of parking, and fierce beach volleyball during the warmer months.

Shelling and Diving

The beaches are uniformly fine white sand, and compared to the beaches to the south, there are few shells in sight. So how can the Emerald Coast be ranked as a top shelling destination? They're offshore—you have to dive for them. Giant sandbars about a mile from shore and a natural coral-encrusted limestone outcropping (the pre-ice age shoreline) three miles out act as natural shovels to collect perfectly formed shells—pastel lion's paws, true tulips, huge queen helmets, and Florida's signature shell, the horse conchs, are there for the picking.

The center of much of this shelling mania is **Sand Dollar City,** an artificial reef complex the county put together about a mile out. It's got six patch reefs placed in a hexagonal pattern around a single center point,

the sunken 1941 tugboat *Mohawk Chief.* The whole area is a fish and shellfish haven, and by extension, a shelling bonanza. **Timber Hole** is another hot spot of shelling and intriguing marinelife observation (sea squirts, four-foot basket sponges, aqua and purple sea whips). It has a natural limestone reef 6-18 feet high and 110 feet deep, as well as sunken planes, ships, and a railroad car. There are loads of natural reefs in this area for shelling, diving, and fishing; **Amberjack Rocks** is one of the area's largest reef systems, within three miles of Destin Pass. About 80 feet deep, it is known for shelling as well as spearfishing for black snapper and amberjack. **Long Reef** features staircase ledges and is known for lobsters and shells. The area also has intriguing wrecks to explore—an air force barge, a Liberty ship, *Butler's Barge,* and the rubble of the Destin Bridge. Divers here often enjoy 40-100 feet of visibility.

For safety reasons, all divers must display a free-flying 12-by-12-inch flag with a white diagonal stripe on a red background— the diver-down flag—where the dive occurs. Divers should stay within 100 feet of the flag, and the flag and diver should never be in areas that might constitute a navigational hazard.

Emerald Coast Scuba (503-B Harbor Blvd., Destin, 850/837-0955, www.divedestin. net) provides scuba instruction and charters. Many other dive shops offer theme excursions like spearfishing, deep sea, shell, and lobster, with certification classes. They will also take you out snorkeling from their boats. If you just want to snorkel on your own, you can do so from the beach at **Destin jetties** or from the **Old Crystal Beach Pier.**

SPORTS AND RECREATION
★ Crab Island

North of the Destin Bridge, **Crab Island** used to be two islands in the middle of nowhere made of sand dredged by the U.S. Army Corps of Engineers from East Pass, complete with sea grass, shrubs, and seabirds. Now it's submerged a few feet and only surfaces

East Pass

Originally the Gulf of Mexico and the Destin Harbor did not connect to the Choctawhatchee Bay, which posed some navigational challenges to the local fishing fleet and some flooding danger to the settlements. In 1926, three local families changed that. The Destins, the Marlers, and the Melvins started digging by hand, making a two-foot-wide ditch across Okaloosa Island. Within two hours, supposedly, the trench was over 100 yards wide. A torrent of water rushed in, creating what is now East Pass. In 1935 the East Pass Bridge was built. To this day, the U.S. Army Corps of Engineers keeps close tabs on the pass, dredging it every two years, and more often in hurricane years, to ensure the water is deep enough for boats to move safely through it.

The East Pass is the only waterway connecting the Choctawhatchee Bay to the Gulf of Mexico for 60 miles in either direction (Pensacola to the west and Panama City to the east each have waterways that connect the bay with the Gulf). The East Pass is essential to the Destin fishing fleet—without it, the town would not be the angler's paradise that draws fisherfolk from around the world. All because of a few shovels.

at low tide. This is where boaters congregate for fun in the sun. People jump off into the three-foot shallows, eat, chat, and drink. Sometimes there's live music on the back of a boat or floating vendors serving food and drinks (often an ice-cream guy) to all the folks gathered.

To get here, you need something that floats—maybe a pontoon boat, or a glass-bottom boat, or a fishing boat, or even a WaveRunner. You can shop at **Boogies Watersports** (16 Harbor Blvd., www.boogieswatersports.com, 850/654-4497) to pick up a rental that suits your budget, skill level, and personal sense of style. Ask the rental place or any local for specific directions. The best time to go is at high tide, when the water is crystal clear. This place becomes a party zone during holidays and summer

weekends, so plan on a different time if you want to beat the crowds.

★ Fishing in Destin Harbor

About 30 miles offshore, 10 miles from Destin's East Pass, the Gulf of Mexico turns from emerald green to deep blue. This point, the 100-Fathom Curve, is suddenly deep water. This curve is closer to Destin than to any other spot in Florida, meaning a fishing charter from Destin is the quickest way out to deep water churning with fish. In spring is the migration of mighty cobia (you can sight-fish for these) and in May come the kingfish (inshore troll). People bottom-fish for grouper, red snapper, triggerfish, and amberjack year-round. In summer, when the waters warm up, it's serious marlin and sailfish (offshore troll) and wahoo and tuna (inshore troll). Destin bills itself as the "Billfish Capital of the World." Billfish is a tuna-like species similar to marlin, sailfish, and spearfish—those fish with the big swordlike bill. Destin is also known as the "World's Luckiest Fishing Village" because its waters harbor four times more types of fresh fish per season than any other Florida destination except Key West. Supposedly, during any given season, there are 20 edible species of game fish.

So come here to fish. Offshore, bottom, inshore, or even surf-casting—there are lots of people here with enormous experience willing to take you out on a saltwater charter or just hook you up with gear. The area's rivers offer freshwater fishing for catfish, bass, and bream, and many restaurants are willing to cook up your fresh catch.

The price of a private charter averages $150-165 per hour for up to six people. Many boats only accommodate six, so make clear how many people are in your party. You can sign up for a group charter, pooling with other people who are looking to go out. The rates are the same, split between all the people on the boat. You have to find others who are fishing for the same thing.

Destin Charter Service (Fisherman's

Wharf, 850/837-1995) is one-stop shopping, with access to 40 of Destin's best charter boats (there are more than 100 vessels for hire around here). These boats offer year-round fishing trips for individuals or groups, from four-hour trips to overnights, either on the Gulf or the bay side. **Harborwalk Fishing Charters** (10 Harbor Blvd., 850/837-2343, www. harborwalkfishingcharters.com, $170 pp for 5 hours, $200 pp for 6 hours, plus customary 15 percent tip), next to Lucky Snapper, off U.S. 98, is another well-regarded local charter company. Staff will clean, fillet, and bag your catch at trip's end.

To get your own boat and go, **Gilligan's Water Sports** (Destin Harbor, 530 Harbor Blvd., 850/650-9000, www.gilligansofdestin. com) rents pontoon boats for reasonable rates ($275-450) for snorkeling, fishing, or just tooling around. You can also head out into the Blackwater, Shoal, or Yellow Rivers in search of bass, bream, and catfish.

No boat is required to fish from the **Okaloosa Island Fishing Pier** (850/244-1023, 24 hours daily Apr.-Sept., 5am-9pm daily Oct.-Mar., $8 adults, $5 ages 6-12, $7 seniors, no license necessary). It's a 1,261-foot pier, lighted at night, with rod holders and benches built into it. You'll catch all kinds of things, including big mahimahi. You can also cast from the area's finger jetties, sandy shores, and the 3,000-foot **Destin Bridge Catwalk** to hook speckled trout, white snapper, and redfish. And there are stocked ponds in the area, such as the 350-acre **Hurricane Lake** in Blackwater River State Park, filled with channel catfish, largemouth bass, bluegill, and shellcracker.

When you want to find out what is biting and where, visit www.gulfcoastangling.com, then plan your fishing accordingly.

Golf

Emerald-green waters mirrored by emerald-green golf courses. There are 1,080 holes of golf in these parts, many of the courses designed by some of the world's best architects:

Robert Cupp of Jack Nicklaus fame, or Finger, Dye, and Fazio. Many of these courses utilize the area's lush natural beauty and surrounding waterways, with contrasts of woods and wetlands, for challenging and memorably beautiful play.

The 18-hole **Regatta Bay Golf Club** (465 Regatta Bay Blvd., Destin, 850/337-8080, www.regattabay.com, par 72, 6,864 yards, course rating 73.8, slope 148, $59-129) was designed by Robert Walker, winding along the shore of Choctawhatchee Bay and carved through wetlands and protected nature preserves. Another popular one, the creation of Fred Couples and Gene Bates, **Kelly Plantation Golf Club** (307 Kelly Plantation Dr., Destin, 850/650-7600, www. kellyplantationgolf.com, par 72, 7,099 yards, course rating 74.2, slope 146, $69-145) utilizes the Choctawhatchee Bay, nestled along its southern edge with rolling greens and beautiful fairways.

Acclaimed by *Golfweek* as one of the 50 Most Distinctive Development Courses in the Southeast, **Emerald Bay** (4781 Clubhouse Dr., Destin 850/837-5197, par 72, 6,802 yards, course rating 73.1, slope 135, $59-129) was designed by nationally recognized architect Robert Cupp. He said of the course, "There is no signature hole, it is—instead—a signature golf course."

At **Indian Bayou Golf and Country Club** (1 Country Club Dr. E., Destin, 850/837-6191, www.indianbayougolf.com, par 72, 7,000 yards, course rating 74, slope 132-142, $45-85) there's an assortment of Earl Stone-designed nines, the Choctaw, Seminole, and Creek, which can be played in any 18-hole combination. The Creek course, the newest, has lots of water that comes into play; the Choctaw is heavily wooded; and the Seminole has wide fairways and large greens.

Also on the banks of Choctawhatchee Bay, **Shalimar Pointe Golf and Country Club** (302 Country Club Rd., Shalimar, 850/651-1416, par 72, 6,765 yards, course rating 72.9, slope 125, $23-49) is a Finger and Dye-designed course that *Links* magazine accused

Eglin Air Force Base

Eglin Air Force Reservation in Fort Walton Beach is the largest air force base in the free world. It's the size of Rhode Island, covering 724 square miles of reservation and 97,963 square miles of water in the Gulf of Mexico. Eglin employs approximately 10,000 each of military personnel and civilians.

Most of Eglin is off-limits. The Mother of All Bombs (MOAB), the most powerful nonnuclear bomb ever created, was tested here, and for years Eglin Air Force Base has been testing depleted uranium (DU), with an estimated 220,000 pounds of DU penetrators expended since 1973. What is accessible to the public is more fun: Eglin has **two 18-hole championship golf courses** (850/882-2949, year-round). The Eglin Golf Course, host of a 2000 U.S. Open qualifier, has a hill on the seventh hole so steep that the course provides a towrope to golfers. An interesting tidbit: Al Capone funded the layout of this course, and Capone's private beach hideout house is now the officers' club at Eglin.

The **Air Force Armament Museum** (850/822-4062, 9:30am-4:30pm Mon.-Sat., free) is just one of many opportunities for visitors. If you go to the **Jackson Guard Office** (107 Hwy. 85 N., Niceville, 850/882-4164), you can get an outdoor recreation permit, a comprehensive map, and a list of regulations. This allows you to explore the area's many activities—hunting, fishing, primitive camping, canoeing, and hiking part of the **Florida National Scenic Trail** (www. floridatrail.org).

Hunting (which accounts for 4,200 of the 12,000 recreation permits granted annually) is for deer, turkey, wild hogs, and small game, seasonally. There's a huge managed quail area, another for "planted" doves, and two duck management units totaling 78,000 acres. There's even an annual hunt open to the mobility-impaired. Fishing in the reservation is on any of 17 stocked ponds, 2 of them fully accessible.

Birders will enjoy the old-growth longleaf pine swath of Eglin reservation that is a designated part of the **Great Florida Birding Trail** (www.floridabirdingtrail.com). You may see the endangered Okaloosa darter, found in only six creek systems in the central portion of the base. It's also got the fourth-largest red-cockaded woodpecker population in the country. The area is home to more than 90 rare or listed plant and animal species. Within the reservation are seven miles of barrier island for swimming and canoeing, with lots of other creeks; enjoy open-water **kayaking** in the Choctawhatchee Bay, Santa Rosa Sound, or the Gulf.

The **Anderson Pond Recreation Area** (off Hwy. 85, 3 miles north of Niceville) is open year-round, with an elevated boardwalk, a picnic shelter, a pier, and a camping area. All the facilities are fully accessible.

of having "Two of the Hardest Holes on the Emerald Coast," the 11th and 17th. It is bordered by rolling white dunes and dense hammocks of pine, oak, and magnolia. Shalimar Pointe has been host to the Emerald Coast Tour.

Beyond these, there's **Shoal River Country Club, Fort Walton Beach Municipal Course,** the two courses at **Eglin Air Force Base** which are open to serving or retired US military and their guests only. Visitors must have military issued ID to enter the base and play the course. There's also the world-class courses at **Sandestin Golf & Beach Resort.**

ENTERTAINMENT AND EVENTS
The Arts

The attractions on the Emerald Coast are mostly outdoors, where the sun, sand, and fish are. While art is not the largest draw for the Emerald Coast, it doesn't disappoint. The **Northwest Florida Ballet** (310 Perry Ave. SE, Fort Walton Beach, 850/664-7787) produces full-length semiprofessional ballets in a number of local venues, including summer ballet in the park and the requisite holiday performance of *The Nutcracker.* **Stage Crafters Community Theatre** (40 Robinwood Dr. SW, Fort Walton Beach,

850/243-1101, www.stagecrafters.com, $20, musicals $25) is a small community troupe that puts on plays like the familiar *Godspell* and the unfamiliar *Meshuggah-Nuns*. The **Northwest Florida State College's Mattie Kelly Fine and Performing Arts Center** (100 College Blvd., Niceville, 850/729-6000, www.mattiekellyartscenter.org) stages community plays and hosts Broadway touring acts and other big ticket performers in its large 1,650-seat main theater, but also hosts dance, opera, the Northwest Florida Symphony Orchestra, and other arts events.

In visual arts, the **Arts & Design Society** (17 1st St. SE, Fort Walton Beach, 850/244-1271, www.artdesignsociety.org), founded in 1956 by a group of local artists, is more of a community art outreach, with classes, lectures, and children's programs, but it also hosts monthly local, regional, and national exhibits that are worth checking out.

Festivals and Events

In the Destin area, there are annual events like the Spring Splash, the Billy Bowlegs Festival, the Sandestin Wine Festival, and the Christmas Boat Parade—but the biggest of them all is the monthlong **Destin Fishing Rodeo** (850/837-6734, www. destinfishingrodeo.org) in October. There are 30 different categories of prizes, with all saltwater game fish eligible—so you'll see people fishing all over the place with a vengeance. There's a more focused, single-species event in March-April with the annual Cobia Tournaments.

NIGHTLIFE

Destin and Fort Walton Beach get lively, and it's quiet to the east in the Beaches of South Walton area; farther east in Panama City Beach it gets hopping. Here, head dockside to **AJ's Club Bimini** (116 Harbor Blvd., 850/837-1913, 11am-4am daily), on the Destin Harbor, 0.25 miles east of the Destin Bridge, for a Bimini Bash, a powerful concoction of cranberry, orange, and pineapple juices with a five-rum roundhouse punch.

Then stop in for a margarita at **Pepito's** (757 Harbor Blvd., Destin, 850/650-7734, until 4am daily), in front of the Destin Cinemas, or get crazy on the dance floor at **Harry T's** (46 Harbor Blvd., Destin, 850/654-4800, 11am-10pm Mon.-Fri., 9am-close Sat.-Sun.) in Harbor Walk village. Opened by a big-top trapeze artist, Harry T's is adorned with circus memorabilia, including a stuffed giraffe, and treasures from the sunken luxury liner *Thracia*. For live music, head to the **Funky Blues Shack Destin** (34902 Emerald Coast Pkwy., 850/424-6650, 4pm-10pm Sun.-Thurs., 4pm-midnight Fri.-Sat.), where you'll find a variety of music, but mostly blues, funk groups, and dueling piano shows.

SHOPPING

On U.S. 98, eight miles east of Destin, near Sandestin Golf & Beach Resort, **Silver Sands Factory Stores** (10562 Emerald Coast Pkwy. W., Destin, 850/654-9771, www. silversandsoutlet.com, 10am-9pm Mon.-Sat., 10am-7pm Sun.) is supposedly the nation's largest designer outlet center, and it keeps growing. Think Off Saks Fifth Avenue, Ann Taylor, Polo Ralph Lauren, Dooney & Bourke, Tommy Hilfiger, Banana Republic, Liz Claiborne, and the like. For shoes, there's Famous Footwear, Nike, Merrell, New Balance, and Converse. More than 100 designer outlet stores are in 450,000 square feet of retail space, drawing six million shoppers annually.

FOOD

The restaurants of Destin, Fort Walton Beach, and Okaloosa Island tend to focus on fish, with lots of casual oyster bars and fish shacks. There are upscale spots around, but the best places are the Southern-style casual seafood joints.

Breakfast

Start your day at the **Donut Hole** (635 U.S. 98 E., Destin, 850/837-8824, 6am-10pm daily, $4-12). It's breakfast all day, with sturdy baked goods and nice people.

Casual

The ★ **Back Porch** (1740 Scenic U.S. 98 E., Destin, 850/837-2022, 11am-9pm daily, $10-25) is a fun cedar-shingled seafood shack, an ideal place to try your first char-grilled amberjack. The view is great—you won't mind waiting because you can hang out right on the beach while they ready a table. It's a notable surf spot, so you can watch surfers paddling out to the break.

AJ's Seafood and Oyster Bar (0.25 miles east of the Destin Bridge, Destin, 850/837-1913, 10am-11pm daily spring-fall, 10am-9:30pm daily winter, no reservations, $9-21) is another longtime waterfront favorite. Overlooking Destin Harbor, AJ's Club Bimini is the place to see the sunset over a plate of Oysters AJ (oysters baked with jalapeños, monterey jack, and bacon). AJ's charter fleet offers daily trips into shallow or deep waters to hunt for grouper, amberjack, and wahoo—the kitchen will cook your catch straight off the line. Try the fried fish sandwiches or the shrimp po'boy.

Don't like fish? **Fudpucker's Beachside Bar & Grill** (20001 Emerald Coast Pkwy., Destin, 850/654-4200, 1318 Miracle Strip Pkwy., Okaloosa Island Boardwalk, Fort Walton Beach, 850/243-3833, www.fudpucker. com, 11am-9pm Sun.-Thurs., 11am-10pm Fri.-Sat., $8-20) is the place for burgers, drinks on the deck, and some of the best bands on the beach.

In Fort Walton Beach, **The Crab Trap** (1450 Miracle Strip Pkwy., Okaloosa Island Boardwalk, Fort Walton Beach, 850/301-0959, 11am-9pm Sun.-Thurs., 11am-10pm Fri.-Sat., $7-25), nestled in the beautiful James Lee County Park and overlooking the water, graciously accommodates the sand between your toes and the whiff of suntan oil. Grouper, tuna, and amberjack are the freshest catches, with lots of fried seafood and all-you-can-eat snow-crab legs (they're not from around here, though). It's casual, but not as casual as the nearby **Angler's Beachside Grill and Sports Bar** (1030 Miracle Strip Pkwy., Okaloosa Island Boardwalk, Fort Walton Beach, 850/796-0260, 11am-8pm Wed.-Thurs., 11am-9pm Fri., 8am-9pm Sat., 10am-8pm Sun., $7-20). You can eat right on the boardwalk or inside with all the games on big TVs.

Fine Dining

Some of the best food in the area is to be had from chef John Sallman at the ★ **Beach Walk Café** (Henderson Park Inn, 2700 U.S. 98 E., Destin, 850/650-7100, www. beachwalkcafe.com, 5pm-8pm Tues.-Sun., $26-54). There is pecan-crusted grouper served over roasted and crisped potato cakes, and classic blue crab cakes. It's one of the best fine-dining experiences in the area, with a spectacular view of the Gulf of Mexico that makes everything taste a little better.

Louisiana Lagniappe (775 Gulf Shore Dr., Holiday Isle, Destin, 850/837-0881, www. thelouisianalagniappe.com, 11am-9pm daily Mar.-Oct., no reservations, $15-26) overlooks Old Pass Lagoon and is a local favorite serving upscale Louisiana-style seafood, like pannéed fillet of grouper topped with lobster medallions, lightly covered with garlic beurre blanc. It traffics in live Maine lobsters and has a beautiful outdoor deck.

Marina Café (404 Harbor Blvd., Destin, 850/837-7960, www.marinacafe.com, 5pm-10pm daily, $17-28) is another special-occasion destination. It's owned by Harbor Restaurant Group, which also owns Destin Chops (a good steak and chop house not far away), with a second Chops location in Seacrest Beach. There's an outdoor dining deck overlooking the Destin Harbor, but inside seating is just as nice. The menu is all over the map, with Cajun and creole dishes, a sushi bar, pizzas, excellent seafood, and steak entrées.

ACCOMMODATIONS
Under $100

Because of spring break maniacs, most of the hotels don't rent to people under 25 unless they're with an "adult." In the Destin area,

there aren't many big hotels on the beach; most lodgings are a bit of a drive. If you are looking for a quiet, independently owned place at water's edge, try **Sea Oats Motel** (3420 Old U.S. 98 E., Destin, 850/837-6655, $90-200), a long low-slung motel right on the sand, offering condo rentals as well.

If you're willing to hop in the car or on a bike to get to the sand, the **Beachside Inn** (2931 Scenic U.S. 98, Destin, 850/650-9099, $85-180), has brightly colored rooms in a modest-size low-rise hotel. **Fairfield Inn and Suites Destin** (19001 Emerald Coast Pkwy., Destin, 850/654-8611, $85-145) is deluxe for a Fairfield Inn. It's got 100 nicely appointed rooms and two pools (one indoors).

$100-200

The **Best Western Summerplace Inn** (14047 Emerald Coast Pkwy., Destin, 850/650-8003, $110-150) is in the heart of Destin, a quick drive to public beach access. There's a decent continental breakfast included, indoor and outdoor pools with a big whirlpool, and free high-speed internet access.

$200-300

There are plenty of condos on the beach, many renting only by the week in spring-summer high season. The **Pelican Beach Resort and Conference Center** (1002 U.S. 98 E., Destin, 888/654-1425, usually 2-night minimum, $150-300) is a big imposing cube. **Hidden Dunes Beach and Tennis Resort** (9815 U.S. 98 W., Destin, 800/225-7652, $130-600) has units in a 20-story tower at water's edge, luxurious three- and four-bedroom villas overlooking the private Hidden Dunes lake, and Carolina-style cottages with private screened porches nestled in a wooded landscape.

Farther east, in the Beaches of South Walton town of Seascape, the **Majestic Sun Resort** (1160 Old U.S. 98, Miramar beach, 850/986-7654, $110-375) is a huge condo tower with beautiful pools, tennis, and

golf just across the street from the beach. **Sandpiper Cove** (775 Gulfshore Dr., Destin, 850/837-9121, www.sandpipercove. com, $150-300) is a Destin landmark, with a 43-acre landscaped property that has 1,100 feet of beach. These are individually owned and decorated condo units, so look at the pictures before deciding what's right for you. The property has five swimming pools and three outdoor hot tubs.

My favorite place to stay in the area is the ★ **Henderson Park Inn** (2700 Scenic U.S. 98, 888/836-1105, www.hendersonparkinn. com, $229-939), northwest Florida's only beachside bed-and-breakfast. Beyond the inn's lovely setting adjacent to the 208-acre Henderson Beach State Park, travelers are spoiled with tidbits like complimentary breakfast and lunch, nightly sunset glasses of wine and beer, an arrival wine and fruit assortment, evening turndown service with sweets, and a stocked kitchen pantry, all included in the room rates. Guests get complimentary use of water-sports equipment, high-speed internet access, and beach service with chair and umbrella setup.

Vacation Rentals

For beach cottages and luxurious condos, **Newman-Dailey Resort Properties** (12815 U.S. 98 W, Suite 100, Destin, 850/837-1071 or 800/225-7652, www.destinvacation.com) is a well-regarded property management and vacation rental company that's been in the area for decades. The website offers virtual tours of properties.

TRANSPORTATION

U.S. 98 runs east-west along the Emerald Coast, edging the Gulf through Destin and Fort Walton Beach. Fort Walton Beach is 60 miles west of Panama City and 35 miles east of Pensacola. The beach of Fort Walton Beach is actually on Okaloosa Island, a barrier island at the southern end of Choctawhatchee Bay. Destin is about five miles east on U.S. 98 (sometimes called the Miracle Strip Pkwy.). To get to this area from

1: Silver Sands Factory Stores **2:** AJ's Seafood and Oyster Bar **3:** the Henderson Park Inn

the north, take U.S. 331 south, then take Highway 85 south at the Alabama-Florida line, straight to Destin and Fort Walton Beach. From I-10, exit onto Highway 85 south at the Fort Walton Beach exit.

The **Destin-Fort Walton Beach Airport** (VPS, 1701 Hwy. 85 N., 850/651-7160), on Eglin Air Force Base, is a small airport served by Delta Airlines, American, United, and Allegiant.

Beaches of South Walton

The long expanses of white-sand beach have been here all along, but the Beaches of South Walton have been developed in the last 25 years. Residents have kept a tight handle on growth, and some of it may feel contrived, like Disney for adults, but the idea of New Urbanism has taken hold in compact mixed-use towns. Visitors have most of what they need within walking distance of where they're staying, and the Gulf of Mexico and Choctawhatchee Bay are soothing backdrops for a restful vacation. Some of these 15 communities actually developed organically, while others were masterminded by architects and savvy developers. From west to east:

Seascape is the closest to Destin, with lakefront and golf villas in an upscale setting. **Miramar Beach** begins at the Gulf along Scenic Gulf Drive and then curves around to join Emerald Coast Parkway. It's mostly condos and private homes and is close to the Silver Sands Factory Stores. Next up is **Sandestin,** probably the most famous of these little communities, overrun with enormous luxury golf and beach resorts, but all tasteful. The **Village of Baytowne Wharf** is here in the style of a wealthy but rustic Southern fishing village.

Dune Allen Beach is a quaint and quiet beach community two miles long with mostly classic wood-sided beach houses, homes on a lake, and smaller-size condo developments. This is where the area's eight-foot-wide offroad bike path begins, winding all the way to Inlet Beach. Fairly developed, **Santa Rosa Beach** has a number of shops and commercial bits, with some golf and beachside amenities. There's a stylish outdoor mall here

with boutiques, bike rentals, medical offices, antiques stores, a market, and a big handful of restaurants. Then there's **Blue Mountain Beach,** the highest point along the Gulf of Mexico; with wonderful views and beautiful sand; it has become attractive as an artists' retreat.

Grayton Beach is the oldest town between Pensacola and Apalachicola. Settled in the early 1900s, it is a tree-lined beach community of old cypress cottages and small narrow streets. There is a great bar called the Red Bar that you shouldn't miss, as well as many fine restaurants.

With Seaside to the east fully built out, builders turned not long ago to neighboring **WaterColor,** which is primarily a residential community. Many of the new stylized Cracker-style buildings are available for rent, and the town has a sleek hotel, the 60-room WaterColor Inn.

The next town over is **Seaside,** an upscale planned beach community of pastel homes and cottages organized around a town square with an outdoor amphitheater, galleries, restaurants, and boutiques. People either love it, using words like "charming" and "picturesque," or hate it and grumble words like "contrived" and "looks like a stage set" (which it technically was, as the shooting location for the movie *The Truman Show*).

Seagrove Beach is next door to the newer and fancier Seaside. This peaceful beach town is tucked between the coast's natural sand dunes and pine trees. Visitors can choose from rambling beach houses, cottages, or condos. The newest community, **WaterSound,** is one of the fanciest, with a resort that is plopped right against a pristine coastal dune lake. Then there's **Seacrest Beach,** a newish beach community made up of cottages and condominiums hidden behind natural dunes.

One of my more favorite communities is **Rosemary Beach.** Like Seaside, it's completely planned in a narrow architectural style, but this time it's all Caribbean-inspired homes connected to the shore by boardwalks and footpaths, with a town square and an exceptional eternity pool.

And finally, **Inlet Beach** is just over the bridge west of Panama City Beach and next to Rosemary Beach. Named for the large lagoon on its eastern shore, Phillips Inlet, the peaceful community is known for its secluded natural areas and minimal development.

SIGHTS
★ Seaside

It used to be that Americans retreated during the summers to simple beachside cottages for months at a time. Every day, after you got your sunburned hide up off the porch, you biked or walked into the little town center to take in a movie or get the local gossip and an ice cream. In 1946, J. S. Smolian bought 80 acres near Seagrove Beach on Florida's Panhandle with this vision in mind—a utopian summer camp for his employees. His grandson Robert Davis was smitten by the same vision, growing up to become an upscale developer in Miami in the 1970s. Still, the sweet seaside summer village eluded him. He infected Miami architects Andrés Duany and Elizabeth Plater-Zyberk with his dream, and they planned a fantasy town based on the northwest Florida architectural style of wood-frame cottages with peaked roofs, deep overhangs, and big windows for cross-ventilation. They traveled through Florida with sketchpads and eyes wide open.

They made it real in the early 1980s, building a small town nestled against an idyllic curve along the Gulf Coast shoreline, against a wide swath of beach and mild emerald waters. There are 200 or so homes now, in a paradigm called New Urbanism, situated around a town square with an amphitheater, restaurants, elegant boutiques, a repertory theater, and the beach off at the edge of it all. There's also a much-lauded charter school, a chapel, and a medical arts building. It's a living laboratory—an experiment in harmonious beachside community life.

You can go to Seaside to visit. If you vacation here, you pull your car in, turn off the ignition, and that's the last you need of it: Everything is within walking distance in what *Time* magazine called "the most astounding design achievement of its era." Panama City is 40 miles east, Destin is 20 miles west—but Seaside seems miles and miles from anywhere.

BEACHES

Of the numerous beaches along the stretch, many have public beach access, with additional beach accesses within the 14 beach communities if you're staying here. From west to east, most with access right along scenic Highway 30A, the beaches are Miramar Beach, Legion Park, Cessna Park (on the Choctawhatchee Bay side), Dune Allen Beach, Ed Walline, Gulfview Heights, Blue Mountain Beach, Grayton Dunes, Van Ness Butler Jr., Santa Clara, Inlet Beach, and Pier and Boat Ramp 331 (bay side). Which is the nicest is hard to say; most are sparsely populated, many have small, no-fee parking lots, and several have restrooms and showers. My favorite is probably **Santa Clara,** with a beautiful stretch of sand and picnic facilities, but the pristine windswept dunes of **Grayton Dunes** make a nice afternoon of exploration.

SPORTS AND RECREATION
Parks and Recreation Areas

There's a large variety of outdoor activities, so bring your most comfortable hiking shoes. At the top of the list is **Grayton Beach State Park** (357 Main Park Rd., 850/267-8300, 8am-sunset daily, $5 per vehicle, $2 pedestrians and bicyclists, camping $24-30, cabins $110-130, $705-775 per week), south of U.S. 98 halfway between Panama City Beach, near the intersection of Highway 30A and County Road 283, with sugar-white sand, emerald-green water, little development, and huge sea oat-covered sand dunes. Foot traffic is prohibited in the dunes and in bird-nesting areas. Despite its natural setting, there are great restaurants and accommodations in nearby Grayton Beach or Seaside. Camping is popular, with 37 campsites and 30 cabins. Make reservations early. Due to the number of endangered plants and animals in the park (like the rare Choctawhatchee beach mouse), pets must be kept on a six-foot leash. If you visit in the fall, you may see the thousands of monarch butterflies resting beachside during their southward migration to Mexico.

Identified as the most pristine piece of coastal property in the state, **Topsail Hill Preserve State Park** (7525 W. Hwy. 30A, Santa Rosa Beach, 850/267-8330, 8am-sunset daily, honor $6 per vehicle, $2 pedestrians and bicyclists, RV camping $42, tent camping $24, bungalows $100-120, cabins $130-145), 10 miles east of Destin, owes its existence to turpentine. More than a century ago, workers turpentined old-growth longleaf pine trees here for caulking the seams of wooden ships, a key mode of transport. Today, it features 1,600 acres of stunning Gulf-front pine forest, nature trails over mountainous sand dunes and two freshwater dune lakes. It is one of only two remaining natural populations of the nocturnal endangered Choctawhatchee beach mice. The park features a 140-acre RV resort as well as tent camping and nice bungalows to rent.

In the southernmost portion of Walton County, the 15,000-acre **Point Washington State Forest** (5865 E. U.S. 98, Santa Rosa Beach, 850/267-8325, 8am-sunset daily, $2 pp, reserved picnic space $20) is home to more than 19 miles of trails and boasts 10 different habitats with rare plant and wildlife species, from gopher tortoises to red-cockaded woodpeckers. For an easy day hike, try the Eastern Lake Trail System, the first trail established in this forest. It consists of three double-track loop trails. The hiker or bicyclist can travel the

Coastal Dune Lakes

When was the last time you saw a freshwater lake right up against a huge body of saltwater, just a little picturesque sea oat-fringed sand dune separating the two? It appears so gloriously natural that it's easy to overlook, but the Emerald Coast's coastal dune lakes are rare enough to be considered imperiled by the Florida Natural Areas Inventory. The 15 in Walton County have sister lakes in just a few other spots along the Gulf Coast, New Zealand, Australia, and Madagascar.

These lakes were formed 2,000-10,000 years ago. Coastal winds and flowing tides have kept these havens separated from the Gulf by ever-changing dune systems ranging 10-30 feet high. Intermittently, when they are swollen with rainwater, the lakes have little wandering fingers that empty into the Gulf, meaning a canoe or kayak can paddle from freshwater to saltwater and back again without a portage. These dune lake areas are also biologically diverse, with fresh, estuarine, and marine all coexisting in this constant state of flux. Migrating birds are drawn to these coastal lakes.

Topsail Hill Preserve State Park has the densest concentration, with Morris, Campbell, and Stalworth Lakes as well as two minor unnamed coastal dune lakes on its property. For more information on the lakes at Topsail Hill Preserve State Park, contact Park Services specialist Leda C. Suydan (850/267-0299, Leda.Suydan@dep.state.fl.us).

3.5-, 5-, or 10-mile loops. Access to the trail system is at the parking lot and trailhead on County Road 395.

Nearby, off U.S. 98 on County Road 395, just north of Seagrove Beach, and worth a stop to see, **Eden Gardens State Park** (181 Eden Gardens Rd., 850/267-8320, 8am-sunset daily, $4 per vehicle, guided tour $4 adults, $2 children), in historic Point Washington on

1: a coastal dune lake at Topsail Hill Preserve State Park **2:** bike rental at Rosemary Beach

the shore of Tucker Bayou, is a beautiful 1895 Greek Revival estate surrounded by gardens of azaleas, camellias, and large moss-draped live oak. This sprawling 12-acre park was once the home of lumber baron William Henry Wesley and his family. Find yourself a picnic spot on the wide, manicured lawn.

Just east of Seagrove Beach, **Deer Lake State Park** (6350 E. Hwy. 30A, Santa Rosa Beach, 850/267-8300, 8am-sunset daily, $3 per vehicle, $2 pedestrians and bicyclists) is the newest park in these parts. It has an excellent beach with a dune walkover boardwalk, from which there are great views of this dynamic dune ecosystem. North of here are acres of hiking trails worth exploring.

To enjoy all this nature on an ecotour or guided adventure, there are plenty of guides in the area. **Old Cypress Canoe Rental** (2728 Traverse Dr., Vernon, 850/388-2072, tours $35-60) offers guided tours and kayak and canoe rentals to explore Holmes Creek and Cypress Springs. And **Big Daddy's Bike Shop** (2217 Hwy. 30A, Santa Rosa Beach, 850/622-1165, 8am-5pm Mon.-Sat.) offers bike rentals for a ride along Highway 30A or through the nearby state forest area.

Seaside Swim & Tennis Club (394 Forest St., at Odessa St., 850/231-2284, 8am-4pm Mon.-Sat., 8am-2pm Sun.) is at the center of lots of the town's activities. It offers private tennis lessons and clinics for kids and adults, shuffleboard and horseshoes, bike rentals (including trikes), and three beautiful croquet courts. There are three pools—the West Side Pool is the largest, with an adult pool at the north end of Seaside Avenue and a family pool at the northeast corner of Seaside.

Seaside has nearby golf, a long biking-walking path, deep-sea fishing, hiking, kayaking, and swimming in the Gulf.

★ Biking Along Scenic Highway 30A

The 19-mile paved **Timpoochee Trail** is one of the longest and most widely used paths in Walton County, winding through 9 of the 14 beach communities and traversing state recreational areas, state parks, dunes, and coastal dune lakes. Named after Timpoochee Kinnard, the most influential chief of the Euchee people, the path runs along Scenic Highway 30A parallel to the Gulf of Mexico. From migrating flocks of birds to blooming wildflowers and trees, the Timpoochee Trail is full of surprises year-round. Hop off the bike for an ice cream. Rent a bike with a basket and pick up some groceries for dinner along the way—a paperback from Sundog Books, maybe a bottle of wine for the sunset.

This is road- or touring-bike territory. For the mountain biker, a 10-mile loop in the Point Washington State Forest, the **Eastern Lake Bike/Hike Trail,** winds through natural vegetation and wildlife habitat. A newer stretch of trail goes to Seagrove, or go in the opposite direction for a scenic ride from Seaside to Blue Mountain Beach. And then there's the **Longleaf Pine Greenway System** (850/231-5800), interlaced through several state parks and forests, with eight miles of trails through different terrain from the Gulf to Choctawhatchee Bay. Most bike shops will equip you with maps of the different cycling possibilities in the area.

Depending on where you're staying, there are several convenient bike rental shops. From west to east: **Seaside Transit Authority Bike Rentals** (87 Central Square, Seaside, 850/231-0035, $30 per day, $60 for 7 days), **Butterfly Bike & Kayak** (3657 E. Hwy. 30A, Seagrove Beach, 850/231-2826, with Caloi off-road bikes, bikes and kayaks $25 per day, $55 per week), and **Bamboo Beach & Bicycle Company** (50 N. Barrett Square, Rosemary Beach, 850/231-0770, bikes $30 per day, $55 per week).

Fishing

Baytowne Marina at Sandestin is a good place to start. **Spitfire Bait and Tackle Store** (Sandestin, 850/267-7777) provides basic boating necessities, and it's a good place to hook up with a fishing guide. Similarly, **Old Florida Outfitters** (WaterColor,

850/534-4343), an Orvis-endorsed guide program, is a great source for specialized fishing charters, located in WaterColor's Town Center.

Not A Dog Charters (850/267-2514, www.notadogcharters.com) heads out from Grayton Beach; after a short boat ride you'll be bottom fishing for red snapper, grouper, and triggerfish, or trolling for king mackerel. In the spring, the target is cobia, right along the beach. **Yellow Fin Ocean Sports** (850/231-9024) in Grayton will take you fishing for redfish or trout in coastal bays or head out into the Gulf for grouper, snapper, or marlin. **Dead Fish Charters** (174 WaterColor Way, Suite 280, Seagrove Beach, 850/685-1092, www.deadfishcharters.com) specializes in Indian Pass half- or full-day trips, and inshore grouper and snapper trips in Grayton Beach.

SHOPPING

Shopping is clustered in a handful of tasteful centers along the Beaches of South Walton. The **Market Shops at Sandestin** (Sandestin Golf & Beach Resort, 9375 U.S. 98 W., 850/837-3077) complex has 30 shops, split between kitchenware, skin care, chocolates, housewares, and more. The **Shops of Grayton** (26 Logan Lane, Grayton Beach) is not as upscale, and here you'll find jewelry, clothing, and antiques. In Seaside there is **Ruskin Place Artist Colony** near the new Seaside Chapel and the rest of the 40 or so **Merchants of Seaside** (63 Central Square, 850/231-5424) for cafés, galleries, clothing, books, and gifts. Head to the Beaches of South Walton, especially Seaside, if you're looking for art. This area is increasingly a hotbed of independent art galleries.

Ruskin Place, named after John Ruskin, the famous supporter of 19th-century art, is the town's center for galleries, with a good coffee shop and a few other diversions. There are plenty of shops worth a bit of exploration in Seaside, but definitely check out the vessels, chandeliers, sinks, and other blown-glass art of **Fusion Art Glass** (55 Central Square, 850/231-5405, www.fusionartglass.com).

Sundog Books (89 Central Square, 850/231-5481) is a great place in the area to spend a few hours. The current fiction is always in stock, along with plenty of art and design books. In Rosemary Beach, you can visit **The Hidden Lantern Bookstore** (84 N. Barrett Square, 850/231-0091) to pick up your next beach read and browse their excellent selection of books about the local area.

FOOD

All of the little communities of South Walton have their own cluster of restaurants, in a range of price points and culinary traditions. A few I would recommend include ★ **Bud and Alley's Restaurant** (2236 E. Hwy. 30A Santa Rosa Beach, 850/231-5900, lunch 11:30am-3pm daily, dinner 5:30pm-10pm daily, rooftop bar 11:30am-2am daily, $20-28), which is actually named after a dog and a cat. It's an upscale yet casual and unpretentious place, with cooking that nods to the coastal Mediterranean, Basque country, Tuscany, and the Deep South. Oysters Seaside are baked beauties with shrimp, scallops, calamari, cilantro, garlic, and lime, and there are tempura-fried soft-shell crabs with rémoulade, or heads-on shrimp with garlic and shallots. The bar has an extensive wine list and is a great spot for conversation with the locals.

Chef Jim Shirley brings his brand of Southern cooking to Seaside at the **Great Southern Café** (83 Central Square, Seaside, 850/231-7327, 8am-9:30pm daily, $10-28). The menu's regional flair includes Gulf shrimp, oysters, and traditional Southern vegetables. It seems like no one talks about the Great Southern Café without mentioning the Grits a Ya Ya, one of the most ordered dishes, with seasoned shrimp in smoked gouda cheese grits topped with cream gravy, bacon, spinach, and mushrooms. **Dawson's Yogurt** (121 Central Square, Seaside, 850/231-4770, 10am-9pm daily) is the place to indulge in your choice of over 20 flavors of yogurt. The Kahlua fudge is a favorite.

Café Thirty-A (3899 E. Hwy. 30A, Seagrove, 850/231-2166, 5pm-9:30pm daily,

$12-34) is another upscale spot, with a large wine list, many selections by the glass. The menu has broad appeal, with dishes such as wood oven-roasted grouper served with baby tiger shrimp and risotto in a sweet carrot sauce or maple barbecue pork chop with fried peaches and corn mashed potatoes on the side. I'm pretty content just to slice up one of the Hawaiian-style wood-fired pizzas.

Next there's **Basmati's Asian Cuisine** (3295 W. Hwy. 30A, Blue Mountain Beach, 850/267-3028, lunch 11am-2:30pm Mon.-Fri., dinner 5pm-10pm daily, $9-28) with a full sushi bar and mostly Japanese fusion dishes served in a beautiful dining room and a nice sheltered deck.

In the Village of Baytowne Wharf, you've got **Graffiti's & The Funky Blues Shack** (34902 Emerald Coast Pkwy., Destin, 850/424-6650, 4pm-10pm Sun.-Thurs., 4pm-midnight Fri.-Sat., $12-23), a folk art-infused restaurant and live blues venue, or **Slick Lips Seafood and Oyster House** (Village of Baytowne Wharf, Sandestin, 850/347-5060, 11am-9pm Sun.-Thurs., 11am-10pm Fri.-Sat., $15-30)—if you've got the seafood jones, head here, especially for the key lime snapper, char-grilled oysters, and fish tacos.

For breakfast, top honors go to Rosemary Beach's **Wild Olives Market** (104 N. Barrett Square, Rosemary Beach, 850/231-0065, 11am-9pm Wed.-Sun.) or **Summer Kitchen Café** (78 Main St., Rosemary Beach, 850/213-0521, breakfast 7:30am-10:30am, lunch 10:30am-3pm, dinner 5pm-9pm Wed.-Mon., $6-10) for pastries, egg dishes, and other healthy choices.

Locals have been flocking to **Wine World** (WaterColor Town Center, 850/231-1323, 10am-8pm daily), a low-key neighborhood wine, beer, and cheese shop that also serves a fine selection of coffees, pizzas, paninis, and tapas. It's right in WaterColor Market in the heart of Town Center, an easy place to hang out and enjoy the effects of a relaxing beach vacation.

ACCOMMODATIONS

Resorts and Vacation Rentals

The **Hilton Sandestin Beach Golf Resort & Spa** (4000 Sandestin Blvd. S., Destin, 850/267-9500, www.hiltonsandestinbeach.com, $189-450) is a beautiful golf-and-spa resort of 598 rooms, the largest beachfront resort hotel in the region. There are 190 spacious standard guest rooms, 22 parlor suites, two presidential suites, and 385 junior suites that feature bunk beds. There are several excellent on-site dining and shopping options, so there's not much reason to leave. The resort provides access to Gulf and bay beaches.

So many of the nicer accommodations here are private homes or condos. There are numerous property management companies—**Beach Rental of South Walton** (850/534-0600) is a good place to start looking for what you want. Many of the swankier communities have their own websites with rental information and slide shows (www.rosemarybeach.com, www.seasidefl.com). My favorite is definitely ★ **Rosemary Beach** (Hwy. 30A, in between Seacrest and Inlet Beach, 850/278-2030, www.rosemarybeach.com, $200-500, many rentals by the week), with one- to five-bedroom Gulf-front and midtown cottages for vacation rentals. All designed in a loose Caribbean style, there are family cottages, carriage houses, flats, and contemporary lofts, all connected to the shore by boardwalks and footpaths. It's a good location for families, because it's farther east than many of the communities, and thus closer to the liveliness of Panama City Beach but still out of the fray.

The **Sandestin Golf & Beach Resort** (9300 Emerald Coast Pkwy. W., Sandestin, 850/267-8000, $172-450) is the premier resort in this area, set on 2,400 beach- and bayfront acres. There are four championship golf courses, 15 world-class tennis courts, a full-service marina, water sports, charter sailing

1: Sundog Books in Seaside **2:** Village of Baytowne Wharf's restaurant-lined streets **3:** the Sandestin Golf & Beach Resort

and fishing, fine and casual dining, a fancy fitness center, a professional salon and day spa, and fun children's programs. It's got 1,350 different rooms and accommodations, with a range of options.

The **Village of Baytowne Wharf** (9300 Emerald Coast Pkwy. W., Sandestin, 850/267-8000, $180-800) is a sweeping pedestrian village right on the beach that rents its own accommodations. There are different choices to stay, grouped into five resort areas: Beachfront, Beachside, Village, Bayside, and Dockside. Each of the five resorts offers a unique flavor as well as a range of rates. Included with a stay at any of the resort accommodations options are free kayak, canoe, and bike rentals.

To **rent a cottage at Seaside,** call 855/882-0283. The tricky part is figuring out what you want—people have built their dream homes in Seaside, and the prices, styles, and sizes are all over the map. It offers over 200 individual accommodations, including private homes, cottages, luxury town houses, penthouses, and beachfront hideaways.

Camping

The only way to spend under $50 around here is by camping—it's warm much of the year, with nice evening breezes, lots of beach, and plenty of fresh air, and it's not so rural that you can't go out for dinner. One of the best places in the area to camp is in the town of Grayton Beach near Seaside at **Grayton Beach State Park** (357 Main Park Rd., 850/267-8300, 8am-sunset daily, $5 per vehicle, $2 pedestrians and bicyclists, camping $24-30, cabins $110-130, $705-775 per week), south of U.S. 98 halfway between Panama City Beach and Destin, near the intersection of Highway 30A and County Road 283. The campground has 34 sites accommodating tents and RVs and is right on the Gulf of Mexico among trees and dunes. It has restrooms, electricity, and hot showers to rinse away those hours of swimming

and wading in the salty warm waters of the Gulf before you roast some marshmallows over an open fire with the waves lapping in the background.

In Sandestin you can camp on the Gulf at **CampGulf RV Park and Campground** (10005 W. Emerald Coast Pkwy., Destin, 850/226-7485, campsites $67-219, cabins $136-325), with an activity center, fishing, cable TV, and full hookups. **Destin RV Beach Resort** (362 Miramar Beach Dr., Destin, 850/837-3529) is one of the nicest RV campgrounds I have come across. The owners call it a "luxury RV resort." It is right across from the beach and has a swimming pool to enjoy.

You can also camp at **Topsail Hill Preserve State Park** (7525 W. Hwy. 30A, Santa Rosa Beach, 850/267-8330, 8am-sunset daily, honor $6 per vehicle, $2 pedestrians and bicyclists, RV camping $42, tent camping $24, bungalows $100-120, cabins $130-145), 10 miles east of Destin, at the Topsail Hill Gregory E. Moore RV Resort, which has the highest possible rating from *Trailer Life* and Woodall's, placing it in the top 1 percent of RV campgrounds in the nation. The campground has 156 stunning RV sites with electricity, sewer, water, and cable. It also offers 22 tent sites with electricity. The park has a swimming pool, restrooms, hot showers, and a camp store with water, other drinks, snacks, and camping items. A tram will give you a lift to the beach. It's definitely set up for RV enthusiasts, but it's a good place to tent camp as well if there aren't any sites left at Grayton Beach State Park.

TRANSPORTATION

The Beaches of South Walton communities are 35 miles west of Panama City Beach along Highway 30A, also called Scenic Highway 30A and Scenic Gulf Coast Drive. Highway 30A splits off from U.S. 98 just before Highway 393 in the west and right after Panama City Beach in the east.

Information and Services

The Emerald Coast area is in the **central time zone.**

VISITOR INFORMATION

To get visitor information, there are several locations, depending on where your base is. For Destin and Fort Walton Beach information, visit the **Emerald Coast Convention & Visitors Bureau** (1540 E. U.S. 98, Fort Walton Beach, 850/651-7131, www.emeraldcoastfl.com, 9am-4pm daily). There's also the **South Walton Visitor Information Center** (25771 U.S. 331, at U.S. 98, Santa Rosa Beach, 850/267-1216, 8am-4:30pm daily) and the **Destin Area Chamber of Commerce** (4484 Legendary Dr., at U.S. 98, 850/837-6241, 8:30am-5pm Mon.-Fri.).

In Panama City Beach, visit the **Panama City Beach Convention & Visitors Bureau** (17001 Panama City Beach Pkwy., 850/233-5070, www.visitpanamacitybeach. com, 8am-5pm daily) for brochures, maps, and information about attractions and accommodations.

POLICE AND EMERGENCIES

In an emergency, dial 911. For a nonemergency police need, call or visit the **Fort Walton Beach Police Department** (7 Hollywood Blvd., Fort Walton Beach, 850/833-9546) or the **Panama City Beach Police Department** (17115 Panama City Beach Pkwy., 850/233-5000).

In the event of a medical emergency, stop into **Sacred Heart Hospital on the Emerald Coast** (7800 U.S. 98 W., Miramar Beach, 850/278-3000) in the western part of the Emerald Coast; in the eastern part, go to **Bay Medical Center** (615 N. Bonita Ave., Panama City, 850/769-1511).

Pensacola

Pensacola is a picture-perfect beach retreat

with deep turquoise waters and fine white sand. Although it's more widely known as a summer vacation destination, the city is also rich in culture, having seen five flags—Spain, France, England, the Confederacy, and the United States—flown in the past four centuries.

The city and the popular beach on the barrier island of Santa Rosa are both much more casual than most areas along the Gulf Coast. There are plenty of upscale resorts and restaurants, but they seem to find a common thread with a laid-back informal style that leaves pretentiousness behind and retains much of the Old Florida charm that has been lost in cities and beaches to the south. Pensacola also has much more Southern culture than areas farther south.

Highlights

Look for ★ to find recommended sights, activities, dining, and lodging.

★ **Historic Pensacola Village:** Stop for refreshments and food downtown before exploring the cluster of 18th- and 19th-century museums and homes (page 334).

★ **National Museum of Naval Aviation:** Find out why Pensacola is called the Cradle of Naval Aviation at this vast and spectacular museum (page 339).

★ **Pensacola Beach and Fishing Pier:** With miles of beautiful coastline and the longest pier on the Gulf of Mexico, festive action-packed Pensacola Beach is a can't-miss. And you don't need a fishing license to wet a line on the pier (page 342).

★ **Gulf Islands National Seashore:** This protected area has miles of beautiful beach habitat along Santa Rosa Island, as well as Fort Pickens and other historic sights (page 342).

★ **Tubing on Coldwater Creek:** In the warmer months, rent tubes for a fun journey down Coldwater Creek (page 346).

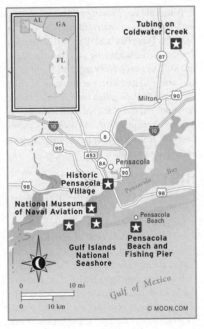

In Pensacola are hospitality and Southern food that is a unique convergence of coastal American, Spanish, and Cajun cultures. You're as likely to find deep-fried mullet with coleslaw, hush puppies, and a tall glass of sweet tea as you are grilled grouper with a mango sauce with a side of black beans and rice or a bowl of spicy New Orleans gumbo with a tray of raw oysters.

And then there are the beaches. Some are developed tourist spots such as Pensacola Beach; others are more uninhabited. The Gulf Islands National Seashore cuts through this area, a 150-mile-long discontinuous string of undeveloped barrier islands that begins at Santa Rosa Island and extends into Mississippi. Santa Rosa Island contains seven beautiful undeveloped miles of beach with clear water, white sand, lots of fish and wildlife, and fewer people crowding the pristine shores.

Pensacola has a strong military presence, with numerous important forts as well as Eglin Air Force Base and the Naval Air Station Pensacola, the launching point for the flight training of every Navy aviator, flight officer, and enlisted aircrew. Because of this, Pensacola is often called the Cradle of Naval Aviation. The free National Museum of Naval Aviation, the third largest in the world, showcases the history of aviation through indoor and outdoor exhibits.

HISTORY

Pensacola has a long history. Native Americans left pottery shards and artifacts in the gentle coastal dunes here centuries before Tristán de Luna arrived with his fellow Spaniards in 1559. Tristán de Luna was the first to attempt a settlement in Pensacola, but violent hurricanes uprooted his effort and sent the Spanish sailing around the peninsula to St. Augustine, where they established North America's first European settlement. Even after this first exploratory settlement didn't

take, Pensacola was settled by Europeans early on. It was one of a handful of colonial communities in the southeastern United States, its Seville Historic District one of the oldest and most intact in Florida. Within this small neighborhood is the 1832 Old Christ Church, Florida's oldest church still standing in situ, and St. Michael's Cemetery, deeded to Pensacola by the king of Spain in 1822. A walk through Historic Pensacola Village provides insight into the area's history.

PLANNING YOUR TIME

The best way to explore Pensacola is by car, but you can get by with public transportation and taxis if you plan to spend most of your time downtown and at Pensacola Beach. If you want to use Pensacola as a base to visit surrounding attractions, you have to rent a vehicle. The most popular area for accommodations is Pensacola Beach. Downtown Pensacola and the Perdido Key are a close second, with downtown more historical, with several excellent bed-and-breakfasts and hotels, and the beaches with mostly chain hotels and high-rise condos. As on most of the Panhandle, high season is April-August. The value season runs roughly August-March. Regardless of when you visit, make reservations in advance. Visitors to the naval base tend to fill the hotels near it.

The Pensacola area can occupy you for three or four days with its historical attractions, beaches, and nature parks. To really explore all the great beaches, plan for a week, or two if you want to spend an extensive amount of time fishing, paddling, or sightseeing in Perdido, Gulf Shores, and Dauphin Island to the west, or the forests, creeks, and rivers to the north. If you fly into Pensacola and rent a car, think about tacking on a couple of extra days to explore the Emerald Coast area to the east.

For camping, head to the Gulf Islands National Seashore at Fort Pickens west of

---

Previous: Pensacola Beach; the historic Pensacola Beach sign; Pensacola Beach ball water tower

Pensacola

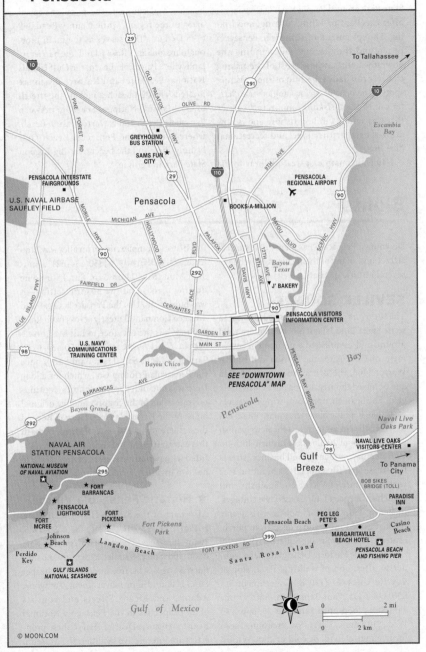

© MOON.COM

Pensacola Beach, north to the Blackwater area around Brewton, and west to Big Lagoon State Park around Perdido. All of these areas offer excellent paddling, fishing, and hiking. The epicenter for fishing is in Pensacola Beach and the marinas surrounding the downtown areas, where most of the fishing charters run daily trips into offshore fishing spots. A favorite of serious anglers is a charter out to the *Oriskany,* an aircraft carrier that was sunk 24 miles offshore and is now utilized as an artificial reef and recreational dive spot.

I-10 is the main east-west highway to the city, with I-110 leading south into downtown Pensacola. U.S. 98 primarily serves the beaches and connects the popular coastal areas of the region, while County Road 399 (Via De Luna Dr.) serves as the main thoroughfare for Santa Rosa Island, the barrier island where Pensacola Beach, the Gulf Islands National Seashore, and Navarre Beach are located. The best beaches include the stretch of Gulf Islands National Seashore between Pensacola Beach and Navarre; Casino Beach, where you find the Pensacola Beach Gulf Fishing Pier; and the beaches at Big Lagoon State Park in Perdido.

Sights

Downtown Pensacola has plenty of historical attractions, many of them clustered in one of several historic districts.

SEVILLE SQUARE

The survivors of an early thwarted attempt to settle Santa Rosa Island moved to more solid ground and established a permanent settlement in 1752. After the French and Indian War of 1763, the British took west Florida and occupied the area, laying out a clean street grid. The Spanish, upon capturing Pensacola after that, kept the old town square intact but renamed the streets to reflect the new Spanish presence. About 20 blocks of historic 18th- to 19th-century residential and business streets have these Spanish names. It's a beautiful area with a mixture of Victorian, Spanish-, and French-influenced Gulf Coast-style cottages, including many 1.5-story houses with steeply pitched gabled roofs and a deep front porch, centered on shady Seville Square Park.

The Seville Historic District makes a wonderful afternoon of walking. First, stop at **Seville Quarter** (130 E. Government St., 850/434-6211, 7am-3am Mon.-Sat., 11am-3am Sun., food until 1am, $10-25, cover $3 Wed., $10 Thurs., $5 Fri.-Sat., free Sun.-Tues.) for live music, food, or cold drinks. Within this historic complex, down an alleyway, stop into **Rosie O'Grady's** (850/434-6211, 7am-3am Mon.-Sat., 11am-3am Sun.) for some dueling pianos and the historic setting—it was built in 1871 as the Pensacola Cigar and Tobacco Company. Directly across from Rosie O'Grady's is the entrance to **Lili Marlene's World War I Aviators Pub** (850/434-6211, 7am-3am Mon.-Sat., 11am-3am Sun.), once the Pensacola Printing Co., which for a long time was the oldest print shop in continuous operation in the country and the original home of the *Pensacola News Journal.* Beyond these, there are several other themed rooms in this entertainment and dining complex, outfitted with period antiques. The complex also has two inviting courtyards and a gift shop.

★ Historic Pensacola Village

Also part of the Seville Historic District, **Historic Pensacola Village** (850/595-5985, 10am-4pm Tues.-Thurs., 10am-7pm Fri.-Sat., noon-4pm Sun., $8 adults, $7 seniors and military, $4 ages 3-14, free under age 3, cheaper Sun.) is bounded by Government, Taragona, Adams, and Alcanz Streets and consists of 20 properties in the Pensacola National Register Historic District. Ten of these properties are interpretive facilities: the Museum

Downtown Pensacola

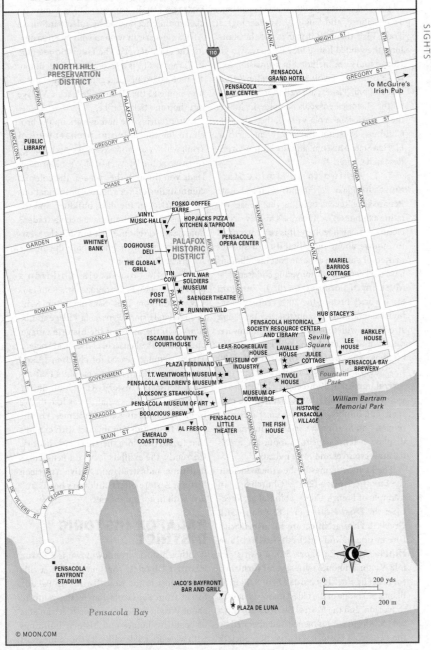

NORTH HILL
PRESERVATION
DISTRICT

PENSACOLA
GRAND HOTEL

PENSACOLA
BAY CENTER

To McGuire's
Irish Pub

PUBLIC
LIBRARY

FOSKO COFFEE
BARRE

VINYL
MUSIC HALL

HOPJACKS PIZZA
KITCHEN & TAPROOM

PENSACOLA
OPERA CENTER

WHITNEY
BANK

DOGHOUSE
DELI

PALAFOX
HISTORIC
DISTRICT

THE GLOBAL
GRILL

MARIEL
BARRIOS
COTTAGE

TIN
COW

CIVIL WAR
SOLDIERS
MUSEUM

POST
OFFICE

SAENGER THEATRE

RUNNING WILD

HUB STACEY'S

PENSACOLA HISTORICAL
SOCIETY RESOURCE CENTER
AND LIBRARY

Seville
Square

LEE
HOUSE

BARKLEY
HOUSE

ESCAMBIA COUNTY
COURTHOUSE

LEAR-ROCHEBLAVE
HOUSE

LAVALLE
HOUSE

PLAZA FERDINAND VII

MUSEUM OF
INDUSTRY

JULEE
COTTAGE

PENSACOLA BAY
BREWERY

T.T. WENTWORTH MUSEUM

PENSACOLA CHILDREN'S MUSEUM

TIVOLI
HOUSE

Fountain
Park

JACKSON'S STEAKHOUSE

PENSACOLA MUSEUM OF ART

MUSEUM OF
COMMERCE

William Bartram
Memorial Park

BODACIOUS BREW

HISTORIC
PENSACOLA
VILLAGE

AL FRESCO

PENSACOLA
LITTLE
THEATER

THE FISH
HOUSE

EMERALD
COAST TOURS

PENSACOLA
BAYFRONT
STADIUM

JACO'S BAYFRONT
BAR AND GRILL

PLAZA DE LUNA

Pensacola Bay

0   200 yds

0   200 m

© MOON.COM

ALCANIZ ST
WRIGHT ST
8TH AVE
GREGORY ST
CHASE ST
FLORIDA BLANCA
MANRESA ST
BRUE ST
TARRAGONA
ALCANIZ ST
JEFFERSON
COMMENDENCIA ST
BARRACKS ST
SPRING ST
PALAFOX ST
BARCELONA ST
GARDEN ST
ROMANA ST
INTENDENCIA ST
GOVERNMENT ST
ZARAGOZA ST
MAIN ST
REUS ST
BAYLEN ST
PALAFOX PL
SPRING ST
S REUS ST
S SPRING ST
W CEDAR ST
S CEDAR ST
S DE VILLIERS ST
WRIGHT ST
GREGORY ST
CHASE ST
110

of Commerce, Museum of Industry, Julee Cottage, Lavalle House, Lear House, Dorr House, Old Christ Church, Weaver's Cottage, Tivoli House, and Colonial Archaeological Trail. Visit them all if you've got the stamina—the guided house tour is the way to go. House tours are included in admission and leave from the Tivoli House at 11am, 1pm, and 2:30pm. Tickets are valid for seven days for the Historic Pensacola complex, including the Historic Pensacola Village, the Pensacola Children's Museum, the T. T. Wentworth Jr. Florida State Museum, and the Hilton-Green Research Center.

T. T. Wentworth Jr. Florida State Museum (Plaza Ferdinand) is an elaborate Renaissance Revival building that houses rotating exhibits on west Florida's history, architecture, and archaeology. It is recommended to inquire about the suitability of subject matter for children as some past installations have not been suitable for young children. The **Museum of Commerce** (201 E. Zaragoza St.) is a brick turn-of-the-20th-century warehouse containing a reconstructed 1890s-era streetscape with a toy store; leather, hardware, music, and print shops; and horse-drawn buggies. The **Museum of Industry** (200 E. Zaragoza St.) houses an exhibit depicting several important 19th-century industries in west Florida: fishing, brick-making, the railroad, and lumber. It was the most recent to reopen and features a variety of interactive displays teaching visitors about the area's natural resources and early industry.

The historic homes in the village include the **Lavalle House** (205 E. Church St.), an example of French Creole colonial architecture; the **Dorr House** (311 S. Adams St.), Greek Revival architecture furnished with fine antiques; and the **Lear-Rocheblave House** (214 E. Zaragoza St.), a two-story folk Victorian home with several furnished rooms. The **Barkley House** (410 S. Florida Blanca St.) is one of the oldest masonry houses in Florida, and the **Mariel Barrios Cottage** (204 S. Alcaniz St.) is owned and operated by the Pensacola Historic Preservation Society

and exhibits household items and furnishings from Pensacola during the 1920s. The **Julee Cottage** (210 E. Zaragoza St.) is a museum classroom once owned by Julee Panton, an African American woman who was free during the era of slavery. The **Tivoli House** (205 E. Zaragoza St.) is a reconstructed version of an 1805 boarding- and gaming house and is now home to the Historic Pensacola Village gift shop and ticket office.

After touring the homes, pick up the brochure for the **Colonial Archaeological Trail,** which was produced by the Archaeology Institute at the University of West Florida; it leads you through the ruins of the colonial commanding officer's house, the foundations of the officer-of-the-day's building, and the remains of what might have been a trader's home and warehouse just outside the western gate of the British fort, built during the American Revolution.

Also, the **Pensacola Children's Museum** (115 E. Zaragoza St., 850/433-1559, 10am-4pm Tues.-Sat., noon-4pm Sun., included in Historic Pensacola Village admission) is in the midst of the historic village, operated by the Pensacola Historical Society. The museum is geared for children 13 and younger, with interactive exhibits that explore Pensacola history. An exhibit on the first floor recreates what it was like to live in Pensacola during colonial times. On the second floor, kids can interact with exhibits that further explore the area's rich history. Currently, the exhibits focus on Pensacola's maritime, industrial, and Native American history. A store offers children's books and toys with historical themes.

PALAFOX HISTORIC DISTRICT

Another historic area downtown is **Palafox Historic District,** contiguous with Seville Square just to the west. It runs up Palafox Street from Pensacola Bay in the south to about Wright Street in the north. It's an area of beautiful homes and historic buildings with wide brick sidewalks. It's the commercial

Downtown Sightseeing Tours

A fun way to explore downtown Pensacola is to take a tour on **Pensacola Pedal Trolley** (225 East Zaragoza St., tours meet in front of the Pensacola Bay Brewery). They offer historic tours ($25 pp), 2-hour pub crawls (Sun.-Thurs. $19 pp, Fri.-Sat. $25 pp), and will book private tours. This pedal-powered ecofriendly trolley cruises through the historic district while the driver narrates the sights along the way.

To explore the history of this area, take a two-hour guided tour on a Segway with **Emerald Coast Tours** (18 E. Garden St., 850/417-9292, call to schedule tour, $45-65 adults, $40-60 students and military). Guide Nic Shuck offers a crash course on operating one of the two-wheeled Segways before you embark on a high-speed excursion that explores the best historical sights and landmarks in downtown Pensacola, including the Plaza De Luna, where the Spanish officially handed over Florida to the United States. It's a great way to get familiar with the lay of the land when you first get into town and perfect for less mobile visitors who would rather not walk the long blocks of downtown. Along the way you'll learn the best spots for good eats and drinks. There are also tours of Pensacola Beach (Mar.-Sept. 15, $55 adults, $50 students and military).

When you're walking to and from Pensacola Bayfront Stadium, or anytime you're downtown and need a quick lift, keep your eye out for **Gopher Carts** (850/792-6565). They offer free rides in golf carts anywhere in the four-mile radius of downtown Pensacola. Their knowledgeable drivers work for tips and can usually give you the rundown about what's happening in the city on any given night. The carts are spacious, clean, and a lot of fun.

heart of Pensacola and houses a couple of the area's big cultural draws.

The **Pensacola Museum of Art** (407 S. Jefferson St., 850/432-6247, 10am-5pm Tues.-Fri., 10am-4pm Sat., noon-4pm Sun., $7 adults, $6 military and seniors, $4 ages 3-14, free under age 3) is right at its center, with a wonderful space and intriguingly diverse exhibits of sculptures, paintings, and photographs, many of them political in nature in recent years. Ask to take a walk through the museum before visiting with small children; you may find some of the material not suitable. The permanent collection has minor works, most on paper, by some mostly 20th-century heavy hitters as well as lots of fine decorative glass. The museum is housed in what was the city jail from 1906 to 1954, so there are sturdy bars on the windows.

Just around the corner you will find the **Vinyl Music Hall** (5 E. Garden St., 850/607-6758, www.vinylmusichall.com, tickets $7-50), the newest music and entertainment venue in town. What was once a historic Masonic Lodge has been restored and remodeled into a hip music venue and bar. The intimate general admission venue is standing room-only and draws large national acts mostly in the blues, rock, and alternative genres.

NORTH HILL PRESERVATION DISTRICT

Before you tire of all this history, another worthy walk is the **North Hill Preservation District,** which occupies 50 city blocks due north of the Palafox District, away from the water, bounded on the west by Reus Street and on the east by Palafox Street. On the National Register of Historic Places, the neighborhood is residential, with great examples of fully restored historic homes. They aren't open for visitors, but some of the current owners are descendants of the original builders—Spanish nobility, lumber barons, French Creole people, and Civil War soldiers.

NAVAL AIR STATION PENSACOLA

Pensacola is known as the Cradle of Naval Aviation, a bold claim that can be authenticated through an exploration of one of the

1

2

3

many sites open to the public at the **Naval Air Station Pensacola** and environs. To reach the historic mainland forts and the National Museum of Naval Aviation from the north, take exit 7 off I-10 onto Pine Forest Road (Hwy. 297), go about 1.5 miles, and take a right onto Blue Angel Parkway. Then drive 12 miles to the west gate of the Naval Air Station. Visitors without military stickers can *depart* only from the main entrance on Navy Boulevard.

★ National Museum of Naval Aviation

If you're only going to see one historic attraction in Pensacola, the **National Museum of Naval Aviation** (1750 Radford Blvd., NAS Pensacola, 850/453-2389 or 800/327-5002, 9am-5pm daily, free) is one of the largest air and space museums in the world, with 160 restored aircraft representing Navy, Marine Corps, and Coast Guard aviation. There's a seven-story glass-and-steel atrium in which four A-4 Skyhawks are suspended in formation. You can stand on the flight deck of the USS *Cabot* and fly an F/A-18 mission in Desert Storm in a motion-based flight simulator. There's an IMAX theater ($9 adults, $8 seniors, military, and ages 5-17, $7 active military, free under age 5) that hosts a rotation of films, usually about aircraft, aviation, and military history, including the long-running feature called *The Magic of Flight.*

If you're in town March-November, don't miss the **Blue Angels** (www.navalaviationmuseum.org, 55-minute practice sessions often 9am or 11:30am Tues.-Wed. Mar.-Nov.), at an outside viewing stand north of museum on the flight line. Check the website to confirm the schedule. Watch the Navy's impressive acrobatic flight squadron of F-18 Hornets perform stunning barrel rolls, high-speed loops, their trademark diamond formation, and other daring flight maneuvers. After practice, spectators often have

the opportunity to talk with the pilots and get their autographs.

Pensacola Lighthouse

Also on the grounds of the Naval Air Station Pensacola, you can climb the 177 steps to the top of the **Pensacola Lighthouse** (Hwy. 292 S., 850/393-1561, 9am-5pm daily, $7 adults, $4 seniors, military, and under age 13), which follows on the heels of other lighthouses erected in this area. The construction of the first Pensacola lighthouse, the Aurora Borealis, was completed in 1824, also the first lighthouse on the Gulf Coast and the second lighthouse in Florida. It stood at the northern entrance of the bay near the present-day Lighthouse Point Restaurant. Unfortunately, trees on Santa Rosa Island obscured the light beam to ships. The present lighthouse was begun in 1856, and it was lit in 1859. At night it still shines for sailors 27 miles out at sea, 171 feet tall and with a first-order Fresnel lens. In 1965 the lighthouse was automated, obviating the need for an on-site keeper. The Keeper's Quarters now house the Navy's Command Display Center, with an exhibit on the lighthouse and the Naval Air Station.

The Forts

Accessed through Naval Air Station Pensacola, the historic forts in this area are actually part of the **Gulf Islands National Seashore** (1801 Gulf Breeze Pkwy., Gulf Breeze, FL 32563, 850/934-2600). The park spans 160 miles from Cat Island, Mississippi, east to the Okaloosa Day Use Area near Fort Walton Beach.

Fort Barrancas sits on a sandy bluff overlooking the entrance to Pensacola Bay. This site has seen three forts—first an earth-and-log Royal Navy Redoubt in 1763, then a Spanish two-part fort with Bateria de San Antonio at the foot of the bluff and Fort San Carlos de Barrancas above. The American brick-and-mortar Fort Barrancas was mostly completed in 1846, boasting 37 guns. During the Civil War, Confederate forces held Fort Barrancas until 1862. It was rearmed in 1890 and used as a training facility briefly during

1: Seville Square 2: Pensacola Lighthouse
3: National Museum of Naval Aviation

the Spanish-American War, after which it was disarmed again and used as an observation and communications post until 1930. Fort Barrancas was deactivated in 1947 and lay unused until it became part of the Gulf Islands National Seashore in 1971. It was entirely restored by 1980 at a cost of $1.2 million. Today, there's a visitors center with exhibits on the history of Pensacola under five flags (1559-1971), with displays of Civil War and coastal artillery artifacts. The visitors center shows a 12-minute video on the fort and offers guided tours daily.

The **Fort Barrancas-Advanced Redoubt** (850/934-2600), 700 yards south, was built 1845-1859 to defend the Pensacola Navy Yard from overland infantry assault. It was only staffed during the Civil War, after which it was deemed obsolete. Scheduled tours of Fort Barrancas are offered throughout the year. The 0.5-mile Trench Trail connects the Advanced Redoubt to the Fort Barrancas Visitor Center.

The largest of the four forts built to defend Pensacola Bay, construction of **Fort Pickens** on Santa Rosa Island began in 1829 and was completed in 1834; the fort was used until the 1940s. It is said to be the only Southern fort not captured by the Confederacy in the Civil War, and that Geronimo surrendered here in 1886, marking the end of the Apache Wars. The park has a visitors center with a great self-guided tour map of the fort. There are also regularly scheduled ranger tours and a little museum with regular interpretive programs. There is year-round **camping** (850/934-2600, reservations 877/444-6777) in the area on the west end of Santa Rosa Island, as well as the Blackbird Marsh and Dune Nature Trails and a fishing pier.

While Fort Pickens is on the western tip of Santa Rosa Island, **Fort McRee** is on a narrow bar of sand on the eastern tip of Perdido Key. Or maybe I should say it used to be there. Once used as the third point of the triangle (with Pickens and Barrancas) by the U.S. Army to defend Pensacola Bay, Fort McRee was built there 1834-1839. It was heavily damaged during the Civil War and then leveled by hurricanes over the years. It is a great sailing day trip to the fort, where you can usually have the beach and surrounding island to yourself and wander through the remnants of the fort and Battery 233.

visitors center, Fort Barrancas

FAMILY-FRIENDLY ATTRACTIONS

There are only so many historic sites a kid can endure. Beyond the area's beaches, there are a couple of fun enticements for young ones. The **Gulf Breeze Zoo** (5701 Gulf Breeze Pkwy., 850/932-2229, 9am-4pm daily Jan.-Feb., 9am-5pm daily Mar.-Oct., 9am-4pm daily Nov.-Dec., $21 adults, $20 seniors, $17 ages 2-12, free under age 2), 10 miles east of Gulf Breeze on U.S. 98, is home to 1,400 animals on a 50-acre wildlife preserve. You can view the free-roaming animals from the boardwalk or from the cute red Safari Line train. The train ride is narrated by a guide who points out African wild dogs, giraffes, pygmy hippos, gorillas, and native wildlife. The zoo also has a tranquil Japanese garden, a gift shop, the Jungle Cafe, and the Whistlestop Snack Bar.

During the last 11 days of October, the **Pensacola Interstate Fair** (6655 W. Mobile Hwy., 850/944-4500, $12 over age 11, $6 ages 4-11, parking $5) is vast, with 147 acres of rides and exhibits. Along with the carnival rides and games, the fair always features headline music acts that have included names like Travis Tritt, Sugar Ray, Grand Funk Railroad, and the White Tie Rock Ensemble. Other attractions include livestock, agriculture, and antique car exhibits.

It's fairly small-scale compared to Disney or Busch Gardens, but **Sam's Fun City** (6709 Pensacola Blvd., 850/505-0800, www.samsfuncity.com, 11am-8pm Sun.-Thurs., 11am-10pm Fri.-Sat. spring-fall, 11am-10pm Sat., 11am-8pm Sun. winter, $8-38), just south of I-10 on U.S. 29, is Pensacola's amusement park. There are a bunch of midway-style rides along with go-karts, bumper boats, and miniature golf. It has a 1,600-square-foot arena for laser tag, a huge game arcade, and **Surf City Water Park** with a wave pool, 15 waterslides, a 1,200-foot-long endless river, spray grounds, water play structures, and kiddie pools. The on-site Bullwinkle's Restaurant is a pleasant, something-for-everyone family eatery.

Beaches

The long stretch of the **Gulf Islands National Seashore** and the **Naval Air Station Pensacola** and **Eglin Air Force Base** farther east have imposed restrictions on commercial growth. The communities in the area set quotas on density and height restrictions on new construction. Thus, the more urban beachfront areas around Pensacola aren't littered with high-rise condos and resort hotels, and there's another six miles of utterly preserved seashore in the park.

Shared with the state of Alabama, **Perdido Key** is the westernmost island in the long chain of barrier islands that line the Panhandle's edge. The developed beach areas are called **Orange Beach** and **Johnson Beach,** and the more natural part is **Perdido Key State Park** (15301 Perdido Key Dr., 850/492-1595, 8am-sunset daily, $3 per vehicle up to 8 people, $2 pedestrians and bicyclists), 15 miles southwest of Pensacola off Highway 292. These beaches provide some of the best swimming in the state—warm clear water, gentle surf, and long stretches of shallows. **Big Lagoon State Park** (12301 Gulf Beach Hwy., 850/492-1595, 8am-sunset daily, $6 per vehicle, $2 pedestrians and bicyclists, $10 boat launch for 1 person and 1 boat, $12 for 2-8 people with boat, camping $20), 15 miles southwest of Pensacola off Highway 292, is just across the bay from Perdido Key and offers tent, camp trailer, and RV sites. The secluded beaches at Big Lagoon State Park are excellent for fishing the flats or just relaxing on the shore of the lagoon's calm waters.

Santa Rosa Island, just to the east, is one of the longest barrier islands in the world, stretching 50 miles from Pensacola Bay on its western side to Choctawhatchee Bay to its east. All the beaches along this stretch of coast have exceptionally beautiful white quartz sand.

For beach sports gear, stop by **Innerlight Surf Shop** (655 Pensacola Beach Blvd., 850/934-9004) to rent surfboards and paddleboards ($15 per hour, $30 for 3 hours, $45 for 10 hours, $60 per day), kayaks ($25 per hour, $45 for 3 hours, $60 for 10 hours, $75 per day). If you're new to surfing, consider getting a lesson with an experienced wave rider (1-hour private lesson $55, 1-hour semiprivate $45, 1 hour group of 5 or more $35) before shredding the surf in the Gulf.

★ PENSACOLA BEACH AND FISHING PIER

Pensacola Beach (800/635-4803, 9am-5pm Mon.-Sat., 10am-3pm Sun.) covers much of the island, with restaurants, shops, and entertainment at their highest density near the **Pensacola Beach Fishing Pier** (24 hours daily, $1.25, fishing $7.50 adults, $4.50 children, free under age 6), which is 1,471 feet long and 30 feet above the water. Crossing the two bridges from Pensacola to Santa Rosa Island, you're on Pensacola Boulevard—it splits left and right, but directly in front is Pensacola Beach. The area is rich with watersports possibilities: parasailing, sailboarding, deep-sea fishing, Jet Skiing, and scuba diving. Pensacola Beach is public, accessible by car or by ECAT bus or trolley. From the fishing pier you're likely to catch flounder, redfish, trout, bluefish, sheepshead, pompano, bonito, Spanish and king mackerel, and possibly cobia. From its end, you're likely to spot dolphins, sea turtles, and the occasional manatee. If you've arrived unprepared, you can buy bait and rent fishing gear (rods $7, carts, coolers, nets, gaffs $6) at the pier.

At the corner of Pensacola Boulevard and Fort Pickens Road, which runs west, is **Casino Beach,** the heart of Pensacola Beach, named for an old beachside casino resort from 1933. The casino is long gone, but its beach-ball water tank is still a landmark. Casino Beach is home to the huge brick Gulfside Pavilion, site of numerous free concerts and events. The

beach has picnic tables, restrooms, restaurants, and souvenir shops. Just past the tollbooth onto the island, **Quietwater Beach,** on the Santa Rosa Sound side, is a gentle shallow beach that's great for kids.

★ GULF ISLANDS NATIONAL SEASHORE

The **Gulf Islands National Seashore** (850/934-2622, $7 pp or 7-day pass $20 per vehicle) has numerous beaches along Santa Rosa Island. At its westernmost edge is **Fort Pickens Park,** maintained by the National Park Service. The road is in a sensitive habitat for nesting sea turtles and colonial shorebirds, so don't park along the sandy shoulder; it's easy to get your vehicle stuck, and to incur a park ranger-issued ticket.

Historic Fort Pickens is open for self-guided tours during daylight hours. There is a fishing pier, and the Fort Pickens campground has 200 campsites, some equipped with water and electricity and others without for tent camping ($26-40). All campers have access to running water, grills, picnic tables, and restrooms with cold showers. Boaters planning to camp can unload passengers and gear near Battery Langdon on the bay side of the island and west of the Ranger Station dock and hike on the bike path or Fort Pickens Road to Loop A. Highway 399 (J. Earle Bowden Way) on Santa Rosa Island connects Pensacola Beach with Navarre Beach.

Within the Fort Pickens area is another beach called **Langdon Beach,** which has picnic tables, restrooms, and outdoor showers. The scenic bike path, from Langdon Beach all the way to the fort, has been restored, as have the Dune Nature Trail and the Blackbird Marsh Nature Trail.

Also part of Gulf Islands National Seashore, **Opal Beach** is three miles east of Pensacola Beach. It is generally less populated, offering restrooms, showers, and picnic pavilions, and is a great stop for hikers and bikers taking in the

---

1: Pensacola Beach Fishing Pier 2: dunes at Gulf Islands National Seashore

Fast Times

Addicted to speed? Pensacola has **Five Flags Speedway** (7451 Pine Forest Rd., 850/944-8400, www.5flagsspeedway.com, $5-20), on Hwy. 297 a mile south of exit 7 on I-10, was built in 1956, one of the oldest established short-track racetracks still in existence. The high-banked asphalt oval is the fastest half-mile track in the country and home to the annual Snowball Derby, usually the first few days of December, the country's premier short-track Super Late Model event. The rest of the season features racing of different kinds, from the fire-breathing fuel-injected winged sprint cars of the United Sprint Car Series, to the Bombers, Spectators, Super Stocks, Vintage, and Pro Late Models. The track has attracted top drivers like Carl Yarborough and Rusty Wallace as well as fans from all over.

Pensacola Greyhound Track and Poker Room (951 Dog Track Rd., 850/455-8595, www.pensacolagreyhoundtrack.com, 7pm Fri.-Sat., 1pm Sun., free), off U.S. 98, offers the thrill of high-speed greyhound racing and the equally thrilling attendant betting. You can watch the races from an air-conditioned restaurant-lounge called the Kennel Club or from rail-side seats. The facility has live and instant replay TVs throughout the complex. Texas hold 'em, seven-card stud, and Omaha poker are played in the newly added **Poker Room** (9am-3am Mon.-Thurs., 24 hours Fri.-Sun., free).

beautiful dune landscape between Pensacola Beach and Navarre Beach on the Seashore Trail or the South Santa Rosa Loop Trail. The Opal Beach area can also be reached by motorists via Highway 399, which runs parallel to the multi-use trail through the national seashore. From Pensacola Beach, drive east toward Navarre Beach on Highway 399. Opal Beach is on the Gulf side (right). From Navarre Beach, drive west toward Pensacola Beach on Highway 399. Opal Beach is on the Gulf side (left).

NAVARRE BEACH

Family-friendly **Navarre Beach,** the eastern-most on Santa Rosa Island, has restrooms, picnic facilities, and a fishing pier. The Navarre Beach County Park is 130 acres of beach, wetlands, and scrub, a third of which is set aside not to be developed in perpetuity. After lolling on the beach, you can follow the multiuse Seashore Bicycle Trail alongside dunes, forests, and the Gulf for a nice array of picturesque scenery.

Sports and Recreation

FISHING AND DIVING

The Three Mile Bridge over Pensacola Bay carries traffic alongside the long-abandoned U.S. 98 bridge, used by local anglers as their huge personal fishing pier prior to Hurricane Ivan. Now much of it lies on the bottom of Pensacola Bay. A new fishing pier runs alongside the Three Mile Bridge, and anglers are back to reeling in their catches. In general, fishing has taken a huge upswing. In 2006 the decommissioned aircraft carrier USS *Oriskany* was sunk as an artificial reef in the Gulf of Mexico 22.5 miles southeast of

Pensacola Pass, the first time a ship of this size had been sunk for this purpose. The decommissioned *Mighty O* (32,000 tons, 911 feet), which saw action in Korea and Vietnam, sits in 212 feet of water. The *Oriskany* is the first navy ship cleaned according to the EPA's 2004 policies to ensure artificial reefs are environmentally safe.

Divers can reach the top of the *Oriskany*'s superstructure or "island" at a depth of 60 feet, while its flight deck sits in 130 feet of water, below the range of recreational divers but within reach of specialty deep-water divers. With water temperatures in mid-80s in summer and mid-60s in winter, visibility is 60-100 feet. It has been used as the site of underwater weddings.

BOAT TOURS AND CHARTERS

Climb aboard a 50-foot Navy launch boat for a two-hour cruise dolphin and sightseeing cruise with **Chase-N-Fins** (655 Pensacola Beach Blvd., 850/492-6337, 10am, 2pm, and 5pm daily, $25 adults, $15 ages 5-12, free under age 5). The boat holds up to 49 passengers. For something less crowded, join **Jolly Sailing** (655 Pensacola Beach Blvd., 850/723-6142, $25-85) for a two-hour dolphin, sunset, or sailing cruise on their 34-foot Pearson sailboat, their 27-foot covered powerboat, or the *Jolly Mon*, a 27-foot sailboat. Snorkeling and stand-up paddleboard tours are also available.

Captain Jeff Lacour pilots the *Dolphin Express* (701 Pensacola Beach Blvd., 850/619-8738, $25 adults, $15 children, free under age 5), a 50-foot vessel with wraparound seating. If you're in town for the Blue Angels air show, call ahead and reserve a seat for a great view. To catch fish in Pensacola Bay, call **Hot Spot Charters** (701 Pensacola Beach Blvd., 850/449-5555, inshore $375-650 for up to 6 anglers, offshore $1,150-1,750 for up to 6 anglers, offshore $1,400-2,500 for up to 10 anglers), or **Bout Time Charters** (715 Pensacola Beach Blvd., 850/380-1671, inshore $450-750 for up to 4 anglers, offshore $500-1,100 for up to 4 anglers). The most common catches are speckled trout, redfish, red snapper, flounder, sheepshead, blue fish, Spanish and king mackerel, grouper, or amberjack.

Just across the bridge to Pensacola Beach, **Key Sailing** (400 Quietwater Beach Blvd., 850/932-5520) rents 22-foot pontoon boats that can hold 11 ($190 for 2 hours, $275 for 4 hours, $450 all-day), Jet Skis ($55-550), kayaks ($15-100 single, $25-135 double), paddleboards ($25-150), as well as 13-foot and 16-foot catamaran sailboats ($60-350). Or climb aboard their glass-bottomed 45-foot catamaran tour boat for a two-hour dolphin cruise ($25 adults, $15 children). For a bird's-eye view of Pensacola Beach, go parasailing ($110 for 2 people, $100 for 1). They take you out on a speedboat and then take you up 500-600 feet above the water for a 10-minute high-flying adventure.

In Navarre, **Navarre Family Watersports** (8671 Navarre Pkwy., 850/939-9923) offers dolphin tours on WaveRunners ($125), WaveRunner rentals ($60 half-hour, $95 per hour), pontoon boat rentals ($275 half-day, $450 full-day), kayak rentals ($15 per hour, $40 for 4 hours, $60 per day), a water park ($20 per hour, $30 for 2 hours, $35 all-day), mini golf ($7 adults, $4 under age 13), and helicopter rides ($50 for 10 miles down the coast, $100 for 20-mile flight to a sunken ship, $358 for 2 passengers for a 40-mile trip over the National Seashore from Navarre to Pensacola Beach, $500 for 2 passengers for a 60-mile flight to Fort Pickens). Military discounts are available.

In Perdido Key, chase fins with **Blue Dolphin Cruises** (29603 Perdido Beach Blvd., 251/981-2774) on their 51-foot covered pontoon boat. Their cruises are some of the most reasonably priced in the area ($15-20 adults, $15 under age 11), and their tour boats have an enclosed area with heating and air-conditioning. The wraparound open-air viewing deck lets you enjoy bay breezes with unobstructed views.

PADDLING

Paddlers can explore one of the finest waterways in the South along the 19-mile **Coldwater Creek Paddling Trail,** which flows south from the Highway 4 bridge, just east of Berrydale and 20 minutes north of Pensacola. It ends at the Highway 191 launch east of Whiting Field. The creek, which is spring-fed and cold, offers the perfect retreat from the hot Florida summer. There are plenty of beaches to camp on along the way, and the swift current will require you to be vigilant for submerged logs. During low flow, paddling the creek may require some portaging.

You can rent a canoe or tube from one of the numerous local outfitters and paddle or float down the calm, sandy-bottomed river along the 31-mile designated **Blackwater River Canoe Trail** (maps at www.floridadep. gov). Blackwater is a winding and often wide river that's dotted with large beaches and high bluffs that are forested with pine and cedar groves. The canoe trail is divided into three sections, and outfitters provide shuttle trips between various launch points. The most popular section for paddlers and tubers is six miles that traverse Blackwater River State Park (40 minutes northeast of Pensacola). Paddlers and tubers begin at the Bryan Bridge Launch on Bryan Bridge Road and end at Deaton Bridge on Deaton Bridge Road, inside the state park. This section can become crowded during the summer and holidays.

★ TUBING ON COLDWATER CREEK

April-September, hundreds of people float the Coldwater Creek in tubes every week. **Adventures Unlimited Outdoor Center** (8974 Tomahawk Landing Rd., Milton, 850/623-6197), a 50-minute drive north of Pensacola, is the most popular outfitter in the area. They provide tubing trips (8am-3pm, 3.5-hour trip, 4 miles, $23 single tube, $12 cooler tube, includes shuttle). The float is a pleasant way to beat the heat and see one of the most beautiful waterways in northwest Florida. Make sure to pack a lunch to enjoy at one of the many sandbars along the creek. Also bring sunscreen and plenty of water.

In addition to tubing trips, Adventures Unlimited provides canoe rentals ($58-68 per canoe for 4-, 7-, or 11-mile trips, $79-90 overnight trip, $90-100 for 2-day trips, $100-111 for 3-day trips), kayak rentals ($42 per kayak for 4-, 7-, or 11-mile trips), campsites ($30 up to 4 people, $5 per additional person) with water and 30-amp electrical hookups, paddleboards ($47), a variety of private cabins ($69-309), and an inn ($129). For an adrenaline rush, try soaring above the forest, beaches, and creeks on their network of zip lines and platforms ($89 for 3 hours, $129 for 5 hours). If you're feeling adventurous, try a one- to three-night paddling trip. Adventures Unlimited takes you, your gear, and your canoes to the launch site to drop you off. After a day of paddling, you stop at a beautiful campsite on a beach. On the last day, they pick you up at the designated site.

Pensacola Bayfront Stadium

HORSEBACK RIDING

The **Coldwater Recreation Area** (Gordon Land Rd., off Hwy. 4), south of Berrydale, is popular for riding, with 50 miles of horse trails, stables, and a campground with electricity and water, as well as restrooms and showers. Call ahead to reserve stable space (877/879-3859).

SPECTATOR SPORTS

Pensacola Wahoos

Pensacola is embracing baseball with open arms at the **Pensacola Bayfront Stadium** (351 W. Cedar St.), a baseball and sports complex that's primarily home to the **Pensacola Wahoos** (850/934-8444, www.milb.com, $13-50), a Cincinnati Reds-affiliated minor-league team, but the stadium also hosts the Argos, the University of West Florida's football team, and occasional concerts. On Pensacola Bay on the outskirts of downtown, near the Three Mile Bridge, the stadium quickly received accolades, including the Best Ballpark of 2012 award from Baseballparks.com. The classic open-air stadium seats 5,038 fans and was designed by the same firm that did the new Yankee Stadium and the renovation of Wrigley Field in Chicago. It's a beautiful coastal setting to spend the evening.

Pensacola Ice Flyers

If you're into ice hockey, **The Pensacola Ice Flyers** (201 East Gregory St., 850/466-3111, $15-35) is the city's professional hockey team, part of the Southern Professional Hockey League. Games are held at the Pensacola Bay Center, and being close to the ice feels great after a long day in the sun at the beach.

Food

DOWNTOWN

Breakfast

Bodacious Brew (407 S. Palafox Place, at W. Main St., 850/434-6300, breakfast 7am-11am Mon.-Sat., coffee, tea, and pastries 7am-8pm Mon.-Sat., $5-10) offers an extensive espresso, coffee, and tea selection. For breakfast, try the jalapeño and cheddar scone or their bodacious gouda grits alongside a veggie quiche. At the long coffee bar, baristas get fancy and prepare java all kinds of ways, including pourovers, Chemex, siphons, and French-press preparations.

A good choice for coffee and pastries near the north end of the business district is **Fosko Coffee Barre** (8 Palafox Place, 850/332-7737, 6:45am-10pm Mon.-Sat., 8am-8pm Sun.). The brick and wood interior is cozy, clean, and gives the place an historic feel. Their iced coffees and frappes are popular during the summer. A small selection of sandwiches and sweet treats has helped make this a popular spot to meet before catching a music show at the nearby Vinyl Music Hall.

Casual

In the same building as Bodacious Brew is the **Bodacious Olive** (10am-6pm Mon.-Fri., 9am-4pm Sat., 9am-2pm Sun.), where you can shop fresh bread, seasonings, artisanal olive oils, and vinegars from around the world. For lunch, grab some healthy greens at their salad bar, **So Chopped** (11am-6pm Mon.-Thurs., 11am-7pm Fri.-Sat., $5-10), where you can build your own salad from their extensive fresh ingredients, or choose a wrap, soup, or salad on their menu. It's the best way to eat healthy while you're downtown, and the prices are reasonable. Go upstairs to **The Wine Shop** (9am-6pm Mon.-Sat., 8am-2pm Sun.) for a wonderful selection of small production wines mostly from France, Italy, California, and New Zealand.

For pizza and beer, go to **HopJacks Pizza Kitchen & Taproom** (10 Palafox Place, 850/497-6073, www.hopjacks.com, $7-20). Pizza is the house pride, along with 150 bottled and 36 beers on tap. Take a seat inside on their plush couches or grab a slice and head out to the outdoor courtyard for an evening under the stars.

Before or after a Wahoos baseball game, slide in to the recently renovated **Doghouse Deli** (30 S. Palafox St., 850/432-3104, 8am-3pm Mon.-Thurs., 8am-9pm Fri.-Sat., 10am-2pm Sun., $5-10) for a hot dog prepared nearly any way imaginable. This longtime Pensacola favorite originally opened in 1977. Favorites include the slaw hound with coleslaw, chili, and cheese, and the Chicago dog piled high with onions, relish, cucumbers, pickles, and tomatoes. Or pick your own toppings from an extensive list on the chalkboard. They also offer nachos, kielbasas, sandwiches, and a full breakfast menu.

Get a little rum or whiskey in your milk shake at the **Tin Cow** (102 S. Palafox Place, 850/466-2103, 11am-11pm Sun.-Thurs., 11am-2am Fri.-Sat., $7-15), along with hearty burgers and canned craft beer. The place is hipster at heart and the burgers are the staple, but they also have a wide array of appetizers, soups, salads, and sliders.

Popular with the lunch and budget-minded crowd, **Al Fresco** (501 S. Palafox Place, $6-15) is a collection of stylish, clean food carts around a classy open-air courtyard with umbrella-covered tables shaded by tall palm trees. It's in the heart of the business district on Palafox Street and perfect to get a quick bite when the weather cooperates. Options include a taco spot called **Calavera Tacos** (11am-8pm Mon.-Thurs., 11am-10pm Fri.-Sat., and 11am-6pm Sun.), an oyster bar called **Shux** (11am-9pm or later daily), **Slims Philly Experience** (11am-7pm Mon.-Thurs., 11am-9pm Fri.-Sat., 11am-5pm Sun.), an Asian fusion spot with pot stickers, popular Chinese dishes, and Thai favorites called **Fusion** (11am-7pm Mon.-Thurs., 11am-9pm Sat., and 11am-5pm Sun.), and **Southpaw Cajun Express** (11am-7pm Mon.-Thurs., 11am-9pm Fri.-Sat. 11am-5pm Sun.), which serves Cajun favorites like red beans and rice and po'boy sandwiches, as well as salads, soups, and seafood platters.

They don't serve food, but if you love craft beer, you should open the taps and try one of the 15 seasonal varieties at **Pensacola Bay Brewery** (225 E. Zaragoza St., 850/434-3353, www.pbbrew.com, noon-9pm Mon.-Thurs., noon-11pm Fri.-Sat., noon-8pm Sun.), ranging from light pilsners to dark oatmeal stouts, all with names that hark back to Pensacola's past. Try a Desoto Berliner Weisse Ale or the Conquistador Dopple Bock, and for a virgin drink, stop in for a delicious Cannonball Root Beer. For a behind-the-scenes glimpse into the world of brew mastery, embark on a brewery tour (3:30pm Fri.-Sat.) and taste a selection of their finest cold ones.

Head to **Jaco's Bayfront Bar and Grille** (997 S. Palafox Place, 850/432-5226, 11am-9pm Mon.-Thurs., 11am-10pm Fri.-Sat., 10am-9pm Sun., $10-20) for a casual dinner or drinks overlooking the Palafox Pier Marina. Their eclectic menu features pizza, pastas, seafood, and steaks. It's American fare with Asian fusion selections and good vegetarian offerings. The wraparound outdoor seating makes this one of the best locations for sunset dining downtown, and the Sunday brunch is popular when the weather is nice. For lunch, try their mahimahi tacos with mango salsa; for dinner dig into the ahi tuna with wasabi mashed potatoes. Brunch favorite include stuffed french toast.

Fine Dining

On the waterfront at the southern end of downtown is ★ **The Fish House** (600 S. Barracks St., 850/470-0003, www.fishhousepensacola.com, 11am-close daily, brunch 11am-2pm Sun., dinner 2pm-close Sun., $13-28), seen on the Travel Channel, in *Food and Wine* magazine, and *Wine Spectator*. Just-off-the-docks seafood, sushi, an award-winning chef, and the Fish House Deck Bar—it's all a hit. From a fire pit conversation area and dining tables to an hors d'oeuvres menu and an outdoor bandstand and sprawling deck for dancing, 3,500 square feet of sun and Gulf breezes offer live music from local and regional bands Friday-Saturday nights.

Popular with locals, **The Global Grill**

(27 S. Palafox Place, 850/469-9966, www.globalgrillpensacola.com, 5pm-9pm Tues.-Thurs., 5pm-10pm Fri.-Sat., $7-30) offers some of the best, and only, tapas in Pensacola. It's a world-beat approach that includes tuna sashimi, crab cakes, and lamb lollipops with an Israeli couscous cake and sun-dried tomato au jus. They also serve larger seafood, beef, and poultry entrées.

The best fine dining in Pensacola is at **Jackson's Steakhouse** (400 S. Palafox St., 850/469-9898, lunch 11am-2pm Mon.-Fri., dinner 5:30pm-10pm Tues.-Sat., brunch 11am-2pm Sat.-Sun., $28-40), an upscale chophouse in an historic and elegant setting. They've won a long list of awards and accolades that include eight Golden Spoons and eight *Wine Spectator* Awards of Excellence. Try the wood-fired filet with lump crab and fried green tomatoes, or the beef brisket in sweet Florida barbecue sauce, and pair it with a glass of vino from their impressive wine list.

EAST HILL

North and east of the North Hill Preservation District, East Hill has a couple of my favorite restaurants. **Jerry's Drive-In** (2815 E. Cervantes St., 850/433-9910, 10am-9:30pm Mon.-Fri., 7am-9:30pm Sat. $5-9) offers killer cheeseburgers, onion rings, and fried okra in a comfy diner setting. It's been here since the 1940s and still has a line at lunch (but it's not actually a drive-in; it's a walk-in).

A local favorite for pastries, macaroons, peanut butter bars, and smiley-face cookies since 1946, the small **J's Bakery** (2014 N. 12th Ave., 850/439-6546, 7am-6pm Mon.-Fri., 8am-6pm Sat., $2-10) is in the heart of East Hill. Also well loved for its fresh baked bread, birthday cakes, and tasty apple, cherry, and pecan pies, during Mardi Gras this is the place to get colorful king cake. They now serve breakfast and lunch sandwiches and salads. Also along 12th Avenue is **Ozone's Pizza Pub** (1010 N. 12th Ave., 850/433-7336, 11am-10pm daily, $10-20), the favorite neighborhood pizza joint. It's a family-friendly place during dinner hours and evolves into

a college-age hangout in the evenings. They serve thick-crusted pizza loaded with a generous amount of toppings. Their specialties include an extensive list of meat-centric and vegetarian pizza options, grinders, salads, and pasta dishes, along with a wide selection of beers.

★ **McGuire's Irish Pub** (600 E. Gregory St., 850/433-6789, 11am-2am daily, $10-30) is the Pensacola restaurant everyone knows about. "Irishmen of all nationalities" sign dollar bills and staple them to the ceiling, beer is brewed on the premises, the gorgeous wine cellar has a capacity of 8,000 bottles, and you can spend an ungodly sum on a burger (accompanied by caviar and champagne). It's a hard place to describe, really, set in Pensacola's original 1927 Old Firehouse. The steaks are good and expensive USDA-certified prime, but it still has a wild-and-woolly Irish pub feel. It's vast, with 400 seats and 200 employees, sprawling through a bunch of curio-packed theme rooms. Just go—it'll be fun.

GREATER PENSACOLA AREA

The **Tuscan Oven** (4801 N. 9th Ave., 850/484-6836, www.thetuscanoven.com, 11am-9pm Tues.-Thurs., 11am-10pm Fri.-Sat., $7-20) serves traditional southern Italian thin-crust pizzas prepared in a hardwood-fired oven shipped straight from Italy. The oven and counter bar that wraps around the kitchen are the centerpiece of the cozy dining room. Chat with the friendly owners and staff while you watch your pizza get prepared. An outdoor patio is great for dining or drinking one of the wines from the selective list. The restaurant is close to Cordova Mall.

If you're staying in a place with a kitchen, pick up some fresh seafood at **Joe Patti's Seafood** (524 S. B St., 850/432-3315, 7:30am-7pm Mon.-Sat., 7:30am-6pm Sun.), a few blocks west of the ballpark. It's a sprawling warehouse facility that has a large selection of seafood, shrimp, oysters, and crabs as well as an impressive on-site sushi stand, seafood restaurant, and upscale deli.

Mariah's Fresh Seafood Market (621 E. Cervantes St., 850/432-4999, 8am-7pm Mon.-Sat., 8am-6pm Sun.) is more centrally located and smaller than Joe Patti's, but still offers all the seafood staples, such as shrimp, snapper, grouper, mahimahi, oysters, crabs, scallops, and more.

PENSACOLA BEACH
Breakfast

For coffee, breakfast, and internet, go to the Drowsy Poet (655 Pensacola Beach Blvd., 850/203-1524, 6am-9pm Mon.-Sat., 6am-2pm Sun., $3-10), on the third floor above Innerlight Surf and Skate. Sip your coffee or smoothie while you enjoy breakfast or lunch with an incredible waterfront view.

For breakfast and lunch, locals head to the Native Cafe (45 Via De Luna Dr., 850/934-4848, 7:30am-3pm daily, $5-12), with all-American breakfast dishes like fried eggs and pancakes along with specials like crab cakes benedict. In the colorful row of businesses near the Gulf Islands National Seashore, it's a close option if you're renting a house on this side of the island. At lunch, fish tacos are the specialty, and New Orleans dishes like gumbo fill out the menu. The walnut-crusted key lime pie ($3.50) is a top pick for dessert. Prices are excellent.

Casual

Greatest oyster bar? ★ Peg Leg Pete's (1010 Fort Pickens Rd., 850/932-4139, 11am-10pm daily, $8-20), my favorite restaurant on Pensacola Beach, offers some of the best prices on the freshest seafood in Pensacola Beach. The little-known secret is that the owner also owns Maria's Seafood, the second-largest seafood distributor in town. The casual pirate-themed atmosphere and the extensive playground make it a great place for families. The menu features local favorites and regional classics like grouper sandwiches, crab claws,

and a perfect cup of seafood gumbo. Take the stairs down to the "under-where?" bar, where they serve cold drinks, raw oysters, and a full menu, with live music on weekends.

On the bay side, Hemingway's (400 Quietwater Beach Rd., 850/934-4747, www.hemingwaysislandgrill.com, 11am-9pm Mon.-Thurs., 11am-10pm Fri.-Sat., 10am-9pm Sun., $8-33) features an open kitchen and two levels of outdoor deck seating. The menu is island-inspired, with roasted corn and crab chowder, Key West ribs, and shrimp basted with dark rum sauce, and the drinks tend toward tropical cocktails and beach favorites.

Also on the bay, Flounders Chowder House (800 Quietwater Beach Rd., 850/932-2003, 11am-10pm Mon.-Thurs., 11am-midnight Fri.-Sat., 10:30am-10pm Sun. winter, 11am-midnight daily summer, $10-20) is a large family-friendly restaurant with a bar. Notice the impressive shrimp boat on the side of the building, and an outdoor stage for live music has a sand pit in front for dancing. Don't miss the confessional booths, taken from a New Orleans church. Steak and seafood are the main attraction, and you can get grouper, mahimahi, and tuna cooked on the wood-fired grill. The flagship dish is flounder stuffed with crabmeat. A new addition is their New Orleans-style snow cone stand (from $3, plus $2 to add alcohol).

Sidelines (2 Via de Luna Dr., 850/934-3660, www.sidelinespensacola.com, 11am-11pm daily, $7-20) is a fun sports bar with an extensive beer selection and excellent chicken wings, burgers, ribs, and the like. The Caribbean chicken sandwich, smothered in honey barbecue sauce, and the Philly cheesesteak, with a hefty portion of thinly sliced beef, are favorites.

Jimmy Buffett fans should stop by Landshark Landing (165 Fort Pickens Rd., 11am-10pm Mon.-Sat., 11am-8pm Sun. Mar.-Oct., $8-15), the casual bar and restaurant next door to the Margaritaville Beach Hotel. The wood and metal-roof building with open sides sits right on the Gulf, so the beach breeze rolls through. It's fun and lively,

---

1: Jaco's Bayfront Bar and Grille on the downtown waterfront 2: fish filets on ice at Joe Patti's Seafood 3: Al Fresco in downtown Pensacola 4: Flounders Chowder House on Pensacola Beach

decorated with all sorts of Buffett memorabilia, and several TVs for watching the game. Live music plays most weekends. The menu offers shrimp, nachos, and burgers, but most people come for the plentiful boat drinks and margaritas, of course.

Wild Roots (5 Via De Luna Dr., 10am-5pm daily, $8-15) is the place for more health-conscious beach bums to eat. Popular with the active crowd, the menu features organic wraps, soups, salads, pizzas, presses, sandwiches, and pastries. For a cold and healthy treat, pop in for an organic frozen beach pop ($3.50), made from fruit juice, veggie juice, nut milks, or ice cream. The 32 flavors keep all the kids happy, and each pop has a paper cup attached at the bottom to contain the melting juice.

Cactus Flower Cafe (400 Quietwater Beach Rd., 850/934-5999, 11am-10pm daily, $8-15) will give you your Mexican food fix while you're out on the beach. At the Quietwater Boardwalk, this Pensacola favorite has expanded to five locations on the Gulf Coast. Their success is a testament to their tasty California-style Mexican menu. They have mainstay tacos, burritos, and quesadillas, but their mahimahi tacos, enchiladas verdes, and traditional chicken posole soup stand out.

Fine Dining

Best sushi on the beach? Views of the Gulf beach make swanky modern **H2O Grill and Bonsai Sushi Bar** (12 Via De Luna Dr., 850/972-1700, 6:30am-10pm daily, $12-26) a perfect spot for date night. The interior is colorful and fun. Choose from classic sushi rolls or build your own. The menu has a mix of seafood, Cajun dishes, Asian fusion, and Mediterranean-influenced selections. After dinner, relax around a conversation fire pit, listen to the waves roll in, and order cocktails from the poolside bar.

Look to the left when you cross the bridge to Pensacola Beach and you'll see **The Grand Marlin** (400 Pensacola Beach Blvd., 850/677-9153, 11am-9pm Mon.-Thurs., 11am-10pm Fri.-Sat., 9am-9pm Sun., $15-30), where you can enjoy fine dining with views of Pensacola Bay and Santa Rosa Sound through floor-to-ceiling windows. Steak and seafood dishes are the main features, including grilled lobster tail drizzled in key lime butter sauce, oysters Rockefeller, or a sugar-cured pork shank with orange mustard glaze. Make sure to see the huge marlin that hangs in the dining room: It's a 1,228.5-pound behemoth that holds the North Carolina record.

Accommodations

UNDER $100

The **Ashton Inn & Suites Pensacola** (910 N. Navy Blvd., 850/455-4561, $60-80) serves the Naval Air Station Pensacola and NTTC Corry Station, and is convenient to the National Museum of Naval Aviation.

A Pensacola Beach favorite is the low-rise ★ **Paradise Inn** (21 Via de Luna Dr., 850/932-2319, www.paradiseinn-pb.com, $69-160), with Old Florida charm. It's on the beautiful sound side, and the Gulf is just a short walk away. With some of the best waterfront rates in town, rooms surround a casual fun bar and restaurant that serves delicious

Southern seafood, American fare, and traditional New Orleans-inspired dishes. A private dock is available for boaters, and the Paradise regularly features live music, mostly blues, reggae, zydeco, and coastal country bands that perform on its waterfront stage. Room specials are often offered for weekdays, so check the rates before you arrive.

$100-200

The **Pensacola Grand Hotel** (200 E. Gregory St., 850/433-3336, $125-145) has a fully equipped and updated gym on the second floor, an extensive library on the first floor, a heated pool, upscale dining in the 1912 Restaurant, and cocktails in the Cavu Club. The downtown location is convenient to the historic areas.

Courtyard by Marriott Downtown (700 E. Chase St., 850/439-3330, www.courtyardpensacoladowntown.com, $134-169) is five stories with 120 spacious rooms combining comfort and functionality, including high-speed internet access, large desks, and ergonomic chairs. Amenities include a restaurant for breakfast, a large fitness room, and a swimming pool with a hydrotherapy spa.

The **Hilton Pensacola Beach Gulf Front** (12 Via de Luna Dr., 850/916-2999, www.hiltonpensacolabeach.com, $109-259) is a large beachfront hotel within walking distance of shopping, dining, and nightlife. Many rooms are Gulf-front with private balconies. H2O, its signature restaurant, features seafood, Asian cuisine, and sushi, and offers a chef's table experience as well as private and semiprivate dining.

In an excellent location in the Seville Square area downtown, offering quick and easy access to the beaches, is **Holiday Inn Express** (101 E. Main St., 850/433-2231, www.hiexpress.com, $90-150). It has a wonderful included breakfast every morning, and rooms are clean, modern, and spacious. Many rooms have nice views of downtown Pensacola and Pensacola Bay.

$200-300

On Pensacola Beach, **Margaritaville Beach Hotel** (165 Fort Pickens Rd., 850/916-9755, www.margaritavillehotel.com, $119-419) offers tropical-themed rooms and suites. There's a beautiful pool and tiki bar, and Frank and Lola Love Pensacola Café serves breakfast, lunch, and dinner. At the Gulf-front Landshark Landing, you'll find nightly entertainment, volleyball nets, a playground, hammocks tied beneath palm trees, and a pared-down menu of mostly American food and lots of Jimmy Buffett's Landshark beer on tap.

Hampton Inn Pensacola Beach (2 Via de Luna Dr., 850/932-6800, www.hamptonpensacolabeach.com, $150-300) has 181 excellent rooms right on the Gulf. The property has a lively tiki bar by the pool where bartenders whip up specialty drinks like the Mojo, Voodoo Juice, or Island Ice Pick. The unmatched location puts you at the center of action on Pensacola beach, just steps from the fishing pier, main beach, restaurants, and bars.

The historic **Lee House** (400 Bayfront Pkwy., downtown Pensacola, 850/912-8770, www.leehousepensacola.com, $150-245) is an upscale bed-and-breakfast in the heart of downtown Pensacola, across from Seville Square Park and less than a mile from the Three Mile Bridge that takes you to Pensacola Beach. Breakfast is wonderful, and each of the eight suites has a unique theme, from the elegant bridal suite with a private jetted tub to a nautical-themed suite. Two cottages offer more privacy.

OVER $300

The upscale **Portofino Island Resort** (10 Portofino Dr., Pensacola Beach, 850/916-5000, www.portofinoisland.com, $380-700) on Pensacola Beach is at the eastern end of seven miles of preserved beach and beautiful dunes of the Gulf Islands National Seashore preserve. There's wonderful flats fishing, kayaking, and boating on Santa Rosa Sound, and the Gulf is just a short walk from the heated pools and hot tubs. The resort offers two- and three-bedroom suites, each equipped with a kitchen, a washer and dryer, and a private balcony.

VACATION RENTALS

Most of the vacation rentals are on Pensacola Beach. There are a large number of condos available for nightly, weekly, and monthly bookings. Many of the homes for rent that line the Gulf shoreline are large four- and five-bedroom homes. For a more affordable stay, the condos and classic cinder-block homes that dot the residential areas of the beach are a great choice. For vacation rentals on

Pensacola Beach, search **Vacation Rentals by Owner** (www.vrbo.com) or **Airbnb** (www.airbnb.com) in the Pensacola Beach and Perdido Key areas. To stay in the more historic downtown or East Hill areas, check out the rental listings offered by **Pensacola Historic Dream Cottages** (850/232-1266, www.pensacoladreamcottages.com).

CAMPING

Near Pensacola Beach, camp at one of 200 campsites ($26-40) in **Fort Pickens National Park** (1400 Fort Pickens Rd., 850/934-2600, $20 per vehicle, $15 motorcycles, $10 pedestrians and bicyclists). Tents and RVs are welcome. Some campsites have water and electricity; those for tent camping do not. Each campsite has fire rings, grills, and nearby restrooms with showers. The Gulf, bay, and historic forts are a short walk from the campground. This is the most affordable way to stay on the beach, and the campground is near the island's tip, a great spot for fishing. The forts are fun to explore for a few hours. You can download a self-guided tour brochure from the National Park Service website (www.nps.gov/guis). The fort held many prisoners when it was operating, the most famous being Geronimo, the Apache warrior captured in the 1880s. Ghost stories around the campfire, anyone?

A fancier option for RV enthusiasts is the **Pensacola Beach RV Resort** (17 Via De Luna Dr., 850/932-4670, www.pensacolabeachrvresort.com, $70-130, $350-650 per week, $1,150-1,750 per month), in the heart of the business district and near Casino Beach, the most popular beach on Santa Rosa Island. The sound-side campground resort features a large clubhouse with showers and an event space, a nice pool for hot summer days, two beaches with beautiful sound views, washers and dryers, and a small on-site shop. This is an exceptionally affordable option if you're looking for a week- or month-long RV site on the beach just a short drive from downtown Pensacola.

On the west side of town, some of the best campsites ($26.70) are just north of Perdido Key at **Big Lagoon State Park** (12301 Gulf Beach Hwy., 850/492-1595, $6 per vehicle with 2-8 people, $4 single occupant, $2 pedestrians and bicyclists, boat launch $10-12). The 655-acre park on Big Lagoon has 75 sites with water, electricity, a picnic table, a fire ring, and a grill. The campground has three bathhouses with showers. With five miles of hiking trails, excellent fishing, paddling around the lagoon and tributaries, boating in the surrounding waters, and close proximity to the Gulf, this park is a gem. Winter and fall are great times to camp, as it's often quiet. There are numerous picnic pavilions, beaches along the Intracoastal Waterway, and birding along the forested trail or shorelines. Kayak, canoe, and paddleboards are available for rent at the ranger's station. Take a short drive up the road and hike the nature trails at **Tarkiln Bayou Preserve State Park** (2401 Bauer Rd., Pensacola, 850/492-1595, www.floridastateparks.org, 8am-sunset, $3 per vehicle, $2 pedestrians and bicyclists).

North of Pensacola is a wealth of camping and outdoor recreation. The landscape changes dramatically to dense pine forests with a network of creeks and rivers. There are 30 campsites ($26.70) at **Blackwater River State Park** (7720 Deaton Bridge Rd., 850/983-5363, $4 per vehicle). Each site has water and electricity, and the bathhouse has hot showers. Rent a canoe or tube from one of the numerous local outfitters and paddle or float down the calm, sandy-bottomed river along the 31-mile designated **Blackwater River Canoe Trail** (maps at www.floridadep.gov).

Blackwater State Forest has several campgrounds, including those listed below. Information on availability and reservations are at the **Florida Forest Service** (850/957-6140). The most popular is **Hurricane Lake** (Hurricane Lake Rd., off Hwy. 4), with two campgrounds, one on the north side of the 318-acre lake, and another on the south side. Bring your pole and tackle for the excellent bass fishing. The sites on the north side are a mix of primitive sites ($10) and sites with electricity and water ($25). The sites on the south end are all primitive. Both campgrounds have faucets, restrooms, and boat ramps to the lake. **Bear Lake Recreation Area** (2.5 miles east of Munson, off Hwy. 4) has campsites ($25) with electricity and water, restrooms, showers, a boat launch, and a pier. There are lots of hiking trail nearby, including the 1.3-mile Sweetwater Trail and the 4-mile Bear Lake Loop Trail.

Karick Lake Recreation Area (7.5 miles north of Baker, east of County Rd. 189) has two campgrounds ($25) with electricity and water on Karick Lake. Restrooms and showers are available, as well as a boat ramp, a pier, and hiking trails nearby. The trailhead for the east end of the Jackson Red Ground Trail, a 21-mile hike that connects to the Red Rocks area of the state forest, is at Karick Lake.

You'll find campsites ($25) on a small 6.5-acre lake at the **Krul Recreation Area** (0.5 miles east of Munson, north of Hwy. 4). The west-end trailhead of the Sweetwater Trail connects to Bear Lake, which makes a nice overnight hike between campgrounds. A swimming area has a net to keep the alligators away, restrooms have showers, and sites have electricity and water.

For something more rugged, backpack through the rolling forest along the 43-mile Blackwater State Forest segment of the **Florida Scenic Trail.** Three access points allow you to plan a backpacking trip along this section that traverses the Hutton Unit, Juniper Creek Trail, Jackson Red Ground Trail, and the Wiregrass Trail. The terrain is mostly flat and easy, with plenty of shade. You traverse paths alongside creeks and the Blackwater River and navigate through pine, oak, cedar, and scrub forests. The bluffs at Red Rocks are one of the highlights. Designated campsites, campgrounds, and shelters along the way provide backpackers with plenty of options.

Information and Services

Pensacola is in the **central time zone.**

VISITOR INFORMATION

Begin a visit with a stop in the **Pensacola Bay Area Convention & Visitors Bureau Information Center** (1401 E. Gregory St., 800/874-1234, www.visitpensacola.com, 8am-5pm Mon.-Fri., 9am-4pm Sat., 10am-4pm Sun.), at the foot of the Pensacola Bay Bridge, to pick up maps, brochures, and a copy of the self-guided historic district tours. There's also a convenient **Pensacola Beach Visitors Information Center** (735 Pensacola Beach Blvd., Pensacola Beach, 850/932-1500, 9am-5pm Mon.-Sat., 10am-3pm Sun.).

POLICE AND EMERGENCIES

In an emergency, dial 911. If you need medical assistance, **Baptist Hospital** (1000 W. Moreno St., Pensacola, 850/434-4011) has full emergency services, as do **Sacred Heart Hospital** (5152 N. 9th Ave., Pensacola, 850/416-7710) and **Gulf Breeze Hospital** (1110 Gulf Breeze Pkwy., Gulf Breeze, 850/934-2000).

Transportation

CAR

The major east-west roads in this area are I-10, U.S. 90, and U.S. 98. Running north-south are U.S. 29 and I-110. To get to Pensacola from I-10, travel south on Highway 85 into Fort Walton Beach, then west on U.S. 98 to Navarre, then west over the Navarre Toll Bridge, and finally west on Highway 399 for 20 miles to Pensacola Beach. Or you can go south on I-110 (there are lots of chain motels along this stretch) or Highway 281, then east on U.S. 98, follow signs to the beaches, and drive over Pensacola Beach Toll Bridge into Pensacola Beach. To get to Perdido Key from Pensacola, go west on Highway 292 to Perdido, and over Perdido Key Bridge onto Perdido Key.

In town, Palafox Street is the major north-south artery, and Garden Street, which becomes Navy Boulevard on the way to the naval station, runs east-west. The historic district to the waterfront is walkable; for the rest of the area, you'll need a car. Naval Air Station Pensacola is southwest of the city, and Pensacola Beach is southeast of the city on Santa Rosa Island. Pensacola is connected to Gulf Breeze by the Pensacola Bay Bridge (also called Three Mile Bridge), which in turn is connected to Pensacola Beach by the Bob Sikes Bridge.

AIR

In Escambia County four miles northeast of downtown Pensacola, **Pensacola International Airport** (PNS, 2430 Airport Blvd., 850/436-5000, www.flypensacola.com) is the biggest airport in northwest Florida, but that's not saying much—it's not huge, with 100 daily flights on American, Delta, Frontier, Silver, Southwest, and United. Delta has the largest number of flights.

Taxis queue up outside the main terminal entrance at baggage claim. Car rental agencies are inside the main terminal entrance across from baggage claim. **Alamo** (800/327-9633), **Avis** (800/831-2847), **Budget** (800/527-0700), **Dollar** (800/800-4000 domestic, 800/800-6000 international), **Hertz** (800/654-3131), and **National** (800/227-7368) are all on the premises. Enterprise and Thrifty are off-site.

BUS AND TRAIN

Amtrak (980 E. Heinberg St., 800/872-7245, www.amtrak.com) has a train station in Pensacola, but it has been closed since Hurricane Katrina damaged the tracks in 2005. Plans are to restore train service, but no date has been given. **Greyhound** (505 W. Burgess Rd., 850/476-4800, www.greyhound.com) offers extensive bus service. The large local military presence ensures decent public transportation. There's a local bus line run by **Escambia County Area Transit** (850/595-3228, www.goecat.com) that includes a University of West Florida (UWF) trolley service and a Pensacola Beach trolley. It is possible to get around without a car, but some of the significant attractions are inaccessible via public transportation. Pensacola Beach has a free seasonal **Island Trolley** (May 22-Labor Day) that runs to all destinations on the beach.

Alabama Gulf Shores

The beaches in Gulf Shores and Orange Beach are just as beautiful and sugar-white as those in Pensacola and Destin. If the famous, ramshackle Flora-Bama wasn't located right on the border crossing, you wouldn't even know that you had just passed into Alabama. This stretch of coast is a natural extension of the Florida Gulf Coast in both geography and culture.

From Orange Beach to Gulf Shores are 32 miles of beautiful shoreline. Orange Beach and Gulf Shores are favored by younger travelers looking for a party as well as families who prefer plenty of entertainment, shopping, and dining options. Several new upscale developments have been built recently on the barrier island. On the western end of Gulf Shores, you'll find the larger and more expensive golf and beach

Highlights

Look for ★ to find recommended sights, activities, dining, and lodging.

★ **Fort Morgan State Historic Site:** This fort, which played a vital role in the Civil War, hosts reenactments throughout the year—including cannon firings (page 362).

★ **Florida Point Beach:** There is 6,000 feet of sugar-white sand for your beach chair and ample free parking. What more could you ask for (page 362)?

★ **Gulf Shores Public Beach:** A cluster of entertainment and restaurants surrounding the sand makes it perfect beach party (page 365).

★ **Hugh S. Branyon Backcountry Trail:** Hike or bike through rare maritime forest habitat and explore beautiful dune and coastal environments on this mostly paved trail system (page 366).

★ **Bon Secour National Wildlife Refuge:** This 7,000-acre preserve provides habitat for migrating birds, sea turtles, and other animals. There are miles of pristine beach and an exceptional network of hiking trails (page 367).

★ **Fishing from Gulf State Park Pier:** The largest pier on the Gulf Coast extends 1,500 feet into emerald waters. It's the best place in the area to reel in Spanish mackerel, bluegill, and more (page 371).

★ **Fort Gaines:** Walk back in time to explore the intricate arched tunnels and high bastions of this fort, which played an integral role in the Battle of Mobile Bay during the Civil War (page 380).

★ **Dauphin Island Audubon Bird Sanctuary:** Walk the boardwalks and trails at this sanctuary, which provides an important habitat for over 370 species of birds on their spring and fall migrations (page 382).

resorts. However, there are still plenty of reasonably priced accommodations, and compared to the Florida Gulf Coast, these two cities are often a real bargain.

For something more laid-back and traditional, take the ferry from the western tip of Gulf Shores and cross Mobile Bay to Dauphin Island, a charming and culturally Southern destination without the traffic jams and beach parties typical of Gulf Shores in the summer. The beaches aren't as nice as those to the east, and the offshore oil rigs are definitely an eyesore, but it's a wonderful place to rent a house for a weekend, a week, or more and spend time with the family enjoying the slow pace of life, quiet beaches, surrounding wilderness and wildlife, and welcoming people who live in this picturesque beach community.

This stretch of coast was settled in the late 1800s by anglers and farmers who were drawn to the undeveloped land and the easy access to a variety of freshwater and saltwater fishing environments. Early farmers grew a variety of crops, predominantly satsuma oranges, which explains the name Orange Beach. However, you won't see many orange trees here today. In 1920 a salesperson peddling orange tree seedlings infected with blight wiped out most of the orange groves. The building of the Intracoastal Waterway in the 1930s brought more commerce and development and made the region a popular vacation spot for residents of the Southeast. Today the region is visited by more than one million travelers a year, most of them coming from Birmingham, Alabama, and New Orleans.

PLANNING YOUR TIME

Travelers typically come to the area for weekend-long vacations, with the number of tourists swelling during the summer holidays. However, there is plenty to keep you busy for a week or more. It's not difficult to find a condo or house that is rented by the day, week, or month. During the slow winter season, you can get exceptional deals on rentals by the month or for the entire season, typically November-March, with prices going up slightly around the winter holidays. The busy season is the hot summer months, mid-May-late September. My favorite time to visit is late fall, October-November, or late spring, mid-March-mid-April.

During fall is cooler weather, less crowded beaches, the fall bird migrations, and better prices on accommodations, activities, and food. June-November is hurricane season, and so the weather can be unpredictable. During this time of the year, I don't recommend booking week- or month-long rentals too far in advance, but if you can escape for a weekend and know the coast is clear of hurricanes, then this is a great time to be here.

The spring is even better. Hurricane season is far away, and summer crowds haven't poured in yet. The weather is cool, and hotels and rentals are less expensive. The result is comfortable warm weather and having the beaches and forests all to yourself. This is the best time to camp and enjoy outdoor activities like paddling and hiking. The bugs, particularly mosquitoes, have just started hatching but are far from intolerable. A main concern when pursuing outdoor activities during this time is afternoon thundershowers. They produce violent lightning storms that are beautiful and thrilling yet extremely dangerous. The thunderstorms happen nearly every day, usually around 2pm.

Transportation
Amtrak (800/872-7245, www.amtrak. com) offers train service as far south as the Hattiesburg, Mississippi, station, 100 miles west of Gulf Shores, but you'll have to drive from there. Amtrak has plans to repair the rail line that runs from New Orleans through the Panhandle, but this route has been out of service since Hurricane Katrina badly damaged the tracks in 2005. Also, **Greyhound**

Alabama Gulf Shores

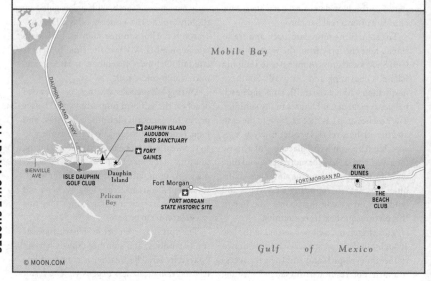

© MOON.COM

(239/774-5660, www.greyhound.com) provides regular service to Mobile and Pensacola, but Greyhound does not have a station in Orange Beach or Gulf Shores. The **Wave Transit System** (251/344-6600) operates a reliable network of city buses ($1.25 fare adults, day pass $3, children 5 and under free).

By air, the closest large airport is **Pensacola International Airport** (PNS, 850/436-5000, www.flypensacola.com), one hour east in Pensacola. **Advantage Airport Shuttle** (850/420-7807, www. advantageairportshuttle.com) provides service from Pensacola Airport to Orange Beach ($60-70) and Gulf Shores ($75-90). There is a smaller regional airport in Mobile, the **Mobile Regional Airport** (MOB, 800/357-5373, www.mobairport.com), with flights on American, Delta, United, and Via Air to Atlanta, Charlotte, Houston, Chicago, and Dallas. Private planes can also fly into Jack Edwards Airport in Gulf Shores, Foley Municipal, and Dauphin Island Airport.

Orange Beach and Gulf Shores

This stretch of Alabama's Gulf Coast is known as "Pleasure Island." It's not a natural island. In 1933 the Intracoastal Waterway was built, which cut the beaches off from the mainland of Alabama and left this 32-mile stretch of beach surrounded on four sides by water. If you visit, you'll understand the "pleasure" part. This has been the go-to destination for Alabamians wanting a beach vacation for generations.

The biggest draw of this area—apart from the miles of sugar-white beaches—is the abundant freshwater and saltwater spring-fed lakes that dot the coast for fishing. Most are found within the 6,150 acres of Gulf State Park, which also features rare maritime forest, coastal beaches, and vital dune habitat. The park is around 900-acre Lake Shelby, and as you drive along the coast, you will discover

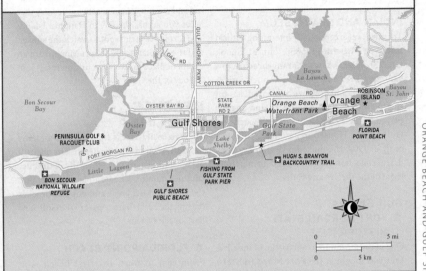

large stretches of beach and dune habitat that are preserved as a part of the Gulf State Park complex. These preserved sections of beach are possibly the only thing that has kept this coastline from becoming entirely developed.

In recent years the laid-back charm of the culture coupled with the exceptional bargains found along this stretch of coast have been drawing record-breaking crowds from all over the country. A boom in development followed Hurricane Ivan in 2004, which expanded capacity for tourism and the development of new entertainment districts like the Wharf in Orange Beach, boasting the tallest Ferris wheel in the Southeast.

If you drive from the north on Highway 59, you literally dead-end at the emerald waters of the Gulf of Mexico. Right in front is The Hangout, a sprawling bar and restaurant favored by the party crowd, and more importantly the Gulf Shores Public Beach, which is the most popular and crowded beach on this stretch of coast. Turn right and head toward the western tip of Gulf Shores, where you'll find several upscale resorts and much quieter beaches. All the way at the western tip of the island is Fort Morgan, a large fort used most famously in the Civil War during the Battle of Mobile Bay. Also at the western tip is the ferry terminal that can transport you and your car over Mobile Bay to Dauphin Island. If you turn right at the end of Highway 59, you drive toward Orange Beach and the Florida border and pass by several excellent beaches with ample parking.

SIGHTS

Orange Beach

COASTAL ARTS CENTER OF ORANGE BEACH

Explore and buy the work of local artists at the **Coastal Arts Center of Orange Beach** (26389 Canal Rd., 251/981-2787, www. orangebeachal.gov, 9am-4pm Mon.-Fri., free). Housed in an old homestead right on Mobile Bay and surrounded by beautiful low-hanging oak trees, this picturesque art center features paintings, crafts, pottery, and glasswork by the area's best local and regional artists. Hands-on workshops suitable for adults and children are offered in many art forms, including glassblowing, and are a great way to spend a rainy day when the beach isn't in the forecast.

INDIAN AND SEA MUSEUM

The small yet exceptionally interesting **Indian and Sea Museum** (25850 John M. Snook Dr., 251/981-8545, www.orangebeachal.gov, 9am-4pm Tues. and Thurs., free) offers insight into the area's history with an emphasis on the role that Native Americans and anglers played in the rich past of Orange Beach and Gulf Shores. Housed in an old schoolhouse built in 1909, the museum contains a wonderful collection of artifacts and memorabilia that fill the shelves and walls.

Gulf Shores
★ FORT MORGAN STATE HISTORIC SITE

One of the most important battles of the Civil War was fought at the **Fort Morgan State Historic Site** (51 Hwy. 180, 251/540-5257, www.fortmorgan.org, 8am-5pm daily, $7 adults, $5 students and seniors, $4 ages 6-12, free under age 6), easily explored on foot. Stop at the visitors center and museum to pick up a self-guided tour brochure. Interpretive plaques along the route give detailed accounts of the construction of the fort and information about life during various wars with an emphasis on the Battle of Mobile Bay.

On the western end of Gulf Shores, Fort Morgan was where Union admiral David Farragut spoke those famous words, "Damn the torpedoes; full speed ahead!" The fort contains more than 40 million bricks and was completed in 1834, seeing action in four wars: the Civil War, the Spanish-American War, and World Wars I and II. It can get a little spooky walking in the enclosed sections of the fort, and young children may not enjoy those parts.

The star-like shape of the fort enabled soldiers to defend the main ship channel into Mobile Bay with a steady stream of artillery fire as attacking ships approached and then moved into the bay. You can also explore the old lighthouse keepers quarters, built in 1872.

Surrounding the fort are great opportunities for fishing, shell searching, or beach walking and relaxing. Also nearby is the ferry that takes you across the bay to Dauphin Island. The fort is a favorite spot to watch the sunset, and the boat launches at Fort Morgan are an excellent place to launch your watercraft into the bay or the Gulf.

BEACHES
Orange Beach

You can easily access the beach from many locations around Orange Beach. The difficult part is finding parking, especially in the busy summer months. The best place to start is at the large parking areas and popular beaches dotting the coast that are part of the Gulf State Park beach system.

★ FLORIDA POINT BEACH

From east to west, the first beach is at **Florida Point,** just 0.3 miles east of the Perdido Pass Bridge. The beach is wide, with 6,000 feet of Gulf shoreline to walk and find that perfect spot in the sugar-white sand. Parking is free, as are restrooms and showers. The beach is on the eastern side of Perdido Pass, so it is not the best spot for swimming due to the strong currents, heavy boat traffic, and higher presence of sharks in the pass. However, it offers an excellent spot to watch incoming charter fishing boats at the end of the day.

ALABAMA POINT BEACH

Cross the Perdido Pass Bridge to reach the beach at **Alabama Point.** Park along the west side of the bridge, and walk down to the sand. This is the site of the ultra-hip Gulf Restaurant, built from two shipping containers. Alabama Point is slated for expansion: A much larger boardwalk complex will include beach and bait shops. Alabama Point has been the most popular spot for surfing, but word on the beach is that the recent dredging by the U.S. Army Corps of Engineers has ruined the break. It's still one of the best spots on the Alabama coast to

Orange Beach

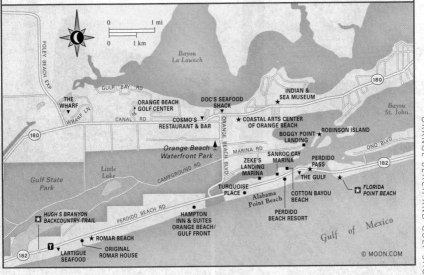

catch a wave, which isn't saying much—this area isn't known for surfing.

COTTON BAYOU BEACH

Just two miles west of Alabama Point at the intersection of Highways 182 and 161 is the Gulf State **Cotton Bayou Beach,** a small beach access point with a parking lot that's easy to miss. It's between two condo developments and a testament to Orange Beach's dedication to providing as much public access to the beach as possible. A small restroom is in the parking lot. Like many of the beaches in this area, Cotton Bayou is an excellent spot for swimming.

ROMAR BEACH

Head two miles west of Cotton Bayou Beach to reach **Romar Beach.** There's only a small amount of free parking here and no restrooms or facilities. However, there are plans for development at this beach, with new pavilions and restrooms in the years to come. Despite the lack of facilities, it's usually pretty busy in the summer and an excellent spot for swimming.

ORANGE BEACH WATERFRONT PARK

The **Orange Beach Waterfront Park** (26425 Canal Rd., 251/981-6039, www.orangebeachal.gov, daily, free) on Wolf Bay is a favorite for families. The beautifully maintained and landscaped park has plenty of outdoor activities to keep the kids entertained. The 400-foot fishing pier extends into Wolf Bay and features covered pavilions with seating. The huge and impressive playground, called the "kid's park," is lit at night. There are plenty of slides, swings, and things to climb on in this castle-themed playground. You'll find grills and picnic tables underneath the covered pavilions and a paved walking path for bikes, jogging, or a leisurely stroll beside picturesque Wolf Bay.

ROBINSON AND BIRD ISLANDS

Ever wanted to hang out on your own island? You can do that in Orange Beach, but you'll need your own boat to get there. In 2003 the city of Orange Beach purchased **Robinson and Bird Islands,** two adjacent small islands just north of Perdido Pass. Their quartz-white

beaches have been a popular destination of boaters for years. On a nice summer day, boats are often crowded around the island as close as possible. On holidays it will most likely be packed with people. If you want the island to yourself head out early morning on a weekday, especially in the late spring after spring break is over, fall, or winter. The official line from the city is that the islands were preserved to protect them from development and to provide a refuge for wildlife, but the most common wildlife you'll see here are locals partying on the beaches.

Gulf Shores

You won't have a hard time finding a great beach in Gulf Shores. Like Orange Beach and Pensacola to the east, this area has plenty of public access points and parking lots. Many of the beaches in Gulf Shores are also a part of the Gulf State Park complex, with three miles of preserved beaches along this stretch of coast. In addition to those listed below, you'll find miles of beaches within **Bon Secour National Wildlife Refuge.**

★ GULF SHORES PUBLIC BEACH

The most popular beach in the area is the **Gulf Shores Public Beach** (100 Gulf Shores Pkwy., 251/968-1420, www.gulfshoresal.gov, daily, parking $5 up to 4 hours, $10 per day). To find huge crowds of beachgoers, just drive to the end of Highway 59. The public beach is where The Hangout is located, impossible to miss. There are volleyball courts, plenty of bars and restaurants, three open-air pavilions, and restrooms with showers. Young beachgoers and the party crowd hang out on this beautiful, well-maintained, and regularly cleaned beach. Lifeguards are here all day during summer, making this an excellent choice for families for swimming, surfing, or boogieboarding. The beach is wide, which makes it easy to find a spot to set up a chair for the day, even when crowds are huge on summer

weekends and holidays. However, you might not find parking during these times. Get here early if you need a parking spot, or ride a bike or walk from your hotel or condo.

Surrounding the main public beach is a cluster of smaller **public access points** (251/968-1420, www.gulfshoresal.gov): **2nd St. Beach Access** (240 W. Beach Blvd., daily, parking $5), **5th St.** (599 W. Beach Blvd., daily, free parking), and the **6th St. Beach Access** (699 W. Beach Blvd., daily, parking $5). If you're staying nearby, you can get to the beach via the crosswalks at 4th Street and 13th Street as well.

THE BEACH AT GULF STATE PARK PIER

For fishing with your beach-lounging, start at the **Gulf State Park Pier** (20800 E. Beach Blvd., 251/967-3474, www.alapark.com, daily, free parking, fishing $9 per day, rod rentals $10 for 4 hours), in Gulf State Park between Gulf Shores and Orange Beach. Hurricane Ivan destroyed the original pier in 2004, and five years later Gulf Shores opened the largest pier on the Gulf, at 1,540 feet long. You can walk the length of the pier or just enjoy the view ($3 adults one trip, $4 all-day). Newly added are indoor seating and air-conditioning to the concession area that sells snacks and drinks, an indoor shop with tackle and bait as well as souvenirs, restrooms at the midway point of the pier, and wheelchair-accessible rail fishing. Parking is free, and the lot can hold over 200 cars. At the base of the pier is a restroom with showers and shaded picnic tables and benches. The pier is impressive, but the wide beach around the pier is just as popular, with plenty of room to spread out and enjoy the sand and surf with the family. The break on both sides of the pier pilings is popular with surfers and boogie boarders, while the rest of the beach is excellent for swimming.

GULF STATE PARK PAVILION AREA

Another top spot to hit the beach is the **Gulf State Park Pavilion Area** (22250 E. Beach Blvd., 251/968-7296, www.alapark.com,

---

1: Coastal Arts Center of Orange Beach **2:** Fort Morgan State Historic Site **3:** Florida Point Beach

Gulf Shores

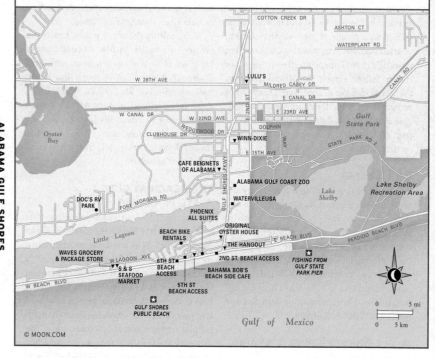

COTTON CREEK DR

ASHTON CT

WATERPLANT RD

CANAL RD

W 28TH AVE

LULU'S

MILDRED CASEY DR

E CANAL DR

W CANAL DR

W 22RD AVE

E 23RD AVE

Gulf
State Park

CLUBHOUSE DR

WEDGEWOOD DR

DOLPHIN

WINN-DIXIE

STATE PARK RD 2

E 15TH AVE

Oyster
Bay

CAFE BEIGNETS
OF ALABAMA ▼

ALABAMA GULF COAST ZOO

Lake
Shelby

Lake Shelby
Recreation Area

WATERVILLEUSA

DOC'S RV
PARK

FORT MORGAN RD

PHOENIX
ALL SUITES

Little Lagoon

BEACH BIKE
RENTALS

ORIGINAL
OYSTER HOUSE

BEACH BLVD

PERDIDO BEACH BLVD

THE HANGOUT

WAVES GROCERY
& PACKAGE STORE

W LAGOON AVE

6TH ST
BEACH
ACCESS

2ND ST. BEACH ACCESS

FISHING FROM
GULF STATE
PARK PIER

S & S
SEAFOOD
MARKET

BAHAMA BOB'S
BEACH SIDE CAFE

W BEACH BLVD

5TH ST
BEACH ACCESS

GULF SHORES
PUBLIC BEACH

Gulf of Mexico

0   5 mi

0   5 km

© MOON.COM

daily, parking $5, large vans $13), six miles east of Highway 59. This beach is usually less crowded than around the pier, and it's popular for surf fishing. Hurricane Ivan destroyed the original pavilion in 2004, but the new pavilion is a major improvement, featuring restrooms with air-conditioning and private showers, a small snack bar, and a fireplace for cold days on the coast. This is a great beach for families who don't mind the crowds on the weekends.

LAKE SHELBY RECREATION AREA

A less crowded beach away from the Gulf is at the **Lake Shelby Recreation Area** (20115 E. Hwy. 135, 251/948-7275, www.alapark.com, 7am-sunset daily, free parking). One mile east of the junction of Highways 59 and 182, the beach can be accessed from the Gulf State Park campground. The 900-acre freshwater lake is open to fishing, boating, kayaking,

and swimming. At the beach you'll find restrooms, showers, picnic tables, and pavilions.

HIKING, BIKING, AND WILDLIFE-WATCHING
Orange Beach
★ HUGH S. BRANYON BACKCOUNTRY TRAIL

Few coastal trail systems in the Southeast are better than the **Hugh S. Branyon Backcountry Trail** (trailheads on Hwy. 182 and Hwy. 161 in Orange Beach, 251/981-1180, www.backcountrytrail.com, sunrise-sunset daily, free), a system of six trails that total 11 miles. The Backcountry Trail is popular with hikers, bikers, and joggers. It's a great way to spend the afternoon exploring the unique maritime forest habitat of Orange Beach. Download the free app on the website to get an up-to-date map with virtual kiosks along the way that give details on the natural surroundings, local lore, Native American heritage, and historical significance of the area. Each trail traverses a unique habitat. The most popular is the Catman Road segment, a paved trail perfect for biking or hiking. It takes you past a screened-in pavilion where you can have a picnic lunch before exploring the butterfly garden, ending at the northern edge of Little Lake. This is a great way to get some exercise and spend a little time in the shade away from the beach.

Rent bikes for the trail at **Beach Bike Rentals** (22989 Perdido Beach Blvd., 251/968-1770, www.beachbikerentalsorangebeach.com, 9am-sunset daily, $20-25 per day). They offer single three-speeds and cruisers as well as tandem cruisers and have daily, weekly, and monthly rates. Locks and helmets are included with rentals.

Gulf Shores
★ BON SECOUR NATIONAL WILDLIFE REFUGE

Some of the best hiking in the area is found at the **Bon Secour National Wildlife Refuge** (12295 Hwy. 180, 251/540-7720, www.fws.gov/bonsecour, 7am-sunset daily, office 9am-2pm Mon.-Fri., free entry, free parking), a 7,000-acre preserve with more than six miles of hiking trails through coastal habitats that include beaches and sand dunes, fresh- and saltwater marshes, freshwater swamps, and upland forests. More than 370 bird species have been seen, including ospreys, great horned and eastern screech owls, yellow-billed cuckoos, and common loons. The refuge is one of the largest undeveloped stretches of land on the Alabama coast and receives more than 100,000 visitors every year, but most get no farther than the popular Gulf-side beach. Once you get out on the trails, you often have the backcountry to yourself. Bon Secour means "safe harbor" in French. While hiking, you're likely to encounter the many migrating and resident birds, and maybe even a red fox or a coyote.

All of the trails are in the preserve's Perdue Unit, with one of the most popular the two-mile-long **Pine Beach Trail,** with a perfect overview of the preserve. The trailhead is near the entrance of the park on the left side of Mobile Street. The hiking is moderately strenuous, especially in the exceptionally sandy areas, where your ankles and calves will get a workout. Hikers traverse the maritime scrub forest and pass between two lakes on the way to the dunes ecosystem that leads to the beach and the Gulf. The most unique and impressive section is along a thin strip of land with the freshwater Gator Lake and the saltwater Little Lagoon on either side. The trail takes two hours, but there's much of interest along the way, so it's easy to spend three or four hours on this hike. It's also easy to make a day of the trip and sit or walk on the beautiful beach at the Pine Beach Trail's southern end.

Another popular trail is the one-mile-long wheelchair-accessible **Jeff Friend Trail** at the eastern end of the preserve's Perdue Unit that loops around the northern edge of Little Lagoon. The hiking is easy, and along the way you'll explore sections of the maritime forest. The **Centennial Trail** connects the Jeff Friend Trail to the Pine Beach Trail and leads through the forest just north of Little Lagoon. Hike the **Gator Lake Trail** to explore the shoreline of freshwater Gator Lake. During the winter this trail is favored by birdwatchers, who spot yellow-rumped warblers and blue-gray gnatcatchers. If you're lucky you might spot an endangered Alabama beach mouse; look for them scurrying across the sand dunes. They play a vital role in the health of the dune ecosystem by distributing seeds for sea oats, grasses, and other vegetation.

The refuge has miles of beaches within the park, and they can be accessed by driving down the main park road, Mobile Street, until it ends at a parking lot on the Gulf, or you can hike the Pine Beach Trail to a more secluded and quiet beach to the east of the main beach area. Once you are on the Gulf, there are miles of beaches to walk and explore. You should be able to find solitude to sit and hear nothing but the waves crashing against the shore.

Walking the beaches on the Gulf side May-October, you may see loggerhead and Kemp's ridley sea turtles that use the beaches of the preserve as a nesting ground.

ALABAMA COASTAL BIRDING TRAIL

If you're into bird-watching, you can find the flocks by following the **Alabama Coastal Birding Trail** (trailheads on Hwy. 182 just across Perdido Pass, 877/226-9089, www.alabamacoastalbirdingtrail.com, sunrise-sunset daily, free). Detailed maps and information on the best places to see seabirds, sparrows, and other species can be found on the website. The site details what birds to expect in different seasons in each location along the trail. The trail extends across much of Alabama. Much of the trail in this area is in the Bon Secour National Wildlife Refuge and around Fort Morgan on the western end of the island. This region draws huge numbers of migrating birds during spring and fall migrations. The birding is exceptional, but you can see even more birds by heading over to Dauphin Island to the west, one of the premier birding spots in the country.

GOLF
Orange Beach

Before you hit the course, practice your swing and get golf gear at the **Orange Beach Golf Center** (4700 Easy St., 251/981-4653, www.obparksandrec.com, 7am-9pm daily, $3 per bucket of 34 balls). This driving range and pro shop have 30 grass tees and 10 covered mat tees. The range is lighted for driving in the cooler nighttime hours during the summer.

Gulf Shores

The Peninsula Golf and Racquet Club (20 Peninsula Blvd., 251/968-8009, www.peninsulagolfclub.com, 7am-7pm daily, greens fees $45-89), a 27-hole championship course designed by Earl Stone, is tucked away beside Mobile Bay and the Bon Secour National Wildlife Refuge. Golfers of all skill levels can enjoy this extremely playable course

with 7,000 yards from the championship boxes. Winding through live oaks and native vegetation, the course attracts a wide variety of birds and wildlife that add nature to the experience. The tennis courts, pools, activities at the clubhouse, and restaurant will keep the family occupied during and after the game.

The **Gulf State Park Golf Course** (20115 Hwy. 135, 251/948-4653, www.alapark.com, from 7am daily, 18-hole $13-27, 9-hole $11-16) is an exceptional value in a beautiful setting. PGA pro Harry Dwyer manages this course, nestled in the middle of a wildlife refuge. Alligators are often spotted on the lakes and water features of the championship course designed by Earl Stone. The fairways are wide, and there aren't many water features, which makes playing easier than on other courses in the area. This a great place to bring the kids for a few rounds.

An exceptionally manicured course with impressively low rates is found at **Kiva Dunes Golf Course** (815 Plantation Rd., Suite 100, 251/540-7000, www.kivadunes.com, from 7am daily, from $69). Designed by Jerry Pate, the course was voted Best New Course by *Golf Digest*. You can stay at the Kiva Dunes Resort and almost walk from your room onto the course. They frequently offer specials at the resort, like a three-night package that includes two days of unlimited golf, breakfast, and cart rentals at a deeply discounted rate, so you can get the most out of a golf vacation on one of the best courses in the area.

The Golf Shores Golf Club (520 Clubhouse Dr., 251/968-7366, www.golf.gulfshores.com, from 7am daily, from $49) is a par-71 course with many bunkers, water features, and fairway enhancements. The ProLink Solutions GPS system allows golfers to quickly get familiarized with the course with five sets of tees that range 4,822-6,856 yards.

The two courses at **Craft Farms Golf Resort** (3840 Cotton Creek Circle, 251/968-7500, www.craftfarms.com, from 7am daily, from $40) were designed by Arnold Palmer. The Cotton Creek Course is a traditional

18-hole 7,000-yard course with rolling fairways and forward tees. Surrounded by lakes and forest, the four-star course has been rated by *Golf Digest* one of the best places to play. Bring your A game and relish in the challenge of the sixth hole, which requires a well-placed tee shot over water. The Cypress Bend Course has staggered tees and is rated 4.5 stars by *Golf Digest*. The sprawling bunkers, wide fairways, and vast landing areas are punctuated with cordgrass lakes that come into play on almost every hole. The fourth hole is the one to watch out for. The dress code is relaxed on both courses: Golfers can wear shorts, and collared shirts and spikes are required. Groups of five are welcomed if they keep up with the pace of play.

CANOEING AND KAYAKING
Orange Beach

The best place for paddlers to start in Orange Beach is a trip down the **Orange Beach Kayak and Canoe Trail.** Download maps of the 10 official launch points along this trail at the Orange Beach Community Website (www. orangebeach.ws). The trail starts at the launch on Gulf Bay Road on Wolf Bay. Paddlers travel east past Waterfront Park and Harrison Park before reaching Arnica Bay and paddling into Bayou St. John, ending at the Boggy Point Boat Launch. There are launch and take-out points along the way if you want to paddle the trail in shorter sections.

If you need a kayak for your own self-guided tour, **Paddled by You Kayak Rentals** (26448 Cotton Bayou Dr., 251/752-9250, http://paddledbyyou.com, 9am-6pm Mon.-Sat., single kayak $50 per day, $25 for 2 hours, double kayak $65 per day, $35 for 2 hours) will rent you a kayak to take down the trail or to launch from wherever you like. They also rent paddleboards and special kayaks outfitted for fishing.

Gulf Shores

A favorite paddling and kayak-fishing spot is the spring-fed freshwater **Lake Shelby,** which can be accessed from the Gulf State Park campground. During large storms and hurricanes, the Gulf will often breach the lake and deposit saltwater fish species. This gives kayak-anglers an opportunity to experience the best of freshwater and saltwater fishing and reel in largemouth bass, speckled trout, redfish, and bluegills. The mile-long **Little Lagoon** offers great paddling, as does nearby **Gator Lake.** Paddlers can launch their kayaks and canoes from the new Lagoon Park.

The legendary **"Ice Box" on the Bon Secour River** is a favorite of paddlers. This spring head stays cold year-round and is the perfect retreat from the summer heat. You can rent a kayak and take an easy self-guided float down the slow river at **Beachnriver Kayak Rentals** (Foley, 251/971-8359, 7am-3pm Tues.-Sun. May-Aug., single kayak $35, double kayak $75 for 7 hours), which launches floats from the river's end just 15 miles north of Gulf Shores. Kayakers must return to the launch site by 3pm. The rental center only accepts cash.

To rent kayaks and paddleboards on the beach, call **GoGo Kayaks** (921 Gulf Shores Pkwy., 251/752-5500, www.gogokayaks.com, 9am-5pm daily, single kayak $60 per day, $115 per week, double kayak $75 per day, $145 per week, paddleboard $165 per week). Pick up your rentals at the shop, or they'll deliver for an extra charge. They can accommodate rentals for groups of 50 or more. Another great place to rent kayaks, or anything else you may need for your beach vacation, is **Gulf Shores Beach Rentals** (3873 Gulf Shores Pkwy., 888/896-9854, www.gulfshoresalbeachrentals. com, daily, single kayak $95 per day, double kayak $125 per day, paddleboard $150 per day, beach umbrella $40 per day). They also rent beach chairs, cribs, bicycles, and more. They will even do your grocery shopping.

FISHING

In addition to the Gulf State Park Pier, you can enjoy surf fishing all along the beaches on the Gulf side, freshwater fishing at the inland lakes, and saltwater light-tackle or flats

fishing in the surrounding bays, bayous, and saltwater lakes.

Orange Beach

Distraction Charters (Orange Beach Marina, 251/975-8111, www.distractioncharters.com, 8am-6pm daily, $1,350 half-day, $2,600 all-day) specializes in deep-sea and inshore charters for up to six people. Charters can be tailored to catch specific fish. If it's running, Distraction Charters will help you get it.

A popular charter company geared for groups of 7-10 is **Intimidator Charters** (Orange Beach Marina, 251/747-2872, www.gulfshoresdeepseafishing.com, 8am-6pm daily, $1,600 for 6 hours). Call **Brown's Inshore Guide Service** (Orange Beach Marina, 251/981-6246, www.brownsinshore.net, 8am-6pm daily, $400 for 4 hours, $600 for 6 hours for 2 people, $50 each additional passenger) if you want to do some light-tackle inshore fishing. The knowledgeable and experienced Captain David Brown takes groups on four- and six-hour fishing trips. All trips include bait, tackle, and fishing licenses.

If you have your own boat, launch at **Boggy Point Boat Launch** (end of Marina Rd., off Hwy. 161, 251/981-6039, www.gulfshores.com, sunrise-sunset daily, free), near the Perdido Pass Bridge, or at the **Cotton Bayou Boat Launch** (Hwy. 182, just east of Hwy. 161, 251/981-6039, www.obparksandrec.com, sunrise-sunset daily, free).

Gulf Shores
★ **FISHING FROM GULF STATE PARK PIER**
The **Gulf State Park Pier** (20800 E. Beach Blvd., 251/967-3474, www.alapark.com, daily, free parking, fishing $9 per day, rod rentals $10 for 4 hours), in Gulf State Park between Gulf Shores and Orange Beach, is the largest pier on the Gulf at more than a quarter mile

long. The pier can get crowded on weekends and holidays, but there is usually a spot available where you can wet your line and reel in ladyfish, king mackerel, Spanish mackerel, cobia, sheepshead, jack crevalle, speckled trout, flounder, redfish, bluefish, and black drum. The octagon-shaped end of the pier is 90 feet wide and offers space for anglers to fish in the 26-foot-deep water of the Gulf. The snack bar, bait and tackle shop, and fish-cleaning facilities are scattered along the pier, which was rebuilt after Hurricane Ivan destroyed the previous pier in 2004. A major improvement is the addition of restrooms at the midway point.

FISHING CHARTERS
The best choice to charter a fishing boat that caters to families is **Miss Brianna Fishing Charters** (26619 Perdido Beach Blvd., 251/747-3126, www.gulfshorefishingcharters.com, 8am-6pm daily, $750-2,200). They offer light-tackle and heavy rod fishing trips that last 4-36 hours. The 36-foot *Miss Brianna* sleeps up to six for longer overnight charters, and the cockpit is comfortable and air-conditioned, with a TV and a satellite dish. On the deck you can grill up your catch on the Big Green Egg grill while you troll the Gulf for yellowfin tuna, swordfish, amberjack, snapper, and more. This charter is a top choice for families and serious anglers alike.

If you want to see the charter boats and meet the captains before you book your fishing trip, head down to **Zeke's Landing Marina** (26619 Perdido Beach Blvd., 251/981-4007, www.zekeslanding.com, daily). Stop by in the morning or around sunset for the chance to look over one of the largest charter fleets on the Gulf Coast. You can also get tackle and pick up your groceries, beer, and just about anything else you need for a day at the beach at **Waves Grocery and Package Store** (1154 W. Beach Blvd., 251/948-4010, 6am-10pm daily).

1: the Hugh S. Branyon Backcountry Trail **2:** golfing **3:** kayaks in Gulf Shores **4:** fishing at the Gulf State Park Pier

ENTERTAINMENT AND EVENTS

Orange Beach

The central spot for entertainment in Orange Beach is unarguably **The Wharf** (4720 Main St., 251/224-1000, www.alwharf.com). Located on the Intracoastal Waterway, also known as Portage Creek, which feeds into Wolf Bay and the Gulf, you won't miss it if you drive down the Foley Beach Expressway. Look for the South's largest Ferris wheel and you'll know you've found the place to do some shopping, catch a movie, see a concert, or eat. The 10 restaurants cater to seafood lovers. From the expansive marina you can boat up and rent a slip for the night or catch a fishing charter and take a sightseeing cruise for dolphins. The Wharf is also home to the popular outdoor **Amphitheater at the Wharf,** which hosts world-class concerts by the likes of Kenny Chesney, Kelly Clarkson, and The Fray; be sure to check the listings. Catch a movie at the state-of-the-art **Rave at the Wharf Orange Beach,** with 15 screens and matinees for rainy days. Also at the Wharf is the indoor laser tag center called **Arena the Next Level,** with 10,000 square feet of obstacles and structures for laser tag or bazooka-ball, a game where players compete at shooting glow-in-the-dark soft foam balls from adjustable-velocity guns. It's great fun and a high-energy game that will get your heart racing.

Over at the SanRoc shopping center, you can take the family on a dolphin sightseeing adventure with **Dolphins Down Under** (Carib Marina, 28101 Perdido Beach Blvd., 251/968-4386, www.dolphinsdownunder.net, 9am-4pm daily, $25 adults, $15 ages 3-10, free under age 3). They specialize in dolphin tours aboard their glass-bottom boats. The knowledgeable staff knows exactly where to go to find dolphins, and often you'll have the opportunity to see the playful mammals jumping out of the water.

If you just have to squeeze in a game of mini golf and go-karts, bring the kids to **Adventure Island** (24559 Perdido Beach Blvd., 251/974-1500, www.adventure-island.

com, 10am-9pm Wed.-Sat. June-Labor Day), where you can see the live erupting volcano. OK, it's a fake volcano in a kitschy mini amusement park, but it's still neat. If that's not enough, they also have laser tag, bumper boats, and paddleboats.

Gulf Shores

Families have a hard time running out of things to do in the Gulf Shores area. For some soaking-wet fun at a classic water park, bring the kids to **WatervilleUSA** (906 Gulf Shores Pkwy., 251/948-2106, www.watervilleusa. com, hours vary, $36, $28 military, $26 seniors and children under 42 inches). It's not large, but the waterslides send you careening down slides at phenomenal speeds. There's a lazy river and other rides found at county fairs, like a carousel and a roller coaster. The indoor arcade offers relief from the heat, and the food prices are extremely reasonable for an amusement park. You can make a day out of it, especially if you break it up with a trip to the beach or a nap for the younger kids, but a half-day is about right for most visitors. The water park is closed for winter, and hours change month to month; check the website for current hours.

A new addition to the Gulf Shores area is the **Hummingbird Zipline Course** (21101 Hwy. 135, 251/948-9494, www. gulfadventurecenter.com, $79-89). A series of high-elevation platforms connect six zip lines, two of which race over the edge of Lake Shelby. If you're not into the high adrenaline of zipping, you can take things a little slower and rent a kayak or paddleboard from the on-site outfitter. For a more classic adventure, take the family to the **Alabama Gulf Coast Zoo** (1204 Gulf Shores Pkwy., 251/968-5731, www.alabamagulfcoastzoo.org, 9am-4pm daily, $11 adults, $9 seniors, $8 ages 3-12, free under age 3), a small zoo just blocks from the beach that houses 290 animals, including a pair of Bengal tigers; this zoo was the first in the country to have tigers from each of the species' four color variations. A mining exhibit allows guests to pan for gemstones and fossils. Along with the tigers you'll enjoy the lions, bears, monkeys, macaws, a petting zoo, a reptile house, and an aviary. In summer, see the daily animal shows. This park makes a great half day of family fun.

The second weekend in October is the **National Shrimp Festival** (along Hwy. 182, 251/968-7220, www.myshrimpfest.com, $59-79), one of the best seafood fests in the country, attracting 250,000 people each year for peel-and-eat or deep-fried decapod fun. Find this area's most celebrated crustacean served any way you like at 250 vendors, along with local artists and musicians and a 10k-5k run in the morning.

Spend the day watching movies at the **Cobb Theaters Pinnacle 14** (3780 Gulf Shores Pkwy., 251/923-0100, www. cobbtheatres.com). Learn about the fascinating history of the area at the small but informative **Gulf Shores Museum** (244 W. 19th Ave., 251/968-1473, www.gulfshoresal.gov, 10am-noon and 1pm-5pm Tues.-Fri., 10am-2pm Sat., free), including fishing history and how Gulf Shores has coped with intense and destructive hurricanes.

SHOPPING
Orange Beach

Shopping is limited to surf shops, beach-goods stores, and souvenir shops along the main drag, but you can find a nicer collection of mostly beach-themed boutiques at **The Wharf** (4720 Main St., 251/224-1000, www. alwharf.com). Another similar development built around a large marina is the **SanRoc Cay Marina Entertainment District** (27267 Perdido Beach Blvd., 251/981-7173, www. sanroccay.com). An extension of the Perdido Beach Resort, this shopping district features concerts by local musicians on weekends in the courtyard. The shops are all locally owned and mostly sell women's beach-themed apparel, art, and gifts. Four restaurants are on-site, and you can rent kayaks and Jet Skis, take fishing excursions, and enjoy dolphin cruises from the marina docks.

For great deals, drive to the **Tanger Outlet**

Center (2601 S. McKenzie St., Foley, 251/943-9303, www.tangeroutlet.com) in Foley, Alabama. This enormous outlet mall features factory stores like Gap, Jos. A. Bank, J.Crew, and more, just 20 minutes (18 miles) from Orange Beach. For groceries, go to **Publix** (25771 W. Perdido Beach Blvd., 251/980-1400, www.publix.com, 6am-11pm daily).

Gulf Shores

All your surf gear and apparel needs can be met at local favorite **Tambo's Surf Shack** (3800 Gulf Shores Pkwy., 251/948-7873, 10am-7pm Sun.-Thurs., 9am-8pm Mon.-Sat., 10am-6pm Sun.), with a large inventory of surfboards, shorts, and wax. For the ultimate selection of bikinis and souvenirs, stop in at **Alvin's Island** (100 W. Beach Blvd., 251/948-3121, www.alvinsisland.com, 9am-10pm daily), a beach-goods megastore with an impressive inventory of everything for a day at the beach. Groceries can be found at **Publix** (160 Cotton Creek Dr., 251/948-1281, 6:30am-10pm daily). They make excellent deli sandwiches to pack for a surfside picnic.

FOOD
Orange Beach

The Gulf (27500 Perdido Beach Blvd., www. thegulf.com, 11am-10pm daily, $8-15) is a good place to stop for a quick bite when you first roll into Orange Beach. The oceanfront restaurant, artfully built from stacked shipping containers, is a masterpiece of modern design. Even if you're not hungry, stop by for a drink and enjoy the excellent view of the Gulf. The menu is a welcome departure from the "fry everything" edict that dominates Orange Beach culinary culture. Burgers and sandwiches keep the less adventurous satisfied, while specials like lobster spaghetti and mahimahi tacos bring fresh seafood flavors.

Hot sauce and raw oyster aficionados will love **Doc's Seafood Shack** (26029 Canal Rd., 251/981-6999, www.docsseafoodshack.com, 11am-10pm daily, $7-16), where everything you need to mix your own custom cocktail-sauce creation is right on the table. Their specialty is oysters on the half shell. Doc's is as casual as a cracker barrel and a favorite of folks who love classic Southern-style fried seafood. If you're into sports, relax and watch the game with the family while you work your way through a pound of shrimp, a tray of raw oysters, and plenty of sweet iced tea.

★ **Cosmo's Restaurant and Bar** (25753 Canal Rd., 251/948-9663, www. cosmosrestaurantandbar.com, 11am-9:30pm Sun.-Thurs., 11am-10pm Fri.-Sat., $15-30) features steak, seafood, and classic New Orleans-style entrées. At lunch, try the pecan-crusted redfish, or keep it simple and savor a crab cake sandwich or shrimp po'boy. At dinner, dig into chef Jack Baker's French influence with the chicken roulade, a chicken breast wrapped in bacon and stuffed with asparagus and gruyère cheese, topped with a sage-and-leek cream sauce. The signature dish is banana leaf-wrapped fish, and the sushi menu is extensive. Make dinner reservations on weekends during summer. If the weather's cool, sit on the outdoor patio. The lines can be long, but the experience is worth the wait.

For fresh and steamed carryout seafood, go to **Lartigue's Seafood Market** (23043 Perdido Beach Blvd., 251/948-2644, www. lartiguesseafood.com, 11am-7pm daily). Raw oysters, fresh Gulf shrimp, snapper, and the like can be found on ice to take home. The family-owned market has been open in Orange Beach since 1979, and they have some of the best prices in the area.

Gulf Shores

Restaurants are plentiful in Gulf Shores, and most are along Highway 182 (Beach Blvd.) and Highway 59 (Gulf Shores Pkwy.). Choose wisely, as there are plenty of places that prey on unsuspecting tourists with low-quality frozen seafood and subpar service. If you only visit one place in Gulf Shores, head to ★ **Lulu's** (200 E. 25th Ave., 251/967-5858, www.lulubuffett.com, 11am-9pm daily, $10-25). It's owned by Jimmy Buffett's sister and is a venerable shrine to the Margaritaville lifestyle, colorful and tropical. The main restaurant and bar is on Portage Creek, surrounded by a sprawling outdoor seating area complete with volleyball courts, a playground, and several smaller bars in Key West-style cottages. Drive in or sail your boat up to the dock. The coconut shrimp coupled with a cheeseburger in paradise and a slice of key lime pie are the perfect pairing with a frozen concoction (with or without alcohol).

The Hangout (101 E. Beach Blvd., 251/948-3030, www.thehangoutal.com, 10:30am-9pm Sun.-Thurs., 10:30am-10pm Fri.-Sat., $10-25), a sprawling, laid-back bar and restaurant on the beach, features live music most nights in summer. Come for a night of dancing or to watch the day game over wings, burgers, and fried shrimp. Before the party crowd arrives, it's an excellent choice for families—kids love playing in the large sand pit. Once the band starts up, the place draws a heavy-drinking college crowd. Expect rock, reggae, country, and alternative bands on two stages. Enjoy the free foosball and table tennis, and on winter nights, the outdoor fire pit.

For fine dining, locals go to **Coast Restaurant and Sushi Bar** (453 Beach Club Trail, 251/948-2111, www.nolansrestaurant. com, from 6pm Tues.-Sat., $18-28), an upscale restaurant that's a great choice for a romantic dinner. In the Beach Club Resort and Spa it specializes in seafood, steaks, and sushi. The atmosphere is bright and clean with beautiful wood trim. The water views of the Gulf add to the wonderful atmosphere. The small bar is a favorite of hotel guests. A sunset dinner is recommended.

There are many options for oysters in Gulf Shores, but not many better than **The Original Oyster House** (701 Gulf Shores Pkwy., 251/948-2455, www.theoysterhouse. com, 11am-9pm daily, $9-20). Oysters are prepared every way you can imagine along with standard seafood options like fried

---

1: the shipping containers making up The Gulf restaurant **2:** hotels in Gulf Shores **3:** The Hangout bar and restaurant **4:** Kiva Dunes Resort and Golf

Welcome to Flora-Bama!

the Flora-Bama

Technically four inches over the Alabama line in Florida's Perdido Key, the **Flora-Bama** (17401 Perdido Key Dr., Perdido Key, 850/492-0611, www.florabama.com) is a ramshackle beachside roadhouse where fun flows as unchecked as the booze. The bartenders are famous—and there are 10 bars, along with three stages for bands, volleyball courts, an oyster bar, a store, and a sprawling beachside patio. But that's just the beginning. Started in 1961, it was a little local bar that has grown over the years. It looks as if it were built from driftwood and scraps of debris left behind by a hurricane.

The third weekend in April it also hosts the international spectacle, the annual **Interstate Mullet Toss,** where contestants grip deceased slippery fish and throw them as far as they can into the state of Alabama. It's a straight distance competition, but you definitely get style points. Football spiral, underhanded, shot put-style—practice at home with a trout or something to hone your craft. Several hundred people compete, and nearly 30,000 people turn out to watch. There's a Ms. Mullet contest, barbecue, crawfish, peel-and-eat shrimp, topless oysters, and a whole lot of cocktails.

The Flora-Bama has a couple of other annual events of note, one of which is the **Polar Bear Dip** on the morning of January 1, an early-morning bar-to-water scramble. After a bracing splash in the Gulf (many "bears" leave behind their clothing entirely), revelers go back to the Flora-Bama for some warming black-eyed peas—and if you find a dime in your peas, it's good luck for the whole year.

flounder, gumbo, and enormous platters of fried seafood ubiquitously known at Gulf Coast seafood restaurants as the fisherman's platter. This popular place is perfect spot for a large family dinner. The peanut butter pie is delicious.

If you didn't get enough of the Margaritaville lifestyle at Lulu's, continue your search for the perfect frozen concoction at **Bahama Bobs Beach Side Café** (601 W. Beach Blvd., 251/948-2100, www.bahamabobs.com, 11am-10pm daily, $10-20). Well-loved for their fried shrimp and po'boys, this small tropical-style café is within walking distance from the beach. The outdoor seating is worth the wait and a better choice than the cramped indoor seating. A great pick from the menu is the shrimp and crab combo with boiled potatoes and corn. It's enough for two if you have a small appetite. Parking is limited.

For a sweet Southern-style treat, stop in at **Café Beignets of Alabama** (200 W. Fort Morgan Rd., 251/948-2311, 7am-noon daily, $5-12), where they serve those delectable puffy, crispy doughnuts covered in powdered sugar. The menu is beignets and coffee, which is sure to satisfy a craving without driving all the way to the French Quarter in New Orleans. Forgo your regular cup of joe and try the café au lait and chicory coffee that has that special Southern flavor. For a little more down-home Southern cookin', you can't go wrong with breakfast, lunch, or dinner at **Kitty's Kafe** (3800 Gulf Shores Pkwy., 251/943-5233, 6am-7pm Mon.-Sat., 7am-2pm Sun., $7-15), where owner Kitty Simpson will appease your craving for fried chicken and the like. They serve breakfast all day, so don't be shy coming in at 1pm for pancakes and bacon after a late night at The Hangout or Flora-Bama.

Tired of paying high prices for a small fillet of broiled snapper but don't quite have the angler's knack? Take the easy road and pick up fresh seafood or order takeout at **S&S Seafood Market** (1154 W. Beach Blvd., 251/968-3474, 11am-8pm daily Mar.-Oct. $5-15). Prices are better than at most of the seafood restaurants in the area, and the spicy fried shrimp, fried grouper, and gumbo are some of the best in Gulf Shores. You can call ahead and place your order. Make sure to ask for a few hush puppies on the side.

ACCOMMODATIONS
Orange Beach
For a great value, stay at the **Hampton Inn and Suites Orange Beach** (25518 Perdido Beach Blvd., 251/923-4400, www.hamptoninn3.hilton.com, $120-240). Breakfast is included, and the suites have fridges, microwaves, modern decor, and comfy beds. The inn offers easy access to a Gulf-front beach, and the ample meeting space makes this property a great choice for conventions and meetings.

At **Perdido Beach Resort** (27200 Perdido Beach Blvd., 251/981-9811, www.perdidobeachresort.com, $120-240) you can choose pool-view or Gulf-front rooms. The lobby has a fun piano bar, and the tiki-style pool bar offers a wonderful view of the Gulf. There is easy access to the beach, an excellent indoor heated pool, four lighted tennis courts, and a spacious fitness center.

The architecturally stunning ★ **Turquoise Place** (26302 Perdido Beach Blvd., 800/210-7914, www.turquoiseplacerental.com, $350-1,200) was featured on the cover of *USArchitecture* magazine. Directly on the Gulf, it has heated indoor pools, an indoor children's pool, seasonally heated outdoor pools, indoor hot tubs, and a 450-foot-long lazy river that winds around the property. Stop in at the poolside tiki bar or spend the day at the full-service spa. The fitness center is top-notch, with an excellent view of the Gulf. The prices are high for Orange Beach, but the resort is luxurious.

For something casual, choose the **Original Romar House** (23500 Perdido Beach Blvd., 251/974-1625, www.theoriginalromarhouse.com, $99-299), a six-room bed-and-breakfast. The spacious back deck has an excellent Gulf view, and the rooms are furnished with antiques. The tropical-themed Parrot House Cottage has a full kitchen and living room. The Captain's Quarters ($99-139) is small and perfect for solo budget travelers. They offer complimentary wine at happy hour, afternoon refreshments, a hot tub, warm hospitality, and a wonderful breakfast.

Gulf Shores
The Gulf Shores area has begun to lean toward high-end development, and for the most part outshines Orange Beach accommodations in this respect. However, there is still a wide variety of accommodation choices. Budget-minded travelers looking for a suitable efficiency can find a great deal at the **Staybridge Suites Gulf Shores** (3947 Gulf Shores Pkwy., 251/975-1030, www.staybridgehotels.com, $95-160). The suites have fully equipped kitchens and are exceptionally spacious for

the rates. A complimentary hot breakfast is served every morning. There are not a lot of frills, but you can't beat the rates for these spacious rooms in a great location.

Enjoy a more upscale experience at the **Courtyard by Marriott Gulf Shores Craft Farms** (3750 Gulf Shores Pkwy., 251/968-1113, www.mariott.com, $100-170). On the Craft Farms Golf Resort, this property is geared to golfers who want to mix business with one of the best courses in the Panhandle. There is an excellent pool, and the public beach is only four miles away.

One of the best golf getaways on the Gulf Coast, **Kiva Dunes Resort and Golf** (815 Plantation Dr., 251/540-7000, www.kivadunes.com, $170-300). is a collection of homes and condos that surround an excellent golf course. It offers 3,000 feet of quiet beach, three outdoor pools, a fitness center, an onsite restaurant, a tiki bar, a golf pro shop, tennis courts, and a spacious fitness center. Go to the website to see photos and rates.

The **Gulf Shores Plantation** (805 Plantation Rd., 251/540-5000, www.gulfshoresplantation.com, $100-400) offers a large variety of cottages and condos. This family-oriented resort has an indoor pool, six outdoor pools, several hot tubs, saunas, horseshoe pits, a putting green, and thousands of feet of Gulf beaches. The resort also has tennis courts, shuffleboard, basketball courts, and a fitness center. All the cottages and condos have full kitchens and either a patio or a balcony.

On the west end of Gulf Shores, ★ **The Beach Club Resort and Spa** (925 Beach Club Trail, 251/224-7684, www.thebeachclub.spectrumresorts.com, $230-600) is a family-oriented resort featuring a collection of cottages and one- to five-bedroom condos. Each has fully equipped kitchens, balconies with views of the Gulf, and a range of styles, sizes, and rates. The cottages offer more privacy and the resort's amenities. Many of the cottages are around a lake, and some have hot tubs and private pools. There are several outdoor pools around the resort, as well as a full-service spa,

hot tubs, an ice cream shop, and organized kid's activities.

Vacation Rentals

Most vacation rental companies in the area deal with properties in both Orange Beach and Gulf Shores. A wide range of homes and condos are available to rent, running the gamut from simple, classic, modest beach cottages to impressively large and fancy beach homes for several families to share. All along the coast are high-rise condo developments. The offerings can be overwhelming, but a few expert rental companies can help you get what you are looking for, whether it is a small condo on the Gulf or a large home tucked away on a wooded lot on Mobile Bay. The two established and trusted rental companies in the area are **Meyer Vacation Rentals** (1585 Gulf Shores Pkwy., Gulf Shores, 251/968-7516, www.meyerre.com) and **Brett/Robinson Vacation Rentals** (3259 Gulf Shores Pkwy., Gulf Shores, 251/968-7363, www.brett-robinson.com). Both have great websites with pictures and rates for all the homes available in the area.

An upscale selection of Caribbean-style cottages and condos can be found at **Martinique on the Gulf** (987 Blvd. Martinique, Gulf Shores, 251/540-2641, www.martinique-gulf.com, $250-575). This premier development is adjacent to the Bon Secour National Wildlife Refuge and offers two- and three-bedroom condos and two- to five-bedroom cottages. It features a phenomenal pool area, a hot tub, a kid's pool, a fitness center, professional tennis courts, and a private boardwalk that leads to the Gulf beaches.

In the middle of town are the **Phoenix All Suites Hotels** (201 E. Beach Blvd., Gulf Shores, 251/968-8300, www.phoenixallsuites.com, $150-300). The west and east towers feature one-bedroom suites with full kitchens, 1 or 1.5 baths, and a balcony with Gulf views. They're no-frills condos, but the nice outdoor pool and the fact that the condos are just 1,500 feet from the public beach make the Phoenix a great value.

Camping

The best camping in the Gulf Shores and Orange Beach area is at ★ **Gulf State Park** (22050 Campground Rd., Gulf Shores, 251/948-7275, www.alapark.com/gulfstate, 7am-sunset daily, campsites $25-69, cabins $115-300). This 496-site campground is along the north shore of Middle Lake and offers many lakefront sites. Sites are close together and best suited for RVs. Some sites offer more privacy and shade for tent camping, but the size of the campground often means a loud experience. If you're a light sleeper, bring earplugs—during the summer months, RV campers run their air-conditioners all night, which can be quite loud. The campground offers direct access to miles of hiking trails, including the Rosemary Dunes Trail, which leads to the Gulf and the Gulf State Park Pavilion Beach. The beach is a 1.5-mile drive from the campground. Amenities include a swimming pool, wireless internet, a clean modern bathhouse with hot showers, full laundry facilities, and water, electric, and sewer hookups at every site. The lake is open for swimming, fishing, and boating, and the campground is within walking distance of the Gulf State Park Golf Course.

The park offers even more comfort in 20 cabin and cottage rentals, mostly one- and two-room buildings that sleep 4-6 people, located along the lakeshore, near the golf course, and a few in a forested area of the campground. The cabins on the lake are some of the best in the park. Each has a private dock, a fish-cleaning bench, and barbecue grills. Each cottage is fully equipped, and linens are provided. The cabins are reserved far in advance, so book well ahead of time to enjoy some of the most comfortable camping you've ever experienced.

On the bay side in Gulf Shores, pull your RV into **Fort Morgan RV Park** (10397 2nd St., 251/540-2416, www.fortmorganrvpark.com, $49-70, $565 per month Oct.-Apr., $700 per month May-Sept.), where 35 sites are spread over six acres right on Mobile Bay. Large oak trees provide ample shade at most campsites, and nearly every site has a water view of the bay. This park is favored by anglers, who fish from the 200-foot pier. Beaches are just 1.5 miles from the park. A new bathhouse and free laundry facilities were added in 2013. Water, sewer, electric, cable, and wireless internet are included with each site.

More tucked away on the northern side of Little Lagoon is **Doc's RV Park** (17595 State Rd. 180, Gulf Shores, 251/968-4511, www.docsrvpark.com, $36-42, $257-265 weekly, $500-640 per month), with 75 RV sites only three miles from the beach. Each site has full electric and sewer hook-ups, wireless internet, and cable. The campground features a swimming pool, a playground, laundry, a bathhouse, a clubhouse, and 14 park-model cabins ($85, $510 weekly) you can rent. This campground is a favorite among long-term campers.

In Gulf Shores, 25 more RV sites can be found at **Bay Breeze RV** (1901 Bay Breeze Pkwy., 251/540-2362, www.baybreezerv.com, $36-48, $216-288 weekly, $528 per month). Beach access on Mobile Bay is just a short walk from the campground. They also offer RV rentals and one cabin to rent. The fishing and boat dock make this campground the choice of boaters. The campground has a bathhouse and laundry facility, making it more comfortable to stay for a longer period.

TRANSPORTATION
Car

The main driving access to the area from New Orleans to the west and Jacksonville and Tallahassee to the east is I-10. From the north, take I-65 from Birmingham or I-85 from Atlanta. All these lead to Mobile, Alabama. To get to the Gulf Shores area from Mobile, it's a 49-mile one-hour drive on Highway 59 South to the Gulf Shores Public Beach, then turn right toward the west end of Gulf Shores or left toward Orange Beach.

From Pensacola, follow U.S. 98 to Highway 292, known as Barrancas Avenue, Gulf Beach Highway, and Sorrento Road at different points along the route. Highway 292 goes through Perdido and right to the Florida-Alabama border, where it becomes Highway 182 once you cross into Alabama and reach Orange Beach.

Air

Advantage Airport Shuttle (850/420-7807, www.advantageairportshuttle.com) provides service from **Pensacola** **International Airport** (PNS, 850/436-5000, www.flypensacola.com), about an hour east, to Orange Beach ($60-70) and Gulf Shores ($75-90).

Thrifty (877/238-0898), **Hertz** (850/432-2345), **Avis** (850/433-5614), **Budget** (850/432-5499), **Enterprise** (850/478-6730), and **Alamo** (888/826-6893) provide rental cars at Pensacola International Airport.

Dauphin Island

To escape the throngs of tourists around Gulf Shores and Orange Beach, load your car onto the ferry at the western tip of Gulf Shores and venture to Dauphin Island, a favorite family destination for people in Mobile and also coveted by anglers due to the easy access to Mobile Bay to the north, Bon Secour Bay to the east, and the Gulf of Mexico to the south. The fishing is exceptional, and the island hosts the largest fishing tournament in the world, the Alabama Deep Sea Fishing Rodeo. Usually a sleepy spot on the Gulf Coast, it's transformed every July into a bustling frenzy of anglers, fishing boats, and 75,000 spectators. If you don't want to deal with crowds, don't visit the island during rodeo time.

The pace of life is usually slow on Dauphin Island, with hardly any shopping unless you're in the market for fresh oysters, shrimp, or blue crab, and the accommodations are remarkably limited, with most visitors renting homes or condos. Dauphin Island is genuinely Southern and a place where the influences of the French and Spanish are in the cuisine, culture, and architecture. To really experience the island, do two things: first, take a boat out on the water, and then just relax.

If you love birds, grab your binoculars and visit in spring to see some of the 347 species reported on this 14-mile-long island, the first piece of land birds reach during their biannual migrations. The island is considered one of the top 10 most significant spots on the planet for birds and was named by *Wild* *Bird Magazine* as one of the top four locations to watch spring migrations in the United States. On the eastern tip of the island is the Audubon Bird Sanctuary, a 164-acre parcel preserved and managed to support the massive spring and fall migrations.

SIGHTS
Indian Shell Mound Park
Visit the **Indian Shell Mound Park** (830 Desoto Dr., 251/861-2882, www.dauphinislandhistory.org, dawn-dusk daily, free) and walk the short trail through the 11-acre park surrounding a massive shell mound left behind by early Native Americans. They roasted boatloads of oysters and threw the shells into a pile that over time grew to the highest point on the island. Almost as impressive as the mound are the enormous oak trees found in the park. Some of the larger ones are more than 800 years old and were mature trees when the Spaniards first visited Dauphin Island.

★ Fort Gaines
Arguably the most historically significant site on Dauphin Island is **Fort Gaines** (51 Bienville Blvd., 251/861-6992, www.dauphinisland.org, 9am-5pm daily, $8 adults, $4 ages 5-12), on the eastern tip of the island. Construction of the fort began in 1821 and was completed in 1861. The fort was used most notably in the Battle of Mobile Bay, a significant clash in the Civil War. During World

Dauphin Island

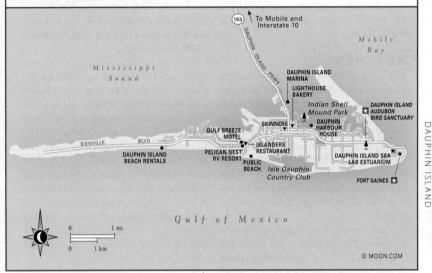

193 To Mobile and Interstate 10

DAUPHIN ISLAND PKWY

Mobile Bay

Mississippi Sound

DAUPHIN ISLAND MARINA

LIGHTHOUSE BAKERY

Indian Shell Mound Park

DAUPHIN ISLAND AUDUBON BIRD SANCTUARY

SKINNERS

GULF BREEZE MOTEL

DAUPHIN HARBOUR HOUSE

BIENVILLE   BLVD.

ISLANDERS RESTAURANT

PELICAN NEST RV RESORT

DAUPHIN ISLAND BEACH RENTALS

PUBLIC BEACH

DAUPHIN ISLAND SEA LAB ESTUARIUM

Isle Dauphin Country Club

FORT GAINES

Gulf of Mexico

0   1 mi

0   1 km

© MOON.COM

War II, the fort became a station for an antisubmarine branch of the U.S. Coast Guard as well as the base for the Alabama National Guard.

After paying the entrance fee at the visitors center, you are free to explore the fort on your own. Constructed with brick and sand mortar, the fort's most notable features are the tall arched tunnels and steep outer walls. In and around the fort are original cannons, a functioning blacksmith shop, kitchens, and an exhibit that includes the original anchor from the USS *Hartford,* where Admiral David Farragut spoke the famous words, "Damn the torpedoes; full speed ahead!" Even though the fort has received substantial damage from the ongoing tropical storms and intense hurricanes, it is still considered one of the best-preserved forts from the Civil War era, with excellent examples of early artillery.

To get here, drive east down Bienville Boulevard to the end of the road, and you'll reach the fort. Take a self-guided tour or drive your vehicle around the fort's outer wall, which runs parallel to the coastline.

Dauphin Island Sea Lab Estuarium

To learn more about the Mobile Bay aquatic environment, visit the **Dauphin Island Sea Lab Estuarium** (101 Bienville Blvd., 919/861-2141, www.estuarium.disl.org, 9am-6pm Mon.-Sat., noon-6pm Sun. Mar.-Aug., 9am-5pm Mon.-Sat., noon-5pm Sun. Sept.-Feb., $11 adults, $9 seniors, $6 ages 5-18). The primary focus of the estuarium is to facilitate Alabama's universities and grade schools with courses, workshops, and graduate programs in marine-science environmental education. Nonstudents can get a glimpse into what life is like below the waters of Mobile Bay, the Tensaw River Delta, and the northern Gulf of Mexico in the indoor visual exhibits here as well as taking a walk on the boardwalk above the surrounding marsh. While exploring the estuarium, you will see alligators, turtles, snakes, gars, oysters, horseshoe crabs, blue crabs, stone crabs, shrimp, octopus, eels, starfish, sea horses, and jellyfish. The highlight of the facility is a touch tank that lets children touch sealife on display. The kid-centric aquarium and environmental education programs will get children of all ages interested in understanding what is happening in Mobile Bay, the fourth-largest estuary system in the United States.

BEACHES

More impressive than the beaches on Dauphin Island is the island's laid-back atmosphere and culture. Don't get me wrong: The beaches are enjoyable, but the beaches in Gulf Shores and Orange Beach are nicer. On Dauphin Island, the offshore oil rigs are close to shore and clearly visible. This might not bother many people, but when I look out across the Gulf, I prefer to see the clean, blue line of the horizon and not the blinking lights of an oil rig platform.

There are three main access points for the beaches on Dauphin Island. The largest and most popular beach is the **Dauphin Island Public Beach Access** (1509 Bienville Blvd., 251/861-3607, www.dauphinisland.org, $5 per car or motorcycle, $2 pedestrians and bicyclists, $20 RVs and buses), which is also the site of the Dauphin Island Fishing Pier. This is a beautiful spot with more than two miles of undeveloped beaches, four large picnic pavilions, restrooms, outdoor showers, and a nice playground for children.

It is a long trek from your car to the edge of the Gulf, where most people prefer to set up their beach chairs and umbrellas. Wear sandals for the long trek out to the water's edge. The beach is good for swimming, but there are no lifeguards, so swim close to shore, look for rip currents, and avoid the Gulf when it's rough if you're not accustomed to swimming in open water.

There is something extremely odd about the fishing pier: It never reaches the water. At one time it was a deep-water fishing pier, but in 2007-2008, Pelican Island was slowly moved toward Dauphin Island by a series of harsh hurricanes and winter storms until they were connected. Now the beach is much larger, but the pier is unfishable.

On the east end of the island, use the **Fort Gaines Public Beach Access.** It's not much of a beach, but the thin strip of sand around the fort area is a convenient place to get close to the water if you're visiting the fort. This beach is excellent for swimming, but there is no lifeguard on duty.

With the pier now out of use at the main public beach, the island authority has decided to open the **West End Public Beach** (far west end of Dauphin Island, 251/861-5525, www.townofdauphinisland.org, 10am-6pm daily, $2 parking plus $3 pp over age 12). This family-oriented beach has a waterslide, beach chair and umbrella rentals, food vendors, snow cones, and cocktails. The waterslide and snow cones are reminiscent of Pensacola Beach in the 1970s and 1980s. The West End beach is nice and wide and known as the place to find the best shells on the island. A lifeguard is on duty in summer, making this the island's best beach for swimming.

SPORTS AND RECREATION
Birding, Hiking, and Biking

Rent a bike or hike the **Island-Long Bike Path.** The seven-mile paved path runs parallel to Bienville Boulevard and traverses most of the island. With such an excellent and accessible bike path, there's no reason why you can't see everything on the island and get a great workout at the same time. The more you hike or bike on the bike path, the more fried shrimp and daiquiris you're allowed to have.

★ DAUPHIN ISLAND AUDUBON BIRD SANCTUARY

The **Dauphin Island Audubon Bird Sanctuary** (211 Bienville Blvd., 251/861-3607, www.dauphinisland.org, dawn-dusk daily, free) was created to accommodate the large number of migrating birds and butterflies that pass over Dauphin Island during their spring and fall migrations. Bring your

1: sea oats in the sugar sands on Dauphin Island
2: a boardwalk at Dauphin Island Audubon Bird Sanctuary 3: Fort Gaines on Dauphin Island

binoculars and explore this 164-acre park on the eastern side of the island that features a wide variety of habitats. Explore freshwater lakes, swamp, beach, coastal dune, pine forest, and hardwood forest on six trails. The park can be accessed from the Dauphin Island Campground as well as from the main parking lot on Bienville Boulevard. Spring is the best time to spot birds, which literally fall out of the sky when a cold front with rain pushes over the island during spring migration. If you're into birding, the Audubon Bird Sanctuary should not be missed.

INDIAN SHELL MOUND PARK

For a more historical experience, hike the trail at the **Indian Shell Mound Park** (830 Desoto Rd., 251/861-2882, www.dauphinislandhistory.org, dawn-dusk daily, free). The short trail leads around an ancient shell mound left behind by early Native Americans who possibly used the island to escape the cold winter weather.

Canoeing and Kayaking

Rent a pontoon boat from the **Dauphin Island Marina** (650 LeMoyne Dr., 251/861-2201, http://dauphinislandmarina.com, 8am-5pm Wed.-Sun., $275 half-day, $400 full-day). Buy bait and tackle here for fishing. They offer guided ecotours and dolphin tours (1pm-5pm) as well as sunset cruises (5pm-8pm) on pontoon boats ($35 adults, $25 ages 6-12, free under age 6).

If you want a kayak or bike delivered to you, call Lynn at **Dauphin Island Kayak and Bicycle Rentals** (251/422-5285, 9am-6pm daily). Single kayaks are $25 for two hours and $60 for a full day. She rents tandems and has the best prices for two or more boats for more than two days. Bicycles are $15 per day. Lynn offers tours of the island by boat or bike, and her tours can include lunch at one of the local restaurants or prepacked picnics.

Now that you've rented a boat, you can launch your watercraft at one of the many boat launches or beaches around the island. On the eastern side of the island, launch at the Dauphin Island Campground or the boat launch at Fort Gaines. These are great launches to paddle out to Sand Island just south of Dauphin Island in the Gulf. The boat launch at the Dauphin Island Marina is centrally located and an excellent launch point into Mobile Bay. It's easy to get into the Gulf from the main public beach, centrally located on the south side of the island.

Fishing

Before you get on the island, pick up all the fishing supplies you need and learn the locals' secrets by stopping in at **Jemison's Bait & Tackle** (16871 Dauphin Island Pkwy., 251/873-4695, 4:30am-9pm daily). The ramshackle store might not look like much, but it offers a wealth of information if you ask the right people. Just past the store, you can put your newly purchased bait and tackle to the test at the **Cedar Point Fishing Pier** (18250 Dauphin Island Pkwy., 251/873-4476, www.fishingpier.net, 24 hours daily, $5). You can buy tackle and bait at the fishing pier's shop as well. A great place to fish late into the night, the pier is the oldest privately owned fishing pier on the Gulf Coast, and it's been getting a lot more business since the Dauphin Island Fishing Pier has become unfishable.

For a pro guide to take you out into Mobile Bay or the surrounding fishing hot spots, set up a fishing charter with **Capt. Mike's Deep Sea Fishing** (650 LeMoyne Dr., 251/861-5302, www.captainmikeonline.com). He is based out of the Dauphin Island Marina and has three boats that range 40-65 feet. They can accommodate trolling and bottom fishing for red snapper, king mackerel, and grouper, or fishing for larger blue marlin and tuna.

FESTIVALS AND EVENTS

The biggest festival on the island is the **Alabama Deep Sea Fishing Rodeo** (251/471-0025, www.adsfr.com). Held in mid-July, this fishing tournament is the largest saltwater fishing tournament in the world, attracting 3,000 anglers and 75,000 spectators every year. It's a ton of fun to watch the boats come in and unload their impressive catches onto the docks. The three-day event awards $400,000 in prizes in 30 categories, including a master junior angler award.

Find out about life during World War II at the **WWII Living History Event** (Fort Gaines, 251/861-6992, www.dauphinisland. org), which takes place in early March and includes live reenactments by soldiers, period craftspeople, and some exciting live cannon firing.

Most people consider New Orleans to be synonymous with Mardi Gras, but the festival actually began in Mobile. Experience Mardi Gras Dauphin Island-style at the **People's Parade** (Bienville Blvd., 251/861-5525, ext. 222, www.townofdauphinisland. org). Always the second parade of the season, usually mid-late January, the parade is much more laid-back than the parades in Mobile or New Orleans. You won't find barricades, but you will see families cooking out and partying along the parade route for the entire day, usually into the late hours. Crowds arrive early along the route to stake out and set up their camps for the day. If you want to catch beads and Moon Pies (those delectable chocolate-covered graham-cracker-and-marshmallow-stuffed treats tossed out at parades), get to the parade early in the morning before the first float rolls past.

SHOPPING

There's not much shopping on Dauphin Island, but there are plenty of island-themed clothing, jewelry, and other beach souvenirs at **The Hippie Fish** (1008 Desoto Ave., 251/656-5696, 10am-5pm Mon.-Sat., 1pm-5pm Sun.). A nice collection of sealife-inspired art, gifts, and clothing can be found at the popular **Dauphin Island Sea Lab Estuarium Gift Shop** (101 Bienville Blvd., 251/861-2141, ext. 7545, www.giftshop.disl.org, 9am-6pm Mon.-Sat., 1pm-6pm Sun.). You don't have to pay the estuarium admission to get into the gift shop, and if you like Gulf-themed housewares, it is worth a stop.

You can find all the groceries and other beach supplies you need at the **Ship & Shore** (401 LeMoyne Dr., 251/861-2262, 5am-10pm daily), just across the bridge on the right as you come onto the island. This grocery store doubles as the town's hardware store. If you're in desperate need of retail therapy, head over to Gulf Shores or Mobile.

FOOD

It's a small island, and the selection of restaurants is limited, with most located right across the Dauphin Island Bridge on LeMoyne Drive and along Bienville Boulevard; choice eateries cluster around the intersection of these roads.

For a delightful breakfast before you hit the beach, visit the ★ **Lighthouse Bakery** (919 Chaumont Ave., 251/861-2253, 6am-3pm Wed.-Fri., 6am-4pm Sat., 9am-3pm Sun., $4-10). This historic home has been turned into a wonderful bakery that serves large flaky croissants and a wonderful selection of fresh-made sandwiches for breakfast or lunch. Eat outdoors at one of the tables that line the front porch or at the picnic tables on the front lawn if the weather is nice. If the bakery is busy, you can browse the interesting and quirky collection of knickknacks and souvenirs for sale that line every square inch of the restaurant walls.

A great place on the island for lunch, dinner, or a drink is **Islander's Restaurant** (1504 Bienville Blvd., 251/861-2225, 11am-9pm daily, $12-20). Formerly the Oarhouse, the new management has turned things around and improved the menu. There are fresh seafood dishes as well as some of the best shrimp po'boys on the island, with excellent, perfectly chewy rolls. The portions are large, and the shrimp and grits and piña coladas are a perfect combo after spending the day on the beach.

For fresh seafood that you can cook at the beach house or condo, stop in at **Skinners Seafood** (1012 Bienville Blvd., 251/861-4221, www.skinnerseafood.com, 8am-6pm Wed.-Mon., 8am-5pm Sun., $7-15). They own a fishing boat, and as a result nearly everything in

the store is brought in fresh daily from the Gulf and bay. Just don't go into the store hungry or you might leave with more raw oysters, shrimp, and red snapper than you can handle. They sell a nice variety of hot sauces, spices, boils, and batters to accompany your effortless seafood catch, and offer an extensive menu of steamed seafood that you can order to go.

ACCOMMODATIONS

Accommodations are extremely limited on Dauphin Island, and most visitors rent beach houses or condos.

Under $100

The best affordable choice on the island is the **Gulf Breeze Motel** (1512 Cadillac Ave., 251/861-7344, www.gulfbreezemotel.info, $74-139). This clean no-frills motel is on the bay side and within walking distance of public beach access. Enjoy views of the bay from the balconies of most of the 32 rooms. Two rooms include full kitchens. The dock behind the motel has boat slips if you want to sail up to your room.

$100-200

The **Dauphin Island Harbour House** (730 Cadillac Ave., 251/861-2119, www.dauphinhouse.com, $110-189) offers an enjoyable bed-and-breakfast experience. The property includes a large deck, a wonderful breakfast each morning, and 10 rooms that vary greatly, some with larger baths or better views of the bay than others. The pier behind the house is a great place to relax or fish for flounder and redfish. If you're sailing, boat slips ($50) are available.

Vacation Rentals

The best way to set up a beach rental is to contact ★ **Dauphin Island Beach Rentals** (800/771-1480, www.dauphinislandbeachrentals.com). They offer a wide variety of homes and condos, with most options family-oriented beach houses of more modest size and style than on the beaches farther east. The homes and condos available reflect the island's laid-back and casual lifestyle. Most homes and condos on the island rent for $100-300, or $700-2,000 per week. Monthly and long-term rentals are available.

Camping

The only campground on the island is the **Pelican Nest RV Resort and Campground** (1510 Bienville Blvd., 251/861-2338, www.dauphinislandcampground.com, $35-80). The campground has 150 sites with access to power and water and 75 sites with RV hookups. In the bathhouse you'll find hot showers and restrooms. A boardwalk takes you from the campground to the beach, and a small store in the campground will keep your cooler stocked with camping and beach supplies. It's free to use the boat launch, and you can explore the nearby Fort Gaines historical site. The campground is only 0.5 miles from the where the ferry departs, great if you want to hitch a ride over to Gulf Shores for the day, but not the best if you are a light sleeper or a tent camper. The ferry arrives early in the morning, and when the ferry horn blows, there is little chance you'll stay asleep. For this reason, the campground is more accommodating for RV campers.

TRANSPORTATION

Car

You can drive to Dauphin Island from Gulf Shores or Orange by heading north to Mobile and then driving south to the island, but the ferry is more fun and often faster. From Gulf Shores or Orange Beach, the quickest way to Dauphin Island is to drive west on I-10 to Highway 193 south, which leads to the island.

Ferry

The **Mobile Bay Ferry** (101 Bienville Blvd., Dauphin Island; 110 Hwy. 180, Gulf Shores, departs every 45 minutes 8am-6pm daily Mar.-Nov., every 90 minutes 8am-6pm daily Nov.-Feb., one-way $16 cars, $35 RVs, $10

1: the Lighthouse Bakery **2:** Gulf Breeze Motel on Dauphin Island.

motorcycles, $12 boats with trailers under 21 feet, $18 boats with trailers over 21 feet, $5 passengers, free under age 6) is more relaxing, and much more fun, than driving. It connects Highway 193 at Dauphin Island on the west side with Highway 180 at Mobile Point on the east. The ferry trip takes 40 minutes each way.

Information and Services

Orange Beach, Gulf Shores, and Dauphin Island are in the **central time zone.**

VISITOR INFORMATION

For visitor information on Gulf Shores and Orange Beach, stop in at the **Orange Beach Welcome Center** (23685 Perdido Beach Blvd., Orange Beach, 251/974-1510, www.gulfshores.com, 8am-5pm daily) or the **Gulf Shores Welcome Center** (3459 Gulf Shores Pkwy., Gulf Shores, 251/968-7511, www.gulfshores.com, 8am-5pm daily) to pick up brochures and maps as well as plenty of great coupons. Their website has a tremendous amount of visitor information.

For more Dauphin Island information, call or visit the **Dauphin Island Chamber of Commerce** (1101 Bienville Blvd., 251/861-5524, www.dauphinislandchamber.com); they share a space with the community library and have free Wi-Fi, computers to use, and all the information and brochures you need to plan your Dauphin Island days.

POLICE AND EMERGENCIES

In an emergency, dial 911. For a nonemergency police need, call or visit the **Orange Beach Police Department** (4480 Orange Beach Blvd., 251/981-9777, www.obpd.org). The **Gulf Shores Police Department** can be reached at 251/968-2431, and the **Dauphin Island Police Department** can be reached at 251/861-5523.

In the event of a medical emergency, stop into the **Orange Beach Medical Center** (4223 Orange Beach Blvd., 251/974-3820) or **Gulf Shores Medical Center** (200 Office Park Dr., 251/968-7379). To fill a prescription, there is a **CVS Pharmacy** in Orange Beach (25761 Perdido Beach Blvd., 251/974-1590). The **Gulf Shores Family Pharmacy** (251 Clubhouse Dr., 251/968-3784) has an antique soda fountain and a Wurlitzer jukebox to play while you wait.

Background

The Landscape

GEOGRAPHY

Florida is bounded on the north by Alabama and Georgia, to the east by the Atlantic, to the south by the Straits of Florida, and to the west by the Gulf of Mexico. The east coast of the state is comparatively straight, extending in a rough line 470 miles long. The Gulf side, on the other hand, has a more curving and complex coastline, measuring roughly 675 miles. In all, Florida's 2,276-mile coastline is longer than that of any other state in the contiguous United States and contains 663 miles of beaches and more than 11,000 miles of rivers, streams, and waterways.

Florida is nearly pancake flat, without notable change in elevation, and young by geological standards, having risen out of the ocean 300-400 million years ago. The state of Florida has six major geographical regions, several of which are represented along the Gulf Coast. First, the **coastal lowlands** encircle the state and extend along the shores inland 10-100 miles. The most recent to emerge from the ocean, the lowlands are covered with forests of saw palmetto and cypress. To the northwest, between the Perdido and Apalachicola Rivers, the **western highlands** are hilly uplands of pine forest. The highlands offer the highest elevation in Florida—345 feet above sea level in the northwestern part of Walton County. Farther east, between the Apalachicola and Withlacoochee Rivers, the **Tallahassee Hills** is a hilly region dotted with live oak and pine forests. It gradually slopes eastward to a plain until it hits the Suwannee River.

The Gulf side of the state has numerous deep-water bays: Tampa Bay, Apalachicola Bay, Charlotte Harbor, and Pensacola Bay. There is also an abundance of rivers (Caloosahatchee, Peace, Withlacoochee, Manatee, Suwannee, Ocilla, Ocklockonee, Apalachicola, Choctawhatchee, Yellow, Escambia, Perdido, and others) and harbors on the Gulf side, and a record-holding number of first-magnitude springs. Thus, the fishing, boating, and swimming along the Gulf Coast are legendary.

Starting in the south, the **Everglades** region consists mainly of submerged sawgrass plains. The water, about knee-deep and with a slight southward current, provides habitat to hundreds of fish species, birds, and small mammals. Some of the Everglades' water is overflow from **Lake Okeechobee,** the second-largest freshwater lake with boundaries entirely in the United States, 30 miles wide and 33 miles long.

North of the lake, extending through De Soto, Manatee, Osceola, and Brevard Counties, is a vast tract of prairie land with large swamp areas. This is where most of the state's cattle are raised. North of that, in Polk, Marion, Orange, Sumter, Lake, and Alachua Counties, there's a little rise along the central ridge (up to 300 feet above sea level), with large and small lakes dotting the fertile, gently rolling terrain. The **coastal plain** that runs along the length of the Gulf Coast is low-lying and sandy, skirted by a dense pine region and marshes in many parts.

Several geographical features and plant communities are common in Florida, such as barrier islands, mangrove islands, marshes, hardwood hammocks, pineland, and flatwoods.

Barrier Islands

Barrier islands are ridges of sand that usually run parallel to the main coast (Sanibel sticks out the other way), separated from the mainland by a bay or lagoon. They are sand deposits of recent geologic origin, in much of the Gulf Coast composed of almost pure milky quartz. Delivered to the Gulf by rivers, this sand is washed and well sorted, resulting in fine, even-grained sand along many Gulf beaches. Buffering the mainland from storms and heavy surf, they are constantly being contoured and molded by wave action and wind. **Sea oats** and other beachside plants provide a little structure and foundation for dunes to develop. They capture and hold the blowing sand—thus, they are to be preserved and nurtured (there's a steep fine for trampling or messing with the sea oats on Gulf Coast beaches). **Swales** are wetlands formed on these islands where the wind has scoured out the sand down to the water table or below, and often a **maritime forest** can be found on the back side of barrier islands behind the secondary dunes.

Mangrove Islands

Along Florida's south coast and halfway up

the peninsula, mangrove swamps hug the shoreline. They create a fringing network around most islands, growing at the high-tide line and helping to stabilize the shore. In the maze of the **Ten Thousand Islands** between Marco Island and the Everglades, you can see entire island ecosystems created by saltwater-tolerant mangroves. These trees send their roots into the shallows, filtering pollution and providing a crucial habitat for fish and wading birds.

Marshes

Marshes make up a large area near the Gulf Coast—spaces that are partially or peri-odically submerged land, where the water table is near the surface of the soil. Water flows into marshes and swamps from rivers, creeks, and bayous, bringing with it rich organic debris that settles and accumulates in the marshes, compacting into peat. Trees in marshes, or in the larger category of **wetlands,** get used to living in standing water. Cypress and tupelo buttress their trunks by sending up "knees" for support (and for absorbing air).

In **salt marshes** there is a clear line drawn between the wetland and upland, because the salt is detrimental to the growth of so many plant species. (From Apalachicola Bay south to Tampa Bay, salt marshes are the main coastal community.) In freshwater wetlands that line is more blurred, with the wetland plants shifting subtly into upland species. In the case of **tidal marshes,** affected by the ebb and flow of tides, the demarcation line is even more pronounced. Many tidal marshes along the Gulf Coast are dominated by stands of black needle rush and saltmarsh cordgrass.

Freshwater and saltwater marshes, as well as a similar community called a **seagrass meadow,** are enormously important to Florida's fish species, providing the shelter as a "nursery" for many species, a safe haven in which to mature among the marsh grasses before adult fish go out into the predator-dense Gulf.

Swamps, certainly a defining feature of Florida, are just forested wetlands. About 10 percent of Florida is covered by forested wet-land bordering rivers or ponds, populated by plant species that tolerate periodic high water levels. For great examples of swamps, visit Fakahatchee Strand State Preserve or Big Cypress National Park.

Hardwood Hammocks

Hardwood hammocks may be the oldest natural community type in Florida, dating back more than 25 million years. There are **upland hardwoods** and **bottomland hardwoods,** the latter being the transition forest between a drier upland area and a wet river floodplain. Either way, the largest mature trees in a hardwood forest (laurel oak, sweetgum, Southern magnolia, and others) tend to hog all the light. The understory, the next level of stratification (trees like dogwood and shrubs like Elliott's blueberry or Florida anise), has to grab whatever light is left over. And then the forest floor (moss and ferns) lives in the low-light murk. Vines and epiphytes have to hoist themselves up on the canopy trees to gain access to light.

Pineland

Longleaf pineland used to cover 70 million acres in the South. Sadly, Florida pineland is an endangered plant community, a habitat that must be burned regularly to thrive. The small remaining pinelands in Florida are gen-erally so close to residential and commercial areas that regular burning programs often aren't feasible. As if that's not bad enough, invading species like the Brazilian pepper are choking native species in these delicate habitats.

Long Pine Key in Everglades National Park is a great example of a pineland, much of it old-growth forest. And along the north-west Panhandle, **Blackwater River State Forest,** along with Conecuh National Forest and Eglin Air Force Base, contains the larg-est holding of longleaf pine trees in the world. Longleaf pine is a long-lived tree, living 350-500 years. A mature longleaf pine forest has an open canopy that allows sunlight to flood

Gulf Coast Temperatures

City	Avg. Low (°F)	Avg. High (°F)
Apalachicola	59	79
Cedar Key	61	83
Fort Myers	64	84
Naples	64	85
Panama City Beach	53	81
Pensacola	59	77
Sarasota	62	83
St. Petersburg	66	82
Tallahassee	56	79
Tampa	63	82

the forest floor, resulting in a forest floor with lots of plant species and grasses.

Flatwoods

Pine flatwoods (also called pine flats or pine barrens), on the other hand, are ubiquitous in Florida, historically covering almost half of the natural land area in the state. They are characterized by low, flat land, an open canopy of slash pine, and an understory dominated by palmetto prairie. Slash pine has historically been used to produce all kinds of commercial goods, from paper products to turpentine and household goods. Additionally, pine flatwoods provide important habitat for many wildlife species.

A **scrub** is a similar plant community—the same pine above with various shrubs and palmetto underneath—but scrubs are found in upland areas that are generally harsher and drier, with no organic matter in the soil. It's an austere habitat, but home to the threatened **gopher tortoises** and the endangered Florida **scrub jay.**

CLIMATE
Heat and Humidity

Florida is closer to the equator than any other continental U.S. state, on the southeastern tip of North America, with a humid subtropical climate and heavy rainfall April-November. Its humidity is attributed to the fact that no point in the state is more than 60 miles from saltwater and no more than 345 feet above sea level. If this thick steamy breath on the back of your neck is new to you, know that humidity is a measure of the amount of water vapor in the air. Most often you'll hear the percentage described in "relative humidity," which is the amount of water vapor actually in the air divided by the amount of water vapor the air can hold. The warmer the air becomes, the more moisture it can hold.

When heat and humidity combine to slow evaporation of sweat from the body, outdoor activity becomes dangerous even for those in good physical shape. Drink plenty of water to avoid dehydration and slow down if you feel fatigued or notice a headache, a high pulse rate, or shallow breathing. Overheating can cause serious and even life-threatening conditions such as heatstroke. The elderly, small children, the overweight, and those on certain medications are particularly vulnerable to heat stress.

During the summer months, expect temperatures to hover around 90°F and humidity to be near 100 percent. The most pleasant times of the year along the length of the Florida peninsula are December-April—not surprisingly, the busiest time for tourism. Along the Panhandle, however, where temperatures are more moderate in the summer and chillier in the winter, the summer sees more tourist action.

The common wisdom is that the hard freeze line in Florida bisects the state from Ocala to Jacksonville. North of that, freezing temperatures rarely last long, and south of that it's just an hour here or there under the freezing point (with serious damage to tropical plants in years when the temperature dips low). The best approach for packing in preparation for a visit to Florida is layering—with a sweater for overly air-conditioned interiors or chilly winds, and lots of loose wicking material for the heat.

Rain

It rains nearly every day in the summer along the Gulf Coast—and not just a sprinkle. Due to the abundance of warm moist air from the Gulf of Mexico and the hot tropical sun, conditions are perfect for the formation of thunderstorms. There are 80-90 thunderstorms each summer, generally less than 15 miles in diameter—but vertically they can grow up to 10 miles high in the atmosphere. These are huge localized thunderstorms that can drop four or more inches of rain in an hour, while just a few miles away it stays dry. The bulk of these tropical afternoon thunderstorms each summer are electrical storms.

Lightning

With sudden thunderstorms comes lightning, a serious threat along the Gulf Coast. About 50 people are struck by lightning each year in the state. Most of them are hospitalized and recover, but there are about 10 fatalities annually. Tampa is the "Lightning Capital" of the United States, with around 25 cloud-to-ground lightning bolt blasts on each square mile annually. The temperature of a single bolt can reach 50,000°F, about three times as hot as the sun's surface. There's not much you can do to ward off lightning except to avoid being in the wrong place at the wrong time. The summer months of June-September have the highest number of lightning-related injuries and deaths. Usually lightning occurs during daylight hours, with the highest concentration 3pm-4pm, when the afternoon storms peak. Lightning strikes usually occur either at the beginning or end of a storm, and can strike up to 10 miles away from the center of the storm. Keep your eye on approaching storms and seek shelter when you see lightning.

Locals use the 30-30 rule: Count the seconds after a lightning flash until you hear thunder. If that number is under 30, the storm is within six miles of you. Seek shelter. Then, at storm's end, wait 30 minutes after the last thunderclap before resuming outdoor activity.

HURRICANES

Hurricanes are violent tropical storms with sustained winds of at least 74 mph. Massive low-pressure systems, they blow counterclockwise around a relatively calm central area called the eye. They form over warm ocean waters, often starting as storms in the Caribbean or off the west coast of Africa. As they move westward, they are fueled by the warm water of the tropics. Warm moist air moves toward the center of the storm and spirals upward, releasing driving rains. Updrafts suck up more water vapor, which further strengthens the storm until it can be stopped only when contact is made with land or cooler water. In the average hurricane, just 1 percent of the energy released could meet the energy needs of the United States for a full year.

In Florida, the hurricane season is July-November, and the seasons can be really destructive, sometimes wreaking havoc on the Gulf Coast in rapid succession. These storms have been named since 1953. At first it was just female names, but since 1978 male names are also used. Really powerful hurricanes' names are retired, kind of like sports greats' jerseys.

Hurricane Safety

Monitor radio and TV broadcasts closely for

Hurricane Lingo

HURRICANE TERMS

- **Tropical depression:** an organized system of clouds and thunderstorms with a defined circulation and maximum sustained winds of 38 mph (33 knots) or less

- **Severe thunderstorm:** a thunderstorm with winds 58 mph (50 knots) or faster or hailstones 0.75 inches or larger in diameter

- **Tropical storm:** an organized system of strong thunderstorms with a defined circulation and maximum sustained winds of 39-73 mph (34-63 knots)

- **Hurricane:** a warm-core tropical cyclone with maximum sustained winds of 74 mph (64 knots) or greater

- **Eye:** the "calm" center of a hurricane with light winds and partly cloudy to clear skies, usually around 20 miles in diameter, but ranging 5-60 miles

- **Eye wall:** the location within a hurricane where the most damaging winds and intense rainfall are found

- **Tornadoes:** violent rotating columns of air that touch the ground; they are spawned by large severe thunderstorms and can have winds estimated at 100-300 mph (87-261 knots). A **tornado watch** means they're possible; a **tornado warning** means they're in your area.

HURRICANE WARNINGS

- **Tropical Storm Watch:** issued when tropical storm conditions may threaten a particular coastal area within 36 hours, when the storm is not predicted to intensify to hurricane strength

- **Tropical Storm Warning:** winds ranging 39-73 mph that can be expected to affect specific areas of a coastline within the next 24 hours

- **Hurricane Watch:** a hurricane or hurricane conditions may threaten a specific coastal area within 36 hours

- **Hurricane Warning:** a warning that sustained winds of 74 mph or higher associated with a hurricane are expected in a specified coastal area in 24 hours or less

HURRICANE SCALE

- **Category 1:** winds 74-95 mph with a storm surge of 4-5 feet and minimal damage

- **Category 2:** winds 96-110 mph with a storm surge of 6-8 feet and moderate damage

- **Category 3:** winds 111-130 mph with a storm surge of 9-12 feet and major damage

- **Category 4:** winds 131-155 mph with a storm surge of 13-18 feet and severe damage

- **Category 5:** winds 156 mph and over with more than an 18-foot storm surge and catastrophic damage

directions. Gas up the car, and make sure you have batteries, a water supply, candles, and food that can be eaten without the use of electricity. Get cash, have your prescriptions filled, and put all essential documents in a large resealable bag. In the event of an evacuation, find the closest shelter by listening to the radio or TV broadcasts. Pets are not allowed in most shelters. There are designated pet shelters, but all animals must be up to date on shots. Alternatively, an increasing number of hotels and motels accept animals for a nominal daily fee.

ENVIRONMENTAL ISSUES
Oil Spills

The *Deepwater Horizon* well off the coast of Louisiana exploded on April 20, 2010, killing 11 workers on the rig and began releasing oil into the Gulf of Mexico. When the well was finally plugged on July 15, it had released an estimated 53,000 barrels of oil a day into the Gulf. According to the Flow Rate Technical Group appointed by BP and the Coast Guard to estimate the extent of the spill, the total volume of oil released into the Gulf over the three months is believed to be at least 205.8 million gallons of crude oil. On September 19, the relief well was finally completed and the Coast Guard declared the well to be officially "dead."

What the oil spill has meant for the ecosystem in the Gulf of Mexico is still largely unknown, as the long-term effects of the largest oil spill in the Gulf are still being studied and documented.

On April 23, 2010, the U.S. Coast Guard began receiving reports that oil was washing up in wildlife refuges and the seafood grounds on the Louisiana coast. By June 21, fully 36 percent of federal waters in the Gulf were closed for fishing, totaling nearly 67,000 square miles and detrimentally impacting the fishing industry. The estimated impact of the oil spill's cost to the fishing industry along the Gulf Coast is over $2.5 billion. More than 8,000 species that inhabit the area were impacted by the oil spill, including 1,200 fish, 200 bird, 1,400 mollusk, 1,500 crustacean, 4 sea turtle, and 29 marine mammal species. According to the 2011 U.S. Fish and Wildlife "Deepwater Horizon Fish and Wildlife Collection Report," 6,918 dead animals had been collected, including 6,147 birds, 613 sea turtles, and 157 dolphins and other mammals.

More than 1.8 million gallons of chemical dispersants were released into the Gulf of Mexico directly at the wellhead source in an effort to break up the oil before it reached the surface. Robert Diaz, a marine biologist at the College of William and Mary, recently said, "The dispersants definitely don't make oil disappear. They take it from one area in an ecosystem and put it in another." University of South Florida researchers are finding that the dispersed oil is having a toxic effect on the Gulf's phytoplankton and bacteria—the microscopic plants that make up the basis of the food chain. The federal Environmental Protection Agency and the National Oceanic and Atmospheric Administration have openly stated that they support the claim that dispersed oil is no less toxic than the oil alone. However, recently reports have contradicted this and claimed that the Corexit dispersants made the oil spill more than 52 times more toxic.

Other Environmental Issues

There are many complex and far-reaching environmental issues in Florida, from declining amphibian populations to an abundance of Superfund sites, paper mill water contamination, saltwater intrusion in the Everglades and other areas, and the quickly disappearing Florida panther population. Millions of acres have been bulldozed to make way for strip malls, condo developments, and all those beautiful golf courses and theme parks. It's the same story that is told of many recently developed natural settings.

Recent drought in Georgia has meant that the U.S. Army Corps of Engineers has repeatedly withheld water to accommodate the needs of greater Atlanta; the Corps uses the Buford Dam to regulate water flow from Lake Lanier, which feeds freshwater into the Apalachicola River and eventually into Apalachicola Bay. Downstream along the Apalachicola River and Apalachicola Bay, the resulting salinity (less freshwater in an estuary means a greater percentage of saltwater) may mean the end of the state's oyster industry, not to mention the destruction of endangered species like Florida sturgeon and several kinds of mussels.

Still, the state's commitment to the environment elevates the situation from hopeless. There's been an enormous grassroots effort in

the past decade in Florida, which has moved into the mainstream after the BP oil spill, of regular people who have stood up against offshore drilling and supported the protection of the abundant and beautiful natural resources that are so directly tied to the quality of life and economy of everyone in the state. If their efforts are successful, the state's natural treasures, as well as its fishing and tourism industries, which make up such a large portion of the Gulf Coast's economy, might be preserved, restored, and possibly even strengthened.

Plants and Animals

The abundance of sunlight and rain and the near absence of the four traditional seasons allow for the successful growth of nearly 4,000 plant species and nearly that many animals in Florida. The lower Gulf Coast's palms, the great cypress swamps, mangroves, and on the Panhandle one of the greatest forested regions in the East—Florida's plantlife is richly diverse, providing a range of habitats. Even nonnative plants and animals flourish in these lush conditions, a fact that troubles Floridian scientists as more invasive species take hold. The trade in exotic pets and plants, as well as the movement of huge numbers of people and vehicles, can bring new species into Florida, devastating native species and invading natural areas.

PLANTS

On March 27, 1513, Easter Day, Ponce de León landed on the coast of Florida and pronounced it a "land of flowers." And it's true, mostly. The subtropical climate is warm, moist, and lush, with the kind of foliage in the summer for which you don't need a stop-action film in order to document growth. There are plants that grow like Audrey II in *Little Shop of Horrors:* fast, loose, and weird. The even greater thing is that many native Floridian and even flourishing nonnative plants have huge advocates and devotees.

Avid clubs are devoted to carnivorous plants, to orchids, to bromeliads, to palms (which are really not trees—despite the fact that the state "tree" is the cabbage palm). It's a gardener's state, but there's a certain humility gardeners bring to the table. It's not generally a state for regimented topiary or manicured rose gardens. Serendipity, chance, and nature's whim play a part in Florida gardening. So much is given, but, as recent hurricane seasons have shown, so much can be taken away.

Trees

Palm trees are practically a Florida cliché. Also known as cabbage palm and palmetto, it's from the **sabal palm** that hearts of palm are harvested. Sabal palm grows in all conditions in the state—wet, dry, coastal, swampy—and it is from the fronds of the sabal that the Seminole people built watertight chickee roofs. In some parts of the Gulf Coast, you'll encounter **royal palm,** identified by its towering 80-foot pale-gray trunk and bright glossy crown shaft. Many of the other palm species associated with Florida are not native—the easily recognized **coconut palm,** the heavy-trunked **Canary Island date palm,** and the slim statuesque **red latan palm.** You'll see them all along the Gulf Coast, but it's what they're in contrast to that gives this subtropical landscaping its own flavor.

Mangroves are often called walking trees because they hover above the water, their arching prop roots resembling so many spindly legs. Seeds sprout on the parent tree and drop off, bobbing in the water until they lodge on an oyster bar or a snag in the shallows. There, the seed begins to grow to a tree, the foundation of a new tiny island. Around its roots, sediment and debris build up to create a

1: hurricane debris from 2018 2: an oil rig near Fort Morgan on the Alabama Gulf Coast

thick layer of peat upon which other plant species begin to grow. This first tree drops more seed tubules, which get stuck in the mulchy ground and create more trees. This is how islands are often created off the Gulf Coast.

There are three types of mangrove along the Gulf: The red mangrove forms a wide band of trees on the outermost part of each mangrove island, facing the open sea. The red mangrove encircles the black mangrove, which in turn encircles the white mangrove at the highest, driest part of each mangrove island. Mangroves are protected by federal, state, and local laws.

Cypress is another oh-so-Florida tree. Forested wetlands in the state are often dominated by cypress trees, located along stream banks and riverbanks or in ponds with slow-moving water. Bald cypresses (they aren't always bald, they just lose their leaves in winter) are the largest trees in North America east of the Rockies. They can live for hundreds of years, quietly ruminating with their roots in water, their "knees" protruding above the soil and waterline. The function of these knees, part of the root system that projects out of the water, isn't fully known, other than that they provide stability and more air for the base of these flood-tolerant trees. The Gulf Coast offers several cypress swamps to explore.

Live oaks are certainly not the sole custody of Florida. Throughout the South these huge semideciduous trees loom, gnarled and woebegone, draped with Spanish moss (which is neither Spanish nor a moss). The Tallahassee area is especially dense with live oaks, but you'll see them all over.

The **gumbo limbo,** native to North America, is common down toward the Everglades. They call it the sunburn tree, as its smooth bark peels off in sheets to reveal a red trunk color beneath. I love these trees, and I love saying their name even more.

Sawgrass

Also a defining feature of the Everglades, sawgrass looks like smooth, soft hay. It dominates wide swaths of marshland in this area, known as "The River of Grass," but sawgrass blades have little sawlike teeth along one side that make walking through it painful.

Epiphytes

Epi means "on" and *phyte* means "plant." Thus, an epiphyte is a plant that grows on another plant. They're sometimes called air plants because they grow above ground, in the air, roots wiggling in the breeze. Host plants support them high off the ground, where they don't need to compete for light and rainwater, and where they don't have to cope with floodwater and marauding animals. Epiphytes generally do no harm to the host plant and get their nutrients from their own photosynthesis and their own water from runoff on their host. Cardinal airplant and resurrection fern are wonderful plants to explore.

Within this category, **orchids** are probably the best known, with more genera than any other plant. They are among the most exotic and delicate flowers in the world, holding a special fascination for collectors, photographers, and hobbyists. Orchids abound in the Everglades' hardwood hammocks, marshes, pineland, and prairies. To see thousands of orchid species, visit the Marie Selby Botanical Gardens in Sarasota.

Bromeliads are another type of epiphyte, members of the pineapple family. They use shallow roots only to anchor themselves to a tree or the ground and absorb through their leaves the water and nutrients they need from the air and from the rain. These leathery, brightly colored tropical plants often collect water in little "tanks" or between their leaves. Of Florida's 16 species of native bromeliads, 13 are not found elsewhere in the United States.

Crops

The citrus fruit industry has been big business

1: oak tree and spanish moss on Orange Beach 2: a gopher tortoise on Cabbage Key 3: an orchid at Marie Selby Botanical Gardens

Gators!

In his excellent memoir, *Totch, A Life in the Everglades*, Totch Brown describes a gator's sounds:

> Gators make three different sounds. One is the "grunt" used by young gators in distress to call their mothers. When you pick up a baby gator it'll start grunting every time. The mother will come to this sound right away. (With practice, you can imitate this "grunt" and often fool a grown gator into coming to you.)
> Then there's a blowing sound gators make when they're more or less hemmed up, or cornered and are good and mad.
> The third sound is the gator bellow—a bloodcurdling sound that can be heard for miles across the Everglades. When one gator bellows, usually another will answer.... When a 12-foot gator bellows, he raises his head up as high as possible, his mouth wide open, and with a full breath, lets out his air. It's a sight to be seen! The bellowing is generally in mating season, the late spring, when the rains are about to start. The gators seem to be asking Mother Nature for a drink of water.

I've seen a gator bellow with his head tipped way back. To me he didn't seem like he was asking anybody for anything other than to buzz off. It's a noise that has the same kind of effect as your first viewing of *Jaws*.

Alligators were first listed as an endangered species in 1967, their numbers threatened by hunting and habitat loss. Then the American alligator was removed from the endangered species list in 1987 after the U.S. Fish and Wildlife Service pronounced a complete recovery of the species. Conservative estimates put the population at over one million in Florida, Louisiana, Texas, and Georgia. Because they can tolerate brackish water as well as freshwater, they can be found in rivers, swamps, bogs, lakes, ponds, creeks, canals, swimming pools, and lots of Florida golf courses.

The American alligator is the largest reptile in North America (distinguished from the American crocodile by its short, rounded snout and black color). They can live 35-50 years in the wild, 60-80

in the state since the 1890s when Chinese horticulturist Lue Gim Gong introduced a new variety of **orange** and a hardier **grapefruit.** Today, citrus is Florida's leading cash crop, with the state producing 90 percent of the country's orange juice (almost all Florida oranges are juiced, not sold whole). Florida is second only to Brazil in orange juice production, and it is the world leader in grapefruit production.

There are about 750,000 acres of citrus groves in the state and more than 100 million citrus trees, mostly in the lower two-thirds of the state. There are about 40 citrus packinghouses and 20 citrus processing plants in Florida. It is estimated that the growing, packing, processing, and selling of citrus generates a $9 billion per year impact on Florida's economy—not surprisingly, the orange blossom is the state flower. Recent cold snaps that devastate the season's yield have posed a major

threat to this Florida industry and the estimated 76,000 jobs in the citrus industry or related businesses.

Beyond citrus, Florida is the "winter salad bowl," providing 80 percent of the fresh vegetables grown in the United States January-March. The Gulf Coast is responsible for lots of tomatoes, peppers, and strawberries—Plant City near Tampa is the state's strawberry capital. There are also exotic tropical fruits and vegetables grown along the Gulf Coast, from smooth-skinned avocados the size of softballs to mangoes (Lee County), guavas, lychees, sapotes, cherimoyas, and others.

ANIMALS
Fish

No other state in the United States and few other countries boast a more varied marine environment. Florida has hundreds of

years in captivity. The average adult male is 13 feet in length (half of the length taken up by the tail), although they can grow up to 18 feet long. Bulls are generally larger than females, weighing 450-600 pounds.

Alligators are cold-blooded. It's a good survival tactic because they don't need to eat as much or as often as their warm-blooded counterparts. In fact, they can't eat unless their internal body temperature is 90 degrees. Thus, they don't eat all winter, and in the spring can be seen in the midmorning basking on the banks in a sunny spot. They're hungry and ready to mate in April-May—a good time to steer especially clear. In the summer the females lay their eggs in a nest (up to 70 eggs) and cover them, then the eggs incubate for 65 days. (As a cool aside, alligators lack sexual chromosomes, so that sex is determined by the temperature at which eggs incubate. Between 90 and 93 degrees, they're all male; between 87 and 89 degrees, they're female.) The mom stays close, carrying the freshly hatched babies to the water. Even

a gator in the Everglades

after they're swimming around, mama is protective for up to the first two years (supposedly she can hear their cry for help up to a mile away). Still, only 1 in 10 alligators survives through the first year.

Alligators are everywhere in Florida, and they eat just about anything. Usually that means lizards, fish, snakes, turtles, even little gators, but they'll also enjoy corgi and terrier if you don't keep your pup on a short leash.

species of fish crowding its waters. There's the Atlantic and the fertile Gulf of Mexico with its hundreds of bays, sounds, inlets, and brackish marshes. But there are also freshwater rivers, lakes, estuaries, and numerous other marine environments.

The **Panhandle** has long stretches of white-sand beaches and ocean that quickly drops off to deep water—boaters in 70 feet of water can often see bathers on the beach. The area is also home to bountiful estuaries (where rivers meet the sea) tucked behind long narrow barrier islands.

From **Apalachicola** to the **Big Bend,** estuaries are protected by oyster bars and rocky islands. Here the water depths drop off gradually. Off the Suwannee River and St. Marks Light, ordinary outboard motorboats can run aground more than three miles from shore. This area has few beaches and is dominated by marshes with vast sea grass beds. Farther south along the Gulf, anglers enjoy a number of exciting species, from huge **tarpon** to tasty **grouper, cobia,** and the fabled **snook.**

In much of this area, freshwater fishing is most productive in the spring, while sportfishing is good all year. But you need a license. An annual nonresident saltwater or freshwater fishing license is $47, a seven-day license is $30, and a three-day license is $17. You need to figure out what you're fishing for before you purchase your license, but either way the revenue goes to the Florida Fish and Wildlife Conservation Commission.

There are also numerous shellfish species: **scallops** in Steinhatchee, **oysters** in Apalachicola, **stone crabs** in Everglades City, **clams** in Cedar Key, and delicious **Florida blue crabs** all over the state.

Birds

With 500 bird species, both those native to the state and those that migrate here, the Gulf Coast is a bird lover's paradise in a range of habitats. Mangrove estuaries are home to many species of **egrets, herons,** and numerous other **wading birds. Waterbirds** occupy interior wetlands, and countless **shorebirds, terns,** and **gulls** populate the white-sand beaches. Unique to the state, the **Florida scrub jay** lives in a small patch of scrub-oak habitat; **ospreys** and **bald eagles** make their large nests all along the Gulf Coast. In the woods you can find **red-shouldered hawks** and endangered **red cockaded woodpeckers.** In backyard ponds you'll see the long, sinuous neck of the **anhinga**— what Native Americans called "snakebirds"— standing in a confident-looking stance with their wings stretched out to dry after a dive for fish. You'll spot **white pelicans,** the second-largest flying bird in North America, sailing low over the Gulf waters, while high above a **frigate** is barely a speck. Your hair might stand on end when you hear the nagging cry of a **little blue heron,** and you may be startled by the trilling call of the enormous **sandhill cranes** that stroll around in small family groups of three.

It's serious birding country, with loads of expert birders to lead you through the prime birding spots. There are numerous birding festivals along the Gulf Coast, and the **Great Florida Birding Trail** (www.floridabirdingtrail.com) for when you want to get out into the wilderness alone.

Large Mammals

After the alligator, the **West Indian manatee** is the Florida Gulf Coast's most famous animal. A manatee is a large, gray aquatic mammal with a body that tapers to a flat, paddle-shaped, beaver-like tail. Completely herbivorous, they are gentle and slow moving, found in shallow rivers, estuaries, saltwater bays, canals, and coastal areas. Manatees are migratory and are concentrated in the warm Florida waterways in the winter.

Most of their time is spent traveling, resting, and eating—they can consume 10-15 percent of their body weight daily in vegetation (a lot, since adult males weigh 800-1,200 pounds). They have no known predators, but habitat destruction and collisions with watercraft propellers have kept this species on the endangered list. There are an estimated 3,500 West Indian manatees left in the United States, many of them convened along the Nature Coast in Homosassa and Crystal River in the winter. Manatees are protected under federal law, and the Florida Manatee Sanctuary Act of 1978 states: "It is unlawful for any person, at any time, intentionally or negligently, to annoy, molest, harass, or disturb any manatee." It's a steep fine and imprisonment, so look but don't touch these guys. In many waterways on the Gulf Coast there are reduced boat speed zones for manatee protection.

Another locally protected animal is the **Florida panther.** They're called Florida panthers, but really they once roamed throughout the Southeast from east Texas to the Atlantic and north to parts of Tennessee. Overhunting, loss of habitat, and reduction of their primary prey reduced their population to just a handful living in southern Florida in pinelands and mixed swamp forests. Fewer than 100 remain in Florida, making them one of the rarest and most endangered mammals in the world. A subspecies of cougar that has adapted to the subtropical environment of Florida, they are still to be found occasionally in Fakahatchee Strand State Preserve and Big Cypress National Preserve, where there is a 26,605-acre **Florida Panther National Wildlife Refuge.** The Florida Fish and Wildlife Conservation Commission monitors panther activity using radio telemetry collars. Florida panthers are tawny and brown with cream or white undersides; adult males average 130-160 pounds with an average length of 6-8 feet.

Cattle were first introduced to North America in 1521, when Ponce de León landed on the Gulf Coast. He brought a small herd of Andalusian cattle, the descendants of which might be the foundation stock of Florida's

piney-woods cattle. Spanish missions had herds of cattle, and the Native Americans learned to raise cattle from the Spanish. British and Creek invasions of Spanish Florida in 1702 and 1704 destroyed the Spanish herds, but the Seminole people kept their own herds intact. During the English occupation of Florida, the British brought their own longhorn and short-horn cattle, which eventually bred with the surviving Andalusians, resulting in a tough, compact cow weighing a scant 600 pounds. A speckled brindle pattern, sharp horns, and a cranky disposition still define the Florida piney-woods cow. Cows used to roam the state freely, branded or earmarked for owner iden-tification. In order to round them up, Florida ranch hands would crack long whips to get them moving. Some people say this is why rural Floridians are called Crackers.

Reptiles and Amphibians

There are so many exciting wild animals in Florida, from alligators to roseate spoonbills, that the little everyday animals often get short shrift. The Gulf Coast is lizard central, with several species duking it out for dominance. The **Cuban knight anole** was introduced into Florida in the 1950s. These and the **brown anole** are hardy and aggressive (although not in any way harmful to humans), and they have displaced the native **green anole** along the Gulf Coast. The green anole is still the top liz-ard species in the state's interior.

Turtles are also plentiful in Florida, with 26 different species. Of the species that pre-fer dry land, there is the **Florida box turtle** common to upland scrub and marshes. They can live up to 100 years but are now protected and uncommon. The **gopher tortoise** you'll see in upland scrub areas. They are protected but occur throughout the state. **Florida snapping turtles** can get up to 70 pounds and are common throughout the state, whereas **alligator snapping turtles** are only found along the Panhandle. Both have powerful jaws that could snap a finger in half. The **Florida soft shell turtle** can be found throughout the state; it has a rubbery

shell to allow it to bury itself in the sand as well as swim fast. The **Florida cooter** lives in large ponds, canals, slow-moving rivers, and lakes—it's historically a delicacy among Floridians, and occasionally you'll still find it on menus on the Gulf Coast.

Over 33 species of frogs inhabit the state of Florida, from the exotic **giant marine toad** once imported to control cane beetles to the ubiquitous **Cuban tree frog,** which has dis-placed many local frog species and has a pretty noxious skin toxin—as well as a number of snakes. The snake that seems to worry everyone is the **Florida cottonmouth**—almost always near water, reaching up to six feet, and highly venomous. You'll often encounter them sun-ning themselves on semisubmerged logs along southern Gulf Coast rivers, whereas Florida's **eastern diamondback,** the largest and most dangerous local snake, is more common in pal-metto flatlands and pine woods. **Black racers** are much more common, most of them fairly small despite their potential to grow to six feet. Common in many Florida gardens, they're nonvenomous but can still bite if cornered.

Spiders and Insects

There are loads of big spiders in Florida too. One of the coolest is the large **golden silk spider** common to wooded areas or groves, but there are also excellent brightly colored **jumping spiders** that don't build webs but instead hunt for their prey and pounce on the unsuspecting. The **black and yellow argiope spider** is another distinctive and fairly common Gulf Coast species—they build big webs with zipper-like zigzag bands of silk at the center.

There are two species of **fire ants** in Florida, the red imported fire ant and the tropical or native fire ant. Either way, their sting is a nasty shock. They form loose, sandy mounds on the ground, and when perturbed, they swarm out of their house to bite you, leaving raised white or red welts that hurt and itch for days. Be aware of where you're stand-ing while visiting Florida, and avoid mounds of loose dirt at all costs.

History

THE GULF COAST'S NATIVE AMERICANS

Twenty-seven thousand years ago, small groups of primitive hunters crossed the Bering Strait from Asia to the Americas. Generation after generation traveled southward until these hunters arrived in what is now Florida—perhaps one of the last places in continental North America to be inhabited by humans. A warm and mild climate, with waters teeming with fish, Florida was a hospitable home for early nomadic Paleo-Indians (circa 12,000-7500 BC). They built small huts of animal fur and lived off the land's bounty, fishing the bays and streams. Between 1000 BC and AD 1500, they developed advanced tools and pottery-making skills. By 1500, Florida's peoples were divided into large groupings, most ethnologically and linguistically related to the Creek family. Each grouping was divided further into small independent villages. Estimates put the total numbers of Native Americans in Florida at 100,000 at that time.

In northwest Florida the **Apalachee people** of the Tallahassee Hills, between the Suwannee and Apalachicola Rivers, and the **Timucua people,** their dominion in the center of the Florida peninsula, between the Aucilla River and the Atlantic and as far south as Tampa Bay, brought farming skills to the area. They cultivated squash, beans, and corn, hunting to supplement their meals with meat. Highly organized and hierarchical nations, they lived in great communal houses and had an absolute ruler (who was assisted by a shaman and a council of noblemen) and a delineated social order. They also built elaborate burial and temple mounds, the ruins of which can still be seen.

Along the southwest Gulf Coast the **Calusa people** dominated, feared because of their fierceness. They were tall, with long flowing hair and simple garb consisting only of breechclouts of tanned deerskin. They were not farmers, living instead off the bounty of the local waters and the wealth of the nearby woods. Forty Calusa villages spread along the Florida Gulf Coast, with Mound Key near the mouth of the Caloosahatchee River the largest village. They had only primitive tools, but the Calusa built huge mounds of shell and deep moats to protect their villages of raised thatch-roofed huts. They practiced sacrificial worship and exhibited little interest in the Spaniards' missionary overtures.

Franciscan friars fared better in bringing Roman Catholicism to the Timucua and the Apalachee, just as the Spanish soldiers were granted permission to steal from the indigenous people. The missionaries taught the converts to read and write, and they became more like Spaniards, leaving their villages to build houses in St. Augustine or carrying corn along the Camino Real connecting St. Augustine with the Tallahassee area.

Both nations lost large numbers to diseases brought by the Spaniards, and then more to the British who tried to raid the Spanish missions and gain control of Florida. The British brought the Yamasee people from South Carolina, and together they destroyed the mission buildings and enslaved many of the indigenous people. In 1763, when the Spanish ceded Florida to the British, the Spanish departed the fort at St. Augustine and took the remaining indigenous people to Cuba. While the Calusa were less amenable to coexisting peacefully with the Spanish, they met the same fate, dying out in the late 1700s. Enemy nations from Georgia and South Carolina began raiding Calusa territory; some Calusa people were captured and enslaved, and the rest likely died of introduced diseases such as smallpox and measles.

The **Seminole people** were originally of Creek stock, hailing from Georgia and Alabama. They moved into Florida during the mid-1700s, occupying the space indigenous

Floridians had left behind. They too ended up being annihilated by disease and the Spanish, British, and American settlers. Their refusal to withdraw to reservations resulted in the Seminole Wars of 1835-1842. By the end of the war, 4,420 Seminoles had surrendered and were deported to the West. Another 300, however, defied every effort of the U.S. government, retreating to the backwoods of the Everglades to hide out. Many of their descendants occupy the area to this day. According to 2000 census data, 581 tribes, bands, and groups are represented in the state's Native American population of 117,880.

In recent years the Seminole Nation, headquartered in Hollywood, Florida, has assumed a higher profile, with more noncontiguous reservations than any Native American nation and lucrative gaming casinos getting larger by the year.

SPANISH EXPLORATION

The southernmost state in the United States, Florida was named in 1513 by **Ponce de León,** clearly taken with the lush tropical wilderness when he visited. This expedition, the first documented presence of Europeans on what is now the U.S. mainland, was ostensibly "to discover and people the island of Bimini." On the return voyage he rounded the Dry Tortugas to explore the Gulf of Mexico, entering Charlotte Harbor. He soon realized that Florida was more than a large island. Near Mound Key he encountered the Calusa people, and while on Estero Island repairing his ship he narrowly escaped capture. Eight years later he returned and headed to the Calusa territory with 500 of his men, aiming to establish a permanent colony in Florida. In an ensuing battle with the Calusa, Ponce de León was pierced in the thigh by an arrow and carried back to his ship. He never returned.

Many of the subsequent explorers' missions were less high-profile. In 1516, **Diego Miruelo** mapped Pensacola Bay. In 1517, **Alonso Álvarez de Pineda** went the length of the Florida shore to the Mississippi River, confirming Ponce de León's assertion that Florida was not an island. In 1520, **Lucas Vázquez de Ayllón** mapped the Carolina coast (which at the time Spain claimed in the vast region they called "Florida").

Pánfilo de Narváez was a veteran Caribbean soldier, hired by Spanish authorities in 1520 to overthrow Hernán Cortés's tyrannical rule. After a lengthy imprisonment by Cortés, Narváez went back to Spain and obtained a grant to colonize the Gulf Coast from northern Mexico to Florida. Together with **Cabeza de Vaca,** an armada of five ships, and 400 soldiers, Narváez landed north of the mouth of Tampa Bay in 1527. Spanish-Native American relations deteriorated quickly during this period; the Spaniards' ruthless hunt for gold and riches met with violence on the part of the locals.

Narváez ordered his ships back to Cuba, while a band of men headed northward to the Panhandle in search of gold. Empty-handed, Narváez finally returned to the Gulf at St. Marks. Assuming Mexico to be only a few days' journey to the west, Narváez had five long canoes constructed, which capsized in a storm off the coast of Texas. Narváez drowned, and only Cabeza de Vaca and four others survived. This little band traveled 6,000 miles and in 1536 reached Mexico City to report on their ill-fated mission.

SPANISH, FRENCH, AND ENGLISH COLONIZATION

Then came **Hernando de Soto.** In spring 1539 he sailed for Tampa Bay with seven vessels, 600 soldiers, three Jesuit friars, and several dozen civilians with the intent of starting a settlement. Where he went exactly is a topic of much debate: Some say he landed in Manatee County; others believe it was in Charlotte Harbor. Like many of the conquistadores before him, De Soto was attracted to the stories of Native American riches to the north, so he sent his fleet back to Cuba, left only a rudimentary base camp on the Manatee River, and set off inland from the coast. He and his group never found what they sought, moving ever northward into Georgia, South

Famous Names in Florida History

- **Pedro Menéndez de Avilés:** founder of St. Augustine
- **William Pope du Val:** first territorial governor
- **Osceola:** Seminole leader
- **David Levy Yulee:** one of Florida's initial U.S. senators and first Jewish American senator
- **Henry B. Plant:** famed Gulf Coast railroad baron of the late 19th century
- **Henry Flagler:** builder of the East Coast Railway, which connected the whole East Coast of Florida
- **Hamilton Disston:** bought four million acres in central Florida and created a canal system
- **Thomas Edison and Henry Ford:** inventors (both only lived here part-time, but they left a big mark)
- **John Ringling:** circus entrepreneur
- **Barron Collier:** southwest Florida landowner and builder of Tamiami Trail
- **A. Philip Randolph:** labor leader

Carolina, Tennessee, Alabama, Mississippi, and Arkansas, where De Soto died of fever.

There were religious missions to the state during the same time—Dominican priest **Luis Cancer,** three additional missionaries, and a Christianized indigenous woman named Magdalene arrived on the beaches outside Tampa Bay in 1549. Given the Native Americans' experience with outsiders, it's no wonder that Cancer was quickly surrounded and clubbed to death. The survivors in his party promptly sailed back to Mexico.

In 1559, the viceroy of Mexico decided a settlement on the Gulf was essential to help shipwrecked sailors and to discourage French trading visits. He hired **Tristán de Luna** to establish this colony. With 1,500 soldiers and 13 ships, De Luna landed at Pensacola Bay. He sent a party to scout out the interior and decided to wait until they returned to unload the supplies from the ship. This proved to be a disastrous move. The scouting party returned after three weeks, only finding one Native American village. But before De Luna and his men could unload the supplies from their ships, a powerful hurricane swept

through on September 19, 1559, and destroyed five of their ships and most of their cargo. The party moved inland to an abandoned Native American village, but their dwindled supplies kept the settlers on the brink of starvation through the winter and spring. In summer 1560, the party moved upriver into what is now north Georgia, where they remained until returning to Pensacola Bay in November 1560. Eventually De Luna was replaced with a new governor in April 1561, but De Luna's impact and legacy as one of the early explorers of the Florida Panhandle remains to this day. (As an aside, in 1992 the Florida Bureau of Archaeological Research found the remains of a colonial Spanish ship in Pensacola Bay that might have been one of De Luna's sunken ships.) Shortly after De Luna's expedition, King Philip II of Spain announced that Spain was no longer interested in promoting colonial expeditions to Florida.

French Protestant Huguenots prepared to challenge Spain's sovereignty in Florida, which ended in failure. **Jean Ribault,** France's most lauded seafarer of the time, set sail for Florida in April 1562, establishing a colony at Port

Royal, South Carolina, that year. It didn't work out, and somehow on his return to Europe, England's Queen Elizabeth had him arrested for establishing a French colony in Spanish territory. Spaniard **Pedro Menéndez de Avilés,** a much-celebrated naval commander, took up where Ribault left off, establishing what is thought of as the first European settlement, in St. Augustine, Florida, in 1565.

The history of Florida during the first Spanish administration (1565-1763) centers along the east coast and St. Augustine. The English neighbors to the north periodically attempted to capture the Florida territory (Governor Moore of South Carolina made an unsuccessful attempt in 1702, and Governor Oglethorpe of Georgia invaded Florida in 1740), and in 1763 Spain ceded Florida to Britain. The British in turn did an equally incomplete job of populating the country and developing its resources, especially in light of the increasingly aggressive Native Americans. The British controlled Florida 1763-1781, at which point the Spanish occupied it again 1783-1821. But in 1821 the Spanish government ratified a treaty turning Florida over to the United States.

STATEHOOD, CIVIL WAR, AND RECONSTRUCTION

After the signing of the Adams-Onis treaty ceding Florida to the United States in 1821, Andrew Jackson was appointed military governor of the territory. Florida's present boundaries were established, with Tallahassee as the new capital and William P. Duval as its first territorial governor. It was an agriculture economy, with settlers expanding ever southward and crowding out the Seminole people. Florida was admitted to the Union in 1845, the 27th state. After Abraham Lincoln's election to the presidency in 1860, Florida seceded from the Union in 1861 and joined the Confederacy. Florida furnished salt, cattle, and other goods to the Confederate army. Relative to population size, Florida furnished more troops than any other Confederate state, participating in the campaigns of Tennessee and Virginia. Florida was represented in the higher ranks

of the Confederate service by major generals Loring, Anderson, and Smith, and brigadier generals Brevard, Bullock, Finegan, Miller, Davis, Finley, Perry, and Shoup. Florida was represented in the Confederate cabinet by Stephen H. Mallory, Secretary of the Navy. The most notable Civil War engagement fought in Florida was the February 20, 1864, Battle of Olustee, a Confederate victory.

After the war, a new constitution was adopted, the Fourteenth Amendment ratified, and Florida was readmitted into the Union in 1868. It took a decade or so for the state to establish social, educational, and industrial health. The state's general level of poverty led to four million acres of land being sold to speculative real-estate promoters in 1881. The discovery of rich phosphate deposits in 1889 improved the state's economy, as did its increasing popularity as a winter resort destination.

FLORIDA'S FIRST BOOM

Along with the phosphate mining in the southwestern part of the state, agriculture (especially citrus) and cattle ranching brought wealth to Florida, as did wealthy tourists who came to relax in the state's natural beauty and mild climate each winter. In the 1870s, steamboat tours on Florida's winding rivers were a popular attraction. Sponge diving around Tarpon Springs, cigar-making around Tampa—industry was booming in the later part of the 19th century even along the less-populated Gulf Coast.

The boom had its roots in the railroad and in road construction, industries that blossomed as a result of the state legislature's passage of the Internal Improvement Act in 1855. It offered cheap or free public land to investors, particularly those interested in transportation. On Florida's east coast, **Henry Flagler** was responsible for the Florida East Coast Railway, completed in 1912 and linking Key West all the way up the eastern coast of Florida. After making his money with Standard Oil, in retirement he realized that the key to developing the state of Florida was to establish an extensive transportation system. Arguably his biggest contribution was converting all of the small railroad lines he purchased to a standard gauge, allowing trains to travel the whole length.

On the Gulf Coast

Another Henry worked his magic on the other coast of Florida: **Henry B. Plant** was largely responsible for the first boom period along the Gulf, using his railroad to open vast but previously inaccessible parts of the state. Henry Plant's rails extended south from Jacksonville along the St. Johns River to Sanford then southwest through Orlando to Tampa. The Plant Investment Company bought up several small railroads with the aim of providing continuous service across the state, his holdings eventually including 2,100 miles of track, several steamship lines at the port of Tampa, and a number of important hotels. The University of Tampa now occupies the lavish hotel Plant built at the terminus of his line. This new rail line not only provided passengers with easy access but also gave citrus growers quick routes to get their produce to market.

Around the same time, in 1911, **Barron Gift Collier** visited Useppa Island off the Fort Myers coast and fell in love with the subtropical landscape. Over the next decade he bought up more than a million acres of southwest Florida, making himself the largest landowner in the state. His holdings stretched from the Ten Thousand Islands northward to Useppa Island and inland from Naples into the Everglades and Big Cypress. He invested millions of dollars to convert this vast wilderness into agricultural land and a vacation paradise. His real gift, however, was his completion of the state's Tamiami Trail, a road that still exists today, linking Tampa with Miami. In gratitude, the state created Collier County in his honor in 1923, with Everglades City as the county seat.

The Roaring '20s were good to Florida. With more Americans owning cars, it became hip to visit the Sunshine State on vacation. Land speculators bought up everything, with parcels being sold and resold for ever-increasing amounts of money. Great effort was expended to drain the Everglades and Florida swampland to create even more viable land for homes and agriculture. The land frenzy reached its peak after World War I in 1925, but a swift bust followed the next year due to a major hurricane, then another one in 1928, and then the Great Depression.

CUBAN REVOLUTION

Ninety miles south of Key West, Cuba has always been closely connected with the affairs of Florida, and vice versa. Under Spanish rule in the late 1800s, Cuban relations with Spain deteriorated, and in 1868 the two countries went to war, with 200,000 Cuban and Spanish casualties. In 1898, the Spanish-American War focused the country's attention on the Gulf Coast city of Tampa, the primary staging area for U.S. troops preparing for the war in Cuba.

During the war, many prominent Cubans fled to Key West, including Vicente Martinez Ybor, who opened a cigar factory, the El Principe de Gales, in Key West in 1869. He eventually relocated the factory to a scrub area east of Tampa in 1886, once Henry B. Plant had completed rail service to aid in shipping and importation. This first factory begat a huge cigar industry in Tampa, with 200 factories at its peak.

The war lasted only a few months after U.S. involvement. Cuba was relinquished to the United States in trust for its inhabitants by the signing of the Treaty of Paris on December 20, 1898. Spanish rule ended January 1, 1899, and U.S. military rule ended May 20, 1902.

Cuban history after that continued to be fractious: Tomás Estrada Palma was the first president of the new republic, but he was ousted in 1906. Again, a provisional American government ruled, then withdrew in 1909. There was a period of prosperity, another revolt, and then General Gerardo Machado was elected president in 1925 and reelected in 1928. During his second term, he suspended the freedoms of speech, press, and assembly, and was forced to flee the country in 1933.

Colonel Fulgencio Batista y Zaldívar, who controlled the army, was elected president in 1940. During his term, Cuba entered World War II on the side of the Allies. Batista was defeated in 1944 by Grau San Martín, and then in 1948 Carlos Prío Socarrás was elected president—but he was overthrown by Batista in 1952. Mayhem ensued, but Batista wasn't taking no for an answer. There continued to be strong anti-Batista resistance, and in 1959 Batista resigned and fled the country. Fidel Castro set up a provisional government with himself as premier. Political refugees from the Cuban revolution poured into Florida by the thousands.

Not long after came the Cuban Missile Crisis of October 1962, precipitated by the Soviets installing nuclear missiles in Cuba. Soviet field commanders in Cuba were authorized to use tactical nuclear weapons unless President John F. Kennedy and Premier Nikita Khrushchev could reach an understanding.

In 1980, more than 100,000 Cuban refugees came to the United States, mostly through Florida, when Castro briefly opened the port of Mariel to a flotilla of privately chartered U.S. ships, and in the early 1990s Florida received refugees from the military coup in Haiti and another wave of refugees from Cuba in 1994. Many of the Cuban expatriates live in Miami and environs, less so on the Gulf Coast. Still, the Cuban influence is robustly felt in areas such as Tampa's Ybor City.

MODERN FLORIDA

While it was the first state to be settled by Europeans, Florida might be the last state to have entered fully into modernity. It remained more or less a frontier until the 20th century, with the first paved road not until 1920. It was really World War II that changed things in the state, prompting a period of sustained growth that lasted more than 50 years. Immigration to the state has resulted in a diversity of ethnic groups, with a dense concentration of Cubans in the Miami area and Mexicans throughout the state.

Tourism has been responsible for much of the growth in modern times, with a serious assist from Walt Disney World, the biggest tourist destination on the planet. There are more hotel rooms in Orlando than in New York City. The beaches have continued to draw multitudes of tourists, and the beaches of the northwestern part of the state have seen a recent surge of interest, with locations such as Seaside and Destin becoming increasingly popular vacation destinations.

handrolling cigars at Ybor City in Tampa

Local Culture

DEMOGRAPHICS

Florida ranks third in the United States in population, behind California and Texas. In 2018, the population was estimated to be 21,312,211, up from 9,746,961 in 1980. According to 2017 population estimates, Miami is the largest metropolitan area, with 6,158,824 residents. On the Gulf Coast, the most populous areas are Tampa Bay (3,091,399), Fort Myers-Cape Coral (739,224), Sarasota-Bradenton (720,042), Pensacola (487,784), and Naples (372,880). Nearly 1,000 people move to Florida every day, and the fastest-growing part of the state is in the Fort Myers-Cape Coral area.

Age

Florida's age distribution over the past several decades has changed very little regarding those 65 years and older. In 1990 there were 3,281,220 Floridians ages 65 and older (17.7 percent of the total population), and in 2018 the estimated number was 3,926,889 (19.4 percent of the total), still the highest percentage of any state in the country.

The Gulf Coast, especially the area around Tampa, has gotten younger in recent years. The youth population (ages 0-19) has shown increasing growth rates over the last 30 years, from 15.5 percent in 1970-1980 to 22.6 percent in 2010.

The median age is at its lowest all along the northern border of the state where it meets Georgia and Alabama and along the Panhandle. Another dense concentration of youth is around Miami and Tampa; St. Petersburg, famously a retirement destination, has also shifted younger demographically. The oldest parts of the state, citizenry-wise, are Sarasota, Naples, and along the Nature Coast.

Race

The population of the Gulf Coast is primarily white (75.7 percent in 2018), with the greatest ethnic diversity in the Tampa Bay area. The African American population is twice that of the Latino population along the Panhandle and the Alabama and Georgia borders, while in the southern part of the state, close to Miami, the correlation is the opposite.

Religion

Gulf Coast residents are primarily Christians. Jewish retirees don't appear to settle along the Gulf Coast, with the exception of Sarasota (9 percent Jewish, compared Coral Gables to Palm Beach on the east coast, which is 13-15 percent Jewish). The southernmost part of the state is predominantly Roman Catholic, as is the area north of Tampa through the Nature Coast. Most Floridians are Protestants, with the percentage increasing the closer you get to the northern border of the state.

SNOWBIRDS

What's a snowbird? It's a temporary resident in Florida, someone who comes from a colder, less hospitable winter climate to bask in the Sunshine State in winter. Snowbirds are usually of retirement age or nearing it. More specifically, New Yorkers account for 13.1 percent of Florida's temporary residents, followed by Michiganders at 7.4 percent, Ohioans at 6.7 percent, Pennsylvanians at 5.8 percent, and Canadians at 5.5 percent. The average length of stay is five months. If Florida has roughly seven million households, there are an estimated 920,000 temporary residents during the peak winter months and another 170,000 during late summer.

CIRCUS PERFORMERS

Most people connect Sarasota with the circus, as it became an official circus town in 1927 when John Ringling brought Ringling Bros. and Barnum & Bailey Circus's winter quarters. Many of the little people who starred in the circus retired in Sarasota (in specially

Who You Calling a Florida Cracker?

That's a good question, really. Many Florida historians are devoted to the theory that the term Florida Cracker originated with the area's cow hunters. As Jesse Otis Beall describes it in the book *Cracker* by Dana Ste. Claire:

> Well, people didn't know what cracker meant and they thought it was just a slang word, you know, for a person. But it was named after the whip, I think, the crackin' whip, as the cowhunters come in. There wasn't cowboys in those days, there was cowhunters, and they used those whips and we'd say, "Yep, here comes the Crackers." That's where the word comes from. I'm always a callin' myself a Cracker.

Pretty convincing, this hypothesis goes back as early as 1810, with John Lambert's *Travels through Lower Canada, and the United States of North America*. But a lot of historians aren't buying it, instead adhering to a different theory. Even Florida cow hunter historian Joyce Peters believes that Florida Crackers got the name because of their diet—poor rural people, they had trouble rounding up enough calories. Cracked corn fit the bill, as it could be roughly stone ground and then made into a paste with water or fat, baked into a hard "cracker," and then either eaten as hardtack or reconstituted in a stew. Still others say, yes, cracked corn is implicated, but in a more nefarious way. These Florida backwoodsmen were known to operate moonshine stills that fermented cracked corn mash into a blisteringly alcoholic "white lightning." Other theories that may or may not hold water: The people were named after the "cracker box" shape of their simple log houses, or they were called *cuaqueros* (Quakers) by the Spaniards, who confused them for a colony of Quakers who settled early on in Florida. And the speculations go on.

The book *Cracker* explores widely what one is, but in the glossary it cuts to the chase: "Cracker—a self-reliant, independent, and tenacious settler of the Deep South, often of Celtic stock, who subsisted by farming or raising livestock and, as a general rule, valued personal independence and restraint-free life over material prosperity. Cracker settlers provided a spirited foundation for the peopling of the rural South and Florida."

These days Florida Cracker is still something a Floridian can call him- or herself, but it's not a moniker to go slinging around lightly. There are still Florida Crackers along the Gulf Coast, and they carry the distinction with pride.

built small houses in an area known as "Tiny Town"). Still, Sarasota doesn't get the title "Showtown USA"; that honor goes to another Gulf Coast town, **Gibsonton,** or Gibtown, as it's affectionately called. It was made famous as a wintering town for sideshow and circus performers as well as garden-variety carnies. Many of them retired permanently to Gibtown and have died off, but they leave the town with a colorful history. It's south of Tampa on U.S. 41, near the town of Riverview.

Gibsonton was home to Percilla "Monkey Girl" Bejano and her husband, Emmitt "The Alligator Skin Man" Bejano (billed as the "World's Strangest Married Couple" on sideshow midways all over). There was Jeanie the Half Girl, Al the Giant, and Grady "Lobster Boy" Stiles Jr. (from a long line of people with

ectrodactyly, or "lobster claw" syndrome); Stiles committed murder but got off with probation because prison wasn't equipped to handle him, only to be murdered himself some years later. The conjoined twin Hilton sisters ran a fruit stand here. Melvin "Rubber Face" Burkhart was the most recent to die, in 2001. His most famous routine was to shove an ice pick and a five-inch nail into his nose.

Gibtown has a post office counter that accommodates little people, and its zoning laws allow residents to keep elephants and circus animals in trailers on their front lawns. It is home to the **International Independent Showmen's Association** (6915 Riverview Dr., 813/677-3590) and a bar called **Showtown USA Lounge** (10902 U.S. 41 S., 813/677-5443) that has rollicking karaoke on

Famous Floridians

It's an incomplete list, but these people were born and raised in the Sunshine State, or at least called it home for a long while.

- **Baseball players:** Buster Posey, Steve Carlton, Dwight Gooden, Barry Larkin, Sammy Sosa

- **Football players:** Emmitt Smith, Mike Ditka, Joe Namath, Daunte Culpepper, Mike Astott, Warrick Dunn, Tony Dungy, Chris Simms

- **Tennis players:** Jennifer Capriati, Martina Hingis, Anna Kournikova, Ivan Lendl, Martina Navratilova, Monica Seles, Andy Roddick, Serena and Venus Williams

- **Wrestlers:** Hulk Hogan, Rick Flair, Dwayne "The Rock" Johnson, Joannie "Chyna" Laurer, Randy "Macho Man" Savage

- **Actors:** Johnny Depp, Kelsey Grammer, Sidney Poitier, Butterfly McQueen, Burt Reynolds, Ben Vereen, Faye Dunaway, Buddy Ebsen, River Phoenix, John Travolta

- **Writers:** Harriet Beecher Stowe, Marjorie Kinnan Rawlings, Zora Neale Hurston, Ernest Hemingway, Carl Hiaasen, Stephen King

- **Artists:** John James Audubon, Winslow Homer

- **Singers:** Jim Morrison, Pat Boone, Jimmy Buffett, Frances Langford, Gloria Estefan, Enrique Iglesias, Lenny Kravitz, Tom Petty, Bo Diddley, the Backstreet Boys, and some of 'N Sync, the brothers Gibb, Beyoncé Knowles, Jennifer Lopez, Scott Stapp

- **Military figures:** Joseph W. Stilwell (Army general), Daniel James (Air Force general)

---

the weekend. A historic eatery called **Giants Camp Restaurant,** opened by Al Tomaini (8 feet, 4 inches tall) and his wife, Jeanie (2 feet, 6 inches tall), has sadly closed.

Even if you can't fit it into your trip, you can get a sense of Gibtown if you watch the "Humbug" episode of the *X-Files* (season 2), in which Mulder and Scully travel to Gibsonton to investigate the death of Jerald Glazebrook, the Alligator Man. In the episode you'll meet Jim Jim, the Dog-Faced Boy, and the Enigma, who is covered in blue puzzle-piece tattoos and eats glass. A 65-minute documentary called *Gibtown* is hard to find but worthwhile. Gibsonton is also home to the largest tropical fish farm in the country, **Ekkwill Waterlife Resources** (813/677-5475, www. ekkwill.com).

MOVIES SET ON THE GULF COAST

Florida has been a film location about as long as there have been movies. Today it is ranked third in the country for film production based on revenue generated. The climate, the scenery, the dense tropical foliage have all sparked the imagination of directors, cinematographers, and actors, standing in for far-flung lands on several continents. The earliest Florida films aren't flights of fancy, however, but rather the 1898 newsreels of U.S. troops in Tampa during the Spanish-American War. The Museum of Florida History in Tallahassee has a collection of movie posters from films shot in the state. Some from this collection, and an assortment of others, all shot along the Gulf Coast:

Hell Harbor (1930), the first full-length "talkie" to be made in the state, was shot in Tampa and depicts the story of the descendants of pirate Henry Morgan. *A Guy Named Joe* (1944), starring Spencer Tracy as a World War II pilot who dies and becomes the guardian angel of a young pilot in love with Tracy's girlfriend, was also shot in Tampa at Drew and MacDill air fields. The Marx Brothers' *The*

Cocoanuts (1929) may be set in Miami, it's not totally clear, but it revolves around Florida's first land boom. *The Yearling* (1946) is educational and an absolute classic starring Gregory Peck; it's based on the Newbery Award-winning book by Marjorie Kinnan Rawlings and was nominated for seven Oscars. Parts of the film were shot at Rawlings's homestead in Cross Creek.

Some camp faves include *Mr. Peabody and the Mermaid* (1948), a William Powell film shot at Weeki Wachee Springs with local mermaids; *Beneath the 12 Mile Reef* (1953), the story of a Greek sponge diver from Tarpon Springs who falls in love with a girl from the rival Key West sponge divers; and the king of Gulf Coast films, *Creature from the Black Lagoon* (1954), filmed in Wakulla Springs and Tarpon Springs and followed by two sequels.

Directed by Cecil B. DeMille and starring Betty Hutton, James Stewart, and Charlton Heston, *The Greatest Show on Earth* (1952) was filmed at the Barnum & Bailey headquarters in Sarasota and required all the actors to do their own stunts. Elvis spent a little time on the Gulf Coast in Pasco County filming *Follow That Dream* (1962)—it's not a well-reviewed film. And Christopher Plummer, Gypsy Rose Lee, and Burl Ives got to hang out in the Everglades for the making of Nicholas Ray's *Wind across the Everglades* (1958), a story about the hardscrabble life in the wilds of south Florida.

Victor Nuñez has done a few excellent movies set along the Gulf Coast, including *A Flash of Green* (1988), based on the novel by J. D. MacDonald about corruption in Sarasota, and *Ruby in Paradise* (1993), a small film about a young woman, played by Ashley Judd, set on the Panhandle. He did the Peter Fonda pic *Ulee's Gold* (1997), a Panhandle family drama about beekeepers, and another not widely released Florida pic called *Coastlines*.

Peter Weir's *The Truman Show* (1998), starring Jim Carrey, is set in the scary-perfect Panhandle town of Seaside; Volker Schlondorff's crime drama *Palmetto* (1998) is set in and around Sarasota; and Spike Jonze's *Adaptation* (2002), a loose interpretation of Susan Orlean's book *The Orchid Thief,* takes place in the mangrove swamps of the Everglades. John Sayles's *Sunshine State* (2002) is set in a fictional town in Florida, which might be the east coast, but it describes the conflicts of early Floridians and new developers so well that it's worth seeing. Kids will recognize Florida as the setting for *Hoot* (2006), Carl Hiaasen's environmental flick filmed in Boca Grande.

GULF COAST CULINARY SPECIALTIES

As you might expect, the Gulf of Mexico supplies most of the unique eats and culinary traditions for the region. When traveling the Gulf Coast, one of the most important questions to ask before you sit down for a meal is if the seafood is fresh. Next, consider what you have already tasted, and then taste something new—stretch the boundaries of what you are willing to eat. You won't know if you like raw oysters smothered in cocktail sauce and piled with horseradish and a squeeze of lemon until you try them, and chances are high that you will love them.

Learn what seafood is harvested in the area and know what fish are typically running and fresh during the time of year that you are visiting a particular region. Find out what seafood festivals occur in the towns you are visiting. This is an easy indicator of what variety of seafood is celebrated, eaten, and harvested in the region (although there are exceptions, such as the Fiddler Crab Festival in Steinhatchee). Eating seafood along the Gulf Coast is as much a part of the culture and experience of the place as staking an umbrella in the sand and spending the day at the beach; don't miss out on either one.

Apalachicola Oysters

You won't get far in Apalachicola without hearing about oysters, the favorite food and once the source of an industry that brought in $6 million each year. Oysters grow many other places along the Gulf Coast, but these became world famous as a result of the huge numbers that used to grow in the surrounding waterways, and because people say they taste better. While they are no longer growing and being harvested in the huge numbers they once were, you may still be able to buy a bag and shuck them yourself. Try them raw, fried, steamed, or stuffed; you'll understand why so many are willing to travel so far to taste them.

Steinhatchee Scallops

Harvesting scallops is as popular as eating them in Steinhatchee. Try both—the harvesting season runs early July-late September. Each person can pull up to 2 gallons per day of scallops from the productive sea grass beds in the bay, and each vessel can have up to 10 gallons on board at a time. The epicenter of scalloping activity in the region is at the picturesque Steinhatchee Landing Resort. Most of the seafood restaurants along the Gulf Coast offer them. I like mine pan-fried and drizzled with fresh garlic and butter.

Cedar Key Clams

The clam industry has been thriving in Cedar Key for a century in clean waters that have given rise to some of the largest clam canneries in the country. Stop in at the Island Hotel and Restaurant to get your Cedar Key Sweet's fix of littleneck clams. They come steamed, sautéed in butter, or in some truly delicious clam chowder ready for all those northern snowbirds that flock down every winter.

Grouper Sandwich

It's a staple on the Gulf Coast for lunch or dinner after a day at the beach or out on the boat. The recipe is simple: Take a huge, flaky slab of grilled, blackened, or fried grouper and put it in between a chewy bun with some premium cheese, fresh tomato and lettuce, and maybe a slather of tartar sauce, and you've got one supreme sandwich sure to leave any coastal sightseer in a state of sublimity. The best I've found is at Peg Leg Pete's on Pensacola Beach or at the Sandbar Waterfront Restaurant

on Anna Maria Island just off the coast of Sarasota.

Shrimp and Grits

What do you get when you combine fresh Gulf shrimp with a truly classic Southern staple? Heaven in a bowl. If the idea of eating grits makes you cringe, then this is the perfect dish for you. One bite of this ultimate seafood fusion specialty is likely to convert even the most adamant opponent to the Deep South's take on porridge into an advocate for the South's newest culinary classic. Usually served with a sprinkling of crumbled bacon and a few fresh green onion slices to give it a little green, you can find the creative combo popping up on menus across the Gulf Coast. However, the farther south you go, the less likely you are to find this tasty treat. For the cream of the crop, cruise on over to The Fish House in Pensacola or the Beach Walk Café at Henderson Park Inn in Destin, or visit celebrity chef Jim Shirley for some Smoked Gouda Grits a Ya Ya at his Great Southern Café in the idyllic coastal town of Seaside on the Emerald Coast.

Fried Mullet

Don't be afraid: Mullet tastes good, especially when fried in a spicy and salty batter and then dipped in tartar sauce. Folks across Florida have developed a taste for it, but you have seen less of it on menus in recent years due to the bad press that cornmeal's better half has unjustly received. For some major-league fried mullet, mosey on over to Posey's Beyond the Bay in Panacea or stop in and celebrate at the Interstate Mullet Toss held in late April every year at the Flora-Bama, a popular restaurant and bar right on the Florida-Alabama state line.

Seafood Bouillabaisse

The culinary traditions of the Gulf Coast are a reflection of the rich history of the place. The French never actually controlled Florida, but they did have short-lived sovereignty over Pensacola and nearby Mobile. The French put their focus on Louisiana and New Orleans to the west, and as a result the Cajun and French culinary traditions are established in the collective Gulf Coast cookbook. Seafood bouillabaisse is one of the favorite French dishes that can be found on the entrée lists of many restaurants in the region. Nearly everyone has a different take on this traditional French fish stew, that is often served with a hodgepodge of fish, shrimp, and mussels. My favorite is the lobster tail, fish, mussels, and shrimp seafood bouillabaisse found at the Beach Bistro on Anna Maria Island.

Essentials

Transportation

GETTING THERE
Air

Tampa International Airport is the largest airport on the Gulf Coast, with 550 flights per day, and has been ranked 19th nationwide in on-time performance. The Northwest Florida Beaches International Airport outside of Panama City is the best way to fly to the popular beaches of South Walton County; it is the first international airport to be built in the United States in over a decade. Generally, the most direct routes and cheapest fares can be found through these airports, but

it's worth pricing flights to Orlando, an hour east of Tampa, with Orlando International Airport and the increasingly popular Sanford International Airport. Gulf Coast airports, from north to south:

- **Pensacola International Airport** (PNS, 4 miles northeast of Pensacola, 850/436-5000)

- **Northwest Florida Regional Airport** (VPS, 1 mile east of Destin, 850/651-7160)

- **Northwest Florida Beaches International Airport** (ECP, 20 miles northwest of Panama City, 850/763-6751)

- **Brooksville Tampa Bay Regional Airport** (BKV, 40 miles north of Tampa, 352/754-4061)

- **St. Petersburg-Clearwater International Airport** (PIE, 7 miles southeast of Clearwater, 727/453-7800)

- **Tampa International Airport** (TPA, 5 miles west of downtown Tampa, 813/870-8700)

- **Sarasota-Bradenton International Airport** (SRQ, 3 miles north of Sarasota, 941/359-2770)

- **Venice Municipal Airport** (VNC, 0.5 miles south of Venice, 941/486-2711)

- **Punta Gorda Airport** (PGD, 3 miles southeast of Punta Gorda, 941/639-1101)

- **Southwest Florida International Airport** (RSW, 10 miles southeast of Fort Myers, 239/590-4800)

- **Naples Airport** (APF, 2 miles northeast of Naples, 239/643-0733)

FROM EUROPE

Most international flights to the Gulf Coast arrive at Tampa or Southwest Florida International in Fort Myers. Additional international flights arrive at Miami, Orlando, and Key West.

CHEAP FARES

Online travel resources (Hotwire, Kayak, Orbitz, Expedia, etc.) offer last-minute specials and weekend deals on travel. The way to get a good fare in advance on air travel or hotel rooms is by traveling outside peak season. That period is different for different parts of the Gulf Coast; each chapter gives the approximate peak season dates in its introduction. For instance, peak season on St. George Island is the middle of the summer, while in Naples summer is the least desirable time to visit, thus the cheapest. Spring break in March-April seems to be the most expensive time to visit much of the Gulf Coast, but bear in mind that in the off-season, hours for restaurants and attractions are sometimes more limited.

Car

The main thoroughfares in Florida include I-95, which crosses the Florida-Georgia border just north of Jacksonville and hugs the east coast of the state all the way down, and I-75, which runs south from Georgia through the state's middle, then to the coast just south of Tampa. I-4 extends southwest across the state from Daytona through Orlando and connects to I-75 in Tampa. On the Panhandle, I-10 is the big east-west road, accessed from the north by U.S. 29, U.S. 231, or U.S. 19. U.S. 98 is a scenic route that hugs the coast along most of the Panhandle.

Boat

Traveling to Florida by boat, the **Gulf Intracoastal Waterway** is a 1,090-mile toll-free East Coast channel that links Norfolk, Virginia, to Miami, Florida, and Carrabelle, Florida, to Brownsville, Texas through gorgeous sheltered waters. There's a noncontiguous section of the waterway connecting Tampa Bay with the Okeechobee Waterway. The Gulf Intracoastal Waterway follows a course of sheltered bays, rivers, and canals along the Gulf of Mexico, which makes it perfect for recreational cruising.

The **Port of Tampa** is a huge home port for a variety of cruise lines (Carnival, Royal Caribbean, Holland America, and Norwegian Cruise Line). Nearly a million passengers pass through its cruise terminals each year.

GETTING AROUND
Car

Florida's Gulf Coast is an ideal destination for those with a poor sense of direction. There are only a few major roads you have to master, and even the urban areas are mostly laid out in a grid. On the Panhandle, I-10 runs inland east to west, while at the coast the major east-west road is U.S. 98. U.S. 98 curves all the way around the Big Bend of the Panhandle into the Florida peninsula, where it is also called U.S. 19. U.S. 19 extends along the coast all the way down to St. Pete. I-75 is the huge north-south artery on the Gulf Coast side of the Florida peninsula, stretching from where it enters the state at Valdosta, Georgia, all the way south to Naples, where it jogs across the state to the east along what is called Alligator Alley. One of the more famous north-south routes in Florida is U.S. 41, also known as the Tamiami Trail, which extends from Tampa to Naples, where it shoots east across the state significantly south of I-75. The Tamiami Trail and I-75 run parallel and close together. Which you choose depends on your preference: I-75 has the speed; Tamiami Trail has the charm.

CAR RENTALS
Alamo (800/462-5266), **Avis** (800/831-2847), **Budget** (800/527-0700), **Dollar** (800/800-4000 domestic, 800/800-6000 international), **Enterprise** (800/736-8222), **Hertz** (800/654-3131), and **National** (800/227-7368) provide rental cars at the major airports on the Gulf Coast. You pay a small premium for the convenience of picking up and dropping off at the airport, and you pay significantly more if you pick up a car in one city and drop it off in another. Most rental car companies insist that the driver be at least 21 years old, some even

older than that—be sure to have your driver's license and a major credit card (even if you aim to pay cash, the rental companies want a credit card for their own peace of mind).

Whether to accept a rental agency's insurance coverage and waivers depends on your own car insurance—before leaving home, read your car policy to determine if it covers you while renting a vehicle. Also, some credit cards cover damages to many basic types of rental cars, so it's worth checking into that as well. If you decline the insurance, rental car companies hold you totally responsible for your rental vehicle if it's damaged or stolen. The rental agency's insurance may add $20-40 per day to your bill.

HITCHHIKING
Florida is not a great hitchhiking state. The law reads: No person shall stand in a roadway for the purpose of soliciting a ride. Clearly, you can't stand *in the road* to thumb a ride, but there's nothing that says you can't stand on the shoulder. Still, police officers don't like it, and most people won't pick you up. Regardless, you will still see people thumbing on the highway, and in all the years I have lived in Florida I have never seen anyone get arrested for attempting to hitchhike or heard of anyone ending up in the slammer as a result of trying to do it. Still, I don't recommend it. Standing on the side of the highway is dangerous. Getting in a car with a stranger is dangerous.

Bus

Greyhound (214/849-8966, www.greyhound.com) service has gotten spottier in recent years, but there are still regular routes that run from Naples through Fort Myers, then up to Tampa and St. Petersburg, and all the way around the Big Bend of the Panhandle to Panama City and Pensacola. If traveling by Greyhound is new to you, here's some general information: There are no assigned seats (do not, under any circumstances, take the seats adjacent to the bathroom—it's olfactory suicide), no smoking, no pets, and no meal service, but there are regular meal stops so you can jump out and buy something. Stopovers at any point along the route are permitted if you've paid a regular fare. The driver gives you a notation on your ticket, or a coupon, and you can get back on whenever you like.

Who rides the bus these days? The elderly, the military, the poor, and people who just don't fly. Regular patrons include children who wish they were somewhere else, and their parents, who also wish their children were somewhere else. There are better ways to see the state, but few that are cheaper, and the Greyhound buses have become much nicer in recent years, and now you can get free internet service on most buses.

Train

Train service is limited along the Gulf Coast. **Amtrak** (800/872-7245, www.amtrak.com)

offers service exclusively up the eastern side of the Florida peninsula and Orlando, with the exception of the Gulf Coast city of Tampa and environs. To give some idea of price, the three-hour trip from Orlando to Jacksonville is usually about $40 one-way. Amtrak service has been greatly improved over the past few years. It now offers free Wi-Fi on some trains, and there is always more legroom on the train than on a plane. Unfortunately, much of Amtrak's service that once existed throughout the length of the Panhandle has been out of commission since Hurricane Katrina destroyed the tracks in New Orleans in 2005. There are plans to restore this service, but the timeline remains unclear. Make sure to check with Amtrak about the availability of any route before you make your travel plans.

Visas and Officialdom

FOREIGN TRAVELERS
Visas

Security is tight for foreign visitors, with procedures constantly in flux. To find up-to-date information on visas and customs, visit www.usa.gov/travel-and-immigration. Keep your passport in a safe place, and make a copy of the passport number and other critical information and keep it elsewhere.

Money

Working with dollars is fairly simple—there's a $1 banknote, the $5, the $10, the $20, and, less common, the $50. Larger bills are seldom used and seldom accepted without a lot of scrutiny. In coins, pennies ($0.01) are pretty much only good for wishing wells; then there's the nickel ($0.05), the dime ($0.10), the quarter ($0.25), the more rare 50-cent piece ($0.50) and dollar ($1) coins.

Foreign currency can be exchanged at a limited number of airports (Tampa, Orlando, Fort Myers) on the Gulf Coast. Exchange money before you arrive. For the most part,

if you have a Visa or MasterCard, put all of your accommodations, restaurant meals, and attractions expenditures on that—an easy way to keep track of how you spent your money on vacation.

Electricity

The United States uses 110-120 volts AC at 60 hertz, as opposed to Europe's 220-240 volts at 50 hertz. For the most part, Gulf Coast hotels will have blow-dryers for your use, so leave yours at home. If you have other electrical devices for which you need a converter, bring one from home.

Telephone Basics

Each urban area along the Gulf Coast has its own area code of three numbers that must be dialed if calling from outside. For example, the area code in Tampa is 813, but you don't need to dial it if you're calling within the area code. If you're dialing another area code, you must first dial 1 (except on cell phones), then the three-digit area code, then the seven-digit phone number. Be aware that cell phones have rendered the pay phone an endangered species. If you don't have a cell phone that works in Florida, you're better off getting a prepaid international calling card. Hotels also charge by the call, so making calling-card calls is often more cost-effective.

Calling from abroad, the international code for the United States is 1. Within the United States, the 800, 833, 844, 855, 866, 877, and 888 area codes are toll-free, meaning they cost you nothing to dial.

Tipping

Service-sector workers expect a tip. It's only in name a "gratuity," meaning an elective gift. In reality it's how they make the bulk of their income. Fifteen percent is pretty much the minimum, whether it's at a restaurant, a hair salon, or in a taxi. Tip bellhops about $1 per bag; tip the valet parking attendant $1-2 every time you get your car. Tip a good waiter or bartender 15-20 percent. But here's some tricky stuff: If the hairdresser or tour operator is the owner of the business, a tip can sometimes be seen as an insult. Keep lots of small bills at the ready for all these situations, but don't ever tip at the movies, a retail shop, the gas station, or at the theater, ballet, or opera.

Metric Conversions

The United States had a failed attempt at going metric in the 1970s. So, you need to know that one foot equals 0.305 meters; one mile equals 1.6 kilometers; and one pound equals 0.45 kilograms. Converting temperatures is a little trickier: To convert Fahrenheit to Celsius temperatures, subtract 32 and then multiply the result by 0.555. Got it?

Travel Tips

WHAT TO PACK

Florida is casual, and what to pack is mostly about being comfortable. If you're spending time in Naples, Sarasota, or Tampa's Hyde Park, bring something a little more formal, preferably in a tropical style, to wear in the evening. Elsewhere, the name of the game year-round is layering. For women, a twin set and slacks is a good dressy outfit; for men, a polo shirt and khakis. You will need several pairs of shoes: something for dinner, sneakers for hiking (ones that can get wet and possibly muddy, repeatedly), and swim shoes or sandals.

Even if you're visiting the Gulf Coast in the summer, bring a sweater. Most places keep the air-conditioner going strong. You'll appreciate this when you first step inside from the relentless heat, but if you plan to spend any length of time indoors, you'll end up getting cold, especially when the cold air-conditioning is coupled with sweat on the skin. In the winter, a long-sleeved pullover with light slacks is usually fine unless you're up north on the Panhandle and in the Tallahassee area, where the temperatures can drop near and very occasionally below freezing during the winter months of January-February. During these times you will want to layer your tops—bring a fleece or other good jacket and a pair of warm pants or jeans.

Bring sunscreen, binoculars, polarized sunglasses (for seeing depth when you fish and to better spot dolphins), a bird book, a snorkel, swim flippers, a good novel, more bathing suits than you think you can use, bug spray, flip-flops or sandals, a digital camera, maybe a disposable waterproof camera, and your cell phone (it will work in almost every part of Florida these days, especially with Verizon service, except a very few rural parts of the Nature Coast).

A car is an essential tool in most of the area, but visitors can also rent bikes, scooters, skates, strollers, beach chairs, boogie boards, surfboards, skimboards, fishing equipment, motorboats, personal watercraft, kayaks, canoes, sailboards, and sailboats.

WHAT IT WILL COST

This information is hard to nail down: What it costs depends on what you're willing to spend. If I averaged the prices at all the restaurants of the Gulf Coast, I'd say a restaurant dinner for one person costs $20. If I were to do the same thing for accommodations, I might find an average hotel room costs $100. But are those numbers really helpful? It's a range, with significant variation, on both counts.

Travel costs are at their most expensive during peak season, which for the Florida peninsula is December-April; for the Panhandle it's June-August. What's helpful to know is that the Gulf Coast is for the most part less expensive the farther north and west you go, and also in Tampa. However, some more rural coastal areas in the Big Bend region of the state such as Carrabelle and Sopchoppy tend to be some of the most affordable places to visit on the entire coast. Top-dollar honors go to **Naples,** where an average dinner for one is about $30 and an average room is about $150 per night mid-season. Then it gets cheaper and cheaper as you drive up I-75 and west along U.S. 98. Cheapest place on the Gulf Coast? **Panama City Beach,** where lots of bargain hotel rooms on the beach bottom out at $30. **Pensacola** is an affordable town and hands down the best value; **Sarasota,** not so affordable.

Beaches on the Gulf Coast are free, with maybe a few dollars' cost for parking and sunblock. What you do at them may cost more—a half-day offshore fishing trip will run at least $250, an ecotour kayak trip around $50, a brief WaveRunner rental $40. Of the attractions, everything pales financially by comparison to a day at Walt Disney World. Still, **Busch Gardens** in Tampa, **Asolo Theatre** tickets in Sarasota, and **snorkel-with-the-manatees** charters in Homosassa are all expensive.

If you can stay for a week, which I recommend, you can cut costs: A totally luxurious multiple-bedroom beach house rental on **St. George Island** or even **North Captiva Island** will cost less per night than a swanky single room in Naples. In a rental house, you can be even more fiscally prudent by preparing your own breakfasts and picnic lunches. Splurge on dinners.

With attractions, check their websites for free or reduced-rate days or nights. Museums tend to admit people free on Thursday nights or Sunday mornings, primarily to lure locals, but you can benefit. It's worth it to visit the local chambers of commerce or convention and visitors bureaus, not only for the information, but also for the coupons.

VISITOR INFORMATION
Maps

Visit Florida (www.visitflorida.com) sends a great map of the whole state with its Visit Florida literature. (And, as always, AAA members should raid the free-map smorgasbord that is their divine right.) The state's tourism office also has several welcome stations near Florida's border (one north of Pensacola on I-10, one off U.S. 231, one in Tallahassee, one in Jennings off I-75, and one on the state's east coast on I-95) that give out good state and regional maps. Some cities (Apalachicola, Naples) can be navigated with only the photocopied map the desk clerk at the hotel hands out; just follow the yellow highlighter marks. In other cities (Tampa), you need a real map. And if you're traveling alone, don't be chintzy—buy the laminated flip map to the area; its ease of use in the car may keep your wheels on the road.

GPS systems and cell phone apps such as Google Maps are absolute godsends for the frequent road-tripper. These portable navigation tools make it easy to plug in addresses and get detailed directions to your destination.

Tourist Offices

Tourist office addresses are listed at the end of each chapter. Most convention and visitors bureaus have extremely helpful websites, and

Vacation Rentals on the Gulf Coast

If you're planning on staying a week or more along the Gulf Coast, or just want more privacy than is usually found at resorts and hotels, you may want to consider renting a privately owned condo or a home. In most areas along the coast, there are companies that specialize in vacation rentals, and the offerings often run the gamut from mega-million-dollar mansions with Gulf-front views to bargain-priced studio efficiencies with tiny kitchenettes. Some tips to help you navigate the process of finding that perfect rental on the Gulf Coast:

USE ALL RESOURCES AVAILABLE

There are lots of options when it comes to finding a vacation rental. Each chapter in this guide highlights some of the best local real estate companies in that area that help match vacation-home owners with renters. Since these companies are tried-and-true trustworthy sources for local vacation rentals, they are often the best way to find a vacation home or condo.

In recent years, however, much of the vacation rental market has moved out of the hands of these brick-and-mortar real estate companies and onto the internet, where owners can cut out the middle man and market their vacation rentals directly to renters. Currently, the top websites online to search for vacation rentals are Airbnb.com and VRBO.com (VRBO stands for Vacation Rentals by Owner). The sites are easy to use, and they have the largest inventories. Tripadvisor.com has recently dipped its toes into the vacation rental market, and its offerings are growing rapidly; check them out as well.

DECIDE WHAT YOU WANT BEFORE YOU START YOUR SEARCH

You can find almost any type of vacation rental you can imagine. In Pensacola you can rent a dome-shaped home that claims to be able to withstand a category 5 hurricane. Determine exactly what it is that you're looking before you call the vacation rental companies. And definitely don't dismiss the resorts, hotels, inns, and bed-and-breakfasts in the area that you are visiting. You might be able to find a great deal on a stay at one of these places, so check what kind of specials they are running before you set your sights on a vacation rental.

---

many will send you a vacation package of information, maps, and coupons free of charge.

ACCESS FOR TRAVELERS WITH DISABILITIES

The more developed parts of the Gulf Coast (Pensacola, Destin, Sarasota, Naples, Tampa) are very accessible to travelers with disabilities. As one would expect, the more remote and rural areas may not have ramps, accessible restrooms, and other amenities. You may want to consider buying a copy of *Wheelchairs on the Go: Accessible Fun in Florida,* an access guide for Florida visitors who use canes, walkers, or wheelchairs. The 424-page paperback covers wheelchair-accessible and barrier-free accommodations, tourist attractions, and activities across the state.

Society for Accessible Travel & Hospitality (212/447-7284, www.sath.org) provides recommendations and resources to help travelers with disabilities plan their vacations, and **Able Trust** (850/224-4493, www.abletrust.org) offers helpful links to disability resources throughout Florida. Most major car-rental companies have hand-controlled cars in their fleets (give them 24-48 hours' notice to locate one). If you need to rent a scooter or wheelchair during your visit, **ScootAround** (888/441-7575, www.scootaround.com) is a mobility enhancement company with scooter and wheelchair rental service in a number of Gulf Coast cities.

Diabetic travelers can call the **American Diabetes Association** (800/342-2383, www.diabetes.org) to get a list of hospitals that provide services to diabetics, or log on to

Keep in mind that the closer you get to the water, the more the rental usually costs. Also, if you are going to be traveling with other families or friends, consider renting one large house that's big enough for everyone. It's a great way to save money on an extended trip. If you want to bring a pet along, you shouldn't have a problem finding pet-friendly rentals.

CLOSELY REVIEW ALL THE LISTINGS

Not all vacation rentals are created equal. While every condo in an entire development may have the exact same layout, the owners will leave their mark on their personal unit. Always look at the pictures of each rental that you're considering. This way you will find exactly what you are looking for.

KNOW WHEN TO WAIT AND WHEN TO BUY

It's a tricky game to play, but sometimes if you time your purchase right, you can often save 10-40 percent. Every

a vacation rental in Homosassa

area has its high season, and these months will be the most expensive time to stay at a vacation rental. However, there are often more rentals available than the market can fill. If you're flexible on what type of rental you want or on what dates you want to vacation, you will often save the most money if you wait until right before you want to rent. There are usually reduced prices being offered on vacation rentals if the available dates are just around the corner. It's a bit of risk versus reward, but if you really want a great deal, try rolling the dice and book at the last minute.

Dialysis Finder at www.dialysisfinder.com. The **American Foundation for the Blind** (800/232-5463, www.afb.org) provides information on traveling with a dog guide.

TRAVELING WITH CHILDREN

The Gulf Coast is the kind of destination suited to a rambling family car trip. But how to face the open road with a carful of antsy travelers? As with a NASA launch, it's all about careful planning and precise execution. Consider yourself lucky that this doesn't mean devising zero-gravity suits and dehydrating food—you just have to keep your astronauts comfortable, fed, and entertained. To that end, consider carrying a master list of all that you've packed. Although it sounds pretty meticulous, it helps to see where your gaps are, it

allows you to easily keep track of things from car to motel to final destination, and if you generate this list on the computer, it can be used as the basis for future trip lists.

The list should be divided into categories: clothes and equipment (these are the things that go in the trunk, to be exhumed at your final destination), and the stuff that makes or breaks your travel time—food, entertainment, and car comfort. Older kids can each be put in charge of a category checklist as the car gets loaded.

For smaller kids, always take a change of underpants or diapers inside the car with you, rather than in the trunk with the luggage. For older kids, encourage a layered approach to dressing—when one child is chilly, donning another layer may be preferable to making everyone endure the car heater.

Think of packing foods that nature has already prepackaged—bananas, oranges, hard-boiled eggs. Avoid things with sauces or drip potential, chips coated with the dreaded nacho cheese orange goo, or things that crumb too easily. And for drinks, carry a large plastic spill-proof cup for each child. This way, you can get juices at convenience stores but you won't be at the mercy of those wide-mouthed, splash-prone glass bottles in the car. Alternatively, bring a bevy of frozen juice boxes. You won't have to wait in line for sodas, and the juice boxes will be nice and cold during the first leg of the trip.

The sight of the golden arches fills most kids with joy and most parents with dread. Fast food is the most common pitfall on long car trips, a wasteland of fat, salt, and sugar. To avoid the tortures of drive-through (it's everywhere, after all), you have to stand firm. Finding other food can be an adventure on long trips. On the Gulf Coast, this is easy: Get off the highway and hunt down an old-fashioned diner, one with counter stools, a good jukebox, and a short-order cook who makes the perfect grilled cheese. In preparation for your trip, research the indigenous foods of the areas you'll be passing through. Use the internet to print out pictures and histories of each city's culinary highlights.

When traveling in the car with small children, allow more time to reach your destination. Count on stopping every hour to stretch your legs and run around. Churches are good stopping spots if rest areas aren't available, as they often have open, grassy areas and playgrounds. Traveling at night or during nap times is a good way to make up time. Put blankets, pillows, and any necessary stuffed animals in the back seat at the ready.

Your local party goods and dollar stores are perfect places to find inexpensive new forms of amusement. Wrap each new toy as a gift, to make the excitement last. Caveat: Do not buy travel games with small pieces sure to get lost immediately under the back seat. Maze books, magic-pen books, stickers, a magnetic puzzle of the United States, even car bingo can keep everyone entertained. For long car trips, the book *Miles of Smiles* is filled with car games. Picture-puzzle books (like *I Spy* and *Where's Waldo*) can be made into games as well: One person names an object for the rest to find in the picture.

Even if you dislike the plugged-in feel of video games, iPods, or DVDs in the car, bringing a stereo headset for each child allows everyone to listen to their first choice, whether that's Taylor Swift or *Goodnight Moon*. You can even make your own books on tape: Record your child's favorite stories on audiotape, and then they can have the stories "read" to them in the car.

Bring lap desks and art supplies for projects. Dated spiral-bound drawing pads can be a nice way to chronicle a trip, with each child keeping the finished pad (parents can annotate as instructed). Encourage older kids to journal with a cool pad and a set of gel pens.

TRAVELING WITH PETS

More and more hotel chains are accepting people's canine companions (other pets, from pot-bellied pigs to naked mole rats, are a harder sell). Best Western, Motel 6, Holiday Inn, and even swanky chains such as Four Seasons often accept pet guests for an additional fee. To get good information, visit www.petswelcome.com.

Flying with your pet to and from Florida can be problematic, as most major airlines have an embargo against pets as checked baggage during the summer months (any day in which the outdoor temperature might reach 90°F), and even for small pets that fit under an airplane seat, the airlines only allow one pet per cabin. The ASPCA strongly discourages pets as checked baggage.

Dogs are prohibited on many walking trails in Florida, as well as most beaches. There are designated dog parks and dog beaches all over the Gulf Coast. Pensacola, Panama City, Tampa, St. Petersburg, Sarasota, and Fort Myers all have designated dog beach parks with amenities such as fenced play areas, dog water fountains, and poop bags. Be aware that

ESSENTIALS HEALTH AND SAFETY

in much of the Gulf Coast's wilderness areas, poisonous snakes and alligators pose more of a threat to your dog than to you.

TRAVELING ALONE

Most activities on the Gulf Coast are well suited to traveling alone. The only exception to that is backwoods camping in the Everglades or deep wilderness, and traveling around high crime areas of the cities on the Gulf Coast. Consider giving rangers your schedule and detailed whereabouts when engaging in these activities. Be vigilant when traveling in urban areas. Look up crime data for the cities you are visiting and avoid the parts of town where most of the crime occurs. I wouldn't hesitate to recommend the Gulf Coast as a spot for quiet solo travel—except, perhaps, during college spring break, and then I would recommend it for loud and lively socializing and partying.

GAY AND LESBIAN TRAVELERS

Miami's South Beach and Key West are the locus of lots of gay travel. Nowhere on the Gulf Coast is the nightlife as trendy, but that said, nothing on the Gulf Coast seems unsuitable for gay or lesbian travel. The Gulf Coast's wealth of outdoor activities seems suitable for any orientation, as do the restaurants and accommodations. It's a fairly nightlife-impoverished area regardless of your orientation, so you may spend your evenings curled up with a good book.

A good resource is the **Gay, Lesbian & Bisexual Community Services of Central Florida** (407/228-8272, www.thecenterorlando.org) for welcome packets and calendars of events, or the **International Gay & Lesbian Travel Association** (954/630-1637, www.iglta.com, $99 annually to join) for a list of gay-friendly accommodations, tours, and attractions.

SPRING BREAK FEVER

Because school schedules vary across the country, spring breakers arrive in Florida at different times. Some come as early as late February, but March and April are the months most colleges and schools release for spring break. Students focus most of their attention on specific cities along the eastern coast of the state (Daytona Beach, Miami Beach), but along the Gulf Coast, Panama City Beach and down by Key West are the big draws.

Health and Safety

Despite what it might look like in the backcountry of the Everglades, Florida is a modern, developed kind of place, with good emergency services and medical care all over the Gulf Coast. From Tampa to Sarasota you'll see more medical facilities, pharmacies, and billboards for MRI scanners than nearly anywhere else, a remnant of the area's recent past as a retirement-age destination (as the Bob Dylan song says, "it's younger than that now").

Still, you want to do what you can to stay healthy during a visit here. The sun is probably the biggest underestimated foe. **Sunburn** can be wicked, so be sure to slather with at least an SPF of 30, and because you'll be in and out of water, and sweating in the steamy humidity, opt for waterproof or water-resistant cream such as Banana Boat Sport Sunblock Lotion (waterproof and sweat-proof, SPF 30). Even better, one of my favorite finds on the Gulf Coast, Avon now makes an SPF 30 Skin So Soft cream with a DEET-free bug repellent in it to cope with the Gulf Coast's other big bully, the **mosquitoes.** DEET-based products are more effective in preventing mosquitoes from landing on you, but I hate to have that poison sitting on my skin all day. Lather up with the Avon product, then apply a DEET-based spray only if the mosquitoes

Alligators: Staying Safe

Florida residents have learned to be blasé about gators. They're an everyday part of living in this subtropical climate. But things are changing. Sanibel Island may be leading the way for a new stance on gators. In the past six years, several people have died in alligator attacks across the state, with several in Sanibel. It's hard to be as sanguine about gator-human relations when people are getting chomped while pruning their gardens.

The problems are not just a function of their large numbers—people feed the gators and thus they have gotten chummy and less fearful of humans, and vice versa. So new policies are being put in place. In many spots along the Gulf Coast, if gators get large (over eight feet), they are taken away and "processed." Smaller ones get relocated. The jury is out on this interspecies relationship.

Here are a few safety tips to keep in mind:

· Don't feed the gators. If you see others doing so, give an alligator in the Everglades them a hard time.

· Don't bug them during their cranky spring mating season.

· Don't bother the babies or come between a mother and her young.

· Closely supervise kids playing in or near fresh or brackish water. Never allow little kids to play by water unattended. The same goes for pets. In fact, just don't let your dog swim in fresh or brackish water in Florida, period.

· Alligators feed most actively at dusk and dawn, so schedule your lake or river swim for another time.

· They don't make good pets. They are not tamed in captivity, and it's illegal.

· If you are bitten, seek medical attention, even if it seems minor. Their mouths harbor infectious bacteria.

· If you see a big one that seems especially interested in humans, call the local police nonemergency number.

· Don't throw your fish scraps and guts back into the water when fishing. This encourages gators to hang around boats and docks.

are bad. Mosquitos in Florida can carry West Nile Virus, Zika Virus, St. Louis Encephalitis, Eastern Equine Encephalitus Virus, Dengue Virus, Chikungunya Virus, and others. There was a Zika outbreak in Florida in 2017 where 81 cases were reported.

Another burning subject is **fire ants.** If you see loose sandy mounds on the ground, do not stand in them. These little devils get incensed at the foot in their house and swarm up

your shoe and beyond to bite, leaving raised white or red welts that hurt and itch for days. There is no known treatment for their bites, but I have found that if you douse the bites with aftershave or just plain alcohol, it helps reduce the itching substantially, though not the burning.

The Gulf Coast's municipal water is perfectly safe to drink, although it tastes a little funky in some areas. A much tastier bet is the food. On the Gulf Coast you'll find one great seafood restaurant after another. Make sure to try some of the most adventurous local foods when you're on the Gulf Coast, as they are usually the most memorable and tasty. Become the Sir Edmund Hillary of food: When asked "Why did you eat that?" answer back a gravelly "Because it was there." Try the oysters and clams raw on the half shell with a splash of Tabasco. For some, this can be dangerous: Pregnant women, young children, the elderly, or anyone with an immune system problem should order all seafood baked, broiled, steamed, or fried. The bacteria *Vibrio vulnificus* can, at the very least, ruin your vacation. For a list of safe and sustainable flatfish, California's Monterey Bay Aquarium's website (www.montereybayaquarium.org) has a useful seafood-watch section.

Many travel articles suggest getting **medical travel insurance.** If you have medical insurance, though, that's probably all the coverage you'll need. The best emergency rooms are listed in each chapter, and you can always dial 911 (a number used nationwide to contact local emergency medical, fire, or police personnel) or the **Centers for Disease Control and Prevention** (800/232-4636, www.cdc.gov) for information on health hazards by region.

Resources

Suggested Reading

NAPLES, THE EVERGLADES, AND THE PARADISE COAST
Travel Guide

Molloy, Johnny. *A Paddler's Guide to Everglades National Park.* Gainesville, FL: University Press of Florida, 2000. Paddling the Everglades is daunting, plain and simple. There are things in there that can kill you, others that can merely maim. This book well describes 53 designated paddling routes, camping spots, places to avoid, and wind and tide issues. Molloy is a serious outdoorsman who has written a handful of well-regarded paddling and camping books for Florida and Colorado.

Memoir

Brown, Loren G. "Totch." *Totch: A Life in the Everglades.* Gainesville, FL: University Press of Florida, 1993. It's my favorite book about this area, told in glorious vernacular by the original Everglades renegade. A seasoned tall-tale teller, Totch harkens back to his days in the Ten Thousand Islands, moonshining, selling gator hides, fishing, smuggling dope, and any other thing he thought might be fun, or lucrative, or both. It's memoirs like this that clinch southwest Florida as this country's final frontier.

Nonfiction

Douglas, Marjory Stoneman. *The Everglades: River of Grass.* Sarasota, FL: Pineapple Press, 50th anniversary edition, 1997. Originally published in 1947, this was a book that actually changed the world. At the time, the Everglades were a worthless swamp that developers were scheming about draining and damming. The publication of this straightforward natural history, heavy on the flora, fauna, and indigenous people, galvanized President Harry Truman to sign the controversial order protecting more than two million acres as Everglades National Park. Douglas has been called the Queen of the Everglades, and her descriptions of the Native Americans, pirates, runaways, and ne'er-do-wells who populated the 'Glades are as compelling as ever.

Orlean, Susan. *The Orchid Thief: A True Story of Beauty and Obsession.* New York: Ballantine Books, 2000. This was the book that the film *Adaptation* was loosely based on. *New Yorker* staffer Susan Orlean wrote an incredible piece on John Laroche, an orchid chaser who was arrested with three Seminole people in 1994 carrying contraband rare orchids and epiphytes from the Everglades. Orlean expanded on the story, writing a book that reveals a whole world of eccentric and brilliant obsession. The Wild West feel of the Everglades and its swampy environs is clear, and the story is at times hilarious and moving. It is definitely one of my favorite books on the area, and you can also learn a lot about orchids. Be careful, though—you might just become obsessed.

Zimmerman, Stan. *A History of Smuggling in Florida: Rum Runners and Cocaine Cowboys.* Charleston, SC: The History Press, 2006. Wander through the Ten Thousand Islands and it becomes clear: This would be a good place to hide, or to get lost, or both. It's this geographic anomaly, plus Floridians' general sense of subversive fervor, that makes Florida a natural spot from which or to which to smuggle drugs, booze, or other contraband.

Fiction

Matthiessen, Peter. *Killing Mister Watson.* New York: Vintage, reprint edition, 1991. It's part of a trilogy, along with *Lostman's River* and *Bone by Bone,* that paints a vivid picture of the early settlers living at the edge of civilization in the Ten Thousand Islands and the Everglades. Drawn from bits of historical fact, Matthiessen creates a fictionalized oral history set in Chokoloskee and other little mangrove islands. Edgar J. Watson, who is said to have gunned down the outlaw Belle Starr, came here to elude the law but instead faced the rough frontier justice of his fellow fugitives. It's an absolute must-read if you plan to spend any time in Everglades City. At age 81, Matthiessen collapsed the three stories into one book (as he originally intended) and released the revision as an 890-page novel called *Shadow Country.* For this work he received his second National Book Award.

FORT MYERS, SANIBEL, AND CAPTIVA
Nonfiction

Smoot, Tom. *The Edisons of Fort Myers.* Sarasota, FL: Pineapple Press, 2004. Lots of biographies cover Edison's public life as a world-famous inventor, but this one explores the big loves of his life: Mina Miller and Fort Myers, Florida. It's an especially fun read preceded or followed by a visit to the Edison estate.

Turner, Gregg. *Railroads of Southwest Florida.* Charleston, SC: Arcadia Publishing, 2000. Turner's written a ton about Florida railroads, so he's something of an expert on the rails. This book covers Henry Plant, the Florida Southern Railway, and all the other railway endeavors that prompted accelerated growth in this part of Florida. The writing isn't super exciting, but there's a lot of good information here. He has a newer one called *Florida Railroads in the 1920s* (2006) about the "Big Three's" race in the state.

Witherington, Blair and Dawn. *Florida's Living Beaches: A Guide for the Curious Beachcomber.* Sarasota, FL: Pineapple Press, 2007. A handy paperback identification guide, it packs in 822 items, 983 color images, and 431 maps describing the state's plants, animals, minerals, and artificially created objects.

Fiction

Hiaasen, Carl. Where do you even put Carl Hiaasen in a guide about the Gulf Coast? He's everywhere in south Florida, bigger than a novelist, bigger than a *Miami Herald* columnist. He's like a rock star around here (he even owns a Fender Strat that Dave Barry helped him pick out), with so many titles it's hard to pick which ones to list. The most recent is *Star Island,* New York: Grand Central Publishing, 2010; before that *Scat, Downhill Life, Flush, Nature Girl, Skinny Dip, Basket Case, Sick Puppy, Lucky You, Stormy Weather, Strip Tease, Native Tongue, Skin Tight, Double Whammy,* and *Tourist Season.* He has a penchant for two-word titles and writes mostly about southern Florida. He likes to write about smart hookers with a heart of gold, finds tough-guy baldies especially amusing, and is a bulldoggish environmentalist. In addition to his novels, Hiaasen has also published two collections of his newspaper columns, *Kick Ass* and *Paradise Screwed,* and an anti-Disney book called *Team Rodent.*

White, Randy Wayne. *Sanibel Flats.* New York: St. Martin's Press, 1991. Randy Wayne White was a fishing guide at Tarpon Bay on Sanibel for 13 years. A prolific mystery novelist, he writes mostly about this part of southwest Florida, with numerous novels featuring super tough-guy Doc Ford solving various mysteries (*Black Widow, Hunter's Moon, The Deadlier Sex, Cuban Death-Lift, The Deep Six, The Heat Islands, The Man Who Invented Florida, Captiva, North of Havana, The Mangrove Coast, Ten Thousand Islands, Shark River, Twelve Mile Limit, Everglades, Tampa Burn,* and *Dead of Night*). In all his books, Florida is one of the main characters, described in all its glory. White is a columnist for *Outside Magazine* and *Men's Health,* and he's written lots of other books of essays and such, including *Batfishing in the Rain Forest* and a fish cookbook.

SARASOTA COUNTY
Photography

Evans, Walker. *Walker Evans: Florida.* Los Angeles: J. Paul Getty Trust Publications, 2000. Everyone knows Walker Evans's gutsy, gripping Depression-era photographs. But for six weeks in 1942, Evans focused his lens on Sarasota for *Mangrove Coast,* a book by Karl Bickel. These are some of the wonderful photos he took during that time of the circus's underbelly, old people, railroad cars, and decrepit Florida buildings. Text is by novelist Robert Plunket.

Nonfiction

Apps, Jerry. *Tents, Tigers, and the Ringling Brothers.* Madison, WI: University of Wisconsin Press, 2006. Apps writes pretty much exclusively about Wisconsin. But this story started there, in Baraboo, Wisconsin, to be exact. It's a wonderful history of the Ringling Circus and the seven brothers who made "The Greatest Show on Earth" from scratch. It's got great photos of early circus life.

TAMPA
Travel Guide

Murphy, Bill. *Fox 13 Tampa Bay One Tank Trips with Bill Murphy.* St. Petersburg, FL: Seaside Publishing, 2004. An offshoot of a television segment Murphy does, the books showcase 52 Florida-based adventures that are all within a full tank of Tampa. It's got lots of off-the-beaten-path attractions, all worthy of your time, from Pioneer Florida Museum in Dade City to the excellent camping at Fort De Soto Park in Pinellas County.

Drama

Cruz, Nilo. *Anna in the Tropics.* New York: Theatre Communications Group, 2003. This play won Cruz the Pulitzer Prize for drama in 2003. It is a romantic drama, loosely a retelling of Tolstoy's *Anna Karenina,* that depicts a Cuban-American family of cigar makers in Ybor City (Tampa) in 1930. It tells the story of the factory's new lector, a person hired to read aloud great works of literature and the day's news to the cigar workers. A beautiful stage play—keep your eyes open for performances during your visit.

ST. PETERSBURG AND PINELLAS COUNTY
Nonfiction

Klinkenberg, Jeff. *Seasons of Real Florida.* Gainesville, FL: University Press of Florida, 2004. *St. Petersburg Times* writer Klinkenberg may have invented the term "Real Florida," which means the Old Florida, without Disney, fancy golf courses, or really anything glamorous. This book is an assemblage of largely humorous essays he's written for the paper that tell great stories about the people, flora, and fauna in west-central Florida. Another collection of essays titled *Pilgrim in the Land of Alligators* was published in 2008 by the University Press of Florida.

Fiction

MacDonald, John. *Condominium.* New York: Fawcett, reissue edition, 1985. For most of his life MacDonald was considered a prolific pulp fiction writer who spent more than half his life in west-central Florida, first in Clearwater, then in Sarasota and Siesta Key. This book still seems fresh, especially in light of 2004's hurricane season. The setting is Golden Sands, a Sunbelt condo in the path of Hurricane Ella. It's a multicharacter disaster book—think something like *The Towering Inferno.* (*Cape Fear,* by the way, was based on a MacDonald book.)

THE NATURE COAST
Nonfiction

Warner, David T. *Vanishing Florida: A Personal Guide to Sights Rarely Seen.* Montgomery, AL: River City Publishing, 2001. I love this book, written by a guy who sounds like a dead ringer for Ernest Hemingway (Papa features occasionally in the book, so maybe Warner fancies a resemblance himself). Some of this book appeared as features in *Sarasota* magazine—mostly it's chapter-long ruminations and odes to small towns along the Gulf Coast (especially good chapters on Cedar Key and other parts of the Nature Coast), with lots of drinking and womanizing thrown into the mix.

Fiction

Cook, Ann. *Trace Their Shadows.* New York: Mystery and Suspense Press, 2001, and *Shadow Over Cedar Key.* New York: Mystery and Suspense Press, 2003. As a baby the author was the model for the original Gerber baby (daughter of cartoonist Leslie Turner, who drew the famous baby head in 1928), but as an adult she has turned to mystery writing. The cool thing about these books is the setting—they are easy, beachy reads with plucky reporter Brandy O'Bannon having exciting adventures all over charming Cedar Key.

THE FORGOTTEN COAST
Nonfiction

Cerulean, Susan, ed. *Between Two Rivers.* Tallahassee, FL: Red Hills Writers Project, 2004. If you can find it—give it a serious college try—you'll be mesmerized by this anthology of 29 writers telling stories about the rich cultural and environmental landscapes of the Red Hills and northern Gulf Coast. (The two rivers in question are the Aucilla to the east and the Apalachicola to the west.) The Red Hills Writers Project is a group of mostly Florida writers with a serious nature and ecological bent to their writing. Editors include Susan Cerulean (biologist, activist, and writer of *Book of the Everglades* and *Wild Heart of Florida*), Southern author Janisse Ray (*Ecology of a Cracker Childhood, Wild Card Quilt*), and Tallahassee poet Laura Newton (poetry editor of the *Apalachee Review*).

Rudloe, Jack. *The Living Dock of Panacea.* New York: Alfred A. Knopf, 1977. Rudloe is one of the contributors to *Between Two Rivers.* He's a longtime Florida naturalist, director of Gulf Specimen Marine Laboratory, and author of nine or so books on the area. He's big into turtles (*Time of the Turtle, Search for the Great Turtle Mother*), but this older book (recently reprinted with a new introduction and called just *The Living Dock*) is a great rumination on the Gulf Coast's marinelife, told from the author's floating dock in the tiny fishing community of Panacea.

THE EMERALD COAST
Travel Guide

Hollis, Tim. *Florida's Miracle Strip: From Redneck Riviera to Emerald Coast.* Jackson, MI: University Press of Mississippi, 2004. This is a nostalgic look at the area that is now the fairly glamorous Panama City Beach, Fort Walton Beach, Destin, and Pensacola Beach, with lots of fun descriptions of the campy Old Florida attractions that used to bring people here—like Castle Dracula and the

Snake-A-Torium. It's got lots of cool vintage photos and postcards.

Fishing

Dew, Gregory. *The Barefoot Fisherman's Guide to the Emerald Coast: From Gulf Shores, Alabama, to Apalachicola, Florida*. Birmingham, AL: Crane Hill Publishers, 1999. It's a little techie, with lots of talk about tackle and rigs, so the beginning angler might just be interested in chapter three, which enumerates 40 or so fabulous fishing spots on this gorgeous stretch of coast. Dew also gives great information on all of the species you're likely to catch here, and then what to do with them if you aim to eat 'em.

Hoskins, Jim. *Fishing the Local Waters: Gulf Shores to Panama City*. Gulf Breeze, FL: Maximum Press, 2006. A guide to angling in Florida's Gulf Coast waters, written by two local anglers, includes LORAN coordinates for 50 tried-and-true spots. Even for the rookie it's a valuable book because it gives a listing of guides and services in the area.

PENSACOLA
Nonfiction

Pensacola Historical Society. *Pensacola in Vintage Postcards*. Charleston, SC: Arcadia Publishing, 2004. It's just a packet of postcards, but a riffle through will give you a sense of the way Pensacola used to be.

ALABAMA GULF SHORES
Nonfiction

Jackson, Harvey. *The Rise and Decline of the Redneck Riviera: An Insider's History to the Florida-Alabama Coast*. Athens, GA: The University of Georgia Press, 2013.

Rogers, William, et al. *Alabama: The History of the Deep South State*. Tuscaloosa, AL: University Alabama Press, 2010. A comprehensive history of the state. The book is divided into three main sections: The first concludes in 1865, the second in 1920, and the third brings the story to the present.

CHILDREN'S BOOKS ABOUT THE GULF COAST
Travel Guides

DeWire, Elinor. *Florida Lighthouses for Kids*. Sarasota, FL: Pineapple Press, 2004. Great pictures and fun stories about Florida's 33 lighthouses (many on the Gulf Coast)—it gives kids something to read in the car and a way to participate in the process of planning a trip.

Lantz, Peggy, and Wendy Hale. *The Young Naturalist's Guide to Florida*. Sarasota, FL: Pineapple Press, 2006. Again, this gives kids a fun window through which to see the kooky plants and animals of the state, with information on careers in the environmental field.

Fiction

DiCamillo, Kate. *Because of Winn-Dixie*. Cambridge, MA: Candlewick Press, 2001. Now a major motion picture, this book about 10-year-old India Opal Buloni and her ugly dog Winn-Dixie (named for where she found him) has captured the attention of lots of families. It's a great story, set in a fictional town of Naomi, Florida (I like to think it's modeled on someplace down toward Port Charlotte). Opal's had kind of a hard life, so it might be too much for a sensitive kid.

George, Jean Craighead. *Everglades*. New York: HarperTrophy, reprint edition, 1997. Geared toward littler kids (maybe 5-8), it tells the story of a man poling through the Everglades and teaching his five young passengers about the 'Glades' sawgrass, hundreds of species of animals, and fragile ecosystem. It's not as preachy as it sounds—the environmental message is light, and Wendell Minor's illustrations are wonderful. Newbery medalist Jean Craighead George has written lots of wonderful children's books with the Florida wilderness at their centers—older kids might like the eco-mystery *The Missing 'Gator of Gumbo Limbo,* New York: HarperTrophy, 1993.

Hiaasen, Carl. *Hoot.* New York: Knopf Books for Young Readers, 2002. Geared for readers 9-12, this Newbery-honor book by Florida great Carl Hiaasen does double duty. As with many of Hiaasen's novels there's a heavy environmental message, this one about protecting rare burrowing owls and their habitat, but it also tells an exciting tale of new kid Roy Eberhardt, who moves to Coconut Grove and gets mixed up in a crazy ecological adventure with Mullet Fingers and bully-beater Beatrice in a fight against Mother Paula's All-American Pancake House. A middle-school mystery, the language and plot are edgy. A second book, *Flush,* New York: Knopf Books for Young Readers, 2005, follows a similar formula: Misunderstood teen iconoclast takes a stand and helps preserve the environment in the face of adults' scheming machinations.

Hogan, Linda. *Power.* New York: W.W. Norton, 1999. In an area that was once populated exclusively by Native Americans, it's exciting to read about what life must have been like before all the development. This is a coming-of-age story about a 16-year-old Native American girl named Omishito, who witnesses the killing of a sacred animal, the Florida panther. It is based on a true story.

Konigsburg, E. L. *T-backs, T-shirts, Coat and Suit.* New York: Aladdin, 2003. A more contemporary book from the author of the classic Newbery winner *From the Mixed-Up Files of Mrs. Basil E. Frankweiler,* this one tells the story of 12-year-old Chloe, who spends the summer in Florida with her wild aunt

Bernadette, who drives a commissary van and sells junk food at roadsides. For ages 9-12.

Rawlings, Marjorie Kinnan. *The Yearling.* New York: Simon Pulse, 50th edition, 1988. Rawlings wrote 10 books while a resident in Cross Creek, Florida, the most popular of which was *The Yearling,* which won a Pulitzer Prize in fiction in 1939. It tells the story of scrappy young Jody Baxter and his pet fawn Flag, who together roam the Florida scrublands wrestling big swamp gators and cavorting with bear cubs. Rawlings's second-best book is called, simply, *Cross Creek,* also with the same earthy Florida Cracker dialect.

Smith, Patrick D. *A Land Remembered.* Sarasota, FL: Pineapple Press, 1998. Beginning with Tobias MacIvey's arrival in Florida in 1858, this young-adult historical novel tells the story of three generations of Floridians carving out a hardscrabble life for themselves in the wilds of central Florida. This sweeping story is rich in Florida history.

GUIDES TO FLORIDA WILDLIFE
Birds

Maehr, David. *Florida's Birds: A Field Guide and Reference.* Sarasota, FL: Pineapple Press, 2005. For birders and rookies alike, birds can be quickly identified in this book via picture (pretty ones with birds grouped by similar species), text, or index. Maps indicate when migratory birds are present or breeding, and where.

Tekiela, Stan. *Birds of Florida Field Guide.* Cambridge, MN: Adventure Publications, 2005. It's a great small-size book organized by bird color. This makes it easy to narrow things down when you've just spotted a flash of wing color in your binoculars.

Even better than these books, though, is the sand- and waterproof *Florida's Gulf Coast Birds* flip map illustrated by Ernest C.

Simmons; visit www.floridabooks.com if you can't find it in area bookstores. It puts birds into rough groups—wading birds, shorebirds, wetland birds, birds of prey, etc. Another great resource is the spring and fall bird migration tables at www.birdnature.com.

Fish

Arnov, Boris. *Fish Florida: Saltwater/Better Than Luck—The Foolproof Guide to Florida Saltwater Fishing.* Houston: Gulf Publishing, 2002. This is a fairly good beginner book: It describes a kind of fish, let's say amberjack, then tells you how it fights (fiercely); appropriate tackle, whether you're spinning or plug casting or fly-fishing; and technique for live bait or light tackle casting. It also gives catch and size limits and other regulations.

Dew, Gregory. *The Barefoot Fisherman's Guide to the Emerald Coast: From Gulf Shore, Alabama, to Apalachicola, Florida.* Birmingham, AL: Crane Hill Publishers, 1999. Flip to chapter three, which enumerates 40 or so fabulous fishing spots on this gorgeous stretch of coast, and what you're likely to catch there.

Mammals

Adams, Alto. *A Florida Cattle Ranch.* Sarasota, FL: Pineapple Press, 1998. You'll learn about Cracker cows, scrub, and the hardscrabble world of Florida ranching.

Maehr, David. *The Florida Panther: Life and Death of a Vanishing Carnivore.* Washington DC: Island Press, 1997. The author makes these endangered cougars spring to life in their last frontier in the Big Cypress National Preserve and around the Okaloacoochee Slough.

Sobczak, Charles. *Alligators, Sharks & Panthers: Deadly Encounters with Florida's Top Predator—Man.* Sanibel, FL: Indigo Press, 2006. It chronicles grisly attacks, but with an underlying environmentalist's message

about humans mucking about in creatures' natural habitats.

Butterflies

Daniels, Jaret. *Butterflies of Florida Field Guide (Our Nature Field Guides).* Cambridge, MN: Adventure Publications, 2003. It's a lovely field guide with great pictures and not-too-Latin text.

Shells

Witherington, Blair and Dawn. *Florida's Seashells.* Sarasota, FL: Pineapple Press, 2007. It's light enough to pack in your beach bag, with good color photos and interesting text about the marine animals.

Where to Find Good Florida Wildlife Books

Haslam's Book Store (www.haslams.com) is a St. Petersburg institution and one of the best bookstores in Florida, while in Tampa **Inkwood Books** (http://inkwoodbooks.com) has a broad Florida nature, wildlife, and gardening section. **Florida Plants Online Bookstore** (www.floridaplants.com) indeed lists lots of excellent books on local flora, but its reach also extends to fauna, highbrow literature, and books for young readers. For rare or out-of-print books, **Grove Antiquarian** (www.abebooks.com) traffics in preowned books, specializing in south Florida and the Caribbean. The bookstore at **Everglades National Park** (www.nps.gov) features a long reading list of Evergladescentric books.

Pineapple Press (www.pineapplepress.com) is the best local small press, producing a handful of books on Florida each year, all of high caliber and many with an environmental bent. The **University Press of Florida** (www.upf.com), the consolidated publishing efforts of all the Florida state universities, groups Florida books by helpful categories (environment, people, arts, and artifacts).

Internet Resources

GENERAL GULF COAST

Visit Florida
www.visitflorida.com
For a good introduction to the Gulf Coast, contact the state's official visitor information organization, Visit Florida (or call 888/7-FLA-USA—888/735-2872), for a copy of its excellent annual *Visit Florida* guide, the *Florida Events Calendar,* or *Florida Trails.* Online resources include a number of electronic travel guides (for which you can order printed versions if you prefer). Visit Florida also has a 24-hour multilingual tourist assistance hotline (800/656-8777).

Florida Secrets, The Insider's Guide to Unique Destinations
www.floridasecrets.com
The graphics have a cheese factor and it's heavy on the advertising, but the site is a treasure trove of little-known destinations in Florida, divided up on the Gulf Coast by southwest, west-central, eastern, and western Panhandle.

FISHING

Florida Fishing
www.floridagofishing.com
It's a clearinghouse of fishing info, sites, guides, fishing charters, and fishing captains in the state.

CAMPING

Florida Association of RV Parks & Campgrounds
www.campflorida.com
It's an easy-to-use comprehensive database of Florida campgrounds, including amenities information for each site. You can also go on this website and order a print version of the guide. To make reservations at a Florida state campground (or in any state), however, you must utilize www.reserveamerica.com.

PARKS AND FORESTS

Florida State Parks Department
www.floridastateparks.org
Find a park, its affiliated camping and lodging, or get a bead on what events are coming up along the Gulf Coast. The site also has maps and directions to Florida's state parks, and it runs an amateur photo contest of state park photography.

Florida Trail Association
www.floridatrail.org
The Florida Trail Association is a nonprofit that builds, maintains, promotes, and protects hiking trails across the state of Florida, especially the 1,400-mile Florida Trail. From this site you can download all kinds of trail maps and park brochures.

SPORTS

Florida Sports Foundation
www.flasports.com
The foundation usually posts the "Grapefruit League" Florida spring-training baseball schedules on its website late in January. Another way to find out about spring training for your favorite team is by visiting the website of Major League Baseball (www.mlb.com).

NAPLES, THE EVERGLADES, AND THE PARADISE COAST

Naples, Marco Island and Everglades Convention & Visitors Bureau
www.paradisecoast.com
A slick website for the area, it features convenient charts for local accommodations, a round-up of attractions and recreation, and well-written background on the area. The only thing that's missing here is detailed restaurant info.

Guide to Southwest Florida
www.florida-southwest.com
Naples and Marco Island enticements are laid

out in categories, and the restaurant write-ups are reliable.

FORT MYERS, SANIBEL, AND CAPTIVA

Lee County Visitor and Convention Bureau
www.fortmyers-sanibel.com
www.leevcb.com

One of the most professional-looking sites around from a convention bureau, its information is helpful, current, and entertainingly written.

Charlotte Harbor and the Gulf Islands
www.charlotteharbortravel.com

This area gets short shrift due to its proximity to better-known vacation destinations. Still, as the website shows, Charlotte Harbor has loads to do and abundant natural beauty. It has an easily downloadable list of local accommodations.

SARASOTA COUNTY

Sarasota Convention & Visitors Bureau
www.visitsarasota.org

The convention and visitors bureau's award-winning site is about as user-friendly as they come, with easily sortable menus of restaurants, accommodations, outdoor attractions, and more. The excellent feature stories on the area's lures are written by local travel writers. The site is offered in English, Spanish, and German. A second site, www.discovernaturalsarasota.org, focuses exclusively on the natural draws of the area, including beaches, parks, gardens, and historic sites.

Anna Maria Island Chamber of Commerce
www.annamariaislandchamber.org

Too far from Tampa in the north and too far from Sarasota to its south, Anna Maria Island doesn't really get covered in other, bigger regional websites. This one doesn't have as many

bells and whistles as other sites, but it's got all the basics of where to stay, what to do, and where to eat.

TAMPA

Tampa Bay Convention & Visitors Bureau
www.visittampabay.com

This is a good site for background on the Bay Area as well as travel strategies and accommodations.

Creative Loafing
www.cltampa.com

The local alternative weekly newspaper has a great website. The writing is provocative and witty and covers politics, arts and entertainment, local events, and regional news.

ST. PETERSBURG AND PINELLAS COUNTY

St. Petersburg/Clearwater Area Convention & Visitors Bureau
www.visitstpeteclearwater.com

Similar to the Tampa Bay Convention and Visitors Bureau site, this one focuses, not surprisingly, on the beaches. It's easy to book a room from this site, and it features excellent downloadable maps.

Tampa Bay Times
www.tampabay.com

The daily metro paper covers local as well as national news. It has a great website, and the paper's movie, book, and pop music reviews are notable. The paper's food-critic column by Laura Reiley is also worth the read for her outstanding, mouthwatering descriptions of the area's best eats.

THE NATURE COAST

Citrus County Tourist Development Council
www.discovercrystalriverfl.com

This is an interactive site with a wealth of information on Homosassa, Crystal River, and environs. It's a good site from which to choose a manatee snorkeling trip or fishing charter.

Citrus County Chronicle
www.chronicleonline.com
For more information about local events, pick up the *Citrus County Chronicle,* the largest daily in the county, or visit the easy-to-use online version.

Cedar Key Chamber of Commerce
www.cedarkey.org
The chamber's site is a fine resource for information specifically about Cedar Key, especially good for local events.

Cedar Key Beacon
www.cedarkeybeacon.com
Explore the *Cedar Key Beacon,* the little island newspaper that directs you to events and activities. Print versions are also available with new editions every Thursday.

Steinhatchee Landing Resort
www.steinhatcheelanding.com
Steinhatchee is one of the Gulf Coast's least-known destinations, and generally the Web doesn't help much to illuminate. This is the best site about the area, brought to you from the most popular upscale resort on the Nature Coast. The recreation section is helpful in planning a trip.

THE FORGOTTEN COAST
Franklin County Tourist Development Council
www.floridasforgottencoast.com
The Development Council's site offers resources for lodging, activities, and attractions throughout Franklin County.

Apalachicola Bay Chamber of Commerce
www.apalachicolabay.org
Straightforward and no-nonsense, this site has good background information on the area and a list of chamber members that actually provides guidance when you're choosing a fishing charter or beach house rental.

THE EMERALD COAST
Beaches of South Walton
www.visitsouthwalton.com
About as nice as a site like this can be, this resource well describes the dozen-plus little communities that make up the area, providing useful insight into where to eat, what to do, and where to stay. (Seaside has its own website, www.seasidefl.com, that is even more impressively stylish.)

Emerald Coast Convention & Visitors Bureau
www.emeraldcoastfl.com
This is a fairly serviceable site that explores the areas of Destin, Fort Walton Beach, and Okaloosa Island. The best feature is the lodging locator, in which you can sort by a long list of amenities.

Panama City Beach Convention & Visitors Bureau
www.visitpanamacitybeach.com
For information specifically on Panama City Beach, this is the best resource. It offers lots of spring break-specific material during March-April. From the site you can also order a 96-page vacation guide that provides helpful and accurate information about activities, entertainment, accommodations, and dining.

PENSACOLA
Pensacola Bay Area Convention & Visitors Bureau
www.visitpensacola.com
All there is to do in Pensacola, Pensacola Beach, and Perdido Key is outlined in an organized fashion, with a special emphasis on the beaches as well as the historical and military attractions.

ALABAMA GULF SHORES

Gulf Shores and Orange Beach Tourism
www.gulfshores.com
This site is a great resource for planning your trip to Gulf Shores and Orange Beach. A daily updated entertainment and event calendar gives you the scoop on what's happening in the area, and a section that features deals and packages is a great place to find specials on lodging, restaurants, and activities here.

South Mobile County Tourism Authority
www.dauphinislandchamber.com
This site provides extensive listings for area restaurants, events, attractions, and lodging.

Index

List of Maps

Photo Credits

Acknowledgments

I'd like to thank everyone at Avalon Travel for all their help in making this project possible, as well as Laura Reiley, author of the first and second editions of *Moon Florida Gulf Coast*.

I'd also like to thank the following people for their time and expertise during the researching of this guide: Sarah Brazwell at Sandestin Golf and Beach Resort; Kelly Grass Prieto at Hayworth Creative; Anita Grove of the Apalachicola Bay Chamber of Commerce; Lee Rose of Lee County Visitor and Convention Bureau; Hue Reynolds at the Florida Department of Education; Bob Thomas at Florida State University; Katie Kole at Visit Tallahassee; Michelle Moran at Sunstream Resorts; Shannon Hagen of the Beaches of South Walton Tourist Development Council; Sandee Harraden at North American Canoe Tours and the Ivey House in Everglades City; Laura A. Lee of the Pensacola Bay Area Convention and Visitors Bureau; Alissa Hopkins at the Morean Arts Center; Josh Hall at the St. Pete and Clearwater CVB; Jamie Veronica at the Big Cat Rescue in Tampa; JoNell Modys of the Greater Naples, Marco Island and Everglades City CVB; Lindsay Bennett at the Panama City CVB; Kelly Robinson of Visit Florida; Shawn Collier and Angie Hester; and all the wonderful people I've met while traveling across the Gulf Coast of Florida.

More from Moon Travel Guides

Want a getaway to the coast, a city adventure, or to see where the road takes you? Moon has a guide to suit your style!

MAP SYMBOLS

═══ Expressway	○ City/Town	✈ Airport	⛳ Golf Course
━━ Primary Road	◉ State Capital	✗ Airfield	🅿 Parking Area
─── Secondary Road	⊛ National Capital	▲ Mountain	⬗ Archaeological Site
┄┄┄ Unpaved Road	★ Point of Interest	✦ Unique Natural Feature	⛪ Church
─── Feature Trail	• Accommodation		🛢 Gas Station
┄┄┄ Other Trail	▾ Restaurant/Bar	⧖ Waterfall	Glacier
┈┈┈ Ferry	▪ Other Location	♣ Park	Mangrove
═══ Pedestrian Walkway	▲ Campground	▪ Trailhead	Reef
▥▥▥ Stairs		⛷ Skiing Area	Swamp

CONVERSION TABLES

°C = (°F - 32) / 1.8
°F = (°C x 1.8) + 32
1 inch = 2.54 centimeters (cm)
1 foot = 0.304 meters (m)
1 yard = 0.914 meters
1 mile = 1.6093 kilometers (km)
1 km = 0.6214 miles
1 fathom = 1.8288 m
1 chain = 20.1168 m
1 furlong = 201.168 m
1 acre = 0.4047 hectares
1 sq km = 100 hectares
1 sq mile = 2.59 square km
1 ounce = 28.35 grams
1 pound = 0.4536 kilograms
1 short ton = 0.90718 metric ton
1 short ton = 2,000 pounds
1 long ton = 1.016 metric tons
1 long ton = 2,240 pounds
1 metric ton = 1,000 kilograms
1 quart = 0.94635 liters
1 US gallon = 3.7854 liters
1 Imperial gallon = 4.5459 liters
1 nautical mile = 1.852 km

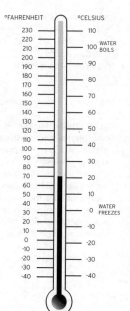

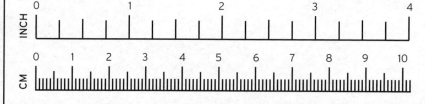

MOON FLORIDA GULF COAST
Avalon Travel
Hachette Book Group
1700 Fourth Street
Berkeley, CA 94710, USA
www.moon.com

Editor: Rachael Sablik
Acquiring Editor: Nikki Ioakimedes
Series Manager: Kathryn Ettinger
Copy Editor: Christopher Church
Graphics Coordinator: Lisi Baldwin
Production Coordinator: Lisi Baldwin
Cover Design: Faceout Studios, Charles Brock
Interior Design: Domini Dragoone
Moon Logo: Tim McGrath
Map Editor: Kat Bennett
Cartographers: Karin Dahl, Brian Shotwell
Indexer: Rachel Kuhn

ISBN-13: 978-1-64049-110-6

Printing History
1st Edition — 2005
6th Edition — October 2019
5 4 3 2 1

Text © 2019 by Joshua Lawrence Kinser & Avalon Travel.
Maps © 2019 by Avalon Travel.
Some photos and illustrations are used by permission and are the property of the original copyright owners.

Front cover photo: Florida coastal inlet at dawn © Dean Fikar/Getty images
Back cover photo: Naples, Florida © dreamstimes.com

Printed in China by RR Donnelley.

Avalon Travel is a division of Hachette Book Group, Inc. Moon and the Moon logo are trademarks of Hachette Book Group, Inc. All other marks and logos depicted are the property of the original owners.